PERGAMON INTERNATIONAL LIBRARY
of Science, Technology, Engineering and Social Studies

*The 1000-volume original paperback library in aid of education,
industrial training and the enjoyment of leisure*

Publisher: Robert Maxwell, M.C.

17.50
70S

Helping People
Change
(PGPS – 52)

THE PERGAMON TEXTBOOK
INSPECTION COPY SERVICE

An inspection copy of any book published in the Pergamon International Library
will gladly be sent to academic staff without obligation for their consideration for
course adoption or recommendation. Copies may be retained for a period of 60 days
from receipt and returned if not suitable. When a particular title is adopted or
recommended for adoption for class use and the recommendation results in a sale
of 12 or more copies the inspection copy may be retained with our compliments.
The Publishers will be pleased to receive suggestions for revised editions and new
titles to be published in this important international Library.

Pergamon Titles of Related Interest

Bellack/Hersen DICTIONARY OF BEHAVIOR THERAPY TECHNIQUES

Blanchard/Andrasik MANAGEMENT OF CHRONIC HEADACHES

Hersen/Kazdin/Bellack THE CLINICAL PSYCHOLOGY HANDBOOK

Karoly/Kanfer SELF MANAGEMENT AND BEHAVIOR CHANGE: From Theory to Practice

Meichenbaum STRESS INOCULATION TRAINING

Pinkston/Linsk CARE OF THE ELDERLY: A Family Approach

Related Journals*

ADVANCES IN BEHAVIOUR RESEARCH AND THERAPY
BEHAVIOUR RESEARCH AND THERAPY
BEHAVIORAL ASSESSMENT
CLINICAL PSYCHOLOGY REVIEW
JOURNAL OF BEHAVIOR THERAPY AND EXPERIMENTAL PSYCHIATRY

*Free sample copies available upon request

AAE-4840

PERGAMON GENERAL PSYCHOLOGY SERIES
EDITORS
Arnold P. Goldstein, Syracuse University
Leonard Krasner, SUNY at Stony Brook

Helping People Change
A Textbook of Methods
Third Edition

edited by
Frederick H. Kanfer
University of Illinois

Arnold P. Goldstein
Syracuse University

PERGAMON PRESS
New York Oxford Toronto Sydney Frankfurt

U.S.A.	Pergamon Press, Maxwell House, Fairview Park, Elmsford, New York 10523, U.S.A.
U.K.	Pergamon Press, Headington Hill Hall, Oxford OX3 0BW, England
PEOPLE'S REPUBLIC OF CHINA	Pergamon Press, Room 4037, Qianmen Hotel, Beijing, People's Republic of China
FEDERAL REPUBLIC OF GERMANY	Pergamon Press, Hammerweg 6, D-6242 Kronberg, Federal Republic of Germany
BRAZIL	Pergamon Editora, Rue Eça de Queiros, 346, CEP 04011, Paraiso, São Paulo, Brazil
AUSTRALIA	Pergamon Press Australia, P.O. Box 544, Potts Point, N.S.W. 2011, Australia
JAPAN	Pergamon Press, 8th Floor, Matsuoka Central Building, 1-7-1 Nishishinjuku, Shinjuku-ku, Tokyo 160, Japan
CANADA	Pergamon Press Canada, Suite No 271, 253 College Street, Toronto, Ontario, Canada M5T 1R5

Copyright © 1986 Pergamon Press Inc.

Second printing 1986
Third printing 1988

Library of Congress Cataloging in Publication Data
Main entry under title:

Helping people change.

    (Pergamon general psychology series ; 52)
    Includes bibliographies and indexes.
    1. Behavior modification. 2. Personality.
I. Kanfer, Frederick H., 1925-   . II. Goldstein,
Arnold P. III. Series. [DNLM: 1. Behavior Therapy.
2. Personality. WM 425 H483]
BF637.B4H45 1985   158   85-6267
ISBN 0-08-031601-8
ISBN 0-08-031600-X (pbk.)

Printed in Great Britain by A. Wheaton & Co. Ltd., Exeter

To Ruby, Ruth, and Larry for their infinite patience,
encouragement, and affection

and

To Susan with love and admiration for her concern
with helping others

Contents

Preface to the Third Edition

Since publication of the second edition, there has been a considerable broadening of the research and conceptual base of behavior change methods, as well as an increase in the types of social and personal problems to which these methods have been applied. The efforts of helpers have previously been heavily concentrated on targeting persons with primarily psychological disturbances. More recently, helpers are increasingly working with populations whose demographic characteristics are associated with special problems. Research and counseling with older persons, with women with conflicting role expectations, with victims of structural unemployment, and with persons at risk for health problems or wishing to adopt health-oriented life-styles illustrate the expanding scope of the range of persons seeking and obtaining counseling and therapy. Despite these expansions in application, there have been relatively few innovations in specific techniques since publication of the last edition. In fact, most of the novel areas of application have utilized clinical procedures that have constituted the main body of behavioral change techniques, as described in the previous edition.

At the theoretical level, multifactor systems-oriented models are tending to displace single-factor mechanisms of etiology and change. As a result, greater individualization of treatment has been widely emphasized in the current literature. Both research publications and other articles emphasize the need to treat each client, not for a specific symptom or behavioral problem, but with careful attention to his or her life setting, personal values, and biological and sociopsychological characteristics.

Social conditions are constantly altering the nature of psychological problems. For example, the current orientation toward healthy life-styles adds to the changing image of the "ideal American." It is surely related to the sudden increase in the variety of complaints brought to the clinician's attention. A variety of serious eating disorders; changes in standards for sexuality, partnership and marriage; and changes in the role that vocations play in overall life satisfactions are some of the cultural factors that are altering the mixture of problems brought to clinicians. A host of sociocultural developments is also contributing to the high incidence of and concern about violence and abuse in personal relationships. Treatment of these and other related problem areas has become the topic of many specialized volumes. Most of them incorporate adaptations of the basic techniques described in this volume. In the present revision, therefore, we have asked contributors to update and expand on these techniques, so that the reader could be prepared to utilize them in many different contexts. We have made no attempt to duplicate description of the methods and programs available to advanced readers in the many volumes on special problem areas.

Since the second edition was published, the trend toward integrating cognitive and behavioral methods and stressing self-management by clients has grown. Recently, attention has also been given to the affective dimension in behavior and the role of emotional variables in modifying cognitive and behavioral events. Despite these growing trends, the last 5 years have not witnessed substantial innovations in treatment methods that would radically alter the efficacy of treatment. As a result of these changes in the field since 1980, revisions of the chapters vary from extensive rewrites in some chapters to minor revisions in chapters on areas in which principles and methods have remained in use without major changes. The addition of new contributors in the third edition inevitably changes the context and presentations from the previous edition. All contributors, who are active researchers and practitioners in their own subspecialties, have revised and updated their chapters to include new research findings, technological advances, and examples of current interest. Feedback from readers of the previous editions has helped us to improve the organization and readability of chapters. The chapter revisions have added new findings and methods without reducing description of the basic principles and procedures that have withstood the test of time. As in previous editions, suggestions for clinical procedures were included only if there existed some empirical evidence in support of their utility. We believe that the book contains, in both depth and breadth, the most important psychological methods that are currently used to help people change.

In preparing the third edition we have been helped by the sincere effort, interest, and dedication of the contributors to this edition. We wish to express our high regard and appreciation to them. Their expertise and concern with providing and applying the best of psychological research and theory toward the increase of human happiness and satisfaction and the decrease of deficiency are what has given this book both its theme and its substance.

Frederick H. Kanfer
Arnold P. Goldstein

1

Introduction

Frederick H. Kanfer and Arnold P. Goldstein

Perhaps the most characteristic feature of our lives during the last few decades has been the rapid increase in the rate of change — in the physical environment, in our technology, and in our social, political, and moral institutions. Bombarded by mass media, by a wealth of available goods and ideas, and by the ever-changing scene to which our senses are exposed, each of us finishes the day having changed for better or worse, even if ever so slightly. A conversation with a friend, an interesting movie or book, a new emotional experience, a political rally, a work of art, or a breathtaking natural scene may all make a deep impression on us and can alter our attitudes about ourselves and about the world. If an experience is sufficiently intense, it can alter our behavior to the extent that our families and friends are surprised at the change. Yet, many persons go through their daily routine given the same exposure to ideas, images, and people as others but remain unable to change their view of themselves or others and unable to give up self-defeating patterns of behavior, even though solutions and opportunities for growth are at an arm's length. Others meet their world in rigid, fearful, or aggressive ways, finding little happiness or satisfaction, yet unable to break the vicious circles they seem to engender. It is these populations, persons who are stymied in resolving their personal and interpersonal problems, who are the focus of our attention as professional helpers.

This book is about psychological methods designed to help people change for the better, so that they can fully develop their potentials and capitalize on the opportunities available in their social environment. The helping methods we will examine share the common goal of promoting change in ways that can lead to greater personal happiness, competence, and satisfaction. Our point of view stresses that a professional or paraprofessional helper can serve as both a consultant and an expert teacher or guide to persons whose discomforts, psychological disabilities, and social inefficiencies have been of sufficient concern to them, or to others in their environment, that the assistance of a trained outsider is deemed necessary.

People help one another in numerous ways in everyday life and, indeed, people do change as a result of such informal assistance. However, several distinct characteristics consistently differentiate the professional or paraprofessional helping relationship from friendship or other helpful interactions. Whether the helping relationship is called psychotherapy, counseling, guidance, behavior modification, or Gestalt therapy, and whether it is conducted by a physician, a psychiatrist, a psychologist, a social worker, a child care worker, a mental health technician, or a hospital nurse or aide, the same features are found in all professional or paraprofessional helping relationships: they are unilateral, systematic, formal, and time limited.

The *unilateral* aspect of the helping relationship reflects the fact that the participants agree that one person is defined as the helper and the other as the client. It is also agreed, explicitly or implicitly, that the focus of the relationship and all its activities is on solving the problems of the client. In this respect, the change process is unlike most other interpersonal interactions. The personal problems, the private affairs, the worries and the wishes of one person, the helper, are intentionally not focused upon. Treatment, therapy, or whatever the helping relationship is called, is one-sided and concentrates exclusively on the client.

The professional or paraprofessional helping relationship is *systematic* in that the participants typically agree at the outset on the purposes and objectives of their interaction, and the helper attempts to plan and carry out procedures that move in an organized fashion toward resolution of the client's problems.

The relationship is *formal*, in that the interaction between helper and client is usually confined to specified times and places. Although the interaction need not always be conducted at the same time of day and in the same office, clinic, or hospital, this usually is the case. The times and places are arranged in such a way that the helper has no other role or duty during meetings with the client. At times, the helper might intentionally create an informal atmosphere. For example, a helping interaction can occur when a child care worker plays checkers or Ping-Pong or takes a walk with a child, or when an adult client is seen in his or her home. However, under these circumstances the child care worker's concern is not with winning the game or getting physical exercise during the walk, nor is the visit in a client's home a social occasion for mutual enjoyment. These are, instead, examples of formal treatment in an informal setting.

Helping relationships are *time limited*. The relationship terminates when the stated objectives and goals are reached. The termination is always considered the final outcome of the relationship and can be based on mutual agreement or on either the helper's or the client's initiative.

If you consider a friendship or an interaction with a colleague or a neighbor for a moment, it will become clear that none of the features listed is common in such relationships. Social relationships are formed for mutual benefit of the participants, there is usually no fixed agenda for what is to be accomplished, the relationship is typically enjoyed for what it is rather than for what it may accomplish, and it is terminated for numerous reasons other than completion of a task.

The history of professional helpers goes back over many centuries. In each age, the predominant theory of human nature determined which professional group was considered the most competent to relieve people's discomforts and psychological problems. In societies in which theological explanations of man dominated, priests, shamans, or witch doctors were given the task of assisting people with their personal problems or rectifying behavioral deviations. More recently, the assumption was accepted in Western societies that behavioral disorders were manifestations of disturbances of the nervous system or the biological structure of the individual. As a result, major responsibility for dealing with psychological problems was given to physicians and, in particular, psychiatrists. Indeed, early suspicions that brain damage or weak nervous system structures were the causes of many behavior disorders resulted in rigorous search for the specific roots of what was then called "mental diseases." Even Freud's comprehensive theory of human behavior was based on the assumption that the driving energy underlying human activity, psychic libido, developed by conversion from physical energy via the nervous system.

In the last 3 decades there has been increasing disenchantment with the view that behavioral problems represent mental illnesses associated with the organism's biological or psychic structures. Alternate models of psychological disturbances have been based on ideas derived from philosophical systems and, increasingly, from scientific psychology. Congruent with this trend, there has also been the recognition that relief of psychological problems can be offered by persons with expertise in nonmedical specialties. Further, the erosion of belief in the infallibility of the authoritative professional has hastened the development of brief training programs that permit many laypersons to participate in the treatment or behavior change process. This expansion of the helper pool has helped reduce the scarcity of assistance available, caused by the small number of highly trained professionals and the large number of persons in need of help. This greatly expanded use of paraprofessional personnel, parents, volunteer workers, and many others as helpers is a development we strongly endorse. Their success with many types of clients with a broad range of problems is already evident.

WHO IS QUALIFIED TO HELP?

Many different professions have as one of their goals the accomplishment of behavior change in their clients. Teachers, physicians, clergy,
social workers, psychologists, and probation officers are among the professionals who offer services designed to change human behavior. Even if
enduring changes in the client's behavior are not the immediate focus of the
professional service, they can still play a role in the total context of the services offered. Attorneys, nurses, dentists, and financial advisors are among
those who can achieve their specifically stated goals more easily if they can
influence their clients to change in ways ranging from minor accommoda-
tions to sweeping changes in their life patterns. For example, the more
effective dentist is one who not only restores tooth damage or applies
preventive treatment in the office, but who is also able to persuade the
patient to alter daily oral hygiene behaviors and, perhaps, even eating
habits sufficiently so that future damage is prevented or retarded. However, not all professionals are equally qualified to deal effectively with psychological problems. Currently, the most acceptable criterion for
qualification in the helping professions has been evidence of successful
completion of specified training programs. Generally, the successful completion of a study program is certified by a degree, and the holder is
regarded as competent to carry out a specified range of professional duties.
Of course, the distinction between meeting requirements in academic
courses and showing the skills needed for professional practice is not
clearly made by degree-granting institutions. In fact, frequent and heated
debates have centered on the type of training that qualifies persons best for
helping professions.

The most widely accepted criteria of professional level competence are
doctoral degrees with specialties in clinical psychology or counseling psychology, medical degrees with residency training in psychiatry, or advanced
degrees in social work. However, there has been a growing recognition that
the management of behavior change programs is not the province of any
single discipline, nor is it necessary to expect every practitioner to be able
to function in all areas within the given discipline. In fact, as treatment
methods for psychological problems have moved away from their earlier
foundations in religious, philosophical, or biological concepts of man, to
encompass psychological, social, economic, and political components as
well, there has been a parallel development that has facilitated the delivery
of effective behavior change programs by persons with much shorter and
less complex formal training than the mastery of 4 to 6 years of postgradu-
ate training that is required of psychologists or psychiatrists. As noted
earlier, such persons can and do make significant contributions to helping
people change. In part, this change in requirements is a result of the divi-

sion of labor now possible because of clearer specification of the ways in which behavior change techniques can be applied. Traditional psychotherapeutic techniques were based primarily on complex and abstract personality theories, and the interpersonal relationship between helper and client was considered to be the primary instrument of change. As a result, it was necessary to train a person first, in depth, in the theories and assumptions of the therapy system. The development of treatment skills was a slow process, mainly by apprenticeship and close individual supervision. In many disciplines, for example, psychoanalysis, the training period might extend until the trainee was in his or her 40s. With the realization that many components of a behavior change program can be learned rather quickly and that complete mastery of the entire field is not essential for participating in some stages of the total program, there has been the increased effort noted earlier to train persons with limited knowledge of change methods (paraprofessionals) to work under the direction of more extensively trained persons.

In a survey of leading writers in the field of behavior modification, Sulzer-Azaroff, Thaw, and Olsen (1974) asked respondents to indicate the type of competency expected of four levels of helpers: behavior analyst, behavior technology coordinator, behavior technologist engineer, and behavior cotechnician. The expectations were quite consistent for the highest level (behavior analyst), who was seen as a person who develops programs, research, and new methods. The lowest level (behavior cotechnician) was not expected to have very specific competencies; most of his or her skills could be obtained in on-the-job training or in relatively few college courses. The behavior technology coordinator was described generally as a skilled person, at the predoctoral level, who could conduct helping programs in schools, institutions, and other facilities, but who was not expected to assume research and administrative roles. The survey clearly showed that persons at different training and skill levels can collaborate successfully in the helping effort.

Supervisors must have skills in evaluating the nature and scope of a person's problems. They must understand the social, biological, and economic context of the problem. They must be skilled in making decisions that would permit them to select among available helping techniques in order to construct a therapeutic program. They must know the methods by which progress in a program can be monitored and under what conditions the helping program can be changed. Finally, they must know the limitations of both their own skills and those of their helpers, and they must have knowledge of resources that can be called upon when the problem falls beyond the limits of their own competence or the resources of their agencies. In this sense, a pyramid operation can be developed with a supervisor or consultant whose role is greatest at the beginning of treatment, who can monitor progress of treatment, and who can offer to the paraprofessional any supervision and advice needed. This concept, developing a team of helpers varying in skill and competence, is also useful because it permits the delivery of psychological services to large numbers of people who previously could not have afforded expensive individual psychotherapy. Thus, qualifications for offering psychological help differ for different levels of helpers. Although it is possible for a person to carry out a well-planned and structured change program under supervision after only a few weeks of training, the total management of a client requires consultation or supervision by a person with thorough familiarity with psychological principles and clinical methods and an awareness of the limitations of his or her own and others' skills. But paraprofessionals with limited training can also make substantial contributions to successful treatment. Durlak (1979) reviewed 42 studies comparing the effectiveness of professional and paraprofessional helpers. He found that paraprofessionals, working in narrowly defined clinical roles with specific client populations, were generally as effective as professional helpers. Their strongest effectiveness was noted in studies in which intervention was directed at such specific target responses as unassertiveness, speech anxiety, and enuresis.

A totally different qualification for a helper concerns personal characteristics. As already indicated, and as discussed in detail in a following section on ethics, it is essential that the helper be motivated primarily by the goal of helping the client rather than furthering his or her own interest. In addition, the helper must be able to discern cues about the impact of his or her own behavior on the client. Which other particular helper characteristics are desirable has been the subject of research and theory for many years. They seem to include, at minimum, helper empathy, warmth, honesty, and expertness. These and other apparently desirable helper characteristics are examined in depth in chapter 2.

Although the helping methods described in the following chapters have been tested and validated to some extent, it cannot be stressed too often that the methods themselves do not guarantee success. It is both skillful *application* (i.e., the judgment of when to apply what methods to which clients) and knowledge about when to *change* a technique or an objective that are essential for successful helping programs. Most of the techniques described in the following chapters are not tied to specific client problems. Thus, they can be used in ameliorating a wide variety of personal, social, sexual, or other problems. When skillfully applied, they are likely to bring about beneficial changes in the client's behavior. But mere acquaintance with a catalog of available therapeutic techniques is insufficient preparation for competent psychological helping.

The problems and dangers of use of psychological helping techniques by persons without proper qualifications are legion. For example, operant techniques applied to continuing physical complaints could reduce the frequency of the complaints. However, such a change could also mask the inroads of a serious medical illness. Increasing assertiveness or feelings of independence in one marriage partner could indeed change the partner's behavior. However, without a thorough assessment and appreciation of the interpersonal context of the problem, an unskilled therapist could also find himself or herself contributing to increasing problems between marriage partners, and perhaps divorce or abandonment by a partner. Treatment for homosexual behavior, even though the client wishes to change his or her sexual orientation, might fail simply because the client might not have a sufficiently strong repertoire of heterosexual behaviors to explore new sexual directions or to achieve sufficient success in sexual and nonsexual activities that can take the place of his or her previous pleasurable experiences. The helper, therefore, must have full awareness of the range of factors that go into designing a treatment program, be aware of his or her own limitations, and work closely with others who can provide the necessary guidance. Premature, clumsy, or ignorant application of behavior change techniques is wasteful and inefficient at best, and harmful at worst.

Summarizing our discussion on the necessary qualifications of the helper, it should be clear that paraprofessionals, students, human service aides, mental health technicians, attendants, nurses, and many other persons without prolonged professional training in psychological services can make major contributions to helping people change. In fact, they are often the persons who can put a conceptual program into actual operation best. In many settings, a paraprofessional worker spends more time with a client than any professional and has, by far, more influence in his or her extensive contact with the client than a senior professional might have in the short time of a diagnostic or therapeutic interview. However, execution and not design is the task of the paraprofessional. Continuous self-monitoring and feedback to a consultant or supervisor are necessary to maintain the efficiency of the program and to protect the client.

WHAT IS A PSYCHOLOGICAL PROBLEM?

Psychological problems, in general terms, are difficulties in a person's relations with others, in his or her perception of the world about him or her, or in his or her attitudes toward himself or herself. Psychological problems can be characterized by a person's feelings of anxiety or tension, dissatisfaction with his or her own behavior, excessive attention to the problem area, inefficiency in reaching desired goals, or inability to function effectively in psychological areas. Psychological problems can at times also be characterized by a situation in which the client has no complaint but others in his or her social environment are adversely affected by his or her behavior or judge him or her to be ineffective, destructive, unhappy, disruptive, or in some other way acting contrary to the best self-interest or the best interest of the social community in which he or she lives. Thus the major characteristics of a psychological problem are in evidence when (a) the client suffers subjective discomfort, worry, or fears that are not easily removable by some action that he or she can perform without assistance; (b) the client shows a behavioral deficiency or excessively engages in some behavior that interferes with functioning described as adequate either by himself or herself or by others; (c) the client engages in activities that are objectionable to those around and that lead to negative consequences either for himself or herself or for others; and (d) the client shows behavioral deviations that result in severe social sanctions by those in the immediate environment.

Psychological problems sometimes are related to problems in other areas. For example, an automobile accident can cause physical disability that in turn leads to psychological difficulties. A person who has lost a job, a marital partner, or life savings might temporarily face psychological difficulties. Sociopolitical climates such as discriminatory practices against a minority member, economic problems, sexual, moral, or religious demands by the environment that are inconsistent with the person's past history, all can cause psychological problems. Very frequently, transient psychological problems can be resolved not by psychological helpers but by resolution of the "source" problem. For example, concern about a medical disability or serious illness is better treated, if treatable, by medical care than by psychological help. Unhappiness over loss of a job is more easily remedied by finding a new job than by resolving psychological problems about the loss. It is incumbent upon the psychological helper, therefore, to analyze the total problem to determine if dealing successfully with at least some aspects of it can be more effectively carried out by someone who is not a psychological helper, whereas those components that comprise the person's attitudes, behaviors, or interactions remain the proper domain for mental health helpers.

THE GOALS AND OBJECTIVES OF HELPING RELATIONSHIPS

A good treatment program is built with a clear conception of treatment goals, developed jointly by the helper and the client. It is possible to differentiate among five long-term treatment objectives: (a) change of a particular problem behavior, such as poor interpersonal skills; (b) insight or a clear rational and emotional understanding of one's problems; (c) change in one's subjective emotional comfort, including changes in anxiety or tension; (d) change in one's self-perceptions, including goals, self-confidence, and sense of adequacy; and (e) change in one's life-style, or "personality restructuring," an objective aimed at a sweeping change in the client's way of living. The selection of any one of these goals does not eliminate the secondary achievement of other objectives. For example, although many of the techniques described in this book are oriented toward change of particular behaviors, such changes often bring with them changes in the person's insights into his or her own actions, modification of attitudes toward himself or herself, and in some cases, a rather sweeping alteration of the person's total life-style. At the same time, therapists who aim for improved insight and major personality changes in their clients might also achieve, during the helping process, change in social behaviors or self-reactions. Thus, treatment objectives are not mutually exclusive, and the listing above is simply intended to indicate that primary emphasis can be given to a particular goal without sacrificing the achievement of others as by-products or secondary outcomes of the change process.

Behavior Change

If the goal of a helping effort is to change a particular behavior, a thorough evaluation of the person's life circumstances is required in order to be sure not only that the target behavior is amenable to change, but also that such a change will lead to a significant improvement in the person's total life situation. A more detailed description of the steps necessary prior to beginning the change program is given below in our discussion of the diagnostic process.

Insight

Insight as a goal has been most characteristic of psychoanalysis and its variations. These helping methods are not covered in the present volume, first because the assumptions underlying psychoanalytic therapy are extensive, and thorough training of therapists in psychoanalytic methods, including personal analysis and long supervision of cases, is usually required. Second, the therapeutic benefits of psychoanalytic and other insight-seeking methods are currently not well-substantiated by empirical research and laboratory findings. They are excessively time consuming and, in our view, rarely represent the treatment of choice. The arguments in the psychological and psychiatric literature concerning the utility of insight versus behavior change, however, have sometimes been overstated. When a motivated client establishes a relationship between current behavior problems and past history, whether or not such a relationship is in fact accurate, the satisfaction of having achieved an explanation for his or her own behavior and the new labels he or she can then attach to emotional experiences can serve as a beginning for change in actual daily behaviors.

Emotional Relief

The reduction of anxiety has long been considered the most critical problem in the management of neurotic disorders.[1] In general, when anxiety reduction or relief of chronic emotional tension is the primary objective of a helping effort, it is assumed that the client will later be able to conduct himself or herself more effectively because (a) he or she already has a repertoire of skills necessary to deal with life situations and (b) his or her use of these skills was previously inhibited by anxiety. If this is not the case (i.e., if the problem involves not only inhibition due to anxiety, but also incompetence due to skill deficiency), changes in particular skill behaviors might be set up as the next goal in the change program. If the problem is both partly emotional and partly related to particular behavior deficiencies, then both the reduction of emotional tension and behavioral skill training could be dual treatment objectives.

Change in the Client's Self-Perception

Techniques for changing a person's self-perceptions and evaluations of his or her own behavior are found in several chapters in this volume. In general, the application of such procedures assumes that a person's improved self-image is sufficient to help him or her perform the constructive behaviors of which he or she is capable. For example, once a person sees himself or herself as competent or perceives herself or himself more realistically in relation to others, she or he might be able to plan and act with greater self-confidence, a greater sense of direction, and greater social effectiveness.

Life-Style Changes

The most ambitious objective for a change program is the attempt to alter the person's total pattern of living. Frequently, this requires not only a change in the client's behavior, but also plans for changing the environment in which he or she lives, his or her circle of friends, his or her place of employment, and so forth. One example might be the client who is a drug addict and whose entire daily routine is subordinated to the procurement of an illegal narcotic. But every change process results in some changes of the person's daily life pattern, if it is at all successful. In some instances, the clarification of the life-style to which the person aspires can itself be a

---

[1]The techniques for reduction of anxiety are described in chapter 5 of this volume.

preparatory part of the change process. In other cases the main objective of treatment is the development of goals in a person who feels "alienated" or complains of a lack of direction and purpose. Thus, all change programs include consideration of the extent to which treatment success would alter the client's life. However, the extent to which these considerations are focal varies from minimal, as in correcting a study habit problem, to maximal, as in treating drug addiction or agoraphobia.

A PRESCRIPTIVE CAUTION

In the early years of psychotherapy research, investigators concerned with its effectiveness typically framed their research questions in global outcome terms, for instance, Does treatment A work? or Is treatment A superior to treatment B? Such questions could be answered affirmatively only in those exceptional instances in which the treatment(s) studied were sufficiently powerful to override the high degree of between-patient, within-conditions heterogeneity. Even then, the generality of such questions often provided little information either about how to improve the effectiveness of the treatment (because the treatment as a whole had been studied, with little or no concern for its separate components) or about how to use the outcome information to help any *individual* patient (because only between-group effects were examined). In attempts to alleviate these weaknesses and to broaden the criteria for assessing treatment effectiveness, researchers now use statistical methods and evaluation procedures that permit examination of the *process* of change in individuals (Barlow, Hayes, & Nelson, 1984) and meta-analyses that evaluate the magnitude of treatment effects across many studies (Glass, McGraw, & Smith, 1981). Analysis of cost-effectiveness is also included in developing guidelines for mental health policies (Kiesler, 1980, 1982). But innovations in statistical techniques still leave unanswered the critical question about what specific mechanisms of change are embedded in various therapies and how their effectiveness is related to specific patient categories and problems (Parloff, 1984).

Investigators now seek to discern which type of patient, meeting with which type of therapist, using which type of treatment, will yield what outcome? This is a prescriptive view of psychotherapy. It holds that most treatments cannot be classified as "good" or "bad" in any comprehensive sense. Instead, this view holds that different treatments and therapists are appropriate for some patients but not for others. This prescriptive view of the therapy enterprise looks toward identifying optimal patient × therapist × treatment matches in designing treatment plans. In both research and practice, a conscious and consistent effort is made to avoid the patient, therapist, or treatment uniformity myths against which Kiesler (1966) has warned.

The implications of this viewpoint for the use of the present book are both clear and major. In each of the following chapters many behavior change procedures are described and explicitly or implicitly recommended for clinical use. Our prescriptive view cautions us that, although each procedure rests, at least to some extent, on supportive empirical research, almost none should be expected to lead to behavior change in all patients, or for all problems of one patient, or at all stages of the treatment process. In the next chapter, for example, the nature and value of therapist empathy is examined. The position taken is that patient perception of therapist-offered empathy is a significant influence upon certain aspects of a positive therapeutic relationship and eventual patient change. Yet we must not assume this to be the case for all patients or at all times. We agree with Mitchell, Bozarth and Krauft (1977) who commented

> . . . empathy, warmth, and genuineness might be used differentially depending on client diagnosis. Clinical wisdom suggests that high levels of empathy might overwhelm a schizophrenic client early in therapy and that, instead, empathy might best be increased slowly over time within the context of uniformly high levels of warmth. On the other hand, with a neurotic, initially high levels of warmth might best be lowered somewhat in the middle phase of therapy in order to heighten negative aspects of the "transference" and increase anxiety sufficiently so it becomes an excellent stimulus for change. (p. 490)

We and others have developed this prescriptive view of psychotherapy in detail elsewhere (Goldstein, 1978; Goldstein & Stein, 1976) for those interested in pursuing its implications further. For our present purpose, its import is to caution the helper that optimal utilization of a technique requires consideration of the joint characteristics of patient, therapist and technique.

DESIGNING A CHANGE PROGRAM

This volume is not intended to provide the helper with in-depth knowledge about diagnostic methods for analyzing the client's problem and designing a treatment program on the basis of this assessment. Nevertheless, the reader should be aware of the importance of an early analysis of the problem as the absolutely essential foundation for the application of any treatment technique. At this time there are few widely accepted principles that can guide a helper through the evaluation and assessment process. There are many books and articles that summarize available psychological tests; some also discuss the most critical features of the person's life situation that should be examined before a decision is made concerning an objective and its associated treatment technique (e.g., Goldfried & Pomeranz, 1968; Gottman & Leiblum, 1974; Kanfer & Grimm, 1977; Kanfer & Saslow, 1969; Lanyon & Goodstein, 1971; Sundberg, 1977). As a minimum requirement for deciding upon the choice of helping methods, the helper must make a thorough analysis of the context in which the problem behavior occurs, the form and severity of the problem behavior, the consequences both to the client and to his or her environment of the problem behavior, the resources of the client and of his or her environment for the promotion of change, and the effects which a change in behavior would have on the client and others. These and other factors comprise the content of what has been called a *functional analysis* of the problem situation. The information necessary to complete such an analysis may come from interviews, from observations, from knowledge of the client's past history, from reports of other persons who know the client, or from any other source that yields reliable information. In some cases, especially when the problem behavior has some physiological components, information about the medical status and physical health of the client is absolutely necessary.

A good functional analysis reveals factors that have contributed to the problem behavior and those that currently maintain it. It also gives some information about what particular stresses and demands are placed upon the client by the environment in which he or she lives. For example, for a complete assessment it is not sufficient to know what a person does and what effects his or her actions have. It is also necessary to have an understanding of what requirements are placed upon him or her by his or her immediate circle of friends, job situation, community, and persons who are important in his or her life. Further, a good functional analysis also yields a list of problematic behaviors that might require attention and information that would assist the helper to set priorities so that he or she can better decide which particular problem(s) to attack. Which items are placed high on the priority list would depend on the individual's life circumstances and initial responses to the change program. For example, any behavior that is self-destructive or has serious social consequences would be the most central initial target. However, in some cases, several problems might have equal priority. In this instance, a decision might rest on which of these problem behaviors are more amenable to solution by the available techniques. The client's conviction that he or she can change and the degree of support from other persons in his or her environment to assist in the change program must also be taken into account.

Another important aspect of the assessment procedure lies in the establishment of some methods and criteria for assessing the client's progress throughout the program. For example, the operant behavior change methods described in chapter 4 are usually applied in conjunction with quantitative records of the frequency, intensity, or duration of the behavior being changed before, during, and after the change program. With other techniques, the evaluation component is not so readily built into the treatment program. For example, relationship methods, group techniques, and attitude change methods often aim to alter more complex behavior patterns and typically do not incorporate a quantitative measurement or monitoring process into the treatment. Nevertheless, the helper should have some record of the patient's problem behaviors, complaints, and expectations prior to the onset of any change program. It is only with such documentation that helper and client can decide whether the change program has been effective, and further decisions about shifting to other objectives or terminating the relationship can be made (Kanfer & Busemeyer, 1982). The evaluation component of the treatment program is of importance not only for assisting the helper and the client in making decisions about progress and termination. It also serves as an incentive for both client and helper by giving them some objective evidence of the progress that has been achieved, and it enables the helper to specify more clearly the areas in which the program may have failed and the reasons for this failure.

ETHICAL CONSIDERATIONS

A helper makes a number of demands on her or his clients, expecting them to be frank in discussing their problems, to be involved in the change program, and to commit themselves to certain requirements of the program such as keeping appointments, paying bills, and carrying out contracted exercises or activities. Because of the very nature of the helping relationship, it is quite obvious that the client's interests must be protected to avoid damage or grief resulting from a helper's ignorance, unscrupulousness, self-serving manipulation of the client, or exploitation of the client's vulnerability.

The use of the helping techniques described in this book should be restricted to situations in which a person *seeks* help from others in a formal way. Thus, the change techniques should not be applied in informal settings in which a person is unaware of the fact that attempts are being made to change his or her behavior; they should not be applied casually in personal relationships with friends or family members; they should not be applied when a client denies the existence of a problem even though it has been pointed out by others. In the latter case, more complex treatment programs would have to be used, even though the change techniques presented here could ultimately comprise part of the total treatment package.

In our discussion of professional qualifications, we pointed to the importance of the helper's training and background for the protection of the client. In this section we will look at a series of ethical considerations that a helper must abide by if he or she is to be helpful to the client and to be accepted by the community in which he or she practices. On some of the matters that follow, there is debate concerning the breadth of action open to the helper. Therefore, the following items range in importance from those for which a breach of ethics can lead to expulsion from professional societies to those items that are primarily a matter of individual conscience.

Exploitation by the Helper

There is no disagreement concerning the absolute requirement that the helper must not utilize the relationship in order to gain social, sexual, or other personal advantage. The self-serving functions of a helper, however, can extend from the slight extension of a treatment program beyond its absolutely necessary duration, in order to provide a helper with financial resources, to the flagrant financial, moral, or sexual exploitation of a client. The helper has access to confidential information that could embarrass or hurt the client. Even subtle pressure implying the use of such information for self-serving purposes is equivalent to blackmail and is clearly unethical.

Deception

The purposes and goals of the interaction should be clear to the client or her or his guardian. The client or guardian should be informed of any hazards or potential aversive consequences that are involved in a treatment procedure, and no exaggerated promises should be made about the likelihood of successful treatment outcome. It is improper to discuss the achievements or objectives of a change program with a third party, be it a marital partner, a parent, or an employer, without communicating such intentions to the client. Similarly, advice and guidance that would force the client into a situation over which she or he has no control would constitute unethical behavior. Advice to engage in illegal behaviors or suggestions of actions that would expose the client to hazards or predictable untoward consequences are examples of deceptive helper maneuvers.

Competence and Appropriate Treatment

It is the responsibility of the helper not only to offer the highest level of service, but also to be aware of his or her own limitations so that he or she can refer the client to someone else when necessary. In addition to referrals to others in the mental health field, it is also the helper's responsibility to be certain that problems outside the area of psychological treatment be properly referred. For example, referral to a physician for medical difficulties, to an attorney for legal problems, or to a social service agency for economic assistance should be made when these problems are evident or likely. Because the helper sometimes is not fully aware of the limitations in his or her own training, it is advisable for a helper to have some professional affiliation that will enable him or her to obtain assistance from colleagues regarding difficult cases. Persons who have paraprofessional training should discuss such problems with their supervisors, under whose direction the change program is conducted.

Principle of Least Intervention

Although it is obvious that almost any person might benefit from psychological counseling or a helping relationship, it is essentially the task of the helper to intervene in the client's everyday life only to the extent that the client desires a change. Once the jointly agreed upon objective is reached, the helper should either terminate the relationship or discuss in detail with the client the possibility of future change programs. Only if the client agrees to additional programs should they be undertaken. A prior problem concerns the question of whether any treatment should take place at all. In some instances, clients seek assistance for problems that actually turn out to be common difficulties in everyday life. In such cases, for example, when a client is experiencing a grief reaction after the death of a close relative, information and reassurance could be sufficient. Similarly, parents might refer a child for assistance when, in fact, the child's behavior is not unusual for his or her age group. In such instances, behavior change programs would not be undertaken, and it could be possible to terminate the interaction when reassurance and information are given to the client.

Some techniques of behavior change, especially those that rest heavily on the alteration of the client's social environment (discussed in chapter 4), could involve the participation of other persons in channeling the client's behavior in a desired direction through the use of rewards and punishments. Programs in institutions such as hospitals, schools, or prisons might involve deprivation of certain privileges in order that they could be used later as rewards for appropriate behaviors. There is intense dispute concerning the appropriateness of such techniques because of their nonvolitional and manipulative aspects. As a result, special caution must be exercised to assure that the client's civil rights are not infringed upon and that the client can make the kinds of choices about participating in a program that would normally be considered reasonable in the institutional setting in which they are introduced. The utilization of aversive stimuli is considered unethical when permission by the client or his or her guardian is not obtained. Other ethical problems associated with this method are discussed in detail in chapter 6.

In general, the helper needs to assure himself or herself continuously that she or he is maintaining the dignity of the client and guarding the confidentiality of information obtained in the helping relationship and that the therapeutic program does not have detrimental effects on either the client or others. It is the helper's responsibility to protect the client's rights and interests so that the change program clearly contributes to the client's welfare, rather than creates new problems and conflicts for her or him.

WHAT IS CONTAINED IN THE FOLLOWING CHAPTERS?

The chapters in this book provide detailed descriptions of different behavior change techniques by professionals who are expert in their respective fields. The techniques are generally appropriate for treatment of persons who show no gross social disorganization or such serious disturbances in their social or personal behavior that they require institutionalization. The techniques are, therefore, most applicable to persons who have difficulties in some areas of their lives but who can function at least marginally well in other areas. The techniques presented here are by no means exhaustive of the field of behavior change. They do constitute the most important methods that have been applied in the treatment of psychological problems. In selecting treatment approaches and techniques, we have chosen only those that are based on psychological theory that is widely accepted and that have as their foundation at least some laboratory research and evidence of effectiveness in application. Many of the methods mentioned here are quite new or still in the exploratory stage. However, we have eliminated from presentation a large number of methods now practiced that are based only on the belief of the practitioner that they are effective but that have no other empirical evidence or theoretical rationale behind them. Anecdotal observation or limited clinical experience that has not been substantiated by research or field studies is insufficient grounds for use of a method. We have eliminated techniques that clients have reported have made them feel better, unless some independent evidence of change is also available. All of the methods that are discussed in the following chapters have been described at considerable length in the professional literature. The reader will find references at the end of each chapter that will guide him or her to additional reading in order to strengthen his or her knowledge of each technique and, consistent with the ultimate goal of this book, more fully aid the helper in helping people change.

REFERENCES

Barlow, D. H., Hayes, S. C., & Nelson, R. O. (1984). *The scientist-practitioner.* Elmsford, NY: Pergamon Press.
Durlak, J. A. (1979). Comparative effectiveness of paraprofessional and professional helpers. *Psychological Bulletin, 86*, 80–92.
Glass, G. V., McGraw, B., & Smith, M. (1981). *Meta-analysis in social research.* Beverly Hills, CA: Sage.

Goldfried, M. R., & Pomeranz, D. M. (1968). The role of assessment in behavior therapy. *Psychological Reports, 23*, 75–87.

Goldstein, A. P. (Ed.). (1978). *Prescriptions for child mental health and education.* Elmsford, NY: Pergamon Press.

Goldstein, A. P., & Stein, N. (1976). *Prescriptive psychotherapies.* Elmsford, NY: Pergamon Press.

Gottman, J. M., & Leiblum, S. R. (1974). *How to do psychotherapy and how to evaluate it: A manual for beginners.* New York: Holt, Rinehart, & Winston.

Kanfer, F. H., & Busemeyer, J. P. (1982). The use of problem-solving and decision-making in behavioral therapy. *Clinical Psychology Review, 2*, 239–266.

Kanfer, F. H., & Grimm, L. (1977). Behavioral analysis: Selecting target behaviors in the interview. *Behavior Modification, 1*, 7–28.

Kanfer, F. H., & Saslow, G. (1969). Behavioral diagnosis. In C. Franks (Ed.), *Behavior therapy: Appraisal and status.* New York: McGraw-Hill.

Kiesler, C. A. (1980). Mental health policy as a field of inquiry for psychology. *American Psychologist, 35*, 1066–1080.

Kiesler, C. A. (1982). Public and professional myths about mental hospitalization. *American Psychologist, 37*, 1323–1339.

Kiesler, D. J. (1966). Some myths of psychotherapy research and the search for a paradigm. *Psychological Bulletin, 65*, 110–136.

Lanyon, R. I., & Goodstein, L. D. (1971). *Personality assessment.* New York: John Wiley.

Mitchell, K. M., Bozarth, J. C., & Krauft, C. C. (1977). A reappraisal of the therapeutic effectiveness of accurate empathy, nonpossessive warmth, and genuineness. In A. S. Gurman and A. M. Razin (Eds.), *Effective psychotherapy: A handbook of research.* Elmsford, NY: Pergamon Press.

Parloff, M. B. (1984). Psychotherapy research and its incredible credibility crisis. *Clinical Psychology Review, 4*, 95–109.

Sulzer-Azaroff, B., Thaw, J., & Olsen, C. (1974). Behavioral competencies for the evaluation of behavior modifiers. Unpublished mimeo, University of Massachusetts, Mansfield Training School.

Sundberg, N. D. (1974). *Assessment of persons.* Englewood Cliffs, NJ: Prentice-Hall.

2

Relationship-Enhancement Methods

Arnold P. Goldstein and Charles R. Myers

Barbara Harris is a 34-year-old woman, a wife, the mother of two children, a part-time office receptionist and, every Tuesday at 10:00 a.m., a psychotherapy patient. Over the course of the past few years, Barbara developed a number of concerns that more and more were interfering with her comfort and happiness. Backaches and a series of vague physical symptoms that seemed hard to cure were the apparent beginning of her change from a relatively problem-free and fully functioning person. Conflicts with her husband began around this time — about money, about sex, and about raising their children. Barbara's physical discomfort, her irritability, and her difficulty in getting along with people all increased as time passed. Eventually, these concerns and behaviors became so troublesome to Barbara and those around her that she contacted a psychotherapist recommended by her physician. She has been meeting with him for about a year now, and both feel she has made substantial progress in dealing effectively with her problems. Her physical complaints have decreased markedly, her relations with others are considerably more satisfying and, in general, Barbara seems well on her way to joining the two-thirds of all psychotherapy patients who apparently benefit from treatment.

In the same city in which Barbara lives there are four other women who have gone through similar difficulties and similar recovery from these difficulties. Yet none of them has ever met with a psychotherapist. What did they do? Pressed by the stress each was experiencing, each sought out a "good listener" or a "friendly problem solver" with whom she felt she could share her burdens. For one, it was a friend; for the second, her minister; for the third, her family physician; and for the last, a "paraprofessional" helper called a "home aide." All five women changed for the better, apparently in large part because of whatever occurred between each and her helper. Barbara's recovery might or might not have been somewhat more complete, or somewhat more rapid, but, for our present purposes, the significant fact is that all the women improved.

These mini-case histories are fictitious, but the facts they portray are all established. Many people do find problem relief, personal growth, and self-understanding as a result of participating in some form of psychotherapy. But many people obtain similar benefits as a result of their interactions with a wide variety of other types of helpers—friends, clergy, bartenders, relatives, counselors, nurses, and so forth. These facts have long intrigued researchers interested in what it is that causes people to change their behavior, emotions, and attitudes. Perhaps, many of these researchers have proposed, some of the causes of such changes can be identified by determining what ingredients successful psychotherapy and successful help from others have in common. If certain procedures, circumstances, or events are clearly characteristic of successful helping of different kinds, then we have the opportunity to use them most effectively in helping others.

Dr. Jerome Frank, in his important book, *Persuasion and Healing* (1961), has made a similar point. He compared psychotherapy, "informal" psychotherapy (from a friend, clergy person, etc.), faith healing, religious revivalism, placebo effects in medical practice, and a host of other activities in which two people, a helper and a client, collaborate to bring about some sort of psychological change in the client. According to Frank, perhaps the major responsible ingredient in determining whether such change occurs is the quality of the helper-client relationship. The same conclusion emerges if one examines descriptions of almost all of the many different approaches to formal psychotherapy. These several approaches vary in many respects—therapist activity and directiveness, how much this focus is upon behavior versus the patient's inner world of feelings and attitudes, whether emphasis is placed upon the patient's present life or childhood history, which aspects of his or her current difficulties are examined, and in a host of procedural ways. Yet, almost every approach to psychotherapy emphasizes the importance of the therapist-patient relationship for patient change. The better the relationship (a) the more open is the patient about this feeling, (b) the more likely he or she is to explore these feelings deeply with the helper, and (c) the more likely he or she is to listen fully to and act upon advice offered by the helper; that is, the more likely the patient is to change.

This remarkably consistent viewpoint, in the psychotherapies and in other approaches to psychological change, has also found consistent support in other fields. How well a variety of medications serve their intended purpose has been shown to be partly a result of the relationship between the drug giver and the drug receiver. Learning in school has been demonstrated to depend in part on the teacher-pupil relationship. The subject's behavior in the experimental laboratory can also be readily influenced by the experimenter-subject relationship. In brief, there now exists a wide variety of research evidence, from several different types of two-person interactions, to indicate that the quality of the helper-client relationship can serve as a powerful positive influence upon communication, openness, persuasibility and, ultimately, positive change in the client. This evidence is also useful in providing information that helps define the term *relationship*. Our definition, it will be noted, emphasizes positive feelings and interpersonal attitudes reciprocally held by the helper and the client: a positive or "therapeutic" relationship can be defined as feelings of liking, respect, and trust by a client toward the helper from whom she or he is seeking assistance, combined with similar feelings of liking, respect, and trust on the part of the helper toward the client.

A number of methods have been identified as ways of making the helper-client relationship a more positive one. Each of these relationship-enhancement methods has been the subject of considerable research. Each has both added to our understanding of what the relationship is and helped explain the usefulness of the relationship for helping people change. These several methods, therefore, form the framework for the remainder of this chapter. We will, in turn, consider several concrete examples of each method, focusing upon how the relationship can be enhanced or improved to the benefit of client change. Figure 2.1 provides an overview of our viewpoint.

The relationship enhancers listed below are the major means currently available for improving the quality of the helper-client interaction. This interaction or relationship can be defined in terms of the three components indicated: liking, respect, and trust. Successful enhancement of these components, in turn, has been shown to lead to greater influenceability and,

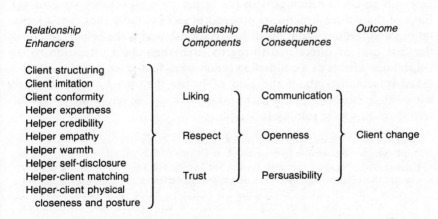

FIGURE 2.1. Progression from Relationship Enhancement to Client Change

subsequently, to greater client change. It should be noted that most psychotherapists and psychotherapy researchers view a positive relationship between helper and client as necessary, but not sufficient, for client change. Without such a relationship, change is very unlikely. With it, the foundation exists for other more specific change procedures (such as those described in subsequent chapters) to yield their intended effects.

ATTRACTION

Laboratory research has developed several procedures for successfully increasing attraction of the experiment's subjects to their experimenter. The present writer (Goldstein, 1971) has shown that many of these attraction-increasing procedures are highly effective in enhancing the helper-client relationship, especially the client's liking of the helper. Three such procedures: structuring, imitation, and conformity pressure are presented below.

Structuring

It is perhaps fitting, in this book in which several dozen procedures for helping people change will be described, that the first procedure to be illustrated is probably one of the least complex. Structuring a client so that he or she will like or be attracted to his or her helper is, quite simply, a matter of (a) telling him or her that he or she will like the helper ("direct" structuring), (b) briefly describing certain positive characteristics of the helper ("trait" structuring), or (c) clarifying what he or she can realistically anticipate will go on in meetings with the helper (role expectancy structuring). Each of these three structuring procedures seeks to mold the client's expectations and feelings about his or her relationship with the helper. In one of the first uses of direct structuring to strengthen client attraction to the helper, new clients at a counseling center were first given certain tests that asked information about the kind of helper they would prefer to meet with — his or her behavior, expectations, goals, and so on. Shortly after this testing, clients were told by the tester

> We have carefully examined the tests you took in order to assign you to a therapist whom you would like to work with most. We usually can't match a patient and therapist the way they want most, but for you we have almost exactly the kind of therapist you described. (The tester then showed the client how well his test results describing his preferred helper apparently matched other information purportedly indicating the actual behavior, expectations and goals of the helper with whom he would be meeting.) As a matter of fact, the matching of the kind of person you wanted to work with and the kind of

person Mr. _____ is, is so close that it hardly ever happens. What's even more, he has often described the kind of patient he likes to work with most as someone just like you in many respects. You two should get along extremely well. (Goldstein, 1971, p. 21)

It should be noted that no actual matching of client preferences with helper characteristics was done here. Clients participated in the structuring procedure we have just described, and then each was assigned to a therapist whose turn it was for a new patient. Nevertheless, such structuring led clients to actually show increased liking of their helpers and increased openness about their problems. Thus, clients' belief that helpers would be the kinds of people they would like was enough to influence their actual attraction toward them.

The enhancing effect on both attraction and openness has been shown to be even stronger when trait structuring of the client is conducted. These are instances in which specific, important qualities of the helper are described to the client before they actually meet. Once again, the effect of these procedures on the actual attraction that develops is quite strong, even though the helper characteristics described might in fact not be present. Which particular helper characteristics are selected to be described to the client is an important matter. In most uses of trait structuring, the two helper traits chosen have been "warmth" and "experience" — the first of which tells the client something important about how comfortable she or he is likely to feel during the helping process, the second of which gives her or him information about the likely positive outcome of this process. Both items of information, therefore, enhance client attraction to the helper. The statement that follows is an example of trait structuring of helper warmth and experience:

> The therapist has been engaged in the practice of therapy for over 20 years and has lectured and taught at some of the country's leading universities and medical schools. Questionnaires submitted to the therapist's colleagues seem to reveal that he is a rather warm person, industrious, critical, practical and determined. (Goldstein, 1971, p. 50)

Trait structuring has also been used successfully "in reverse" to increase helper attraction toward the client. With this, qualities of the client are emphasized that lead the helper to anticipate that the client will be "a good patient." The type of problem the client supposedly has, the diagnosis, and his or her motivation to work hard to improve are some examples of positively structured traits of the client that have been communicated to the helper.

A great deal of psychological research has been conducted on the effects of leading a person to believe she or he is similar to a stranger in important attitudes, background, or values and on her or his liking that person when they meet. This research convincingly shows that the greater the structured similarity, the greater the attraction to the other person. This positive effect of structured similarity on attraction has also been found to operate in the helper-client relationship. It is largely for this reason that great use has been made in recent years of certain types of "paraprofessional" helpers, that is, persons who are lacking in certain formal training or degrees but who possess beliefs, personal backgrounds, and life-styles quite similar to those of the persons they are seeking to help. These similarities between paraprofessional helpers and the people they serve, like *structured similarity*, enhance the quality of the therapeutic relationship.

We have seen thus far that direct structuring and trait structuring for warmth, experience, and similarity can each have attraction-increasing effects. So, too, can the final type of structuring we wish to present — role expectancy structuring. Whereas direct and trait structuring mostly concern telling the client something about the kind of person the helper *is*, role expectancy structuring focuses on what the helper (and what the client) actually will *do* when they meet. If, because of misinformation or lack of information about what to expect, the client later experiences events during these meetings with the helper that surprise or confuse him or her, negative feelings will result. Events that confirm his or her expectancies serve to increase his or her attraction to the helper. For example, many new psychotherapy patients come to therapy with expectations based primarily on their past experiences in what they judge to be similar relationships, such as what happens when they meet with their medical doctors. During those visits, the patient typically presented a physical problem briefly, was asked a series of questions by the physician, and was then authoritatively told what to do. Now, however, when the client with such "medical expectations" starts psychotherapy, he or she is in for some surprises. The client describes a psychological problem and sits back awaiting the helper's questions and eventual advice. The helper, unlike the general physician, wants the client to explore his or her feelings, to examine his or her history, to speculate about the causes of the problem. These are not the client's role expectations, and when such important expectations differ, the relationship clearly suffers. These are but a few of the several ways in which client and helper can differ in their anticipations of how each will behave. Prior structuring of such expectations has been shown to be an important contributor to increased attraction and a more lasting and fruitful helper-client relationship. This structuring can be provided by having new clients listen to a tape recording of a typical helper-client meeting. More commonly, role expectancy structuring has been accomplished by providing the client with a structuring interview (also called an *anticipatory socialization interview* or a *role induction interview*) before the first meeting with the helper. The following is an excerpt from such an interview in which a helper explains to the prospective client what he or she can expect to occur in psychotherapy:

Now, what is therapy about? What is going on? Well, for one thing, I have been talking a great deal; in treatment your doctor won't talk very much. The reason I am talking now is that I want to explain these things to you. There is equally good reason that the doctor in treatment does not say much. Everyone expects to tell the psychiatrist about his problem and then have him give advice which will solve everything just like that. This isn't true; it just doesn't work like that . . . Before you came here you got advice from all kinds of people . . . If all of the advice you have received had helped, odds are that you wouldn't be here. Your doctor wants to help you to figure out what you really want to do — what the best solution is for you. It's his job not to give advice but to help you find out for yourself how you are going to solve your problem.

Now, what goes on in treatment itself? What is it that you talk about? What is it that you do? How does it work? Well, for one thing, you will talk about your wishes, both now and in the past. . . . You will find that with your doctor you will be able to talk about anything that comes to your mind. He won't have any preconceived notions about what is right or what is wrong for you or what the best solution would be. Talking is very important because he wants to help you get at what you really want. . . . The doctor's job is to help *you* make the decision . . . most of us are not honest with ourselves. We try to kid ourselves, and it's your doctor's job to make you aware of when you are kidding yourself. He is not going to try to tell you what he thinks but he will point out to you how two things you are saying just don't fit together.

. . . the patient . . . sometimes feels worse and discouraged at some stages of treatment. You know, you'll feel you're not getting anywhere, your doctor is a fool, and there's no point in this, and so on. These very feelings are often good indications that you are working and that it's uncomfortable. It is very important that you don't give in to these temporary feelings when they come up.

. . . say whatever comes to your mind, even if you think it is trivial or unimportant. It doesn't matter. It is still important to say it. And if you think it is going to bother your doctor, that doesn't matter either; you still say it.

So, just like the [keeping of] appointments, we make an absolute rule not to think ahead about what you'll say and therefore protect yourself from facing important things. Say whatever is on the top of your mind, no matter what.[1]

We may note then, in summary of our presentation thus far, that structuring can lead to increased attraction by the client toward the helper, whether such structuring is a simple matter of a straightforward statement of probable liking (direct structuring), a description of certain of the helper's positive qualities or of helper-client similarity (trait structuring), or an explanation of the events and behaviors one should expect in the relationship (role expectancy structuring). Whether a given structuring statement of any of these kinds actually does increase client attraction depends in part on matters other than the structuring itself. These statements tend to be

---

[1]From "Anticipatory socialization for psychotherapy" by M. T. Orne and P. H. Wender, 1968, *American Journal of Psychiatry, 124*, pp. 1202–1212. Copyright © 1968 the American Psychiatric Association. Reprinted by permission.

most effective when the person doing the structuring is perceived as trust-worthy, and when the client is experiencing distress or discomfort from her or his problems.

Imitation

As we have just described, attempts to increase client attraction by struc-turing typically rely on statements about the helper presented to the client. A second approach to attraction enhancement, that is, to the liking compo-nent of the helper-client relationship, has relied on different procedures, those based on research concerned with imitation. Essentially, increasing attraction to the helper through imitation involves exposing the client to a person (the *model*) who plays the part of a client who likes the helper and clearly says so. This approach is also called *modeling* or *observational learning*. In the typical use of imitation, an audiotape or videotape of the attracted model client is played to the real client. The content of such tapes is usually part of an actual or constructed counseling or psychotherapy ses-sion between the model and the helper. The client simply listens to or observes the tape(s) and then later meets with the helper. The following is an excerpt from such an attraction-imitation tape, a tape that in its entirety contained a dozen such high-attraction statements by the model client:

> How would I like my parents to be different? Well, I think mostly in the fact that they could've cared more, that they could have showed it, you know, been warmer and not so cold. That's mainly it. . . . You know, I guess I said this before, but *even though all you've been doing the past 5 or 10 minutes is ask-ing me questions, I still for some reason or another feel comfortable talking to you and being honest about myself. I feel that you're warm and that you care.*
> (Goldstein, 1973, p. 216)

As suggested in our discussion of structuring, a change-enhancing rela-tionship involves *both* client attraction toward the helper and helper attrac-tion toward the client. The more reciprocal or mutual the positive feelings, the more likely the progress toward rapid client change. For this reason, imitation has also been used to increase helper attraction to the client. The following transcript is part of a modeling tape designed for this purpose, a tape used successfully with helpers of several kinds. Each statement in italics depicts a model helper expressing attraction, liking, or positive evalu-ation toward a client, that is, expressing the behaviors we were training the listening helpers to imitate.

> *Therapist:* Since this is our first interview, I'll be asking you about a number of different areas of your life. Why don't we start off by your telling me about your family?
>
> *Patient:* My family. Well, you know sometimes — sometimes I think my family could do — just as well without me. You know. Like I'm a — a useless sort of

object that sort of sits around the house. When I — come home from work it's like — like there's nothing there.

Therapist: You don't feel that your family looks forward to your coming home at night?

Patient: Sometimes it — sometimes it seems that they don't even know when I'm home. Kids'll be running around and — my wife — well sometimes the way she acts it would be better if I just stayed out. Some of the things that she gets into — MMMMMMMMMMM.

Therapist: I'm not clear why your wife would act that way. I find you a rather easy person to talk with. . . . . What kind of things does your wife get into?

Patient: — I don't know. She's always yelling and screaming — wants me to do things when I come inside — always telling me I have this to do and that to do. She doesn't realize I just wanna come home and I wanna relax a little bit. Nah — I don't know how she can push me all the time — do this — do that — all the time.

Therapist: Sounds like marriage has been a lot of trouble for you.

Patient: — Yeah. Yeah — really it — it was different before. When we first got married it was — it was nice. We went out and saw different people, did . . . did some things together. Got along pretty good too. Didn't have all this that's going on now.

Therapist: From our meeting so far, I'm finding it rather easy to get along with you too. . . . . I guess things aren't going very well with your wife now.

Patient: No — my wife changed. She got — she got different. Things started — you know — she started not to care about things. We couldn't go out as much. Then — then the babies came and then — wow — feeding them and taking care of them and doing all those things. Never had any time to do the things that we used to do together. — You know, it's usually hard for me to talk about things like this, but it's easy talking to you. Like — you know when I'd come home from work — my wife — she'd be running around the house after the kids — and when I'd come in the door I'd get ignored you know. No one says hello — no one asks you how you are.

Therapist: — Somehow all this seemed to happen around the time the children came?

Patient: It — seems that way. Before we had the kids we didn't have these problems. Now it — it's just not the same.

Therapist: What about your parents, did your father — drink?

Patient: Oh, yeah. He — could down them with the best of them. My old lady will tell you that. Yeah, he really knew how to drink. Used to get into some terrible fights with my old lady though. Boy — he'd come home — have a little too much in him — she'd really let him have it. I'd have to — pull the pillow up over my head so I wouldn't hear the noise. Couldn't get to sleep.

Therapist: Your mother was very hard on your father then.

Patient: Yeah. She really used to get mad at him. You know, for drinking and all that. She used to yell at him. Get on his back all the time. Really be nasty to him. Maybe that's one of the reasons why he's six feet under right now.

Therapist: Sort of like the same thing your wife is doing to you?

Patient: Yeah. You're right. You really hit the nail on the head. You really understand what's going on. There's a lot of things about the two that are kind of the same. I think she's trying to do the same thing to me that my mother did to my father. — Yell and fight — the yelling and carrying on. They'll both do it. Scream at you — and call you a drunk. Telling me I can't take on any responsibility. Always yelling about something. Money. Why don't you have more of it? Why can't we buy this? Why can't we buy that? I'm working — as hard as I can — and she does — she doesn't realize that. She thinks all I have to do is work — all the time. She thinks it's — it's easy for me to — to work every day. — Always pushing me. I don't like to be pushed. I get — I'll get things done. But I have to work — at my own pace, otherwise — it just doesn't matter if I work or not, if I can't work at my own pace.

Therapist: You seem to be really trying to make your marriage work. I respect people who really try like that. . . . It sounds like your wife and you just — don't do things the same way.

Patient: Yeah. She's in her own world. — She doesn't care about anything that I do — or say. She doesn't care about me or anyone else. Sometimes I just feel like getting up and leaving. There's nothing there any more.

Therapist: You'd like to just go away?

Patient: Mmhmm.

Therapist: Have you ever done this?

Patient: Not for any long time. Used to — get away for a couple of days by myself. But I always ended up coming back because I had no one else to go to.

Therapist: Well, now when you feel like that you can come see me. . . . You don't like being alone.

Thus, imitation is a second established path to attraction enhancement. Yet matters are not quite this simple. Each of us observes many people every day, but most of what we observe we do not imitate. We see expensively produced and expertly acted modeling displays of people buying things on television commercials, but much more often than not we do not imitate. People imitate others only under certain circumstances. We tend to imitate others with whom we can identify, thus, to encourage imitation, the taped model should be the same sex and approximate age as the viewing client whose attraction we are seeking to increase. We are especially prone to imitate behavior we see leading to rewards that we too desire. Therefore, the most successful attraction-enhancing modeling tapes are those on which the attracted model is rewarded by having his or her problems resolved. Further, it is not by accident that television commercials so frequently involve extensive repetition (particularly of the product's name), because imitation often increases with the repetition of the modeling display. Finally, imitation will be more likely if the viewer is encouraged to rehearse or practice what he or she has seen. In short, repetitive watching of a rewarded model of the viewer's age and sex, and rehearsing the observed behaviors, will all increase the amount of imitation that occurs.

Conformity Pressure

People with problems often have problems with people. Clients often seek help in the first place because of difficulty in getting along with others, and this difficulty can be reflected in *low* attraction (dislike, suspiciousness, ambivalence) toward the helper. Under such circumstances, trying to increase attraction by telling (structuring) or showing (imitation) him or her appropriate materials might not work. More powerful procedures could be required. If so, conformity pressure is one such possibility. In the typical use of conformity pressure in the research laboratory, a group of individuals meet and each member in turn is required to make a judgment aloud — about which of two lines is longer, or whether a dot of light moved, or which social or political viewpoint is more correct, or some other matter of judgment. However, unknown to one member of the group, all the other members are actually accomplices of the group leader and are told in advance to respond to his or her requests for their judgments in a predetermined and usually unanimous or near-unanimous manner. In at least a third of the groups arranged in this manner, the nonaccomplice member conforms to the majority judgment — even when it is (to the outsider) obviously incorrect. Research conducted by one of the present writers in counseling settings indicates that similar use of conformity pressure can indeed serve as a powerful attraction-enhancer. After hearing a taped session between a helper and client, 3 members (accomplices) of a group of 4 "clients" rated aloud the helper as attractive in a variety of ways. The real client conformed to this pressure and did likewise. Of greatest interest, in other groups, different real clients also rated the taped helper as highly attractive after conformity pressure from accomplices, even when the taped helper being rated was (again to outside observers) highly *un*attractive in several important respects.

HELPER CHARACTERISTICS

Expertness and Status

Our definition of relationship emphasized reciprocal liking, respect, and trust. Seeking to improve the relationship by focus upon attraction enhancement is equivalent to emphasizing the liking component of this definition. Relationship can also be enhanced by procedures relevant to the respect component. A major means of enhancing client respect for the helper concerns the helper's real or apparent expertness and status. In general, we may assume that the greater the helper's expertness, the greater the client's respect for her or him.

In psychotherapy, there is much about the psychotherapist, his or her behavior, and his or her physical surroundings that testifies to his or her apparent expertness and authority. Haley (1963) commented in this regard:

> The context of the relationship emphasizes the therapist's position. . . . Patients are usually referred to him by people who point out what a capable authority he is and how much the patient needs help. Some therapists have a waiting list, so that the patient is impressed by standing in line to be treated, while others may imply that patients with similar symptoms were successfully treated. Furthermore, the patient must be willing to pay money even to talk to the therapist, and the therapist can either treat him or dismiss him, and so controls whether or not there is going to be a relationship. Not only the therapist's prestige is emphasized in the initial meeting, but also the patient's inadequacy is made clear. The patient . . . must emphasize his difficulties in life to a man who apparently has none. The physical settings in which most therapists function also reinforce their superior position. In many instances the therapist sits at a desk, the symbol of authority, while the patient sits in a chair, the position of the suppliant. In psychoanalytic therapy the arrangement is more extreme. The patient lies down while the therapist sits up. His chair is also placed so that he can observe the patient's reactions, but the patient cannot observe him. Finally, the initial interview in therapy usually makes quite explicit the fact that the therapist is in charge of the relationship by the rules for treatment he lays down. He suggests the frequency of interviews, implies he will be the one who decides when treatment will end, and he usually instructs the patient how to behave in the office. He may make a general statement about how the patient is to express himself there, or he may provide specific instructions as in the analytic situation where the patient is told he must lie down and say whatever comes to mind. (pp. 71–73)[2]

What else is there that distinguishes the expert helper from the inexpert? In our own research, as will be seen shortly, the level of apparent helper expertness was varied by altering the external trappings surrounding the helper—his or her title, books, office, diploma, and so on. Research reported by Schmidt and Strong (1970) showed that clients also judge expertness to a large extent from the observable behavior of their helpers. According to their results, college students describe the expert and inexpert counselor quite differently:

> *The expert* shakes the student's hand, aligning the student with himself, and greets him with his first name. He seems interested and relaxed. He has a neat appearance but is not stuffy. . . . He talks at the student's level and is not arrogant toward him. The expert assumes a comfortable but attentive sitting position. He focuses his attention on the student and carefully listens to him. He has a warm facial expression and is reactive to the student. His voice is inflective and lively, he changes his facial expressions, and uses hand gestures. He speaks fluently with confidence and sureness. The expert has prepared for the interview. He is informed as to why the student is there and is familiar with

---

[2]From *Strategies of psychotherapy* by J. Haley (1963). New York: Grune & Stratton. Copyright 1963 by Grune & Stratton, Inc. Reprinted by permission.

the student's test scores, grades, and background. . . . He asks direct and to-the-point questions. His questions are thought-provoking and follow an apparently logical progression. They seem spontaneous and conversational. The expert is willing to help determine if the student's decisions are right, but does not try to change the student's ideas forcefully. He lets the student do most of the talking and does not interrupt him. The expert moves quickly to the root of the problem. He points out contradictions in reasoning, and restates the student's statements as they bear on the problem. . . . He makes recommendations and suggests possible solutions.

The *inexpert* is awkward, tense, and uneasy. He seems to be afraid of the student. He does not greet the student by name to put him at ease. . . . He is not quite sure of himself or of some of his remarks. He seems too cold, strict and dominating, and too formal in attitude and action. His gestures are stiff and overdone. . . . The inexpert slouches in his chair. He is too casual and relaxed. . . . His voice is flat and without inflection, appearing to show disinterest and boredom. . . . The inexpert comes to the interview cold. He has not cared enough about the student to acquaint himself with the student's records. The inexpert asks vague questions which are trivial and irrelevant and have no common thread or aim. His questioning is abrupt and tactless with poor transitions. He asks too many questions like a quiz session, giving the student the third degree. . . . The inexpert is slow in getting his point across and is confusing in his discussion of what the student should do. . . . The inexpert does not get to the core of the problem. . . . He just doesn't seem to be getting anywhere. (p. 117)[3]

These descriptions were then used by the investigators (Strong & Schmidt, 1970) as the script outline in a study examining the effects of status on a helper's influence. Counselors taking the role of expert and inexpert were thoroughly rehearsed in the behaviors described above. The former were introduced to clients with the statement

> The person you will be talking with is Dr. _____ , a psychologist who has had several years of experience interviewing students.

The inexpert helper was, contrastingly, introduced with the statement

> We had originally scheduled Dr. _____ to talk with you but unfortunately he notified us that he wouldn't be able to make it today. In his place we have Mr. _____ , a student, who unfortunately has had no interviewing experience and has been given only a brief explanation of the purpose of this study. I think he should work out all right, though. (Strong and Schmidt, 1970. p. 83)

Analysis of the helper-client interviews that were then held revealed, as predicted, greater positive change in those clients structured and in fact seen by the "expert" helper.

---

[3]From "Expert and inexpert counselors" by L. D. Schmidt and S. R. Strong (1970). *Journal of Counseling Psychology, 17,* pp. 115–118. Copyright 1970 by the American Psychological Association. Reprinted by permission.

It thus seems that the greater the change-agent's expertness, the greater his or her effectiveness in altering the behavior and beliefs of the target. Laboratory research strongly supports this contention. A substantial number of investigations confirm the fact that a statement is more fully accepted and acted upon when the recipient believes it comes from an expert or high-status person than when its apparent source is a person of low or unknown expertise.

The first evidence we obtained in support of the relationship aspect of this finding was obtained almost accidentally (Goldstein, 1971). We conducted a study whose purpose was to determine if client attraction to the helper would increase if the helper went out of his way to do a small favor or extend an extra courtesy to the client. The courtesy involved was offering the client coffee and a doughnut, not a usual event in counseling or psychotherapy. Although this procedure did improve their relationship, attraction increased even more at those times when the helper made it clear that the coffee and doughnut were for himself, and not for the client! We had not predicted this result, and only half-jokingly speculated that perhaps attraction increased because anyone behaving so boorishly must be an important person. That is, perhaps attraction increased here because, in the client's eyes, the helper had increased his status. We tested this notion more directly in our next investigation (Sabalis, 1969). Sabalis had four groups of clients, two of whom were seen by what appeared to be a high-status helper, two by a low-status helper. Not all persons, we predicted, are attracted to high-status persons. Authoritarian persons, those rigidly respectful of authority, seem to be highly responsive and attracted to such persons, whereas more equalitarian individuals are less drawn to experts and similar sources. Thus, in this study, it was predicted that a high-status helper would increase the attraction-to-helper of high authoritarian clients but not of equalitarian clients.

The clients (of both kinds) in the high-status groups each received a postcard indicating the time of the interview. The interviewer was "Dr. Robert Sabalis." When each client arrived for the interview, the interviewer introduced himself as "Dr. Sabalis, a member of the faculty of the Psychology Department." A "Dr. Robert Sabalis" nameplate was on the interviewer's desk, and the office itself was a large, well-furnished one belonging to a faculty member. The interviewer was neatly dressed in a business suit. The session began with some test taking by the client, which the interviewer described as tests on which he was doing research. As the client filled out the test forms, the interviewer opened a text and began to jot down notes from it, indicating to the client as he did that he was preparing an examination for one of the classes he taught.

For the low-status groups, the interviewer's name on the postcard and in his introduction upon meeting was "Bob Sabalis." He described himself to clients as a senior undergraduate psychology major who was meeting with them as a requirement for one of his own courses. His attire was consistent with the typical undergraduate's. The interview office was quite small and sparsely furnished. As the test taking commenced, he began note taking from a text again, but this time indicated he was preparing for an examination he had to take.

The predicted effect of status on attraction was obtained. That is, high authoritarian clients became significantly more attracted to the interviewer after the high-status, but not the low-status, procedures.

As described above, Strong and Schmidt showed the positive effect of expertness by training counselors to behave as either expert or inexpert. Sabalis used one interviewer, who served as both the high- and the low-status helper. The positive effect on the helper-client relationship was obtained again. Streltzer and Koch (1968) implemented expertness in yet another way. Their research concerned the effects role-playing the part of lung cancer patients would have on persons needing to reduce their smoking. Participating "patients" role-played a series of scenes involving meeting the doctor, the doctor's giving the diagnosis, treatment plans, and advice to quit smoking immediately. Half of the "patients" enacted their role with a "doctor" who was a 21-year-old female psychology major. She used no title. The other smokers met with a 32-year-old male physician who introduced himself as "Doctor." Both types of smokers decreased in smoking more than persons not participating in the role-playing. Those role-playing with the real expert, furthermore, showed by far the greatest negative change in their attitudes toward smoking.

Similar findings have been reported by other researchers. Corrigan, Dell, Lewis, and Schmidt (1980) have provided an especially comprehensive review of these recent studies, examining the array of evidential, reputational, and behavioral cues to helper expertness and status that have been shown with reliability to have substantial attraction-enhancing potency. In general, it may be concluded that helper expertness and status serve to increase client respect, which in turn leads to the client's being more open to the helper's attempts to influence him or her and, subsequently, more likelihood of client change.

Credibility

The respect component of the helper-client relationship is also influenced by helper credibility. The greater the level of credibility, the greater the client's respect for the helper. Johnson and Matross (1977) defined helper credibility as his or her perceived ability to know valid information and his or her motivation to communicate this knowledge without bias. As Johnson (1972) observed, empirical evidence exists demonstrating that credibility is determined by several helper characteristics: (a) *expertness* as defined above, and as signified by title, institutional affiliation, and other indexes of academic and professional achievement; (b) *reliability* as an information source, that is, dependability, predictability, and consistency; (c) *motives and intentions* of the helper — the clearer it is to the client that it is his or her interests, and not the helper's own, toward which the helper is working, the greater the helper's credibility; and (d) *dynamism* of the helper, his or her apparent confidence, forcefulness, and activity level.

Empathy

We have just examined the positive effects on the helper-client relationship of the real or apparent expertness and status of the helper, as well as her or his perceived credibility. There are several other helper qualities of importance in this regard, and the present section will focus upon one of these — empathy. The level of empathy offered by the helper and its effects on the client has been the object of considerable research and theory. This research has consistently shown that a helper's empathy with the client's feelings strongly influences the quality of the helper-client relationship that develops and, subsequently, the degree of client change, at least with a substantial proportion of psychotherapy clients.

Truax and Carkhuff (1967) are two researchers who have been quite active in studying the effects of empathy on the helper-client relationship. They commented, as a beginning definition of *empathy*,

> As we come to know some of his wants, some of his needs, some of his achievements and some of his failures, we find ourselves as therapists "living" with the patient much as we do with the central figure of a novel. . . . Just as with the character in the novel, we come to know the person from his own internal frame of reference, gaining some flavor of his moment-by-moment experience. We see events and significant people in his life as they appear to him — not as they "objectively are" but as he experiences them. As we come to know him from his personal vantage point we automatically come to value and like him. . . . We begin to perceive the events and experiences of his life "as if" they were parts of our own life. It is through this process that we come to feel warmth, respect and liking. . . . (p. 42)

These same researchers have also developed a more detailed definition of empathy, which is quoted in full below. Described in the statement that follows is their Empathy Scale, consisting of levels of empathy that a helper can provide a client — graduated from very low (level 1) to very high (level 5).

EMPATHIC UNDERSTANDING IN INTERPERSONAL PROCESSES

A Scale for Measurement

Level 1
The verbal and behavioral expressions of the helper either do not attend to or detract significantly from the verbal and behavioral expressions of the client(s)

in that they communicate significantly less of the client's feelings and experiences than the client has communicated himself.

Example. The helper communicates no awareness of even the most obvious, expressed surface feelings of the client. The helper may be bored or disinterested or simply operating from a preconceived frame of reference which totally excludes that of the client(s).

In summary, the helper does everything but express that he is listening, understanding, or being sensitive to even the most obvious feelings of the client in such a way as to detract significantly from the communications of the client.

Level 2
While the helper responds to the expressed feelings of the client(s), he does so in such a way that he subtracts noticeable affect from the communications of the client.

Example. The helper may communicate some awareness of obvious, surface feelings of the client, but his communications drain off a level of the affect and distort the level of meaning. The helper may communicate his own ideas of what may be going on, but these are not congruent with the expressions of the client.

In summary, the helper tends to respond to other than what the client is expressing or indicating.

Level 3
The expressions of the helper in response to the expressions of the client(s) are essentially interchangeable with those of the client in that they express essentially the same affect and meaning.

Example. The helper responds with accurate understandings of the surface feelings of the client but may not respond to or may misinterpret the deeper feelings.

In summary, the helper is responding so as to neither subtract from nor add to the expressions of the client. He does not respond accurately to how that person really feels beneath the surface feelings; but he indicates a willingness and openness to do so. Level 3 constitutes the minimal level of facilitative interpersonal functioning.

Level 4
The responses of the helper add noticeably to the expressions of the client(s) in such a way as to express feelings a level deeper than the client was able to express himself.

Example. The helper communicates his understanding of the expressions of the client at a level deeper than they were expressed and thus enables the client to experience and/or express feelings he was unable to express previously.

In summary, the helper's responses add deeper feeling and meaning to the expressions of the client.

Level 5

The helper's responses add significantly to the feeling and meaning of the expressions of the client(s) in such a way as to accurately express feelings levels below what the client himself was able to express or, in the event of ongoing, deep self-exploration on the client's part, to be fully with him in his deepest moments.

> *Example.* The helper responds with accuracy to all of the client's deeper as well as surface feelings. He is "tuned in" on the client's wave length. The helper and the client might proceed together to explore previously unexplored areas of human existence.

> In summary, the helper is responding with a full awareness of who the other person is and with a comprehensive and accurate empathic understanding of that individual's deepest feelings. (pp. 174–175)[4]

A great deal of research has been done on the effects of high levels of helper empathy in counseling, guidance, and psychotherapy. Certain effects on the client regularly occur in these studies. Feeling understood, that someone has been able to truly perceive his or her deeper feelings, the client's liking of the helper increases. In a sense, the client also comes to trust himself or herself more under these circumstances, for one regular result of high helper empathy is deeper and more persevering *self-exploration* by the client. In several of these studies, greater client change is a clear result. High levels of helper empathic responding can, therefore, be viewed as a necessary (but probably not sufficient) condition for client change. Carkhuff (1969) is, we feel, largely correct in his comment:

> Empathy is the key ingredient of helping. Its explicit communication, particularly during early phases of helping, is critical. Without an empathic understanding of the helpee's world and his difficulties as he sees them there is no basis for helping. (p. 173)

A more concrete understanding of helper empathy, and its effects upon client behavior, is provided by the specific examples that follow. The first is drawn from a psychotherapy session. Note how all helper statements are at least level 3, and often higher:

> *Helpee:* Um. I don't know whether, whether I'm right or wrong in feeling the way I do, but, uh, I find myself withdrawing from people. I don't care to go out and socialize and play their stupid little games any more. Um, I get very anxious and come home depressed and have headaches—it seems all so superficial. There was a time when I used to get along with everybody; everybody

---

[4]From *Toward Effective Counseling and Psychotherapy* by Charles B. Truax and Robert R. Carkhuff, 1967, Chicago: Aldine. Copyright © by Charles B. Truax and Robert R. Carkhuff. Reprinted by permission of the authors and Aldine Publishing Company.

said, "Oh, isn't she wonderful! She gets along with everybody; she's so nice and everybody likes her," and I used to think that was . . . that was something to be really proud of, but, oh, but, I think that only told how I, or who I was at that time, that I had no depth. I was sort of whatever the crowd wanted me to be, or the particular group I was with at the time. Um, I know it's important for my husband's business that we go out and socialize and meet people and make a good impression and join clubs and play all those stupid little games—Elks, and, you know, bowling banquets, and, uh, fishing trips and fraternity-type gatherings. Um, I . . . I just don't care to do it any more, and, um, I don't know if that means that I'm a . . . that there's something wrong with me psychologically, or, uh, or is this normal. I mean . . . uh . . . people don't really know who I am and they really don't care who one another, who the other person is. They . . . it's all at such a superficial level.

Helper: You're darn sure of how you feel, but you really don't know what it all adds up to. Is it you? Is it the other people? What are the implications of your husband's business? You? Where is it all going?

Helpee: Uh, huh. It's an empty life. It's, um, there's, uh, no depth to it at all. I mean, you just talk about very, very superficial things, and the first few times, it's O.K. But then after that, there's nothing to talk about. So you drink and you pretend to be happy over silly jokes and silly things that people do when they all, uh, are trying to impress one another, and they're very materialistic, and, uh, it's just not the route I want to go.

Helper: So your feelings are so strong now that you just can't fake it any more.

Helpee: That's right, so what do you do? People say, "Oh, there's something wrong with you," then, "You need to see a psychiatrist or something," because you . . . you know the thing in society is that the normal person gets along with people, and, uh, can adjust to any situation. And when you . . . when you're a little discriminating, maybe very discriminating or critical, then that means there's something wrong with you.

Helper: While you know how strongly you feel about all these things, you're not sure you can really act in terms of them and be free.

Helpee: I don't know if I'm strong enough. The implications are great. It may mean, uh, a break up of the marriage, uh, and it means going it alone, and that's too frightening. I don't think I have the courage. But I do feel like I'm in sort of a trap.

Helper: You know you can't pretend, yet you're really fearful of going it alone.

Helpee: Yes, there's nobody I can really talk to, I mean, you know, it's one thing if you have a . . . like your husband . . . if you can share these things, if he can understand it at some level, but . . . um . . . he can't.

Helper: It's like, "If I act on how I really feel, though, it frightens the people who mean most to me. They won't understand it, and I sure can't share that with them."

Helpee: (Pause) So what do you do. (Pause) I mean . . . I . . . you know. I find myself going out and telling the people who I really feel about, about different topics and getting into controversial issues, and, uh, and that's, that's too anxiety provoking for me. I can't, because then you get into arguments and I don't want to do that either, that leads nowhere. I just get frustrated and anxious and upset and angry with myself for getting myself into the situation.

Helper: You know that doesn't set you free, you know . . .

Helpee: No, it bottles me up.

Helper: That only causes you more problems, and what you're really asking about is, how you can move toward greater freedom and greater fulfillment in your own life.

Helpee: I . . . I think I know who I am now, independent of other people, and, uh, which people aren't and . . . um . . . there's no room for that kind of person in this society.

Helper: There's no room for me out there!

Helpee: (Pause) So what do I do?

Helper: We run over and over the questions that . . . you end up with. "Where do I go from here? How do I act on this? I know how I feel, but I don't know what'll happen if I act on how I feel."

Helpee: I . . . have an idea of what'll happen.

Helper: And it's not good!

Helpee: No! It means almost starting a whole new life.

Helper: And you don't know if you can make it.

Helpee: Right, I know what I've got here, and if I don't make it all the way with the other, then I'm in trouble.

Helper: While you don't know what'll happen if you act on your feelings, you know what the alternatives are if you don't. And they're not good either. They're worse.

Helpee: I . . . I don't have much choice. (pp. 219–220)[5]

A second series of examples is drawn from our own research (Goldstein, 1973), in which we sought successfully to increase helper empathy by a set of training procedures rather different from Truax and Carkhuff's. Our trainees were nurses and attendants employed in state mental hospitals. Part of our training sequence involved exposing them to a number of different examples of highly empathic responses to difficult or problematic patient behaviors and statements. These examples included[6]

1. *Nurse:* Here is your medicine, Mr. _____ .

    Patient: I don't want it. People here are always telling me to do this, do that, do the other thing. I'll take the medicine when *I* want to.

    Nurse: So it's not so much the medicine itself, but you feel you're bossed around all the time. You're tired of people giving you orders.

---

[5]From *Helping and human relations* by R. R. Carkhuff, 1969, New York: Holt, Rinehart & Winston. Copyright 1969 by Holt, Rinehart & Winston. Reprinted by permission.

[6]From *Structured learning therapy* by A. P. Goldstein, 1973, New York: Academic. Copyright 1973 by Academic Press. Reprinted by permission.

2. *Patient:* I can't leave the hospital, I'm still sick. What will I do when I get home?

   Nurse. You just don't feel ready to go yet, and wonder if you're up to being home.

3. *Patient:* I don't know why they keep giving me this medicine. I've taken it for weeks and I don't feel any better. I've told this to Dr. _____ twice already.

   Nurse: Not only doesn't the medicine seem to work, but the doctor doesn't seem interested in doing anything about it.

4. *Patient:* I was in the hospital before. Things were really bothering me. Finally, I just couldn't take it anymore. I left home, didn't show up at work, and somehow ended up in the hospital.

   Nurse: Things just piled up and up, from bad to worse, and you wound up here.

5. *Patient:* Sometimes I think my family could do just as well without me. It's like I almost don't exist as far as they're concerned. They almost never come to see me.

   Nurse: You'd really like them to visit, but they don't really seem to care about you.

6. *Patient:* My father and mother used to get into terrible fights. He'd come home and they'd really go at it. I'd have to pull the pillow over my head so I wouldn't hear the noise.

   Nurse: It sounds like something that would be really upsetting, especially to a child.

7. *Patient:* I'd really like to know about their school, their friends, things like that. You know, the things a father is interested in. My youngest son, he's on a football team, but he never invited me to a game. He never cared if I was there or not. I don't understand it.

   Nurse: It must hurt very deeply when he doesn't let you be a part of his life.

8. *Patient:* I don't like talking to the psychologist. He's OK but I've been asked *all* the questions many times already.

   Nurse: You're just good and tired of going through the whole procedure.

9. *Patient:* It's just not fair that I have to stay on the ward because of last weekend. My husband was nasty. He made me very nervous. It wasn't my fault. Can't I please go off the ward?

   Nurse: You feel the trouble at home was really your husband's fault, and now you're being punished for it.

10. *Patient:* I can't stand her anymore. She never shuts up, talk, talk, talk. She talks more than any other patient here. I don't want to sit near her or be near her.

    Nurse: She's really very annoying to you. You'd like to have nothing to do with her.

A similar set of high-empathy examples was used to train a different type of helper, home aides. These are persons trained to provide psychological and physical assistance to elderly, disabled, psychiatric outpatients, and similar persons in their own homes. Some of these examples were

1. *Patient:* The old age home was really different from this apartment building. All my friends are still there. I don't even know anyone here.

   Home Aide: Sounds like you're lonely in your new home. Kind of like a stranger in a new place. I can see how it's pretty depressing missing all your friends.

   Patient: I sure *am* lonely. Every friend I have is still at the home. And it's so hard living all alone with three whole rooms to myself. I even get sad listening to people's voices in the other apartments.

   Home Aide: You'd like to get out of your three lonely rooms and meet some of the other people in the building. You'd be happier if you made some new friends.

2. *Patient:* I don't like. . . . It makes me feel silly for you to wash and feed me.

   Home Aide: It makes you uncomfortable when someone takes care of you. You feel like you should be doing things on your own and you shouldn't need me.

   Patient: Mm hm. I feel like a baby when someone's helping me. But I know I can't do stuff myself now 'cause I've tried.

   Home Aide: You feel foolish when you have to rely on other people since you should be helping yourself. But you know that you need other people's help now for your own well-being.

3. *Patient:* I think about things like falling down the stairs, or dropping my cigarette in bed, or a stranger coming to my house late at night. . . . I don't really know what I'd do . . .

   Home Aide: You're worried about whether you could handle an emergency all alone.

   Patient: Yeah, I worry, *a lot.* . . . I remember how scary it was the time I fainted and nobody was here to help me.

   Home Aide: It would be nice to be able to count on somebody's help when something goes wrong, and you're not sure you can take care of things all by yourself.

4. *Patient:* All I seem to do is care for these kids 25 hours a day! Which is a lot for a mother to do by herself!

   Home Aide: Sounds as if you'd like more time to yourself or someone to help you. That's a lot for one person to do and you seem angry about it.

   Patient: Why shouldn't I be angry! It's a lot to expect one person to change diapers, tie shoelaces, fix meals, yank the kids out of the mud, wash their filthy faces, constantly run to drag their stupid toys out of the road . . .

   Home Aide: You get pretty angry when you constantly have to watch over those kids. It's like the more demands they make on you, the less time you have to do things for yourself.

5. *Patient:* My kids couldn't care less if I exist. They're only in Rochester, but somehow that's too far away to visit me.

   Home Aide: You'd like them to visit, but somehow they don't seem interested enough.

   Patient: Yeah, you got the idea. If they were interested in me they'd make the short trip to come to see me. But they don't even call. And I'll be damned if I'll invite them one more time.

   Home Aide: You're not about to beg them to visit you if they aren't interested. But you seem pretty hurt that your own children don't seem to care about you.

6. *Patient:* (Bashfully looking down). Do you think you could maybe show me how to, um, wash myself alone, instead of you helping me. The nurses helped me in the hospital when I had arthritis. . . . Well . . . I still shake so much I'm afraid I'll drop the soap or fall down.

   Home Aide: It's kind of embarrassing to need someone to help you wash. Even though right now it's probably safer that way, you'd really rather do it yourself.

   Patient: You're not kidding. I can't tell you how I hated bathtime in the hospital. It was so embarrassing to have the nurse see me, you know, naked. But maybe it had to be that way. Like you say, it was safer. And also a lot cleaner than if I did it myself.

   Home Aide: So even though you don't like people to see you naked, maybe it would make you feel more comfortable if I helped you while the arthritis is still bothering you.

7. *Patient:* This apartment's *nothing* like the old age home. There I had people to take care of me, and there was always something to do, and my room was arranged differently there . . .

   Home Aide: It's hard getting used to a brand new home which doesn't even seem like your home yet.

   Patient: But you know, I remember being afraid I wouldn't get used to the old age home, and I did. So, even if it's hard now in this new place, I guess I'll get used to it.

   Home Aide: Even though it's a little hard and scary at first, it's comforting to know you got used to a new home before and you can probably do it again.

8. *Patient:* (Annoyed) I wish you wouldn't put things away in my house any way you feel like it!

   Home Aide: I'm just barging right into your house, doing whatever I want with your things—as though I don't respect you.

   Patient: Yeah! I keep my things in certain places for certain reasons and I don't like anyone moving them without asking me.

   Home Aide: You're used to living a certain way and all of a sudden I come in and put things where *I* think they should go. I can understand that you'd be angry with me for barging in.

9. *Patient:* (Hectically) Oh! I'm really sorry about that chair! I was planning to reupholster it last week! And that lightbulb just blew out yesterday.

(Heavily, shaking head in hand) Oh-h-h I'm sorry. . . . This place is a rathole.

Home Aide: It's kind of embarrassing when someone comes to your house for the first time and sees it looking like a mess.

Patient: Well, *you'd* be embarrassed, wouldn't you? The furniture is a wreck, the walls are shabby, some of the lights don't work. . . . I don't even want you to see the kitchen. . . . I feel terrible that you have to see everything like this!

Home Aide: You're ashamed that everything in your house seems to be dirty or broken and you feel like apologizing for the mess.

10. *Patient:* The only reason I called Home Aides is that the doctor recommended it and he was standing right there. I really don't want you to take care of me. I don't need help.

Home Aide: You feel that you can take care of yourself, and you resent it when I come in and start doing things for you.

Patient: Yes, I *can* take care of myself! . . . Except, I guess I could use some help now that I don't see so good.

Home Aide: You still feel up to taking care of things like before, but you realize it's a little harder now . . . Even so, you don't like to ask for help.

The significance of helper empathy in the helping enterprise has been emphasized in our earlier discussion, and we have now provided several examples. It will be useful to close this section with a listing of the guidelines, provided by Carkhuff (1969), for helpers wishing to become proficient in offering these levels of empathic responses to clients.

1. The helper will find that he is most effective in communicating an empathic understanding when he concentrates with intensity upon the client's expressions, both verbal and nonverbal.

2. The helper will find that initially he is most effective in communicating empathic understanding when he concentrates upon responses that are interchangeable with those of the client (Level 3).

3. The helper will find that he is most effective in communicating empathic understanding when he formulates his responses in language that is most attuned to the client.

4. The helper will find that he is most effective in communicating empathic understanding when he responds in a feeling tone similar to that communicated by the client.

5. The helper will find that he is most effective in communicating empathic understanding when he is most responsive.

6. The helper will find that he is most effective in communicating empathic understanding when, having established an interchangeable base of communication (Level 3), he moves tentatively toward expanding and clarifying the client's experiences at higher levels (Levels 4 and 5).

7. The helper will find that he is most effective in communicating empathic understanding when he concentrates upon what is not being expressed by the client and, in a sense, seeks to fill in what is missing rather than simply dealing with what is present.

8. The helper will find that he is most effective in communicating empathic

understanding when he employs the client's behavior as the best guideline to assess the effectiveness of his responses.

Further useful rules for the effective communication of helper empathy, and examples thereof, are presented in the work of Egan (1976), Goldstein (1981), Goldstein and Michaels (1985), Guerney (1977), and Ivey and Authier (1971).

Warmth

As was true of empathy, warmth is appropriately considered a central ingredient of the helping relationship. Whatever specific change methods the helper uses, their likelihood of success seems in large measure to be a result of the relationship base on which she or he and the client are interacting. Helper warmth is a highly important aspect of this base. Without it, specific helping procedures can be technically correct but therapeutically impotent.

Helper warmth is also important in relationship terms because it appears to beget reciprocal warmth from the client. Truax and Carkhuff (1967), in fact, commented that "It is a rare human being who does not respond to warmth with warmth and to hostility with hostility. It is probably the most important principle for the beginning therapist to understand if he is to be successful in the therapeutic relationship." This contention received ample support in a research program conducted by one of the present writers (Goldstein, 1971). When liking of A toward B (helper or client) was increased by structuring, status-enhancement, or other procedures, B's liking of A reciprocally increased — even though we had applied no procedures whatsoever to B directly. Several other researchers have reported the same reciprocal result. The Truax and Carkhuff definition of this helper quality, and their examples of its occurrence in counseling and psychotherapy, help clarify the nature and significance of helper warmth.

The dimension of nonpossessive warmth or unconditional positive regard ranges from a high level, where the therapist warmly accepts the patient's experience as part of that person without imposing conditions, to a low level, where the therapist evaluates a patient or his or her feelings, expresses dislike or disapproval, or expresses warmth in a selective and evaluative way.

Level 1

The therapist is actively offering advice or giving clear negative regard. He or she could be telling the patient what would be "best" for him or her, or in other ways actively approving or disapproving of his or her behavior. The therapist's actions make him or her the locus of evaluation; he or she sees himself or herself as responsible for the patient.

Example

Patient: . . . and I don't. I don't know what sort of a job will be offered me, but — eh . . .

Therapist: It might not be the best in the world.

Patient: I'm sure it won't.

Therapist: And, uh . . .

Patient: . . . but . . .

Therapist: But if you can make up your mind to stomach some of the unpleasantness of things.

Patient: Um hm.

Therapist: . . . you have to go through — you'll get through it.

Patient: Yeah, I know I will.

Therapist: And, ah, you'll get out of here.

Patient: I certainly, uh, I just, I just know that I have to do it, so I'm going to do it but — it's awfully easy for me, Doctor, to (sighs) well, more than pull in my shell. I — I just hibernate. I just, uh, well, just don't do a darn thing.

Therapist: It's your own fault. (Severely)

Patient: Sure it is. I know it is. (Pause) But it seems like whenever I — here — here's the thing. Whenever I get to the stage where I'm making active plans for myself, they say I'm high. An . . .

Therapist: In other words they criticize you that . . .

Patient: Yeah.

Therapist: So tender little lady is gonna really crawl into her shell.

Patient: Well, I — I'll say "okay."

Therapist: If they're gonna throw, if they're gonna shoot arrows at me, I'll just crawl behind my shell and I won't come out of it. (Forcefully)

Patient: That's right. (Sadly)

Therapist: And that's worse. (Quickly)

Patient: (Pause) But why don't they let me be a little bit high? Why — right now I'm taking . . .

Therapist: (Interrupting) Because some people . . .

Patient: (Talking with him) . . . 600 milligrams of malorin, whatever that is, malorin.

Therapist: . . . because a lot of people here don't know you very well at all. And because people in general, at times, you have to allow that they could be stupid. You too. I mean you're stupid sometimes, so why can't other people . . .

Patient: So much of the time.

Therapist: Why can't other people? I mean, you're an intelligent person and are stupid. Why, why can't you allow that other intelligent people can also be stupid? When it comes to you they don't know very much.

Patient: Mmm. (Muttering)

Level 2

The therapist responds mechanically to the client, indicating little positive regard and hence little nonpossessive warmth. He or she might ignore the patient or his or her feelings or display a lack of concern or interest. The therapist ignores the client at times when a nonpossessively warm response would be expected; he or she shows a complete passivity that communicates almost unconditional lack of regard.

Example

Patient: (Speaking throughout in a woebegone voice) You don't have to sit down and, and, and write like that but I thought he'd answer my letter. I thought, I didn't think he'd answer the letter, I thought he'd come up.

Therapist: Um, hm.

Patient: . . . and, and visit me; it's only 50, he hasn't been to visit me yet. It's only been about, uh, it's only about 50, 60 miles from here.

Therapist: Uh, hm.

Patient: And I kind of expected him last Sunday but he didn't . . .

Therapist: You were just sort of looking for him but he . . .

Patient: (Interrupting insistently) Well, I wasn't, I wasn't, I was looking for him, I wasn't looking for him. I had a kind of a half-the-way feeling that he wouldn't be up here. I know him pretty well and he's—walks around, you know, and thinks and thinks and thinks and—maybe it'll take him two or three weeks an' all of a sudden he—he'll walk in the house (laughs)—"Let's go see—so and so." (Nervous laughter) He's a—he's a lot like I am—we're all the same, I guess. He probably—read the letter and—probably never said very much, walked out, forgot about it (laughing nervously), then all of a sudden it dawned on 'im (nervous laughter) and, ah, that's, ah, that's about, about the size of it, as far as that goes. And, uh, uh, so as I say, I—I wouldn't be, I wasn't—too overly disappointed when he, when he didn't ah, ah, ah. ah, answer it or come to see me. He probably will yet. (Laughs) I'm an optimist, I always have been, he'll probably come and visit me some day. May he'll come and let me go down there 'n live. Maybe he won't, won't make much difference (laughs) one way or another.

Therapist: Hmmm. You can sort of . . .

Patient: Yeah.

Therapist: . . . take things as they come. (Brightly)

Level 3

The therapist indicates a positive caring for the patient or client, but it is a semipossessive caring in the sense that she or he communicates to the client that her or his behavior matters to the therapist. That is, the therapist communicates such things as "It is not all right if you act immorally," "I want you to get along at work," or "It's important to me that you get along with the ward staff." The therapist sees herself or himself as responsible for the client.

Example

Patient: I still, you sorta hate to give up something that you know that you've made something out of, and, and, uh, in fact, it amounts to, uh, at least, uh, what you would, uh, earn working for somebody else, so . . .

Therapist: (Enthusiastically) O.K. What, well, eh, why don't — why don't we do it this way? That, uh I'll kind of give you some homework to do. (Laughs) And when you're going home these weekends, um, really talk to your wife, and, ah, think yourself about pretty specific possibilities for you, considering the location and considering what time of year it is and, what you can do and things like this, and, eh, then we can talk it out here and really do some, some working on this in earnest, and not just talk plans. . . . (Patient answers "yeah" after every phrase or so.)

Patient: (Interrupting) Well, I actually, I'd almost feel gettin' out right away but I, somethin' sort of holds me back, yet the season isn't — there (*Therapist:* Uh, huh) and I don't know if it's good for me or not (*Therapist:* Uh, huh), but I, ah . . .

Therapist: O.K., but at least this next couple of months we can use in — trying at least to set something up or, or . . .

Patient: Cuz I feel that I, I don't know, I — feel I just want to do things again.

Therapist: (Um, hm). Uh, 'cuz the longer you stay away from work, I was just reading about that psychologist James here the other day, an' it seems like if once you get into things and work, you feel better (*Patient:* Sure) . . . and you don't uh, it seems like, uh the further you stay away from things, eh, you, well, eh, you sort'a think about it, put it that way. Um, hm. O.K. So, ah — in our thinking about it, though, that next few weeks, let's get closer to the doing of them. O.K.? (Warmly)

Patient: Well, yes, that's — what . . . .

Therapist: Sound okay to you?

Patient: Yes. It sounds okay to me.

Therapist: Good enough. (Amiably)

Level 4

The therapist clearly communicates a very deep interest and concern for the welfare of the patient, showing a nonevaluative and unconditional warmth in almost all areas of functioning. Although there remains some conditionality in the more personal and private areas, the patient is given freedom to be himself or herself and to be liked as himself or herself. There is little evaluation of thoughts and behaviors. In deeply personal areas, however, the therapist might be conditional and communicate the idea that the client may act in any way he or she wishes — except that it is important to the therapist that he or she be more mature, or not regress in therapy, or accept and like the therapist. In all other areas, however, nonpossessive warmth is communicated. The therapist sees himself or herself as responsible to the client.

Example

Therapist: One thing that occurs to me is I'm so glad you came. I was afraid you wouldn't come. I had everything prepared, but I was afraid you wouldn't come. (Pause)

Patient: What—would you have thought of me then? I guess maybe I shouldn't have, but I did anyway. (Rapidly)

Therapist: Is that—like saying, "Why or What?" But, partly you feel—maybe you shouldn't have come—or don't know if you shouldn't or "not should." There's something about—feeling bad that could make you—not want to come. I don't know if I got that right, but—because if you feel very bad then—then, I don't know. Is there anything in that?

Patient: Well—I've told you before, I mean, you know, two things that, when I feel bad. I mean one that always—I feel that there's a possibility, I suppose, that you know, that they might put me back in the hospital for getting that bad.

Therapist: Oh, I'd completely forgotten about that, yeah—yet, and that's one thing—But there is another?

Patient: Yeah, I already told you that, too.

Therapist: Oh, yeah, you sure did—I'd forgotten about it—and the other you've already said, too?

Patient: I'm sure I did tell it. (Pause)

Therapist: It doesn't come. All I have when I try to think of it is just the general sense that if you feel—very bad, then it's hard or unpleasant to—but I don't know—so I may have forgotten something—must have. (Pause)

Patient: You talk—you always, hear what I'm saying now, are so good at evading me, you always end up making me talk anyway.

Therapist: You're right.

Patient: You always comment on the question or something, and it just doesn't tell me.

Therapist: (Interjecting) Right, I just instinctively came back—to you when I wondered—what, I, well like saying, because—that's what I felt like saying. You mean to—you mean to say that a few minutes ago we had decided that I would talk . . .

Patient: Well, you—you mentioned it, but (*Therapist:* Right) that's as far as it got.

Therapist: You're right—and I just—was thinking of what you're asking—I'm more interested in you right now than anything else.

Level 5

At stage 5, the therapist communicates warmth without restriction. There is a deep respect for the patient's worth as a person and his or her rights as a free individual. At this level the patient is free to be himself or herself even if this means that he or she is regressing, being defensive, or even disliking or rejecting the therapist. At this stage the therapist cares deeply for the patient as a person, but it does not matter to him or her how the patient chooses to behave. The therapist genuinely cares for and deeply prizes the patient for his or her human potentials, apart from evaluations of his or her behavior or thoughts. The therapist is willing to share equally the patient's joys and aspirations or depressions and failures. The only channeling by the therapist might be the demand that the patient communicate personally relevant material (Truax & Carkhuff, 1967, pp. 58–68).

Example

Patient: . . . . ever recovering to the extent where I could become self-supporting and live alone. I thought that I was doomed to hospitalization for the rest of my life and seeing some of the people over in, in the main building, some of those old people who are, who need a lot of attention and all that sort of thing, is the only picture I could see of my own future. Just one of (*Therapist:* Mhm) complete hopelessness, that there was any —

Therapist: (Interrupting) You didn't see any hope at all, did you?

Patient: Not, not in the least. I thought no one really cared and I didn't care myself, and I seriously — uh — thought of suicide; if there'd been any way that I could end it all completely and not become just a burden or an extra care, I would have committed suicide, I was that low. I didn't want to live. In fact, I hoped that I — I would go to sleep at night and not wake up, because I, I really felt there was nothing to live for. (*Therapist:* Uh, huh [very softly]) Now I, I truly believe that this drug they are giving me helps me a lot, I think, I think it is one drug that really does me good. (*Therapist:* Uh, hm).

Therapist: But you say that, that during this time you, you felt as though no one at all cared, as to what (*Patient:* That's right) . . . what happened to you.

Patient: And, not only that, but I hated myself so that I didn't, I, I felt that I didn't deserve to have anyone care for me. I hated myself so that I, I, I not only felt that no one did, but I didn't see any reason why they should.

Therapist: I guess that makes some sense to me now. I was wondering why it was that you were shutting other people off. You weren't letting anyone else care.

Patient: I didn't think I was worth caring for.

Therapist: So you didn't ev- maybe you not only thought you were — hopeless, but you wouldn't allow people . . . (Therapist statement is drowned out by patient).

Patient: (Interrupting and very loud) I closed the door on everyone. Yah, I closed the door on everyone because I thought I just wasn't worth bothering with. I didn't think it was worthwhile for you to bother with me. "Just let me alone and — and let me rot that's all I'm worth." I mean, that was my thought. And I, I, uh, will frankly admit that when the doctors were making the rounds on the ward, I mean the routine rounds, I tried to be where they wouldn't see me. The doctor often goes there on the ward and asks how everyone is and when she'd get about to me, I'd move to a spot that she's already covered. . .

Therapist: You really avoided people.

Patient: So that, so that she wouldn't, uh, talk with me (*Therapist:* Uh, hm) and when — the few times that I refused to see you, it was for the same reason. I didn't think I was worth bothering with, so why waste your time — let's just . . .

Therapist: Let me ask you, ask you something about that. Do you think it would have been, uh, better if I had insisted that, uh, uh, you come and talk with me?

Patient: No, I don't believe so, doctor. (They speak simultaneously.)

Therapist: I wondered about that; I wasn't sure . . . (Softly)

Patient: I don't — I, I, I . . .

Raush and Bordin (1957) helped define warmth further. Helper warmth they held, has three components.

Commitment. The therapist demonstrates some degree of willingness to be of assistance to the patient. This assistance may vary in degree of activity and concreteness. For example, the therapist may offer help in the form of setting limits, breaking limits, or actively collaborating with the patient in the solution of an external problem, or he may offer help only by committing his time. At any given moment, the therapist occupies some point along a continuum representing degree of commitment. . . . The therapist most typically commits a specified amount of time to the patient; he commits, for the patient's use at those times, a private meeting place which will remain relatively undisturbed by extraneous factors, he commits his skills and his efforts at understanding and aiding the patient; he also commits to the patient a relationship in which the patient's needs and interests are dominant, and in which the therapist's personal demands are minimized. For the patient also there are commitments: to honor appointments, to pay fees regularly, to avoid conscious inhibitions of associations, to discuss impending decisions, and so forth.

Effort to understand. The therapist shows his effort to understand by asking questions designed to elicit the patient's view of himself and the world, by testing with the patient the impressions that he, the therapist, has gained of these views, and by indicating, by comments or other forms of action, his interest in understanding the patient's views. At the other extreme, aside from absence of the kind of behavior we have just described, the therapist tends to act as though he had a preconceived view of the patient, his actions, and his feelings. . . . Certainly, it is the therapist's efforts at understanding which produce the first major emotional tie between patient and therapist in most forms of psychotherapy . . . this effort on the part of the therapist will be a major determinant of "rapport" and of communication between patient and therapist. Such an effort on the part of the therapist may be communicated in many ways: by attentive and unintrusive listening, by questions indicative of interest, by sounds of encouragement, by any of the verbal or nonverbal cues which say in effect, "I am interested in what you are saying and feeling — go on." But whatever the manner of communication, the effort at understanding on the part of the therapist is communication of warmth. . . . The patient's gratification and his willingness to communicate more freely under these circumstances . . . are "natural" responses to warmth, in the sense that both children and adults feel gratified when their serious communications are listened to seriously.

Spontaneity. The least spontaneous therapist is guarded, either consciously or unconsciously masking all of his feelings. These masked feelings may be intimately related to the underlying needs and feelings of the patient, or they may be those which occur as part of the natural interaction between any two people. Such a therapist maintains an impressive mien and is likely to be inhibited in all of his motor expressions, such as gestures. His verbal communications are marked by stereotype, formalism, and stiffness. The least spontaneous therapist may, however, seem to act impulsively. Such impulsivity will have a compelled, unnatural quality. . . . "Simply going through the motions of psychotherapy is not enough," is, and must be, emphasized by supervisors of students of the process. The therapist must be capable of expressing something of himself. . . . Observation of different therapists indicates considerable variability in the amount of affect expressed. Some therapists seem always to have a tight rein on themselves; they are or seem to be emotionless. Others seem to feel much freer to express themselves; they seem more "natural." (p. 352)[7]

Similar behaviors represent warmth in yet other research. In one we read: "During a warm interview the interviewer smiled, nodded her head, and spoke warmly. During a cold interview she spoke unsmilingly, she did not nod her head; and she kept her voice drab and cold." As in much of this type of research, these investigators found that interviewees talked significantly more to the warm interviewer.[8] Another study with a similar result used a helper speaking in a "soft, melodic and pleasant voice" versus speaking in a "harsh, impersonal, and business-like voice" for the comparison of warm versus cold helpers. In a successful repeat study, the same researcher elaborated his definition of warmth in a manner akin to Raush and Bordin's "commitment" and "effort to understand." Specifically, in addition to the voice qualities, the warm helper "showed interest, concern, and attention," whereas his "cold" counterpart displayed "disinterest, unconcern, and nonattentiveness."

Though it is clear that helpers can be trained to reliably show the behavior described above, and these helper behaviors have been shown to affect what the client does, the reader must be cautioned against a too rigid adoption of "a warm stance." Smiling, a pleasant voice, and the like can indeed represent warmth. But if warmth at root is, as Raush and Bordin suggested, commitment, effort to understand and spontaneity, warmth can also be represented behaviorally by directiveness, assertiveness, autonomy-enhancing distancing, and even anger. To a large extent, it is the context and content of the helper-client interaction that will determine if a given instance of

---

[7]From "Warmth in personality development and in psychotherapy" by H. L. Raush and E. S. Bordin, 1957, *Psychiatry, 20*, pp. 351–363. Copyright 1957 by *Psychiatry*. Used with permission.

[8]The term *significantly* will be used throughout this book in its common statistical usage, that is, a statistically significant result is a "real" one, one that might happen by chance only 5 times in 100.

helper behavior is perceived by the client as warmth. Carkhuff and Berenson (1967) made a similar observation when they commented: ". . . it is not always communicated in warm, modulated tones of voice; it may be communicated, for example, in anger. In the final analysis, it is the client's experience of the expression that counts" (p. 28).

Self-disclosure

The trust component of the helper-client relationship (see Figure 2.1) can be positively influenced by helper self-disclosure (Bierman, 1969; Johnson, 1972; Jourard, 1964). Johnson and Matross (1977) described a trust-enhancing, self-disclosure sequence in which (a) the client disclosed personal information about his needs, problems, history, relationships; and (b) the helper responded by offering facilitative conditions and reciprocated in self-disclosure by revealing such information as his views of the client, his reactions to the unfolding therapy situation, and information about himself.

A number of investigations have consistently shown that helper self-disclosure does function to elicit reciprocal client self-disclosure and ratings of greater helper trustworthiness (Bierman, 1969; Drag, 1968; Sermat & Smyth, 1973).[9]

MISCELLANEOUS METHODS

We have seen so far in this chapter that the helper-client relationship can be enhanced by direct statements to the client about the helper's likability (structuring); by the client's observation of a counterpart expressing attraction to a helper, or helper observation of a counterpart expressing attraction to a client (imitation); by a client's hearing other clients rate a helper as attractive (conformity pressure); by describing the helper to the client as someone of considerable expertness, experience, and accomplishment, or by surrounding the helper with various signs and symbols of such expertness and achievement (status); by helper believability and openness about himself or herself; by helper credibility and self-disclosure; or by the facilitative conditions of helping behaviors actually offered the client by the helper (e.g., empathy and warmth). These several approaches can be considered the major methods of relationship enhancement currently available, because of the amount and conclusiveness of research on each. However,

---

[9]Simonson has shown in a number of studies that these positive effects are optimized when the content of what the helper discloses about himself or herself is private (background, preferences, views) but not relevant to the helper's own, personal problems (Simonson & Apter, 1969; Simonson & Bahr, 1974.)

certain other means of improving the nature of the helper-client interaction have also appeared in the professional literature. Each of these should be viewed by the reader as somewhat more tentative or speculative than those just considered, because the amount or quality of supporting research evidence for each is still rather small.

Helper-Client Matching

This approach to the helping relationship, in contrast with those just considered, typically does not seek to alter anything in the helper or client in order to enhance the goodness of their fit. Instead, an effort is made to (a) identify real characteristics of helpers and clients that are relevant to how well they relate, (b) measure helpers and clients on these characteristics, and (c) match helpers and clients into optimal (for client change) pairs based on these measurements. Much of the research on matching is conflicting or inconclusive, but some of it does lead to useful, if tentative, conclusions. The following are frequent characteristics of an optimal helper-client match.

1. Helper and client hold congruent expectations of the role each is to play in the relationship. They understand and agree upon their respective rights and obligations regarding what each is expected to do and not to do during their interactions.
2. Helper and client are both confident of positive results from their meetings. Each anticipates at least a reasonably high likelihood of client change.
3. Helper and client come from similar social, cultural, racial, and economic backgrounds.
4. Helper and client are similar in their use of language, conceptual complexity, extroversion-introversion, objectivity-subjectivity, flexibility, and social awareness.
5. Helper and client are complementary or reciprocal in their need to offer and receive inclusion, control, and affection. The need for inclusion relates to associating, belonging, and companionship versus isolation, detachment, and aloneness. Control is a power or influence dimension, and affection refers to emotional closeness, friendliness, and the like. Helper and client are complementary or reciprocal on these dimensions if the level of inclusion, affection, or control that one member needs to offer approximates the level of that dimension that the other member needs to receive.

Obviously, no given helper and client can be paired on all of these dimensions. However, the greater the number of them reflected in a particular pairing, the more likely that a favorable relationship will develop.

Proxemics

Proxemics is the study of personal space and interpersonal distance. Is there a connection between how far apart two persons sit and their posture, on the one hand, and the favorableness of their relationship on the other hand? First, it does appear that liking in an interview setting leads to physical closeness and a particular type of posture. In an experiment by Leipold (1963), one group of college students were told, "We feel that your course grade is quite poor and that you have not tried your best. Please take a seat in the next room and Mr. Leipold will be in shortly to discuss this with you." Other groups heard neutral or positive statements about their course performance. Those receiving praise subsequently sat significantly closer to the interviewer; those who were criticized chose to sit farther away.

A second study also suggests that increased liking leads to decreased physical distance. Walsh (1971) used imitation procedures to successfully increase how attracted a group of patients were to an interviewer. Before each interview, the office was arranged so that the patient's chair was physically light, on wheels and located at the other end of the room 8 feet from where the interviewer would be sitting. Upon entering the room, the interviewer suggested to the patient that he "pull up the chair." Attracted patients pulled the chair significantly closer to the interviewer than did unattracted patients.

Our concern, of course, is the other way around, that is, relationship enhancement. Does close sitting and certain posturing *lead to* a favorable relationship? This notion was tested in one of our modeling studies. For some patients, the interviewer not only sat close by (27 inches), but also assumed a posture shown in other research to reflect liking. Specifically, he leaned forward (20°) toward the patient, maintained eye contact 90% of the time, and faced the patient directly (shoulder orientation of 0°). Very different distance and posture were involved in the contrasting condition. The interviewer was 81 inches from the patient, leaned backward 30°, showed eye contact 10% of the time, and faced partially away from the patient with a shoulder orientation of 30°. Results of this research did in part show that distance and posture can indeed influence the patient liking that develops. As was true in the case of helper-client matching, relevant proxemic research is not great. Tentatively, however, we may begin to view close distance and "interested" posture as probable relationship enhancers.

Conversational "Dos" and "Don'ts"

A step-by-step, relationship-building "cookbook" is neither possible nor desirable. Obviously, each helper-client pair is different enough from others, so that what we have provided in this chapter should be read and used as *general* suggestions only. How, when, and where a given procedure is used, and what specific form it takes, must be left to the good judgment of each helper. This same proviso applies to the material that follows. Wolberg (1967) has provided a listing of what he views as helper behaviors to include or avoid when trying to build a favorable helper-client relationship. Most of this listing, and the examples he provided, are reproduced below. His suggestions should be taken as guidelines only, and not as a recipe to be applied verbatim.

Avoid exclamations of surprise.

Patient: I never go out on a date without wanting to scream.

Unsuitable responses.

Therapist: Well, for heaven's sake!
Therapist: That's awful!
Therapist: Of all things to happen!

Suitable responses.

Therapist: I wonder why?
Therapist: Scream?
Therapist: There must be a reason for this.

Avoid expressions of overconcern.

Patient: I often feel as if I'm going to die.

Unsuitable responses.

Therapist: Well, we'll have to do something about that right away.
Therapist: Why, you poor thing!
Therapist: Goodness, that's a horrible thing to go through.

Suitable responses.

Therapist: That must be upsetting to you.
Therapist: Do you have any idea why?
Therapist: What brings on this feeling most commonly?

Avoid moralistic judgments.

Patient: I get an uncontrollable impulse to steal.

Unsuitable responses.

Therapist: This can get you into a lot of trouble.
Therapist: You're going to have to put a stop to that.
Therapist: That's bad.

Suitable responses.

Therapist: Do you have any idea of what's behind this impulse?
Therapist: How far back does this impulse go?

Therapist: How does that make you feel?

Avoid being punitive under all circumstances.

Patient: I don't think you are helping me at all.

Unsuitable responses.

Therapist: Maybe we ought to stop therapy.
Therapist: That's because you aren't cooperating.
Therapist: If you don't do better, I'll have to stop seeing you.

Suitable responses.

Therapist: Let's talk about this; what do you think is happening?
Therapist: Perhaps you feel I can't help you.
Therapist: Is there anything I am doing or fail to do that upsets you?

Avoid criticizing the patient.

Patient: I just refuse to bathe and get my hair fixed.

Unsuitable responses.

Therapist: Are you aware of how unkempt you look?
Therapist: You just don't give a darn about yourself, do you?
Therapist: That's like cutting off your nose to spite your face.

Suitable responses.

Therapist: There must be a reason why.
Therapist: Do you have any ideas about that?
Therapist: How does that make you feel?

Avoid making false promises.

Patient: Do you think I'll ever be normal?

Unsuitable responses.

Therapist: Oh, sure, there's no question about that.
Therapist: In a short while you're going to see a difference.
Therapist: I have great hopes for you.

Suitable responses.

Therapist: A good deal will depend on how well we work together.
Therapist: You seem to have some doubts about that.
Therapist: Let's talk about what you mean by normal.

Avoid threatening the patient.

Patient: I don't think I can keep our next two appointments, because I want to go to a concert on those days.

Unsuitable responses.

Therapist: You don't seem to take your therapy seriously.

Therapist: If you think more of concerts than coming here, you might as well not come at all.

Therapist: Maybe you'd better start treatments with another therapist.

Suitable responses.

Therapist: I wonder why the concerts seem more important than coming here.

Therapist: Maybe it's more pleasurable going to the concerts than coming here.

Therapist: What do you feel about coming here for therapy?

Avoid burdening the patient with your own difficulties.

Patient: You look very tired today.

Unsuitable responses.

Therapist: Yes I've been having plenty of trouble with sickness in my family.

Therapist: This sinus of mine is killing me.

Therapist: I just haven't been able to sleep lately.

Suitable responses.

Therapist: I wouldn't be surprised, since I had to stay up late last night. But that shouldn't interfere with our session.

Therapist: I've had a touch of sinus, but it's not serious and shouldn't interfere with our session.

Therapist: That comes from keeping late hours with meetings and things. But that shouldn't interfere with our session.

Avoid displays of impatience.

Patient: I feel helpless and I think I ought to end it all.

Unsuitable responses.

Therapist: You better "snap out of it" soon.

Therapist: Well, that's a nice attitude, I must say.

Therapist: Maybe we had better end treatment right now.

Suitable responses.

Therapist: I wonder what is behind this feeling.

Therapist: Perhaps there's another solution for your problems.

Therapist: You sound as if you think you're at the end of your rope.

Avoid political or religious discussions.

Patient: Are you going to vote Republican or Democratic?

Unsuitable responses.

Therapist: Republican, of course; the country needs good government.

Therapist: I'm a Democrat and would naturally vote Democratic.

Suitable responses.

Therapist: Which party do you think I will vote for?

Therapist: Have you been wondering about me?

Therapist: I wonder what you'd feel if I told you I was either Republican or Democrat. Would either make a difference to you?

Therapist: I vote for whoever I think is the best person, irrespective of party, but why do you ask?

Avoid arguing with the patient.

Patient: I refuse to budge an inch as far as my husband is concerned.

Unsuitable responses.

Therapist: It's unreasonable for you to act this way.

Therapist: Don't you think you are acting selfishly?

Therapist: How can you expect your husband to do anything for you if you don't do anything for him?

Suitable responses.

Therapist: You feel that there is no purpose in doing anything for him?

Therapist: Perhaps you're afraid to give in to him?

Therapist: How do you actually feel about your husband right now?

Avoid ridiculing the patient.

Patient: There isn't much I can't do, once I set my mind on it.

Unsuitable responses.

Therapist: You don't think much of yourself, do you?

Therapist: Maybe you exaggerate your abilities.

Therapist: It sounds like you're boasting.

Suitable responses.

Therapist: That puts kind of a strain on you.

Therapist: Have you set your mind on overcoming this emotional problem?

Therapist: You feel pretty confident once your mind is made up.

Avoid belittling the patient.

Patient: I am considered very intelligent.

Unsuitable responses.

Therapist: An opinion with which you undoubtedly concur.

Therapist: The troubles you've gotten into don't sound intelligent to me.

Therapist: Even a moron sometimes thinks he's intelligent.

Suitable responses.

Therapist: How do you feel about that?

Therapist: That's all the more reason for working hard at your therapy.

Therapist: That sounds as if you aren't sure of your intelligence.

Avoid blaming the patient for his failures.

Patient: I again forgot to bring my doctor's report with me.

Unsuitable responses.

Therapist: Don't you think that's irresponsible?
Therapist: There you go again.
Therapist: When I tell you the report is important, I mean it.

Suitable responses.

Therapist: I wonder why?
Therapist: Do you know why?
Therapist: Perhaps you don't want to bring it.

Avoid rejecting the patient.

Patient: I want you to like me better than any of your other patients.

Unsuitable responses.

Therapist: Why should I?
Therapist: I don't play favorites.
Therapist: I simply don't like a person like you.

Suitable responses.

Therapist: I wonder why you'd like to be preferred by me.
Therapist: Perhaps you'd feel more secure if I told you I liked you best.
Therapist: What do you think I feel about you?

Avoid displays of intolerance.

Patient: My wife got into another auto accident last week.

Unsuitable responses.

Therapist: Those women drivers.
Therapist: Women are sometimes tough to live with.
Therapist: The female of the species is the most deadly of the two.

Suitable responses.

Therapist: How does that make you feel?
Therapist: What do you think goes on?
Therapist: How did you react when you got this news?

Avoid dogmatic utterances.

Patient: I feel cold and detached in the presence of women.

Unsuitable responses.

Therapist: That's because you're afraid of women.
Therapist: You must want to detach yourself.
Therapist: You want to destroy women and have to protect yourself.

Suitable responses.

Therapist: That's interesting; why do you think you feel this way?

Therapist: How far back does this go?

Therapist: What feelings do you have when you are with women?

Avoid premature deep interpretations.

Patient: I've told you what bothers me. Now what do you think is behind it all?

Unsuitable responses.

Therapist: Well, you seem to be a dependent person and want to collapse on a parent figure.

Therapist: You've got an inferiority complex.

Therapist: You never resolved your Oedipus complex.

Suitable responses.

Therapist: It will be necessary to find out more about the problem before I can offer a valid opinion of it.

Therapist: We'll continue to discuss your attitudes, values and particularly your feelings, and before long we should discover what is behind your trouble.

Therapist: That's for us to work on together. If I gave you the answers, it wouldn't be of help to you.

Avoid the probing of traumatic material when there is too great resistance.

Patient: I just don't want to talk about sex.

Unsuitable responses.

Therapist: You'll get nowhere by avoiding this.

Therapist: You must force yourself to talk about unpleasant things.

Therapist: What about your sex life?

Suitable responses.

Therapist: It must be hard for you to talk about sex.

Therapist: All right, you can talk about anything else you feel is important.

Therapist: Sex is always a painful subject to talk about.

Avoid unnecessary reassurance.

Patient: I think I'm the most terrible, ugly, weak, most contemptible person in the world.

Unsuitable responses.

Therapist: That's silly. I think you're very good looking and a wonderful person in many ways.

Therapist: Take it from me, you are not.

Therapist: You are one of the nicest people I know.

Suitable responses.

Therapist: Why do you think you feel that way?

Therapist: How does it make you feel to think that of yourself?

Therapist: Do others think the same way about you?

Express open-mindedness, even toward irrational attitudes.

Patient: I think that all men are jerks.

Unsuitable responses.

Therapist: That's a prejudiced attitude to hold.
Therapist: You ought to be more tolerant.
Therapist: With such attitudes you'll get nowhere.

Suitable responses.

Therapist: What makes you feel that way?
Therapist: Your experiences with men must have been disagreeable for you to have this feeling.
Therapist: Understandably you might feel this way right now, but there may be other ways of looking at the situation that may reveal themselves later on.

Respect the right of the patient to express different values and preferences from yours.

Patient: I don't like the pictures on your walls.

Unsuitable responses.

Therapist: Well, that's just too bad.
Therapist: They are considered excellent pictures by those who know.
Therapist: Maybe your taste will improve as we go on in therapy.

Suitable responses.

Therapist: Why?
Therapist: What type of pictures do you like?
Therapist: What do you think of me for having such pictures?

Make sympathetic remarks where indicated.

Patient: My husband keeps drinking and then gets violently abusive in front of the children.

Unsuitable responses.

Therapist: Why do you continue living with him?
Therapist: Maybe you do your share in driving him to drink.
Therapist: He's a no-good scoundrel.

Suitable responses.

Therapist: This must be very upsetting to you.
Therapist: It must be very difficult to live with him under these circumstances.
Therapist: You must find it hard to go on with this kind of threat over you.
(pp. 584-590)[10]

---

[10]From *The technique of psychotherapy.* 2nd ed. by L. R. Wolberg (1967). New York: Grune & Stratton. Reprinted by permission of Grune & Stratton, Inc. and the author.

The "Resistive" Client

In chapter 1 we entered a prescriptive caution, holding that the diverse change procedures examined in this book are optimally implemented in a differential, tailored, or prescriptive manner. No change-relevant procedures fit all clients; all change-relevant procedures fit some clients. The same statements are also true of relationship-enhancing techniques. The several procedures described and illustrated in the present chapter as potentially relationship enhancing should be viewed as potentially powerful interventions that, nevertheless, are in no instance applicable to all clients. A ready example of this prescriptive perspective concerns empathy. Research of the past decade confirms not only that high levels of perceived helper empathy are facilitative with some client subsamples and irrelevant with certain others, but also that such helper behaviors can function as a negative influence upon the therapeutic relationship in certain other samples of clients. As we have recently noted elsewhere,

> While it is perhaps the most widely held (non-prescriptive) belief in contemporary psychotherapies of all types that an empathic and genuine therapist-patient relationship is a necessary and at times even sufficient facilitator of patient change (Patterson, 1966; Rogers, 1957; Truax & Carkhuff, 1967), the possibility that this generalization might not hold with at least some subtypes of juvenile delinquents has appeared sporadically in the delinquency literature for at least the last 25 years (Goldstein, Heller, & Sechrest, 1966; Lambert, DeJulio, & Stein, 1978; Redl & Wineman, 1957; Schwitzgebel, 1961; Slack, 1960). Characteristic of this perspective is the early statement by Redl and Wineman (1957) specifically warning against overwhelming the delinquent with a close therapeutic relationship and recommending instead that a benevolent but somewhat impersonal and objective style of interaction might more likely lead to favorable therapeutic events, especially in the early stages of treatment. An identical perspective has been operationalized in such therapies as Schwitzgebel and Kolb's (1964) "experimenter-subject psychotherapy," Slack's (1960) "streetcorner research," Stollak and Guerney's (1964) "minimal contact therapy," Sechrest and Strowig's (1962) recommended use of teaching machines, and our own suggestions in this context regarding the likely prescriptive utility of impersonal, machine, and action therapies. (Goldstein et al., 1966)

It is not only the delinquent youngster for whom less, or at least different, might be better than more for relationship-enhancement purposes. DeVoge and Beck (1978) described a broad range of potential clients for whom the closeness, friendliness, and submissiveness of a "typical" therapist-patient relationship could be highly aversive.

> We contend that with many clients, the therapeutic situation is a more complex, perhaps even a grim atmosphere which neither elicits nor offers support for such behaviors from a therapist. We refer to persons predisposed toward hostility, people who tend to prefer noncompliance or resistance toward a therapist. (p. 235)

Munjack and Oziel (1978) assumed a similar position in their valuable explication of diverse types of resistive client behavior. From them, as well as from the several sources mentioned in the last Goldstein quote, it seems clear that substantial numbers of clients exist who, from one perspective, can be viewed as resistive to typical therapist relationship-enhancing behaviors. Rather than view such thwarting as "resistive," we prefer to conclude that such relationship offerings are simply prescriptively less than optimal and often functionally counterproductive. What then ought to be offered to such clients, beyond the general "impersonal and objective" stance described above? Stated otherwise, are there currently available, prescriptively useful means of enhancing the quality of the therapeutic relationship with what might be termed "low relatability" clients? Although this is clearly not a matter that has received considerable empirical scrutiny, given the sheer numbers of such persons, it clearly should. Potentially effective relationship-enhancing techniques for use with such persons are already apparent, and they include employing a less authoritative structure, maintaining patient permission, and acceding to patient need for autonomy and even power (Beutler, 1982); providing patients with a high degree of choice with minimal justification, seeking initial compliance under conditions of low external pressure, and using reattributional training to enhance self-attribution of responsibility (Willis, 1982); using interpretive modeling, antisabotage procedures, paradoxical prescriptions (Spinks & Birchler, 1982); building upon patient variability, acknowledging patient beliefs while challenging them, selectively using initial overnurturance (Wachtel, 1980); and other social-psychological (West & Higginbotham, in press), paradoxical (Bogden, 1982), and eclectic (Lambert, 1982) procedures. Again we stress: The need is considerable, the potential relationship-enhancement technology for such clients contains many good leads at present, the empirical work remains largely undone.

SUMMARY

For whom is this chapter written? Who should our helpers be? Relationship-enhancing procedures, as well as the many helper methods described in the chapters that follow, are not the private property of a chosen few who happen to have earned certain professional credentials. Certainly, such training can lead to skills of considerable positive consequence for client change. But at least as important is the kind of person the helper is. We are in strong agreement with Strupp (1973), who observed

> It seems that there is nothing esoteric or superhuman about the qualities needed by a good therapist! They are the attributes of a good parent and a decent human being who has a fair degree of understanding of himself and his interpersonal relations so that his own problems do not interfere, who is reasonably

warm and empathic, not unduly hostile or destructive, and who has the talent, dedication, and compassion to work cooperatively with others. (p. 2)

Thus, the potential helper's personal background, degree of self-understanding, maturity, typical ways of relating, and concern for others are all as crucial to the outcome of her or his helping effort as is her or his formal training as a helper.

We have held throughout this chapter that, without a favorable helper-client relationship, client change will rarely occur. With such a relationship, client change is possible, or even probable, but not inevitable. Other, more specific, change measures must typically be utilized in addition. We leave to the chapters that follow the task of fully describing and illustrating these specific procedures.

REFERENCES

Beutler, L. E. (1982). *Eclectic psychotherapy*. Elmsford, NY: Pergamon Press.

Bierman, R. (1969). Dimensions for interpersonal facilitation in psychotherapy and child development. *Psychological Bulletin, 72*, 338-352.

Bogden, J. L. (1982). Paradoxical communication as interpersonal influence. *Family Process, 21*, 443-452.

Carkhuff, R. R. (1969). *Helping and human relations*. New York: Holt, Rinehart, & Winston.

Carkhuff, R. R., & Berenson, B. G. (1967). *Beyond counseling and therapy*. New York: Holt, Rinehart, & Winston.

Corrigan, J. D., Dell, D. M., Lewis, K. N., & Schmidt, L. D. (1980). Counseling as a social influence process: A review. *Journal of Counseling Psychology, 27*, 395-441.

DeVoge, J. T., & Beck, S. (1978). The therapist-client relationship in behavior therapy. *Progress in Behavior Modification, 6*, 203-248.

Drag, L. R. (1968). *Experimenter-subject interaction: A situational determinant of differential levels of self-disclosure*. Unpublished master's thesis, University of Florida, Gainesville, FL.

Edelman, E., & Goldstein, A. P. (1984). Prescriptive relationship levels for juvenile delinquents in a psychotherapy analog. *Aggressive Behavior, 10*, 269-298.

Egan, G. (1976). *Interpersonal living*. Monterey, CA: Brooks/Cole.

Frank, J. D. (1961). *Persuasion and healing*. Baltimore: Johns Hopkins Press.

Goldstein, A. P. (1971). *Psychotherapeutic attraction*. Elmsford, NY: Pergamon Press.

Goldstein, A. P. (1973). *Structured learning therapy toward a psychotherapy for the poor*. New York: Academic Press.

Goldstein, A. P. (1981). *Psychological skill training*. Elmsford, NY: Pergamon Press.

Goldstein, A. P., Heller, K., & Sechrest, L. B. (1966). *Psychotherapy and the psychology of behavior change*. New York: John Wiley.

Goldstein, A. P., & Michaels, G. Y. (1985). *Empathy: Development, training and consequences*. Hillsdale, NJ: Erlbaum.

Guerney, B. G. (1977). *Relationship enhancement: Skill training program for therapy, problem-prevention, and enrichment*. San Francisco, CA: Jossey-Bass.

Haley, J. (1963). *Strategies of psychotherapy*. New York: Grune & Stratton.

Ivey, A. E., & Authier, J. (1971). *Microcounseling*. Springfield, IL: Charles C Thomas.

Johnson, D. W. (1972). *Reaching out: Interpersonal effectiveness and self-actualization*. Englewood Cliffs, NJ: Prentice-Hall.

Johnson, D. W., & Matross, R. (1977). Interpersonal influence in psychotherapy: A social psychological view. In A. S. Gurman and A. M. Razin (Eds.), *Effective psychotherapy: A handbook of research*, pp. 395-432. Elmsford, NY: Pergamon Press.

Lambert, M. J. (1982). *Psychotherapy and patient relationships*. Homewood, IL: Dow Jones-Irwin.

Leipold, W. E. (1963). *Psychological distance in a dyadic interview*. Unpublished doctoral dissertation. University of North Dakota, Grand Forks, ND.

Munjack, D., & Oziel, J. L. (1978). Resistance in the behavioral treatment of sexual dysfunctions. *Journal of Sex and Marital Therapy, 42*, 122-138.

Orne, M. T., & Wender, P. H. (1968). Anticipatory socialization for psychotherapy. *American Journal of Psychiatry, 124*, 1202-1212.

Patterson, C. H. (1966). *Theories of counseling and psychotherapy*. New York: Harper & Row.

Raush, H. L., & Bordin, E. S. (1957). Warmth in personality development and in psychotherapy. *Psychiatry, 20*, 351-363.

Redl, F., & Wineman, D. (1957). *The aggressive child*. Glencoe, IL: Free Press.

Rogers, C. R. (1957). The necessary and sufficient conditions of therapeutic personality change. *Journal of Consulting Psychology, 21*, 95-103.

Sabalis, R. F. (1969). *Subject authoritarianism, interviewer status, and interpersonal attraction*. Unpublished master's thesis, Syracuse University, Syracuse, NY.

Schmidt, L. D., & Strong, S. R. (1970). Expert and inexpert counselors. *Journal of Counseling Psychology, 17*, 115-118.

Schwitzgebel, R. (1961). *Streetcorner research: An experimental approach to the juvenile delinquent*. Cambridge, MA: Harvard University Press.

Sechrest, L. B., & Strowig, R. W. (1962). Teaching machines and the individual learner. *Educational Theory, 12*, 157-169.

Sermat, V., & Smyth, M. (1973). Content analysis of verbal communication in the development of a relationship: Conditions influencing self-disclosure. *Journal of Personality and Social Psychology, 26*, 332-346.

Simonson, J., & Apter, S. (1969). *Therapist disclosure in psychotherapy*. Paper presented at the meeting of the Eastern Psychological Association, Philadelphia, PA.

Simonson, N., & Bahr, S. (1974). Self-disclosure by the professional and paraprofessional therapist. *Journal of Consulting and Clinical Psychology, 42*, 359-363.

Slack, C. W. (1960). Experimenter-subject psychotherapy: A new method of introducing intensive office treatment for unreachable cases. *Mental Hygiene, 44*, 238-256.

Spinks, S. H., & Birchler, G. R. (1982). Behavioral-systems marital therapy: Dealing with resistance. *Family Process, 21*, 169-185.

Streltzer, N. E., & Koch, G. V. (1968). Influence of emotional role-playing on smoking habits and attitudes. *Psychological Reports, 22*, 817-820.

Strong, S. R., & Schmidt, L. D. (1970). Expertness and influence in counseling. *Journal of Counseling Psychology, 17*, 81-87.

Strupp, H. H. (1973). On the basic ingredients of psychotherapy. *Journal of Counseling and Clinical Psychology, 41*, 81-87.

Truax, C. B., & Carkhuff, R. R. (1967). *Toward effective counseling and psychotherapy*. Chicago: Aldine.

Wachtel, P. L. (1980). What should we say to our patients?: On the wording of therapists' comments. *Psychotherapy: Theory, Research and Practice, 17,* 183–188.

Walsh, W. G. (1971). *The effects of conformity pressure and modeling on the attraction of hospitalized patients toward an interviewer.* Unpublished doctoral dissertation, Syracuse University, Syracuse, NY.

West, S., & Higginbotham, N. (1985). *Psychotherapy and the psychology of behavior change* (Vol. 2). Elmsford, NY: Pergamon Press.

Willis, T. A. (1982). *Basic processes in helping relationships.* New York: Academic Press.

Wolberg, L. R. (1967). *The technique of psychotherapy* (2nd ed.). New York: Grune & Stratton.

3

Modeling Methods

Martha A. Perry and M. Judith Furukawa

INTRODUCTION

Imagine the following series of events. While watching some children skateboarding down a steep hill, a boy sees one child fall and badly scrape her leg and arm. He decides to go bike riding instead. Back at home, his little sister and brother dress up in their mother's and father's clothes and play house. His older sister, who just bought her first car, is watching her father demonstrate how to change a tire. The children's mother is cooking a fancy French dinner using a recipe she saw Julia Child prepare on television. The evening paper reports a crime similar to one in a movie that was recently in town. Coming home on his bike, the boy pauses to survey a bumpy, muddy path across a vacant lot. Seeing several other children on bikes successfully navigate the path, the boy decides to take this shortcut home.

What do these events have in common? In each instance, the actions or behavior of an individual or group influenced the behavior of another. Many different terms have been offered to account for this process, including *imitation, copying, mimicry, identification,* and *modeling.* In this chapter we will use the term *modeling* to refer to the process of observational learning in which the behavior of an individual or group—the model—acts as a stimulus for similar thoughts, attitudes, or behaviors on the part of another individual who observes the model's performance.

In psychology, the study of imitation was almost totally neglected until the pioneering work by Miller and Dollard (1941). These authors reviewed the theories existing at the time and formulated their own analysis of imitation using a behavioristic framework. Over 20 years passed before the significance of imitative learning for social learning and personality development was highlighted in an important book authored by Bandura and Walters (1963). Since that time, the name of Bandura has become almost synonymous with the study of observational learning and its effects upon social behavior. The term *modeling* has come to replace imitation as a general term encompassing a variety of observational learning processes.

Although there are a number of conflicting theories concerning the nature and operation of the modeling process, the position adopted by Bandura (1977) seems to be the most widely accepted. According to Bandura, the first stage in observational learning is *acquisition*, or learning, of a response. In order to learn, a person must attend to and accurately perceive the important features of a model's behavior. It is assumed that, during the process of observation, the observer acquires images and verbal representations (cognitions) of the model's behavior that are then coded, organized, or rehearsed to facilitate their storage in memory. It is not necessary that the observer be reinforced during the acquisition phase or engage in any overt practice for observational learning to occur.

The second phase of this process concerns *performance* of the modeled behavior by the observer. For performance to occur, the individual must be capable of initiating appropriate actions from the stored symbolic representations and must be motivated to perform. The distinction between acquisition and performance of a modeled response is an important one, for it is often the case that a response acquired through observation is never actually performed by the observer. For example, you might have observed the behavior of a sky diver by watching detailed films of the jumps to the extent that you *learned* what steps are involved in the activity (acquisition phase), even though you have yet to jump out of a plane in an attempt to perform this behavior yourself.

Reinforcement and punishment can play roles both in the acquisition and the performance of modeled behavior. Consequences to the model can serve to selectively focus the observer's attention on the modeled behavior. Further, consequences to the model serve an informative function, notifying the observer of what results might be expected if the behavior were performed. The nature of the consequences motivates the observer to perform or not perform the modeled behavior. There are a variety of other factors that can determine whether a behavior that has been acquired through observational learning is subsequently performed by the observer. Many of these factors will be described in the discussion of the practical application of modeling principles that follows. Once the behavior is performed, consequences to the observer upon performance inform him or her about the adequacy or appropriateness of the behavior and influence further performance.

Before beginning the discussion of how modeling methods can be applied in the clinical setting, it would be helpful to briefly review the *effects* of observational learning. Bandura (1969) outlined three major effects of modeling, each of which has an important counterpart in clinical application. The first involves both the acquisition of new skills and the performance of them. The second effect involves behaviors that have been acquired and performed and that are under some form of inhibition (either personal or social). In these cases, the desired effect of modeling can be either to disinhibit performance (to remove the restraints and increase the level of performance) or to further inhibit performance. The final effect of modeling is to facilitate the performance of previously learned behaviors that, though under no constraints, are not performed at all or are performed only at a low rate.

The learning of new behaviors or of newly integrated patterns of behavior is termed the *observational learning effect*. An example of this effect is a girl's learning to change a tire by watching her father demonstrate the skill. This effect lends itself to a variety of applications, such as teaching basic social skills to withdrawn or socially inept clients, training autistic or mentally retarded children in the basic fundamentals of speech, and instructing hospitalized psychotic patients in skills needed upon their return to the community.

The second effect of modeling occurs when behaviors are under some form of inhibition or restraint for the observer. The observer has already learned how to perform the behavior prior to exposure to the model, and the effect of modeling is to either increase or decrease the rate of performance of this behavior by the observer. In these cases, observation of the consequences experienced by the model following his or her performance is of particular importance. This observation provides an expectation of what might happen to the observer when performing the same behavior. Behaviors exhibited by the model that are followed by positive consequences are likely to produce an increase in the performance of these behaviors by the observer. When this increased performance involves behaviors that were previously under inhibition, a *disinhibitory effect* is said to occur. In the case of the boy who was uncertain about riding his bike on the muddy path, the effect of observing other children successfully negotiating the path served to disinhibit his own behavior. On the other hand, if another bike rider had been observed to slip and fall in the mud (a negative consequence), the boy might have wished to seek a safer route home. In this latter case, an *inhibitory effect* is involved. If the boy had observed children trampling a neighbor's flowers and then being punished, this observation would have had an inhibitory effect. Inhibitory effects decrease the likelihood of performance of the behavior.

Many of the clinical applications of modeling principles fall within the category of disinhibitory effects. Behaviors that have been inhibited by the presence of strong fears or anxiety, as in phobic disorders, have been successfully treated by having phobic individuals witness models who engage in these feared behaviors and experience positive or safe consequences. Some attention has also been paid to the use of inhibitory effects in the clinical setting. Clients who engage in unrestrained behaviors that are socially disapproved (e.g., alcoholics or delinquents who have difficulty in controlling impulsive behavior) might be able to strengthen their own inhibitions against such behaviors by observing a model experience negative consequences for performing those same actions.

The third effect of modeling is termed the *response facilitation effect*. In this case, the effect of modeling is to increase behaviors that the observer has already learned and for which there are no existing constraints or inhibitions. The effect of the model is simply to provide an information 'cue"

Table 3.1. Factors Enhancing Modeling

I. Factors enhancing acquisition (learning and retention)
  A. Characteristics of the model
    1. Similarity of sex, age, race and attitudes
    2. Prestige
    3. Competence
    4. Warmth and nurturance
    5. Reward value
  B. Characteristics of the observer
    1. Capacity to process and retain information
    2. Uncertainty
    3. Level of anxiety
    4. Other personality factors
  C. Characteristics of the modeling presentation
    1. Live or symbolic model
    2. Covert model
    3. Multiple models
    4. Mastery model versus coping model
    5. Graduated modeling procedures
    6. Instructions
    7. Commentary on features and rules
    8. Summarization by the observer
    9. Rehearsal
   10. Minimization of distracting stimuli
II. Factors enhancing performance
  A. Factors providing incentive for performance
    1. Vicarious reinforcement (reward to the model)
    2. Self-reinforcement
    3. Vicarious extinction of fear of responding (no negative consequences to the model)
    4. Direct reinforcement
    5. Imitation of children
  B. Factors affecting quality of performance
    1. Rehearsal and feedback
    2. Participant modeling
  C. Transfer and generalization of performance
    1. Similarity of training setting to everyday environment
    2. Repeated practice affecting response hierarchy
    3. Incentives for performance in natural setting
    4. Learning principles governing a class of behaviors
    5. Provision of variation in training situations

that triggers similar behavior on the part of the observer. For example, the first person to leave a party might prompt everyone else to leave as well. Assuming that almost everyone at the party has the social skills needed to excuse himself or herself and depart, and that for few people are there inhibitions to this behavior, the effect of the first person's leaving is simply to facilitate this response in others.

In the next section a review of factors that enhance modeling is presented. This section is divided into those factors that primarily facilitate acquisition of new responses and are particularly relevant to observational learning effects, and those that enhance performance of behaviors that may be either newly learned or already in the observer's repertoire. It must be noted that, although this section simplifies and organizes a multitude of factors, the effects of those factors are not necessarily so well delineated. Many of the factors that foster acquisition have some effect on performance as well. In like manner, factors affecting performance can affect acquisition. Further, the independent contributions of each factor to a treatment effect have not been clarified. Currently, because the importance of the various factors is already acknowledged, treatment planning frequently relies on "packages" that include as many of the factors as possible in an attempt to insure success. Table 3.1 is an abbreviated checklist of these factors, corresponding to the text presentation. It is provided as a reference to be used in developing modeling programs after becoming familiar with the more specific content of the next section.

The last section of this chapter provides a number of detailed examples of modeling as applied to specific client populations and problem areas. The use of modeling with fear-related behaviors is described first. Next a discussion of modeling as it is most typically used with children is presented. Modeling programs that have been used with clinical populations including developmentally delayed adults and children, psychotic adults, delinquents, drug addicts, and alcoholics follow. Modeling as a training method for helping parents modify their children's behavior and for helping professionals and paraprofessionals is considered last.

FACTORS ENHANCING MODELING

Factors Enhancing Acquisition

According to Bandura, for acquisition to occur, the observer must attend to the relevant behaviors of the model and process and retain the observations. The clinician can do much to assure that conditions facilitate this process by his or her choice of model and model behaviors, by attention to characteristics of the observer, and by careful structuring of the way in which the model and behaviors are presented. In the following sections, suggestions regarding these factors are presented. Table 3.1 summarizes these suggestions in a checklist that can serve as a quick guide for the helping professional who is planning a modeling program.

Characteristics of the Model

Who should play the role of the model? What characteristics of a model are most likely to produce imitative effects? A great deal of research has been conducted on these questions. Reviews by Bandura (1969) and Flanders (1968) summarized much of the early research. More recent studies have expanded this literature and acknowledged the sometimes complex relationships among the model characteristics, the observer characteristics, and the skill or problem that needs to be addressed (Bauer, Schlottmann, Bates & Masters, 1983; Bussey & Perry, 1982; Chartier & Ainley, 1974; Davidson & Smith, 1982; Strichart, 1974). Thus, the appropriate answer to these questions depends on the nature of the problem to be treated, the observer characteristics, and the interaction between them. The following guidelines can be helpful, however, in selecting models.

A model who is similar to the observer in sex, age, race, and attitudes is more likely to be imitated than a dissimilar model. With similarity, the observer is assured that behaviors shown are both appropriate to and attainable by someone like himself or herself. Models who possess prestige in the eyes of the observer are generally more likely to be emulated than low-prestige models; this is especially true when the observer is anxious about her or his performance. It is important, however, to avoid models whose status level is so prestigious that the observer sees their behavior as an unrealistic guide for his or her own behavior.

The effect of competence level of the model in comparison with that of the observer is a complex one. In general, the discrepancy between the model's competence and the observer's perceived competence should not be so great that the observer rejects the model's example. The person might attribute "magical powers" to the performer or feel totally unable to match the model's superior performance. One study, looking at children, found that children who saw an adult superior model lowered their standards, children who saw a peer model matched the standards, and children who saw an inferior model revised their standards downward (Davidson & Smith, 1982). Probably the best choice of model is someone who is just one or two steps advanced from the position of the observer, or one who proceeds from a position of relative similarity to the observer to one of greater proficiency.

Warmth and nurturance on the part of the model also facilitate modeling effects. An unfamiliar model who realistically portrays warmth would be an appropriate choice, as would a model who has previously developed a friendly relationship with the observer. A model who has been associated with reward to the observer is also likely to be one who captures the observer's attention.

Characteristics of the Observer

What factors relating to the observer are of importance in modeling? Bandura (1977) discussed determinants of the modeling effect that reside in the observer. Heller and Marlatt (1969), Marlatt (1972), and Rimm and Medeiros (1970) also pointed out relationships between characteristics of the observer and the modeling effect. Clinicians must attend to attributes of the observer and either alter the state of the observer in order to facilitate modeling or structure the situation in such a way as to best match its demands to the existing capabilities and state of the observer.

The observer's capacity to process and retain information is of primary importance to modeling. The clinician must be aware of the observer's intellectual strengths and weaknesses and alter the modeling situation accordingly. For example, the child with an attention deficit disorder will need his or her attention focused through such techniques as simplification, minimization of outside distractions, and use of a commentary accompanying the modeling display. A mentally retarded person might need a great deal of repetition. An autistic child or schizophrenic adult might need to be taught rudimentary observation and imitation skills before more complex behaviors could be demonstrated. The clinician must also be sensitive to the effects that medications can have on a patient's intellectual processes.

Several characteristics of an observer in a particular situation affect learning. Uncertainty is such a characteristic. An observer who is unsure about the appropriateness of her or his behavior is more likely to attend to a model. In this case, the behavior of the model provides needed information. When an individual is faced with choosing among several behavioral alternatives and the situation itself is ambiguous, a model's behavior and its consequences can serve as a direct signpost for the observer. At a formal dinner party, for example, guests who are uncertain about the function of a finger bowl will watch the host carefully to learn its proper use. One might use this factor clinically by creating doubts in the client's mind about appropriate behaviors and creating a need for information. The person who then demonstrates the appropriate behaviors for the situation will command the attention of the observer.

Anxiety is another observer characteristic that affects learning. Too much anxiety on the part of the observer can interfere with observation, processing, or retention of the model's behavior. It might be necessary to train the observer in relaxation techniques prior to model presentation and instruct him or her to relax during the model's actual performance. This procedure is similar to desensitization therapy, in which it is assumed that relaxation will counter the anxiety response. Although the effectiveness of relaxation training in modeling treatment programs has yet to be fully determined, its use could prove helpful for observers who are unusually apprehensive.

Other personality factors or individual characteristics can contribute to or detract from the effectiveness of modeling. For example, research has shown that impulsive children observing reflective models are more likely to change their behavior than reflective children with impulsive models (Ridberg, Parke, & Hetherington, 1971). Socially isolated children labeled *peer-oriented* increase their social interactions significantly more than nonpeer-oriented children after observing a modeling film (Evers-Pasquale & Sherman, 1975). Zigler and his associates (Turnure & Zigler, 1964; Yando & Zigler, 1971) have found that mentally retarded persons with no identifiable damage or genetic abnormality are more outer directed than children of average intelligence. That is, they look to others for cues about how to solve problems facing them. This suggests that modeling would be an especially effective training technique for these individuals. However, the self-image of the individual can also be important, as subjects with more positive self-images, even subjects who are mentally retarded, show less imitation (Leahy, Balla, & Zigler, 1982). Other characteristics of the observer such as dependency, self-esteem, perceived level of personal competence, socioeconomic status, racial status, and sex interact to determine the effectiveness of the modeling procedure in a given situation. Specific guidelines for each situation cannot be given, but the clinician should consider the possible interaction of these characteristics with the training procedures.

Characteristics of the Modeling Presentation

How should the model be presented to the observer? What instructions or commentary can be given to enhance learning from the model? What behaviors on the part of the observer contribute to learning and retention of the modeled behaviors? A number of authors have provided summaries of these considerations (Bandura, 1969; Goldstein, 1973; Goldstein, Sprafkin, & Gershaw, 1976), and many research studies have been conducted evaluating the use of the following techniques.

There are several forms of model presentation from which to choose. The first involves the use of a *live model* who performs the behavior in the presence of the observer. This approach has a number of advantages. A live model is inherently more interesting than a symbolic one to many people, focusing and sustaining their attention. In addition, a live model can alter his or her performance to simplify or show another way of performing the behavior. The use of live models does carry certain risks, however, in that the model's behavior cannot be exactly predicted or controlled. It would be disastrous, for example, if the model in a phobic treatment procedure began to exhibit increasing anxiety. If this were to happen, the treatment would backfire and the client would be likely to show an increase in fear — an inhibition effect instead of a disinhibition effect.

For many applications of modeling, the therapist might prefer to use a *symbolic model* consisting of representations of the model's behavior in the form of films, videotapes, audiotapes, cartoons, or even written scripts. The medium chosen for presentation of a symbolic model depends on the behavior to be changed and on other practical considerations. Research evidence (reviewed by Bandura, 1969; Thelen, Fry, Fehrenbach, & Frautschi, 1979) suggests that symbolic models can be successfully used in many circumstances. Symbolic models offer several advantages over live models. The model's recorded behavior can be controlled and edited to highlight the relevant portions of the model's behavior. Modeling tapes or films can also be kept on hand for repeated use in a clinical setting and can more easily be used in a group treatment situation.

A *covert model*, a variation sometimes used, is one that is imagined by the learner (Cautela, 1976; Harris & Johnson, 1980; Kazdin, 1976). The therapist describes and instructs the client regarding the learning situation and the appropriate skills and behaviors. The client is then asked to imagine the other person, a model, performing the behaviors. The procedure can also have the client imagine herself or himself as the model. Whether the client is able to use imaginal processes is important and must be assessed before use of this procedure.

Often the modeling procedures can be improved through the use of *multiple models*, some of whom are similar to the observer and others of whom vary along such dimensions as age, sex, and race. Using different models enhances the presentation by showing both the generality of the behavior and its appropriateness for the particular observer. Multiple models naturally show some variability in their performance of the behavior, thereby suggesting alternatives to the observer and increasing his or her flexibility in other situations. Not only do multiple models enhance the modeling effect for a single observer, but they are also especially important for group treatment. Multiple models increase the probability that at least one of the models will be perceived as similar to him or her by each of the members of the group. One caution in using multiple models emerges from a study by Fehrenbach, Miller, and Thelen (1979) that demonstrated that if multiple models were inconsistent in their behavior, little imitation of any model occurred.

A characteristic of the modeling presentation that has received considerable attention has to do with *coping* versus *mastery* performance (Ginther & Roberts, 1982; Klorman, Hilpert, Michael, LaGana, & Sveen, 1980; Meichenbaum, 1972; Sarason, 1975). The distinction is between a model who begins performance at a level of proficiency similar to that of the observer and progresses to competent performance and a model who performs competently at the outset. A coping model might initially show lack of performance skills and affect (anxiety, lack of confidence) that interfere with performance. The model then verbalizes her or his own initial feelings and subsequent problem-solving or coping strategies (*cognitive modeling*) while improving behaviorally. Although the evidence is not all in favor of a coping model, this is an approach that should be considered, particularly for hesitant or anxious clients or those whose problem-solving skills are deficient.

Graduated modeling procedures can also be used when demonstrating complicated skills or behaviors. The skills are presented and mastered first in their component parts. Then the entire behavior sequence is reconstructed. When teaching motor behaviors such as driving an automobile or playing a musical instrument, for example, it is advisable to break the sequence into simple components and present the basic steps individually before demonstrating the entire chain of responses. The degree to which one must simplify depends on the complexity of the skill and on the capabilities of the observer.

The use of *instructions* or other commentary should also be considered as part of the modeling presentation. Initial instructions that explain what the observer will see in the modeling display and tell the observer that he or she will be expected to reproduce the modeled behavior increase the observer's attention to the model. The instructions "prime" the observer to watch for particular aspects of the model's performance, thus establishing an appropriate instructional set. The importance of the behavior to be observed can be further emphasized by having the narrator point out the functional relevance of the behavior for the observer.

In cases in which the modeled behavior is particularly complicated or abstract, learning and retention can be facilitated by having either the model or a narrator comment on the important features of the modeled behavior and on the general principle or rule governing the model's performance. As an example, suppose a model were demonstrating assertive behavior to a withdrawn, socially inept observer. The scene involves ordering dinner in a restaurant and discovering that the steak is too tough to eat. The model exhibits an assertive response in this situation by requesting the waitress to bring another steak. The model can comment at this point

> That was an example of an assertive response. I was entitled to a good steak and was willing to pay for it. I explained the difficulty in an open and friendly manner to the waitress and asked her to bring me another steak. Afterwards I felt good about myself and enjoyed my meal.

By listening to the model highlight the essential characteristics of an assertive response, the observer is more likely to remember the behavior and is in a better position to apply this form of response in a variety of different situations. As an additional aid to retention, the observer can be asked by the therapist to summarize the main features and general rules associated with the model's behavior. Several studies (e.g., Bandura, Grusec, & Menlove, 1966) have found that observers who actively summarize the model's behavior are better able to learn and retain this information.

Retention is also aided by having the observer rehearse the modeled behavior either during the modeling presentation itself or at one or more times following the demonstration. *Rehearsal* can be active, that is, actual performance of the behavior, or covert, in which case the observer imagines performing the behaviors. *Covert rehearsal* serves as an aid for coding the modeled behavior, whereas active rehearsal helps in both coding and developing the necessary motor and verbal skills required to perform the behavior smoothly.

Attention should also be paid to designing the modeling situation in a way that minimizes distractions to learning. For example, in a film or videotape presentation, the room should be darkened and noise kept to a minimum in order to focus on the display itself. Attention to an audiotaped model can be improved by presenting it to the observer through earphones. When live models are used, particularly in a naturalistic setting, every attempt should be made to reduce the distracting influence of other individuals or environmental events.

We can see that there are many factors that can affect the processes of acquisition and retention. Although not all of them might be under the control of the individual planning the modeling procedure, careful consideration of those that are will lead to more successful intervention. The goal is to produce the best possible modeling package within the constraints imposed by a particular setting. In the next section, we focus on those aspects of the modeling procedure that relate to performance.

Factors Enhancing Performance

Beyond learning a behavior and retaining cognitions about its nature and its appropriateness for a particular situation, a person must also actually produce that behavior when the right conditions present themselves. Bandura separates this performance phase of modeling from the acquisition phase discussed in the previous section. In the clinical situation, treatment is not considered successful until the modeled behavior is performed. The clinician can design modeling programs that provide incentives for performance, enhance the quality of performance, and facilitate transfer and generalization of performance. Table 3.1 summarizes the suggestions that follow.

Factors Providing Incentives for Performance

How can the therapist build *incentives* into the modeling presentation that will motivate the observer to perform these same responses? A variety of experimental studies reveal that, when a model's behavior is rewarded, or even when the consequences of his or her actions simply are not aversive, the probability that the observer will match these behaviors is significantly increased. Observation of a model who is punished for his or her behavior, on the other hand, usually produces a decrease in performance of the modeled behavior.

Observation of the reinforcing consequences to the model's behavior involves the process of *vicarious reinforcement*. This procedure is to be distinguished from *direct reinforcement*, in which the observer is reinforced for the performance of an imitative response. Vicarious reinforcement has two main effects. It provides the observer with both information concerning the relevant features of the model's performance and an incentive or inducement to copy the model's behavior. As an example, suppose a model is shown engaging in a series of trial-and-error behaviors while attempting to solve a difficult puzzle. He or she discovers a response that leads to a correct solution. At this point, the model is rewarded by an onlooker who says, "Good! You solved the puzzle by that last move!" By seeing the model receive social approval at that particular moment, the observer gains both information concerning the most effective response in that situation (the reinforcement identifies the correct response) and an incentive to perform the same behavior in order to receive a similar reward. In the absence of an extrinsic source of reinforcement, similar effects can be obtained by having the model reward himself or herself for the desired behavior. An example of verbal self-reinforcement is "Wow! I solved the puzzle by myself — good for me!" The use of self-reinforcement by the model has an additional advantage in that, not only is the desired behavior demonstrated, but a method of self-control is also shown.

In some situations, for example the treatment of fear-related behaviors, the fact that the model experiences no negative consequences for her or his behavior operates in a manner similar to vicarious reinforcement. The safe consequences contrast sharply with the unpleasant ones imagined by the fearful observer and encourage her or him to try the same behaviors.

Direct reinforcement to the observer for performing a modeled behavior increases the probability that the behavior, once performed, will be repeated. During practice sessions the therapist can greatly augment the effects of treatment by encouraging and rewarding the observer for successful performance. The direct experience of reinforcement is likely to be at least as effective as, if not more effective than, vicarious reinforcement. In participant modeling programs (to be explained in the next section), the model provides rewards directly to the observer as he or she performs along with the model. The principles of vicarious and direct reinforcement have been well documented in the modeling literature (Bandura, 1971; Kanfer, 1965).

Some special procedures might be helpful in facilitating children's performance of modeled behaviors. Having the model first imitate the child's behaviors can increase the child's subsequent imitation of the model. Although the factors relating to this effect have still to be clarified, researchers (Kaufman, Kneedler, Gamache, Hallahan, & Ball, 1977) have suggested that being imitated is reinforcing to children and provides an incentive for their later imitation of the model, although children respond more favorably to peer models if they perceive the model's imitation of them as coincidental rather than deliberate (Thelen, Miller, Fehrenbach, & Frautschi, 1983).

Factors Affecting Quality of Performance

Given that an observer performs at least an approximation of a modeled behavior, in what ways can the therapist help to make the behavior more acceptable or of better quality? The fact of having observed and learned about a behavior does not assure that one can perform that behavior correctly. The more complex the behavior, for example learning to play the piano, the more likely that its performance will be initially inaccurate.

Active rehearsal of a modeled behavior interspersed with repeated modeling displays is one way to give the observer multiple opportunities to compare performance with the standard and make modifications that improve quality. *Feedback* as to the adequacy of the behavioral attempts facilitates this process. As part of the feedback, the therapist might also wish to utilize verbal prompts or "coaching" if the observer fails to respond or responds incorrectly. The therapist could say, for example, "Well, that was a good try, but you didn't get it exactly right that time because. . . . Okay, let's try it again and see if you can do it the way I suggested," or "Let's watch it and look closely at those places where you didn't get it quite right."

A procedure closely related to rehearsal is *participant modeling*. Originally developed by Ritter (1968, 1969) as a treatment method for phobic disorders, this procedure involves direct interaction between the model and the observer. After demonstrating the desired behavior, the model guides the observer through the steps involved, offering physical assistance if necessary. It is easy, during the procedure, for the model to provide immediate feedback about response accuracy and to selectively reinforce more correct performance as the observer improves. The essential features of participant modeling as applied to the treatment of fears are found in Bandura, Blanchard, and Ritter (1969) and Klingman, Melamed, Cuthbert, and Hermecz (1984).

Transfer and Generalization of Performance

Of most interest to therapists using modeling training programs is insuring that clients perform the trained behaviors in their daily settings—on the ward, at school, in the community. How can training be structured so as to foster transfer and generalization? Goldstein, Sprafkin, and Gershaw (1976) summarized applicable principles and demonstrated in Structured Learning Training programs the incorporation of these principles into training.

The therapist can provide training in situations most like those that the client encounters in daily living. The people with whom the observer usually interacts can be involved in the training process. Ward staff, for example, can be asked to participate in training sessions, so that the patients are able to practice with them. Or, training can take place in the actual physical setting in which the behavior should occur. The more similar the training setting to the natural setting in which the behaviors should eventually occur, the more likely that observers will transfer performance of learned behaviors to that setting.

Repeated practice is a very important factor in facilitating transfer. When an individual is faced with a commonly occurring situation, the most likely behaviors to be displayed are those that are highest in the individual's response hierarchy. Although behaviors might be correctly performed in a training situation, if they have not been practiced frequently enough to make them more familiar than the old, well-established behaviors, they are unlikely to be exhibited outside of the training setting.

Just as incentives for performance are important in the training setting, so are they needed in the natural setting. Reinforcement increases the likelihood that a behavior will be transferred and will continue to be performed. Often the naturally occurring consequences for a behavior are quite different from the training consequences for the same behavior, even to the point that a desirable behavior is discontinued in the everyday setting. Children with newly learned compliance or helping behaviors, for example, can have those behaviors inadvertently extinguished by parents or teachers who take good behavior in children for granted and therefore fail to reinforce such behaviors. Involving parents and teachers in the training process and helping them continue to provide appropriate consequences for performance of desirable behaviors helps foster the transfer of these behaviors to the natural setting.

Many of the suggestions made for enhancing the acquisition of behaviors are also applicable to fostering generalization. Learning the rules and principles that govern a behavior rather than simply learning to copy the behavior in isolation gives the observer a way of thinking about a new situation and deciding whether a behavior from that general response category is appropriate. For example, when teaching an observer to assert himself or herself in a restaurant when unacceptable food is served, one can also teach the principle that the person as a consumer is entitled to acceptable goods in general and can pleasantly but firmly demand his or her rights. Then, when the client faces a different situation in which assertion is appropriate, he or she will be more likely to produce behavior from the overall category of assertive responses under those circumstances as well. An observer who has simply had rote practice sending back unacceptable food is far less likely to make this generalization. A training procedure that presents general principles is therefore helpful, as is discussion of those principles with the observer and asking the observer to summarize characteristics of the overall class of behaviors.

Training for generalization can be expanded beyond cognitive training to the performance sphere. Rather than modeling and providing practice in one instance of a behavior, the therapist can present multiple situations that demonstrate variations of a single behavior. A client can observe and practice an assertive response in a restaurant, in a store, with a door-to-door salesperson, with a man or a woman, with a submissive other or an argumentative other, and so on. Such variety helps the observer to develop her or his own general principles and permits her or him to gain practice and performance feedback under a variety of conditions. The real world is likely to produce fewer surprises for the observer when training has been diverse.

It is clear that a training program that focuses only on the learning and performance of specific behavior in the training setting is incomplete. Transfer of behaviors to the everyday setting and generalization of behaviors to new situations that might arise are just as important. In addition, clients should either be taught variations on the modeled behavior or principles governing the class of behaviors, so that generalization in terms of form of response will also occur.

We now turn to specific examples of the application of modeling procedures to a variety of settings with diverse client or patient populations.

APPLICATIONS OF MODELING METHODS WITH SPECIFIC POPULATIONS

Modeling in the Treatment of Fear-Related Behaviors

A common use of modeling in clinical settings has been in the treatment of behaviors that are under the inhibition of fear or anxiety. Although early research in this area often focused on fears such as snake phobia (Bandura, Blanchard, & Ritter, 1969) that have little relevance to everyday life, more recent research has looked at the use of modeling with fear of dental procedures, operations, testing situations, and even commonly encountered animals such as cats and dogs.

Klingman, Melamed, Cuthbert, and Hermecz (1984) used a videotape to present two methods of dealing with fear of dental procedures (in this case, more specifically, injections). Thirty-eight children, screened to select those with preexisting dental fear, observed both a male and a female peer demonstrate the use of controlled breathing and imagery distraction to counteract fear. One group of children, in addition to observing the film, had an opportunity to practice these techniques briefly after they were demonstrated. A variety of measures were used including self-report; physiologic measures of skin resistance, heart rate, and respiration; and dentist's and observers' ratings of fear and cooperation. Because these researchers were already confident of the efficacy of modeling in reducing fears, they chose to look at the differences between the group exposed to modeling alone and the group that also practiced the skills. The results gave support to the efficacy of adding periods of active practice to modeling for the learning and utilization of coping skills. Two incidental findings pointed out the importance of individual differences: "Children who reported greater self-control to begin with tended to show lower fear after participant modeling than those lower in self-control," and "Children high in defensiveness recalled less information after peer film viewing and were rated as more fearful than children lower in defensiveness" (p. 421).

In an earlier study, Melamed and Siegel (1975) investigated the use of modeling in reducing the anxiety of children who were facing surgery. Anxiety on the part of children scheduled for hospitalization and surgery is felt to create problems on several levels. Preoperative anxiety has been suggested as a significant factor in impeding recovery from surgery. Behavior problems, either transient or long-term in nature, have been observed in children hospitalized for surgery. Melamed and Siegel studied 60 children between the ages of 4 and 12 who were scheduled for elective surgery (tonsillectomies and hernia or urinary-genital tract repair). Thirty of these children saw a modeling film immediately prior to hospital admission. The other 30 viewed a control film about a boy on a nature trip in the country. In the following excerpt, Melamed and Siegel described the modeling film:

The experimental film, entitled *Ethan Has an Operation*, depicts a 7-year-old white male who has been hospitalized for a hernia operation. This film, which is 16 minutes in length, consists of 15 scenes showing various events that most children encounter when hospitalized for elective surgery from the time of admission to time of discharge, including the child's orientation to the hospital ward and medical personnel such as the surgeon and anesthesiologist; having a blood test and exposure to standard hospital equipment; separation from the mother; and scenes in the operating recovery rooms. In addition to explanations of the hospital procedure provided by the medical staff, various scenes are narrated by the child, who describes his feelings and concerns . . . at each stage of the hospital experience. Both the child's behavior and verbal remarks exemplify some anxiety and apprehension, [yet] he is able to overcome his initial fears and complete each event in a successful and nonanxious manner. (p. 514)

The investigators used multiple measures of situational and trait anxiety to study the children's response both preoperatively and postoperatively. Some of these involved observer ratings, others involved self-ratings, and some were physiologic measures. The children were also rated on number and degree of behavior problems. The efficacy of preoperative preparation using a modeling film was demonstrated on all measures of situational anxiety. In addition, children viewing the modeling film did not show any increase in behavior problems from the preoperative to postoperative assessment periods. This was in contrast with the children who saw the nature film (control group). These differences are of particular interest because *all* children received the usual hospital-initiated preoperative counseling and demonstration procedures. Any changes produced by the film were therefore above and beyond those produced by hospital staff efforts.

Four weeks later, the children returned to the hospital for postsurgery examinations. This provided a test of generalization of film effects because it was a similarly stressful event that was not specifically depicted in the modeling film. Group differences were maintained on all measures of situational anxiety. In addition, children who had viewed the modeling film showed a significant reduction in anxiety-related behaviors as compared with their prefilm ratings.

Although both of the previous studies point out the usefulness of modeling in alleviating children's fears, modeling, either alone or in conjunction with other techniques, has proven valuable with adults as well. Ladouceur (1983) worked with 36 adults ranging in age from 21 to 62 whose "lives were markedly restricted by their phobias" (p. 942) of dogs and cats. In this study, as with many of the more recent studies, the focus was on discovering the most effective treatment package rather than on examining the role of modeling per se. Three treatment groups were compared with a placebo (discussion) treatment. Each group received participant modeling training that involved 20 progressively more difficult tasks with the feared animal. The participant modeling had the therapist first perform a task, followed by the subject attempting the same. If the subject was unable to do so, the therapist would aid the subject by breaking the task down into small steps or by physically assisting the subject in carrying out the task. Components designed to change fearful cognitions were added to two of the groups (self-verbalization and self-instructional training).

Immediately after training, which could last up to a maximum of eight 1-hour sessions, all treatment groups showed an equal amount of improvement in their behavior in relation to the feared animal and an equal increase in their self-efficacy. At follow-up 1 month later, the participant-modeling-only group and the participant-modeling-with-self-verbalization group still showed less fearful behavior when compared with the control group. The participant-modeling-with-self-instruction group, however, no longer showed an improvement in their behavior. These authors concluded that the cognitive portion of their treatment package did not add to the effectiveness of the participant modeling and might, in fact, have actually detracted from learning in the case of the group that had self-instruction training. Interestingly, behavior changes were not accompanied by lowered self-ratings of anxiety, although subjects did feel more able to handle their anxiety (increased self-efficacy).

Covert modeling has also been a component of treatment programs for anxieties. Harris and Johnson (1980) assigned 48 test-anxious subjects to one of three treatment groups or to a waiting list control. The treatments included a study skills training group in which a variety of self-management and study skills were taught; a self-control desensitization group that incorporated the study skill training as well as desensitization including relaxation training and hierarchy construction; and an individualized covert modeling group. The latter group received the study skills training, and they developed hierarchies of anxieties; they did not receive training in relaxation. Instead, they were helped to establish personal images of their own competency based on past experiences and then to use these coping images of themselves as models as they worked through their anxiety hierarchies.

The individualized covert-modeling-plus-study-skills group was shown to be significantly improved on most self-report measures of test anxiety; they also showed improved academic performance in a subsequent school quarter. The self-control-desensitization-plus-study-skills group showed an equal improvement on test anxiety, but they did not show improvement in academic performance. The group receiving study skills training alone showed less improvement on the anxiety measures and no change in academic performance. The waiting list control group showed no change on anxiety measures but a significant decrease in academic performance. When the covert desensitization treatment was provided for the control group at a later time, however, the original findings were replicated. This study provides one of the strongest supports for the usefulness of covert modeling but clearly emphasizes its use within a context that provides many other aids to behavior change, including training in self-management, identification of anxiety-arousing situations, and pairing of coping images with a hierarchical arrangement of anxiety images.

As can be seen, the trend in the treatment of phobias is toward combining several techniques into a treatment package. The theoretical distinctions

among techniques, which seemed clear when behavioral programming was
in its infancy, have blurred with the passage of time, but the end result
looks to be more efficacious interventions.

The Use of Modeling with Children

Modeling has come to be a common technique for teaching a wide variety of skills to children, perhaps because the elements of a modeling package, including various symbolic representations of models, role-playing,
and other practice procedures, are concrete, developmentally appropriate,
and appealing to children. The majority of the current literature focuses on
social skills training and includes attention to both the teaching of cognitive
problem-solving skills and the performance aspect of social behavior.
Spence (1983), in a review of social skills programs, pointed out that the
traditional components of such training include instructions and discussion, modeling, role-playing, coaching, feedback, social reinforcement,
and homework. She pointed out the usefulness of modeling for the facilitation of existing skills but emphasized the importance of coaching when new
skills are being taught.

Several recent books provide concrete guidelines for the professional
who would set up skill training programs for children. Cartledge and Milburn (1980), for example, reviewed skill training methods and presented a
list of resources including puppets, books, films, and filmstrips to be used
in modeling and role-play games. McGinnis and Goldstein (1984) likewise
gave concrete steps for the trainer who would use Structured Learning for
teaching prosocial skills to children. Structured Learning includes the elements of modeling, role-playing, performance feedback, and transfer of
training.

Modeling certainly can be and is used by parents and others in informal
social situations. The examples at the beginning of this chapter demonstrated the pervasiveness of modeling as an informal training procedure.
Other examples might include the parent who demonstrates (models) a variety of home behaviors such as making a bed, setting a table, washing the
hands; the sibling who demonstrates how to play a game or throw a ball;
and the coach who demonstrates a catcher's stance.

Considerable modeling also goes on in classrooms. The teacher often
demonstrates the academic skills that students are expected to perform. For
example, 2 x 2 = 4 is written on the board. "Now, class, you do the problem on your work sheets like this one I've shown you," or

Johnny (reading aloud): Bob and his brother looked in the . . . uh . . .
the . . .

Teacher: . . . window . . .

Johnny: . . . the window of the pet shop.

The teacher is not the only model available in the classroom. Several examples show how peers, paraprofessionals, and filmed models could be used effectively in schools.

Csapo (1972) solicited the help of 6 normal primary schoolchildren to be models of appropriate classroom behavior to 6 emotionally disturbed classmates. The peer models were to sit with the emotionally disturbed children for 3 weeks to show the right kind of behavior for school. The emotionally disturbed peer was told to watch his or her partner and to try to do what that child was doing. The peer model gave tokens to the partner whenever he or she was doing things right.

The target behaviors for each child were defined. Inappropriate behaviors to be modified included such things as speaking out of turn, sucking the thumb, and poking others. Each emotionally disturbed child exhibited fewer inappropriate behaviors and more appropriate behaviors over the course of the program. In addition, it is reported anecdotally that peer models developed more positive attitudes toward their partners and that peer relationships in general improved.

What is important to note here? *First*, once the intervention procedures are initiated, the teacher can proceed with the regular academic program for all children. She or he need not interrupt the entire class to attend to misbehavior. *Second*, not only do target students gain, but the models might show important gains as well. And *third*, the fact that such young children can successfully participate in this type of program suggests that almost any mature-for-age child could serve as an effective peer model. Variations of this plan would permit simultaneous modeling to a number of children by one model or one-to-one peer modeling to just one child in a classroom who might need special help. Several children could be selected to model a single behavior for one child or to model different behaviors for the same child.

Sometimes, however, peer or teacher modeling is an inappropriate choice for treatment. Ross, Ross, and Evans (1971) reported the modification of behavior by modeling and guided participation of an extremely withdrawn 6-year-old child. Because of the severity of the child's problem, using the teacher as a therapist was not feasible. The child needed so much attention that the teacher would have had to ignore the rest of the class to attend to him. Because the child avoided his peers, they could not serve as models for him either.

In this study, an experimenter (psychologist) and a model (undergraduate student) conducted a 7-week treatment program in the preschool. Although such personnel might not be routinely available, a program could be conducted by trained paraprofessionals such as willing mothers or other volunteers. This program was designed, first, to establish generalized imitation of the model, that is, to get the child to copy or imitate any model

behaviors. Second, the program used modeling to eliminate fear and avoidance behaviors and to teach social interaction and motor and game skills.

In the first phase, lasting four sessions, M (model) was paired with a variety
of tangible and social rewards; was positive and demonstrative to S (subject)
and rewarded him for imitative responses; and was immediately responsive to
S's bids for attention, help, and approval. When M was absent E (experimenter) encouraged S to reproduce M's behaviors and rewarded him for imitative responses. By the end of this phase, the facilitating effect of nurturance on
imitation was confirmed. S was strongly attached to M: he talked constantly
about M to E, reproduced many of M's verbal and nonverbal behaviors, and
waited eagerly at the door of the preschool for M to come. (Ross et al., 1971,
p. 275)

Now that the model had become valued to the child and was imitated by
him, the second phase of the program was initiated. This phase had several
steps.

1. The model demonstrated social interactions with other children. These
   were graduated in degree of approach and interaction. If the child did
   not watch, as sometimes happened, a commentary by either the
   experimenter or the model was given.
2. Pictures, stories, and movies of children approaching and relating to
   other children were shown to the child and discussed with him by the
   model or the experimenter (symbolic modeling).
3. Reluctant peer interactions were modeled, and the model received reassurance and encouragement from the experimenter. This step was taken
   to create similarity between the child and the model and to show
   progression in social interaction.
4. The model and/or the experimenter modeled appropriate social behaviors in humorous situations. The child was drawn into these sessions.
5. The model and the child together participated in a graduated series of
   social interactions.
6. The model demonstrated, and helped the child practice, games and
   other preschool appropriate skills.
7. The child was tested outside of the school setting (e.g., sent into a group
   of strange children in a park). He received encouragement and reward
   from the model or the experimenter for his performance on these occasions. In addition, these situations provided material for additional
   role-play.

After treatment, according to the measurements used in this study, the
child's behaviors were very similar to those of the socially competent children in the classroom. Thus, through the help of outside personnel, major
changes can be brought about within the naturalistic school setting, using
models and guided participation. Note that this program made use of both

live and symbolic models, of guided participation, of prompting, of direct reinforcement, and of training for generalization.

Treatment approaches need not be directed at only one child at a time. Mitchell and Milan (1983) worked with 6 preschool children in an inner-city child care center. Their treatment employed symbolic modeling through the use of cartoon models. The cartoon characters, including Wonder Woman and Superman, showed such appropriate classroom behaviors as cleaning up and group-time behavior. The authors reported that these procedures were successful in creating behavior change.

Another example of a group procedure was presented by Goodwin and Mahoney (1975). These authors used modeling techniques to increase the amount of nondisruptive behavior demonstrated by 3 hyperactive, impulsive boys in their classroom. These boys, who were between the ages of 6 and 11, showed a marked inability to cope with verbal aggression. The modeling procedure involved a verbal taunting game in which one child stands inside a circle 2 feet in diameter while other children taunt him from the perimeter of an outer circle 6 feet in diameter. The 3 boys observed a 3-minute videotape of a 9-year-old male model participating in this game. According to Goodwin and Mahoney,

> In addition to remaining ostensibly calm, looking at his taunters, and remaining in the center of the circle, the model was portrayed as coping with verbal assaults through a series of covert self-instructions. These thoughts, which were dubbed in on the tape, consisted of statements such as "I'm not going to let them bug me" and "I won't get mad." (p. 201)

One week later, the three boys saw the videotape again, but this time the coping thoughts and actions of the model were pointed out and discussed. After viewing the videotape, the boys were asked to recall as many of the coping responses as they could.

The boys played the taunting game before seeing the model, in between the two modeling sessions, after the second session, and subsequently at follow-up. The boys made very few coping responses before observing the model. Interestingly, their behavior remained unchanged after the first modeling session. After the second session, however, which included discussion and rehearsal of coping responses, their performances improved dramatically and were maintained at follow-up. Of more importance than their improvement in playing the taunting game was the change in the boys' classroom behavior. Prior to participation in the modeling procedure, the three boys were observed to display nondisruptive behavior 50%, 64%, and 54% of the time. At follow-up, their rates of appropriate classroom behavior had increased to 86%, 91%, and 91%, respectively.

McGinnes and Goldstein (1984) provided a step-by-step guideline to trainers for setting up Structured Learning for a variety of skills. One of their transcripts gives the feel of how a training session might proceed.

After some procedures designed to enhance the students' motivation to learn the skills of this session, and after formulation of the skills for the session, a modeling situation was set up. The leader, Mr. Jennings, related the skill to the children in the group and then reviewed the steps to dealing with it.

> *Mr. Jennings:* Okay, we have the steps to the skill of Dealing with Your Anger. And many of you came up with problems you have where Dealing with Anger could help you. Tom, you get in trouble with your mom. Chris, you've tried ignoring and that hasn't seemed to work for you. And Michelle, you said that when you get mad and yell, then you get in trouble. Ms. Benson and I are going to act out the skill steps to Dealing with Your Anger. Ms. Benson will be sitting at this desk working and I'll walk by her desk. I'm going to knock her papers on the floor. I want you to all watch very carefully to see if Ms. Benson follows all the steps. What is the first step Ms. Benson needs to do?

> *Tammy:* (Looking at the steps written on the chalkboard.) Stop and count to ten.

> *Mr. Jennings:* Good. The next step.

> *Willie:* Think of your choices.

> *Mr. Jennings:* Yes. And what are her choices?

> *Chris:* Talk to the person in a friendly way.

They go on to finish listing all the choices.

> *Mr. Jennings:* Great. Now let's watch to see if Ms. Benson follows all the steps. (Ms. Benson is sitting at a desk near the group and begins to work. Mr. Jennings walks by and knocks her papers to the floor.)

> *Ms. Benson:* He did it again. (She sighs.) Boy, that makes me angry! But I won't let him know that he's getting to me. So, first I have to stop and count to ten. One . . . two . . . three . . . four . . . five . . . six . . . seven . . . eight . . . nine . . . ten. Now I think of my choices. I could walk away, but he's done this before and I've already tried that. I could do something I like to do, but I have to get this work done. I think I'll try talking to him. Maybe if I tell him I have to get my work done, he'll stop doing this. Mr. Jennings, I've been trying to get this work done and now my papers are all messed up. Would you help me pick them up so I can get this project done?

> *Mr. Jennings:* Oh, well, I'm sorry. I guess I did mess things up for you.

> *Ms. Benson:* Yes, but I'd appreciate it if you'd help me.

> *Mr. Jennings:* Okay . . . sorry. (He assists Ms. Benson in picking up her papers.)

> *Ms. Benson:* Well, how did I do? Did I follow the first step?

> *Chris:* Yeah. You counted to 10.

> *Mr. Jennings:* Yes, you did a good job of stopping and counting to 10 to control your anger. Did she follow Step 2?

> *Tom:* Yes.

> *Mr. Jennings:* How do you know?

> *Tom:* She said she was thinking about what to do.

Mr. Jennings: Good. She thought about her choices out loud so we would know what she was thinking. What about Step 3?

Michelle: Yeah. She talked to you . . . told you why she was mad.

Mr. Jennings: Right. Overall, how did Ms. Benson do? (pp. 174–176)

The transcript goes on to demonstrate preparation for and performance of role-playing, providing feedback, and assigning homework.

The examples provided have demonstrated the use of single and multiple models; live and symbolic modeling presentation; peer, paraprofessional, and professional models; coping and mastery models; overt and covert models. In all cases the modeling was combined with other procedures designed to underscore the important aspects of the modeling and to provide practice and feedback. Academic skills, appropriate classroom behavior, social interaction skills, and self-management skills are all reasonable targets to be addressed by these procedures. The possibilities are limited only by the imagination of the person designing such programs.

Modeling in the Training of Developmentally Delayed Adults and Children

Modeling, both alone and in combination with other techniques, has been used to teach a variety of behaviors to developmentally delayed individuals, ranging from a behavior as relatively simple as the correct use of the telephone to a behavior as complex as language. Developmentally delayed individuals, perhaps more than any other group, often have difficulty following and responding to verbal instructions. It is not surprising, therefore, that helpers have intuitively demonstrated what they wanted done when instructions have not brought about the correct response. Researchers, in turn, have questioned the effectiveness of modeling with this population and have provided us with a better understanding of when this technique proves useful, both in the laboratory and in naturalistic settings.

Teaching mentally retarded adults to use the telephone has frequently been the object of treatment programming. A recent study (Matson, 1982) looked not only at the usefulness of modeling in teaching telephone skills, but also at a treatment package that the author called "independence training." In addition to modeling, this package incorporated instructions, shaping, feedback, social reinforcement, self-monitoring, and evaluation. Modeling was found to be more effective than no treatment both immediately after training and 3 months later. Even more effective, however, was the independence training package. In studies such as this, the effectiveness of each of the elements of the package was not determined nor is it known whether the effects were additive.

Earlier studies, such as that by Stephan, Stephano, and Talkington

(1973), give us a detailed look at the modeling procedure. In this study, developmentally delayed girls 16 to 22 years of age (mean age 19) with IQs of 55 to 85 (mean IQ 64.9) participated in the training. Of interest to these experimenters was the comparison of training using a live model with training through the use of videotapes.

Procedures for training programs such as this can be quite simple. In this case, some of the girls were introduced to a model (female college student) and told: "This lady is going to show you how to use the telephone. Watch closely as you will have to use the telephone in the same way as shown" (p. 65). Other girls were asked to watch a videotape on the use of the telephone. They were told: "The girl on the videotape is going to show you how to use the telephone. Watch closely as you will have to use the telephone in the same way as the girl on the videotape" (p. 65). In both cases, the model then identified six parts of the telephone, demonstrated how to make a phone call to the police, and demonstrated how to answer the phone and take a message for a person who is not at home. The girls were then asked to perform the tasks. The demonstration-test sequences were presented three times.

Findings encouraged the continued development of training programs for retarded persons that incorporate the use of modeling. The two modeling groups just described performed significantly better than a control group that saw no model. The group that observed a live model, however, was not significantly different in performance from the group that watched the videotape. This suggested that the use of a series of training videotapes could be an effective timesaving method of training moderately mentally retarded individuals to perform certain basic skills.

A group training procedure used by Perry and Cerreto (1977) also demonstrated the usefulness of videotape modeling and a treatment package for training developmentally delayed individuals. In this study, a broad spectrum of social skills was taught, including mealtime behaviors and social interaction skills such as meeting and conversing with people, offering to help with a task, and responding to a minor social accident. The participants were adult group-home residents, most of whom were moderately mentally retarded. The training program incorporated the following features: verbal summarization of important aspects of the modeling display, model presentation of component parts of a behavior as well as the complex reconstructed skill, rehearsal of behavior, and feedback and reinforcement from group members and leaders. During rehearsal, behavioral sequences were practiced both exactly as they had been modeled and with variations proposed by the group members. Observations of the residents in their usual mealtime setting and in a simulated setting in interaction with a stranger indicated that the behaviors practiced in the training setting had been successfully transferred to the home environment.

Modeling as a tool to teach language has been used with children labeled as autistic and/or as severely mentally retarded. A recent study by Beisler and Tsai (1983) demonstrated the direction in which such training is proceeding. They worked with 5 boys aged 36 to 68 months. The IQs of the boys ranged from 63 to 116 on the Merrill-Palmer Scale of Mental Tests (4 of the 5 boys' scores were above 90) or 65 to 136 on the Leiter International Performance Scale, and all of the children used some language prior to training. The concern was not to teach these children to simply repeat words or respond to direct questions but to teach them language as a "communicative exchange," that is, "requesting, informing, seeking information, greeting, and commenting on the environment" (p. 288). The appropriate language response was modeled several times, and then the trainer paused, waiting for the child to come up with the response. Little in the way of fading or prompting was needed. Of particular interest in this study was the lack of extrinsic reinforcers used. Beisler and Tsai found that fulfilling the communicative intent of the language spoken (e.g., giving the child what he asked for, doing what he asked be done) was a sufficient reinforcer to produce improvement in language. They referred to this form of reinforcement as the "natural consequences of communicative exchange" (p. 298). Training was done over a 6-week period as part of an inpatient program. All 5 boys were reported to have improved their language skills, based on several measures of language development.

Clearly these autistic children were not as impaired initially as many are. Frequently, *no* spontaneous imitation is seen, in both the autistic and the severely mentally retarded populations. Hintgen, Coulter, and Churchill (1967) provided a detailed description of how one might begin to teach imitation to one of these severely impaired children. In this case the children were a $6\frac{1}{2}$-year-old autistic boy by the name of Sonny, who spent most of his day ritualistically manipulating objects or playing with his fingers and spitting, and Becky, a $5\frac{1}{2}$-year-old autistic girl, who spent her time rocking. Both children were mute. The program proceeded as follows:

> . . . the child was isolated in an 8 × 15 room, 24 hours per day for 21 consecutive days. Throughout this time the child received all food, water, and social contact from adults (two in the case of Sonny, six in the case of Becky) contingent upon the emission of specific behaviors. During an average of 6 hours of daily training sessions spread over a 12-hour period, food, water, and release from physical restraint (all paired with verbal approval) were used to reinforce three types of imitative responses. (p. 37)

1. Individual and combinational uses of body parts — for example, holding up one finger, clapping hands, touching parts of the body, various hand, tongue, and mouth positions, running, jumping, etc. . . . (p. 37)
2. Simple and complex use of objects — for example, dropping a ball in a bucket, hooking a toy train together, buttoning, line drawing, brushing teeth, playing appropriately with toys, cutting with scissors, etc. . . . (p. 38)

3. Vocal responses—for example, the imitation of vowel and consonant sounds with a gradual progression to words. (p. 38)

Some examples give the flavor of the procedures of the training sessions:

Imitation of vocal responses—blowing. During an 80-minute session on the third day of Sonny's isolation, he was placed on a chair sitting directly in front of and facing E-1 (the first experimenter), and was physically restrained from getting off the chair. During this session a blowing response was to be imitated in preparation for the later imitation of forcing air for the "puh" sound. Sonny had been observed making a blowing sound spontaneously during rituals, but never in imitation of an adult model. Because Sonny did blow on a harmonica in imitation of an adult during the use of objects session, E-1 started the session by blowing on a large toy harmonica, which Sonny imitated very consistently. With each imitation response, E-1 pulled the harmonica slightly away from Sonny's mouth, so that Sonny was required to blow harder to get the musical tone. Then E-1 took Sonny's hand and blew on it and asked Sonny to imitate that response. After presenting over 30 models, Sonny had not attempted to blow on his own hand, and after 15 minutes, E-1 left the room and E-2 (the second experimenter) entered. E-2 then attempted to have Sonny imitate the blowing of a pinwheel, although no response was emitted during 15 minutes of continuous models. In the next 30 minutes, E-2 alternated between presenting models of blowing on the harmonica and blowing on the pinwheel. Sonny became very agitated during this period and emitted much of the avoidance behavior that was typical during the first few days of intensive training. He cried, pinched, hit, hugged, laughed, giggled, and teased in attempting to avoid making the blowing response. As his avoidance behavior increased in intensity, E-2 increased the amount of physical restraint used. Finally, Sonny made an excellent blowing response, and was rewarded by E-2 with a partial release from physical restraint and lavish praise. E-1 then entered the room again, replacing E-2, and tried to get a consistent blowing response. After 10 minutes of crying and squirming by Sonny, which necessitated E-1 reinstating the physical restraint, Sonny made another excellent blowing response. E-1 rewarded Sonny by releasing the physical restraint and swinging him up in the air. During the last 5 minutes of this period Sonny made 33 blowing responses in imitation of E-1. Then E-2 came in for 5 minutes more and obtained 32 blowing responses from Sonny. No food was used as a reward during this session, and all imitative responses were rewarded by the release of physical restraint and the presentation of social reinforcers. (pp. 38-39)

Imitation of use of objects—scissors. During one session in Becky's third day in the room, a pair of children's scissors were taped to the thumb and middle finger of Becky's hand. Holding scissors in her own hand, E then presented a model of opening and closing the hand. With some help Becky was able to imitate the response. By the end of the 45-minute session Becky was beginning to make small cuts in a thick piece of paper in imitation of E. (p. 39)

Obviously the treatment of Sonny and Becky was an intensive and time-consuming one-to-one approach. Because of the degree of deficit in the functioning of these children, it is perhaps inevitable that such must be the case.

The use of peers as models appears frequently in the modeling literature in general, but, for obvious reasons, more rarely in the literature dealing with the developmentally delayed population. In a now classic study, Whalen and Henker (1969, 1971) made use of both modeling and reinforcement as training procedures for a "therapeutic pyramid" program in an institution for the mentally retarded. In their program, teenagers with IQs in the 40s to high 60s were first trained in behavior modification techniques by the experimenters. Modeling was a major component of this training of assistants or tutors, as shown in the following excerpts:

> During the initial session, the tutor received a brief orientation to the goals and procedures of the project. He was told he had been selected to be a "special teacher" for a younger child. He then observed an experienced behavior therapist begin to teach a trainee to imitate a particular response. Following this brief observation, the beginning tutor practiced the technique with the same trainee. The experimenter remained in the room with the dyad and closely supervised all interactions. In his supervising role, the experimenter provided the tutor with frequent verbal evaluations (feedback) regarding his performance and suggestions for improvement. In addition to verbal feedback, further demonstrations were provided when the tutor failed to understand or remember the technique and when each new phase of the program (e.g., gaining attention, extinguishing tantrums, shaping imitative speech and action) was introduced.
>
> The experimenter's use of modeling and feedback was gradually decreased as the tutor became increasingly confident and adept. The goal was to withdraw supervision progressively so that the tutor would learn to assume increasing responsibility for the training of his child. The tutors also began to teach each other, spontaneously modeling for and providing feedback to the "colleagues." (p. 332)

When their training was complete, the tutors began to work with their charges. Again modeling and reinforcement techniques were used.

> The initial focus of training was on extinguishing tantrums and establishing eye contact. The next phase consisted of teaching the trainees to imitate simple sounds and gestures. The tutor first demonstrated the behavior he was attempting to teach the trainee. If the trainees failed to imitate, attention getting prompts were employed to elicit the desired responses. For example, in verbal imitation training the tutor would hold the reward (food) next to his mouth as he pronounced the stimulus word so that the trainee, whose attention had been focused by the reward, would see how the word was formed on the tutor's lips. When necessary, sounds were prompted by manipulating the child's mouth and lips. Analogously, the tutor prompted gestures by moving the trainee's limbs. The prompts were "faded" as rapidly as the trainee's performance allowed. . . . After the trainee performed an accurate imitative response or an adequate approximation, the tutor rewarded him with food, praise, and physical affection. (p. 333)

How successful was this program? After 25 sessions, one child "now has an imitative vocabulary of about 400 words and can understand and follow

several directions, such as 'turn off the light' and 'touch your nose'"
(p. 334). His tutor "has demonstrated his ability to function relatively independently as a tutor. Moreover, he is quite adept at prompting and evaluating the performance of his fellow tutors" (p. 334).

Modeling is now widely accepted as an important component in the
training of developmentally delayed children and adults. Models and
trainers can be other mentally retarded persons, or, if available, other non-
professional helpers can be trained as tutors. The use of modeling enhancement principles such as prompting and reinforcement maximizes the
training effects. These findings are important in this field, which has few
effective training techniques. So many developmentally delayed individuals, particularly those in institutions, have not had the benefit of training
programs due to limited staff and resources. However, if nonprofessionals
can be trained as tutors and if presentation of filmed models as well as
group training are effective in teaching new skills, training can be accomplished without the addition of large numbers of staff and without overbur-
dening those who are already working with this population. Although the
use of modeling becomes more problematic with those who are so severely
impaired as to lack imitative skills, we can see from the previously cited
research and from reports of other programs with severely and profoundly
mentally retarded individuals and autistic children (Baer, Peterson, & Sherman, 1967; Lovaas, Freitag, Nelson, & Whalen, 1967) that modeling can be
used successfully as part of the treatment programming even in these cases.

Modeling in the Treatment of Psychotic Adults

The deficits of some psychotic adults resemble the deficits found in autistic children. In severely disturbed schizophrenic patients, for example,
behavioral repertoires are extremely limited and can be characterized by
lack of speech and social withdrawal. It is not surprising that applications
of modeling to the treatment of psychotic adults are very similar to programs discussed in the previous section. One difference, however, is that, in
training autistic children, we are usually concerned with the observational
learning of new skills, because the child might not have previously learned
or performed the target skills. With psychotic adults, on the other hand,
the intent might be to reinstate the use of skills that were in the patient's
repertoire at some time in the past.

Social skills training has been the focus of most of the recent studies
using modeling with adult psychiatric patients. Monti, Curran, Corriveau,
DeLancey, and Hagerman (1980) used a 20-hour social skills training package with 23 male patients involved in treatment at a Veterans Administration hospital. The package included reading of a treatment manual,
discussion, modeling of appropriate and inappropriate behaviors, response

practice, coaching, and feedback from both the therapist and fellow patients. This was contrasted with a standard sensitivity training package given to an additional 23 patients. All patients continued to participate in the regular treatment program. Patients were assessed immediately posttreatment and again at a 6-month follow-up. Both self-report and observational measures were used. The authors concluded that "overall, the results very strongly support the efficacy of doing social skills training with psychiatric patients in a day hospital setting." (p. 247)

Earlier studies by Gutride, Goldstein, and Hunter (1973, 1974) provide us with detailed examples of the modeling aspects of such programs. In the first of these studies, four modeling videotapes were used for training.

> . . . the first tape contained enactments indicating how one individual (the model) can interact with another individual who approaches him. The second, how an individual (the model) can initiate interaction with a second person. The third, how an individual (the model) can initiate interaction with a group of people. Finally, continuing this progression reflecting increasing complexity of social interaction, the fourth tape depicted how an individual (the model) can resume relationships with relatives, friends and co-workers from outside the hospital. (Gutride et al., 1973, p. 410)

These authors considered many modeling-enhancement factors in the design of their videotapes, including,

> . . . portrayal of several heterogeneous models; the introduction and summarization of each tape by a high status narrator (hospital superintendent and clinic director), who sought by his introduction to maximize observer attention and by his summary to re-emphasize the nature of the specific, concrete social interaction behaviors; portrayal of the model's characteristics as similar to that of most participating study patients (age, sex, patient status); and frequent and readily observable reward provided the model contingent upon his social interaction behavior. (p. 410)

Note in the following excerpts from the modeling tapes the attention given to the modeling-enhancement variables.

Tape 1

Narrator's introduction

Hello, I'm Dr. Turner from Denver State Hospital. You are now going to see some very important movies which will show you how some patients at another hospital were able to get to know and talk to another person who came over to them. I want you to pay close attention to these movies and notice what these patients did in order to get to know the person who came over to them.

The narrator went on to give reasons (to feel better and to be happier) for people to know and talk with others. He stated four important points to be noticed about how the model would respond. He then reviewed the points made and the reasons for interacting. Finally, he directed the viewer's attention to the task.

> Since we want you to feel better and since we also want you to be happier, we want you to do all these things, just like the patients in the movies. So pay close attention and learn what to do. Thank you.

Scene 1

M (model) is seated by himself, doing nothing.

P (patient): Hello, my name is Tom. What's your name? (extends hand)

M: I'm Steve. (shakes his hand and looks at P)

P: How are you today?

M: Fine thanks, and you?

Conversation continued for a few more interchanges, with M being reinforced for his friendly behaviors.

> *P:* . . . I'm really happy to meet you. It's always nice to meet new people and to have new friends to talk to, too.

Other scenes continued to model both verbal and nonverbal interaction patterns and to provide reinforcement to the model for his efforts.

Scene 3

The model is seated alone, reading a newspaper.

P: Can I see a section of the newspaper?

M: Sure, which section would you like? (looks at P)

P: The sports page if you've finished it already. Do you read the sports page?

M: Yes I do. I like reading about football and hockey. I've finished that section so here it is. (looks at and leans toward P)

P: Thanks a lot. That's nice of you to share your newspaper. I also like to follow the football and hockey scores.

M: Good. . . . Maybe then we can talk about our favorite teams after you've read the sports news. Who do you think will go to the superbowl this year?

P: I don't know but I think it'll be Dallas again. Say, y'know, I really like talking to you about sports.

After 10 scenes, the narrator returned to sum up the films just seen.

> You just saw some very important movies which showed you how some patients were able to get to know and talk to another person who came over to them.

The narrator again reviewed the material stated in the introduction. Then:

> Because these patients were able to get to know and talk with the person who came over to them they felt much better and they were happier. When we talk

with people, we are healthier and we have more fun. We want you to feel better and be happier too, so now we want you to do all the things you saw the patients in the movies do, right here with the other people in your group. Thank you.

As is suggested in the narrator's last statement, the training did not end with the presentation of the models. The patient group then discussed and role-played the scenes they had seen. They received feedback and reinforcement for their own efforts at imitation of the roles played by the model.

The second study (1974) focused on training in specific skill deficit areas, for example,

Narrator's introduction

Hello, I'm Dr. K. . . .
This week we are starting with the absolute basics of social interaction —
simple eating behavior. . . . Watch this tape carefully as it demonstrates eating behaviors that can really affect your sociability.

Scene 1

Narrator: Put your napkin on your lap.

Patient A sits down at dining hall table, takes his napkin off the table, unfolds it, puts it on his lap.

Narrator: Good.

Patient A smiles.

Patient B sits down at dining hall table, takes his napkin off the table, unfolds it, puts it in his lap.

Narrator: Good.

Patient B smiles.

Narrator continues with patient C.

Narrator: Also use your napkin during the meal when you need it.

Patients A and B perform.

Patient C, eating, takes napkin off his lap, wipes his mouth, puts his napkin back in his lap.

Narrator: Very good.

Patient C smiles.

Narrator: That was good, that's how to use your napkin.

After another scene, the narrator summed up the action:

Now that you've seen the actors demonstrate the importance of good eating posture and using your napkin, fork and knife properly, you will have a chance to do it yourselves, and by seeing yourselves on television learn just how sociable you can look through good eating habits. Sit up straight, use your napkin, hold your knife and fork properly, and I guarantee that you will not only look good, but feel good as well. "Try it, you'll like it."

The examples cited above show that procedures that incorporate modeling as a major part of training are effective in treating some of the behavioral deficits of psychotic adults. In general, however, results are better for simple than for complex skills, and they are better for acute patients than for chronic patients. As is usually true, generalization of behaviors to other settings is a problem. Training of hospital personnel to prompt and reinforce trained behaviors on the ward and in the general hospital environment might be good supplements to any training program for psychotic adults.

Modeling in the Rehabilitation of Alcoholics, Delinquents, and Addicts

A recent review of models and methods in prevention and intervention in alcohol relapse (Donovan & Chaney, 1985) noted the use of a variety of performance-based cognitive behavioral interventions both to train alcoholics in social skill deficit areas and to enhance their perceived self-efficacy. Included among such interventions is problem-solving training, training to recognize warning signs of relapse, and training in appropriate behaviors in response to the warning signs. A variety of cognitive and behavioral interventions are used for these purposes.

Outcome studies such as the one by Chaney, O'Leary, and Marlatt (1978) package a variety of behavioral techniques to address the deficits and behavioral tendencies of the problem drinker. This study, for example, in its skill training group, combined modeling, role-playing, and coaching techniques to train alcoholics to go through the problem-solving steps of problem definition and formulation, generalization of alternatives, and decision-making. Once alternatives were chosen, the behaviors necessary for following those alternatives were modeled and practiced. The skill training group, as compared with a discussion and a no-treatment control group, showed significantly improved performance on a verbal role-play measure of responses to situations associated with drinking and relapse. These gains had decreased by the 4-month posttest, suggesting the need for a stronger intervention. Measures of actual drinking behavior at a 1-year follow-up, however, showed the skill training group to be significantly different from the controls on days drunk, total number of drinks, and average drinking period length.

Just as alcoholics might be lacking in their behavior repertoires, the problems of other individuals such as delinquents and addicts are often related to deficits in social behaviors. These individuals have not learned socially approved ways of handling everyday situations, and they often have not learned appropriate problem-solving methods that allow them to analyze and determine how they should approach a situation. How can modeling be used to help such individuals? Several examples are presented next.

Sarason (Sarason, 1968; Sarason & Ganzer, 1973) developed a program of social skill training for use with institutionalized male delinquents. Some of the problem situations modeled are very similar to those encountered by alcoholics. In the following example, Tom, a newly paroled youth, is pressured to go out drinking:

(George knocks on the door and Tom answers.)

Tom: Hi, George, how're you doing?

George: Hey, Man, we're glad to see you back. Gotta celebrate your return. We got a couple of cases of beer out in the car. Come on, we're gonna have a party.

Tom: Oh, you know I got to stay clean.

George: What do you mean, you gotta stay clean? Come on, this party was planned just for you. We even got a date with Debbie lined up for you. It won't hurt just this once.

Tom: Well you know I'm on parole. I can't go drinking. . . . I might get caught and if I get caught now, I'll really get screwed.

George: Oh, Man, we won't get caught. We never get caught doing anything like that.

Tom: Well, maybe you guys have never gotten caught, but the night I got in trouble I was out drinking and ended up stealing a car. (pause) You know, I just got back.

George: Look Man, you don't have to drink. Just come to the party and have a little fun. What are we going to tell Debbie anyway?

Tom: You know being there is the same as drinking to the fuzz. And Debbie won't have any trouble finding someone else.

George: Boy, I sure don't understand you. You sure changed since you got back from that place. You trying to kiss us off?

Tom: No, that's not it, Man. If you want to do something else where we wouldn't get into trouble, (pause) like go to a show, the dance or something, that would be okay but . . . well . . . I know some guys who were in there for a second or third time and they don't get breaks anymore. You know what it is to be on parole.

George: Okay, look, let's just have one quick beer out in the car, okay? For old time's sake.

Tom: No, Man. I know where that leads. Then it would be just one more and then pretty soon we'll be drunk. I can't do it, Man.

George: Jeez! What is the matter with you, Man? Just one beer?

Tom: Maybe another night. My old man expects me to help him work on the boat tonight anyway. I'll be in trouble with him if I take off. Look, I'm sorry, maybe some other time, okay?

George: Okay. Can't be helped, I guess. Look, we'll be at John's place. Come on over later if you can.

Tom: Sure. See you tomorrow anyway. (Sarason & Ganzer, 1971, p. 139)

Other vignettes covered such topics as how to apply for a new job, how to resist social pressure from peers to engage in antisocial behaviors, and how to delay immediate gratification in order to reach more culturally accepted goals in the future. In each of the modeling groups, which consisted of 4 to 5 adolescents, two models acted out a script that demonstrated appropriate behavior in one of the problem situations. Following the modeling sequence, the observers were called upon to summarize and explain the main points made in the vignette. Each group member then rehearsed the same scene with either another group member or a model as a partner.

Sarason and his colleagues compared the effectiveness of this modeling procedure with a traditional group-discussion approach. The modeling treatment package was found to be highly effective, as assessed by a variety of attitudinal and behavioral adjustment measures.

A similar approach to the teaching of prosocial skills to adolescents who need remedial training has been described in detail by Goldstein, Sprafkin, Gershaw, and Klein (1980). They provided skill checklists, step-by-step procedures for training in individual skills, sample transcripts of group sessions, and ideas for managing behavior problems that might arise in the groups. The leader of adolescent groups would do well to study the structured learning programs provided by these authors.

Reeder and Kunce (1976) used modeling procedures with heroin addicts in a residential treatment program. These investigators chose to depict problem situations that residents and staff felt created the most difficulty for addicts both during and following treatment. The areas selected for modeling presentation were

> (a) accepting help from others—necessary for residential and follow-up phases of the program; (b) capitalizing on street skills—identifying skills that the addict has and helping him to apply them legitimately; (c) job interviewing—necessary in order to know the expectancies of the potential employer; (d) employer relations—important for retaining a job; (e) free-time management—necessary for maintaining drug abstinence; and (f) new life-style adjustment—enabling the addict to successfully cope with "old friends" from the drug culture. (p. 561)

Ex-addict paraprofessional staff and selected residents served as models for the videotaped presentations. In addition to demonstrating specific skills, the videotapes were designed to teach a general coping approach that could be applied to any problem situation the addict might face. Initially, the model was shown to have ineffectual behavioral skills in the problem area and to be pessimistic about his ability to improve. The model would then reflect upon the problem and discuss it with a peer or staff member. Following reflection and discussion, the model would try out new problem-solving abilities and behavioral skills. At the close of the vignette, the model was able to handle the situation effectively and independently.

After viewing a modeling sequence, residents engaged in a focused discussion of the presentation. Group members were encouraged to project themselves into the situation and to describe what they would do if confronted with a similar problem.

Reeder and Kunce compared this group, which viewed and discussed the videotaped modeling presentations, with a similar group that saw videotaped lectures on the same topics. Follow-up data on vocational status at 30, 90, and 180 days after release from treatment showed that subjects who participated in the modeling treatment group had substantially better outcomes than those who participated in the video-lecture treatment.

These studies suggest that modeling can be used effectively to teach new behavioral repertoires to individuals who have previously engaged in socially disapproved behaviors. Modeling, as a treatment modality, would appear to have many advantages over the more coercive forms of behavior change that are frequently (and often unsuccessfully) used with individuals demonstrating deviant and antisocial behavior patterns.

Modeling in the Training of Parents and Helpers

Modeling is an effective technique for behavior modification of persons of all ages (children, adolescents, adults), of many classifications (normal, delinquent, developmentally delayed, psychotic), and with many different problems (fear, behavior deficits, behavior excesses). Modeling can be equally effective when used to train persons whose concerns are with behavior change. These include parents who are seeking help in becoming modifiers of their own children's problems and professionals and paraprofessionals who seek to become change agents, such as the readers of this book.

Numerous investigations have explored the use of various procedures and media for teaching parents to use behavioral techniques with their children (Flanagan, Adams, & Forehand, 1979; Nay, 1975; O'Dell, Mahoney, Horton, & Turner, 1979; O'Dell et al., 1982; Webster-Stratton, 1981, 1984).

A large study by O'Dell et al. (1982) used careful experimental controls. Reinforcement skills were taught to 100 parents through one of five procedures: (a) minimal instructions, (b) a written manual that included descriptions of scenes of parents and children, (c) an audiotape that was a reading of the written manual, (d) videotaped modeling that included a narrator and varied models acting the parent-child scenes, and (e) live modeling by a graduate student and rehearsal with the parents' own child, assisted by prompting and shaping. All of the training methods, which had identical content, proved to be superior to the minimal instructions. The written manual, videotape modeling, and live modeling produced behavioral results essentially equivalent to each other. The authors, however, noted that the videotape training appeared to be more helpful for a wider range of parents.

Webster-Stratton (1981) has presented guidelines for developing and using videotape modeling programs as a method of parent education:

1. In order for parents in the program to relate positively to the models, they are told that the parent models in the videotapes are not actors but actual parents who have, in fact, attended a parenting course similar to the one they are taking. In addition the models selected for the videotapes are representative of white and black families, in all social classes, and include fathers as well as mothers. Parent models also have children of the same age as do the parents attending the program.

2. The parent models in the videotapes are frequently shown receiving praise from the therapist for appropriate parenting behaviors. In addition, the parent model is considered to have been rewarded when he or she is able to get from their child appropriate and pleasurable behaviors or a reduction in a child's misbehaviors.

3. In order to be sure parents watching the videotapes do not get distracted, their attention is directed to the models' behaviors in the following way. They are shown vignettes of parent models interacting with their children in appropriate and inappropriate ways. After each presentation of a particular parent-child vignette, the videotape is stopped and the parents are given a chance to report their observations and to "discover" the appropriate behaviors. If any disagreement occurs among the parents or if parents miss a crucial feature of the incident, the scene is replayed for further discussion. This contrast between the parental interactions presumed appropriate and those judged inappropriate serves to clarify and emphasize the desired behaviors.

4. The parents attending the videotape program do not have the opportunity to directly practice under supervision what they observe on videotapes and therefore they receive no direct reinforcement or feedback from the educator. However, parents are given a homework assignment to play for 10 minutes a day with their child in order to practice the skills they have learned in the program. The play periods are designed to minimize the possibility of negative exchanges and maximize the possibility of positive exchanges between parent and child. It is felt that parents are reinforced in these play periods by seeing improvements in their children's behaviors. In addition, because these parents are watching the program in groups, the resulting expressions of support and enthusiasm by other parents act as powerful reinforcements.

5. Finally, in order to further generalization of the effects of the videotape program to home settings, the educator helps the parent groups discuss how the techniques demonstrated by the model on the videotape might apply to their own situations. This results in the parents becoming active participants in the educational process, thus facilitating learning. The group process cannot be minimized; the group is a source of extensive ideas and abundant social reinforcement for every parent's achievements. (pp. 94–95)

The content of the parent-training programs used by Webster-Stratton includes (a) effective play techniques, (b) setting limits, (c) handling misbehavior, and (d) communication and feelings.

Webster-Stratton (1984) recently compared the effects of this videotape parent training program with individual therapy using live modeling, role-playing, rehearsal, and feedback. The subjects of her study were the mothers of 35 conduct-disordered children. She found that 1 month after a 9-week training program, the parent behaviors and attitudes were significantly improved over those of a nontreated control group. The children of the treated mothers decreased in noncompliance. These findings continued at 1-year follow-up. There were no significant differences in outcome between the two treatment groups, leading the author to suggest that the cost-effectiveness of the videotape modeling (therapist time 48 hours versus therapist time for the individual treatment 251 hours) argues for videotape treatment.

We turn now to a consideration of some applications of modeling to the training of helping personnel. The training of ministers to be more empathic in their responses to a counselee was the focus of a study by Perry (1975). An empathic model was presented to the ministers on an audiotape. Subjects were told that the counselor they would hear was a minister who has been doing a great deal of therapeutic counseling in his ministry for the past 4 years and was highly thought of by his colleagues for the quality of his counseling (same sex and occupation as subjects, high status, experienced). In the modeled interactions between the minister (model) and the client, the client periodically rewarded the minister (as indicated by the italicized statements).

Patient: Well—I've been drinking quite a few years I guess. I think—I can't figure out the exact time. It just happens you know, you—you don't really know when you start, when you—start drinking—there's no big change in your life. You know I—I really don't drink that much I—have a few drinks now and then—but not that many.

Therapist: You don't think that drinking's the big problem.

Patient: Probably every guy I know drinks more than I do. My wife thinks I drink a lot though—she's—boy, you talk to her you'd think I was the biggest bum on skid row. *My wife doesn't understand me the way you do.*

Therapist: Sounds like she nags you about drinking as well as money.

Patient: You do—do understand. . . . (Perry, 1970, p. 90)

And later:

Patient: . . . I'm no superman—I just—do the work I'm supposed to do. Or try to do it anyway. You seem to understand that. I wish everybody understood me the way you do. I really like you. But. . . . (p. 96)

Subjects heard 12 scenes between the minister and his client. At the end of each scene, the subject was requested to respond empathically to the client's last statement as he would if he were counseling.

Subjects who heard a high-empathy model, as in the examples above, gave responses to the standard interview that were significantly higher in empathy than subjects who heard no model or heard a model who was low in empathy. When the minister subjects were asked to conduct an actual interview with an alcoholic client-actor, those who heard the high-empathy model still tended to offer higher levels of empathy than those who did not. The results for the interview, however, were not as strong as those from the immediate posttest. This is common in studies of training and therapy and suggests the need to program more aggressively for generalization.

Some authors have suggested that instructions explaining empathy and its importance in counseling, particularly when accompanied by varied examples of empathic responses and comments about what makes the responses empathic, could increase generalization. In the following study, the usual modeling procedures have been expanded in this manner. The trainee has also been given immediate feedback and reinforcement, providing an opportunity for developing discriminations between empathic and nonempathic responses.

Goldstein and Goedhart (1973) offered a 2-day, 10-hour training course to nurses in a psychiatric hospital. Their training program consisted of the following:

1. A presentation and discussion of the meaning and nature of empathy and its importance for patient change, nurse skill development, and hospital climate.
2. Distribution and discussion of the Carkhuff empathy scale (Carkhuff, 1969) highlighted with concrete examples of the five levels represented.
3. Discussion of such supporting topics as (a) means for identifying patient feelings, (b) means for communicating to patients that their feelings are understood, (c) empathy versus sympathy, (d) empathy versus diagnosis or evaluation, (e) empathy versus directiveness or questioning, and so forth. (p. 169)

Following the introductory group discussion, the modeling and role-playing phases of the training were initiated. Thirty situations were enacted by the group leaders in which the nurse-model offered empathic responses to each patient statement. During each situation enactment, group members were requested to refer to the empathy scale after each patient statement and to silently role-play their own responses prior to hearing the model's response. The 30 situations were then repeated, with group members offering responses after each patient statement. Finally, an extended role-play was initiated that started with one of the standard situations but moved on to wherever the actors took it. Feedback and further modeling from other group members and from leaders were given.

After training, nurses responded in a more empathic manner to situation items than before training. One month later, higher levels of empathic response continued. As an added bonus in this study, head nurses who were participant members and observers in the original training groups became trainers for a second group. Their nurse trainees increased in empathy as well. Thus, not only were intensive modeling and role-playing techniques effective in altering the nurses' verbal behavior, but these techniques were also effective in teaching trainers to produce positive changes in other trainees. In an extension and replication of the above study, Goldstein added on-the-ward feedback and training for the psychiatric hospital personnel. Results showed that the trainees used their new skills on the ward as well as in the testing situations.

SUMMARY

This chapter described the use of modeling as a technique that can be used to modify behavior in a wide variety of settings. The term *modeling* refers to the process by which the behavior of one individual or group, the model, acts as a stimulus for similar thoughts, attitudes, and behavior on the part of another individual, the observer. Some of the basic concepts that apply to modeling were discussed in the first major section of the chapter. An important distinction was drawn between the acquisition phase of modeling, in which the model's behaviors are first acquired or learned by the observer, and the performance phase, in which the observer subsequently performs the behavior demonstrated by the model. Three effects of modeling on behavior were described: (a) the observational learning effect, in which observers both acquire and perform new responses; (b) the disinhibitory/inhibitory effect, in which performance of previously learned but inhibited behavior is either disinhibited (increased) or inhibited even further (decreased) and; (c) the response facilitation effect, in which the performance of an already learned behavior, which is not under existing restraint or inhibition, is increased.

A review of those factors contributing to the successful use of modeling procedures was presented in the second section, divided into a discussion of those factors that primarily facilitate acquisition of new responses and those factors that enhance performance of responses (either newly learned or previously acquired). Considered under factors enhancing acquisition were characteristics of the model, characteristics of the observer, and characteristics of the modeling presentation. Incentives for performance, factors affecting quality of performance, and transfer and generalization of performance were among the topics discussed in the second half of this section. Table 3.1 presents these factors in checklist form and is meant to serve as a guideline for those who are creating modeling programs.

The last part of the chapter described the use of modeling with a variety of populations and problem areas. This section began with examples of the application of modeling to fear-related behavior. At first, modeling had been used extensively in the treatment of snake phobias. More recently, this form of treatment has also been used to help alleviate fears of children facing surgery or hospitalization, reduce test anxiety, and help control fear of commonly encountered animals.

Next, examples were given in which teachers, peers, and nonprofessionals acted as models, teaching new behaviors to socially disturbed and withdrawn children and normal children. Modeling also has proven effective in the treatment of developmentally delayed individuals. Basic survival skills, such as the use of a telephone, can be taught to retarded individuals by the use of either live or videotaped models. Success has also been reported in training more intellectually competent retarded youths to serve as models for the less able. More severely impaired children have been taught basic imitation skills as well as beginning language skills.

Modeling has also been used successfully in the treatment of psychotic adults. In contrast with the treatment of autistic children, where the aim of treatment is to develop new behaviors, the goal of modeling treatment methods with psychotic patients often is to reestablish previously learned, but no longer performed, responses. Examples presented in this section showed how modeling can be introduced as a method of teaching psychotic adults appropriate interpersonal behaviors to use upon their return to the community.

The training of new interpersonal skills has also been emphasized by those working with alcoholics, delinquents, and addicts. One problem common to each of these groups seems to be the inability to resist social pressure. Many other skills have received attention and have been effectively taught by modeling.

Modeling can also be used to teach behavior change methods and therapeutic skills. An example was presented that compared different procedures for training parents to reinforce their children's behaviors. A videotape program for parent education also was included. In another example, the modeling of empathy was shown to lead to a changed therapist-client interaction. In one study, a combination of methods (instructions, modeling, feedback, reinforcement, and role-playing) was incorporated into a training program for nurses to increase their empathic level of responding when working with their patients.

It can be seen in reviewing recent studies, in comparison with earlier ones, that the trend is toward treatment packages that include modeling as one component rather than the only component. Such "package" programs not only enhance the learning and performance of behaviors, but are also likely to increase generalization of treatment effects as well. Modeling has become an established procedure in behavioral treatment.

REFERENCES

Baer, D. M., Peterson, R. F., & Sherman, J. A. (1967). The development of imitations by reinforcing behavioral similarity to a model. *Journal of the Experimental Analysis of Behavior, 10*, 405-416.

Bandura, A. (1969). *Principles of behavior modification.* New York: Holt, Rinehart & Winston.

Bandura, A. (Ed.). (1971). *Psychological modeling: Conflicting theories.* Chicago: Aldine-Atherton.

Bandura, A. (1977). *Social learning theory.* Englewood Cliffs, NJ: Prentice-Hall.

Bandura, A., Blanchard, E. E., & Ritter, B. (1969). Relative efficacy of desensitization and modeling approaches for inducing behavioral, affective, and attitudinal changes. *Journal of Personality and Social Psychology, 13*, 173-206.

Bandura, A., Grusec, J. E., & Menlove, F. L. (1966). Observational learning as a function of symbolization and incentive set. *Child Development, 37*, 499-506.

Bandura, A., & Walters, R. H. (1963). *Social learning and personality development.* New York: Holt, Rinehart & Winston.

Bauer, G. P., Schlottmann, R. S., Bates, J. V., & Masters, M. A. (1983). Effect of state and trait anxiety and prestige of model on imitation. *Psychological Reports, 52*, 375-382.

Beisler, J. M., & Tsai, L. Y. (1983). A pragmatic approach to increase expressive language skills in young autistic children. *Journal of Autism and Developmental Disorders, 13*, 287-303.

Bussey, K., & Perry, D. G. (1982). Same-sex imitation: The avoidance of cross-sex models on the acceptance of same-sex models. *Sex Roles, 8*, 773-784.

Carkhuff, R. F. (1969). *Helping and human relations.* New York: Holt, Rinehart & Winston.

Cartledge, G., & Milburn, J. F. (1980). *Teaching social skills to children: Innovative approaches.* Elmsford, NY: Pergamon Press.

Cautela, J. R. (1976). The present status of covert modeling. *Journal of Behavior Therapy and Experimental Psychiatry, 6*, 323-326.

Chaney, E. F., O'Leary, M. R., & Marlatt, G. A. (1978). Skill training with alcoholics. *Journal of Consulting and Clinical Psychology, 46*, 1092-1104.

Chartier, G. M., & Ainley, C. (1974). Effects of model warmth on imitation learning in adult chronic psychotics. *Journal of Abnormal Psychology, 83*, 680-682.

Csapo, M. (1972). Peer models reverse the "one bad apple spoils the barrel" theory. *Teaching Exceptional Children, 4*, 20-24.

Davidson, E. S., & Smith, W. P. (1982). Imitation, social comparison, and self-reward. *Child Development, 53*, 928-932.

Donovan, D. M., & Chaney, E. F. (1985). Alcohol relapse prevention and intervention: Models and methods. In G. A. Marlatt & J. R. Gordon (Eds.), *Relapse prevention: A self-control strategy for the maintenance of behavior change.* New York: Guilford.

Evers-Pasquale, W., & Sherman, M. (1975). The reward value of peers: A variable influencing the efficacy of filmed modeling in modifying social isolation in preschoolers. *Journal of Abnormal Child Psychology, 3*, 179-189.

Fehrenbach, P. A., Miller, D. J., & Thelen, M. H. (1979). The importance of consistency of modeling behavior upon imitation: A comparison of single and multiple models. *Journal of Personality and Social Psychology, 37*, 1412-1417.

Flanagan, S., Adams, H. E., & Forehand, R. (1979). A comparison of four instructional techniques for teaching parents the use of time out. *Behavior Therapy, 10*, 94-102.

Flanders, J. P. (1968). A review of research on imitative behavior. *Psychological Bulletin, 69,* 316–337.

Ginther, L. J., & Roberts, M. C. (1982). A test of mastery versus coping modeling in the reduction of children's dental fears. *Child and Family Behavior Therapy, 4,* 41–52.

Goldstein, A. P. (1973). *Structured learning therapy: Toward a psychotherapy for the poor.* New York: Academic Press.

Goldstein, A. P., & Goedhart, A. (1973). The use of structured learning for empathy enhancement in paraprofessional psychotherapist training. *Journal of Community Psychology, 1,* 168–173.

Goldstein, A. P., Sprafkin, R. P., & Gershaw, J. (1976). *Skill training for community living: Applying structured learning therapy.* Elmsford, NY: Pergamon Press.

Goldstein, A. P., Sprafkin, R. P., Gershaw, N. J., & Klein, P. (1980). *Skillstreaming the adolescent: A structured learning approach to teaching prosocial skills.* Champaign, IL: Research Press.

Goodwin, S. E., & Mahoney, M. J. (1975). Modification of aggression through modeling: An experimental probe. *Journal of Behavior Therapy and Experimental Psychiatry, 6,* 200–202.

Gutride, M. E., Goldstein, A. P., & Hunter, G. E. (1973). The use of modeling and role playing to increase social interaction among asocial psychiatric patients. *Journal of Consulting and Clinical Psychology, 40,* 408–415.

Gutride, M. E., Goldstein, A. P., & Hunter, G. E. (1974). The use of structured learning therapy and transfer training in the treatment of chronic psychiatric inpatients. *Journal of Clinical Psychology, 32,* 277–279.

Harris, G., & Johnson, S. B. (1980). Comparison of individualized covert modeling, self-control desensitization, and study skills training for alleviation of test anxiety. *Journal of Consulting and Clinical Psychology, 48,* 186–194.

Heller, K., & Marlatt, G. A. (1969). Verbal conditioning, behavior therapy and behavior change: Some problems in extrapolation. In C.M. Franks (Ed.), *Behavior therapy: Appraisal and status.* New York: McGraw-Hill.

Hintgen, J. N., Coulter, S. K., & Churchill, D. W. (1967). Intensive reinforcement of imitative behavior in mute autistic children. *Archives of General Psychiatry, 17,* 36–43.

Kanfer, F. H. (1965). Vicarious human reinforcement: A glimpse into the black box. In L. Krasner & L. P. Ullman (Eds.), *Research in behavior modification.* New York: Holt, Rinehart & Winston.

Kaufman, J. M., Kneedler, R. D., Gamache, R., Hallahan, D. P., & Ball, D. W. (1977). Effects of imitation and nonimitation on children's subsequent imitative behavior. *Journal of Genetic Psychology, 130,* 285–293.

Kazdin, A. E. (1976). Effects of covert modeling, multiple models, and model reinforcement on assertive behavior. *Behavior Therapy, 7,* 211–222.

Klingman, A., Melamed, B. G., Cuthbert, M. I., & Hermecz, D. A. (1984). Effects of participant modeling on information acquisition and skill utilization. *Journal of Consulting and Clinical Psychology, 52,* 414–421.

Klorman, R., Hilpert, P. L., Michael, R., LaGana, C., & Sveen, O. B. (1980). Effects of coping and mastery modeling on experienced and inexperienced pedodontic patients' disruptiveness. *Behavior Therapy, 11,* 156–168.

Ladouceur, R. (1983). Participant modeling with or without cognitive treatment for phobias. *Journal of Consulting and Clinical Psychology, 51,* 942–944.

Leahy, R. L., Balla, D., & Zigler, E. (1982). Role-taking, self-image, and imitativeness of mentally retarded and nonretarded individuals. *American Journal of Mental Deficiency, 86,* 372–379.

Lovaas, O. I., Freitag, L., Nelson, K., & Whalen, C. (1967). The establishment of imitation and its use for the development of complex behavior in schizophrenic children. *Behaviour Research and Therapy, 5,* 171–181.

Marlatt, G. A. (1972). Task structure and the experimental modification of verbal behavior. *Psychological Bulletin, 78,* 335–350.

Matson, J. L. (1982). Independence training versus modeling procedures for teaching phone conversation skills to the mentally retarded, *Behaviour Research and Therapy, 20,* 505–511.

McGinnes, E., & Goldstein, A.P. (1984). *Skill-streaming the elementary school child: A guide for teaching prosocial skills.* Champaign, IL: Research Press.

Meichenbaum, D. H. (1972). Examination of model characteristics in reducing avoidance behavior. *Journal of Behavior Therapy and Experimental Psychiatry, 3,* 225–227.

Melamed, B. G., & Siegel, L. J. (1975). Reduction of anxiety in children facing hospitalization and surgery by use of filmed modeling. *Journal of Consulting and Clinical Psychology, 43,* 511–521.

Miller, N. E., & Dollard, J. (1941). *Social learning and imitation.* New Haven, CT: Yale University Press.

Mitchell, Z. P., & Milan, M. A. (1983). Imitation of high-interest comic strip models' appropriate classroom behavior: Acquisition and generalization. *Child and Family Behavior Therapy, 5,* 15–30.

Monti, P. M., Curran, J. P., Corriveau, D. P., DeLancey, A. L., & Hagerman, S. M. (1980). Effects of social skills training groups and sensitivity training groups with psychiatric patients. *Journal of Consulting and Clinical Psychology, 48,* 241–248.

Nay, R. W. (1975). A systematic comparison of instructional techniques for parents. *Behavior Therapy, 6,* 14–21.

O'Dell, S. L., Mahoney, N. D., Horton, W. G., & Turner, P. E. (1979). Media-assisted parent training: Alternative models. *Behavior Therapy, 10,* 103–110.

O'Dell, S. L., O'Quin, J. A., Alford, B. A., O'Briant, A. L., Bradlyn, A. S., & Giebenhain, J. E. (1982). Predicting the acquisition of parenting skills via four training models. *Behavior Therapy, 13,* 194–208.

Perry, M. A. (1970). *Didactic instructions for and modeling of empathy.* Unpublished doctoral dissertation, Syracuse University, Syracuse, NY.

Perry, M. A. (1975). Modeling and instructions in training for counselor empathy. *Journal of Counseling Psychology, 22,* 173–179.

Perry, M. A., & Cerreto, M. C. (1977). Structured learning training of social skills for the retarded. *Mental Retardation, 15,* 31–34.

Reeder, C. W., & Kunce, J. T. (1976). Modeling techniques, drug-abstinence behavior, and heroin addicts: A pilot study. *Journal of Counseling Psychology, 23,* 560–562.

Ridberg, E. H., Parke, R. D., & Hetherington, E. M. (1971). Modification of impulsive and reflective cognitive styles through observation of film-mediated models. *Developmental Psychology, 5,* 369–377.

Rimm, D. C., & Medeiros, D. C. (1970). The role of muscle relaxation in participant modeling. *Behaviour Research and Therapy, 8,* 127–132.

Ritter, B. (1968). The group treatment of children's snake phobias using vicarious and contact desensitization procedures. *Behaviour Research and Therapy, 6,* 1–6.

Ritter, B. (1969). Treatment of acrophobia with contact desensitization. *Behaviour Research and Therapy, 7*, 41-45.

Ross, D. M., Ross, S. A., & Evans, T. A. (1971). The modification of extreme social withdrawal by modeling with guided participation. *Journal of Behavior Therapy and Experimental Psychiatry, 2*, 273-279.

Sarason, I. G. (1968). Verbal learning, modeling, and juvenile delinquency. *American Psychologist, 23*, 254-266.

Sarason, I. G. (1975). Test anxiety and the self-disclosing coping model. *Journal of Consulting and Clinical Psychology, 43*, 148-153.

Sarason, I. G., & Ganzer, V. J. (1971). *Modeling: An approach to the rehabilitation of juvenile offenders*. Final report to the Social and Rehabilitation Service of the Department of Health, Education, and Welfare.

Sarason, I. G., & Ganzer, V. J. (1973). Modeling and group discussion in the rehabilitation of juvenile delinquents. *Journal of Counseling Psychology, 20*, 422-449.

Spence, S. H. (1983). Teaching social skills to children. *Journal of Child Psychology and Psychiatry, 24*, 621-627.

Stephan, C., Stephano, W., & Talkington, L. W. (1973). Use of modeling in survival social training with educable mentally retarded. *Training School Bulletin, 70*, 63-68.

Strichart, S. S. (1974). Effects of competence and nurturance on imitation of nonretarded peers by retarded adolescents. *American Journal of Mental Deficiency, 78*, 665-673.

Thelen, M. H., Fry, R. A., Fehrenbach, P. A., & Frautschi, N. M. (1979). Therapeutic videotape and film modeling: A review. *Psychological Bulletin, 86*, 701-720.

Thelen, M. H., Miller, D. J., Fehrenbach, P. A., & Frautschi, N. M. (1983). Reactions to being imitated: Effects of perceived motivation. *Merrill-Palmer Quarterly, 29*, 159-167.

Turnure, J., & Zigler, E. (1964). Outer-directedness in the problem solving of normal and retarded children. *Journal of Abnormal and Social Psychology, 69*, 427-436.

Webster-Stratton, C. (1981). Videotape modeling: A method of parent education. *Journal of Clinical Child Psychology, 10*, 93-98.

Webster-Stratton, C. (1984). Randomized trial of two parent-training programs for families with conduct-disordered children. *Journal of Consulting and Clinical Psychology, 52*, 666-678.

Whalen, C. K., & Henker, B. A. (1969). Creating therapeutic pyramids using mentally retarded patients. *American Journal of Mental Deficiency, 74*, 331-337.

Whalen, C. K., & Henker, B. A. (1971). Pyramid therapy in a hospital for the retarded: Methods, program evaluation, and long-term effects. *American Journal of Mental Deficiency, 75*, 414-434.

Yando, R., & Zigler, E. (1971). Outer-directedness in the problem-solving of institutionalized and noninstitutionalized normal and retarded children. *Developmental Psychology, 4*, 277-288.

4

Operant Methods

Paul Karoly and Anne Harris

INTRODUCTION AND PRELIMINARY CONSIDERATIONS

Throughout the 1950s and 1960s the behavior therapy movement distinguished itself from other therapeutic schools by its application of the principles of classical and operant conditioning to the treatment of various forms of problem behavior. It is apparent now that behavior therapy need not be narrowly defined, either theoretically or methodologically. Nevertheless, the operant perspective, in all its variations, remains essentially unchanged since its introduction.

B.F. Skinner (1938) proposed the term *operant conditioning* to emphasize the active nature of the organism; that it must operate on the environment in order to change that environment to its own advantage. Skinner also argued that operant behaviors, unlike responses that had been studied earlier in classical conditioning paradigms, were freely emitted behaviors. An operant is any of a class of behaviors that produces a common effect on the environment. For example, a bar press by a rat, reinforced by the experimenter, is an operant behavior regardless of whether the rat pushes the bar with its front paw, its hind paw, or its nose. Similarly, disruptive classroom behavior and volunteering a correct answer can be indistinguishable operants as defined by their functional effects, if the teacher responds to both behaviors with attention. The operant behavior therapist is, therefore, most concerned with the "controlling consequences" of human action.

Operant approaches assume that behavior is lawful and that the specific form, force, or duration of the behavior (its topography) is largely irrelevant to methods for its change or modification. Quite simply, operant approaches assume that, by manipulation of the consequences of a behavior, change can be assured or (to be more precise) that the probabilities of any given behavior will change. Behaviors that in the past have been followed by positive consequences will be strengthened or will increase in frequency. Behaviors that are not followed by positive consequences will tend to become relatively weaker and eventually be replaced by those behaviors that are followed by positive consequences. Although the term *free operant* has been used to emphasize the absence of constraints on responding, in fact there often are constraints on the kinds of behaviors that an organism may emit. For example, it is virtually impossible to teach a pigeon to press a bar for a food reward. Environmental constraints can also limit the range of possible behaviors. Tantrum behavior, involving the breaking and throwing of toys, can only occur in the presence of breakable, throwable toys. Most organism-environment contexts actually include *limiting features* that set natural boundaries on the quality and quantity of behaviors emitted, thus underscoring the interdependence of the individual and the environment — a recognition that is central to the Skinnerian world view.

Before examining operant behavior change techniques in detail and the domain of problem behaviors to which they are best applied, some preliminary considerations will be addressed. First, the effective application of an operant strategy depends initially upon *precise specification* of the behavior to be changed, the so-called goal or target of treatment. Sometimes this goal involves strengthening or increasing the frequency of a "desirable" behavior (e.g., responding assertively, engaging in regular exercise, or increasing time spent studying). In some cases, the target might never occur in the subject's existing repertoire, and it might be necessary to seek to construct the required behavior from existing, similar behaviors. The goal of other interventions might be to weaken (or eliminate) a problem behavior (e.g., smoking, tantrums, or epileptic seizures). At other times, the frequency of the behavior is not of primary concern, but rather the therapeutic goal is to change the circumstances under which the behavior is exhibited. All of these treatment goals can be accomplished through the application of operant conditioning techniques.

It should also be noted that, although the application of the procedures discussed in this chapter can be viewed as following from a rather value-free interpretation of theoretical principles, the specification of the target behavior is clearly a value-laden decision. Parents often seek treatment for their child to reduce the child's noncompliant behavior (i.e., to insure the child's obedience). Most behavior therapists would consider such a treatment goal to be potentially inappropriate without close examination of other aspects of the situation. For example, the parents could be making unreasonable demands, given the child's level of prior knowledge and experience.

Another preliminary consideration is the *level* at which measurement of the target behavior is accomplished. A central feature of traditional learning theory approaches is their insistence on overt, quantifiable behaviors as the only targets appropriate for scientific consideration. Traditional operant approaches have declined to consider hypothetical, covert, or internal processes that have no overt referents. Measurement must, therefore, be precise; and a target behavior is described so as to be specific, observable, and objective (Favell, 1977, p. 17). For example, Eyberg and Robinson (1981) have defined noncompliant behavior as involving a failure to begin to obey a parental command within 5 seconds, or when the child begins an incompatible activity following a command (p. 73). Similarly, constructs such as sulking or depression would need to be redefined with reference to associated overt behaviors within an operant behavior change approach. The insistence on the three criteria of specificity, objectivity, and observability is not simply a theoretical quirk. They make possible the continual reevaluation of therapeutic efficacy. The three criteria cited have also prompted critics of the operant approach to label it "superficial" (concerned only with surface manifestations of people's problems). Therefore, it shall be pointed out that it is only *radical behaviorism* that seeks to rule out private events (like thoughts or images) from experimental analysis. *Methodological behaviorists*, on the other hand, seek only to "objectify" events that are usually covert and unobservable. Thus, many contemporary advocates of the operant approach (often called *applied behavior analysts*) take the position that private events are subject to the same causal laws as are overt (observable, countable) occurrences. Thoughts, self-instructions, feelings, and the like are considered "elements in chains that begin with observable environmental events and end with observable responses by the organism" (Baer, 1982, p. 278). The reader is urged to consider that the discussion in this chapter is potentially compatible with the perspectives presented in the chapters by Kanfer and Meichenbaum (despite the apparent philosophical differences).

As with other behavior therapy techniques, baseline (before-treatment) measurements of problem behaviors are an essential part of the problem definition and the selection of goals for therapy. Obviously, in order for baseline measures to be useful as standards against which to assess change or to evaluate maintenance of therapeutic gain, these measurements must be reliable. Specificity, objectivity, and observability tend to enhance reliability.

INCREASING BEHAVIOR RATES

Positive Reinforcement

Assume that these preliminary considerations have been addressed in the intake session: The target behavior has been carefully defined, baseline data have been gathered, and an increase in behavior frequency has been agreed upon by the therapist and the client as the treatment goal. The application of positive reinforcement, contingent upon the exhibition of the target behavior, could well suggest itself as a treatment strategy. Casual observation, as well as Skinner's more scientific approach, have demonstrated that behaviors that are followed by favorable consequences are likely to be repeated. The definition of the term *reinforcement* is any consequence that tends to increase the probability of a preceding response. When *positive reinforcement* is used, this is accomplished by *adding* something to increase the probability of the behavior. The nature of the positive reinforcer can differ from person to person and often must be empirically described. Primary reinforcers include those things that satisfy basic biological needs of the organism such as food, water, and air. Lovaas (1977) has been successful in using primary reinforcers to increase verbal and social behaviors in severely withdrawn, autistic children. Of course, in certain circumstances, even primary reinforcers can lose their ability or potency to influence behavior. It is doubtful, for example, whether a doughnut would be a positive reinforcer for someone who has recently finished eating Thanksgiving dinner. Secondary reinforcers have, through earlier association with primary reinforcers, acquired the capacity to increase the probability of a given behavior. Secondary reinforcers include such things as money and social approval, and they have obviously been shown to be quite effective in influencing behavior. Geller (1983) reported that, when the awarding of prizes was made contingent on wearing seat belts, seat belt use by munitions plant employees increased from the baseline measurement of 17.3% to 55.5% of all departing drivers. Secondary reinforcers can enhance the maintenance and generalization of behavior change, because secondary reinforcers are similar to naturally occurring rewards.

A number of different theories exist on the mechanism or explanatory principle behind reinforcement. One of these theories is of particular interest in situations where, for some reason, finding an effective reinforcer is problematic. David Premack (1959) proposed the theory of response as reinforcement. He argued that a behavior can itself reinforce another behavior if the former is the stronger of the two responses. Relative strength can be estimated by the amount of time that the individual freely spends engaging in a behavior. Simply by discovering the activities in which the client engages during free time, the clinician might be able to identify a potentially powerful positive reinforcer. The opportunity to engage in the more frequent behavior can be made contingent upon the exhibition of the low-frequency (but desirable) target behavior. Favell (1977) cited the case of a client who regularly took a shower before going to bed. The behavioral goal or target in this case was to increase the amount of time the client spent studying. The opportunity to take a shower was therefore made contingent upon time spent studying. As a result, study time increased.

Negative Reinforcement

Other methods can be used to *increase* the probability of a given response. When *negative reinforcement* is used, it involves the termination (or avoidance) of a consequence. Remember, in positive reinforcement something is added to increase the probability of a behavior. In negative reinforcement something is removed following a desired response, in order to increase the probability of a behavior. Negative reinforcers are generally unpleasant or "aversive," so that the individual is motivated to exhibit a desired (target) behavior in order to "turn off," avoid, or escape from the unpleasant condition. The individual who contingently nags at his or her spouse to put the top back on the toothpaste tube could be attempting to use the principles of negative reinforcement to change behavior. That is, he or she will stop nagging when the desired behavior is emitted. This approach can be more or less effective, depending on several factors (as discussed later). Though it is considered more extensively later in this chapter, it is worth noting here that the objective in *punishment* is a *decrease* in the probability of a response; and this is typically accomplished by the presentation of an aversive consequence contingent upon the occurrence of the target behavior to be weakened. However, unlike reinforcement, which produces learning (conditioning), punishment procedures are generally described as temporarily suppressing a response and not, as might be assumed, producing permanent "unlearning."

In general, positive reinforcers and aversive consequences exert their greatest effect on behavior when they are delivered or removed contingently (that is, dependent upon a particular behavior), with minimal delay, and with consistency. The number of times a response is reinforced and the quantity of reinforcers per response are related to the strength of the behavior in a *negatively accelerated function*. That is, small increases in number or magnitude of reinforcers will result in large increases in response strength (rate, speed, probability of occurrence), until the response reaches a plateau (also called an *asymptotic level*), after which the net addition to response strength declines (Deese & Hulse, 1967).

Reinforcement Schedules

Consistency of application seems to suggest that a behavior should be reinforced each time it occurs in order for learning to be maximized. Brief reflection could lead to reconsideration of this proposition. It is apparent that few behaviors learned outside a clinical setting are (or can be) reinforced every time they occur (continuous reinforcement). Skinner and his colleagues (e.g., Ferster & Skinner, 1957) pioneered the study of reinforcement schedules: the precise specification of contingencies in terms of responses emitted or the time elapsed after response or reinforcement.

There are four simple schedules of noncontinuous or partial reinforcement: fixed-ratio, variable-ratio, fixed-interval, variable-interval. Each schedule is associated with distinctive patterns of responding. The interval schedules require the passing of time before the possibility of reinforcement will again be available to the responding organism. Fixed-interval schedules employ a set time period. In variable-interval schedules the time periods vary around an average value, with some being quite short and others longer. The timing interval begins from the moment the last reinforcer is delivered. The behavior obtained on the fixed-interval schedule shows a characteristic scallop shape, with responding dropping off immediately after reinforcement has been delivered and increasing as the end of the reinforcement-free interval nears. The study habits of most college students with prescheduled midterm and final exams illustrate the effect on behavior of such a reinforcement schedule. Variable-interval schedules are associated with more constant rates of responding across the intervals. Teachers often resort to unannounced "pop quizzes" for this very reason.

With ratio schedules, reinforcement is dependent upon a number of responses emitted rather than upon an interval of time. Fixed-ratio schedules, in which reinforcement occurs only after a fixed number of responses have been emitted, tend to produce high and stable rates of responding. The piecework system employed in some industries is an example of a fixed-ratio schedule of reinforcement. With variable-ratio schedules, the responses-to-reinforcement ratio varies around an average value. Variable-ratio schedules produce high, almost constant rates of responding. Slot machines employ variable-ratio schedules of reinforcement.

As was noted earlier, one reason these partial-reinforcement schedules are of interest in clinical application is that they enhance maintenance of treatment gains by increasing resistance to extinction. Commonsense reasoning might suggest that the more reinforcement given for a response, the stronger the response, and the more responses one should observe when a reinforcement is discontinued (extinction). In fact, exactly the opposite is true. Partial-reinforcement schedules increase the resistance of a response to extinction. This principle is known as *Humphrey's Paradox* (for an extended discussion see Rachlin, 1970, pp. 119–122). Continuous reinforcement is best employed in the early stages of conditioning until the response is reliably exhibited. Then, a partial-reinforcement schedule should be implemented, to help insure maintenance of the behavior outside the therapy situation. Bornstein et al. (1983) reported on the successful application of a variable-ratio schedule of positive reinforcement for the treatment of encopretic behavior.

Positive Reinforcement Illustrated

The use of positive reinforcement to increase the frequency of desired behaviors has perhaps the longest history of any operant technique. An enormous empirical literature exists. Recently reported applications of reinforcement procedures have mirrored the recent changes in the types of problems addressed by applied behavior analysts. For example, medically related problems and problems of the elderly are two of the areas of recent emphasis. Contingent positive reinforcement of certain behaviors (e.g., finger movements) with access to hearing musical selections has been suggested as both an assessment (prognostic) and a treatment strategy in comatose patients (Boyle & Greer, 1983). There is a large literature on the use of positive (and negative) reinforcement in the effective treatment of myopia and for achieving improvements in visual acuity (e.g., Blount, Baer, & Collins, 1984; Rosen, Schiffman, & Cohen, 1984). In geriatric psychology, reinforcement has proven to be an effective technique in managing urinary incontinence among nursing home residents, often a significant problem in that setting (Schnelle et al., 1983).

Recommendations:

1. Identify reinforcers by observing their functional effects on behavior rather than assuming that what is a reward for one individual will serve the same function for another.
2. Identify activity reinforcers after systematic observation of the individual across and within a variety of natural settings.
3. Deliver reinforcers immediately, contingently, and consistently to maximize response strengthening.
4. Use a variety of different reinforcers to minimize loss of potency due to repeated presentation of a single reinforcing stimulus or event.
5. Reinforce behavior often while bringing it to optimal frequency, then thin out reinforcement to minimize loss of potency due to repeated presentation of a single reinforcing stimulus or event.
6. Use social reinforcement (the verbal and nonverbal behavior of people) whenever feasible to permit the developing behavior to be maintained across settings. If necessary, develop social reinforcer effectiveness by fading the use of primary reinforcers.

Negative Reinforcement Illustrated

Negative reinforcement is most often used for strengthening adaptive avoidance responses (e.g., learning to give up smoking, drinking, or fattening foods). It should be clear, however, that the use of negative reinforcement in a controlled setting (the animal laboratory or a therapist's office) constitutes an aversive approach to behavior change, with many of the potential drawbacks associated with punishment procedures (see the present discussion of punishment and also chapter 6).

Penick, Filion, Fox, and Stunkard (1971) employed a "symbolic" aversive stimulus in a negative self-reinforcement program for weight control. The behaviors to be accelerated were associated with dieting. Although weight reduction can be thought of as resulting in the positive consequence of looking and feeling better, the subjects also arranged for a negatively reinforcing event to occur contingent upon weight loss. The dieters each stored a large piece of pork fat in their refrigerators equal in amount to the excess weight to be lost. The investigators simply instructed their subjects to remove the bags of fat contingent upon proportional weight loss. This technique, in combination with others, seemed very effective. Of course the nature of the aversive stimulus, the delay of removal, its "self-mediation," and the absence of any warning stimulus made the weight control program quite unlike most of the laboratory-derived techniques currently in use. However, negative reinforcement is sometimes effective for the treatment of such problems as drug addiction, alcoholism, smoking, and obesity, for which the acquisition of avoidance responses seems clinically desirable and is an expressed goal of the patient. In general, escape or avoidance conditioning (as the sole intervention method) has not produced unequivocally positive outcomes.

Recommendations:

1. When using negative reinforcement to teach avoidance, provide an incompatible, alternate approach response. In treating an alcoholic, for example, one might arrange for shock during alcohol consumption to be terminated by a response that causes some other beverage to be delivered.

2. The termination of the aversive stimulus should be contingent, immediate, and consistent.

3. Remember that, in avoidance conditioning, two events are connected — the aversive stimulus and the cue to the onset of the aversive stimulus (called the *conditioned aversive stimulus*, or CAS). The individual who learns to avoid or remove himself or herself from a situation containing the CAS also causes the association of the CAS and the aversive event to be weakened. Thus, avoidance might also start to weaken. As conditioning proceeds, it is advisable to pair the CAS and the aversive stimulus on an intermittent basis with decreasing frequency.

4. The time between escape or avoidance trials must not be too brief. The aversive stimulus should be off long enough to make the relief enjoyable.

5. If, over time, the individual is not making reliable avoidance or escape responses, bring the training to a halt and determine if unknown contin-

gencies outside of therapy are interfering with the program or if the aversive consequences are, indeed, functionally aversive.

Prompting and Fading

It is, of course, generally simplistic to seek to help a client increase the frequency of a behavior without consideration of the situational factors involved. Few behaviors are fully appropriate in every situation. A *discriminative stimulus* is a cue that functions to signal that a behavior is situationally appropriate and that the potential for reinforcement exists with its occurrence. The ringing of a telephone is, for example, a discriminative stimulus, not compelling a behavior but serving as a cue that reinforcement (or punishment) is likely to occur in its presence. Maladaptive behavior is often the result of responding to an inappropriate stimulus (i.e., the form of the behavior is correct, but it is emitted at the wrong time or place) or of failure to respond to the appropriate cue. Prompting and fading techniques are, therefore, often used, in combination with reinforcement techniques, to bring a client's responses under the influence of verbal or nonverbal signals.

Prompts are behavioral interventions that direct the learner's attention to the required behavior. They can be verbal, physical, or environmental cues. The prompt must initially be effective in provoking the response every time it is presented. At the start of treatment a large or conspicuous prompt might be necessary to satisfy this requirement, for example, physically guiding an autistic client through the application of a deodorant (Tomporowski, 1983) or moving a child's limbs through a series of orthopedic exercises. The prompt should be gradually removed or *faded*, and finally eliminated. At the conclusion of training, the target response should reliably occur without prompting. It is important to note that, although prompts are to be gradually faded, contingent reinforcement should continue. If responding ceases during fading, then an earlier prompt should be reinvoked until responding is once again reliably established. Fading can then proceed at a slower pace or in more gradual steps. Throughout this procedure, reinforcement remains contingent on the exhibition of the target behavior.

Verbal prompting in combination with positive reinforcement has been shown to be an effective method of increasing verbal interaction among socially isolated mentally retarded adults. Kleitsch, Whitman, and Santos (1983) reported a significant increase in verbal interactions from the baseline measurement of no verbal interactions. This verbal behavior apparently generalized to the subject's nonparticipating peers, and a 4-month follow-up suggested that the behavior change was maintained following the conclusion of the training program.

Herbert Terrace demonstrated in research with pigeons (1963) that "errorless learning" was possible through the uses of prompting and fading and that such procedures produced more rapid learning than traditional trial-and-error training procedures. Since that time, errorless learning designs have proven to be an efficient educational strategy with human subjects and have been used, for example, to teach sight words to trainable mentally retarded subjects (Walsh & Lambert, 1979).

Fading and prompting are methods for bringing behavior under *stimulus control*. Stimulus control refers to the general process of manipulating the antecedent conditions that set the stage for reinforced or reinforceable responding. In many therapeutic situations, it is easier, cheaper, faster, or more efficient to program antecedent stimuli for appropriate behavior than to alter the situational contingencies of reward or punishment. Including the antecedent cue or discriminative stimulus in a general formula, along with the operant response (the target) and the contingent consequences (reward or punishment) yields the basic road map of operant psychology — the "Three term contingency":

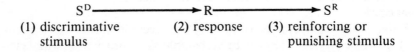

$$S^D \longrightarrow R \longrightarrow S^R$$

(1) discriminative   (2) response   (3) reinforcing or
      stimulus   punishing stimulus

Stimulus control procedures have been effectively employed in complex settings involving such treatment resistant problems as obesity, alcoholism, and smoking. For example, as one component in their successful behavioral program for weight control, Stuart and his colleagues (Stuart & Davis, 1972) taught their clients to strengthen the antecedents of appropriate eating. For example, dieters were urged to provide themselves with an assortment of acceptable foods and to monitor their cumulative consumption on pocket record sheets. In essence, the dieter restricts his or her environment or arranges it to maximize success. Because eating is often cued by the physical characteristics of food (size, texture, color, etc.), the dieter is also taught to employ low-calorie garnishes, such as parsley and paprika.

Another method of stimulus control, sometimes employed in conjunction with provision of cues for appropriate behavior, is the weakening of cues for inappropriate behavior. Nolan (1968) reported on the use of stimulus control procedures in the reduction and ultimate elimination of smoking behavior. In this case report, the client was instructed to smoke only while seated in one particular chair. The chair faced a corner, and other behaviors, such as reading and talking with family members, were prohibited while the client was seated in the chair. (In a second phase of treatment the chair was removed to the client's basement.) This procedure effectively reduced the range of cues that preceded smoking and limited the external reinforcement for the undesirable behavior.

Recommendations:

1. To use stimulus control effectively, identify by observation (not deduction) the functional links between antecedent cues and behaviors to be accelerated.
2. Identify the cues for inappropriate behavior.
3. Remove cues for inappropriate behavior.
4. Make cues for appropriate responding more conspicuous. If certain individuals serve as S^Ds for the appropriate behavior of others, then arrange to have the facilitating persons occupy a more central place in the environment.
5. Do not overwork stimulus control. Remember, each nonreinforced presentation of a stimulus weakens its power to evoke responding.
6. If an arbitrary cue has been established as a discriminative stimulus, gradually fade in natural antecedents in order to foster generalization to the posttreatment environment.
7. Train the individual to take over the cue control of his own behavior.

Shaping

Fading and prompting can also be used effectively when the target behavior is not currently in the client's repertoire, and it must be constructed through a procedure known as *shaping*. Shaping is sometimes referred to as the method of successive approximations. In application, shaping is not dissimilar from the children's "hot and cold" guessing game. Shaping involves initially reinforcing an existing behavior that is different from, but similar to, the target behavior. The criterion for reinforcement changes throughout training, so as to select and reinforce only those behaviors that are increasingly similar to the desired target behavior.

Skinner, for example, once proposed the use of pigeons in the nose cones of guided missiles as part of the control system. He used shaping procedures to teach the pigeons to peck at the center of a ship pictured on a display screen. When electrodes were attached to the pigeons' beaks, the course of the missile could be electronically corrected on a continuous basis to insure a "direct hit." Lovaas (1977) has long employed shaping to establish verbal behavior (and social behavior) in autistic children. In his approach, the therapist initially reinforces any vowel-like sound that happens to be emitted by the child. A physical prompt, such as manual positioning of the child's lips, is sometimes used to let the natural release of air produce a particular vocalization, which can then be immediately reinforced. Once reliable responding has been obtained, the criterion can be shifted a bit; the therapist can choose to reinforce a vocalization only if it occurs within 5 seconds after a verbal prompt. No reward would be administered if a sound occurred 6 seconds after the prompt (extinction). After reliably bringing verbalization under discriminative control, the therapist might next try to elicit imitation on the part of the child, only reinforcing accurate matching.

Recommendations:
The steps in behavior shaping are as follows.

1. Begin by observing the individual whose behavior repertoire is considered deficient. What responses occur at high frequency? Identify the antecedent and consequent (reinforcing) environmental stimuli associated with these high frequency behaviors. Note the variability in topography (form, force, or duration) of the available responses.

2. Based upon the observational data, decide whether a desired terminal response can be differentiated out of existing behaviors and if so, what a first approximation to the end goal should be.

3. Establish the criterion for the first approximation. As Blackwood (1971) pointed out: "In setting the criterion, we are dividing the responses into two classes; responses most like those we want and responses least like those we want. Notice here that the criterion must be set low or all responding will be extinguished" (chapter 7, p. 6).

4. Arrange the setting for maximum likelihood of response emission. If the desired response involves other people or particular stimuli, arrange to have them present during shaping.

5. Differentially reinforce (with the most powerful reinforcers at your disposal — food, praise, physical affection, etc.) variants of ongoing behavior that may be crude first approximations of the desired response. Withdraw reinforcement from variants that are incompatible with the desired end goal. For example, in shaping her son to pay attention to her demonstrations of proper dressing behavior, a mother talks to her child affectionately when he looks in her direction, but is silent when the child turns away, closes his eyes, screams, and so on.

6. Observe the shift in the direction of the goal behavior and shift the criterion accordingly. If repeated reinforcement fails to reliably establish a response, the criterion might need to be lowered. When a behavior is established at a high, stable rate with little fluctuation (e.g., a child's verbalization of "da" occurs to the cue "Say da" 95% of the time), the criterion can be shifted in the direction of the desired response (reinforce only two consecutive "da" responses; reinforce two consecutive "da" responses separated by a maximum of two seconds of silence; then one second, etc.).

7. Use verbal or gestural cues or instructions at all stages of the process, even though the cues do not at first reliably elicit the behavior being shaped. At the onset of the shaping procedure, the child's behavior will determine what cues the shaper will use (step 1). That is, if the child

spontaneously says "goo," the shaper will reinforce the sound and then attempt to establish stimulus control by instructing the child, "Say goo" and rewarding compliance.

Extinction

Operant conditioning techniques can also be employed to reduce the likelihood of excessive or objectionable behavior. This goal is generally accomplished most effectively when applied in tandem with the positive reinforcement of an appropriate substitute behavior. The most obvious way to accomplish such an end would be to do the *opposite of reinforcing the behavior*. Most deviant behaviors are, in fact, maintained by external reinforcement. Attention, whether positive or negative, is often contingent upon the exhibition of a problem behavior. Indeed, social attention is a powerful reinforcer despite any aversive consequences that might follow it, particularly when it occurs contingently.

In terms of its effects on behavior, *extinction* can be considered the procedure most nearly opposite to reinforcement. It consists of terminating or withholding reinforcement for the problem behavior. Many parents unwittingly condition behaviors such as whining by attempting to comfort and console their children contingent upon the whining. Although this can have the immediate effect of decreasing the whining (and incidentally, therefore, positively reinforcing the parent for this behavior control strategy), it will also almost certainly increase the probability of the child's whining in future situations. Extinction is the simplest procedure to reduce this and other simple problem behaviors.

The effectiveness of extinction depends on the therapist's ability to identify *and* eliminate the reinforcement that maintains the behavior. When implementing extinction procedures, it is important to recognize a phenomenon referred to as the *extinction burst*. Before being extinguished, a behavior might actually increase in frequency or intensity (particularly at the beginning of treatment). In other words, behavior will probably get worse before it gets better. For this reason, extinction procedures are often inappropriate when the problem behavior is physically harmful or extremely destructive. Some behaviors such as head banging or finger flapping appear to be self-stimulating (reinforcing) behaviors and, as such, tend to undercut the therapist's success in eliminating their reinforcing components. Extinction is generally ineffective in the elimination of this type of activity (Rincover, 1978). However, Rincover and his colleagues (Rincover, 1978; Rincover, Cook, Peoples, & Packard, 1979) have demonstrated in several studies that, when a sensory feature known to be reinforcing a particular behavior can be discovered through careful observation (for example, the sound of a spinning plate), extinction, specifically sensory extinction, can be effectively used in eliminating the behavior in question.

The rate at which a behavior is extinguished has been shown to be a function of the reinforcement schedule maintaining it. Behaviors maintained under partial reinforcement schedules (sometimes the parent ignores the whining child, sometimes comforts or bribes him or her) are generally more resistant to extinction than those continuously reinforced.

Illustration

Ayllon and Michael (1959) provided one of the first demonstrations of the efficacy of extinction in the treatment of "psychotic talk" by hospitalized patients. Prior to the enactment of behavioral interventions, the ward nurses conducted systematic observations of patient behavior. Data were collected on the frequency of problem behavior, on the kind and frequency of naturally occurring reinforcement, and (a step often neglected by untutored behavior modifiers) on the frequency of incompatible behavior that could be used to displace the deviant responding. The results indicated that much of the undesirable patient behavior was being maintained by the contingent social approval and attention of the nursing staff. Subsequently, the nurses, who served as the behavioral engineers or change agents, were instructed in the use of extinction (being asked, for example, to "ignore the behavior and act deaf and blind whenever it occurs").

The goal for Helen, a patient described as delusional, was the extinction of her "psychotic talk." More than 90% of Helen's conversation focused on her illegitimate child and the men who were after her. After the nurses were instructed to use extinction plus reinforcement of other conversational topics, the sick talk dropped steadily — to a low of less than 25% relative frequency on the 10th week (the delusional talk had persisted for 3 years previously). When the psychotic talk appeared again at higher frequency, it was discovered that Helen was obtaining "bootleg" reinforcement from individuals unfamiliar with the extinction program. The power of extinction was, nonetheless, clearly demonstrated. The reader is referred to Ayllon and Azrin (1968) for further illustrations of the use of extinction with hospitalized patients, to O'Leary and O'Leary (1977) for examples of classroom applications, to Harris and Ersner-Hershfield (1978) for a discussion of extinction with severely disturbed and mentally retarded populations, and to Melamed and Siegel (1980) for applications to medical problems.

Recommendations:

1. Use extinction of inappropriate responding in conjunction with positive reinforcement for incompatible or appropriate behavior.
2. Extinction is effective only if the behavioral engineer has correctly identified the reinforcing stimulus to be withheld. Difficulties and failures in the use of extinction can be minimized by careful and reliable observation of the problem situation, with an eye toward identifying all possible

reinforcers contingent upon undesirable behavior, and by interviewing the target person to ascertain (e.g., through the use of a reinforcer survey) the current effective reinforcers in his or her life.

3. Extinction works best if all those who are potential reinforcers of inappropriate behavior work toward withholding the payoff. Thus, teachers might need to work with parents, hospital personnel need to be coordinated, and, in general, every available resource person needs to become involved in the extinction program. Failing this, the deviant response will be intermittently reinforced, making it resistant to extinction.

4. Prepare those involved with the client, especially program implementers, for the initial increase in the frequency of the undesirable response when extinction begins.

5. Extinction, as the exclusive change method, is inappropriate when the behavior must be stopped at once because it is physically harmful to the client or to others (as in the self-mutilation of children, assaultive behavior, or fire setting); when the frustrating effects produced by reward removal cue other behaviors that are dangerous and potentially uncontrollable (i.e., behaviors for which the cues and reinforcement contingencies are unknown or unmanageable); and when the withholding of rewards for inappropriate behavior also requires the withholding of rewards for desirable responses.

Differential Reinforcement of Other (or of Incompatible) Behavior

Differential reinforcement of incompatible (DRI), but appropriate, behavior is often employed in combination with extinction procedures. DRI can be used in circumstances where it is possible to identify a behavior that is truly incompatible with the problem behavior. In a frequently cited case report, Allen, Hart, Buell, Harris and Wolf (1964) described a 4-year-old girl who spent almost no time interacting with other children in the nursery school setting, but whose behavior elicited almost constant adult attention. The treatment strategy consisted of making adult attention contingent upon her interaction with other children and concurrently ignoring the child during periods of social isolation or during her attempts to elicit adult attention only.

Stuart (1967) reported on his novel treatment of a deeply religious, depressed woman. Stuart had the client "translate" biblical passages whenever she felt particularly depressed, because the woman had indicated to him that it was impossible for her to simultaneously feel depressed and to "revel in the glory of God." Similarly, a physician known to one of the authors often passes out sticks of chewing gum to his young patients prior to giving them injections, based upon his observation of the physical impossibility of chewing gum and crying at the same time.

A slightly different approach to decreasing a problem behavior involves reinforcing the client for exhibiting any behavior other than the problem behavior during a specified period of time. This approach is referred to as differential reinforcement of other behavior (DRO). As a component of a larger treatment package, Favell, McGimsey, and Jones (1978) used DRO procedures to reduce the frequency of self-injurious behavior in an 8-year-old retarded boy. Most of the clinical reports of the use of DRO concern its application in the reduction of self-injurious behavior (Repp & Deitz, 1974; Spiegler, 1983; Weiker & Harmon, 1975).

Recommendations:

1. Use DRO schedules in concert with other nonaversive change methods such as extinction and verbal prompting.
2. When the target (undesirable) behavior occurs at high rates, it might be necessary to prompt the "other" or incompatible response.
3. Employ brief time intervals for initial reinforcement of the desirable response, to permit the learner to earn sufficient reward for its emission.
4. Be sure to avoid reinforcing "other" behaviors that themselves are apt to become problematic to the client in the long run.
5. Use DRO schedules consistently to eliminate the undesirable behavior in as many contexts as it is likely to occur in.
6. Avoid sole use of DRO procedures if the response to be eliminated is life threatening and must be rapidly suppressed.
7. Try to select an incompatible response for DRI contingencies that is already in the client's skill repertoire and that is likely to be maintained in the natural environment (see Sulzer-Azaroff & Mayer, 1977, for further discussion of DRO and related methods).

Satiation and Restraint

Satiation, which involves providing the client with an overabundance of activities (response satiation) or of reinforcing commodities (stimulus satiation), can be used to weaken a problem behavior. It may be recalled from the earlier discussion of positive reinforcement that, at times, a reinforcer can lose potency, particularly after repeated presentations. Food, for example, becomes a less potent reinforcer as hunger is relieved. Although this feature is sometimes problematic in positive reinforcement designs, satiation can be effectively employed to reduce the strength of an inappropriate behavior. In a now classic study, Ayllon (1963) used satiation to decrease the towel-hoarding behavior of a psychiatric patient. Ayllon instructed the ward staff to give the patient towels noncontingently, rather than trying to prohibit the patient's efforts at acquiring them. After she had accumulated approximately 635 towels in her room, the woman voluntarily removed all of them, and the hoarding behavior was permanently discontinued.

Although a classic, Ayllon's is not a case of pure satiation treatment, because the reinforcer was delivered noncontingently. The satiation approach to the treatment of cigarette smoking, however, requires that smokers engage in the response continuously and experience the outcome until the process becomes intolerable. Schmale, Lichtenstein, and Harris (1972) have reported that stimulus satiation, combined with having to inhale either warm smoky air or mentholated air, rapidly reduced smoking behavior to zero, with approximately 60% of subjects still abstaining after 6 months.

Satiation is a rather infrequently applied operant procedure, perhaps because of some of the difficulties soon to be noted. Satiation cannot be used in situations where it is not possible to identify and manipulate the reinforcing stimulus. Additionally, sometimes even when the reinforcer can be identified and manipulated, the potentially harmful effects of the reinforcer could raise both ethical and practical concerns. Using satiation, for example, to decrease the eating of sweets by a diabetic patient seems ill advised to say the least. Finally, social reinforcement might not be subject to the effects of satiation.

Response reduction can also be accomplished through physical restraint. In severe or extreme cases involving dangerous or life-threatening behavior, the individual might need to be confined or physically restricted. Typically, the effects of restraint are short lived. Its utility lies in the possibility that it will be sufficiently aversive (see later on) to reduce dangerous activity while enhancing attention to discriminative stimuli for appropriate responding. Nonetheless, the use of restraint is recommended in the use of restraint! The procedure has the potential to backfire on the inexperienced behavior analyst (see Favell et al., 1978, for an example).

Our recommendation is to use satiation and restraint sparingly and to routinely seek ethical consultation before applying these procedures.

Time Out

Time out (TO) refers to time out from reinforcement or to a specified period of time during which no reinforcement is administered. Time-out procedures can be more effective than extinction in producing rapid decreases in problem behaviors (Patterson, 1971). Time out is particularly well suited for use in those situations where it is difficult for the applied behavior analyst to identify and/or control the reinforcers maintaining the problem behavior and in group or institutional settings (such as classrooms or hospital wards), where it is sometimes easier to deal with disruptive individuals than with a large group. For time-out procedures to be effective, they must be used consistently and upon each occurrence of the problem behavior. It is also important to insure that reinforcements are truly absent from the time-out situation. Sending a child to his or her bedroom, in many cases a room well equipped with toys and other amusements, does not constitute such a situation. Patterson (1971) has suggested the bathroom as an appropriate location for time out. Others (e.g., Eyberg & Robinson, 1982) recommend using a chair facing a corner for very young children.

Rather brief time-out periods, 1 to 5 minutes, have been shown to be as effective with children as 20 to 30 minutes (Patterson & White, 1969). In most time-out programs, a brief explanation is given before the person is placed in time out, for example, "You didn't do what I told you to do so now you'll have to sit in the chair. Stay in the chair until I tell you you may get up" (Eyberg & Robinson, 1982). This "signal" should follow the problem behavior as closely as possible. Most frequently the time-out period is terminated when both the predetermined time period has expired *and* the individual is relatively quiet (to avoid reinforcing crying, tantrums, etc. with the termination of time out) (Hobbs, Forehand, & Murray, 1978).

Illustrations

Wong, Gaydos, and Fugua (1982) reported on the application of modified time-out procedures in the treatment of pedophilia. Their subject was a mildly mentally retarded group-home resident who had previously been accused of several sexual offenses. Baseline data on the subject's approaches to young girls, young boys, and adults was covertly gathered during his walks through the neighborhood surrounding the group home. During treatment, the subject's approaches to young girls and subsequently to young boys precipitated the subject's return by the observer to the group home and his restriction there. This approach was effective in selectively reducing the subject's approaches to young boys and girls, leaving the more appropriate behaviors intact.

In recent years the TO procedure has sometimes been misrepresented and misapplied. Some institutions have used time-out procedures to justify extreme and unethical practices such as isolation and extreme deprivation. For this reason, modified time-out procedures have been proposed in which reinforcement, particularly social reinforcement, is temporarily terminated, though the subject is not physically removed from the situation (nonexclusionary time out). Foxx and Shapiro (1978) described the potential advantages and disadvantages of such a procedure. Foxx, Foxx, Jones, and Kiely (1980) reported on the use of nonexclusionary time out in the reduction of episodes of intransigent aggressive behavior. The subject of their report was an institutionalized, psychotic-like, mentally retarded adult male. The time-out procedure was only one aspect of a treatment package, which also included increased reinforcement for appropriate behavior and relaxation training. The time-out procedure involved the elimination of all social interaction with the subject for 24 hours following an aggressive episode, though the subject was not physically removed from the regular environment. The effectiveness of this treatment was evaluated using several different measures, all of which indicated a highly significant reduction in aggressive behavior.

Recommendations:

1. Use time out in conjunction with positive reinforcement of desirable and incompatible behaviors.
2. Arrange the time-out area to be free of attractive or distracting activities. It should be small but well ventilated. Arrange the area in which appropriate behavior is desired in as attractive a manner as possible (with reinforcing activities and objects immediately available for appropriate behavior). Absence of effects for TO are often attributable to the relatively low magnitude of payoff for correct responding.
3. The majority of successful programs with children employ TO durations of between 5 and 20 minutes. Long durations are undesirable because the individual is removed from opportunities to learn more adaptive responses. One should experiment with short durations of TO first and, if need be, work up to longer durations. Starting out with long durations and subsequently shortening them is not recommended (White, Nielson, & Johnson, 1972).
4. In keeping with TO duration requirements, the distance and travel time to the TO area should be short.
5. If possible, monitor the individual's behavior while in TO. The child who can make a "game" out of TO does not benefit from it.
6. Try not to reinforce any behaviors (either with positive attention or with a display of anger or disappointment) while going to or returning from the TO area.
7. Use verbal and/or nonverbal signals before initiating TO. The chain of behaviors leading up to the TO signal should include a "stop cue," which, if noticed, might come to suppress the disruptive behavior at lower magnitudes.
8. Never use TO if the situation from which the individual is being removed is primarily an unpleasant one. Individuals will simply turn TO into an escape or avoidance opportunity, and the behavior upon which TO is contingent will increase in frequency.

Overcorrection, Positive Practice, and Habit Reversal

Azrin and his colleagues (e.g., Azrin & Nunn, 1973; Foxx & Azrin, 1972) have proposed "positive practice" procedures as additional methods for reducing unwanted behavior. *Habit reversal* and *overcorrection* are two other terms used to refer to this group of procedures. Azrin and Powers (1975) compared the efficacy of the overcorrection procedure with two other procedures (warnings and contingent loss of recess) in reducing disruptive classroom behavior. They concluded that overcorrection was superior. Overcorrection actually involves two fundamental components: restitution and positive practice. Restitution requires that, if misbehavior has led to environmental disruption, the responsible person must repair or restore the behavior setting to a state better than it was before the disruption. If an individual has angrily hit and insulted another person in a group, the restitution might call for an apology to the injured party as well as to everyone else who was present at the time of the misbehavior. Positive practice requires repeated practice of adaptive prosocial behaviors. Thus, the aggressor in the previous example might be required to practice complimenting or praising his or her associates in a group, and for appropriate reasons. Overcorrection could be of particular value when misbehaviors occur at high rates, when there are few alternative behaviors available to reinforce, and when there are few effective reinforcers to remove contingent upon inappropriate responding.

When the behavior to be decreased does not cause environmental disruption, the restitution component is no longer appropriate, and positive practice alone can be used. Thumb sucking might be seen as an example of this type of problem situation. Azrin, Nunn, and Frantz-Renshaw (1980) compared the effectiveness of painting the thumbnail with a bitter-tasting substance to habit reversal (essentially a positive practice procedure) for the treatment of thumb sucking in a sample of 30 children. Their results indicated that habit reversal was the more effective behavior change method. Approximately 92% of the habit reversal group stopped the thumb sucking, in comparison with only 35% of the subjects in the other group. The habit reversal reductions in thumb sucking were maintained throughout a 20-month follow-up period. Azrin, Nunn, and Frantz (1980) likewise demonstrated that habit reversal was superior to negative practice in the treatment of nail biting. Habit reversal has also been shown to be useful in the treatment of teeth grinding, or bruxism (Rosenbaum & Ayllon, 1981b), neurodermatitis (Rosenbaum & Ayllon, 1981a), and nocturnal head banging (Strauss, Rubinoff & Atkeson, 1983).

Recommendations:

1. Overcorrection, positive practice, or habit reversal procedures should be applied as quickly as possible after a misbehavior.
2. Overcorrection is particularly useful in dealing with behavior that tends to infringe upon the rights of others (cf. Spiegler, 1983, pp. 155–156).
3. Try to insure that the restitution and positive practice components focus upon actions that are (or will be) beneficial to the client, rather than

upon actions that are merely unpleasant or embarrassing (and that can be interpreted as punitive).

4. Use these procedures only with clients capable of understanding them or of cooperating with their intended educational function.
5. Use these procedures in concert with reinforcement for appropriate behaviors.
6. Be on the lookout for changes in other inappropriate nontargeted behaviors during and subsequent to overcorrection periods.

Response Cost

Response cost (RC) represents a form of punishment in which previously acquired reinforcers are forfeited, contingent upon the occurrence of an undesirable response. For example, locking up the bicycle of a child who repeatedly rides on busy streets despite being instructed not to is properly described as response cost. Obviously, before this procedure can be implemented, the client must possess reinforcers that can be contingently removed. Speeding tickets and fines for overdue library books are other common examples of response-cost procedures (Reese, 1978).

Response cost (loss of free time) has been used to decrease the off-task behaviors of boys with attention deficit disorder with hyperactivity (Rapport, Murphy & Bailey, 1982). A within-subject design ($N = 2$) suggested that response-cost procedures were superior to methylphenidate (Ritalin) in promoting the appropriate behavior change.

Boudin (1972) reported the use of a response-cost contract in the outpatient treatment of amphetamine abuse. His patient, a female graduate student, had been using amphetamines for 3 years prior to treatment. She had resorted to lying and stealing in order to obtain drugs and was panic-stricken at the thought that she had become an addict. Although the treatment plan involved such elements as stimulus control, verbal encouragement, and aversive techniques, it also included a "stiff" response-cost arrangement wherein the client established a joint bank account with her therapist that included all of her capital ($500). The client signed ten $50 checks, which needed only the therapist's signature to be valid. It was agreed that each drug use or suspected drug use would result in the loss of one check. The RC contingency was used only once during the 3-month contract violation. The client (who was black) was told that valid checks would be sent to the Ku Klux Klan.

Recommendations:

1. Use response-cost procedures in conjunction with positive reinforcement for appropriate and incompatible behaviors.
2. Before establishing an RC system, determine if the potentially lost reinforcers are indeed valued. They must be genuine reinforcers in the sense

that individuals will work to earn them and will spend them on items not otherwise available.

3. Arrange the overall earnings-cost program so that items lost or forfeited cannot be easily or rapidly replaced.
4. Arrange the overall earnings-cost program in such a manner that "fines" are realistic (neither bankrupting the individual in a single trial nor making so little dent in her or his savings that the loss goes unnoticed).
5. Institute the fine as soon as possible after a misbehavior.
6. For individuals who have not earned them, it may be necessary to supply reinforcers noncontingently at first. RC procedures can then be applied.
7. If RC is paired with verbal criticism, it is possible to fade out the punishment contingency and bring disruptive behavior under the verbal control of change agents (therapists, teachers, parents, aides, etc.).
8. With highly motivated clients, it is conceivable that imagined rather than actual reinforcer loss can be used as a punishment procedure (Kazdin, 1972; Weiner, 1965).

Response-Contingent Aversive Stimulation

The final operant method for decreasing problem behaviors to be discussed, response contingent aversive stimulation (RCAS), has probably provoked more ethical (and legal) debate than any of the other operant procedures. RCAS is punishment as it is usually conceived and, therefore, has some serious practical limitations. Punishment procedures, as has been noted, only temporarily suppress responding. They are relativley uninformative, in that they only indicate what not to do (and sometimes the substitute behavior that emerges is as problematic as the behavior being treated). Because of generalization processes, the person administering RCAS and the situation in which it is administered can themselves become classically conditioned aversive stimuli. For these and other related reasons, RCAS is often proposed as a treatment strategy of last resort.Like other procedures used to weaken a behavior, RCAS is most effective when used in combination with procedures designed to strengthen alternative behaviors.

Typically, the aversive stimulus is intended to be perceived by the client as painful, unpleasant, or noxious. However, it is important to recognize that punishment, like reinforcement, is correctly defined solely in terms of its effect on behavior. A punishing stimulus is anything that *decreases* the probability of the particular behavior upon which it is contingent. Both primary and conditioned punishing stimuli can be identified. When behaviors involve immediate physical danger to the client or to others in the environment, or when misbehavior cannot be controlled through the use of antecedent cues or reinforcing consequences, then RCAS might be the treatment of choice.

Sajwaj, Libet, and Agras (1974) reported on the effective application of RCAS in the treatment of ruminative vomiting in a 6-month-old infant. The aversive stimulus was a squirt of lemon juice in the infant's mouth as soon as the motor precursors of the vomiting were noted. The A-B-A-B design employed by the authors supported the effectiveness of the RCAS procedure. The ruminative regurgitation had ceased completely by the twelfth day of treatment.

RCAS is most commonly used in the suppression of self-injurious behavior and in situations "where the use of a relatively small pain in the present can prevent a relatively large pain in the future" (Lovaas & Newsome, 1976). Although self-injurious behavior is reported to occur more often in combination with mental retardation and psychosis, Altman, Haavik, and Higgins (1983) reported on the effective use of RCAS (Tabasco sauce) in eliminating persistent and severe finger biting in an infant with spina bifida (and diminished pain sensitivity) who was intellectually normal.

Recommendations:

When positive control and nonphysical forms of punishment are ineffective in changing behavior, the use of response-contingent aversive stimulation is best carried out in keeping with the following guidelines:

1. Use RCAS in conjunction with positive reinforcement of appropriate behavior and extinction of inappropriate responding.
2. Deliver RCAS as soon as possible after a misbehavior.
3. The duration of RCAS need not be very long (with moderate electric shocks, a duration of 0.1 second has proven effective).
4. Deliver RCAS on a continuous schedule until the response is suppressed or eliminated.
5. The materials used to deliver RCAS should be checked often for safety and reliability (see Butterfield, 1975).
6. Different individuals should be involved in the delivery of RCAS. If possible and necessary, persons with whom the client will have contact outside of therapy should be involved in the delivery of RCAS.
7. Be on guard for negative side effects.
8. Avoid extended periods of RCAS.
9. The individual who delivers RCAS should do so only if he or she is in agreement with the clinical decision that dictates its use.
10. Effective and acceptable alternatives to shock and intense auditory stimulation should be sought. For example, shaking, pinching, hand slapping, and even tickling can suppress behavior in youngsters for whom shock would appear to caretakers as unduly harsh or untenable.
11. Use fading techniques to bring punished responses under discriminative control (e.g., use a warning cue).
12. Inform the client of the nature of the RCAS contingency.

13. Do not apply positive reinforcers in close proximity to the delivery of RCAS.

COMPLEX BEHAVIORS

Operant methods are most closely associated with those situations in which the target behaviors are relatively simple, discrete, stimulus-response units. However, operant procedures can also be used in the management of complex behaviors and behavior sequences. Two additional operant procedures, chaining and the token economy, combine procedures already discussed to develop and manage complex forms of behavior.

The use of *chaining* is indicated when the behavior to be learned is composed of several different elements that must be performed sequentially. Complex motor skills such as swimming or serving a tennis ball are often learned in this way. Tooth brushing, vocational skills, and social skills have also been developed using this procedure. Each component behavior of the chain acts as both a cue (discriminative stimulus) for the next behavior in the sequence and a reinforcer for the preceding behavior (i.e., a conditioned reinforcer). Chaining can proceed in either a forward or a backward direction. That is, the first behavior to be conditioned through positive reinforcement can be either the first behavior in the chain or the final behavior in the chain. Backward chaining is often considered to be the more effective procedure. However, Walls, Zane, and Ellis (1981) compared the effects of whole-task training, forward chaining, and backward chaining in teaching assembly tasks in a vocational rehabilitation setting. They concluded that, with respect to accuracy of assembly, both chaining methods were superior to whole-task training but did not differ from each other.

Recommendations:
The basic rules for teaching behavior chains are to

1. Divide the desired behavior sequence into component units. Size of units should be determined by demands of the individual case.
2. Determine which members of the to-be-continued chain already exist and which will need to be individually shaped.
3. Shape the chain members that are at low strength (low probability of emission) or at zero strength.
4. Begin the chaining procedure by strengthening the final member. Do so in a distraction-free environment.
5. Bring the final member under reliable stimulus control. The accomplishment of this and the preceding step is aided by the use of strong reinforcers (determined by observing the client and asking what he or she likes), consistently, immediately, and frequently given, contingent

upon emission of the desired response. Social reinforcers should also be used (e.g., smiles and praise).

6. Add the next-to-last member of the behavior already acquired. Add each remaining member, working backward to the first response in the chain. For example, a three-member chain can be diagrammed as follows:

$$S_1^D \rightarrow R_1 \rightarrow S_1^R$$
$$S_2^D \rightarrow R_2 \rightarrow S_2^R$$
$$S_3^D \rightarrow R_3 \rightarrow S_3^R$$

(Start here)

Let us assume that we are dealing with the last three members of a toothbrushing chain; (R_3) is brushing reinforced by (S_3^R) the delightful-tasting toothpaste. The cue for brushing (S_3^D) is the toothbrush in hand. Holding the toothbrush will eventually take on reinforcing power. When holding the toothbrush reliably predicts brushing, we can expect toothbrush holding (S_3^D) to reinforce (S_3^D is also S_2^R) toothbrush lifting (R_2). The cue for toothbrush lifting (S_2^D) could be the sight of the toothbrush. Eventually, seeing the toothbrush will reinforce (S_1^R) the first response in our mini-chain (R_1), which is switching on the light in the bathroom.

7. When an error occurs during performance of a chained sequence, correct the error as soon as possible and require the performer to go back as far as possible in the chain and start over.
8. When errors occur in a learned sequence, it might be necessary to punish them. One might need to punish errors that occur early in the chain, because disruption of the initial behaviors undercuts acquisition and can have adverse effects on the learner's motivation.
9. In teaching chained sequences (such as proper dressing, toileting, bathing, and eating behavior) it is helpful and necessary to physically guide the performer through the sequence. The teacher can also demonstrate (model) appropriate behavior.
10. Fading and prompting techniques can also be useful in establishing effective chains.

The effectiveness of token economy programs (TEPs) has now been evaluated for more than a decade (Ayllon & Azrin, 1968). They have been used with a variety of populations and in a number of different settings including educational, rehabilitative, and therapeutic. Their use with chronic institutionalized psychiatric patients has perhaps become the treatment of choice with this population. Kazdin (1982) has reviewed the research on token economy programs and has noted that they have recently been employed with acute psychiatric disorders (Gershone, Errickson, Mitchell, & Paulson, 1977) and in the areas of behavioral medicine (e.g.,

Ferguson & Taylor, 1980), community psychology (Glenwick & Jason, 1980), and geriatric psychology (e.g., Hussian, 1981).

A token is a conditioned reinforcer that can be exchanged at a later time for consumable items or desired privileges (called *backup* reinforcers). Backup reinforcers are determined jointly by the client and the therapist and are referred to as the *reinforcement menu*. In most token economy programs, a client receives tokens for engaging in predetermined "required" behaviors. Some programs also use a response-cost feature that allows tokens to be forfeited contingently upon the exhibition of maladaptive behavior. The advantages of token economy programs over simple positive reinforcement approaches include the following: the capacity for immediate reinforcement, less possibility for satiation (menu items can be changed frequently), and the token program's usefulness in shaping uninterrupted chains of behavior.

Token economy programs have often been less successful in practice than in theory. Some commentators have noted the failure of the newly acquired behaviors to persist outside of the original therapeutic setting. It is important to recognize that TEP is not designed to be continued indefinitely, but should be used to develop or improve behavior, and then be gradually faded out, allowing the natural environmental contingencies to maintain the behavior change. The successful establishment and maintenance of a token economy program is difficult, requiring much forethought and planning and a certain amount of ongoing trial and error. As Kazdin (1982) has noted, initially successful token economy programs have often deteriorated after the planners and researchers departed and the necessary flexibility was lost.

Woods, Higson, and Tamahill (1984) reported longitudinal data (5 years) on 6 patients who participated in a token economy program that targeted self-help skills, domestic activities, and social activities. They concluded that for half the patients the TEP was an effective behavior change strategy and that the behavior changes were maintained following the conclusion of the treatment program. However, the program was apparently ineffective in producing behavior change in the other three patients. Page, Stanley, Richman, Deal, and Iwata (1983) designed a rather complex token economy program combining DRO (eating), response cost, and positive reinforcement of exercise and weight loss for a Prader-Willi adult patient. Hyperphagia, associated with morbid obesity, is a symptom of this genetic syndrome and can be life-threatening. Of particular importance is the fact that the weight loss through this program was maintained by the patient and actually continued in the absence of structured intervention.

In sum, the token economy approach can be viewed as a potentially powerful behavior change technique, but it should not be viewed as invariably effective or as a method to be indefinitely employed. The token approach is best used by experienced and sensitive clinicians who appreciate its limits (cf. Kazdin's discussion of failures in token economies, 1983).

MAINTENANCE AND GENERALIZATION

Of the many and varied forms of therapeutic intervention currently in use, the operant approach is perhaps most dependent upon technological skill in both assessment and application. Although the technology continues to develop, a new set of concerns — humanitarian in nature — has also emerged, including cost-effectiveness, public acceptability, client perceptions of treatment efficacy, and the question of durability (maintenance and generalization) of treatment gain. Space limitations preclude a consideration of all of these issues. However, in briefly considering the last issue, we touch upon all of them to some extent.

A paradox of operant technology is that its power to affect change in specific behaviors or behavior patterns is often bought at the expense of generalization to related responses or persistence of treatment gains over time. It comes as no surprise that, when discriminative stimuli and reinforcement contingencies differ (as is usually the case when we move from the clinic or consulting room to the "real world"), behavior patterns differ.

Recently, Lund and Kegeles (1984) reported on their attempt to increase fluoride mouth-rinsing behavior in 514 seventh graders over a 2-year period. Recognizing that contingency management programs tend to yield large initial success rates but gradual returns to pretreatment levels of maladaptive behavior, the authors sought to prevent relapse through schedule thinning (i.e., moving from saturated to partial reward schedules) and by means of what they called "self-management instruction" (see also the chapters by Kanfer, Davison, and Meichenbaum in this volume). Unfortunately, the hoped-for beneficial results did not accrue. Initial changes did *not* persist. As the authors noted,

> Neither the partial schedule of reward nor the presence of self-management instruction prevented this effect. If the goal is to obtain long-term behavior through relatively short-term education/intervention, it is clear that we do not currently know how to achieve it. . . . (p. 366)

We can only speculate on the reasons why this carefully conducted treatment program failed to achieve its objectives, despite the initial sensitivity to the durability issue. Perhaps operant theory and methodology should not be expected to achieve long-term, real world behavior change without a careful consideration of larger systems issues (cf. Leventhal, 1984). Or perhaps the initial problem (adolescents' lack of preventative dental health behaviors) was inadequately analyzed, the wrong reinforcers identified, or a particularly complex and intractable target selected (cf. O'Leary, 1984).

Although no easy resolution to the thorny issue of treatment maintenance and generalization has been forthcoming, it is noteworthy that researchers and clinicians have taken note of it and have increasingly sought solutions, both conceptual and technical (see Conway & Bucher, 1976; Foa & Emmelkamp, 1983; Goldstein & Kanfer, 1979; Karoly & Steffen, 1980; Kirschenbaum & Tomarken, 1982; Marlatt & Gordon, 1985; Spiegler, 1983).

RECENT DEVELOPMENTS

The introduction of the principles of operant conditioning to the treatment of psychological problems was a revolution staged, and largely won, in previous decades. Operant methods are now recognized by most as powerful behavior change strategies. The methods themselves have changed little since their original development in animal research. Their use in the therapeutic context was, for a time, limited by circumscribed definitions of psychological problems and appropriate therapeutic settings. The recent advances in the area of operant methods have not been concerned with the methods, but rather with the redefinition of legitimate psychological problems and therapeutic settings.

Among the important new directions taken by advocates of the experimental analysis of behavior is that represented by applications to traditional *medical* problems. The use of operant technology in health settings includes the design of behavioral assessment procedures (Karoly, 1985; Keefe, 1979) and the implementation of behavior change programs for such diverse problems as patient noncompliance with medical recommendations (Stuart, 1982), children's fear of surgical procedures (Melamed & Siegel, 1980), rehabilitation of brain-injured patients (Zahara & Cuvo, 1984), management of addictive disorders (Brownell, 1984), treatment of essential hypertension (Wadden, Luborsky, Greer, & Crits-Christoph, 1984), and diagnosis and management of patients with chronic pain (e.g., Fordyce, 1976; Turk, Meichenbaum, & Genest, 1983).

Increasingly, complex behaviors are receiving attention as potential targets of operant procedures. The development of social skills in children (LeCroy, 1983) and in schizophrenic patients (Liberman et al., 1984) are two areas of emerging emphasis. Training efforts have also been extended to include not only the identified client but also parents, peers, and paraprofessionals.

Throughout his career, Skinner (e.g., 1948, 1972) has been concerned with methods of social reform. The application of operant procedures on a larger social scale is also being pursued with vigor. Operant techniques are not only finding application in educational and vocational settings (Azrin, Flores, & Kaplan, 1975) but also in such "nontraditional" areas as pollution and litter control (Witmer & Geller, 1976), energy conservation (Hayes

& Cone, 1977; Palmer, Lloyd, & Lloyd, 1977), and prevention of maladjustment (Maher & Barbrack, 1982).

SUMMARY

This chapter has provided a broad overview of the applied science of operant conditioning known as the experimental analysis of behavior. The defining characteristics of this approach include (a) focus on precise definition and measurement of observable behaviors, (b) functional analysis of environmental antecedents and consequences that control maladaptive responding, (c) use of principles derived from experimental studies of learning in the design of treatment interventions, and (d) continuous evaluation of behavior change.

But it is not just technology that sets an operant approach apart from the traditional insight-oriented systems of psychotherapy. The techniques described here for establishing new behaviors, accelerating personally and interpersonally desirable behaviors, decelerating maladaptive modes of responding, and maintaining treatment-induced learning are all applied in the context of an objective and nonjudgmental view of human action. A behavior is not selected for change because it is unconventional, contrary to someone's view of human nature, or listed in a catalog of symptoms. Rather, when the relationship between an individual's behavior, or pattern of behaviors, and the effective environment is consistently disruptive of that individual's pursuit of personal objectives, of her or his ability to adjust to her or his life circumstances or of her or his sense of comfort, satisfaction, or freedom *and*, when the behavioral clinician is technically and ethically able to intervene, then the two will embark jointly on a venture in behavior modification. In the case of behavior modification with problem children, the negotiating client might be the parents or the teacher, but the behavior change objective must, in fact, be in the adaptive interests of the child.

REFERENCES

Allen, K. E., Hart, B., Buell, J. S., Harris, F. R., & Wolf, M. M. (1964). Effects of social reinforcement on isolate behavior of a nursery school child. *Child Development, 35,* 511–518.

Altman, K., Haavik, S., & Higgins, S. (1983). Modifying the self-injurious behavior of an infant with Spina Bifida and diminished pain sensitivity. *Journal of Behavior Therapy and Experimental Psychiatry, 14,* 165–168.

Ayllon, T. (1963). Intensive treatment of psychotic behavior by stimulus satiation and food reinforcement. *Behaviour Research and Therapy, 1,* 53–62.

Ayllon, T., & Azrin, N. H. (1968). *The token economy: A motivational system for therapy and rehabilitation.* New York: Appleton-Century-Crofts.

Ayllon, T., & Michael, J. (1959). The psychiatric nurse as a behavioral engineer. *Journal of the Experimental Analysis of Behavior, 2,* 323–334.

Azrin, N. H., Flores, T., & Kaplan, S. T. (1975). Job finding club: A group assisted program for obtaining employment. *Behaviour Research and Therapy, 13,* 17–27.

Azrin, N. H., & Nunn, R. (1973). Habit reversal: A method of eliminating nervous habits and tics. *Behaviour Research and Therapy, 11,* 619–628.

Azrin, N. H., Nunn, R., & Frantz, S. E. (1980). Habit reversal vs. negative practice treatment of nailbiting. *Behaviour Research and Therapy, 18,* 281–285.

Azrin, N. H., Nunn, R., & Frantz-Renshaw, S. E. (1980). Habit reversal treatment of thumbsucking. *Behaviour Research and Therapy, 18,* 395–399.

Azrin, N. H., & Powers, M. A. (1975). Eliminating classroom disturbances of emotionally disturbed children by positive practice procedures. *Behavior Therapy, 6,* 525–534.

Baer, D. M. (1982). Applied behavior analysis. In G. T. Wilson & C. M. Franks (Eds.), *Contemporary behavior therapy.* New York: Guilford Press.

Blackwood, R. O. (1971). *Operant control of behavior.* Akron, OH: Exordium Press.

Blount, R., Baer, R., & Collins, F. (1984). Improving visual acuity in a myopic child: Assessing compliance and effectiveness. *Behavior Therapy, 22,* 53–57.

Bornstein, P., Bullegueg, B., McLellern, R., Wilson, G., Sturm, C., Andre, J., & VandenPol, R. (1983). The "bathroom game": A systematic program for the elimination of encopretic behavior. *Journal of Behavior Therapy and Experimental Psychiatry, 14,* 67–71.

Boudin, H. M. (1972). Contingency contracting as a therapeutic tool in the deceleration of amphetamine use. *Behavior Therapy, 3,* 604–608.

Boyle, M., & Greer, R. (1983). Operant procedures and the comatose patient. *Journal of Applied Behavior Analysis, 16,* 3–12.

Brownell, K. D. (1984). The addictive disorders. In G. T. Wilson, C. M. Franks, K. D. Brownell, & P. C. Kendall (Eds.), *Annual review of behavior therapy* (Vol. 9). New York: Guilford Press.

Butterfield, W. H. (1975). Electric shock safety factors when used for the aversive conditioning of humans. *Behavior Therapy, 6,* 98–110.

Conway, J. B., & Bucher, B. D. (1976). Transfer and maintenance of behavior change in children: A review and suggestions. In E. J. Mash, L. A. Hamerlynck, & L. C. Handy (Eds.), *Behavior modification and families.* New York: Brunner/Mazel.

Deese, J., & Hulse, S. H. (1967). *The psychology of learning.* New York: McGraw-Hill.

Eyberg, S. M., & Robinson, E. A. (1981). *Dyadic parent-child interaction coding system: A manual.* Unpublished manuscript.

Eyberg, S. M., & Robinson, E. A. (1982). Parent-child interaction training: Effects on family functioning. *Journal of Clinical Child Psychology, 11,* 130–137.

Favell, J. E. (1977). *The power of positive reinforcement.* Springfield, IL: Charles C Thomas.

Favell, J. E., McGimsey, J. F., & Jones, M. L. (1978). The use of physical restraints in the treatment of self-injury and as positive reinforcement. *Journal of Applied Behavior Analysis, 11,* 225–241.

Ferguson, J. M., & Taylor, C. B. (Eds.). (1980). *The comprehensive handbook of behavioral medicine.* Englewood Cliffs, NJ: Prentice-Hall, Spectrum.

Ferster, C. B., & Skinner, B. F. (1957). *Schedules of reinforcement.* New York: Appleton-Century-Crofts.

Foa, E. B., & Emmelkamp, P. M. G. (Eds.). (1983). *Failures in behavior therapy.* New York: John Wiley.

Fordyce, W. E. (1976). *Behavioral methods for chronic pain and illness*. St. Louis: C. V. Mosby.

Foxx, R. M., & Azrin, N. H. (1972). Restitution: A method of eliminating aggressive-disruptive behavior of retarded and brain-damaged patients. *Behaviour Research and Therapy, 10*, 15-27.

Foxx, C., Foxx, R. M., Jones, J. R., & Kiely, D. (1980). Twenty-four hour social isolation. *Behavior Modification, 4*, 130-144.

Foxx, R. M., & Shapiro, S. T. (1978). The time out ribbon: A nonexclusionary timeout procedure. *Journal of Applied Behavior Analysis, 11*, 125-136.

Geller, E. S. (1983). Rewarding safety belt usage at an industrial setting: Test of treatment generality and response maintenance. *Journal of Applied Behavior Analysis, 16*, 189-202.

Gershone, J. R., Errickson, E., Mitchell, J. E., & Paulson, D. A. (1977). Behavioral comparison of a token economy and a standard psychiatric treatment ward. *Journal of Behavior Therapy and Experimental Psychiatry, 8*, 381-387.

Glenwick, D., & Jason, L. (Eds.). (1980). *Behavioral community psychology: Progress and prospects*. New York: Praeger.

Goldstein, A. P., & Kanfer, F. H. (Eds.). (1979). *Maximizing treatment gains: Transfer enhancement in psychotherapy*. New York: Academic Press.

Harris, S. L., & Ersner-Hershfield, R. (1978). Behavioral suppression of seriously disruptive behavior in psychotic and retarded patients: A review of punishment and its alternatives. *Psychological Bulletin, 85*, 1352-1375.

Hayes, S. C., & Cone, J. D. (1977). Reducing residential electrical energy use: Payments, information and feedback. *Journal of Applied Behavior Analysis, 10*, 425-436.

Hobbs, S. A., Forehand, R., & Murray, R. (1978). Effects of various durations of time-out on the noncompliant behavior of children. *Behavior Therapy, 9*, 652-656.

Hussian, R. A. (1981). *Geriatric psychology: A behavioral perspective*. New York: Van Nostrand Reinhold.

Karoly, P. (1985). The logic and character of assessment in health psychology. In P. Karoly (Ed.), *Measurement strategies in health psychology*. New York: John Wiley.

Karoly, P., & Steffen, J. J. (Eds.). (1980). *Improving the long-term effects of psychotherapy: Models of durable outcome*. New York: Gardner Press.

Kazdin, A. E. (1972). Response cost: The removal of conditioned reinforcers for therapeutic change. *Behavior Therapy, 3*, 533-546.

Kazdin, A. E. (1982). The token economy: A decade later. *Journal of Applied Behavior Analysis, 15*, 431-445.

Kazdin, A. E. (1983). Failure of persons to respond to the token economy. In E. B. Foa & P. M. G. Emmelkamp (Eds.), *Failures in behavior therapy*. New York: John Wiley.

Keefe, F. J. (1979). Assessment strategies in behavioral medicine. In J. R. McNamara (Ed.), *Behavioral approaches to medicine: Applications and analysis*. New York: Plenum.

Kirschenbaum, D. S., & Tomarken, A. J. (1982). On facing the generalization problem. The study of self-regulatory failure. In P. C. Kendall (Ed.), *Advances in cognitive-behavioral research and therapy* (Vol. 1). New York: Academic Press.

Kleitsch, E., Whitman, T., & Santos, J. (1983). Increasing verbal interaction among elderly socially isolated mentally retarded adults: A group language training procedure. *Journal of Applied Behavior Analysis, 16*, 217-233.

LeCroy, C. W. (Ed.). (1983). *Social skills training for children and youth*. New York: Haworth Press.

Leventhal, H. (1984). Rewards and adolescent health behavior: Promise or promise missed. *Health Psychology, 3*, 347-349.

Liberman, R., Lillie, F., Falloon, I., Harpin, R., Hutchinson, W., & Stoute, B. (1984). Social skills training with relapsing schizophrenics. *Behavior Modification, 8*, 155-179.

Lovaas, O. I. (1977). *The autistic child*. New York: Lexington Books.

Lovaas, O. I., & Newsome, C. (1976). Behavior modification with psychotic children. In H. Leitenberg (Ed.), *Handbook of behavior modification and behavior therapy*. Englewood Cliffs, NJ: Prentice-Hall.

Lund, A. K., & Kegeles, S. S. (1984). Rewards and adolescent health behavior. *Health Psychology, 3*, 351-369.

Maher, C. A., & Barbrack, C. R. (1982). Preventing high school maladjustment. Effectiveness of professional and cross-age behavioral group counseling. *Behavior Therapy, 13*, 259-270.

Marlatt, G. A., & Gordon, J. R. (Eds.). (1985). *Relapse prevention*. New York: Guilford Press.

Melamed, B. G., & Siegel, L. J. (1980). *Behavioral medicine: Practical applications in health care*. New York: Springer.

Nolan, J. D. (1968). Self-control procedures in the modification of smoking behavior. *Journal of Consulting and Clinical Psychology, 32*, 92-93.

O'Leary, K. D. (1984). Commentary on rewards and adolescent health behavior. *Health Psychology, 3*, 377-379.

O'Leary, K. D., & O'Leary, S. G. (Eds.). (1977). *Classroom management*. Elmsford, NY: Pergamon Press.

Page, T., Stanley, A., Richman, G., Deal, R., & Iwata, B. (1983). Reduction of food theft and long-term maintenance of weight loss in a Prader-Willi adult. *Journal of Behavior Therapy and Experimental Psychiatry, 14*, 261-268.

Palmer, M., Lloyd, M., & Lloyd, K. (1977). An experimental analysis of electricity conservation procedures. *Journal of Applied Behavior Analysis, 10*, 665-671.

Patterson, G. R. (1971). *Families: Applications of social learning to family life*. Champaign, IL: Research Press.

Patterson, G. R., & White, G. D. (1969). It's a small world. The application of "time out" from positive reinforcement. *Oregon Psychological Association Newsletter* (Supplement), *15*, 2.

Penick, S. B., Filion, R., Fox, S., & Stunkard, A. J. (1971). Behavior modification in the treatment of obesity. *Psychosomatic Medicine, 33*, 49-55.

Premack, D. (1959). Toward empirical behavior laws: I. Positive reinforcement. *Psychological Review, 66*, 219-233.

Rachlin, H. (1970). *Introduction to modern behaviorism*. San Francisco: W. H. Freeman.

Rapport, M., Murphy, H. A., & Bailey, J. (1982). Ritalin vs. response cost in the control of hyperactive children. *Journal of Applied Behavior Analysis, 15*, 205-216.

Reese, E. P. (1978). *Human behavior: Analysis and application*. Dubuque, IA: Wm. C. Brown.

Repp, A. C., & Deitz, S. M. (1974). Reducing aggressive and self-injurious behavior of institutionalized retarded children through reinforcement of other behavior. *Journal of Applied Behavior Analysis, 7*, 313-325.

Rincover, A. (1978). Sensory extinction: A procedure for eliminating self-stimulatory behavior in autistic children. *Journal of Abnormal Child Psychology, 6,* 299-310.

Rincover, A., Cook, R., Peoples, A., & Packard, D. (1979). Sensory extinction and sensory reinforcement principles for programming multiple adaptive behavior change. *Journal of Applied Behavior Analysis, 12,* 221-233.

Rosen, R., Schiffman, H., & Cohen, A. (1984). Behavior modification and the treatment of myopia. *Behavior Modification, 8,* 131-154.

Rosenbaum, M., & Ayllon, T. (1981a). The behavioral treatment of neurodermatitis through habit reversal. *Behaviour Research and Therapy, 19,* 313-318.

Rosenbaum, M., & Ayllon, T. (1981b). Treating bruxism with the habit reversal technique. *Behaviour Research and Therapy, 19,* 87-96.

Sajwaj, T., Libet, J., & Agras, S. (1974). Lemon juice therapy: The control of life-threatening rumination in a six-month-old infant. *Journal of Applied Behavior Analysis, 7,* 557-563.

Schmale, D., Lichenstein, R., & Harris, D. (1972). Successful treatment of habitual smokers with warm smoky air and rapid smoking. *Journal of Consulting and Clinical Psychology, 38,* 105-111.

Schnelle, J., Traughber, B., Morgan, D., Embry, J., Bimon, A., & Coleman, A. (1983). Management of geriatric incontinence in nursing homes. *Journal of Applied Behavior Analysis, 16,* 235-241.

Skinner, B. F. (1938). *The behavior of organisms: An experimental analysis.* New York: Appleton-Century-Crofts.

Skinner, B. F. (1948). *Walden two.* New York: Macmillan.

Skinner, B. F. (1972). *Beyond freedom and dignity.* New York: Vintage Books.

Spiegler, M. D. (1983). *Contemporary behavioral therapy.* Palo Alto, CA: Mayfield.

Strauss, C., Rubinoff, A., & Atkeson, B. (1983). Elimination of nocturnal head banging in a normal 7-year-old girl using overcorrection plus rewards. *Journal of Behavior Therapy and Experimental Psychiatry, 14,* 269-273.

Stuart, R. B. (1967). Case work treatment of depression viewed as an interpersonal disturbance. *Social Work, 12,* 27-36.

Stuart, R. B. (Ed.). (1982). *Adherence, compliance, and generalization in behavioral medicine.* New York: Brunner/Mazel.

Stuart, R. B., & Davis, B. (1972). *Slim chance in a fat world.* Champaign, IL: Research Press.

Sulzer-Azaroff, B., & Mayer, G. R. (1977). *Applying behavior analysis procedures with children and youth.* New York: Holt, Rinehart & Winston.

Terrace, H. (1963). Discrimination learning with and without "errors." *Journal of the Experimental Analysis of Behavior, 6,* 1-27.

Tomporowski, P. (1983). Training an autistic client: The effects of brief restraint on disruptive behavior. *Journal of Behavior Therapy and Experimental Psychiatry, 14,* 169-173.

Turk, D., Meichenbaum, D., & Genest, M. (1983). *Pain and behavioral medicine.* New York: Guilford Press.

Wadden, T. A., Luborsky, L., Greer, S., & Crits-Christoph, P. (1984). The behavioral treatment of essential hypertension: An update and comparison with pharmacological treatment. *Clinical Psychology Review, 4,* 403-429.

Walls, R., Zane, T., & Ellis, W. (1981). Forward and backward chaining and whole task methods. *Behavior Modification, 5,* 61-74.

Walsh, B., & Lambert, F. (1979). Errorless discrimination and picture fading as techniques for teaching sight words to TMR students. *American Journal of Mental Deficiency, 83,* 473-479.

Weiker, R. G., & Harmon, R. E. (1975). The use of omission training to reduce self-injurious behavior in a retarded child. *Behavior Therapy, 6,* 261-268.

Weiner, H. (1965). Real and imaginal cost effects upon human fixed interval responding. *Psychological Reports, 17,* 659-662.

White, G. D., Nielson, G., & Johnson, S. M. (1972). Time out duration and the suppression of deviant behavior in children. *Journal of Applied Behavior Analysis, 5,* 111-120.

Witmer, J. F., & Geller, E. S. (1976). Facilitating power recycling: Effects of prompts, raffles, and contests. *Journal of Applied Behavior Analysis, 9,* 315-322.

Wong, S., Gaydos, G., & Fugua, R. W. (1982). Operant control of pedophilia. *Behavior Modification, 6,* 73-84.

Woods, P. A., Higson, P. J., & Tamahill, M. (1984). Token economy programs with chronic psychotic patients. *Behaviour Research and Therapy, 22,* 41-51.

Zahara, D. J., & Cuvo, A. J. (1984). Behavioral applications to the rehabilitation of traumatically head injured persons. *Clinical Psychology Review, 4,* 477-491.

5

Fear Reduction Methods

Richard J. Morris*

Much of the effort of psychotherapists is directed toward helping people overcome their fears of situations, other people, animals, and objects. Fear is a very strong emotion and is associated with many signs of anxiety, for example, pallor, rapid pulse rate and a "pounding heart," very tense muscles, perspiring in a room of average temperature and humidity, "butterflies" in the stomach, irritability, feelings of panic, inability to concentrate, dizziness, and headaches. These reactions can be placed in three categories. *Motoric reactions* involve avoidance of the feared stimulus, object, or event or at least a very cautious and prudent approach toward the stimulus. *Cognitive reactions* involve unpleasant subjective feelings or cognitions associated with the feared stimulus, including feelings or cognitions of muscular tenseness ("I'm tense"), panic ("I have to get out of here or I will collapse!"), irritability ("I don't like it here and I wish I hadn't agreed to come"), and losing control ("What if something happens to me . . . can I be sure?"). *Physiological reactions* involve rapid breathing, pallor, increased heart rate, pupillary dilation, and a desire to urinate (e.g., Marks, 1969; Morris & Kratochwill, 1983b).

When someone experiences fear in a situation where there is no obvious external danger, the fear is irrational and is called a *phobia*. Table 5.1 lists a number of common phobias that people experience. When a person begins to avoid a nondangerous feared situation—even though she or he realizes that such behavior is foolish or irrational—the fear becomes a *phobic reaction*. In differentiating between a fear and a phobia, Marks (1969, p. 3) suggested that a phobia is a subcategory of fear that

1. Is out of proportion to demands of the situation
2. Cannot be explained or reasoned away

---

*The author wishes to express his gratitude to Hal Arkowitz for his critical commentaries regarding various aspects of this chapter.

Table 5.1. Selected Phobias that People Experience

TECHNICAL NAME	FEAR
Acrophobia	Heights
Agoraphobia	Open places
Aichmophobia	Sharp and pointed objects
Aquaphobia	Going into water
Claustrophobia	Enclosed places
Mikrophobia	Germs
Menophobia	Being alone
Nyctophobia	Darkness
Ochlophobia	Crowds
Pyrophobia	Fires
Thanatophobia	Death
Xenophobia	Strangers
Zoophobia	Animals

3. Is beyond voluntary control
4. Leads to avoidance of the feared situation

To these criteria, Miller, Barrett, and Hampe (1974) added that a phobia "persists over an extended period of time . . . is unadaptive . . . (and in the case of children) is not age or stage specific" (p. 90).

Phobic reactions are among the most common forms of maladaptive behaviors in people. They occur in children, adolescents, and adults. Some phobias, because of their high incidence, are considered "normal" in children, whereas others are viewed as "normal" in adults. For example, fear of dogs and other animals, the dark, ghosts, strangers, and being alone are among the more common childhood phobias; fear of heights, public speaking, spiders and other bugs, and snakes frequently occur in adults. Some irrational fears are transitory whereas others persist over a long time.

When fears become intolerable, professional help is sought. Over the past 75 years, various procedures have been used in the treatment of fears. Psychoanalysis, Adlerian therapy, client-centered therapy, and other forms of verbal therapy have been utilized, as well as drugs, hypnosis, electroconvulsive shock treatment, and certain forms of brain surgery (e.g., leucotomy). In general, these methods have been found to be only moderately successful.

Some therapy procedures, however, have been found to be much more effective. These procedures are based on the learning theory positions of, for example, Skinner (1938, 1953), Pavlov (1927), Hull (1943), and Bandura (1969, 1977; Bandura & Walters, 1963). Though the specifics of each therapy method differ, they do share certain general underlying assumptions: (a) Phobias and the avoidance reactions that accompany them are learned by the individual, (b) phobias do not occur as a result of innate factors, and (c) phobias are not the result of an underlying psychic or psychological disturbance (see, for example, Morris & Kratochwill, 1983b).[1] The present chapter will discuss two therapy procedures that have been found to be effective in the treatment of phobic reactions and fears: *systematic desensitization* and *flooding-related therapies.*

Variations of these methods will also be discussed. Each method will be described in detail, and case examples will be presented that demonstrate its use. The discussion will focus primarily on fear reduction methods with adults. For a thorough discussion of fear reduction methods with children and adolescents, the reader is referred to Morris and Kratochwill (1983a, 1983b, 1985), Kratochwill and Morris (1985), and Kratochwill, Morris, McGrogan, and Ramirez (in press).

SYSTEMATIC DESENSITIZATION

Systematic desensitization was developed in the early 1950s by Joseph Wolpe (e.g., Wolpe, 1958). The basic assumption of this technique is that a fear response (for example, a fear response to heights) is learned or conditioned and can be inhibited by substituting an activity that is antagonistic to the fear response. The response that is most typically inhibited by this treatment process is anxiety, and the response frequently substituted for the anxiety is relaxation and calmness. For example, if a person has a fear of heights and feels very anxious and uncomfortable each time he or she enters an office building and takes an elevator higher than the third floor, we would help this person inhibit the anxiety in this situation by teaching him or her to relax and feel calm. Thus we would *desensitize* the person or *countercondition* his or her fear of heights.

Desensitization is accomplished by exposing an individual, in small, graduated steps, to the feared situation while the person is performing the activity that is antagonistic to anxiety. The gradual exposure to the fear stimulus can take place either in the person's fantasy, where she or he is asked to imagine being in various fear-related situations, or it can occur in real life (i.e., in vivo). Wolpe termed the principle that underlies the desensitization process *reciprocal inhibition.* He described this principle in the following way: "If a response inhibitory to anxiety can be made to occur in

---

[1]An alternative learning theory view on the etiology of fears has been developed by Seligman (1971). He does not completely agree with each of these assumptions. Seligman has incorporated the notion of *biological preparedness* into his theory and states that people, for example, are "prepared" to develop particular fears based on the biological and evolutionary significance of certain stimuli and situations that are tied to their struggle for survival.

the presence of anxiety-evoking stimuli, it will weaken the connection between these stimuli and the anxiety responses" (Wolpe, 1958, p. 562).

The Initial Interview

Before initiating the desensitization procedure, or any of the other fear reduction methods discussed in this chapter, the therapist must first identify the client's fear or phobia and the circumstances under which the fear occurs. This is not an easy assignment. The interview must be conducted within a therapeutic atmosphere of respect for the client, sensitivity to and understanding of the client's difficulties, and genuine concern for the client's overall well-being. The therapist has to probe thoroughly into the client's life history to make sure both therapist and client have a clear understanding of all aspects of the client's fear and of those factors that have contributed (and are contributing) to the fear or phobia.

The goal of the interview, however, is not to identify the causal factor that is responsible for the client's fear or phobia. Therapists who use fear reduction methods generally accept the premise that people's learning histories are very complex, and to assume that a time-limited retrospective account of one's past will uncover the factor or factors that caused a fear or phobia is a fruitless endeavor. The best that an interview can be expected to accomplish is to provide the therapist with a comprehensive picture of who the client is, what kind of environment the client comes from, how the client came to be what she or he is today, and what the circumstances that led to the initial occurrence of the fear or phobia were. The interview will also help the therapist support or refute various hypotheses about the client's problem, specify the goals of therapy, determine which fear reduction method is most appropriate for the client, and assess whether the treatment objectives can be accomplished within the limitations set by the client and her or his life situation (Kanfer & Grimm, 1977). It is therefore quite likely that the initial interview will last over a number of sessions. Though there is neither a standardized approach nor a standard set of questions used in the initial interview, most therapists explore the following topic areas with clients.

Identification of the Target Behavior

This involves not only helping the client identify what is specifically troubling him or her but also trying to determine the types of situations and circumstances in which the fear or phobia occurs. In addition, the therapist asks how long the client has had the fear, whether it has gotten better or worse with the passage of time, and the types of situations in which it seems to be better or worse than "usual." It is also desirable to ask the client about his or her thoughts and feelings concerning the fear.

General Background Information

Discussion centers on the date and place of the client's birth, number and age of siblings, where the client stands in the family birth order, and a retrospective account of the types of interactions the client had with siblings, parents, and significant other persons while growing up. Inquiry is made into which of the children was favored in the family, as well as how the client viewed the manner in which she or he was treated by each of the parents relative to the other children. The therapist should also discuss other items regarding the parents such as who did the disciplining in the family, how the client was punished for misbehavior during childhood and adolescence, and which characteristics in each parent were liked and which disliked the most by the client. It is also important to know the manner in which the parents interacted with each other and to determine what type of role models they provided for the client. For example, did they generally like one another; did they fight, and, if so, was it usually in front of the children and was the fighting verbal or physical; did they ever talk about divorce or separation; and did one parent try to use one or all of the children against the other parent?

For many clients, a favorite aunt, uncle, grandparent, neighbor, or friend may have been as important as, or even more important than, their parents during childhood. These "significant others" should also be discussed, to determine the unique contribution of such people in the client's life.

One additional aspect of the individual's background information involves the fears that were experienced during childhood. The therapist should not only determine the particular childhood fears but also when they occurred, if and when they ended, and whether any of them continued into the adult years.

School and Job Information

For this category, inquiry should be made into the client's likes and dislikes in elementary school, high school, and college; the best and least liked subjects, what the client did after school, the client's extracurricular activities, and so forth. Moreover, the therapist should discuss the client's friendships in and out of school, for instance, whether the client had any close friends and if these friendships were maintained over the years.

The client's work experience should also be brought into this discussion, the therapist asking how far the client went in school and, if appropriate, why he or she did not continue. Particular attention should be paid to the client's work history, likes and dislikes about a job, ability to advance, and consistency of the present job with the client's goals and desires.

Dating and Marriage Information

The therapist explores the client's dating pattern during the teenage and adult years. In addition, the client's sexual experiences before and after marriage are discussed. If appropriate, difficulties in the marriage are discussed, relationships with in-laws and children are explored, and the environment in which the client lives is looked at. Because these are very sensitive topics for some people, they should be explored within a nonjudgmental framework that demonstrates understanding and acceptance of the client.

A summary of a suggested guide for the initial interview is presented in Table 5.2. As the reader has no doubt already determined, the information gained in the initial interview is quite extensive. Some therapists use tape recorders to record this information, whereas others take notes on the client's answers. Still others ask their clients to fill out a standard background information packet that contains many of the same types of questions as those outlined in Table 5.2.

An excerpt from part of the first session of an initial interview with a recently divorced 35-year-old woman illustrates the manner in which an interview is conducted.[2]

Therapist: What is the difficulty that you are having?

Client: I can't fly in airplanes or go up in elevators . . . at least not higher than the third floor, though I am still nervous even then.

Therapist: Let's talk about the airplane difficulty first. What about flying makes you feel uncomfortable?

Client: Well, watching a plane take off is fearful, though as a child I did take lessons in flying and was not afraid. (*Pause*) It's the feeling of being suspended in air and immobile, and of being trapped and feeling that I can't get out.

Therapist: When do you remember this fear beginning?

Client: It started about 10 years ago. My husband had to fly as part of his job with his company, and I would go with him on a number of occasions. Then the fear began getting worse as I would fly more, and about 5 years ago I began having difficulty looking down [out the window]. Now I can't look down at all or even out the window—even if I got up enough nerve to fly in a plane.

Therapist: Can you think of any situation regarding flying that doesn't make you feel uneasy?

Client: Yes (*laughs*), if I don't think about it, it doesn't bother me.

Therapist: Let's be a little more specific. If we could rate your level of fear about airplanes on a 10-point scale, what about flying would be most anxiety provoking to you; that is, a 10 for you?

---

[2]Throughout this chapter the case transcripts, case descriptions, and hierarchies have been changed slightly to protect the anonymity of the clients involved.

Client: Flying over the ocean.

Therapist: What would be a zero?

Client: Being at the airport to pick someone up.

Therapist: What would be a five?

Client: The plane taking off.

Therapist: So, your fear is related to all aspects of your actually flying in a plane. What about seeing a plane on television or in a movie, for example, seeing one in the air?

Client: That bothers me, too . . . especially watching a movie of a plane which was filmed from another plane, and especially when the plane banks.

Therapist: What number would this be on the rating scale?

Client: A five or six.

Therapist: Are there any reasons that you can think of, or ideas that you might have, concerning the development of your fear?

Client: Not really, except that around the time my nervousness began my husband was seeing another woman, and sometime during that period the fear developed . . . I guess I was feeling very threatened that we would break up.

Therapist: What was your relationship with your husband like during this time?

Client: Very poor . . . a lot of fighting and yelling.

Therapist: Any talk of divorce at that time?

Client: No, not really. I guess we both knew that the marriage was shaky, but that we would stay together at least until the children got older.

Therapist: And what about your fear of elevators? When did it begin?

Client: (*Pause*) I think it goes back almost 20 years ago. I remember being in a tall building in Chicago . . . don't remember why . . . and getting a feeling of fright in an express elevator. But I guess you can say I became really scared about 5 years ago. And, it became very bad 3 years ago, right after I took an express elevator to the 20th floor of the Acme building and threw up as I came out, after feeling so nervous and nauseous while going up.

Therapist: Is there anything about riding in an elevator or about elevators in general that doesn't make you feel uncomfortable?

Client: Walking past an elevator with someone and knowing that I don't have to go in.

Therapist: What about going past it, and you're by yourself?

Client: It bothers me a bit. It's at the point now where just walking by one by myself makes me feel uncomfortable.

Therapist: How much — using for a moment our 10-point rating scale?

Client: About one.

Therapist: What would be zero?

Client: Walking past it with someone and knowing I don't have to take it.

Therapist: What would be a 10?

Client: (*Laughs and then pauses*) Being stuck in the elevator and alone by myself.

Therapist: Any thoughts about what events contributed to this fear?

Client: None. I can't figure it out, unless it's related to my airplane fear. But I don't know how.

Therapist: Let's hold on that for a bit and talk a little more about your background. Where were you born and in what year?

Client: In Chicago. . . .

At the end of the first or second session, the therapist often gives the client some questionnaires to fill out at home for the next session. They are used to help the therapist gain additional information about the client which was or could have been missed during the initial interview. Three of the most popular questionnaires appear in the chapter appendix and are briefly discussed next.

- - - -

Table 5.2. Suggested Guide for the Conduct of the Initial Interview

A. *What is the problem behavior? . . . What seems to be troubling you?*
  1. How long have you had this difficulty?
  2. When does this fear or thought usually come into your mind? When does this problem seem to occur the most? In what types of situations or circumstances does the problem occur? Are there any reasons you can think of for its occurrence?
  3. Has the problem been the same all along—or has it gotten better or worse?
     (a) Is there any situation that you can associate with it getting better or worse?

B. *General Background*
  1. When born? Where?
  2. How many brothers and sisters do you have?
     (a) Where are you in the birth order?
     (b) How much older is your eldest or youngest same sex sibling?
     (c) How did (do) you get along with him (her)?
  3. Parents—are they still alive? When did each die?

C. *Father*
  1. What kind of person was (is) he—especially during your childhood?
  2. Was he interested in you? Were you interested in what he had to say?
  3. Did he ever punish you?
  4. Did he play favorites with the children? How did you feel about this?

D. *Mother*
  Same questions asked about the father

E. *Parents*
  1. Did they like each other? Did they like you?
  2. Did they behave toward you as though they liked you?
  3. Did they get along together?
     (a) Fight much? . . . Divorce threats? etc.
     (b) Did they fight in front of children or in privacy?

F. *Significant others*
  1. Were there any other adults who played an important part in your life?
  2. Describe what they were like and how they played an important role in your life.

continued

Table 5.2. continued

G. *Fears during childhood*
   1. Any particular fears?
   2. When did they occur?
   3. Do you still have some of these? When did they stop?

H. *School*
   1. Like school?
   2. Best liked subjects? Least liked subjects?
   3. Sports — Did you participate in them or watch them?
      (a) How were you in them?
   4. Friends
      (a) Did you make any friends at school (college)?
      (b) Any close ones?
      (c) Do you maintain any of those friendships today?
      (d) Anyone at school (college) that you were afraid of? Was the person the same sex
          as you? Were you afraid of any teachers? Why?
      (e) How far did you go in school? Why did you stop your education?
   5. What did you do after you stopped school?

I. *Job*
   1. What kind of work do you do?
   2. Do you like your job? What do you like the best/least about your job?
   3. Any thoughts about quitting?
   4. What other types of jobs have you had? Why did you leave them?
   5. If client is a housewife, ask: How do you like being a housewife?
                                    What do you specifically like about it?
                                    Was it your choice to be a housewife?
                                    Would you like to be doing something else? What?

J. *Sex*
   1. At what age did you begin to have any kind of sexual feelings?
      (a) If client has problem in answering, ask: Well, roughly, were you 10, 15,
          20 . . . more or less?
      (b) or go to the following: Before 10? . . . Before 15? . . . Before 20? . . .
   2. In what kind of situation did you have your first sexual feelings?
      For example, was it out with boys? . . . (girls?) . . . At a movie house? Or what?
   3. At this stage, did you date several boys (girls) or just one at a time?
      (a) Did you go to parties?
      (b) What was the pattern of your dating? . . . Always movies? . . . Dinners?
   4. When did you especially become interested in anybody?
   5. Was there anyone else whom you became interested in?
   6. When did you become really serious? (implying steady dating, become engaged, etc.)
      Or, have you ever become serious with anyone?
      (a) What did you like about him (her)?
   7. Have you ever petted (made out) with anyone? Did you ever masturbate? Any feel-
      ings of guilt or fear about doing (not doing) either of these?
   8. Have you ever had intercourse? Have you ever wanted to? What stopped you?
   9. (If married, ask: Did you ever have intercourse before you were married?)

K. *Marriage*
   1. When did you meet your husband (wife)?
      (a) What did you like about him (her)?
   2. When did you feel that you were ready to marry him (her)?
   3. Was he (she) interested in marrying you?
   4. Since (or while) you were married, did you ever become interested in other men
      (women)?

continued

Table 5.2. continued

---

5. Is (was) your marriage satisfying? What about it makes it satisfying? What about it doesn't make it satisfying? In what way would you like to change your marriage?
6. If divorced and remarried, how about with your second husband (wife)? Is this marriage satisfying?
   (a) How is he (she) different from your first husband (wife)?
   (b) How soon after the divorce did you remarry?
   (c) Was he (she) married before?

L. *Sex and Marriage*
   1. How is the sexual side of your marriage (dating)? How about the sexual side of your second marriage?
   2. Do you have orgasms?
      (a) How often?
   3. Are you happy with your marriage (the person you are dating)?
      (a) Any complaints?
   4. Do the two of you fight with each other? That is, are there arguments?
      (a) What do you usually fight about?
      (b) How long do they usually last?
      (c) How are your fights usually resolved?
   5. Any plans for marriage (thoughts of divorce)?

M. *Children*
   1. How many children do you have? (Do you plan to have children? How many?)
   2. Do you like all of your children? Any favorites?
      (a) Are they all well?
   3. How old is each?
   4. Were they each planned?

N. *Environment*
   1. Do you like where you are now living?
   2. Anything that you are not satisfied with?
   3. What's your religion?
      (a) Is it important to you? In what way?
      (b) How religious are you? . . . not at all, mildly, moderately, or extremely?
      (c) Do you spend a lot of time in church activities?

Fear Survey Schedule (See Appendix 1)

This 5-point rating scale asks the client to rate the amount of fear or discomfort caused by each of the things and events listed in the questionnaire from *Not at All* to *Very Much*.

The Willoughby Questionnaire (See Appendix 2)

This questionnaire also uses a 5-point rating scale. It contains questions about how the client reacts in various situations. The client must respond with one of the following answers: *Never*, *Not at All*, *No*, *Practically Always*, or *Entirely*.

The Bernreuter Self-Sufficiency Inventory (See Appendix 3)

The Bernreuter lists a number of questions regarding self-sufficiency. The client is asked to circle *Yes* if the question applies to her or him, *No* if it does not apply, or the question mark if she or he is not sure whether it applies.

In addition, it is a good idea for the therapist to ask the client to write out a paragraph or two about his or her fears or phobias, describing each of them, any reasons why the client feels they occur, and any thoughts about them. An example of this type of write-up appears below, written by a 42-year-old male who was the vice-president of a large corporation.

> For as long as I can remember, I have been aware and concerned about other people and their estimation of me or how they thought I was doing and whether they liked me. The other part of this has to do with my perception that everyone that I know (my boss, my wife and children, my colleagues, and the people who work for me) expects me to succeed in every aspect of my work. This makes me very nervous and scared that I won't live up to their estimation and expectations of me — and that they are constantly making judgments on what I am doing.
>
> Now I know that I'm not good at everything that I do (in spite of what others think), so I try to avoid as much personal and social contact with people as I can — going to as few company functions as is possible and not going to parties with friends if I can avoid it.
>
> This is all very frustrating to me. Objectively, I know I do well. I make a very good living and have been promoted in my company many times, and have a great deal of responsibility for the manufacturing of our products. But, I am so damned concerned about what others are thinking and saying about me that I go out of my way to be Mr. Nice Guy to make sure that they say good things about me. I don't want to be worried all the time about how I am doing with people at work, with my wife and with my children, and with friends. I want to stop being concerned with how people judge me.
>
> Maybe my mother and father started it all when I was young with always drilling me about doing better in school — even when I got Bs — about watching how I act and what I say to people. I don't know.

The information gained from the interview, personal statement, and questionnaires should provide the therapist with a thorough analysis and understanding of (a) the client's life situation, (b) the circumstances and situations under which the client's fear or phobia occurs, and (c) the relative intensity in various situations of the feelings associated with the fear and the degree to which the client will actively avoid the feared situation. The general assumption is that a person's fear or phobia is learned and that it can be unlearned by applying procedures based on theories of learning (Morris & Kratochwill, 1983a, 1983b).

The therapist must remember, however, that in an interview the client is also assessing the therapist. The client is concerned with whether the therapist understands the nature of his or her problem, whether the therapist is concerned with his or her welfare, whether he or she feels comfortable talking with the therapist, and so forth. The interview, therefore, should not be so mechanical and matter-of-fact that the client as a person is disregarded. The therapist should take care that the amount of detailed information gained from the interview not be obtained at the expense of the client's comfort. This is where the therapeutic relationship and rapport with the client are important. The therapist might even want to anticipate some of the client's concerns by informing him or her that some of their discussions will involve detailed questioning, explaining that details provide the therapist with a thorough understanding of his or her problem, which is necessary for successful therapy (Goldfried & Davison, 1976).

Specific questions are asked, and extensive discussion occurs in the interview because the goal of therapy is very specific, namely, the reduction of the person's fear or phobia. Because of this, it is important to learn as much about the nature of the problem and the circumstances under which it occurs as is reasonably possible. No attempt is made in therapy to reorganize the client's personality, nor is there any general goal of helping the client achieve a higher level of emotional and psychological functioning. The only goal is to reduce the client's fear or phobic reaction, using a procedure best suited for the client, to a point where she or he can carry on daily activities without being bothered by the fear.

If the therapist believes it possible that the client is suffering from a physical disorder that could be causing the problem or that could interfere with treatment, he or she should refer the client to a physician for a thorough examination before proceeding further.

The Desensitization Procedure

After obtaining all of the relevant information about the client, the therapist then decides on the treatment procedure and discusses with the client what will take place next. If systematic desensitization is used, the therapist briefly explains the rationale behind the treatment procedure and describes the various stages in the treatment process. For example, the therapist might say the following:

> The emotional reactions that you experience are a result of your previous experiences with people and situations; these reactions oftentimes lead to feelings of anxiety or tenseness which are really inappropriate. Since perceptions of situations occur within ourselves, it is possible to work with your reactions right here in the office by having you . . . [imagine] or visualize those situations. (Paul, 1966, p. 116)

The therapist would then mention that a technique called *systematic desensitization* is going to be used with the client, and that it consists of two primary stages.

The first stage consists of relaxation training where I am going to teach you how to become very relaxed — more relaxed than you have probably felt in a very long time. Once you have learned to relax, we will then use this relaxed state to counter the anxiety and tenseness that you feel whenever you are in the feared situation(s). We will do this by having you imagine — while you are still very relaxed — a series of progressively more tension-provoking scenes which you and I will develop . . . and which are directly related to your fear. We will thus counter-condition your fear or desensitize your tenseness to the feared situations(s).

This procedure has been found to be very effective in the treatment of many types of fears, and we have used it successfully in the past with people who have fears like yours. We will start the procedure by first teaching you how to become more relaxed and then asking you to practice the procedure at home.

Do you have any questions? (Adapted from Paul, 1966)

Before proceeding further, the therapist should answer any questions that the client has about the procedure or his or her expectations regarding treatment.

Throughout this initial period, as well as during the remainder of therapy, the therapist should make sure that she or he has established a good relationship with the client. The therapist should behave in a way that conveys warmth and acceptance of the client. Many writers (e.g., Goldfried & Davison, 1976; Morris & Magrath, 1983; Wilson & Evans, 1977) have suggested that desensitization procedures should be conducted within the context of a sound therapist-client relationship. In fact, therapist warmth was found by Morris and Suckerman (1974a, 1974b) and Ryan and Moses (1979) to be a significant factor in the outcome of systematic desensitization. (The reader is referred to chapter 2 by Goldstein and Myers for a detailed discussion concerning methods of enhancing the therapeutic relationship and to Morris and Magrath, 1983, for a discussion of the therapeutic relationship in behavior therapy).

There are essentially three steps in the use of systematic desensitization: (a) relaxation training, (b) development of the anxiety hierarchy, and (c) systematic desensitization proper. Because therapists differ from one another in regard to some of the details of systematic desensitization, what is described here is the manner in which the present author conducts this therapy.

Relaxation Training

The therapist begins desensitization by training the client to relax. This training should take place in a quiet, softly lighted room located in a building where there is a negligible amount of outside noise (where possible, the therapist should use the same room as the one in which the initial interview took place). Besides comfortable office furniture, the therapist should have either a couch or a recliner chair in the room, so that relaxation can be facilitated by having the client lie down.

The first step in the procedure is to have the client lean back in the chair or lie down on the couch and close his or her eyes. The therapist then says the following:

> I am going to teach you how to become very relaxed. In doing this I am going to ask you to tense up and relax opposing sets of muscles — proceeding through a series of these. That is, I am going to ask you to tense up and relax different sets of muscles so that there is a cumulative effect of relaxation over your whole body. (*Pause*) Okay, now, I would like you to. . . .

The relaxation steps presented in Table 5.3 are then initiated. These steps represent a modified version of a technique developed by Jacobson (1938) for inducing deep muscular relaxation. The procedure should be presented in a very quiet, soft, and pleasant tone of voice. Each step should take about 10 seconds, with a 10- to 15-second pause between each. The whole procedure should take 20 to 25 minutes.[3]

During the first relaxation training session, it is often helpful for the therapist to practice the relaxation procedure with the client, so that the client can observe (whenever necessary) how to perform a particular step. It is also advisable for the therapist to pace the presentation of each step to the client's ease of performing the steps.

It is not uncommon for clients to feel uncomfortable during the first relaxation session and to not achieve a very deep relaxation level. But over a few sessions, the client will become more comfortable and will be able to reach deep relaxation more easily. The client should also be encouraged to practice the relaxation at home alone, preferably twice a day for 10 to 15 minutes. To enhance the client's practice at home, some therapists record the relaxation procedure on cassette tapes and have the client play the tape while practicing each day. Others give the client an outline of the muscle groups to be relaxed. Both could be done. The most important goal is to teach the client how to relax by himself or herself with a fair degree of ease.

In most cases relaxation training will last for about two or three sessions and will usually overlap with part of the initial interview. Throughout this training, it is a good idea to repeat such phrases as "Breathe normally," "Smooth, even breathing," "Keep your (*particular muscle group*) relaxed," "Just let your body relax . . . and become more and more relaxed."

It is also helpful throughout relaxation training to point out to the client

---

[3]Before initiating the relaxation procedure, it is often helpful, as a precaution, to ask the client if any physical problem exists that might interfere with the tensing and relaxing of various muscles. If the client mentions a problem area, the therapist should omit this muscle group from the procedure and not request the client to strongly tense this set of muscles.

Table 5.3. An Introduction to the Relaxation Training Steps of Systematic Desensitization

Steps in Relaxation
1. Take a deep breath and hold it (for about 10 seconds). Hold it. Okay, let it out.
2. Raise both of your hands about half way above the couch (or, arms of the chair), and breathe normally. Now, drop your hands to the couch (or, down).
3. Now hold your arms out and make a tight fist. Really tight. Feel the tension in your hands. I am going to count to three and when I say "three," I want you to drop your hands. One . . . Two . . . Three.
4. Raise your arms again, and bend your fingers back the other way (toward your body). Now drop your hands and relax.
5. Raise your arms. Now drop them and relax.
6. Now raise your arms again, but this time "flap" your hands around. Okay, relax again.
7. Raise your arms again. Now, relax.
8. Raise your arms above the couch (chair) again and tense your biceps until they shake. Breathe normally, and keep your hands loose. Relax your hands. (Notice how you have a warm feeling of relaxation.)
9. Now hold your arms out to your side and tense your biceps. Make sure that you breathe normally. Relax your arms.
10. Now arch your shoulders back. Hold it. Make sure that your arms are relaxed. Now relax.
11. Hunch your shoulders forward. Hold it, and make sure that you breathe normally and keep your arms relaxed. Okay, relax. (Notice the feeling of relief from tensing and relaxing your muscles.)
12. Now turn your head to the right and tense your neck. Relax and bring your head back again to its natural position.
13. Turn your head to the left and tense your neck. Relax and bring your head back again to its natural position.
14. Now bend your head back slightly toward the chair. Hold it. Okay, now bring your head back slowly to its natural position.*
15. This time bring your head down almost to your chest. Hold it. Now relax and let your head come back to its natural resting position.*
16. Now open your mouth as much as possible. A little wider, okay, relax. (Mouth must be partly open at end.)
17. Now tense your lips by closing your mouth. O.K., relax. (Notice the feeling of relaxation.)
18. Put your tongue at the roof of your mouth. Press hard. (Pause) Relax and allow your tongue to come to a comfortable position in your mouth.
19. Now put your tongue at the bottom of your mouth. Press down hard. Relax and let your tongue come to a comfortable position in your mouth.
20. Now just lie (sit) there and relax. Try not to think of anything.
21. To control self-verbalization, I want you to go through the motions of singing a high note — Not aloud! Okay, start singing to yourself. Hold that note, and now relax.
22. Now sing a medium note and make your vocal cords tense again. Relax.
23. Now sing a low note and make your vocal cords tense again. Relax. (Your vocal apparatus should be relaxed now. Relax your mouth.)
24. Now, close your eyes. Squeeze them tight and breathe naturally. Notice the tension. Now relax. (Notice how the pain goes away when you relax.)
25. Now let your eyes relax and keep your mouth open slightly.
26. Open your eyes as much as possible. Hold it. Now, relax your eyes.
27. Now wrinkle your forehead as much as possible. Hold it. Okay, relax.
28. Now take a deep breath and hold it. Relax.
29. Now exhale. Breathe all the air out . . . all of it out. Relax. (Notice the wondrous feeling of breathing again.)
30. Imagine that there are weights pulling on all your muscles making them flaccid and relaxed . . . pulling your arms and body into the couch.

continued

HPC–F*

Table 5.3. continued

31. Pull your stomach muscles together. Tighter. Okay. Relax.
32. Now extend your muscles as if you were a prize fighter. Make your stomach hard. Relax. (You are becoming more and more relaxed.)
33. Now tense your buttocks. Tighter. Hold it. Now, relax.
34. Now search the upper part of your body and relax any part that is tense. First the facial muscles. (Pause . . . 3–5 sec.) Then the vocal muscles. (Pause . . . 3–5 sec.) The neck region. (Pause . . . 3–5 sec.) Your shoulder . . . relax any part that is tense. (Pause) Now the arms and fingers. Relax these. Becoming very relaxed.
35. Maintaining this relaxation, raise both of your legs (to about a 45° angle). Now relax. (Notice that this further relaxes you.)
36. Now bend your feet back so that your toes point toward your face. Relax your mouth. Bend them hard. Relax.
37. Bend your feet the other way . . . away from your body. Not far. Notice the tension. Okay, relax.
38. Relax. (Pause) Now curl your toes together—as hard as you can. Tighter. Okay, relax. (Quiet . . . silence for about 30 seconds.)
39. This completes the formal relaxation procedure. Now explore your body from your feet up. Make sure that every muscle is relaxed. (Say slowly)—first your toes, . . . your feet, . . . your legs, . . . buttocks, . . . stomach, . . . shoulder, . . . neck, . . . eyes, . . . and finally your forehead—all should be relaxed now. (Quiet—silence for about 10 seconds.) Just lie there and feel very relaxed, noticing the warmness of the relaxation. (Pause) I would like you to stay this way for about 1 more minute, and then I am going to count to five. When I reach five, I want you to open your eyes feeling very calm and refreshed. (Quiet—silence for about 1 minute.) Okay, when I count to five, I want you to open your eyes feeling very calm and refreshed. One . . . feeling very calm; Two . . . very calm, very refreshed; Three . . . very refreshed; Four . . . and, Five.

Note: Adapted in part from Jacobson (1938), Rimm (1967, personal communication), and Wolpe and Lazarus (1966).

*The client should not be encouraged to bend his or her neck either all the way back or forward.

the changes she or he will be experiencing in bodily sensations. For example, the therapist might say: "Notice the warm, soft feeling of relaxation"; "Notice how your (*particular muscle group*) now feel . . . they are warm, heavy and relaxed"; "Notice how relaxed your (*particular muscle group*) feel in contrast to when you were tensing them"; "Notice how you are becoming more and more relaxed—feeling relaxation throughout your whole body."

For various reasons, a few clients have difficulty relaxing with this procedure. No matter how motivated they are, they just find it difficult to respond. They have learned over the years *not* to relax, to be tense, and it might take time for them to change. For example, some have difficulty closing their eyes for longer than a few seconds, some feel uneasy when they lie back in a recliner chair or on a couch while someone is watching them. A few have even reported being afraid to relax. In an attempt to deal with this problem effectively, some writers (Brady, 1966, 1972; Friedman, 1966) have recommended the use of drugs like Brevital (sodium methahexital) to help their clients relax during relaxation training and desensitization. Others have suggested the use of hypnosis or carbon dioxide-oxygen (Wolpe, 1982; Wolpe & Lazarus, 1966), a shaping procedure (Morris, 1973), or biofeedback-assisted relaxation (Javel & Denholtz, 1975; Reeves & Maelica, 1975).

Development of the Anxiety Hierarchy

Upon completion of the initial interview and during the relaxation training phase, the therapist begins planning an anxiety hierarchy with the client for each of the identified fears. This hierarchy is based on the fear that the therapist and client have agreed upon as requiring change and that the therapist has consented to treat and the client has agreed to work on. The therapist should not impose treatment on a client for a fear that the client has not agreed is in need of being reduced.

At the end of the first relaxation training session (assuming the initial interview has now been completed), the client is given ten 3" × 5" index cards and asked to come to the next session with the cards filled out, each containing a description of a situation that produces a certain level of anxiety. Specifically, the client is asked to identify on the cards those situations that are related to the fear and that produce increasingly more anxiety and tension. The client is asked to divide up the fear on a 0 to 100 scale and assign an anxiety-provoking situation to every 10th value (100 representing the most anxiety-provoking situation). Examples of some initial anxiety hierarchies are listed in Table 5.4.

The exact nature of a hierarchy varies, depending on the client's particular fear and perception of the various situations. For example, someone who has a fear of being criticized might describe a number of very different situations when this fear occurs, each differing in the level of fear that it arouses. Someone else might have a very specific fear, where the descriptions of the increasing anxiety-provoking situations differ on a spatiotemporal dimension. This was the case of the woman in Table 5.4, who had a fear of leaving her house. The hierarchy can also vary in terms of the number of people present in a particular situation (e.g., an elevator), the perceived attitudes of others toward the client, and a combination of some of these dimensions (see the fear of flying hierarchy in Table 5.4).

When the client returns with the prepared hierarchy, the therapist goes through it with him or her and adds intermediary items where it seems appropriate. The final hierarchy should represent a slow and smooth gradation of anxiety-provoking situations, each of which the client can easily imagine. Most hierarchies contain 20 to 25 items. It is not unusual, however, for those hierarchies that represent a very specific fear (e.g., driving on the highway at night) to contain fewer items, whereas those representing a more complex fear (e.g., fear of being alone, fear of evaluation, fear of open spaces) contain more items. In Table 5.5 we have listed an example of a final hierarchy.

The therapist should also determine what the client considers a relaxing scene, one that would be 0 on the hierarchy. This is often called the *control scene*. The scene should be unrelated to the client's fears and totally satisfying and comforting. Some common "0-level" scenes are the following:

- Walking through the forest on a nice sunny day with my wife (husband).
- Lying on the beach by the ocean on a sunny, warm day.
- Lying in bed and reading an interesting novel.
- Sitting in a lounge chair in my backyard on a beautiful spring day, watching the clouds go by.
- Lying on the couch and watching a good movie on TV.

Hierarchy development usually occupies at least part of two or three sessions, though less time can be spent with those cases that involve a single phobia.

Systematic Desensitization Proper

Desensitization proper usually begins about three or four sessions after the completion of the initial interview. By this time the client has had the opportunity to practice relaxation at home as well as in the therapist's office and has been able to construct the anxiety hierarchy. If the client has developed a number of hierarchies, the therapist should first work on the one that is most distressing and troublesome to the client. If time allows, the therapist can also work on other hierarchies during the hour but probably should not expose the client to more than three different hierarchies in a given session.

The first desensitization session starts with having the client spend about 3 to 5 minutes relaxing himself or herself on the couch or in the recliner chair. During this time, the therapist suggests to the client that he or she is becoming increasingly more relaxed and is achieving a deeper and deeper level of relaxation. The therapist might add the following comments during this phase:

> Your whole body is becoming heavier . . . all your muscles are relaxing more and more. Your arms are becoming very relaxed. (*Pause*) Your shoulders. (*Pause*) And your eyes . . . very relaxed. Your forehead . . . very relaxed . . . noticing that as you become more relaxed you're feeling more and more calm (*Pause*) Very relaxed . . . relaxing any part of your face that feels the least bit tense. (*Pause*) Now, back down to your neck . . . your shoulders . . . your chest . . . your buttocks . . . your thighs . . . your legs . . . your feet . . . very, very relaxed. (*Pause*) Feeling very at ease and very comfortable.

The client is also asked by the therapist to indicate, by raising his or her right index finger, when he or she has achieved a very relaxing and comfortable state.

Table 5.4. Samples of Initial Anxiety Hierarchies

Fear of being alone

10. Being with a group of people at the lab either at night or during the day.
20. Being alone in a room with another female.
30. Thinking about the possibility of being alone in my house during the day.
40. Walking in class early in the morning when there are few people outside.
50. Actually alone in my bedroom at home and it's daylight.
60. Driving a car alone at night and feeling a man is following me.
70. Walking alone on a city street downtown at night with a girlfriend.
80. Being alone in a house with a young child for whom I am babysitting.
90. Thinking about being alone at night a few hours before I will actually be alone.
100. Sitting alone in the living room of my house at night with the doors closed.

Fear of driving in high places

10. Entering a ramp garage on ground level.
20. Going up to third level of the garage from the second level.
30. Riding with a friend in a car and approach the bridge over the Chicago River on Michigan Avenue.
40. Driving a car with a friend and begin to approach the bridge over the Chicago River.
50. Driving my car over the Chicago River bridge.
60. Driving with a friend and crossing the bridge over the Mississippi River near Moline.
70. Driving my car on the bridge over the Mississippi River near Moline.
80. Driving my car with a friend on a hilly road in Wisconsin.
90. Driving my car with a friend on a hilly road in Wisconsin going halfway up a fairly steep hill.
100. Driving my car with a friend up to the top of a fairly steep hill. We get to the top and get out of the car and look around at the valley below . . . then go into a restaurant nearby — and later drive back down the hill.

Fear of flying in airplanes

10. Watching a movie of a plane moving up and down and banking.
20. Sitting in a private plane — on the ground with the motor idling.
30. Sitting in a private plane on the ground and the pilot begins to taxi down the runway.
40. Sitting in a private plane on the ground, taxiing, and the pilot revs the engine.
50. Planning a trip with a friend on a commercial jet and it's three months before the trip.
60. One month before the trip by jet.
70. Three weeks before the trip by jet.
80. Three days before the trip by jet.
90. In a private plane at take-off.
100. In a commercial jet over land.

Fear of leaving the house

10. Going out the front door to my car to go to the store.
20. Getting in the car and starting it up.
30. In the car and pulling out of the driveway.
40. On the street and pulling away from my house.
50. Two blocks from my house on way to the store.
60. Arrive at the store and park.
70. Enter the store.
80. Get a shopping cart and begin looking for items on my list.
90. Have all the items and go to check-out counter.
100. Have all the items and have to wait in a long slow line to go through check-out.

After the client signals, the therapist asks him or her to visualize a number of scenes from the hierarchy that the two of them developed over the past few sessions. The therapist asks the client to imagine each scene as

Table 5.5. Sample of Final Hierarchy

Elevators
  *1. At my (therapist's) office and seeing the elevator as you walk down the stairs.
   2. Pushing button to summon elevator at my office (on second floor).
   3. Elevator comes to second floor . . . doors open . . . and you go inside and down to first floor.
  *4. In the new elevator with others at the Acme building below the fourth floor—going down.
   5. You enter the elevator at my office, the doors close, and there is a slight pause before it begins going down.
   6. Alone in the elevator in my office building going up from the first to the third floor.
  *7. In a new elevator alone at the Acme building, going up between the first and fourth floors.
  *8. In the new elevator with others at the Acme building going down between the 15th and 4th floors (15 story building).
   9. In the elevator at my office going down. As the elevator reaches the first floor there is a slight pause before the doors open.
 *10. In a new elevator with others at the Acme building and going up between the 4th and 15th floors.
  11. In the elevator alone at the Acme building, going up between the 4th and 15th floors and as you reach the 12th floor to get out there is a momentary pause before the doors open.
 *12. You're on the fifth floor of the Marshall building (a very familiar old building to the client) and you enter the elevator alone, push the button, and it starts to go down to the first floor.
  13. As you are going down in the elevator you begin hearing a few noises from the elevator machinery.
 *14. You enter the Marshall building and walk up to the elevator, step inside, and press the button to go up to the fifth floor.
 *15. You enter the elevator alone in the Ajax building (30 floors) and you take it up to the 10th floor.
  16. . . . to the 15th floor.
  17. . . . to the 20th floor.
 *18. You enter the elevator alone in the Thomas building (50 floors) and you take it to the 20th floor.
  19. . . . to the 30th floor.
  20. You are in the elevator alone in my office building and press the button to go up to the fifth floor, and it doesn't stop until the seventh floor.
  21. You are in the elevator alone at the Marshall building, going down to the first floor, and it stops between the second and first floors. You press the first floor button again and the elevator goes to the first floor.
 *22. You are in an elevator alone in the Thomas building going up to the 45th floor and it gets stuck between the 20th and 21st floors—and then starts up a while later after you have pressed the alarm button.

*Original items that client developed.

clearly and as vividly as possible—"as if you are really there"—while still maintaining a very relaxed state. If the client feels the least bit of anxiety or tension when he or she imagines a particular scene, he or she is told to signal immediately with the right finger.

At this point, the therapist asks the client to indicate with an index finger if she or he is still feeling very calm and relaxed. If the client signals, the therapist presents the control scene. If the client does not signal, the therapist reviews with the client the earlier relaxation sequence until she or he no longer signals feeling tense.

The control scene is presented for approximately 15 seconds. The therapist then proceeds with the desensitization procedure. Here is an example of a desensitization session with a test-phobic individual.

> Now stop imagining that scene and give all your attention once again to relaxing. . . . Now imagine that you are home studying in the evening. It is the 20th of May, exactly a month before your examination. (Pause of 5 seconds) Now stop imagining the scene. (Pause of 10–15 seconds) Stop imagining the scene and just think of your muscles. Let go, and enjoy your state of calm. (Pause of 15 seconds) Now imagine again that you are studying at home a month before your examination. (Pause of 5–10 seconds) Stop the scene and think of nothing but your own body. (Pause of 15 seconds) (Wolpe, 1969, p. 126. Material in parentheses added by present author)

Each hierarchy scene is presented three to four times with a maximum exposure time of 5 seconds for the first presentation and a gradual increase up to 10 seconds for subsequent presentations. The hierarchy items are presented first, in ascending order starting with the lowest feared item first, with relaxation periods between each scene varying from 10 to 15 seconds. In most cases, three to four different scenes are presented per session. This means that a particular desensitization session will last between 15 and 20 minutes. The remainder of the hour can be devoted to discussing issues related to the client's fear (e.g., what occurred during the week regarding the fear), to the desensitization of another fear hierarchy, or to working on some other problem with the client.

After the last scene is presented for a particular session, and if the decision is to go onto another hierarchy, the therapist usually asks the client to relax for a short period of time. The therapist then starts the ending phase of the session by saying the following:

> Just relax . . . feeling very comfortable and at ease. I would like you to stay this way until I count to five. When I reach five, I want you to open your eyes feeling very calm and refreshed. (*Pause*) One . . . feeling very calm; two . . . very calm, very refreshed; three . . . very refreshed; four . . . ; and, five.

The same general format is followed for all subsequent desensitization sessions. The scenes should not be presented in a rapid manner; rather, they should be presented in a conversational manner that conveys both understanding and concern for the client. In order to keep track of which scenes the client passes, how many times a scene has been passed, and where on the hierarchy each session started and stopped, it is advisable to follow a procedure on each hierarchy card like the one outlined in Table 5.6. The date on each card refers to when the scene was presented. The words *stopped* and *started* indicate whether the session stopped or started with the scene. The hash marks help the therapist recall how often the scene was presented, one mark representing each presentation. The circle through the mark indicates that the client signaled anxiety and that the scene was stopped and followed by a relaxation period of the number of seconds indicated next to the circle. Comments are also made at the bottom of the card about the client's observed comfort level while imagining the scene.

The therapist should present each scene until the client has two consecutive failures (indications of anxiety). The therapist should go back to the previous successfully passed scene and work back up again. If failure persists, the previously successful scene should be presented again, so that the client ends the session with a positive experience. The ending phase of the procedure should then begin. The problems associated with the difficult scene should be discussed with the client and modifications made either in the scene or in other aspects of the desensitization procedure.

Even if a client does not signal anxiety, it is often helpful during the conduct of desensitization (especially during the first few sessions) to determine if the client was disturbed by a particular scene, whether the client was able to fully imagine the scene, and if the client continues to feel very relaxed. To do this, the therapist asks between scene presentations "If you were not the least bit disturbed by that scene ("If you were able to imagine that scene very clearly," or "If you continue to feel very relaxed") do nothing; otherwise raise your right index finger." If the client raises his or her finger, the therapist then takes appropriate action, which might entail going through additional relaxation-enhancing suggestions or presenting either the problematic scene or the control scene again and suggesting that the client imagine it in detail. If, after reintroducing a particular scene, the client indicates again that she or he was disturbed by it or could not vividly imagine it, the session is stopped, using the ending phase described above. The therapist then explores in detail the difficulty the client is having and makes any modifications necessary in the hierarchy or relaxation procedure.

A second useful procedure involves assessing the client's overall level of relaxation before, during, and after a particular desensitization session. This usually takes place after desensitization has been completed for the day. The client is asked to rate his or her relaxation level on a 10-point scale, where 0 is *extremely relaxed* and 10 is *not at all relaxed*. This approach not only gives the therapist information regarding the client's relative change in relaxation level from pretreatment to posttreatment across sessions, but also provides feedback to the client regarding his or her own progress.

Table 5.6. Suggested Notational System

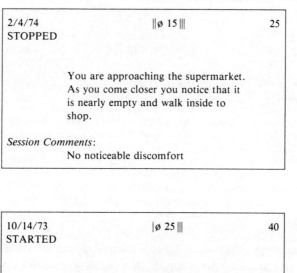

| 2/4/74 | ‖∅ 15 ‖‖ | 25 |
| STOPPED | | |

You are approaching the supermarket.
As you come closer you notice that it
is nearly empty and walk inside to
shop.

Session Comments:
No noticeable discomfort

| 10/14/73 | |∅ 25 ‖‖ | 40 |
| STARTED | | |

At the Tango Bar and you leave your
table for 5 minutes with your drink on
it, and come back and start drinking
from your glass again.

Session Comments:
Moving around in chair at first

Additional Considerations

Throughout desensitization proper, the client should be watched for
signs of fatigue. In this regard, it may be helpful to ask the client whether
she or he feels too many scenes (or hierarchies) are being presented at each
session. It is also advisable to be sensitive to any discomfort the client is
showing during either relaxation training or desensitization proper. Some
of the ways clients express discomfort while lying on the couch or sitting
back in a recliner are the following: moving their bodies around as if to find
a comfortable position, moving their eyelids rapidly; yawning excessively;
or, making unsolicited verbalizations while their eyes are closed.

Occasionally, as in the following example, discomfort can be unrelated
to the client's fear.

Mrs. Farber was well into her fifth desensitization session, progressing slowly
but steadily up her hierarchy concerned with a fear of being alone in her

house. She fluttered her eyelids sporadically, but did not indicate any anxiety about the scenes being presented. During subsequent relaxation-enhancing instructions, she began crossing her legs and shifting her body around. Just as the therapist was about to inquire about her relaxation level, she opened her eyes, sat up in the recliner chair, and said, "You'll have to excuse me. I had a lot to drink today and must go to the washroom. I forgot to go before I came here."

At other times, as in the next example, deep relaxation might set the occasion for very tense clients to begin thinking about their problem.

Mr. Martin had difficulty learning how to relax. Several sessions passed with him unable to achieve a relaxation level lower than 4 on the 10-point self-report relaxation rating scale. In the fourth session, a relaxation enhancing technique was used. He became very relaxed, more relaxed than on previous occasions, and seemed to be pleased with his success. Within a few minutes, he began moving his head from one side to the other, and tears began falling down his cheeks. He then started crying and said that this was the first time he has ever "let . . . (himself) really think about" the difficulties he has had with his impotence "and all the turmoil it has caused in my life."

Similar events can also contribute to a client's repeated failure of an item in a session. In the following example, the particular hierarchy item did not produce the signaled anxiety; rather, the anxiety was triggered by a telephone call that day from an old friend of the client.

Mrs. Carol was progressing steadily through her agoraphobia hierarchy over the first eight desensitization sessions. During the ninth session, an item was presented concerned with driving by herself nine miles to the therapist's office. As soon as the item was presented, she signaled anxiety and repeated this action until the session was stopped. Upon inquiring about her repeated signaling, she began crying and said she had received a telephone call that day from an old college friend with whom she was very close but whom she had not seen for 10 years. The friend had an unexpected 3-hour layover at the airport and decided to call Mrs. Carol and ask her to come out to see her (a distance of 20 miles). Mrs. Carol wanted to go very, very much but was afraid to take a chance and declined, but she did talk to her friend on the telephone for a long time. She felt terrible and angry at herself for having such a "stupid problem."

Another reason for repeated failure of a hierarchy item could be the psychological distance between the last passed item and the next failed one. Two examples of this situation are the following:

Item passed. Flying in the plane after leveling off at 30,000 feet and not hearing any change in the sound of the engines. (#60 on the hierarchy)

Item failed. Feeling the tilt of the plane as it is banking, and not hearing any change in the sound of the engines. (#65 on the hierarchy)

Item passed. Planning a trip on an airplane with a close friend to the Bahama Islands 9 months before the trip. (#20 on the hierarchy)

Item failed. Reviewing plans of airplane trip to the Bahamas with close friend, 1 month before the trip. (#25 on the hierarchy)

In the first example, the client and the therapist decided on an intermediary scene that described a change in the noise of the airplane engines that the client could hear just before she felt the plane banking. A temporal dimension, on the other hand, was inserted between the two scenes in the second example. Specifically, three additional scenes were developed: 6 months before the planned trip, 4 months before, and 2 months before. In both cases these additions to the respective hierarchies facilitated successful passage of the heretofore failed items.

Just as some clients signal repeated difficulty with one or more hierarchy scenes, others never signal anxiety about particular scenes. In some cases, this is good because it suggests that the hierarchy represents a smooth, even gradation of the client's fear. In other cases, this means that the client feels reluctant to signal that anxiety is indeed being experienced. To reduce the possibility of the client's not signaling anxiety when, in fact, she or he should, it is a good idea for the therapist to mention at various times throughout the session: "Remember to signal whenever you feel the slightest amount of anxiety." The therapist should also make every effort to convey neither dissatisfaction with a client's signaling of anxiety nor satisfaction that a client did not signal anxiety at all during a particular session. In both instances, the client might begin to feel that the therapist does not really want any signaling of anxiety.

It is also important for the therapist to end each desensitization session with a positive experience for the client (i.e., ending on a hierarchy item that was passed successfully). Moreover, the therapist should leave sufficient time at the end of the session (as well as before the session begins) to discuss any issues or concerns that the client has or to discuss how things went during the week.

Most desensitization sessions last from 30 minutes to 1 hour, depending on the number of different hierarchies presented. Some researchers, however, have reported successfully treating a phobia by conducting a massed desensitization session that lasted 90 minutes (Wolpin & Pearsall, 1965), whereas others (Richardson & Suinn, 1973) have reported success after a 3-hour massed session. The spacing of most desensitization sessions varies from once a week to twice a week, though Wolpe (1982) reported that some clients have received two or more sessions per day.

Finally, during the initial stages of systematic desensitization, the client is encouraged to avoid the temptation of entering the actual feared situation. Because this could be an unrealistic request for some clients, they are asked to try to avoid entering the feared situation at "full throttle." As desensitization progresses, however, they are encouraged to enter aspects of the feared situation that correspond to lower hierarchy items that have been passed successfully and for which they now feel little, if any, tension or anxiety.

Variations of Systematic Desensitization

Various alternatives to systematic desensitization have been proposed by researchers. In *in vivo desensitization* (e.g., Kipper, 1980; Levine & Wolpe, 1980; Schneider, 1982; Sherman, 1972), the client is exposed to the items on the hierarchy in the real situation rather than through imagination. Relaxation training is not used as the counterconditioned response to the situation. Instead, those feelings of comfort, security, and trust that the client has developed for the therapist (that have emerged from the therapeutic relationship) are used as the counterconditioning agent. The therapist goes into the real-life situation with the client and urges him or her to gradually go through each item on the hierarchy. An example of this procedure is the following:

> Mr. Kay is a very successful salesman in a large metropolitan area. But he is extremely afraid of elevators. Lately his fear has become so intense that he has avoided attending meetings that occur on a level higher than the fourth floor. In vivo desensitization entailed having Mr. Kay and the therapist approach various elevators throughout the city, ride up and down in them, and purposely get stuck in them, following a hierarchy sequence developed earlier with the therapist. Mr. Kay was also encouraged to go up in elevators, etc., on his own while the therapist waited for him at various floors.

A similar technique called *contact desensitization* (e.g., Morris & Kratochwill, 1983b; Ritter, 1968, 1969a, 1969b) is used with both children and adults. This technique also involved a graded hierarchy but adds to it a modeling, touch, information/feedback, and practice component in addition to the therapist's interpersonal relationship with the client. The procedure is outlined in the next example from Bandura:

> In the application of this method to the elimination of snake phobia, at each step the experimenter himself performed fearless behavior and gradually led subjects into touching, stroking and then holding the snake's body with first gloves and then bare hands while he held the snake securely by the head and tail. If a subject was unable to touch the snake after ample demonstration, she was asked to place her hand on the experimenter's and to move her hand down gradually until it touched the snake's body. After subjects no longer felt any apprehension about touching the snake under these secure conditions, anxieties about contact with the snake's head area and entwining tail were extinguished. The experimenter again performed the tasks fearlessly and then he and the subject performed the responses jointly; as subjects became less fearful the experimenter gradually reduced his participation and control over the snake until subjects were able to hold the snake in their laps without assistance, to let the snake loose in the room and retrieve it, and to let it crawl freely over their bodies. Progress through the graded approach tasks was paced according to the subjects' apprehensiveness. When they reported being

able to perform one activity with little or no fear, they were eased into a more difficult interaction. (1969, p. 185.)[4]

A third variation is very similar to desensitization proper, but it involves the use of a tape recorder and/or computer. It is called *automated desensitization* (e.g., Biglan, Villwock, & Wick, 1979; Migler & Wolpe, 1967; Thomas, Rapp, & Gentles, 1979). In this procedure, the client goes through the desensitization process by listening to a series of tape-recorded scene presentations or reading series of hierarchy items displayed on the computer screen, prepared by the therapist with the client's assistance. Developed by Lang (Wolpe, 1969) and later used by Migler and Wolpe (1967), this procedure allows the client to pace himself or herself in the desensitization process and to become desensitized at home. This method has been found to be as effective as live desensitization. A variation of this automated procedure is called *self-directed desensitization* (Baker, Cohen, & Saunders, 1973; Krop & Krause, 1976; Rosen, 1976; Rosen, Glasgow, & Barrera, 1976). In this procedure, clients use instructional materials typically provided them by the therapist and conduct the treatment at their own pace. In some cases the therapist continues to function as a consultant, whereas at other times the therapist sees the client only once for the initial structuring of treatment. The major difference between this procedure and automated desensitization is that with the latter the client uses equipment to mechanically present the treatment package to himself or herself. An interesting fading procedure that makes use of both automated and self-directed methods of fear reduction has been discussed by Öst (1978a). He reports that this procedure is as effective as live desensitization (Öst, 1978b).

Another variation is *self-control desensitization* (Deffenbacher & Michaels, 1981; Deffenbacher, Michaels, Michaels, & Daley, 1980; Goldfried, 1971). In this approach the desensitization procedure is construed as training the client in coping skills, that is, desensitization treatment is viewed as teaching the client to cope with anxiety. Clients are told, for example, to apply relaxation training whenever they become aware of an increase in their feelings of anxiety and tension. They are also encouraged, during the desensitization proper phase, to continue imagining a scene that produces anxiety and to "relax away" the anxiety and/or imagine themselves becoming fearful and then seeing themselves coping with the anxiety and tenseness that they feel. This variation is based on the view that clients

---

[4]From *Principles of behavior modification* by A. Bandura, 1969, New York: Holt, Rinehart & Winston. Copyright 1969 by Holt, Rinehart & Winston. Reprinted by permission.

will not always be in a position where they can readily leave a fearful and anxiety arousing situation, that they must learn to cope with the situation on their own. Rehearsal for this possibility, therefore, should take place in therapy. In this regard, it is not important for the anxiety hierarchy to be theme oriented as in standard systematic desensitization (Goldfried & Goldfried, 1977). The hierarchy need only be composed of situations arousing increasing amounts of anxiety, independent of theme. The following rationale for clients has been suggested by Goldfried:

> There are various situations where, on the basis of your past experience, you have learned to react by becoming tense (anxious, nervous, fearful). What I plan to do is help you to learn how to cope with these situations more successfully, so that they do not make you as upset. This will be done by taking note of a number of those situations which upset you to varying degrees, and then having you learn to cope with the less stressful situations before moving on to the more difficult ones. Part of the treatment involves learning how to relax, so that in situations where you feel yourself getting nervous you will be better able to eliminate this tenseness. Learning to relax is much like learning any other skill. When a person learns to drive, he initially has difficulty in coordinating everything, and often finds himself very much aware of what he is doing. With more and more practice, however, the procedures involved in driving become easier and more automatic. You may find the same thing occurring to you when you try to relax in those situations where you feel yourself starting to become tense. You will find that as you persist, however, it will become easier and easier. (1971, p. 231)

A fourth variation is called *group systematic desensitization* (see e.g., Deffenbacher & Kemper, 1974a, 1974b; Snyder & Deffenbacher, 1977). This procedure involves the same basic phases as individual systematic desensitization, but the phases are adapted for group administration. Groups of five to eight persons are usually treated in this procedure, with each group member having the same fear. Relaxation training is conducted on a group basis, with members of the group reclining on patio chaise lounges or on foam rubber mats on the floor. Hierarchy construction occurs in one of two ways: (a) The therapist and group members develop the hierarchy items together, and then the group rank orders the items; or (b) the therapist brings to the group a potential set of hierarchy items—like the ones presented in Table 5.7—and the group determines which ones are appropriate and/or need modification and what ranking should be assigned to each.

The desensitization proper phase is also conducted in a slightly different fashion than in individual systematic desensitization. In the group approach, this phase is geared to the slowest progressing person in the group. For example, if one person in a group of test-anxious college students is reporting anxiety over the imagination of a particular hierarchy item, the other people in the group would be told to continue relaxing or, in some cases, to imagine their neutral scene. The therapist would then go through repeated presentations of the particular hierarchy item and/or previously passed hierarchy items until the person successfully imagined the difficult scene without reporting anxiety. A variation of group systematic desensitization, called *group vicarious desensitization* (e.g., Altmaier & Woodward, 1981) has clients observe videotapes of people undergoing systematic desensitization for the same fear as that reported by the clients.

FLOODING-RELATED THERAPIES

Like systematic desensitization, flooding methods use the imaginal presentation of anxiety-provoking material. But, unlike the desensitization methods, flooding-related therapies from the very beginning have the client imagine a fearful and threatening scene of high intensity for a prolonged period of time, without any previous relaxation training. The purpose of flooding methods, therefore, is to produce a frightening imaginal experience in the client of such magnitude that the experience will actually result in a reduction in his or her fear or phobia rather than a heightening of it. Two major types of flooding therapy have been discussed in the literature: implosive therapy and flooding. These two methods have many common characteristics.

Implosive Therapy

Developed by psychologist Thomas G. Stampfl (Stampfl, 1961; Stampfl & Levis, 1967), this method utilizes principles from both learning theory and psychodynamic theory (e.g., Sigmund Freud's psychoanalytic theory). Though Stampfl maintains that fears and their associated anxiety are learned, he does not assume that such fears can be most effectively reduced by using a counterconditioning approach. Rather, he believes that a person can best unlearn a fear by using a procedure based on an *extinction model*. Here extinction refers to the gradual reduction in the occurrence of an anxiety response, as a result of the continuous presentation of the fear-producing stimulus in the absence of the reinforcement that perpetuates the fear. In therapy, this extinction process is accomplished by having the therapist " . . . represent, reinstate, or symbolically reproduce the stimuli (cues) to which the anxiety response has been conditioned . . . " without presenting the concomitant reinforcement that maintains the response (Stampfl & Levis, 1967, p. 499).[5]

---

[5]In this statement, Stampfl and Levis are using the term *reinforcement* in the classical conditioning sense of the word, that is, the procedure of following a conditioned stimulus (CS) with an unconditioned stimulus (UCS).

Table 5.7. Possible Items for a Test Anxiety Hierarchy

You hear about a friend who has a test soon.

On the first day of class, the teacher announces the number of tests she will be giving during the first grading period.

Your teacher announces that there will be a test in one week.

It's a couple of days before the test and you still have a lot to study. You know that you will be able to prepare adequately for the exam only if you work steadily and efficiently.

You start studying for the test.

You are studying and wondering how you will remember everything for the test.

It's the night before the exam and you're reviewing everything.

You get ready for your class and it's a few minutes before you have to leave for school.

You're at school and you walk to your class where you have to take the test, and you're thinking about the test.

You enter the classroom where the exam is given.

You take your seat and wait for the teacher to come to you with the test.

Others around you are talking about the material being covered on the test, and you're trying to answer their questions to yourself.

You see the teacher handing out the exams, and you watch others get their copy of the test.

You get your copy of the exam and look it over.

You see a lot of questions you think you should know, but you can't remember the answers to them.

You start the test and wonder how well you are doing compared with the others in your class.

You get to your class expecting a routine discussion or lecture and the teacher passes out a surprise quiz.

You come to an ambiguous question. You think you know the answer, but the question can be interpreted in more than one way.

While answering an essay question, you realize that what you are writing is incorrect and that you will have to cross out what you have written and begin again.

The teacher has just told the class that only half the time remains for you to complete the exam. You have completed less than half of the test and realize that you will have to work more rapidly in order to finish the exam.

You see others finish the test and hand in their papers, and you aren't finished yet.

There are two minutes remaining in the test. If you work very quickly, you will be able to answer all the questions.

You turn in the exam and hear others talking about the test. You didn't answer the questions the same way they did.

Note: Adapted in part from *A comparison of self-control desensitization with systematic desensitization in the reduction of test anxiety* by L. Martinez, 1978. Unpublished dissertation, Syracuse University.

Development of the Avoidance Serial Cue Hierarchy

From information gathered during the initial interview, the therapist develops hypotheses as to what the important cues involved in the client's fear or phobia are. Many of these cues are situational events in the client's life and can be readily identified. For example, in the case of people who have a fear of heights, situational events could be the sight of high-rise office and apartment buildings, winding roads in the mountains, airplanes, bridges, and so forth.

The remaining cues are formulated by the therapist and are based on psychodynamic theory and on the therapist's knowledge of common reactions by clients with similar problems. They are derived from the client's statements in the initial interview and from the client's nonverbal behavior, and they represent those psychodynamic areas that the therapist believes are relevant to the client's fear. These cues are usually related to themes of aggression and hostility, oral and anal activity, sexual activity, punishment, rejection, bodily injury, loss of impulse control, and guilt. For example, Stampfl and Levis (1967) described four of the hypothesized dynamic cues in the following manner:

Aggression. Scenes presented in this area usually center around the expression of anger, hostility, and aggression by the patient toward parental, sibling, spouse, or other significant figures in his life. Various degrees of bodily injury are described including complete body mutilation and death of the victim.

Punishment. The patient is instructed to visualize himself as the recipient of the anger, hostility, and aggression of the various significant individuals in his life. The punishment inflicted in the scene is frequently a result of the patient's engaging in some forbidden act.

Sexual material. In this area a wide variety of hypothesized cues related to sex are presented. For example, primal and Oedipal scenes and scenes of castration, fellatio, and homosexuality are presented.

Loss of control. Scenes are presented where the patient is encouraged to imagine himself losing impulse control to such an extent that he acts out avoided sexual or aggressive impulses. These scenes usually are followed by scenes where the individual is directed to visualize himself hospitalized for the rest of his life in a back ward of a mental hospital as a result of his loss of impulse control. This area is tapped primarily with patients who express fear of "becoming insane" or concern about being hopeless and incurable. (p. 501)[6]

Those cues that are lowest on the hierarchy are assumed to be the situations and events that the client can associate with his or her fear or phobia. The highest cues are those internal dynamic cues that the therapist believes are closely associated with the client's basic psychological problem. The particular dynamic themes emphasized in the hierarchy depend on the client's problem and the information obtained in the initial interview.

The hierarchy scenes are developed by the therapist after the initial interview is completed. They are not developed jointly by the client and the therapist, as in systematic desensitization. Overall, the hierarchy is quite

---

[6]From "Essentials of implosive therapy: A learning-based-psychodynamic behavior therapy" by T. G. Stampfl and D. J. Levis, 1967, *Journal of Abnormal Psychology*, *72*, 496–503. Copyright 1967 by American Psychological Association. Reprinted by permission.

different from the one developed in systematic desensitization. For example, the Avoidance Serial Cue Hierarchy contains only items that are thought to be capable of producing a maximum level of anxiety in the client. This is not the case with the desensitization hierarchy. The latter hierarchy is developed for a different reason, namely, to proceed gradually up the hierarchy in order to minimize the possibility that the client will experience any anxiety. The Avoidance Serial Cue Hierarchy starts with items that produce anxiety in the person and proceeds from external stimuli that evoke anxiety to hypothesized internal stimuli that also produce maximum levels of anxiety.

An example of this type of hierarchy concerned with a fear of enclosed spaces is described by Stampfl:

> . . . [The client] is instructed to imagine that he is entering a closed room. He remains there and is instructed to imagine that he is slowly suffocating to death. . . . [the therapist supplies many details about suffocation and then, based on information obtained in the interview, might present] scenes involving wrongdoing, with a parental figure supervising confinement to the closed space as a punishment. The parental figure might beat and scold the patient while he suffocates. Early traumatic incidents that appear to be related to the phobia may also be introduced, as represented in teasing sequences by being covered and held under blankets. If the patient appears to have been involved in a typical Oedipal situation in childhood, the therapist may suggest scenes that include sexual interaction with a mother figure followed by apprehension by a father figure, who places the patient in a closed space and castrates him . . . the cues related to bodily injury are vividly described (1970, pp. 199–200).[7]

Implosive Therapy Proper

After the hierarchy has been planned, the therapist describes implosive therapy to the client. This usually occurs at the beginning of the third session. It involves telling the client that a number of scenes will be presented to him or her, and that he or she is to sit back in the recliner chair and make every effort to lose himself or herself in that part of the scene that is being imagined. In addition, the client is told to "live" the scenes with genuine emotion and feeling. The goal then is "to reproduce in the absence of physical pain, as good an approximation as possible, the sights, sounds, and tactual experiences originally present in the primary" situation in which the fear was learned (Stampfl & Levis, 1968, p. 33).

The client is neither asked to accept the accuracy of what he or she is

---

[7]From "Implosive therapy: An emphasis on covert stimulation" by T. G. Stampfl, in D. J. Levis (Ed.), *Learning approaches to therapeutic behavior change.* Chicago: Aldine. Copyright 1970 by Aldine Press. Reprinted by permission.

imagining nor to agree that the scenes are representative of his or her fear. The scenes are then described by the therapist and are elaborated on in vivid detail. The more dramatic the presentation of the scenes, the easier it is for the client to participate fully in the experience. Then, as Stampfl and Levis (1967) stated,

. . . an attempt is made by the therapist to attain a maximal level of anxiety evocation from the patient. When a high level of anxiety is achieved, the patient is held on this level until some sign of spontaneous reduction in the anxiety-inducing value of the cues appears . . . the process is repeated, and again, at the first sign of spontaneous reduction of fear, new variations are introduced to elicit an intense anxiety response. This procedure is repeated until a significant diminution in anxiety has resulted. (p. 500)

One way of determining if the scenes are producing anxiety in the client is to observe if the client is flushing, sweating, grimacing, moving his or her head from side to side, or increasing motoric activity in the chair. The implosion procedure is maintained for about 30 to 40 minutes. After a scene has been presented a few times and the client is observed to experience anxiety to this scene, she or he is given the opportunity to present the scene to herself or himself through imagination and is encouraged to act out fully participation in the scene. The therapist continues to monitor the presence of anxiety and aids the client by suggesting that she or he imagine the scene vividly. Sometimes during treatment the client mentions to the therapist a few additional situations or events that produce fear. These should be noted by the therapist and included in the next implosive therapy session.

The session ends after 50 to 60 minutes and after the client has demonstrated a diminution in his or her anxiety response to the implosive scene. The client is then told to practice imagining the implosive scenes at home about once a day until the next session. This practice not only extends treatment outside the therapist's office and therefore aids in the generalization of the treatment effects, but it also helps the client realize that he or she can effectively deal with his or her fears or phobia by using the implosive therapy procedure. In fact, it "is hoped that at the termination of treatment the patient will be able to handle new anxiety-provoking situations without the therapist's help" (Stampfl & Levis, 1967, p. 500).

The following excerpt from a therapy session with a snake-phobic woman demonstrates how implosive therapy has been used. The reader will notice that external stimuli associated with the fear are first introduced into the imagined scene.

Close your eyes again. Picture the snake out in front of you, now make yourself pick it up. Reach down, pick it up, put it in your lap, feel it wiggling around in your lap, leave your hand on it, put your hand out and feel it wiggling around. Kind of explore its body with your fingers and hand. You don't like to do it, make yourself do it. Make yourself do it. Really grab onto the snake. Squeeze it a little bit, feel it. (Hogan, 1969, p. 179)

In the next excerpt, the client's level of anxiety is increased by including material in the imagined scene that is based on hypothesized internal stimuli that are contributing to the fear.

Okay, now put your finger out towards the snake and feel his head coming up. Now, it is in your lap, and it is coming up. Its head [is] towards your finger and it is starting to bite at your finger. Let it, let it bite at your finger. Let the snake kind of gnaw at your finger. Feel it gnawing, look at the blood dripping off your finger. Feel it in your stomach and the pain going up your arm. Try to picture your bleeding finger. And the teeth of the snake are stuck right in your finger, right down to the bone. (Hogan, 1969, p. 180)

In the next excerpt, the psychodynamic interpretation of the fear or phobia is presented.

Therapist: I want you to picture yourself getting ready to get into your bed and there in your bed are thousands of snakes. Can you see them there crawling around in your bed? I want you to lay down with them. Get down with them. Feel yourself moving around with the snakes and they are crawling all over you. And you are moving and turning in bed and they are touching you. Feel them crawling on you, touching you, slimy and slithering. Feel yourself turn over in your bed, and they are under you and on you and around you, and touching your face and in your hair. And they are crawling across your face. Can you feel them touch you? Describe the feeling.

Subject: Kind of cold.

Therapist: Feel, you are now cold and clammy like a snake and they are touching you with their cold, clammy, wet, slimy, drippy, cold bodies that are wiggling and touching your skin and feel them. Uhhh how can you feel them touch you? They are touching you. Can you feel them touch you? Move around so you can get greater contact. Move your body like that woman in the Sealy [mattress] ad and feel them touch you, uhh, wiggly and slimy, they are crawling on you, on your face. Uhhh! (Hogan, 1969, p. 181)

Flooding

The major difference between flooding and implosive therapy is in the type of scenes to which clients are exposed. Instead of exposing clients to horrifying scenes to imagine, in which certain aversive consequences occur (e.g., eating flesh, castrating people, death), scenes are described in which the feared external stimuli are presented for an extended period of time (e.g., Chambless, Foa, Groves, & Goldstein, 1982; Chaplin & Levine, 1981; Fairbank & Keane, 1982). For example, compare the previous implosive therapy excerpt with the following scene from an imaginal flooding procedure:

Imagine that you are going out of the front door of this house. You walk through the front garden and then you are in the street. You turn left and walk in the shopping center where you have to go and buy something. Imagine it as well as you can: the houses you walk past, the cars that rush past you. You are walking there alone and you are going in the direction of the railway crossing. The bars are down and you have to wait. A group of people is standing there waiting and they look at you. You find it very disturbing, this waiting, and you hop a bit from one leg to the other. At last the bars are going up, you walk on, and arrive in the shopping center. It is fuller there; there are more and more people. You begin to feel rather bad now. You become dizzy. You feel it in your legs. But you nevertheless walk on, because there is nowhere you can go there on the street, you cannot flee inside anywhere. Now you have to cross the street. There is a string of cars and you run between them. On the other side of the street there are still more people. Now you are feeling completely dizzy. Your legs are heavy. But there you are walking in the middle of the pavement and there is nowhere you can go. You begin to panic and you think, "I want to go away," "I want to go home," but you cannot go home. You hold onto a gate for a while, but you can't manage anymore. You are sweating terribly, you take another couple of steps and then you fall. You fall there in the middle of the street. People come and stand all around you and are wondering what has happened. And there you lie, in the middle of the street. (Emmelkamp, 1982, p. 61)

Thus, psychodynamic cues and/or interpretations are not used in the formulation of the flooding scenes; rather, the therapist uses only the external cues and vividly describes the scenes for the client to imagine. Scenes are presented for about the same period of time as in implosive therapy, with some research suggesting that continuous exposure of a flooding scene is superior to interrupted exposure (e.g., Chaplin & Levine, 1981; Stern & Marks, 1973).

A variation of the flooding procedure is called *in vivo flooding* (e.g., Emmelkamp, 1982; Emmelkamp & Wessels, 1975; Marshall, Gauthier, Christie, Currie, & Gordon, 1977). In this procedure, the client is exposed in real life to the flooding procedure involving the actual feared situation, event, or object. For example, Yule, Sacks, and Hersov (1974) placed an 11-year-old boy with a noise phobia (i.e., the noise associated with the bursting of balloons) in a small room filled with 50 balloons. The therapist began popping some of the balloons, and the child did the same thing. In the next session, the child was surrounded by 100 to 150 balloons and encouraged to pop them with prompting by the therapist. After two sessions there were no signs of a balloon phobia, and at a 25-month follow-up period there was no indication of any recurrence of the phobia.

Emmelkamp (1982) has suggested that this real life flooding approach is far more effective than the imaginal flooding procedure. *In vivo* flooding, however, could be too terrifying for some clients. Some researchers (e.g., Marshall et al., 1977) have therefore suggested adding a brief real-life exposure component to an imaginal flooding procedure following the end of each treatment session.

A second variation of flooding is called *self-directed in vivo flooding* (see, for example, Emmelkamp, 1982; Mavissakalian & Michelson, 1983). With this method, the client is encouraged to enter actual phobic situations and to remain in these situations until his or her anxiety or discomfort decreases to a fairly comfortable level. The particular conditions, however, under which this or the *in vivo* procedure should be used, or with which types of phobias, have not been specified in the literature.

Limitations of Flooding-Related Therapies

With regard to implosive therapy, Stampfl and Levis (1967) stated that "the more accurate the hypothesized cues and the more realistically they are presented the greater the extinction effect . . . will be" (p. 499). This statement suggests that the therapist should be quite knowledgeable in psychodynamic theory, especially psychoanalytic theory. If the therapist is not, she or he should probably refrain from using this approach. Furthermore, some writers (Marshall et al., 1977; Redd, Porterfield, & Andersen, 1979) have suggested that imaginal exposure to horrifying situations might, under certain conditions, strengthen a client's fear. Other writers (e.g., Emmelkamp, 1982) have concluded that the inclusion of horrifying situations during imaginal flooding does not enhance the effectiveness of the method and that imaginal flooding with pleasant scenes could be more effective, "at least with respect to anxiety reduction" (Emmelkamp, 1982, p. 67). Even though the flooding-related therapies appear to be effective in reducing fears and phobias in people, it appears that this method should be used with caution. The therapist should be very familiar with identifying anxiety cues and formulating highly anxiety-provoking scenes and capable of dealing with a client who might have a very negative experience with the anxiety-provoking scenes presented.

CONCLUSION

The two methods discussed in this chapter have been widely used in the reduction of fears and phobias in adults. Each of these fear reduction methods has in common the *exposure* of the client to the feared situation, event, or object. The exposure can be either imaginal or in vivo or it can be either graduated along a hierarchy or involve the immediate presentation of the most noxious aspects of the fear or phobia. No definitive statement can be made at this time regarding which of the latter exposure methods when combined is more effective than any of the other combined exposure methods for the vast array of fears and phobias that people experience, even though the outcome of some research comparing these different exposure methods has been published (see, for example, Bernstein & Kleinknecht, 1982; Biran & Wilson, 1981; Cullington, Butler, Hibbert, & Gelder, 1984; Emmelkamp, 1982; Howard, Murphy, & Clarke, 1983; Mavissakalian & Barlow, 1981; Shaw, 1979; Williams, Dooseman, & Kleifield, 1984). Thus, a major question still exists regarding the treatment of fears and phobias, namely, which fear reduction method should be used, under what conditions, and for which type of fear? This question cannot be easily answered at this time.

Without a doubt, the most heavily researched fear reduction method is systematic desensitization and its variants. It has been shown in many studies to be very effective in reducing various types of fears. The prime limitation of systematic desensitization treatment is that it is extremely time consuming to conduct, especially when the client has a large number of fears needing reduction. Flooding methods have also been found to be effective in reducing fears and phobias. A flooding approach could be used for those clients who can tolerate being exposed initially to some of the major noxious aspects of their fears or phobias, either imaginally or in real life. This, however, raises an interesting ethical question. Given that we cannot state at the present time which fear reduction method is the treatment of choice for a particular fear or phobia, and given that flooding methods expose clients initially to noxious aspects of their fears, whereas desensitization methods use a graduated exposure approach, should a client have a choice in determining which fear reduction method will be used on him or her? Again, this is not an easy question to answer.

In summary, because of the active clinical research that has been conducted over the last 2 decades in the area of fear reduction methods, we find that some very promising treatment methods have emerged. The next step should be a detailing of the conditions under which each method is effective and for which types of fears or phobias.

APPENDIX 1

FEAR SURVEY SCHEDULE

The items in this questionnaire refer to things and experiences that may cause fear or other unpleasant feelings. Write the number of each item in the column that describes how much you are disturbed by it nowadays.

	Not at All	A Little	A Fair Amount	Much	Very Much

1. Open wounds
2. Dating
3. Being alone
4. Being in a strange place
5. Loud noises
6. Dead people
7. Speaking in public
8. Crossing streets
9. People who seem insane
10. Falling
11. Automobiles
12. Being teased
13. Dentists
14. Thunder
15. Sirens
16. Failure
17. Entering a room where other people are already seated
18. High places on land
19. Looking down from high buildings
20. Worms
21. Imaginary creatures
22. Strangers
23. Receiving injections
24. Bats
25. Journeys by train
26. Journeys by bus
27. Journeys by car
28. Feeling angry
29. People in authority
30. Flying insects
31. Seeing other people injected
32. Sudden noises
33. Cockroaches
34. Crowds
35. Large open spaces
36. Cats
37. One person bullying another
38. Tough looking people
39. Birds
40. Sight of deep water
41. Being watched working
42. Dead animals
43. Weapons
44. Dirt
45. Crawling insects
46. Sight of fighting
47. Ugly people

continued

FEAR SURVEY SCHEDULE continued

	Not at All	A Little	A Fair Amount	Much	Very Much
48. Fire					
49. Sick people					
50. Dogs					
51. Being criticized					
52. Walking on dark streets alone					
53. Being in an elevator					
54. Witnessing surgical operations					
55. Angry people					
56. Mice					
57. Blood					
(a) Human					
(b) Animal					
58. Parting from friends					
59. Enclosed places					
60. Prospect of a surgical operation					
61. Feeling rejected by others					
62. Airplanes					
63. Medical odors					
64. Feeling disapproved of					
65. Harmless snakes					
66. Cemeteries					
67. Being ignored					
68. Darkness					
69. Premature heart beats (Missing a beat)					
70. Nude men (a) Nude women (b)					
71. Lightning					
72. Doctors					
73. People with deformities					
74. Making mistakes					
75. Looking foolish					
76. Losing control					
77. Fainting					
78. Becoming nauseous					
79. Spiders (harmless)					
80. Being in charge or responsible for making decisions					
81. Sight of knives or sharp objects					
82. Becoming mentally ill					
83. Being with a member of the opposite sex					
84. Taking written tests					
85. Being touched by others					
86. Feeling different from others					
87. A lull in conversation					
88. Laboratory rats					
89. Taking any type of test					
90. Public speaking (speaking in front of groups)					
91. Looking down from high places					

Note: Adapted from *The practice of behavior therapy* (2nd ed.) (pp. 283–286) by J. Wolpe, 1973, Elmsford: Pergamon Press. Copyright 1973 by Pergamon Press, Inc. Used with permission.

APPENDIX 2

REVISED WILLOUGHBY QUESTIONNAIRE FOR SELF-ADMINISTRATION

Instructions. The questions in this schedule are intended to indicate various emotional personality traits. It is not a test in any sense because there are no right and wrong answers to any of the questions. After each question you will find a row of numbers whose meaning is given below. All you have to do is to draw a ring around the number that describes you best.

0 means "No," "never," "not at all," etc.

1 means "Somewhat," "sometimes," "a little," etc.

2 means "About as often as not," "an average amount," etc.

3 means "Usually," "a good deal," "rather often," etc.

4 means "Practically always," "entirely," etc.

1. Do you get anxious if you have to speak or perform in any way in front of a group of strangers? — 0 1 2 3 4
2. Do you worry if you make a fool of yourself, or feel you have been made to look foolish? — 0 1 2 3 4
3. Are you afraid of falling when you are on a high place from which there is no real danger of falling — for example, looking down from a balcony on the tenth floor? — 0 1 2 3 4
4. Are you easily hurt by what other people do or say to you? — 0 1 2 3 4
5. Do you keep in the background on social occasions? — 0 1 2 3 4
6. Do you have changes of mood that you cannot explain? — 0 1 2 3 4
7. Do you feel uncomfortable when you meet new people? — 0 1 2 3 4
8. Do you daydream frequently, i.e. indulge in fantasies not involving concrete situations? — 0 1 2 3 4
9. Do you get discouraged easily, e.g. by failure or criticism? — 0 1 2 3 4
10. Do you say things in haste and then regret them? — 0 1 2 3 4
11. Are you ever disturbed by the mere presence of other people? — 0 1 2 3 4
12. Do you cry easily? — 0 1 2 3 4
13. Does it bother you to have people watch you work when you do it well? — 0 1 2 3 4
14. Does criticism hurt you badly? — 0 1 2 3 4
15. Do you cross the street to avoid meeting someone? — 0 1 2 3 4
16. At a reception or tea do you go out of your way to avoid meeting the important person present? — 0 1 2 3 4
17. Do you often feel just miserable? — 0 1 2 3 4
18. Do you hesitate to volunteer in a discussion or debate with a group of people whom you know more or less? — 0 1 2 3 4
19. Do you have a sense of isolation, either when alone or among people? — 0 1 2 3 4
20. Are you self-conscious before "superiors" (teachers, employers, authorities)? — 0 1 2 3 4
21. Do you lack confidence in your general ability to do things and to cope with situations? — 0 1 2 3 4
22. Are you self-conscious about your appearance even when you are well-dressed and groomed? — 0 1 2 3 4
23. Are you scared at the sight of blood, injuries, and destruction even though there is no danger to you? — 0 1 2 3 4
24. Do you feel that other people are better than you? — 0 1 2 3 4
25. Is it hard for you to make up your mind? — 0 1 2 3 4

APPENDIX 3

BERNREUTER S-S SELF-SUFFICIENCY INVENTORY

---

1. Yes No ? Would you rather work for yourself than carry out the program of a superior whom you respect?
2. Yes No ? Do you usually enjoy spending an evening alone?
3. Yes No ? Have books been more entertaining to you than companions?
4. Yes No ? Do you feel the need of wider social contacts than you have?
5. Yes No ? Are you easily discouraged when the opinions of others differ from your own?
6. Yes No ? Does admiration gratify you more than achievement?
7. Yes No ? Do you usually prefer to keep your opinions to yourself?
8. Yes No ? Do you dislike attending the movies alone?
9. Yes No ? Would you like to have a very congenial friend with whom you could plan daily activities?
10. Yes No ? Can you calm your own fears?
11. Yes No ? Do jeers humiliate you even when you know you are right?
12. Yes No ? Do you think you could become so absorbed in creative work that you would not notice the lack of intimate friends?
13. Yes No ? Are you willing to take a chance alone in a situation of doubtful outcome?
14. Yes No ? Do you find conversation more helpful in formulating your ideas than reading?
15. Yes No ? Do you like to shop alone?
16. Yes No ? Does your ambition need occasional stimulation through contacts with successful people?
17. Yes No ? Do you have difficulty in making up your mind for yourself?
18. Yes No ? Would you prefer making your own arrangements on a trip to a foreign country to going on a prearranged trip?
19. Yes No ? Are you much affected by praise, or blame, of many people?
20. Yes No ? Do you usually avoid taking advice?
21. Yes No ? Do you consider the observance of social customs and manners an essential aspect of life?
22. Yes No ? Do you want someone with you when you receive bad news?
23. Yes No ? Does it make you uncomfortable to be "different" or unconventional?
24. Yes No ? Do you prefer to make hurried decisions alone?
25. Yes No ? If you were to start out in research work, would you prefer to be an assistant in another's project rather than an independent worker on your own?
26. Yes No ? When you are low in spirits do you try to find someone to cheer you up?
27. Yes No ? Have you preferred being alone most of the time?
28. Yes No ? Do you prefer traveling with someone who will make all the necessary arrangements to the adventure of traveling alone?
29. Yes No ? Do you usually work things out rather than get someone to show you?
30. Yes No ? Do you like especially to have attention from acquaintances when you are ill?
31. Yes No ? Do you prefer to face dangerous situations alone?
32. Yes No ? Can you usually see wherein your mistakes lie without having them pointed out to you?
33. Yes No ? Do you like to make friends when you go to new places?
34. Yes No ? Can you stick to a tiresome task for long without someone prodding or encouraging you?
35. Yes No ? Do you experience periods of loneliness?

continued

BERNREUTER S-S INVENTORY continued

36.	Yes No ?		Do you like to get many views from others before making an important decision?
37.	Yes No ?		Would you dislike any work which might take you into isolation for a few years, such as forest ranging, etc.?
38.	Yes No ?		Do you prefer a play to a dance?
39.	Yes No ?		Do you usually try to take added responsibility upon yourself?
40.	Yes No ?		Do you make friends easily?
41.	Yes No ?		Can you be optimistic when others about you are greatly depressed?
42.	Yes No ?		Do you try to get your own way even if you have to fight for it?
43.	Yes No ?		Do you like to be with other people a great deal?
44.	Yes No ?		Do you get as many ideas at the time of reading as you do from a discussion of it afterwards?
45.	Yes No ?		In sports do you prefer to participate in individual competitions rather than in team games?
46.	Yes No ?		Do you usually face your troubles alone without seeking help?
47.	Yes No ?		Do you see more fun or humor in things when you are in a group than when you are alone?
48.	Yes No ?		Do you dislike finding your way about in strange places?
49.	Yes No ?		Can you work happily without praise or recognition?
50.	Yes No ?		Do you feel that marriage is essential to your happiness?
51.	Yes No ?		If all but a few of your friends threatened to break relations because of some habit they considered a vice in you, and in which you saw no harm, would you stop the habit to keep friends?
52.	Yes No ?		Do you like to have suggestions offered to you when you are working a puzzle?
53.	Yes No ?		Do you usually prefer to do your own planning alone rather than with others?
54.	Yes No ?		Do you usually find that people are more stimulating to you than anything else?
55.	Yes No ?		Do you prefer to be alone at times of emotional stress?
56.	Yes No ?		Do you like to bear responsibilities alone?
57.	Yes No ?		Can you usually understand a problem better by studying it out alone than by discussing it with others?
58.	Yes No ?		Do you find that telling others of your own personal good news is the greatest part of the enjoyment of it?
59.	Yes No ?		Do you generally rely on your judgment?
60.	Yes No ?		Do you like playing games in which you have no spectators?

Note: From *The practice of behavior therapy* (3rd ed.) (pp. 344–346) by J. Wolpe, 1982, Elmsford: Pergamon Press. Copyright 1982 by Pergamon Press, Inc. Used with permission.

REFERENCES

Altmaier, E. M., & Woodward, M. (1981). Group vicarious desensitization of test anxiety. *Journal of Counseling Psychology, 28,* 467–469.

Baker, B. L., Cohen, D. C., & Saunders, J. T. (1973). Self-directed desensitization for actrophobics. *Behaviour Research and Therapy, 11,* 79–89.

Bandura, A. (1969). *Principles of behavior modification.* New York: Holt, Rinehart & Winston.

Bandura, A. (1977). *Social learning theory.* Englewood Cliffs, NJ: Prentice-Hall.

Bandura, A., & Walters, R. H. (1963). *Social learning and personality development.* New York: Holt, Rinehart & Winston.

Bernstein, D. A., & Kleinknecht, R. A. (1982). Multiple approaches to the reduction of dental fear. *Journal of Behavior Therapy and Experimental Psychiatry*, *13*, 287–292.

Biglan, A., Villwock, C., & Wick, S. (1979). The feasibility of a computer controlled program for the treatment of test anxiety. *Journal of Behavior Therapy and Experimental Psychiatry*, *10*, 47–49.

Biran, M., & Wilson, G. T. (1981). Treatment of phobic disorders using cognitive and exposure methods: A self-efficacy analysis. *Journal of Consulting and Clinical Psychology*, *49*, 886–899.

Brady, J. P. (1966). Brevital-relaxation treatment of rigidity. *Behaviour Research and Therapy*, *4*, 71–77.

Brady, J. P. (1972). Systematic desensitization. In W. S. Agras (Ed.), *Behavior modification: Principles and clinical applications*. Boston, MA: Little, Brown.

Chambless, D. L., Foa, E. B., Groves, G. A., & Goldstein, A. J. (1982). Exposure and communication training in the treatment of agoraphobia. *Behaviour Research and Therapy*, *20*, 219–231.

Chaplin, E. W., & Levine, B. A. (1981). The effects of total exposure duration and interrupted versus continuous exposure in flooding therapy. *Behavior Therapy*, *12*, 360–368.

Cullington, A., Butler, G., Hibbert, G., & Gelder, M. (1984). Problem-solving: Not a treatment for agoraphobia. *Behavior Therapy*, *15*, 280–286.

Deffenbacher, J. L., & Kemper, C. C. (1974a). Counseling test-anxious sixth graders. *Elementary School Guidance and Counseling*, *7*, 22–29.

Deffenbacher, J. L., & Kemper, C. C. (1974b). Systematic desensitization of test anxiety in junior high students. *School Counselor*, *22*, 216–222.

Deffenbacher, J. L., & Michaels, A. C. (1981). Anxiety management training and self-control desensitization – 15 months later. *Journal of Counseling Psychology*, *28*, 459–462.

Deffenbacher, J. L., Michaels, A. C., Michaels, T., & Daley, P. C. (1980). Comparison of anxiety management training and self-control desensitization. *Journal of Counseling Psychology*, *27*, 232–239.

Emmelkamp, P. M. G. (1982). *Phobic and obsessive-compulsive disorders*. New York: Plenum.

Emmelkamp, P. M. G., & Wessels, H. (1975). Flooding in imagination vs. flooding in vivo: A comparison with agoraphobics. *Behaviour Research and Therapy*, *13*, 7–15.

Fairbank, J. A., & Keane, T. M. (1982). Flooding for combat-related stress disorders: Assessment of anxiety reduction across traumatic memories. *Behavior Therapy*, *13*, 499–510.

Friedman, D. E. (1966). A new technique for the systematic desensitization of phobic symptoms. *Behaviour Research and Therapy*, *4*, 139–140.

Goldfried, M. R. (1971). Systematic desensitization as training in self-control. *Journal of Consulting and Clinical Psychology*, *37*, 228–234.

Goldfried, M. R., & Davison, G. (1976). *Clinical behavior therapy*. New York: Holt, Rinehart & Winston.

Goldfried, M. R., & Goldfried, A. P. (1977). Importance of hierarchy content in the self-control of anxiety. *Journal of Consulting and Clinical Psychology*, *45*, 124–134.

Hogan, R. A. (1969). Implosively oriented behavior modification: Therapy considerations. *Behaviour Research and Therapy*, *1*, 177–184.

Howard, W. A., Murphy, S. M., & Clarke, J. C. (1983). The nature and treatment of fear of flying: A controlled investigation. *Behavior Therapy*, *14*, 557–567.

Hull, C. L. (1943). *Principles of behavior.* New York: Appleton-Century-Crofts.

Jacobson, E. (1938). *Progressive relaxation.* Chicago: University of Chicago Press.

Javel, A. F., & Denholtz, M. S. (1975). Audible GSR feedback and systematic desensitization: A case report. *Behavior Therapy, 6,* 251–254.

Kanfer, F. H., & Grimm, L. G. (1977). Behavioral analysis: Selecting target behaviors in the interview. *Behavior Modification, 1,* 7–28.

Kipper, D. A. (1980). In vivo desensitization of nyctophobia: Two case reports. *Psychotherapy: Theory, Research, and Practice, 17,* 24–29.

Kratochwill, T. R., & Morris, R. J. (1985). Conceptual and methodological issues in conducting research on children's fears. *School Psychology Review, 14,* 94–107.

Kratochwill, T. R., Morris, R. J., McGrogan, H. J., & Ramirez, S. Z. (in press). Fears and phobias in children and adolescents. In G. L. Adams (Ed.), *Behavior disorders: Theories and characteristics.* Englewood Cliffs, NJ: Prentice-Hall.

Krop, H., & Krause, S. (1976). The elimination of a shark phobia by self-administered systematic desensitization: A case study. *Journal of Behavior Therapy and Experimental Psychiatry, 7,* 293–294.

Levine, B., & Wolpe, J. (1980). In vivo desensitization of a severe driving phobia through radio contact. *Journal of Behavior Therapy and Experimental Psychiatry, 11,* 281–282.

Marks, I. M. (1969). *Fears and phobias.* New York: Academic Press.

Marshall, W. L., Gauthier, J., Christie, M. M., Currie, D. W., & Gordon, A. (1977). Flooding therapy effectiveness, stimulus characteristics, and the value of brief *in vivo* exposure. *Behaviour Research and Therapy, 15,* 79–87.

Mavissakalian, M., & Barlow, D. H. (Eds.) (1981). *Phobia: Psychological and pharmacological treatment.* New York: Guilford Press.

Mavissakalian, M., & Michelson, L. (1983). Self-directed *in vivo* exposure practice in behavioral and pharmacological treatments of agoraphobia. *Behavior Therapy, 14,* 506–519.

Migler, B., & Wolpe, J. (1967). Automated self-desensitization. A case report. *Behaviour Research and Therapy, 5,* 133–135.

Morganstern, K. P. (1973). Implosive therapy and flooding procedures: A critical review. *Psychological Bulletin, 79,* 318–334.

Morris, R. J. (1973). Shaping relaxation in the unrelated client. *Journal of Behavior Therapy and Experimental Psychiatry, 4,* 343–353.

Morris, R. J., & Kratochwill, T. R. (1983a). Childhood fears and phobias. In R. J. Morris & T. R. Kratochwill (Eds.), *The practice of child therapy.* Elmsford, NY: Pergamon Press.

Morris, R. J., & Kratochwill, T. R. (1983b). *Treating children's fears and phobias: A behavioral approach.* Elmsford, NY: Pergamon Press.

Morris, R. J., & Kratochwill, T. R. (1985). Behavioral treatment of children's fears and phobias: A review. *School Psychology Review, 14,* 84–93.

Morris, R. J., & Magrath, K. H. (1983). The therapeutic relationship in behavior therapy. In M. Lambert (Ed.), *The therapeutic relationship in systems of psychotherapy.* Homewood, IL: Dorsey Press.

Morris, R. J., & Suckerman, K. R. (1974a). Automated systematic desensitization: The importance of therapist warmth. *Journal of Consulting and Clinical Psychology, 42,* 244–250.

Morris, R. J., & Suckerman, K. R. (1974b). The importance of the therapeutic relationship in systematic desensitization. *Journal of Consulting and Clinical Psychology, 42,* 148.

Mowrer, O. H. (1950). *Learning theory and personality dynamics.* New York: Roland Press.

Öst, L. G. (1978a). Fading: A new technique in the treatment of phobias. *Behaviour Research and Therapy, 16,* 213–216.

Öst, L. G. (1978b). Fading vs. systematic desensitization in the treatment of snake and spider phobias. *Behaviour Research and Therapy, 16,* 379–390.

Paul, G. L. (1966). *Insight in psychotherapy.* Stanford, CA: Stanford University Press.

Pavlov, I. P. (1927). *Conditioned reflexes.* London: Oxford University Press.

Redd, W. J., Porterfield, A. L., & Andersen, B. L. (1979). *Behavior modification.* New York: Random House.

Reeves, J. L., & Maelica, W. L., (1975). Biofeedback: Assisted cue-controlled relaxation for the treatment of flight phobias. *Journal of Behavior Therapy and Experimental Psychiatry, 6,* 105–109.

Richardson, F. C., & Suinn, R. M. (1973). A comparison of traditional systematic desensitization, accelerated massed desensitization, and anxiety management training in the treatment of mathematics anxiety. *Behavior Therapy, 4,* 212–218.

Ritter, B. (1968). The group desensitization of children's snake phobias using vicarious and contact desensitization procedures. *Behaviour Research and Therapy, 6,* 1–6.

Ritter, B. (1969a). Treatment of acrophobia with contact desensitization. *Behaviour Research and Therapy, 7,* 41–45.

Ritter, B. (1969b). The use of contact desensitization, demonstration-plus-participation and demonstration-alone in the treatment of acrophobia. *Behaviour Research and Therapy, 7,* 157–164.

Rosen, G. (1976). *Don't be afraid: A program for overcoming your fears and phobias.* Englewood Cliffs, NJ: Prentice-Hall.

Rosen, G. M., Glasgow, R. E., & Barrera, M., Jr. (1976). A controlled study to assess the clinical efficacy of totally self-administered systematic desensitization. *Journal of Consulting and Clinical Psychology, 44,* 208–217.

Ryan, V., & Moses, J. (1979). Therapist warmth and status in the systematic desensitization of test anxiety. *Psychotherapy: Theory, Research, and Practice, 16,* 178-184.

Schneider, J. W. (1982). Lens-assisted *in vivo* desensitization to heights. *Journal of Behavior Therapy and Experimental Psychiatry, 13,* 333–336.

Seligman, M. E. P. (1971). Phobias and preparedness. *Behavior Therapy, 2,* 307–320.

Shaw, P. (1979). A comparison of three behavior therapies in the treatment of social phobia. *British Journal of Psychiatry, 134,* 620–623.

Sherman, A. R. (1972). Real-life exposure as a primary therapeutic factor in the desensitization treatment of fear. *Journal of Abnormal Psychology, 79,* 19–28.

Skinner, B. F. (1938). *The behavior of organisms.* New York: Appleton-Century.

Skinner, B. F. (1953). *Science and human behavior.* New York: Macmillan.

Snyder, A. L., & Deffenbacher, J. L. (1977). Comparison of relaxation as self-control and systematic desensitization in the treatment of test anxiety. *Journal of Consulting and Clinical Psychology, 45,* 1201–1203.

Stampfl, T. G. (1961). *Implosive therapy: A learning theory derived psychodynamic therapeutic technique.* Paper presented at the University of Illinois, Champaign-Urbana, IL.

Stampfl, T. G. (1970). Implosive therapy: An emphasis on covert stimulation. In D. J. Levis (Ed.), *Learning approaches to therapeutic behavior change.* Chicago: Aldine.

Stampfl, T. G., & Levis, D. J. (1967). Essentials of implosive therapy: A learning-based psychodynamic behavioral therapy. *Journal of Abnormal Psychology, 72,* 496–503.

Stampfl, T. G., & Levis, D. J. (1968). Implosive therapy: A behavioral therapy? *Behaviour Research and Therapy, 6,* 31–36.

Stern, R., & Marks, I. (1973). Brief and prolonged flooding. *Archives of General Psychiatry, 28,* 270–276.

Thomas, M. R., Rapp, M. S., & Gentles, W. M. (1979). An inexpensive automated desensitization procedure for clinical application. *Journal of Behavior Therapy and Experimental Psychiatry, 10,* 317–321.

Williams, S. L., Dooseman, G., & Kleifield, E. (1984). Comparative effectiveness of guided mastery and exposure treatments for intractable phobias. *Journal of Consulting and Clinical Psychology, 52,* 505–518.

Wilson, G. T., & Evans, I. M. (1977). The therapist-client relationship in behavior therapy. In A. S. Gurman & A. M. Razin (Eds.), *Effective psychotherapy: A handbook of research.* Elmsford, NY: Pergamon Press.

Wolpe, J. (1958). *Reciprocal inhibition therapy.* Stanford, CA: Stanford University Press.

Wolpe, J. (1962). The experimental foundations of some new psychotherapeutic methods. In A. J. Bachrach (Ed.), *Experimental foundations of clinical psychology.* New York: Basic Books.

Wolpe, J. (1969). *The practice of behavior therapy.* Elmsford, NY: Pergamon Press.

Wolpe, J. (1973). *The practice of behavior therapy* (2nd ed.). Elmsford, NY: Pergamon Press.

Wolpe, J. (1982). *The practice of behavior therapy* (3rd ed.). Elmsford, NY: Pergamon Press.

Wolpe, J., & Lazarus, A. A. (1966). *Behavior therapy techniques.* Elmsford, NY: Pergamon Press.

Wolpin, M., & Pearsall, L. (1965). Rapid deconditioning of a fear of snakes. *Behavior Research and Therapy, 3,* 107–111.

Yule, W., Sacks, B., & Hersov, L. (1974). Successful flooding treatment of a noise phobia in an 11 year old. *Journal of Behavior Therapy and Experimental Psychiatry, 5,* 209–211.

6

Aversion Methods

Jack Sandler

INTRODUCTION

The use of unpleasant or aversive stimuli to change behavior is as old as the history of mankind. In their conventional form, such "punishment" practices are typically designed to terminate or reduce undesirable behavior. An infinite number of examples are available from our daily experiences: Parents spank children for aggressive behavior, teachers require unruly students to remain after school, judges fine traffic violators, and on and on. The general principle underlying each of these examples is that such aversive experiences serve to deter the future occurrence of the problem behavior. Borrowing from this principle, similar techniques and procedures have also been reported in the clinical literature. These procedures are variously termed *aversive therapy*, *punishment procedures*, *reduction programs*, and other terms and are here grouped together under the term *aversion therapy* to designate their use in treatment settings, that is, to accomplish clinically useful objectives.

Both the popular and the clinical uses of aversive procedures to change behavior have been the subject of considerable controversy, The issues raised by the critics are quite complex, and a comprehensive analysis of their arguments is beyond the scope of the present review. Suffice it to say that aversive procedures have been questioned on ethical, theoretical, and practical grounds. On the other hand, a number of authorities have responded to these concerns by emphasizing the therapeutic value of aversive procedures (Baer, 1970; Johnston, 1972; Solomon, 1964). Essentially, the view expressed in the latter case defends the clinical use of aversive procedures on the same grounds that unpleasant and even painful events are often also associated with medical and dental treatment. In each of these cases, the decision to use aversive procedures is made on the basis of the risk-to-benefit ratio. Thus, the pain and discomfort associated with surgery is justified on the basis of the greater health benefits to be realized by the patient. Simultaneously, ethical guidelines governing the use of aversive procedures to change problem behavior have slowly emerged that also offer the behavioral practitioner a general frame of reference for determining the risk-to-benefit ratio. These guidelines can be summarized as follows.

1. Minimally intrusive and low-risk forms of intervention should always be considered before resorting to more intrusive, higher risk procedures. Thus, nonaversive procedures are generally favored over aversive procedures and (as detailed later in the chapter) aversive procedures themselves can be ordered from the least intrusive to the most intrusive.
2. The severity of the problem condition in terms of its physical and psychological impact should be taken into account. In this context, less serious problem behaviors would rarely, if ever, be treated aversively, but severe problem behaviors representing a clear threat to the individual's health and psychological welfare would be regarded as immediate targets for aversion therapy.

In actual practice, the guidelines suggest, for example, that mild nuisance behavior should be dealt with by nonaversive methods (as described in other chapters) or, at most, by mild forms of aversive procedures; whereas severe self-injurious behavior as in head banging, eye gouging, hair pulling, and so on (often observed in, but not restricted to, severely mentally retarded or emotionally disturbed individuals) would represent immediate targets for aversion therapy, especially if less intrusive techniques had already been unsuccessful. Within this framework, the decision to use aversion therapy can be made on the basis of scientific evidence rather than on the basis of preconceived biases (Baer, 1970). This is the position advocated in the present chapter. It should be noted that these guidelines represent a general framework for considering the use of aversion therapy, but individual circumstances will probably be the determining factors in any given case.

General Description

At the practical level, a description of aversive procedures appears to be relatively straightforward and uncomplicated. For the most part, as we have seen, such arrangements involve an undesirable and/or maladaptive behavior on the part of the patient or client and the presentation of an unpleasant stimulus in close time relationship with the behavior. Almost all examples of aversive procedures reflect these characteristics, whether the purpose is to terminate a commonplace problem behavior, as in the case of a parent who spanks a child for playing with matches, or whether the purpose is to produce a clinical outcome, as in the case of administering shock to the fingertips of a child molester while he is handling children's clothing.

If terminating or disrupting undesirable behavior were the only question to be considered, we could simply detail the circumstances under which such effects can be optimized and treat all problem behaviors in this fashion. Unfortunately, the use of aversive procedures is much more complex than would seem to be true on the basis of casual observation. First, as we have seen, deciding when to use aversive procedures is no simple matter, and secondly, even when this decision is relatively clear-cut, there are many additional issues that must be taken into account including the durability of the therapeutic effects, the risk of undesirable side effects, and the general impact of such treatment on overall psychosocial adjustment.

It is only relatively recently that a clearer understanding of the complexity of aversive procedures has begun to emerge, primarily as a result of laboratory studies with animals and clinical applications with actual cases. A framework for understanding these issues can be formulated by briefly reviewing the two major theories that have attempted to explain the effects of aversive stimuli on behavior. Although there are areas of overlap between the two theories, they start with different assumptions, rely on different experimental procedures, and generate different treatment practices. Most of the aversion therapy reports in the literature reflect either one or the other of these theoretical biases, although in actual practice the difference between the two is often blurred.

The first of these two theories emerged out of Pavlov's well-known research on conditioned responses in dogs. In this model, a previously neutral stimulus such as a buzzer or light is presented in close temporal contiguity with an unconditioned stimulus, that is, a stimulus that naturally elicits a reflex reaction such as a tap to the knee eliciting the patellar reflex. After a sufficient number of such pairings or trials, the previously neutral stimulus acquires the power to elicit the reflex. Thus, when an organism is exposed to an aversive stimulus, certain physiological reflexes are elicited (rapid heart rate, increased perspiration, etc.) that are typically regarded as correlates of the fear response.

Extraneous stimuli that are also present at the time acquire the power to evoke the same or a similar reaction. In this fashion, the fear response is "conditioned" to these previously neutral stimuli. Although this is by necessity an oversimplification of the conditioned fear hypothesis, the principle underlying Pavlov's work has been invoked to explain both the manner in which certain maladaptive behaviors such as phobias are acquired and the manner in which undesirable behaviors can be changed in treatment programs. For example, if an alcoholic is required to drink liquor while exposed to a painful stimulus, after a sufficient number of such "trials," the fear response elicited by the painful stimulus will become conditioned to the liquor. Subsequently, the sight, taste, and smell of liquor will elicit the physiological reactions associated with the painful stimuli, and the patient will be repelled by such substances. In fact, procedures of this type have been employed in a variety of problem conditions with varying degrees of success.

The second theory emphasizes the consequences of behavior to explain the effects of aversive stimuli on behavior (Skinner, 1953) rather than on the association between stimuli that precede a response. In this *operant* theory (see chapter 4 for a more detailed description of operant conditioning) virtually all behaviors, abnormal and normal, are considered to be heavily influenced by the consequences of the behavior. Thus, behaviors are acquired and/or maintained because they are rewarded (positive reinforcement) or because they terminate or postpone unpleasant events (negative reinforcement). Conversely, responses that are followed by unpleasant events (punishment) or by no consequences (extinction) decline in frequency. In the example of the alcoholic just noted, shock administered "contingent" on the drinking response (e.g., just as the patient reaches for the drink) will suppress the drinking rate. The effectiveness and/or durability of the suppression effect depends upon a number of variables. Some of these variables are associated with the aversive event (e.g., the intensity and the frequency of the unpleasant stimulus); some of the variables are associated with the history of the response targeted for change (e.g., duration of the response, magnitude of reinforcing events). In operant conditioning procedures, "naturally" occurring response-consequence relationships are favored over Pavlovian discrete trial procedures.

It should be emphasized that these descriptions are based largely on laboratory procedures. Applied situations can reflect a considerable departure from these examples such that attributing clinical outcomes to either one of these explanations is precluded. Thus, in actual practice, Pavlovian procedures can be inadvertently combined with operant procedures and vice versa. Consequently the reasons for any observed changes in client behavior cannot be completely determined. In the example of the alcoholic, a Pavlovian procedure might dictate pairing shock on each trial independent of the patient's behavior. In the actual arrangement, however, the shock might not be administered if the patient declines to make the relevant response (e.g., to drink the liquor), thereby introducing operant effects. Similarly, the circumstances surrounding the operant training procedure can be interpreted within the context of Pavlovian theory. Thus, punishment might be administered contingent on the drinking response in a *free operant* procedure, but the systematic programming of the relevant events could reflect the characteristics of a trial-by-trial procedure as in Pavlovian conditioning.

Although the aversion therapy literature continues to expand at a rapid rate, many additional questions remain unanswered. Thus, a great deal of the clinical work is reported in the form of uncontrolled case studies, or involves a combination of treatment procedures in uncontrolled ways, or fails to provide follow-up information. Although these problems are often the result of practical and ethical constraints, they make analysis of treatment efficacy difficult. Nevertheless, some tentative observations can be made, especially where a treatment outcome has been heavily replicated.

In reviewing this literature, an operant framework will be used, for the most part, because this theoretical position has the clearest relevance to clinical phenomena, the majority of the studies reported in the area of aversion therapy were formulated in this context, and the general methodology employed has been quite satisfactory.

Maximizing the Effects of Aversion Therapy

Once the decision to use aversion therapy has been made, it is the therapist's responsibility to apply the chosen technique in the most efficient manner possible, that is, his or her efforts should include all of the ethical and scientific safeguards that are part of any therapeutic procedure. Ideally, then, the procedure should be designed to eliminate the problem condition permanently, as quickly as possible, and without undesirable residual effects.

As indicated, in operant terms, there are two major sets of variables to take into account in this connection: those variables associated with the aversive events, and those that relate to the problem behavior. An excellent description of the former is available in Azrin and Holz's (1966) summary.

First and foremost, at least at the beginning of treatment, the aversive event should be completely coincident with the problem behavior. That is, it should be administered each time the response occurs, and it should not be administered in the absence of the response. This rationale stems from research that indicates that response reduction occurs most rapidly when the aversive stimulus follows the response whenever it occurs.

In many instances this principle can be easily applied without fear of error because of the specific characteristics of the response. A pronounced facial tic, for example, is usually easily identified (i.e., has discrete and relatively invariant characteristics) and is of brief duration. With such a problem behavior it is a relatively easy task to insure that the aversive event will be paired with each response and that it will never be presented under other circumstances.

A slightly more complex situation is encountered with head banging, which can actually encompass a variety of responses with different topographies and durations. Thus, the head banger can involve different muscle groups from time to time; he or she may move the head forward, backward, or from side to side or strike with different intensity. Furthermore, the head banging response also involves components of normal head movement that might be misinterpreted as precursors to the head banging. In actual practice, such subtle variations could result in the delivery of stimulation when unwarranted or in failure to deliver such stimulation when appropriate.

Even more difficulties are presented by the aversive treatment of alcoholism, which involves elaborate response chains that are subject to considerable variation from time to time and place to place.

One way to resolve these problems is to circumscribe the variability of the behavior, for example, in head banging, by applying a mechanical device that enables only a forward thrust of the head, thus increasing the reliability of treatment. The disadvantage of this approach is that the treatment regime becomes somewhat artificial because it differs from the natural circumstances under which the response occurs. This problem is dealt with in detail later on.

A second recommendation for maximizing treatment is to continue treatment until the problem behavior is no longer evident, thus enhancing the durability of the effect. This might appear to be so obvious as to require no elaboration. The fact of the matter, however, strongly suggests that aversion therapy is frequently ineffective precisely because the clinician has failed to continue treatment beyond some limited time range. How long therapy should be maintained can only be answered empirically; that is, it could be terminated after some reasonable length of time has elapsed (2 weeks, 6 months), during which time the response has not occurred under nonclinical circumstances. A good criterion (and one that, unfortunately, is rarely employed) is the appearance of adaptive behavior under circumstances in which the problem behavior had previously occurred.

A third recommendation is to employ a stimulus or an event that is in fact aversive (in the sense that it would ordinarily be avoided) and not merely a stimulus that is alleged to be aversive on the basis of some a priori consideration. Again, the obvious requires explanation. Many ostensibly aversive stimuli can lose their noxious qualities with repeated occurrences. In fact, under special circumstances, they can even acquire reinforcing properties, thereby producing an effect that is directly opposite to the goal of aversion therapy. For example, there are numerous instances in the clinical literature referring to individuals who continually expose themselves to normally painful stimuli. Such "masochistic" behavior has been the subject of considerable interest in clinical psychology (Sandler, 1964). In general, most socially offensive stimuli such as threats, ridicule, insults, and menacing gestures are characterized by such limitations, but even physically painful stimuli can on occasion become reinforcing. It is probably for this reason that a number of aversion therapists have advocated the use of electric shock. The advantages of shock have been described on numerous occasions and require little elaboration (Azrin & Holz, 1966). Suffice it to say that electric shock can be considered an almost universal aversive stimulus when used appropriately.

Paradoxically, shock can actually serve to minimize the criticisms associated with conventional physical punishment such as paddling, beating, or slapping.

More recently, the search for equally effective nonphysical aversive events has produced several new techniques, some of which represent extensions of traditional fines and penalties. Again, however, the efficacy of these techniques depends upon the extent to which the critical variables can be appropriately applied.

With regard to the variables governing the targeted behavior in question, several suggestions are readily available. First, the events that reinforce or maintain the behavior should be eliminated or administered only for adaptive responses. Second, in general, treatment efficacy is enhanced by dealing with responses of short history rather than those of long history (thus, the longer or more chronic the problem behavior, the more resistant to change).

In general then, aversion therapy is most effective when dealing with a problem behavior of relatively short history, when the circumstances (consequences) that maintain the behavior are only available contingent on adaptive behavior, when a genuinely aversive event is administered on each occurrence of the response (at least during the initial stages of treatment), and all of these circumstances are continued until there is good evidence that a durable effect has been achieved.

There are, of course, many other aspects of aversion therapy procedures that enhance their effectiveness, especially when they are combined with other techniques, as described in a later section. To paraphrase Johnston (1972), the successful use of aversion therapy cannot be reduced to a concise summary of principles; the basic principles must be expanded in application to a variety of procedural details, the importance of any one of which will vary with each situation. Ignoring any of these variables will not doom necessarily any particular therapeutic endeavor; rather the probability of maximal effectiveness is increased to the extent that such factors are carefully considered in the therapeutic attempt (Johnston, 1972).

PROCEDURES AND TECHNIQUES

Pavlovian Procedures

Although many examples of aversion therapy formulated within the Pavlovian model have been reported, as indicated earlier they are subject to a variety of criticisms (Feldman, 1966; Franks, 1963; Kushner & Sandler, 1966; Rachman, 1965).

We have already mentioned the major difficulty in this connection, that is, applying the Pavlovian model to problem behaviors that have pronounced operant components. In addition, Franks (1963) has argued that some Pavlovian procedures (especially those used in the treatment of alcoholism) might not be as durable as those generated by means of operant conditioning procedures. For these reasons, the current review is restricted to only several examples that have been interpreted as examples of Pavlovian conditioning.

One of the most extensive bodies of literature based on Pavlovian aversive methods has been reported by investigators concerned with alcoholism. Of these, Lemere and Voegtlin (1950) presented the most extensive and systematic series of observations. In their procedure, patients are administered emetine or apomorphine (unconditioned stimuli), which frequently elicits nausea and vomiting within 30 minutes. Shortly before vomiting occurs, the patient is instructed to drink his or her preferred alcoholic beverage. This procedure is repeated several times each day for 10 days. Occasional "booster" sessions are administered after the patient is discharged. Voegtlin (1947) reported that about half of the patients treated in this fashion remained abstinent for at least 2 years.

The Pavlovian rationale is evident in the procedure. Ostensibly, after a sufficient number of trial pairings with emetine, the taste, sight, and smell of liquor should elicit nausea and vomiting. A similar rationale is offered in the treatment of alcoholism with antabuse, a drug that causes a violent physiological reaction when mixed with alcohol. Obviously, the validity of the rationale depends upon how closely these procedures approximate the Pavlovian paradigm. In fact, it would appear that such techniques involve considerable departure from the classical conditioning procedure (Franks, 1963). Moreover, if a patient responds very quickly or very slowly (and this is hard to determine with certainty), the alcohol can be delivered too early or even after the patient experiences nausea, representing a further departure from the Pavlovian paradigm.

More recently, Wiens and Menustik (1983) summarized the effectiveness of a similar aversive Pavlovian conditioning program for 312 alcoholics who were treated during a 12-month period at the Raleigh Hills Hospital in Portland, Oregon. Of the 278 patients who completed the entire program and were available for follow up, 190 patients (63%) were still abstinent for 12 months subsequent to their discharge from the hospital. The inpatient phase of the Wiens and Menustik treatment program typically lasts 14 days, with an intervening day between each of five aversion conditioning sessions. Despite the apparent Pavlovian emphasis, it is interesting to note that the procedure is described as one in which "the approach response to alcohol is punished immediately by an aversive reaction, and the patient is expected to transfer the resulting avoidance of alcohol from the clinical situation to all other occasions when he or she has the opportunity or desire to drink" (Wiens & Menustik, 1983, p. 1090).

Aversive Pavlovian procedures have also been reported in treatment programs for sexual deviancy, drug addiction, compulsive gambling, cigarette smoking, kleptomania, and others. For example, Laws, Meyer, and Holman (1978) reported a successful outcome using an olfactory aversion procedure with an institutionalized sexually sadistic 29-year-old male. Sexual arousal (as measured by a penile plethysmograph) to sadistic stimuli was reduced to near-zero levels by the end of treatment. In virtually all of these above procedures, however, the investigators failed to control for operant conditioning effects. For this reason, such effects are reviewed in the next section.

Operant Procedures

The second major category of aversion therapy techniques generally reflects the characteristics of the operant model. The rationale here stems from the assumption that behavior that results in unpleasant consequences will decrease in frequency. Although there are important exceptions to this rule, the assumption has been well documented in both laboratory and applied circumstances.

As we have seen, there are a number of conditions that must be taken into account, perhaps the most important of which is the close temporal relationship between the response and the aversive event (the contingency). For this reason, operant conditioners frequently describe such arrangements as examples of *response produced* aversive stimulation, even when the noxious event is administered by an external agent.

This requirement can be properly implemented in the laboratory situation when the appropriate procedural controls are available. In clinical practice, however, limitations arise that frequently require some departure from the laboratory procedures. The degree of departure depends upon a variety of circumstances, the most important of which is the nature of the problem condition. For example, if therapy is designed to reduce the frequency of a writer's cramp, then the real-life circumstances in which such behavior occurs can be reasonably represented in the clinic, enabling the use of a contingency with the same or a similar response. The situation changes quite drastically, however, in the case of other problem conditions. For example, it is difficult (but not impossible) to create a reasonable approximation of the real-life circumstances related to alcoholism, and even greater problems are encountered with certain sexual deviations and aggressive behavior. Consequently, practitioners have devised a number of methods designed to circumvent this problem. For example, homosexuals are provided with problem-related stimuli such as pictures of same-sex nudes. They are then shocked in the presence of these stimuli. Or patients are asked to imagine real-life scenes and then shocked when they signal the imagined presence of the scene. Although such techniques are by now almost standard practice, it must be acknowledged that these procedures involve (perhaps, at best) problem-related events rather than the actual problem behaviors themselves. That is not to imply that such techniques are therefore ineffective; on the contrary, many of these efforts have resulted in important therapeutic effects. The reasons for the success, however, remain to be identified, because these procedures involve processes beyond those specified by a strict response-consequence model.

This section describes a number of aversive procedures that have been used in therapeutic circumstances. They vary in degree of intrusiveness from those generally considered to be relatively mild (for example, time out) to maximally intrusive procedures (shock).

Time Out from Positive Reinforcement

Over the last few years, increasing attention has been focused on an aversive technique that has been termed *time out* from positive reinforcement (TO). This procedure assumes that a decrease in frequency can be effected if the opportunity to obtain positive reinforcement is denied the individual on the basis of some target behavior, for example, separating a child from the opportunity to receive peer reinforcement contingent on show-off behavior.

There are two major TO procedures: (a) removing the reinforcer from the individual, and (b) removing the individual from the reinforcing system. In most instances, the choice is made on the basis of practical considerations. In the first case, the major changes involve the removal of reinforcement, with little change in the individual's status. A commonplace example is turning off the TV set as a result of an argument between children over a program preference. This makes the reinforcement inaccessible for a while. Or, in the case of a clinical example, turning away from a child during a rewarding activity when the child begins to engage in a temper tantrum. Thus, the adult's potential reinforcing stimuli are temporarily removed.

In the second case, the major changes usually involve the physical removal of the individual from the potentially available reinforcers. The teacher who isolates an aggressive child from the reinforcing effects of peer attention exemplifies a commonplace use of TO.

TO can be applied successfully with individuals of differing ages, personal characteristics, and problem conditions. Several examples are given in a later section of this chapter. In each case, the successful use of the technique depends upon (a) identifying the positive reinforcement, and (b) insuring that the interruption of positive reinforcement is immediately and precisely contingent on the target behavior. In other words, before considering the use of TO, the practitioner must specifically isolate the positive reinforcement and develop a procedure that insures the response-contingent nature of the arrangement. When these rules are neglected in actual practice, the effectiveness of TO is reduced. The teacher who removes an aggressive child from a class activity that the child dislikes is not fulfilling the requirements of TO. Moreover, if the child is sent to the office and becomes the target of individual attention on the part of the guidance counselor or principal, the undesirable behavior could increase rather than decrease in frequency. Similarly, the parent who sends a misbehaving child to a room in which there are a TV, games, and toys has not deprived the child of positive reinforcement and has therefore failed to maximize TO.

Some question has also been raised regarding the duration of TO. That is, once the undesirable response-reinforcement relationship has been determined, how long should the individual remain in TO? Although there is no simple rule of thumb, the duration should be established on the basis of combining practical and behavioral criteria. If a child is placed in TO, for example, in general she or he should remain there until she or he has lost several reinforcement opportunities and the undesirable behavior has stopped. In actual practice, it is probably best to limit TO to 10 to 15 minutes (although occasionally longer durations are required initially) and then to gradually reduce the duration, thus more clearly defining the response-consequence relationship.

In some cases, the difference between TO and an extinction procedure (see chapter 4 for a detailed discussion) is obscure. For example, the popular current practice of turning away from a child during a temper tantrum is frequently regarded as an attempt to extinguish such behavior, but it can also be regarded as time out, primarily depending upon whether or not the reinforcement is completely withdrawn, as in extinction, or is merely withheld, as in TO. Obviously, in actual practice, it is difficult to distinguish between such arrangements.

In any event, the TO technique makes available to the clinician concerned with reducing the frequency of undesirable behavior an important addition to the more conventional aversive methods. When used as described above, there are many clinical problems amenable to such treatment.

Response Cost

A second aversive procedure that has received increasing attention has been termed *response cost* (Weiner, 1962). These aversion arrangements are analogous to the conventional penalty technique in which an individual is fined for undesirable behavior. The major difference between the two is in terms of the systematic nature of response cost. Thus, driving illegally can occasionally result in a fine under the assumption that the loss of money will serve as a deterrent to such future behavior. The fact of the matter is, however, that these efforts frequently do not produce the desired outcome or are effective for only a limited duration.

Response cost, on the other hand, requires a clear explication of the relationship between each undesirable response and the appropriately assigned penalty. When these requirements are maximized, the effectiveness of response cost as a deterrent is maximized. Perhaps for this reason, the clinical application of response cost has usually involved a loss of rewards earned for appropriate behavior.

For example, hospitalized patients might be operating under a token economy in which several different dimensions of constructive behavior earn tokens exchangeable for tangible rewards or privileges. Additional rules could be involved in which behavioral infractions resulted in the loss of tokens. Such combined reward, response-cost arrangements are usually very effective in generating desirable changes in constructive behavior.

On the other hand, if the ratio between amount earned and amount lost results in an overall deficit, the incentive of working for reinforcement decreases and the system can break down. It is important, then, for the practitioner to continuously monitor the effects of response cost in relation to earnings and to adjust the values of each accordingly.

Feedback

Several behavior modification techniques include the monitoring of behavior for the purpose of recording the frequency of a response. The monitoring procedure can take a variety of forms, which range from a patient observing her or his own heart rate on an oscilloscope to the mere act of making a mark on a sheet of paper, as in the case of an individual recording the number of cigarettes smoked.

Under such circumstances, and independent of any formal treatment, the mere act of alerting the individual to the response occurrence can influence the rate of the response (see discussion of self-monitoring in chapter 8). Such effects have been termed *feedback* because they essentially provide information not ordinarily available to the person that a particular response has occurred. With certain problem conditions, feedback can result in a decrease in the frequency of a response. Although the causes of these effects are not well understood, the changes produced can have implications for aversion therapy.

Thus, a number of investigators have suggested procedures designed to enhance the effectiveness of feedback in reducing the frequency of a response. There are several examples in the behavior modification literature that demonstrate that self-charting has resulted in a reduction in the frequency of smoking, drinking, overeating, or arguing. In these cases, it would appear that merely bringing attention to the high incidence of the behavior in question was sufficient to effect a constructive change. The client who suddenly realizes she or he is smoking three packs per day, rather than the two initially reported, must make an adjustment to this new information.

In still other situations, the effectiveness of feedback can be enhanced if it is systematically presented in connection with an appropriate change in behavior. Several investigators, for example, have found that stuttering rates can be suppressed if each dysfluency is immediately followed by delayed auditory feedback (Siegel, 1970). In these cases, because delayed auditory feedback is regarded as aversive by most individuals, the procedure seems to be analogous to the punishment paradigm described in greater detail later in the chapter.

There are still many questions that remain to be answered about the effectiveness of feedback techniques. Their major role in the treatment would seem to be largely in terms of generating initial changes, but these changes are probably transitory unless used with other techniques.

Overcorrection

A relatively new addition to the list of operant aversive techniques has been termed *overcorrection*. Foxx and Azrin (1973) identified two components of the overcorrection procedure: (a) restitutional overcorrection, and (b) positive practice. The first component requires the individual to "overcorrect" the effects of inappropriate behavior (e.g., retrieve a book thrown in anger as well as straightening up other objects in the room). The second component requires the individual to practice the "correct" behavior that is incompatible with the inappropriate behavior. Overcorrection can be used to accomplish several objectives including the suppression of undesirable behavior and for this reason is often considered a punishment procedure.

Despite its relative recency, the overcorrection procedure has achieved rapid popularity, judging by the increasing number of such reports in the applied operant literature (Foxx & Azrin, 1973). The reasons for this enthusiasm are due, no doubt, to the advantages offered by overcorrection. For one, it represents a viable alternative to more intrusive approaches. For another, it can be applied to a wide variety of problem behaviors from the commonplace (e.g., rude table manners) to the most severe (e.g., head banging). A third advantage involves the educative function and the opportunity to reward constructive changes offered by the positive practice component. Finally, overcorrection skills are easily acquired by behavior change agents.

As we shall see in the following survey, overcorrection has been successfully used to change a wide range of problem behaviors.

Physically Aversive Stimuli

By far the bulk of the operant aversion therapy literature involves the use of stimuli that are physically unpleasant or even painful. In these techniques, the noxious event occurs in a response-produced or response-correlated arrangement. A wide variety of stimuli have been employed for this purpose, most of which would ordinarily elicit the withdrawal response (for example, water spraying, visual screening, foul odors, uncomfortable sounds, and painful stimuli such as slaps, hair pulls, and electric shock applied to an area of the limbs). Sometimes these stimuli have been paired with explicit conditioned stimuli such as shouts, reprimands, and disapproving gestures and facial expressions.

Although the search for low-risk physically aversive stimuli continues, the vast majority of these efforts have employed shock, because it complies with the requirements for maximizing the effects of aversion therapy as described earlier. In addition, the intensity and duration of shock can be adjusted in the light of treatment requirements. For these reasons, the current review is largely restricted to shock procedures.

The usual procedure in the employment of shock involves the following sequence of events before initiating treatment:

1. An analysis of the history of the problem condition clearly documenting the ineffectiveness of less severe procedures.
2. An analysis of the problem condition in terms of how often it occurs, when it occurs, where it occurs, and any other relevant circumstances.
3. Involvement of qualified professionals familiar with shock procedures and the ethical guidelines that obtain under such circumstances.

A number of shock delivery devices are commercially available for use in aversion therapy, the most practical of which are battery operated, portable instruments. The responsible practitioner should insure that the device incorporates appropriate safeguards as well as those features that will facilitate a successful outcome. Thus the device should be purchased from a reputable vendor with a complete description of its safety features. The electrode unit (typically attached to a limb) should be small, comfortable, and unobtrusive, thereby minimizing interference with normal routine.

The shock control unit should provide easily identified controls and offer a variety of shock intensities and durations, with the lowest ranges below detectable thresholds. Prior to the use of the device with a client, the clinician should self-administer the shock, starting at the lowest level and gradually increasing the intensity up to the point of discomfort.

The initial treatment session should be conducted in accord with the information obtained from the prior analysis. For example, with a child who displays a high rate of head banging, the child should be moved to a quiet, isolated room and restraints removed. An observably safe intensity level and duration (e.g., 0.05 sec) of shock is applied to the limb each time the response occurs. In addition, a high density of tangible reinforcers should be provided in the absence of the head banging response. The initial session should usually last about 30 minutes, after which the child is returned to the prevailing routine. This is repeated each day until the behavior no longer occurs during the treatment session. These effects are generally observed within three to four sessions. As aversive control over the behavior is acquired, additionally relevant circumstances are generally incorporated into the procedure for the purpose of generalizing the effects over a wider range of circumstances. In the typical case, by the fourth or fifth session, merely strapping on the electrodes is sufficient to control the behavior. Once the effect has generalized over all the relevant circumstances, the electrode routine is gradually faded so that the ultimate control over the behavior falls completely under the positive contingencies and the shock procedure can be abandoned. Occasional "booster" sessions might be required if the problem condition recurs.

Considerable research with shock, both in the laboratory and in clinical situations, has been conducted, providing good descriptions of the manner in which the effectiveness of shock can be maximized.

In order to achieve the optimal aversion therapy effect, initially the shock should be delivered at a safe, but very unpleasant intensity (rather than gradually increased), relatively briefly (0.5 sec, for example), and coincident with the onset of each target response (Azrin & Holz, 1966). Appropriate levels of shock intensity are typically described in equipment manuals provided by the manufacturer. At some later stage in treatment, a shift to a variable schedule of shock delivery (see chapter 4 on operant conditioning) might be considered in order to enhance the durability of the suppression effect.

The variety of problem conditions that have been treated via such procedures ranges across a wide behavioral spectrum, from relatively commonplace responses, such as cigarette smoking, to broad dimensions of complex pathological behaviors, such as child molesting and disturbing obsessions. A review of several clinical investigations and case studies is presented in the section entitled Practical Applications.

Combining Aversion Therapy with Other Techniques

This section is concerned with the manner in which the techniques just described can be used with additional procedures in order to maximize treatment effectiveness. Although they are usually a part of any behavior change program (and as such they are also described in other chapters), the emphasis here is upon their use in conjunction with aversion therapy.

There are two reasons for including such practices. *First*, practically speaking, as we have seen, any attempt to apply a laboratory procedure to clinical situations usually results in some departure from the use of the technique under "pure" circumstances. *Second*, there is increasing evidence that the effects of aversion therapy can be enhanced if the practitioner systematically includes other learning techniques. This is, a more rapid and longer lasting reduction of the undesirable behavior can be achieved under such circumstances than would be true if time out, response cost, and other techniques were used alone.

Including Response Alternatives

Several studies have shown that a change in target behavior can be expedited if an alternative response is available to the patient. In some cases, the therapist can explicitly encourage such "new" learning, and if this technique is combined with a procedure designed to eliminate an undesirable response, positive treatment results can be maximized. Although such procedures have been variously termed *counterconditioning*, *differential reinforcement of other behavior* (DRO), or *reinforcement of incompatible behavior*, they share the practice of concurrently manipulating more than one response dimension in a treatment program. Thus, a counterconditioning program might involve shock contingent on an undesirable response such as aggressive behavior and, at the same time, provide positive reinforcement for an adaptive alternative response, for example, cooperative behavior.

Although it can be assumed that some new response will emerge in every aversive procedure, the response alternative technique requires that the alternative response be identified prior to treatment. For this reason, we distinguish between those programs that formally and explicitly incorporate a response alternative and those procedures in which this process might have occurred but was not planned for. Obviously, the clinician interested in such techniques must acquire an in-depth understanding of general learning principles that include the full range of other techniques in addition to aversive conditioning.

The advantages of the response alternative procedure are numerous: It can be used with all of the techniques described above; it enhances the treatment process, thereby reducing the number of aversive experiences required to modify behavior; it enhances the durability of the effect; and, perhaps most important of all, it offers an adaptive alternative to the individual that might generalize outside the clinic arena. The common practice of substituting candy for cigarettes reflects some of the features of the response alternative technique.

Fading

As we have seen, constructive changes that occur in one situation do not necessarily generalize to other situations. The child who is trained to cooperate in the classroom may continue to be aggressive at home or on the playground. Such "limited" change effects are particularly characteristic of attempts to treat certain problem conditions such as alcoholism. It is not unusual, for example, for patients in a hospital treatment program to show a reduction in alcoholic behavior while in the hospital, only to break down soon after return to the environment in which the original drinking behavior occurred. The problem can be construed as an example of different reactions to different circumstances.

Obviously, then, the most effective treatment is that which accomplishes the greatest generality of change and the *fading technique* offers distinct advantages in this connection (also described in conjunction with operant methods in chapter 4).

Essentially, fading involves a gradual change in the treatment situation such that either (a) reduction in undesirable behavior is maintained in the presence of new (and preferably more "relevant") circumstances, or (b) new circumstances are introduced in order to enhance changes in behavior. Such techniques have been used informally for many years.

A growing practice in penology, for example, involves a gradual series of *discharge experiences*, in which a prisoner is first placed on a work-release program for limited duration, while readjusting to the requirements of normal life. The prisoner might also at first see his or her parole officer perhaps several times a week. If successful, he or she could be advanced to a halfway house, and the number of parole visits would be reduced. In this fashion, the transition from prison life to normal life is gradually effected, under the assumption that constructive changes in behavior are better maintained in the process.

Similarly, improving psychiatric hospital patients are first allowed several weekend passes at home, and, if no problems arise, advance to a month's "trial visit." This can subsequently be extended, depending upon the patient's adjustment outside the hospital.

The difference between these practices and a fading technique involves the greater degree of detail and rigor in the latter case. An ideal fading technique would provide for a gradual exposure to the patient's real-life physical and social stimuli, so that all of the natural events relevant to the problem behavior are ultimately reflected in the treatment situation.

The closer the fading technique approaches the ideal, the greater the generality of treatment effects. One growing practice in the modification of children's behavior involves first instructing parents in the treatment skills and then gradually increasing their share of responsibility for treatment. Similarly, in aversion therapy, parents are instructed in the use of a shock procedure to be applied in the home situation. In this fashion, the fading technique incorporates those individuals and those situations that ultimately determine the durability of any constructive changes that first occurred in the treatment setting.

Schedules

Another technique that in some respects resembles fading involves changes in the schedule of the relevant events. It was mentioned earlier that treatment is initially most effective if the aversive event is applied to each instance of the undesirable response, because this results in the most rapid reduction of behavior. Greater durability of the desired reduction, however, can probably be achieved if the schedule of aversive events is unpredictable, that is, every third or fourth response on an average. The frequency of aversive stimulation can be further gradually reduced if desired, although at some stage the practitioner will obviously be dealing with events that occur only infrequently. Thus, a cigarette smoker might initially receive 10 shocks distributed over 30 cigarettes per day, but, as the smoking rate declined to perhaps 3 or 4 cigarettes per day, adjustments in the shock schedule would also be required.

Use of Significant Others

Where possible and appropriate, individuals who bear an important relationship to the patient can be incorporated into the treatment program. The rationale here again is similar to that underlying the use of fading, that is, enhancing the durability of the change. Some instruction is obviously necessary, including specifically designating a time-out area, a response-cost system and even the use of response-contingent shock. We shall see in the next section where this has been attempted and, depending upon the degree of instruction and preparation, the results have been most impressive. For example, self-injurious behavior in disturbed children is very effectively controlled when parents are instructed to use the treatment technique in the home environment.

Self-Control

Finally, and perhaps most important, considerable attention has increasingly been focused on the use of techniques designed to make the patient responsible for change (see chapter 8 on self-management). The rationale here scarcely requires any explanation, although this is a development representing, in many respects, a radical departure from some conventional treatment practices that covertly, if not overtly, place the major responsibility for change on the therapist.

Techniques of this sort were first initiated in conjunction with problem behaviors that were difficult to analyze publicly such as cigarette smoking, drinking, obsessions, and compulsions. More recently, self-control techniques have been employed with a wider variety of problem behaviors, including aggression, family arguments, and temper tantrums. Essentially, the procedure requires instructing the patient in a variety of techniques designed to alter one or more of the following: (a) typical undesirable reactions to particular occasions, (b) the sequence of responses constituting the aggregate response (breaking up the chain), and (c) the consequences of the undesirable behavior.

Thus, an analysis of the relevant components of an undesirable behavior might reveal that it occurs under certain identifiable circumstances; that it is comprised of several discrete responses; and that it produces certain reinforcing events. Cigarette smoking, for example, usually occurs at regular intervals and in typical stimulus situations. This would provide a picture of the frequency of the smoking behavior. The chain for one smoker might be characterized by removing the package from the shirt pocket, withdrawing a cigarette with the right hand, tapping it on a hard surface, inserting it in the mouth, lighting it, taking several deep drags, keeping it dangling from the lips, alternating between deep drags and knocking off the ashes, and smoking it down rapidly to a short butt before extinguishing the cigarette. This would provide a picture of the topography of the response. Finally, an attempt might be made to analyze the response-reinforcement relationship.

With this information, the patient can be instructed in self-control techniques that enhance the aversion therapy effects. For example, the patient might be instructed to avoid some of the circumstances in which smoking occurs with high frequency, or he or she might be instructed to change some of the components of the chain, such as holding the cigarette in the left hand, placing the cigarette in an ashtray between drags, smoking less rapidly, and so forth. Finally, the patient might also be instructed in the self-administration of aversive events, which could range anywhere from accumulating all the butts and inhaling the stale aroma and placing a picture of a diseased lung in the pack, to self-imposing fines, denying privileges, and delivering shock.

Kanfer and Grimm (1980) offered a learning theory analysis of the issues related to self-control processes. Among other things, they suggested the manner in which seven relevant phases can be employed to enhance clinical objectives. They pointed out the necessity for increasing client motivation, for example, through contractual negotiation of treatment objectives between the client and the therapist; for monitoring progress; and for programming generalization of the effects. There are probably additional procedures that should be considered along with those. In practice, there is sufficient overlap between the techniques such that the distinctions between them are often blurred. For the most part, the practitioner need not be concerned with the theoretical "purity" of the technique. Again, what is probably more important is that as many as possible should be employed in a systematic fashion, thereby optimizing the chances of a successful outcome.

SUMMARY

In brief, the information advanced in the preceding sections suggests several important steps that the therapist must take in any program using aversion methods. First, the therapist should provide evidence that the event to be employed is indeed aversive, that it be applied on a response-contingent basis, and that it be maintained long enough to suppress the behavior for as long as possible.

Furthermore, durable changes can be insured if an alternative (adaptive) response is available; if ordinary, real-life circumstances are represented in the treatment setting; and if self-control techniques are integrated into the treatment program.

PRACTICAL APPLICATIONS

Until now, the discussion has focused on general principles and guidelines. Representative applications from the operant aversion therapy literature will be described in the present section.

An arbitrary distinction is offered between (a) those problem conditions that are relatively "circumscribed" and easily defined and, (b) problem behaviors that are more complex in their response dimensions and less accessible to a "public" analysis. The term *compulsion* has been traditionally applied to many of the problem behaviors in the latter category, under the assumption that there is an internal drive that compels an individual to engage in such behavior despite the maladaptive consequences. The behavior modification movement has called this assumption into question.

In any event, there is some reason to believe that, at least with our present state of knowledge, greater success has been realized with problems in the first category. This conclusion must be qualified by the fact that aversion therapy is still a relatively new approach, and by the fact that successful treatment is determined not only by the complexity of the problem condition but also by the precision and rigor of the treatment technique. Where possible, examples contrasting each major aversion therapy technique within a problem condition are described.

Discrete or Easily Defined Problem Conditions

Self-Injurious Behavior
One of the problem behaviors frequently encountered in extreme forms of pathology is various forms of self-injurious behavior (SIB). Although many other problem conditions such as smoking, alcoholism, and gambling reflect similar characteristics, the SIB label is usually reserved for those behaviors that, if left unchecked, would shortly threaten the biological wel-

fare of the individual. Thus, they require immediate intervention including physical restraint. Unfortunately, most of these interventions are temporary and ineffective.

In the clinical literature, the term SIB usually implies the involvement of the voluntary motor-response system as manifested by head banging, self-mutilation, pulling one's hair out, and so on. The present review also includes examples possibly involving involuntary (or autonomic) processes.

Head Banging, Self-Biting, and Similar Problem Behaviors

By far the most extensive application of aversion therapy with discrete problem conditions has involved the use of painful shock, contingent on head banging and self-mutilation in children. There are now a sufficient number of observations that confirm the effectiveness of such procedures, especially when compared with nonaversive techniques, in terms of rapid suppression of the behavior. Furthermore, when additional measures are incorporated into the procedure (for example, treatment administered by parents of SIB children in the home), the suppressive effects generalize, enabling the emergence of other more productive responses.

Perhaps the most impressive evidence of the efficacy of aversion therapy in such cases is provided by Lovaas and Simmons (1969). In this study, 3 severely mentally retarded children displaying extreme forms of SIB (thereby requiring long periods of time in physical restraints) were exposed to response-contingent shock. In each case, SIB was effectively and completely suppressed in the treatment setting after only a few shocks. The same treatment was also successfully applied by other individuals in other situations in order to maximize the generality of the effects.

Similar results have been reported by a number of other investigators. Tate and Baroff (1966) administered response shock to a blind 9-year-old boy who employed a wide assortment of SIB (head banging, face slapping, self-kicking, etc.). During 24 minutes prior to the treatment condition, 120 instances of SIB were recorded. For the next 90 minutes, a half-second shock was administered for each SIB, and only five SIB responses occurred. The child was also praised for non-SIB. As the treatment progressed, the child was moved from restraints for increasing time intervals (fading). The rate of SIB continued to decline, and no such responses were observed for 20 consecutive days. Interestingly enough, an increase in prosocial behavior emerged during this time.

Risley (1968) attempted to eliminate dangerous climbing behavior in a 6-year-old mentally retarded girl who was constantly injuring herself through numerous falls. After several other techniques proved to be ineffective (DRO and TO), the use of response shock combined with verbal reprimands completely eliminated the climbing behavior in the treatment setting. After instruction, the child's mother employed the same technique in the home setting, with the result that climbing behavior declined from about 20 responses to 2 responses per day. Once again, these changes were accompanied by a concurrent increase in constructive behavior in terms of attending and responding to social stimuli.

These efforts have been followed by a host of similar procedures with highly successful outcomes. Corte, Wolf, and Locke (1971) almost immediately and completely reduced SIB (including self-slapping, eye poking, hair pulling, and scratching the skin) in four mentally retarded adolescents with response contingent shock, after an extinction procudure and a DRO procedure proved ineffective. Again, the treatment had to be applied outside the first treatment setting to enhance generalization.

A similar procedure was employed by Scholander (1972) for reducing a response in which a 14-year-old male continuously placed his hands around his neck. This behavior (which evidently emerged out of an epileptic condition) occurred with such high frequency that it was interfering with many normal ordinary activities such as eating and dressing. The shock procedure resulted in a change from about 25 responses per day to 0 in 4½ weeks, after which the shock apparatus was removed. No further responses occurred during a 9-month follow-up.

Merbaum (1973) reduced SIB (beating face with hands) in a psychotic boy from an average of about 221 responses per 10-minute period to virtually 0 in a 2-hour treatment period. Similar results were obtained by the child's teacher and mother, who were also instructed in providing positive reinforcement for non-SIB (differential reinforcement for other behavior or DRO). These effects were maintained over a 1-year follow-up period and were accompanied by improvement in a variety of behavioral dimensions.

As suggested earlier, the search for effective but less intrusive procedures continues. One such possibility has been advanced by Lutzker (1978). In this case, self-injurious behavior (head and face slapping with hands and fists) in a 20-year-old mentally retarded client was treated by "facial screening" for 30-minute periods over 30 consecutive days. After each instance of SIB, the trainer would hold a large, loosely tied bib over the client's face and in back of the head until the SIB had stopped for 3 seconds. The problem behavior decreased to 0 levels within five sessions after the facial screening procedure was implemented.

Rapoff, Altman, and Christopherson (1980) examined the effectiveness of several alternative procedures including DRO, overcorrection, lemon juice, and aromatic ammonia on severe, high-rate self-injurious behavior (self-poking of the facial area) in a profoundly mentally retarded, nonambulatory 5-year-old boy. "Lemon juice therapy" involved squirting 5 cc of lemon juice into the child's mouth contingent on the poking response; the ammonia procedure involved placing an ammonia capsule under the child's nose for 3 seconds immediately following the target response. Of the various procedures attempted, the ammonia treatment proved to be the most effective, reducing the SIB response to zero rates in the treatment setting and at home.

An excellent example of combining several treatment procedures in a systematic approach was provided by Wesolowski and Zawlocki (1982). The subjects in this study were two 6-year-old identical twin girls diagnosed as totally blind and profoundly mentally retarded. Both subjects frequently pushed their fingers up into their eye sockets, causing tissue damage around their eyes. The first attempt to reduce this behavior involved time out from auditory stimuli. This was administered by placing soundproof earmuffs over the subjects' ears for 2 minutes following each eye-gouging response. This technique reduced the response rate to 0 levels within 12 sessions, but the effect was not maintained. This was then followed by five training sessions combining both auditory time out and response interruption, that is, holding the subjects' hands down in their laps for 2 seconds. Again, responding quickly decelerated, and the effect was maintained for about 2 months. The third and last procedure involved auditory time out plus a reward of 20 cc of apple juice contingent upon a 2-minute interval in which the SIB response did not occur (DRO procedure). Response rates declined to 0 within 2 weeks after this procedure was instituted. Follow-up observations 1 year later revealed that eye gouging was no longer a matter of concern for either subject.

Another problem condition that is related to SIB and is also frequently observed in mentally retarded and emotionally disturbed individuals is excessive self-stimulation and stereotypic behavior. These terms encompass a wide variety of repetitive, idiosyncratic activities that can involve such responses as hand movements (e.g., finger flipping), lip "strumming," continuous rubbing of a part of the body, nonfunctional vocalizations, and jumping or hopping. Such high-frequency inappropriate responses sometimes "blend" with self-injurious behavior and are obviously incompatible with adaptive behaviors. Consequently they represent a prominent target for behavior change procedures. Here again, aversive approaches have proved to be particularly effective. McGonigle, Duncan, Cordisco, and Barrett (1982), for example, used a visual screening procedure to suppress a variety of stereotypic responses in four moderately retarded children. After analysis of the frequency of the responses, the visual screening procedure was implemented. This involved placing one hand over the child's eyes for a minimum of 5 seconds, contingent on the inappropriate behavior. Treatment was continued until self-stimulatory behavior was either substantially reduced or eliminated from each child's repertoire. In all four cases, follow-up data (at least 6 months after treatment) revealed no evidence of stereotyped behavior in any of the four children.

Epstein, Doke, Sajwaj, Sorrell, and Kimmer (1974) used an overcorrection procedure to treat self-stimulatory behavior in 2 children who revealed a wide range of dysfunctional behaviors. After earlier efforts to control the self-stimulatory behavior by means of time out or instruction had failed, a series of overcorrection procedures was administered during daily 30-minute training sessions. When a target response was emitted, the child was instructed or physically guided to engage in a 2.5-minute series of physical exercises. The results revealed a drastic reduction to near 0 rates of stereotyped behavior in both children within five sessions of the treatment program. Furthermore, one of the children showed a spontaneous and concurrent increase in appropriate play behavior that was correlated with the treatment procedure.

This survey represents only a small sample of the wide variety of aversion therapy applications with SIB. Suffice it to say that, in this area, aversion therapy has been highly successful not only in rapidly reducing the frequency of undesirable behavior but also in establishing long-term constructive changes. We have also seen that some of the reservations regarding the use of shock procedures are not supported by the evidence. On the contrary, it would appear that, once control over the SIB is established, the path is clear for the development of other more adaptive responses.

Self-Induced Vomiting

Perhaps as a result of the growing confidence in aversion therapy with SIB, several clinicians have attempted to use similar procedures with other serious problem conditions that have been traditionally resistant to treatment.

One potentially dangerous but fortunately rare problem behavior involves self-induced vomiting. This is a condition characterized by the absence of physiological determinants as well as resistance to drug therapy, thus suggesting the influence of psychological factors. In extreme cases such conditions can result in a severe loss of weight, retarded development, and even loss of life. For these reasons, immediate intervention is required, and three studies report the successful cure of excessive nonorganically determined vomiting behavior.

Luckey, Watson, and Musick (1968) employed a response contingent shock with a chronic 6-year-old mentally retarded vomiter, after standard medical treatment had failed to produce any constructive changes. The child was observed throughout the day, and 1-second uncomfortable shock was administered whenever vomiting or its precursors occurred. By the 5th day, the treatment was reduced to 2 hours at each meal. Further reductions were introduced at later stages as the frequency of the behavior decreased.

Except for a minor reversal several days after the treatment was initiated, no evidence of vomiting was observed on the last 9 days of the treatment. Again, this marked reduction in maladaptive behavior was accompanied by improvement in a variety of prosocial and self-care dimensions.

Lang and Melamed (1969) employed a similar procedure with a 9-month-old chronic vomiter whose life was threatened by continuation of the behavior. In this case, the vomiting act was preceded by sucking behavior and accompanied by vigorous throat movements. The aversion therapy procedure involved a 1-second shock administered as soon as vomiting occurred and continued until the response was terminated. The vomiting response was substantially reduced after two brief sessions, and, by the third session, only one or two responses occurred. These changes were accompanied by a substantial weight gain and increased alertness and responsiveness to the environment. After approximately 3 weeks, the child was discharged from the hospital and was continuing to do well 1 year after treatment.

Kohlenberg (1970) reported similar success in treating excessive vomiting in a 21-year-old severely mentally retarded female. In this case, shock was administered contingent on the presence of stomach tensions that served as the precursor to the vomiting response.

Finally, Marholin, Luiselli, Robinson, and Lott (1980) showed that a taste aversion (lemon juice, Tabasco sauce, etc.) procedure could successfully reduce ruminative vomiting in two profoundly retarded youngsters. In both of these cases the problem behavior was of a long-standing and life-threatening nature. Complete cessation of the vomiting responses occurred 40 days after the treatment program was initiated. Follow-ups conducted 1½ to 2½ months later revealed no evidence of relapse.

Another problem behavior that is related to ruminative vomiting sometimes occurs in certain eating disorders, particularly anorexia nervosa and bulimia. Anorexia nervosa is a condition most often observed as severe reduction in food intake, sometimes serious enough to warrant hospitalization. Bulimia is characterized by the *binge-purge syndrome*, typically superimposed over an anorexic pattern. Here, reduction in food intake alternates with periodic excessive eating episodes (binge eating) followed by self-induced vomiting (purging). This form of vomiting is clearly different from the ruminative vomiting behavior described earlier inasmuch as the latter typically occurs after each meal and does not reflect the more "voluntary" quality of the purging response. A number of behavioral treatments emphasizing the reacquisition of more normal dietary patterns (see chapter 4) have been successful with eating disorders. In such cases, the vomiting component of bulimia is treated "indirectly" rather than as a specific change objective, as in aversion therapy. Thus, as the more normal eating pattern emerges, the desire to engage in the binge-purge sequence spontaneously declines, although, conceivably, this component of the bulimia could also be treated adjunctively by aversive procedures.

Seizures

As in the case of vomiting, seizures are generally considered to be the result of some physiological dysfunction. However, some investigators have argued that such conditions might also be induced or influenced by external factors. In any event, if left unchecked, the frequency and severity of seizures can constitute a serious threat to the individual, and a report by Wright (1973) suggested that at least some forms of seizure-related events can be suppressed by aversion therapy, resulting in a decrease in seizure activity.

Wright worked with a 5-year-old mentally retarded boy who induced his own seizures by moving his hand back and forth before his eyes and blinking while looking at a light source. Observation and EEG recordings confirmed the correlation between these events and seizure episodes. They further revealed the occurrence of several hundred self-induced seizures per day.

Consequently, shock was delivered contingent on each "hand–eye" response in five 1-hour sessions extending over a 3-day period. All responses were suppressed by the third session. However, 5 months later the child was again inducing as many as 400 seizures per day by blinking. Shock was then administered contingent on the blinking response, resulting in a substantial reduction of seizures by the fourth session. A 7-month follow-up revealed a 90% decrease from the pretreatment frequency of hand-eye responses.

Enuresis

Several examples of aversion therapy have also been employed for the purpose of reducing nocturnal bed wetting (enuresis). Tough, Hawkins, McArthur, and Ravenswaay (1971) found that a cold bath contingent on bed wetting, plus praise for bladder control (DRO), completely eliminated the enuresis problem in a mentally retarded 8-year-old boy but was less effective for his younger brother.

Atthowe (1972) found that a combination of aversive events could reduce enuresis in even severely disabled elderly patients. Chronically enuretic patients (who otherwise participated in a token reward program) were moved to a generally aversive environment: crowded ward, lights turned on for 10 minutes four times each night, and patients escorted to the bathroom for 10 minutes. These procedures were maintained for 2 months, after which continence was rewarded (DRO), whereas incontinence resulted in loss of reward (response cost). By the 8th month of the program all of the patients were continent, including some who were severely neurologically disabled, an effect that was maintained almost 4 years after the study was initiated.

By far the largest number of successful attempts to treat enuresis have used a variety of the *Mowrer alert system*, in which bed wetting results in a signal that arouses the individual. After a number of such experiences, most children begin to wake up prior to wetting the bed and are then encouraged to urinate appropriately.

When the apparatus was first described by Mowrer (Mowrer & Mowrer,

1938), he invoked a Pavlovian model to explain the effectiveness of the technique. Thus, the distended bladder served as the conditioned stimulus (CS), which was paired with the unconditioned stimulus (UCS, the alerting stimulus). By means of Pavlovian conditioning, the CS alone would result in arousal. More recently, Jones (1960) has suggested that the technique relies upon an operant aversion therapy model.

Sneezing

Kushner (1970) has shown that excessive sneezing can also be controlled by means of aversion therapy. This case involved a 17-year-old girl who had been vigorously and rapidly sneezing (approximately one response per 40 seconds) for 6 months with no relief. Extensive medical examinations had failed to isolate the cause of this condition, and a variety of treatment techniques had not produced any substantial improvement.

During treatment, a microphone was placed around her neck that was connected to a voice key and a shock source. Each sneeze activated the voice key and automatically delivered a shock to the fingertips (response-contingent shock). Following an adjustment of the shock procedure, in which the electrodes were taped to her arm, thereby insuring better contact, the patient stopped sneezing after 4 hours of treatment. There was no evidence of a relapse during a 13-month follow-up period.

Functional ("Hysterical") Paralysis

In an unpublished study conducted at the Veteran's Administration Hospital in Miami, Florida, a modified aversion therapy program was employed for the purpose of treating a functional paralysis. The patient was a middle-aged male whose complaint was a loss of feeling and impaired locomotion in the lower half of the left leg, causing him to be confined to a wheelchair. Extensive neurological examination ruled out the possibility of any organic dysfunction. The aversion therapy procedure was conducted as follows: Electrodes were placed on the patient's leg and on two fingertips. He was then informed that a mild shock would be administered to his leg, followed in 5 seconds by a stronger shock to his fingers. If he felt the leg shock he was to press a switch that he held in his hand. No further instructions were provided, although each switch response enabled the patient to avoid the shock to the fingers.

This procedure was presented for three trials in the first session, during which time no avoidance responses occurred. The second session was interrupted after the first trial because the patient became nauseated. In the third session, the patient emitted two switch-press responses and verbally indicated that feeling had returned to his leg, whereupon the electrodes were removed and the patient walked back to the ward. He was discharged several days later without complication. Although the results in this case were successful, the procedure employed represents a departure from the typical response-contingent paradigm and seems to be more similar to the *anticipatory avoidance* procedure described more fully in the next section.

Writer's Cramp

Two studies have appeared that report attempts to treat various forms of writer's cramp by means of aversion therapy. This form of motor impairment is usually characterized by muscular contractions or spasms and prevents the individual from continuing tasks that require the use of hand muscles such as writing and typing. The condition is usually attributed to fatigue or emotional problems. In any event, sufferers of writer's cramp are frequently capable of performing other tasks even though such tasks involve the operation of the same or similar hand muscles.

Liversedge and Sylvester (1955) identified 39 cases of writer's cramp as a function of either hand tremors or muscular spasms; each of these conditions was separately treated with a different apparatus. The tremor patients were required to insert a metal stylus into a series of progressively smaller holes in metal chassis. Deviations (striking the side of the hole) resulted in shock. The contraction response was treated by delivering shock to the patient whenever excessive thumb pressure (as measured by a gauge) was applied to a pen. Normal writing was regained after 3 to 6 weeks of treatment in 24 of the patients. These improvements were maintained for up to 4½ years.

Kushner and Sandler (1966) used a similar procedure for treating a hand contraction response in a 42-year-old male teletype operator. The patient was required to operate a typewriter in the clinic, and pretreatment observation revealed a high frequency of rapid spasmodic contractions of the right hand, resulting in errors at the keyboard. The patient was then seen for twelve 30-minute sessions, with shock delivered contingent on each contraction response. The electrodes were removed during the next three sessions, and no contractions were observed. Shortly thereafter, however, the contraction response recurred, and his performance remained erratic and gradually declined through the 46th session. Consequently, the number of weekly sessions was increased. No contractions were observed by the 61st session, and the patient was then switched to a teletype machine. Almost immediately, he was functioning effectively, even when the electrodes were removed.

Stuttering

The behavior modification literature reveals a long and continued interest in the use of aversive techniques for improving the speech of stutterers. Numerous response-contingent events have reduced the frequency of stuttering, including delayed auditory feedback, response-cost arrangements, time-out arrangements, and electric shock. Because only a brief overview of these efforts is provided in the present account, the interested reader is referred to Siegel's comprehensive review (Siegel, 1970). In each of the studies described, stuttering is defined in terms of the frequency of speech dysfluencies (repetitions, interjections, prolongations, interruptions, etc.).

Adams and Popelka (1971) employed a time-out technique with eight young adult stutterers. Essentially, the procedure imposed a nonspeaking period contingent on each dysfluency, under the assumption that the opportunity to speak was positively reinforcing. Although the dysfluency rate decreased during the TO condition, it seems apparent that the results are subject to alternative explanations.

Kazdin (1973) compared the relative effectiveness of response-cost, loud response-contingent sound, and feedback on the suppression of dysfluent speech in 40 mentally retarded patients. In the response-cost procedure, tokens that could be exchanged for tangible rewards were removed upon the occurrence of dysfluencies. In the second condition, a loud noise was presented contingent on each dysfluency, and, in the feedback condition, each dysfluency was marked by a light being turned on. The results indicated that both response-cost and aversive stimulation procedures reduced dysfluencies, but response cost was more effective in every respect including generalization of treatment effects during a posttest.

Delayed auditory feedback (DAF) has also been studied in this connection because such events seem to reflect aversive properties. Typically, the DAF procedure involves a brief delay of the dysfluency and is then transmitted through the client's earphones during a speech task. This requires the individual to reduce her or his verbal rate while simultaneously speaking and listening for dysfluencies. Goldiamond (1956) has shown that such treatment produces fluent and rapid speech. Soderberg (1968) obtained similar results with 11 student stutterers, and, in addition, observed that these effects generalized beyond the experimental condition.

Finally, Daly and Frick (1970) employed a shock procedure with 36 adult male stutterers. Stuttering expectations and actual stuttering responses were treated independently in some patients and simultaneously in others. The results indicated that shocking stuttering expectancies did not reduce the frequency of stuttering responses, but the other conditions did produce a constructive change. Furthermore, these effects were maintained during a 20-minute posttest period.

Complex Problem Conditions

General Compulsions

As noted, there is by now an extensive literature describing attempts to deal with chronic, long-standing, compulsive-type problem conditions via aversion therapy. Perhaps it is natural for behavior therapists to turn in this direction, because most conventional treatment efforts in this area have not been very successful. The literature is replete with examples of treated alcoholics who have fallen off the wagon, dieters who eat more after treatment than before, cigarette smokers who quit during treatment only to smoke again at higher rates after discharge, and so on.

One of the problems encountered with some of these conditions (especially the first of the following three) is that they are directly promoted and reinforced in certain (sometimes many) circumstances. Drinking and smoking are for the most part socially acceptable and, in fact, abstinence can even result in social disapproval. Eating, of course, is a biological necessity, and the rewards are built in to the response. It is only when they occur at excessive frequency or under inappropriate circumstances that they represent problem behaviors. Under these circumstances, such conditions are considered a breakdown in discrimination. The current review is not an attempt to survey the entire range of activity, but rather a sampling of representative efforts.

Alcoholism

The history of the aversive treatment of alcoholism surprisingly stretches back to the Roman era. It is only within recent years, however, that these techniques have achieved an advanced level of sophistication. Starting in the early and middle 1960s, behavior therapists began to employ aversive controls under carefully planned conditions. As indicated, many of the early studies clearly reflected a Pavlovian methodology, but the more recent investigations are more congruent with operant procedures. Furthermore, they are characterized by attempts to find alternatives to shock, and, in some cases, the objectives are to establish controlled (moderate, socially appropriate) drinking rather than complete abstinence. A study by Blake (1965) is perhaps representative of the earlier aversion therapy efforts involving operant processes. In this procedure, electric shock was presented at the same time the patient complied with instructions to sip his drink. The shock was increased until the patient spat out the drink, thus terminating the shock (escape behavior). In addition, the shock was presented only 50% of the time in a random manner. When this treatment was combined with relaxation training, Blake found that approximately 50% of the 37 patients in the program remained abstinent 1 year after follow-up.

In a similar procedure, Vogler, Lunde, Johnson, and Martin (1970) served liquor to alcoholic patients in a simulated bar arrangement. Each drinking response was accompanied by a shock, which was maintained until the patient spat out the drink. Although, again, it is difficult to isolate the punishment effects (the shock for drinking) from the escape effects (the cessation of shock contingent on spitting the drink out), these investigators did include several control conditions and also provided for "booster" treatments after discharge. The results indicated that abstinence was engendered by the treatment.

The Vogler technique, in which treatment was conducted in a naturalistic setting, represents an important development and is evidently being used with increasing frequency. Wards are converted so that they reflect many of the characteristics of settings in which the drinking response actually occurs. Obviously, the effects produced under these conditions stand a better chance of generalizing to the patient's real-life situation than would seem to be true when more artificial circumstances are used.

More recently, Cannon, Baker, and Wehl (1981) reported the results of an aversion procedure that involved either emetic aversion or shock aversion embedded in a broad-spectrum approach to treatment. The subjects were male chronic alcoholics who were already participating in a multifaceted program that consisted of psychotherapy, vocational rehabilitation, alcohol education, and other elements. Their findings suggested that the taste-aversion approach (emetic procedure) was more effective than the shock aversion procedure, although neither of the approaches produced significant changes 1 year after treatment was terminated.

Another, more clearly operant, approach has been reported by Davidson (1973). Actual alcohol-related responses are assessed by an automated device that dispenses 2 cc of preferred liquor per 30 responses in a half-hour period. The patient is given the opportunity to drink the liquor at each delivery interval. Once his or her response rate stabilizes, the patient receives a shock as he or she actually picks up the drink. Shock intensities are maintained until the effects at a given intensity (whether an increase or decrease in response rates) can be reliably demonstrated, and then a new and higher shock intensity is employed until the patient's response rate is completely suppressed. Once this criterion is achieved, the patient is allowed to respond to liquor in the absence of shock (the electrodes are removed). Following these observations, the patient is discharged and requested to make follow-up visits, during which time measurement is continued. Over 80% of the patients declined to respond for alcohol in the follow-up visits, and information from the patients and other sources suggested a substantial reduction in drinking behavior in over 65% of the patients for at least 1 year after discharge. One major limitation in this procedure involves the relatively high level of shock required to achieve response suppression.

Cigarette Smoking

Almost from the beginning, in the 1960s, therapists have revealed a strong interest in the use of aversive methods for cigarette smoking. By now, the number of suggested techniques that incorporate some form of aversive control probably runs into the thousands. Unfortunately, this burgeoning development has not been accompanied by a comparable effort in providing evidence to support the efficacy of the various techniques. Probably everyone knows someone who has tried to stop smoking, even through various aversive means, only to have failed. Unfortunately, without a proper scientific analysis, it is impossible to assess the effectiveness of any of these techniques. In a recent issue of a major psychological journal devoted entirely to the topic of behavioral approaches to smoking, a review of a variety of treatment efforts (including aversive methods) found that at least 75% of the individuals treated had started to smoke again after treatment was terminated (Hunt & Matarazzo, 1973). With this concern over poor long-term effects in mind, let us consider several aversion therapy procedures that have been used in this area.

In an early study, Gendreau and Dodwell (1968) applied an "increasing shock-escape response" technique to reduce the frequency of cigarette smoking. Patients received shock as soon as they complied with instructions to light up a cigarette. Shock intensity was gradually increased until the patient extinguished the cigarette. Differences in smoking rates between treated and nontreated smokers were observed both at the end of treatment and 2 years later.

By the late 1960s, a whole series of studies was reported that involved techniques and equipment designed to enhance the effects of shock aversion therapy with smokers. Perhaps the most sophisticated of these involves a portable shock apparatus that automatically administers shock at some point during the cigarette smoking period. The assumption that seems to underlie such efforts is that if the patient complies with the instructions he or she will receive response shock contingent on each smoking response, and in every smoking situation. This will result in a satisfactory treatment outcome. Although the assumption is a reasonable one, appropriate controls have not been exercised, and the assumption remains to be verified. The limitation of these procedures is that they rely completely upon the cooperation and reliability of the individual patient.

In one of the best controlled studies in the area of cigarette smoking, Dericco, Brigham, and Garlington (1977) assessed the effectiveness of three aversive treatment programs — satiation, cognitive control, and response-contingent shock. The subjects were 24 volunteers varying in age, socioeconomic background, and smoking rates. In the satiation procedure, subjects were instructed to smoke continuously for 30 minutes. In the cognitive control procedure, the subjects reclined in a lounger and heard two recorded messages, one of which associated pleasant images with continuous smoking. The subjects were also instructed to imagine the pleasant scene before smoking and the unpleasant scene after smoking. In the contingent shock procedure, 25 painful shocks were administered to subjects' forearms at various (unpredictable) times throughout the smoking sequence. The subjects were contacted 6 months after the treatment was terminated in order to assess the long-term effects of the three procedures over the other two procedures. The results clearly demonstrated the superiority of the shock procedure over the other two procedures in producing long-term effects. Though the bewildering assortment of aversive treatment programs that have been applied to cigarette smoking demonstrates only limited success, the Dericco et al. study does suggest that if a response shock procedure is employed that involves frequent, intense, and extended shock, success rates increase and relapse rates are reduced.

The Dericco et al. study represents the more recent focus in this area, that is, the development of aversive procedures that not only result in immediate reduction in cigarette smoking but that also produce long-term abstinence. One promising approach has been termed the *rapid smoking/ blown smoky air* procedure (Lichtenstein & Rodrigues, 1977). This procedure combines two aversive conditions: (a) continuous, rapid smoking concentrated over a short time period until the subject can no longer tolerate lighting up another cigarette; while (b) simultaneously, and for the same time period, the subject is exposed to a high density of cigarette smoke directed at the face. Lichtenstein and Rodrigues reported a 34% abstinence rate for subjects 2 to 6 years after they had undergone the treatment procedure.

Lando and McGovern (1982) have suggested that abstinence rates can be further enhanced by combining such aversive approaches with several long-term, broad-spectrum forms of intervention including contracts, booster sessions, and group support. Indeed, their results reveal better than 40% abstinence rates for 12 to 36 months following treatment termination.

These and other developments, especially in the self-control literature, offer a cautious note of optimism for dealing with one of our most resistant problem behaviors.

Overeating

As with cigarette smoking, prematurely applied aversive treatment methods are now widely used for the treatment of obesity, resulting in the emergence of questionable practices and undocumented claims of effectiveness. Again, because of the lack of rigorous studies, only several examples from the aversion therapy literature are presented.

Perhaps the earliest example of a response-contingent shock procedure with two overweight women is described by Meyer and Crisp (1964). Temptation food (food for which the patient had most craving as distinguished from food on a prescribed diet) was displayed for increasing periods of time, and the patients received shock for approach responses. The shock contingency was gradually faded while weight changes were constantly monitored. Any increase in weight resulted in a return to the treatment regime. Although the results for one patient were highly satisfactory (a weight reduction of about 75 lb during 6 months, which was maintained almost two years after discharge), no durable constructive change was observed in the second patient.

Although this procedure appears to have been adapted by a substantial number of behavior therapists, an alternative approach is offered by other investigators employing physically nonpainful aversive events. Ferster, Nurnberger, and Levitt (1962) described a procedure that involved a variety of techniques including emphasizing the ultimate aversive consequences of overeating. Obese women met in groups and discussed the expected outcome of their problem behavior (putting on weight, undesirable appearance, etc.). In addition they were required to monitor their own food intake and weight changes. All of the women reported weight losses, although these effects were not maintained for any great length of time.

As is true in the treatment of cigarette smoking, popularized versions of aversion therapy for overeating have found expression in numerous commercial weight control programs. In some of these cases, aversive stimuli such as foul odors and even shock have been administered contingent on the excessive eating response. A number of authorities, however, have criticized such approaches because of their poor long-term effects (Brightwell & Sloan, 1977).

More promising approaches involving a combination of treatment procedures, however, might produce longer lasting effects. Rodriguez and Sandler (1981), for example, used a variation of the response-cost technique to enhance gradual and consistent reductions in weight. In this case volunteer subjects were required to deposit 10 valuable items, which were only returned to them if they met an individually designed eating standard. Gradual change objectives of specific eating patterns were formulated on a week-by-week basis, and, if the subject failed to meet the agreed-upon objective, the valuable for that week was donated to an undesired organization. All of the subjects in the treatment group showed a gradual and systematic weight loss during the 10-week treatment program that continued over a 6-month follow-up period. Thus, it appeared that the changes in eating patterns induced by the treatment program continued to be used by the subjects even in the absence of formal treatment procedures.

Other Compulsive Conditions

Other investigators have reported the successful treatment of gambling (Barker & Miller, 1968), shoplifting (Kellam, 1969), and idiosyncratic rituals. Barrett, Staub, and Sisson (1983), for example, used visual screening to suppress two ritualistic behaviors in a developmentally disabled 4½-year-old boy. Both of these responses involved heavy preoccupation with shoes, which dominated his daily routine and interfered with the acquisition of adaptive skills. The visual screening procedure used was essentially similar to that of McGonigle et al. (1982) described earlier. Each time the response occurred, the therapist verbalized the inappropriate behavior and placed one hand over the child's eyes for a minimum of 30 seconds while holdling the back of the child's head with the other hand. The procedure was first implemented during free-play activities and later in a classroom setting. The results revealed an almost immediate decrease in the ritualistic behavior in the treatment settings, which generalized and was maintained to the home setting for 12 months after formal treatment was discontinued.

Matson, Coleman, Dilorenzo, and Vucelik (1981) have also reported the successful reduction of stealing behavior in five emotionally disturbed children through the use of overcorrection. Although the characteristic of the target behavior in this study might not satisfy the clinical definition of *kleptomania* (compulsive and habitual stealing), the procedures used might also be useful even in such extreme cases. In the present study, the stealing behavior was part of a general pattern of inappropriate behavior. The children in the study were inpatients in a psychiatric facility. Each child resided in an individual room, and a daily inventory of his possessions was made. This enabled the staff to determine the frequency of stolen items. Restitution overcorrection was administered each time a stolen item was discovered. This consisted of returning the stolen item, apologizing, and being assigned cumulative cleanup work time. The cleanup activity was cumulative, that is, two stolen items resulted in 10 minutes of punishment, four items in 20 minutes, and so on. Although the children differed considerably in the frequency of pretreatment stealing behavior (e.g., from 4 stolen items per day to 40 items per day), dramatic reductions occurred in each case within 5 days of the start of the overcorrection procedure. Two- and 4-month follow-up inquiries revealed 0 instances of the problem behavior in the home.

"Covert" Problem Conditions
Another interesting development that has emerged over the last several years involves the use of aversion therapy in the treatment of covert problem conditions. In such cases, the patient's verbal complaint is usually regarded as the external concomitant of disturbing thoughts frequently involving sexual or aggressive ideations. Despite this commonly accepted assumption, the following review suggests that such conditions are also amenable to aversion therapy.

Kushner and Sandler (1966) used a shock procedure for treating suicidal thoughts in a 48-year-old male. These obsessions were characterized by persistent, daily ruminations focusing upon six different suicidal images. The patient was instructed to imagine a particular scene and received shock upon a signal that the image was clear. Fifteen to 20 such trials were presented in each session, and, after the 12th session, the patient reported that only one image was still present. Treatment was temporarily discontinued after three more sessions because of a death in the family but reinstated after his return. (No suicidal ruminations occurred during this time). Treatment was terminated after five more sessions and a total of 350 trials. A 3-month follow-up revealed no recurrence of the former problem.

Bucher and Fabricatore (1970) employed a self-shock procedure in an attempt to reduce the frequency of hallucinations in a 47-year-old hospitalized patient diagnosed as a paranoid schizophrenic. The hallucinations were described as frequent, obscene, and critical voices that occurred from four to seven times per day and lasted for as long as 20 minutes.

The patient was supplied with a portable shock device and instructed to administer shock to himself at the onset of the hallucinations. This resulted in an apparent immediate and virtually complete cessation of hallucinatory episodes during 20 days, after which the shock device was abruptly removed, and the patient was unfortunately discharged without his consent. He was returned to the hospital 2 weeks later, the voices apparently having "returned."

Haynes and Geddy (1973) showed that hallucinations could also be suppressed by means of a time-out procedure. The patient was a 45-year-old hospitalized female diagnosed as schizophrenic. She showed a high incidence of loud and incomprehensible verbal behavior that was considered to be evidence of hallucinations. During treatment, each hallucinatory episode resulted in a staff member informing the patient that she had to go to the TO room because she was talking to herself, then leading the patient to the TO room, closing the door, and opening the door 10 minutes later. Two treatment periods were separated by a nontreatment interval, to observe the effects of discontinuing treatment.

The results indicated that the hallucinatory behavior decreased by about one-half during the two TO procedures. Even more pronounced changes were produced in a second patient displaying similar problems.

Reisinger (1972) showed that depression-related behavior could be treated by a physically nonaversive treatment procedure. The patient in this case was a 20-year-old institutionalized female diagnosed as anxiety-depressive. Her behavior was characterized by a high frequency of crying without any apparent provocation and little or no positive emotional behavior. The treatment consisted of presenting tokens (exchangeable for tangible rewards) contingent on smiling and removing tokens contingent on crying. Thus, the procedure involved a DRO plus response-cost arrangement. Two treatment periods were interspersed with a reversal condition in which the contingencies were withdrawn. Appropriate changes in both response systems accompanied the various conditions. Finally, the tokens were faded and ultimately replaced by social reinforcement (praise, compliments, etc.), in order to maintain the positive changes under more natural conditions.

Sexual Deviation

An extensive variety of aversion therapy techniques has been employed for the purpose of modifying deviant sexual behavior. The work in this area has been particularly singled out for criticisms as described in the introduction to this chapter. Once again, many of these criticisms do not appear to be warranted in the sense that a large number of previously unhappy individuals have achieved a more satisfactory level of sexual adjustment as a consequence of such treatment. Nevertheless, the concern for better controlled observations is genuine, and one can only hope that this will be resolved by future research.

As was true in the case of alcoholism, many of the earlier aversive procedures were formulated in the context of the Pavlovian model, although it shortly became apparent that operant processes (frequently uncontrolled) intruded into the procedures. The major value of this earlier work is more of a heuristic and historic nature than of a contribution of hard knowledge to theory and practice. Moreover, the initiative displayed by these investigators in attacking complex problems via previously suspect methods, thereby challenging many prevailing myths, should not pass unmentioned.

One of the first attempts to apply an operant aversion therapy procedure with sexual deviations is reported by Blakemore, Thorpe, Barker, Conway, and Lavin (1963). Prior to this study, most efforts used nausea-producing drugs to produce a conditioned aversion in the presence of stimuli related to the deviant practices.

The particular problem condition treated in the Blakemore study was a long-standing transvestism. A variety of such activities, which usually led to sexual gratification, was reported by the patient. Marital and legal circumstances served as the impetus for his seeking assistance.

The treatment was conducted in a private room of a hospital, which housed a full-length mirror and an electric grid floor. The patient's "favorite outfit" of female clothing was placed on the chair.

The procedure involved a series of trials in which the patient was instructed to start dressing in the female clothes. At some point during a trial, he received a signal to start undressing. The signal was either a buzzer or a shock to the feet. These were randomly presented and occurred at varying time intervals while all the female clothes were being removed. Following a 1-minute rest, the procedure was repeated for a total of five trials in each treatment session. A total of 400 trials was administered over 6 treatment days. Because no transvestite behavior was reported 6 months after treatment, the procedure was evidently successful.

It is difficult to classify the Blakemore procedure because it involves mixed components of different paradigms. It seems clear that a response contingency was involved, because shock occurred in connection with at least some transvestite responses and the patient could escape shock by undressing. In any event, this study represented a transition procedure from earlier aversion therapy efforts with sexual deviations, and within the next several years a host of similar efforts was reported.

Thorpe, Schmidt, Brown, and Castell (1964) applied an *aversion relief* procedure to a variety of sexual problems including homosexuality (in individuals who desired to change) and transvestism. This technique relies upon the "relief" experienced by an individual who has escaped a painful event. Furthermore, if an aversive stimulus, such as shock, is removed in the presence of another stimulus, the latter stimulus could acquire positive properties in the process. In the Thorpe study a series of words related to problem behavior was presented, followed by shock. At the end of the series, an opposite and "normal" stimulus (e.g., female breasts) was presented that was not accompanied by shock and therefore produced "relief." Although the procedure is a complicated one, the constructive changes in the patient's sexual behavior could be at least partially attributed to the use of response-contingent shock.

During the 1960s, several studies employing aversion therapy exclusively with homosexuals (who desired to change their sexual preferences) were also reported. Again, although the procedures were complicated and therefore make analysis difficult, the results ranged from moderately to highly successful. Perhaps the most extensive of these efforts was reported by Feldman and MacCulloch (1965) and MacCulloch, Birtles, and Feldman (1971). Their procedure, termed *anticipatory avoidance*, involved response-contingent shock, negative reinforcement (avoidance of shock), fading, and probably DRO. In any event, anywhere from 50% to 70% of the patients treated showed complete cessation of homosexual behavior and an increase in heterosexual behavior during therapy. Moreover, these effects were maintained for as long as 24 months.

Additional reports have also suggested that fetishism (Kushner, 1965), exhibitionism (Kushner & Sandler, 1966), and voyeurism (Bancroft, Jones, & Pullan, 1966) can all be reduced or eliminated via the "shock-contingent-on-fantasy" procedure.

A more clearly operant procedure was reported in the treatment of pedophilia (i.e., child molesting) that was so serious that the patient was being considered for brain surgery (Bancroft et al., 1966). The procedure attempted to re-create the natural conditions in which the pedophilia-related behaviors occurred. Pictures of young girls were presented to the patient, and, when a penile reaction occurred (as measured by the penile plethysmograph), a painful shock was administered to the arm. These were continued until there was a reduction in the response. Each trial lasted 10 minutes, with no shock administered in the absence of a criterion response. Six to eight trials were administered each day over a period of 8 weeks for a total of 200 shock trials. In addition, on every fourth trial, the shock apparatus was disconnected, and the patient saw photographs of adult women while being encouraged to engage in normal sexual fantasies.

Although the investigators did not consider their results to be a complete therapeutic success, there was a marked reduction in pedophilia-related activites and an increase in normal heterosexual behavior.

A more successful outcome using a similar procedure for a client with a similar problem condition has been recently reported by Josiassen, Fantuzzo, and Rosen (1980). In this case, the patient was a 37-year-old single male with a long history of pedophiliac activities. Significant reductions in arousal to deviant stimuli in the treatment setting generalized to the patient's natural environment. Training in appropriate heterosexual skills further facilitated the treatment outcome. By the 18th week of treatment, the patient reported virtually no instances of pedophiliac arousal.

Perhaps the most convincing evidence for the efficacy of aversion therapy with child molesters was recently provided by Quinsey, Chaplin, and Carrington (1980). Eighteen inpatient residents with well-defined child molester histories served as the subjects in this clinical study. Treatment involved 10 sessions of biofeedback plus an aversion therapy component in which sexual arousal to inappropriate stimuli (slides of children) was accompanied by shock. Almost all the subjects showed considerable improvement in terms of their prior inappropriate sexual age preferences. The durability of these effects was also impressive. Thirty child molesters, previously treated in the same manner, were followed for an average of 29 months. Only six of these subjects subsequent to treatment committed child-molesting offenses.

These studies represent the continued refinement of aversion therapy procedures with sexual deviations. Thus, the mechanisms that could mediate treatment effects are becoming more clearly identified. Recently, for example, McConaghy, Armstrong, and Blaszczynski (1981) used aversive procedures with 20 adult males who had requested therapy to reduce compulsive homosexual urges. After a 1-year follow-up, about half of their subjects reported a definite reduction in homosexual feelings and behavior, and approximately 25% of the group reported complete cessation of homosexual behavior. Their findings suggested that aversion therapy in such cases does not reorient homosexual preferences, but rather enables better self-control over various aspects of homosexual behavior that the individual had previously considered to be beyond control.

Generalized Asocial Behaviors

The last problem condition to be considered represents a category that encompasses a wide variety of socially deviant acts, from mild forms of nuisance and asocial behaviors to dangerous acts of aggression directed at objects and other people. The literature in this area is quite extensive and only a brief overview is presented here.

There are by now a whole series of studies indicating the effectiveness of time out for reducing a wide assortment of aggressive, asocial, negativistic behaviors. In addition, these studies have been conducted with a wide variety of people of various ages and sexes in a diversity of institutional settings. Bostow and Bailey (1969), for example, reduced severe disruptive and aggressive behaviors (loud abusive vocalizations, attacks on others) in two mentally retarded female adults by making brief TO contingent on such responses. White, Nielsen, and Johnson (1972) extended these observations to 20 mentally retarded children. Ramp, Ulrich, and Dulany (1971) reduced out-of-seat behaviors and inappropriate talking in a classroom situation, and Wahler (1969) demonstrated that similar techniques could be employed in the home environment through parental instruction. Tyler and Brown (1967) found that aggressive asocial behavior (throwing objects, physical assault, etc.) in 15 adolescent males could be similarly treated.

Aggressive behavior has also been effectively reduced by means of response cost. Winkler (1970), for example, suppressed episodes of violence and loud noise in chronic psychiatric patients by removing tokens contingent on such responses. Kazdin (1972) provided a review of the relevant literature, in which he described the variety of problem behaviors successfully treated by response cost (smoking, overeating, stuttering, psychotic talk); the durability of such procedures in terms of long-range effects; and several aspects of response-cost procedures that could enhance their efficacy.

Finally, response-contingent shock has also been employed, especially when the problem behaviors are highly dangerous. In this fashion, Bucher and King (1971) suppressed the rate of highly destructive acts in an 11-year-old psychotic boy in the treatment setting and at home when the treatment was continued by the child's parent. Royer, Flynn, and Osadca (1971) also used a shock procedure to reduce the frequency of fire setting in a severely regressed disorganized psychiatric patient. In this case, shock correlated with arson-related words had no effect on the patient's actual behavior. Subsequently, the patient was required to rehearse a series of fire-setting activities, with shock administered on a response-contingent basis. This procedure resulted in a marked reduction of the problem behavior and a complete absence of such acts during a 4-year follow-up assessment.

SUMMARY

During the last 10 years, considerable progress has been made in the development of effective aversively based procedures for changing maladaptive behavior in terms of expanding the range of problem behaviors treated, and of enhancing the durability of the effects beyond simply reducing target behaviors during intervention. Perhaps most important, several well-controlled, large studies have been reported that provide good support for the efficacy of such approaches. A number of studies have systematically combined aversive procedures with other forms of intervention, thereby enhancing treatment effectiveness. The search for minimally intrusive techniques is also reflected in the recent literature. Finally, further refinement of ethical and practical guidelines continues to be a focus of attention.

As a consequence of these developments, aversion therapy is rapidly achieving the status of respectability in the total range of services to be considered by professionals concerned with behavior change objectives. Moreover, many of the earlier criticisms that have been raised regarding the use of such procedures have not been confirmed. That is not to say, however, that all of the concerns and questions have been resolved. On the contrary, future work might be directed at comparing the relative effectiveness of different aversive procedures, at relating treatment outcome measures and relapse with specific patient characteristics, and at expanding the variety of problem behaviors that are amenable to aversion therapy. Perhaps answers to these questions will be forthcoming in the next decade.

REFERENCES

Adams, M. R., & Popelka, G. (1971). The influence of "time out" on stutterers and their dysfluency. *Behavior Therapy, 2*, 334–339.

Atthowe, J. M., Jr. (1972). Controlling nocturnal enuresis in severely disabled and chronic patients. *Behavior Therapy, 3*, 232–239.

Azrin, N. H., & Holz, W. C. (1966). Punishment. In W. K. Honig (Ed.), *Operant behavior: Areas of research and application.* New York: Appleton-Century-Crofts.

Baer, D. M. (1970). A case for the selective reinforcement of punishment. In C. Neuringer & J. L. Michael (Eds.), *Behavior modification in clinical psychology.* New York: Appleton-Century-Crofts.

Bancroft, J. H., Jr., Jones, H. G., & Pullan, B. R. (1966). A simple transducer for measuring penile erection with comments on its use in the treatment of sexual disorders. *Behaviour Research and Therapy, 4*, 239–241.

Barker, J. C., & Miller, M. E. (1968). Aversion therapy for compulsive gambling. *Journal of Nervous and Mental Disorders*, *146*, 285-302.

Barrett, R. P., Staub, R. W., & Sisson, L. A. (1983). Treatment of compulsive rituals with visual screening: A case study with long-term follow-up. *Journal of Behavior Therapy and Experimental Psychiatry*, *14*, 55-59.

Blake, B. G. (1965). The application of behavior therapy to the treatment of alcoholism. *Behaviour Research and Therapy*, *3*, 75-85.

Blakemore, C. B., Thorpe, J. G., Barker, J. C., Conway, C. G., & Lavin, N. I. (1963). The application of faradic aversion conditioning in a case of transvestism. *Behaviour Research and Therapy*, *1*, 29-34.

Bostow, D. E., & Bailey, J. B. (1969). Modification of severe disruptive and aggressive behavior using brief time-out and reinforcement procedures. *Journal of Applied Behavior Analysis*, *2*, 31-38.

Brightwell, L. R., & Sloan, L. L. (1977). Long-term results of behavior therapy for obesity. *Behavior Therapy*, *8*, 899-905.

Bucher, B., & Fabricatore, J. (1970). Use of patient-administered shock to suppress hallucinations. *Behavior Therapy*, *1*, 382-385.

Bucher, B., & King, L. W. (1971). Generalization of punishment effects in the deviant behavior of a psychotic child. *Behavior Therapy*, *2*, 68-77.

Cannon, D. S., Baker, T. B., & Wehl, C. K. (1981). Emetic and electric shock alcohol aversion therapy: Six and twelve month follow-up. *Journal of Consulting and Clinical Psychology*, *49*, 360-368.

Corte, H. E., Wolf, M. M., & Locke, B. J. (1971). A comparison of procedures for eliminating self-injurious behavior of retarded adolescents. *Journal of Applied Behavior Analysis*, *4*, 201-215.

Daly, D. A., & Frick, J. V. (1970). The effects of punishing stuttering expectations and stuttering utterances: A comparative study. *Behavior Therapy*, *1*, 228-239.

Davidson, R. S. (1973). Alcoholism: Experimental analyses of etiology and modification, Personal communication.

Dericco, D. A., Brigham, T. A., & Garlington, W. K. (1977). Development and evaluation of treatment paradigms for the suppression of smoking behavior. *Journal of Applied Behavior Analysis*, *10*, 173-181.

Epstein, L. H., Doke, L. A., Sajwaj, T. E., Sorrell, S., & Rimmer, B. (1974). Generality and side effects of overcorrection. *Journal of Applied Behavior Analysis*, *7*, 385-390.

Feldman, M. P. (1966). Aversion therapy for sexual deviation: A critical review. *Psychological Bulletin*, *65*, 65-79.

Feldman, M. P., & MacCulloch, M. J. (1965). The application of anticipatory avoidance learning to the treatment of homosexuality. I. Theory, technique and preliminary results. *Behavior Research and Therapy*, *2*, 165-183.

Ferster, C. B., Nurnberger, J. L., & Levitt, E. B. (1962). The control of eating. *Journal of Mathetics*, *1*, 87-109.

Foxx, R. M., & Azrin, N. H. (1973). The elimination of autistic self-stimulatory behavior by overcorrection. *Journal of Applied Behavior Analysis*, *6*, 1-14.

Franks, C. M. (1963). Behavior therapy: The principles of conditioning and the treatment of the alcoholic. *Quarterly Journal of Studies on Alcohol*, *24*, 511-529.

Gendreau, P. E., & Dodwell, P. C. (1968). An aversive treatment for addicted cigarette smokers: Preliminary report. *Canadian Psychologist*, *9*, 28-34.

Goldiamond, I. (1965). Stuttering and fluency as manipulative operant response classes. In L. Drasner & L. P. Ullman (Eds.), *Research in behavior modification*. New York: Holt, Rinehart & Winston.

Haynes, S. M., & Geddy, P. (1973). Suppression of psychotic hallucinations through time-out. *Behavior Therapy, 4*, 123-127.

Hunt, W. A., & Matarazzo, J. D. (1973). Three years later: Recent developments in the experimental modification of smoking behavior. *Journal of Abnormal Psychology, 81*, 107-114.

Johnston, J. M. (1972). Punishment of human behavior. *American Psychologist, 27*, 1033-1054.

Jones, H. G. (1960). The behavioral treatment of enuresis nocturna. In H. J. Eysenck (Ed.), *Behavior therapy and the neuroses.* Oxford: Pergamon Press.

Josiassen, R. C., Fantuzzo, J., & Rosen, A. C. (1980). Treatment of pedophilia using multistage aversion therapy and social skills training. *Journal of Behavior Therapy and Experimental Psychiatry, 11*, 55-61.

Kanfer, F. H., & Grimm, L. G. (1980). Managing clinical change: A process model of therapy. *Behavior Modification, 4*, 419-444.

Kazdin, A. E. (1972). Response cost: The removal of conditioned reinforcement for therapeutic change. *Behavior Therapy, 3*, 533-546.

Kazdin, A. E. (1973). The effect of response cost and aversive stimulation in suppressing punished and non-punished speech dysfluencies. *Behavior Therapy, 4*, 73-82.

Kellam, A. P. (1969). Shoplifting treated by aversion to a film. *Behaviour Research and Therapy, 7*, 125-127.

Kohlenberg, R. J. (1970). The punishment of persistent vomiting: A case study. *Journal of Applied Behavior Analysis, 3*, 241-245.

Kushner, M. (1965). The reduction of a long-standing fetish by means of aversive conditioning. In L. Ullmann & L. Krasner (Eds.), *Case studies in behavior modification.* New York: Holt, Rinehart & Winston.

Kushner, M. (1970) Faradic aversive controls in clinical practice. In C. Neuringer & J. L. Michael (Eds.), *Behavior modification in clinical psychology.* New York: Appleton-Century-Crofts.

Kushner, M., & Sandler, J. (1966). Aversion therapy and the concept of punishment. *Behaviour Research and Therapy, 4*, 179-186.

Lando, H. A., & McGovern, P. G. (1982). Three year data on a behavioral treatment for smoking: A follow-up note. *Addictive Behaviors, 7*, 177-181.

Lang, P. J., & Melamed, P. G. (1969). Case report: Avoidance conditioning therapy of an infant with chronic ruminative vomiting. *Journal of Abnormal Psychology, 74*, 1-8.

Laws, D. R., Meyer, J., & Holmen, M. L. (1978). Reduction of sadistic arousal by olfactory aversion: A case study. *Behaviour Research and Therapy, 16*, 281-285.

Lebow, M. D., Gelfand, S., & Dobson, W. R. (1970). Aversive conditioning of a phenothiazine-induced respiratory stridor. *Behavior Therapy, 1*, 222-227.

Lemere, F., & Voegtlin, W. L. (1950). An evaluation of aversion treatment of alcoholism. *Quarterly Journal of Studies on Alcohol, 11*, 199-204.

Lichtenstein, E., & Rodriguez, M-R. P. (1977). Long-term effects of rapid smoking treatment for dependent smokers. *Addictive Behaviors, 2*, 109-112.

Liversedge, L. A., and Sylvester, J. D. (1955). Conditioning techniques in the treatment of writer's cramp. *Lancet, 2*, 1147-1149.

Lovaas, O. I., & Simmons, J. Q. (1969), Manipulation of self-destruction in three retarded children. *Journal of Applied Behavior Analysis, 2*, 143-157.

Luckey, R. E., Watson, C. M., & Musick, J. K. (1968). Aversive conditioning as a means of inhibiting vomiting and rumination. *American Journal of Mental Deficiency, 73*, 139-142.

Lutzker, J. L. (1978), Reducing self-injurious behavior by facial screening. *American Journal of Mental Deficiency, 82*, 510-513.

MacCulloch, M. J., Birtles, C. J., & Feldman, M. P. (1971), Anticipatory avoidance learning for the treatment of homosexuality: Recent developments and an automated aversive therapy system. *Behavior Therapy, 2*, 151-169.

Marholin, II, D., Luiselli, J. K., Robinson, M., & Lott, I. T. (1980). Response contingent taste aversion in treating chronic ruminative vomiting of institutionalized profoundly retarded children. *Journal of Mental Deficiency Research, 24*, 47-56.

Matson, J. L., Coleman, D., Dilorenzo, T. M., & Vucelik, I. (1981). Eliminating stealing in developmentally disabled children. *Child Behavior Therapy, 3*, 57-66.

McConaghy, N., Armstrong, M. S., & Blaszczynski, A. (1981). Controlled comparison of aversive therapy and covert sensitization in compulsive homosexuality. *Behaviour Research and Therapy, 19*, 425-434.

McGonigle, J. J., Duncan, D., Cordisco, L., & Barrett, R. P. (1982). Visual screening: An alternative method for reducing stereotypic behaviors. *Journal of Applied Behavior Analysis, 15*, 461-467.

Merbaum, M. (1973). The modification of self-destructive behavior by a mother-therapist using aversive stimulation. *Behavior Therapy, 4*, 442-447.

Meyer, V., & Crisp, A. (1964). Aversion therapy in two cases of obesity. *Behaviour Research and Therapy, 2*, 143-147.

Mowrer, O. H., & Mowrer, W. M. (1938). Enuresis. A method for its study and treatment. *American Journal of Orthopsychiatry, 8*, 436-459.

Quinsey, V. L., Chaplin, T. C., & Carrigon, W. F. (1980). Biofeedback and signaled punishment in the modification of inappropriate sexual age preferences. *Behavior Therapy, 11*, 567-576.

Rachman, S. (1965). Aversion therapy: Chemical or electrical? *Behaviour Research and Therapy, 2*, 289-300.

Ramp, E., Ulrich, R., & Dulaney, S. (1971). Delayed timeout as a procedure for reducing disruptive classroom behavior: A case study. *Journal of Applied Behavior Analysis, 4*, 235-239.

Rapoff, M. A., Altman, K., & Christopherson, E. R. (1980). Suppression of self-injurious behavior: Determining the least restrictive alternative. *Journal of Mental Deficiency Research, 24*, 37-46.

Reisinger, J. J. (1972). The treatment of "anxiety-depression" via positive reinforcement and response cost. *Journal of Applied Behavior Analysis, 5*, 125-130.

Risley, T. R. (1968). The effects and side effects of punishing the autistic behavior of a deviant child. *Journal of Applied Behavior Analysis, 1*, 21-34.

Rodriguez, L., & Sandler, J. (1981). The treatment of adult obesity through direct manipulation of specific eating behaviors. *Journal of Behavior Therapy and Experimental Psychiatry, 12*, 159-162.

Royer, F. L., Flynn, W. F., & Osadca, B. S. (1971). Case history: Aversion therapy for fire-setting by a deteriorated schizophrenic. *Behavior Therapy, 3*, 229-232.

Sandler, J. (1964). Masochism: An empirical analysis. *Psychological Bulletin, 62*, 197-204.

Scholander, T. (1972). Treatment of an unusual case of compulsive behavior by aversive stimulation. *Behavior Therapy, 3*, 290-293.

Siegel, G. M. (1970). Punishment, stuttering, and disfluency. *Journal of Speech and Hearing Research, 13*, 677-714.

Skinner, B. F. (1953). *Science and human behavior*. New York: Macmillan.

Soderberg, G. A. (1968). Delayed auditory feedback and stuttering. *Journal of Speech and Hearing Disorders, 33*, 260-267.

Solomon, R. L. (1964). Punishment. *American Psychologist, 19*, 239-253.

Tate, B. G., & Baroff, G. S. (1966). Aversive control of self-injurious behavior in a psychotic boy. *Behavior Therapy, 4*, 281-287.

Thorpe, J. G., Schmidt, E., Brown, P. T., & Castell, D. (1964). Aversion-relief therapy: A new method for general application. *Behaviour Research and Therapy, 2*, 71-82.

Tough, J. H., Hawkins, R. P., McArthur, M. M., & Ravenswaay, S. V. (1971). Modification of neurotic behavior by punishment: A new use for an old device. *Behavior Therapy, 2*, 567-574.

Tyler, V. O., Jr., & Brown, G. D. (1967). The use of swift, brief isolation as a group control device for institutionalized delinquents. *Behaviour Research and Therapy, 5*, 1-9.

Voegtlin, W. L. (1947). Conditioned reflex therapy of chronic alcoholism. Ten years' experience with the method. *Rocky Mountain Medical Journal, 44*, 807-812.

Vogler, R. E., Lunde, S. E., Johnson, G. R., & Martin, P. L. (1970). Electrical aversion conditioning with chronic alcoholics. *Journal of Consulting and Clinical Psychology, 34*, 302-307.

Wahler, R. G. (1969). Oppositional children: A quest for parental reinforcement control. *Journal of Applied Behavior Analysis, 2*, 159-170.

Weiner, H. (1962). Some effects of response cost upon human operant behavior. *Journal of the Experimental Analysis of Behavior, 5*, 201-208.

Wesolowski, M. D., & Zawlocki, R. J. (1982). The differential effects of procedures to eliminate an injurious self-stimulatory behavior (Digito-Ocular Sign) in blind retarded twins. *Behavior Therapy, 13*, 334-345.

White, G. D., Nielsen, G., & Johnson, S. M. (1972). Timeout duration and the suppression of deviant behavior in children. *Journal of Applied Behavior Analysis, 5*, 111-120.

Wiens, A. N., & Menustik, C. E. (1983). Treatment outcome and patient characteristics in an aversion therapy program for alcoholism. *American Psychologist, 38*, 1089-1096.

Winkler, R. C. (1970). Management of chronic psychiatric patients by a token reinforcement system. *Journal of Applied Behavior Analysis, 3*, 47-55.

Wright, L. (1973). Aversive conditioning of self-induced seizures. *Behavior Therapy, 4*, 712-713.

7

Cognitive Change Methods*

David A. Haaga and Gerald C. Davison

INTRODUCTION

Cognitive change methods constitute one of the liveliest areas of recent clinical theory and research, though its roots can be traced back a number of years (viz., Bandura, 1969; Beck, 1967; Davison, 1968; Ellis, 1962; Kelly, 1955; London, 1964; Mischel, 1968; Rotter, 1954). As our chapter will show, there are numerous members in the family of cognitive behavior therapy, but they all share the central assumption that emotions and behavior are primarily a function of how environmental events are construed. The therapeutic implication of this assumption is that clinical improvement can be achieved, at least with some human problems, by directly altering people's constructions of their world. "We tell ourselves stories in order to live," suggested Joan Didion (1979, p. 11). Cognitive behavior therapists believe that some stories are better than others. The purpose of this chapter is to review the kinds of stories cognitive change specialists encourage their clients to tell themselves so that they might live a little better.

Our focus is primarily on therapeutic practice, but we will attend briefly as well to the theories of psychopathology associated with each approach. These theories are often discussed with clients as a way of orienting and motivating them, and successful practice is no doubt facilitated by an understanding of the rationale behind one's approach. However, we will not undertake extensive critiques of theories. Contemporary cognitive theories of psychopathology surely do not capture the whole truth (e.g., Arnkoff & Glass, 1982; Coyne, 1982; Zajonc, 1984). Our concern is much

*Preparation of this chapter was facilitated by a Predoctoral Merit Fellowship to the first author from the Graduate School of the University of Southern California and by NIH Grant 1R01HL31090-01 to the second author.

more with the *utility* of the therapy systems they have spawned. Just as data supporting the efficacy of a therapy provide no information about etiology of the problems treated (Davison, 1968), so too the utility of a treatment approach can survive research that calls into question a theory from which it derives.

We should note that "cognitive" change methods do not entail an abandonment of procedures typically associated with behavior therapy. The uniqueness of the therapies we will describe lies more in how they conceive of the change process than in the actual techniques employed. Indeed, there is fairly widespread agreement that behavioral procedures are especially effective in bringing about the cognitive changes sought by these therapies. Bandura (1977) hypothesized, for instance, that "cognitive processes mediate change but that cognitive events are induced and altered most readily by experience of mastery arising from effective performance" (p. 191).

In keeping with our emphasis on the utility of therapies as opposed to the adequacy of their underlying theories, we try to emphasize the utility or adaptiveness of various thoughts and attitudes more than their rationality or accuracy. Definitions of rationality are elusive and debatable (Cohen, 1981; Mahoney, 1980). Indeed, perhaps what we really mean when we call clients "rational" is that they think like the psychologist making the judgment. And thoughts that might not be strictly accurate perceptions of one's environment could be adaptive in that they help to maintain a positive, coping orientation (Lazarus, 1980). Arnkoff and Glass (1982) pointed out that even the loathsome "musts" targeted by rational-emotive therapists can be adaptive for some people in some circumstances. For instance, a professional who thinks "I must be competent and highly achieving" may therefore work harder, achieve high goals, and be quite happy and well-adjusted. Rather than assuming that all musts or all reality distortions are to be eradicated, cognitive therapists would do well to consider the potential utility of such thoughts. Perhaps some degree of nonveridical thinking is necessary, for "to stay 'sane' you commonly have to doctor the books" (Gagnon & Davison, 1976, p. 534).

A Clinical Caveat

The purpose of this chapter is to outline the essentials of cognitive change methods. Descriptions of techniques and how they are sequenced could unintentionally convey the impression that therapy proceeds smoothly, is always orderly, and is inevitably goal directed. Such is seldom the case, as any reasonably experienced clinician knows. One backslides, stumbles, guesses, intuits, errs, but one also moves forward with a client unexpectedly quickly, enjoys breakthroughs, and the like. Therapists also listen with what Reik long ago called "the third ear." They use their own reactions as clues to what could be going on with the client. They sometimes doubt what the client is saying (one need not be a graduate of a psychoanalytic institute to have such doubts now and again). Above all, therapists are fallible problem solvers, and their positive movement with clients is seldom as unidirectional as might appear from even honestly written case reports and especially from a chapter such as this one.

We shall now review theory and research bearing on the rational-emotive therapy of Albert Ellis, the cognitive therapy of Aaron T. Beck, social problem solving, and attribution therapy.

ELLIS'S RATIONAL EMOTIVE THERAPY

The essence of Ellis's (1984) rational-emotive theory of psychopathology is that activating events (A) do not directly cause emotional or behavioral consequences (C). Rather, our beliefs (B) about these activating events are the most direct, most important causes of how we feel and act.

Rational-emotive therapy (RET) emphasizes disputation (D) of certain beliefs, namely irrational beliefs (IBs). IBs are considered irrational on the grounds that they are unlikely to find empirical support in a person's environment and do not promote survival and enjoyment. The list of IBs is open-ended,[1] but they can be classified as follows:

1. *Awfulizing statements.* These IBs are self-statements to the effect that some situation is awful, worse than merely inconvenient, for example, "It's awful when things are not the way I'd like them to be" (Walen, DiGiuseppe, & Wessler, 1980, p. 78).
2. *Shoulds, oughts, and musts.* Emotional upset can be mediated by a belief that some unfortunate situation should or must not exist. RET considers this brand of thinking in the face of real inconveniences to be illogical because the situation does exist, and none of us is able to see to it that what we wish to avoid must not occur.[2] The belief that "I must be loved and approved of by every significant person in my life" (Walen et al., 1980, p. 77) would fall into this category.
3. *Evaluations of human worth.* Ellis (1977) considers all global evaluations of persons counterproductive and illogical. They are counter-

---

[1] There is no satisfactory rationale for a finite list of IBs, specified by content, that we can safely presume to be important for most clients and always maladaptive (Arnkoff & Glass, 1982; Kendall & Bemis, 1983). It might be better to think about the forms or types of beliefs that could be maladaptive for many people, then, rather than of a list of specific beliefs, as in some of Ellis's earlier writings (e.g., 1962).

[2] This is not to deny that it *would be nice* if it did not occur. The should-would distinction is important in rational-emotive therapy, as will be seen.

productive because they generate self-blame when one performs poorly, anxiety over possible future self-blame when one performs well. These evaluations are illogical because no objective scale for measuring global human worth exists. All people have strengths and weaknesses, each one of which varies over time and in different situations, and it makes little sense to suppose that these diverse qualities are best described by a single judgment along some yardstick of worth. An example of this type of IB would be "I am not worthwhile unless I am thoroughly competent, adequate, and achieving at all times, or at least most of the time in at least one major area" (Walen et al., 1980, p. 79).

4. *Need statements.* These IBs involve elevating a wish into an absolute need or demand, for instance, "I need someone stronger than myself on whom to depend or rely" (Walen et al., 1980, p. 84).

Labeling these types of beliefs *irrational* on the basis of empirical and pragmatic criteria has been criticized (Eschenroeder, 1982). Many IBs (e.g., I must be loved and approved of by everyone in my environment; I must be thoroughly competent) express value judgments and are not susceptible to empirical confirmation or disconfirmation. If irrationality is ascribed on pragmatic grounds (e.g., whatever makes you upset is irrational), RET becomes circular as a theory of psychopathology; irrational beliefs supposedly cause negative emotions but are simultaneously defined by the presence of these emotions.

As noted, we emphasize the utility of beliefs more than their empirical status. Regardless of whether an IB finds empirical support in a client's environment, RET could be presented with the rationale that subscribing to certain demanding, absolutistic beliefs could lead to dissatisfaction and low self-esteem and might therefore be worth changing.

Therapeutic Procedure

Rational-emotive therapists desire to get to the point quickly with clients; they discourage dwelling on childhood memories or endless outpourings of feelings. The therapist takes an active, directive stance and does a large share of the talking in early sessions (Ellis, 1984).

Asking about a client's expectations regarding therapy could be a good place to start, as many clients enter psychotherapy expecting to express pent-up feelings or to obtain sympathy from a therapist. These misconceptions (as far as this approach to therapy is concerned) can impede progress unless they are handled early (Walen et al., 1980).

Next, an RET therapist would elicit a description of A, the activating event. The therapist would not typically wish to hear great detail about A but rather to find out quickly how the client perceived the situation.

Emotional-behavioral consequences (Cs) of a client's problems are usually quite accessible. Sometimes, though, clients feel ashamed of their reactions and therefore have trouble expressing them. Therapists can attend to nonverbal cues or have clients monitor their emotions in response to situations, recording characteristics of the situations and completing sentences beginning "I feel _____" in response to each (Walen et al., 1980). It should be noted that RET treats emotions as indisputable facts about a client's experience and disputes only the irrational beliefs that produce maladaptive emotions.

RET therapists remain alert to the possibility that a C can become an A, that is, that a client could be worried about being anxious or upset about being depressed (Ellis, 1984; Walen et al., 1980). If this problem becomes apparent, the therapist would address its accompanying IBs (e.g., "I should not be depressed. It's awful that I'm always so anxious, and it makes me a worthless person.") before turning to the external event the client perceives as causing the initial distress.

The next phase of RET involves determining the beliefs lying between the A and C discussed so far and teaching clients the difference between rational (productive, nonabsolutistic) and irrational beliefs. Clients might initially respond to questions about beliefs with statements about emotions (e.g., "I was thinking that I was anxious"), but therapists need to persist in explaining the difference between Bs and Cs. To elicit beliefs rather than emotions, it is useful to ask such questions as, What were you telling yourself when _____? and Were you aware of any thoughts in your head when _____? (Walen et al., 1980).

First responses often consist of rational beliefs. For instance, if a man were upset after losing a satisfying job he had held for several years, he might describe his belief about it as "I was telling myself that it would probably be difficult to find another job as good as that one." According to RET, though, this belief is rational and would lead to moderate disappointment or sadness, not the kind of emotional state that has brought him into therapy. To determine beliefs mediating more extreme and debilitating emotional arousal, it is necessary to probe further and see if the client actually tells himself something more like, "It's unlikely that I'll get as good a job as I had before, and that's awful. I must have a very good job, or I can't stand it."

Once the IBs underlying a client's emotional troubles have been identified, the real business of RET, disputation, can begin. Walen et al. (1980) described a sequence of disputation in which the therapist begins by pointing out to a client the advantages of giving up IBs and substituting rational beliefs (RBs). Negative emotional and behavioral consequences of holding one's current IBs are discussed. Then the client is provided with RBs that could replace them and is asked to imagine how she or he might feel if the RBs were truly believed.

After this motivational phase, the therapist begins to attack the client's specific IBs, primarily by requesting evidence in support of them. If the belief is truly irrational, such evidence will not be forthcoming or will be incorrect, for instance, it might be evidence that would support a rational belief (this situation is inconvenient for me) but not an irrational one (this situation is awful and unbearable).

If a client's IBs are "awfulizing" statements, it might help to ask about worst cases, that is, "What if _____?" What is the worst that could happen, and how catastrophic would that be?

Once the evidence for IBs has been exposed as missing or at least questionable, the therapist can ask how this analysis has made the client feel. If there is improvement, this positive feeling should be emphasized by the therapist and used to encourage further effort at disputation by the client. The therapist should also insure that the client attributes feeling better to having disputed IBs and not to, for example, having gotten problems off of his or her chest.

RET assigns homework for clients to perform between sessions. These assignments can include reading popular works on RET (e.g., Ellis & Harper, 1975), listening to tapes of therapy sessions, and monitoring attempts to use RET disputations of IBs when confronted with troubling situations. Also, RET encourages behavioral experiments. Clients are urged to take risks, to perform behaviors they regard as impossible or as leading to awful consequences in order to gain evidence in support of rational assessments and against their previous IBs.

Following through on homework during subsequent sessions provides reinforcement for carrying out the assignments and can also yield clues regarding the client's progress in acquiring a rational philosophy and applying it to daily life. In sessions it can sometimes be difficult to tell whether clients have actually learned RBs or are simply agreeing with the therapist's statements in order to secure approval (Walen et al., 1980). Besides monitoring clients' homework, therapists can address this issue by checking with significant others in the client's environment to see if they have noticed any change in the client. Clients may be asked at various points in the disputation sequence to rate their moods on 0 to 100 scales to see if presentation of RBs and disputation of IBs actually improve mood. And clients should be asked to express disputations in their own words, to see if they truly understand them.

Throughout the course of therapy, RET practitioners take care not to make rationality yet another must or should (e.g., "Now that I've had RET, I must never subscribe to irrational beliefs and make myself upset again"). If a client seems to hold such a belief, it is examined and disputed just as any other IB would be. Along the same lines, therapists can disclose their own (occasional) slips and irrationalities to make it less likely that a client will irrationally come to view them as faultless masters on whom one must permanently rely or emulate (Prochaska, 1984).

Applications

Ellis (1984) hypothesized that RET works best for clients in reasonably good contact with reality, generally speaking, the kind of person one sees in outpatient settings. Those who are more seriously disturbed present a greater challenge because their irrational tendencies are especially deeply ingrained. Still, even psychotic clients can worry unduly about their disorders (Walen et al., 1980). RET would address this aspect of the problem. Ellis and Bernard (1983) suggested that RET can be useful even with children, particularly as a preventative measure.

RET is not necessarily restricted to clients with high IQ (Lipsky, Kassinove, & Miller, 1980). A below-average group of adult outpatients (Mean = 94) learned RET concepts as well and improved as much on depression and anxiety measures, as did an above-average group (Mean = 110).

Empirical Status

Theory

Some correlational data have accumulated in support of the RET notion that irrational beliefs are associated with emotional arousal, though it cannot be determined from these data whether irrational beliefs actually caused the negative emotions. IBs have been found to correlate with measures of social anxiety (Davison & Zighelboim, 1984; Goldfried & Sobocinski, 1975; Sutton-Simon & Goldfried, 1979), test anxiety (Goldfried & Sobocinski, 1975), speech anxiety (Goldfried & Sobocinski, 1975), fear of heights (Sutton-Simon & Goldfried, 1979), lack of assertiveness (Alden & Safran, 1978; Lohr & Bonge, 1982), and depression (Nelson, 1977; Vestre, 1984).

Therapy

Perhaps because of the provocative writings of Ellis, RET has generated a great deal of interesting philosophical debate. This debate is not matched by a like quantity of empirical work with clinical groups (Kendall, 1984), but some has appeared.

Group RET improved speech-anxious students' scores on a self-report measure of speech anxiety and on the Irrational Beliefs Test (IBT; Jones,

1968) significantly more than did relaxation or no-treatment controls (Trexler & Karst, 1972). Behavioral measures showed less convincing results. Ten sessions of group RET helped subjects who had been an average of 25 lb overweight reduce to about 16 lb overweight at the end of treatment and only 6 lb overweight at an 18-week follow-up (Block, 1980). These results were significantly superior to those for a no-treatment control or a relaxation condition. The lack of relapse, indeed continued weight loss after therapy, was seen as an unusually impressive result.

Finally, Smith (1983) reanalyzed the Lipsky et al. (1980) data alluded to earlier and determined that improvement on their dependent measures was correlated with declining irrational beliefs scores (rs mostly in the $-.5$ range). Such a correlation is a minimal requirement if we are to suppose that the process hypothesized by RET theory (decrease in irrationality) actually mediates change in RET.

Variations on a Theme: Systematic Rational Restructuring

Standard RET eschews excessive therapist warmth and often entails pressuring clients to acknowledge their irrational ideologies.[3] It has been suggested that this style could induce reactance from clients (Goldfried & Davison, 1976). Systematic rational restructuring (Goldfried, Decenteceo, & Weinberg, 1974) has been proposed as an alternative model of rational restructuring, similar in many ways to standard RET but featuring less aggressive cajoling and disputing.

The essence of systematic rational restructuring (SRR) is the use of a hierarchy of upsetting situations, generally similar to that employed in Wolpe's technique of systematic desensitization (Wolpe, 1958). The principal difference is that, instead of muscle relaxation to inhibit or to reduce the emotional arousal elicited by a fearsome imaginary scene, rational self-statements are encouraged.

The self-statements are evaluated in terms of both the accuracy of the

---

[3]This is a very complex matter. In teaching RET to graduate students for a number of years, the second author has often commented on the distinction between the style that Ellis and many of his followers adopt and the substance of the therapy itself. Put another way, do RET therapists *have* to be less empathic than, say, client-centered therapists or many cognitive-behavioral therapists in order to maximize the efficacy and efficiency of the implementation of Ellis's ideas? Ellis has asserted that therapist warmth could actually compromise client progress. If this is really so — and no research thus far has systematically addressed the issue — then therapists operating within the RET framework would do well to (we almost said "should") moderate their empathy in favor of a more directive, even businesslike, approach to clients.

client's perception of A and the implications the client draws from that perception (the B). For example, consider a client who is thrown into a panic if his boss greets him grouchily in the morning. In a fashion similar to what Beck suggests (to whose work we turn in the next section), the client is encouraged to consider how likely it is that the boss was actually angry with *him*, rather than, for example, being preoccupied with a situation that day having little if anything to do with the client. By considering that the perception of A may be more ominous than the true nature of A, the client might be able to reduce his arousal. However, as Ellis argues, one can assume the worst, that is, that the boss is, in fact, angry at the client. The task then is to "de-catastrophize" the situation for the client, working not on the A but on the B, the client's beliefs about the significance of A. This combination of Beck and Ellis is done in the client's imagination, along a graduated hierarchy of anxiety-arousing situations, with the therapist helping the client along the way to reconstrue the events themselves (the A) and/or the implications drawn by the client (the B). The following transcript illustrates the technique in the treatment of a client with speech anxiety:

Therapist: I'm going to ask you to imagine yourself in a given situation, and to tell me how nervous you may feel. I'd then like you to think aloud about what you might be telling yourself that is creating this anxiety and then go about trying to put your expectations into a more realistic perspective. From time to time, I will make certain comments, and I'd like you to treat these comments as if they were your own thoughts. OK?

Client: All right.

Therapist: I'd like you to close your eyes now and imagine yourself in the following situation: You are sitting on stage in the auditorium, together with the other school board members. It's a few minutes before you have to get up and give your report to the people in the audience. Between 0 and 100 percent tension, tell me how nervous you feel.

Client: About 50.

Therapist: [*Now to get into his head.*] So I'm feeling fairly tense. Let me think. What might I be telling myself that's making me upset?

Client: I'm nervous about reading my report in front of all these people.

Therapist: But why does that bother me?

Client: Well, I don't know if I'm going to come across all right . . .

Therapist: [*He seems to be having trouble. More prompting on my part may be needed than I originally anticipated.*] But why should that upset me? That upsets me because . . .

Client: . . . because I want to make a good impression.

Therapist: And if I don't . . .

Client: . . . well, I don't know. I don't want people to think that I'm incompetent. I guess I'm afraid that I'll lose the respect of the people who thought I knew what I was doing.

Therapist: [*He seems to be getting closer.*] But why should that make me so upset?

Client: I don't know. I guess it shouldn't. Maybe I'm being *overly* concerned about other people's reactions to me.

Therapist: How might I be overly concerned?

Client: I think this may be one of those situations where I have to please everybody, and there are an awful lot of people in the audience. Chances are I'm not going to get everybody's approval, and maybe that's upsetting me. I want everyone to think I'm doing a good job.

Therapist: Now let me think for a moment to see how rational that is.

Client: To begin with, I don't think it really is likely that I'm going to completely blow it. After all, I have prepared in advance, and have thought through what I want to say fairly clearly. I think I may be reacting as if I already have failed, even though it's very unlikely that I will.

Therapist: And even if I did mess up, how bad would that be?

Client: Well, I guess that really wouldn't be so terrible after all.

Therapist: [*I don't believe him for one moment. There is a definite hollow ring to his voice. He arrived at that conclusion much too quickly and presents it without much conviction.*] I say I don't think it'll upset me, but I don't really believe that.

Client: That's true. I would be upset if I failed. But actually, I really shouldn't be looking at this situation as being a failure.

Therapist: What would be a better way for me to look at the situation?

Client: Well, it's certainly not a do-or-die kind of thing. It's only a ridiculous committee report. A lot of the people in the audience know who I am and what I'm capable of doing. And even if I don't give a sterling performance, I don't think they're going to change their opinion of me on the basis of a five-minute presentation.

Therapist: But what if some of them do?

Client: Even if some of them do think differently of me, that doesn't mean that *I would* be different. I would still be me no matter what they thought. It's ridiculous of me to base my self-worth on what other people think.

Therapist: [*I think he's come around as much as he can. We can terminate this scene now.*] With this new attitude toward the situation, how do you feel in percentage of anxiety?

Client: Oh, about 25 percent.

Therapist: OK, let's talk a little about some of the thoughts you had during that situation before trying it again. (Goldfried & Davison, 1976, pp. 172–174).

As with RET, the client is encouraged to practice what she or he has learned in therapy, keeping records of attempts to rationally reevaluate situations and the emotions thereby experienced. The therapist might need to emphasize that one needs to be persistent and not become discouraged upon experiencing some setbacks. Irrational thinking is often a long-standing habit, and it takes practice to replace it with rational thinking.

Empirical Evaluation

SRR appears to be a promising alternative to RET. It was effective in reducing test anxiety (Goldfried, Linehan, & Smith, 1978; Wise & Haynes, 1983) and social anxiety (Kanter & Goldfried, 1979; Malkiewich & Merluzzi, 1980) and added to the effectiveness of a behavior rehearsal program to increase assertiveness (Linehan, Goldfried, & Goldfried, 1979). The effectiveness of SRR appears to be due not solely to exposure to previously upsetting situations on the hierarchy (Goldfried et al., 1978). Although they did not test SRR proper, Lipsky et al. (1980) found that rational–emotive imagery (REI; Maultsby, 1977) added to the impact of RET on anxiety, supporting the use of imagery to facilitate rational restructuring.

Some Critical Considerations in Rational Restructuring

Rational restructuring approaches, as well as other cognitive therapies, have been criticized for overemphasizing the control, as opposed to the experiencing, of emotions (Mahoney, 1980). Many people are in distress precisely because they are alienated from their emotions; they should be encouraged to feel and acknowledge them more, not eliminate them through logical analysis (Prochaska, 1984).

In reply, Ellis would point out that RET does not seek to eliminate all experiencing of emotion. RET opposes only "frequent, prolonged, or intense negative or self-defeating emotional states, such as dysfunctional anxiety . . . and senseless hostility" (Ellis, 1962, p. 333). The client after RET does not become unemotional or passive but does calmly accept those situations he or she perceives as unchangeable and experiences only moderate negative emotion in most unpleasant situations (Walen et al., 1980).

RET practice has also been faulted for being overly directive (Bernard, 1981). Private thoughts, those which are deep seated and difficult for clients to verbalize right away, could be what matter most in determining responses to various situations. The RET approach, in which the therapist begins disputing a client's self-verbalizations as soon as she or he can come up with any, might not permit these private thoughts to emerge. RET therapists might do well to spend more time assessing and elaborating thoughts that clients initially have trouble expressing before examining and disputing the irrational notions that RET theory indicates as causing their problems.

Ellis (1962), however, did not see his approach as overly directive. He agreed that the ideologies and assumptions that generate emotional disturbance are typically outside a client's awareness but believed they are "not deeply hidden but can, in almost all instances, be quickly brought to consciousness" (p. 174).

In teaching RET and other behavioral therapies over the past several years, the second author has emphasized to graduate students the importance of Rogerian interviewing techniques in helping clients elaborate their perceptions of their problems and exploring the dimensions of their psychological suffering. The text and workbook of Gerard Egan (1982a, 1982b) have proven to be of significant value in sensitizing student therapists to the complexities involved in achieving an adequate understanding of the client's phenomenological world.

Ethics

RET frankly concerns itself with clients' values, the idea being that absolutistic values engender self-blame and cause much emotional disturbance. Indeed, "emotional disturbance, I must keep insisting, largely consists of the individual's acquiring and reindoctrinating himself with illogical, inconsistent and unworkable values; and effective therapy must partly consist of helping him deindoctrinate himself so that he acquires a saner and more constructive set of values" (Ellis, 1962, p. 366).

Ellis has placed particular emphasis on long-range hedonism. The justification for this value, as well as for showing consideration for others, is that these values work out best for the individual in the long run. One had better seek one's own satisfactions while "keeping in mind that one will achieve one's own best good, in most instances, by giving up immediate gratifications for future gains and by being courteous to and considerate of others, so that they will not sabotage one's own ends" (Ellis, 1962, p. 134).

The RET value system, however, can be criticized on several grounds. Its relativism and individualism leave it with little to say about someone who derives long-term satisfaction from harming others who cannot retaliate. Second, it seems inconsistent to ignore the possibility that someone might derive hedonic satisfaction from living in accord with absolutistic standards. Herein lies a paradox. RET takes the clinical observation that many make themselves miserable by blaming themselves for not living up to absolute standards and then constructs a general principle that people *should* not hold absolutistic values! Finally, the RET emphasis on the individual as self-sufficient (recall that "I need someone stronger than myself on whom to depend or rely" is considered an IB), though it might sometimes promote clients' efforts in therapy, can also foster the "ethic of the lonely struggle" (Wachtel, 1977, p. 288). This model might imply to clients that they can be (and ought to be) tough enough to negotiate their way through life without needing love and support from others. Some might be better served by bearing in mind that "it is, after all, just as human to be able to turn to others as it is to stand alone" (Wachtel, 1977, p. 290).

Still, though some of us may find bones to pick with RET's ethical stance, it is greatly to Ellis's credit that RET is so forthright about values.

It has been argued that psychotherapy is inherently a moral enterprise, and failure to acknowledge the ethical aspects of one's therapeutic program can itself be challenged on ethical grounds (Davison, 1976).

RET as a Humanistic Therapy

RET, like other cognitive therapies, overlaps humanistic therapies in the sense of emphasizing not the world as an objective observer could verify it but instead the client's phenomenological world (Davison & Neale, 1982). In recognition of the humanistic outlook in RET, Albert Ellis won the Humanist of the Year award in 1973. Ellis (1984) has noted that RET shares with client-centered therapy the goal of showing unconditional acceptance of a client, regardless of his or her actions. Both therapies attempt to discourage clients from making global self-ratings based on their behavior. Though differing very much at the level of techniques by being considerably more directive than client-centered therapy, RET does share with humanistic and existential modes of therapy emphasis on personal freedom, individuality, present experience, responsibility, and the growth potential inherent in each person. Clients are exhorted to budge from their sad, sometimes self-pitying doldrums. They may have played a role in getting into their current predicaments — maybe, for current research on biological factors in a range of mental-behavioral problems must not be ignored — and they can now play a role in getting out of their mess. Their existence is formed in large measure by their constructions. RET invites them to test these limits and encourages them to construe their lives differently, in a way that demands less perfection from them and from others, in a way that fosters tolerance of human foibles.

BECK'S COGNITIVE THERAPY

Cognitive therapy (CT) has been described as "an active, directive, time-limited, structured approach used to treat a variety of psychiatric disorders (for example, depression, anxiety, phobias, pain problems, etc.)" (Beck, Rush, Shaw, & Emery, 1979, p. 3). CT was initially developed as a treatment for depression, though; as it has been most fully described and evaluated in that context, CT with depression will be our focus here.

Beck's cognitive model holds that depression results primarily from pervasive, negative misinterpretations of experience (Hollon & Beck, 1979). These misinterpretations give rise to a negative cognitive triad, that is, a negative view of oneself, one's world, and one's future. Depressed people are thought to view themselves as having lost something of value and as being in general "losers" who lack the attributes necessary to attain contentment. They see their worlds as containing insurmountable obstacles preventing them from achieving satisfaction. They believe the future holds no hope of improvement.

Cognitive Distortions

A depressed person's belief in the negative triad can be preserved in spite of contrary evidence, because of the negatively biased manner in which he or she processes this evidence. Beck and his colleagues have identified a number of common distortions in information processing. It should be remembered, though, that assessment for CT ought to be idiographic; no particular distortions are presumed to characterize a client's thinking.

Typical distortions include

1. *Selective abstraction*—a tendency to form conclusions based on an isolated detail of an event, even if this means ignoring much contradictory evidence. For instance, an assembly line worker might produce 100 perfect pieces of equipment followed by 1 bad one and conclude on the basis of the single defective item that she or he is a bad worker.
2. *Arbitrary inference*—making conclusions in the absence of any relevant evidence. A worker might start a new job in a brand new field convinced of becoming a failure at it.
3. *Overgeneralization*—holding extreme beliefs based on particular events and inappropriately applying them to dissimilar settings. A student might have difficulty in math and conclude that he or she will do very poorly in all subjects.
4. *Personalization*—a tendency to relate events to oneself even when there is no connection. Someone might plan a barbecue, find that the event is ruined by a rainstorm, and conclude that she or he did a poor job and was at fault for the failure of the event.
5. *Polarized thinking*—tending to think in all-or-none terms, categorizing experiences only in one of two extremes, with no middle ground acknowledged. An instance of this distortion might be a belief that there are two kinds of people, competent and incompetent.
6. *Magnification/exaggeration*—overestimation of the significance of negative events. The magnifier might arrive for an appointment a minute late and think that she or he has committed a gross impoliteness that could never be forgiven.

Cognitive Schemata

Negative thoughts engendered by the distortions just discussed directly depress mood and lead to behavioral passivity, which helps to maintain depressed mood. These distortions of experience are maintained despite their being dysfunctional and perhaps unrealistic because they are controlled by dysfunctional schemata, fairly stable cognitive patterns dictating the manner in which someone will interpret data from a set of situations (Beck et al., 1979). The negative schemata that influence thinking patterns of depressed persons are probably learned early in life and can be thought of as rules or assumptions for making sense of one's environment. Examples of such dysfunctional assumptions or schemata include (a) "In order to be happy, I have to be successful in whatever I undertake"; (b) "If I make a mistake it means that I am inept"; and (c) "My value as a person depends on what others think of me" (Beck et al., 1979, p. 246).

The distinctions among these various categories of thoughts can seem a bit murky. A useful system for thinking about them was outlined by Marzillier (1980), who distinguished three types of cognitions discussed in cognitive therapy: cognitive events, cognitive processes, and cognitive structures. Cognitive events are "thoughts and images occurring in the stream of consciousness" (p. 252). The events emphasized in Beck's model are "automatic thoughts," which may be verbal or pictorial (images) and which seem to occur rapidly and automatically. Cognitive processes "transform and process environmental stimuli" (p. 252). These include attention, abstraction, and encoding of information. Beck's model posits that the cognitive processes depressed persons use to interpret experience are distorted in the ways described earlier. Finally, cognitive structures are general, long-term cognitive characteristics, including beliefs and attitudes. These are rules and principles governing interpretation of events. In Beck's model, dysfunctional schemata characteristic of depressed people are the prominent cognitive structures.

Our account of Beck's cognitive model in terms of Marzillier's classificatory system is illustrated in Table 7.1, using the example of a person who feels bad as a result of thinking that he or she has failed as a parent.

Table 7.1. Types of Cognitions in Cognitive Therapy

MARZILLIER (1980) SCHEME	CORRESPONDING BECKIAN CATEGORY	EXAMPLE
1. Cognitive event	Automatic thought	I'm a lousy parent. How terrible!
2. Cognitive process	Distorted information processing	Selective abstraction; e.g., I love my kids very much, but yesterday I lost my temper and yelled at them. On the basis of this one incident, I conclude I am no good as a parent.
3. Cognitive structure	Dysfunctional schemata	I must always be competent in every area of life.

Therapeutic Procedure

CT is typically conducted in 15 to 25 sessions, perhaps twice a week for the first 4 weeks and weekly thereafter (Beck et al., 1979). An important first step is to clarify a client's expectations regarding the treatment. Many have been in therapy previously or have otherwise formed expectancies about it that do not fit CT practice. For instance, a client expecting to discuss at length childhood troubles might be disappointed to find that developmental issues are brought up in CT only "if they are relevant to the patient's current difficulties, but the basic model of treatment does not demand that such issues surface in every case" (Bedrosian & Beck, 1980, p. 129). In addition to correcting any misconceptions about CT, a therapist can use this questioning to begin to present the CT rationale. If, say, a client felt anxious or pessimistic before coming to a first CT interview, a therapist might ask what thoughts the client was having at the time and use this information to illustrate the impact of thoughts on feelings and to demonstrate that other thoughts about the same event (e.g., "I'm looking forward to making progress in this therapy program") would have led to quite different feelings.

Behavioral Techniques

Beck et al. (1979) suggested that behavioral techniques are especially important early in therapy with severely depressed clients. The therapist needs to disrupt the depressive cycle of reduced level of activity — sense of incompetence — discouragement — increased immobility — lack of satisfaction and self-esteem or esteem from others — lower mood. Increased activity is not an end in itself, however, but a means toward effecting cognitive change. The results of behavioral interventions can serve as powerful evidence helping to correct the depressed client's negative expectancies and the client to see that pessimism contributes to his or her immobility. It is important, though, not simply to assume that cognitive changes will follow behavioral changes. The therapist needs to find out how a client interprets such changes and to emphasize exactly how the results of behavioral experiments contradict the client's prior beliefs or predictions. Specific behavioral procedures employed in CT are discussed next.

Scheduling Activities. Especially with an extremely inactive client, the therapist collaborates to draw up an hour-by-hour plan of what the client will do, featuring relatively easy tasks at first. The client is then encouraged to continue creating such a plan each evening for the following day. The technique is explained as an experiment to see if increasing activity level will improve mood, perhaps by decreasing the amount of time spent on negative rumination. The client is therefore asked to monitor which tasks she or he performed and whatever thoughts and feelings she or he experienced while carrying out the planned activities.

Activity scheduling is done with a low-pressure set. One might point out that nobody accomplishes all he or she plans, that there is no need to worry if not all activities are carried out. The technique begins as observation, gathering data for planning treatment, rather than as an evaluation of the client's performance. Clients are encouraged to plan for *types* of activity (e.g., I will work on a cognitive change methods chapter from 11 a.m. to noon Tuesday), not for the amount they hope to accomplish (I will write four pages), because amount accomplished often depends on factors outside of our control (noise, coffee supply, etc.). Finally, a client should not expect immediate symptomatic relief from increased activity. The goal is only to do the assignment; subjective relief might not come until later, and, if it is lacking, this does not mean the assignment (or client!) failed.

As with other homework assignments, the data from an activity schedule should be discussed at the next session and can be used to point out that some activities alleviate depressed mood at least temporarily, something the client might not have heretofore believed. Negative thoughts while carrying out the assignment can be elicited and discussed (see Cognitive Techniques section later in the chapter).

Mastery and Pleasure Techniques. Some depressed clients do many things but fail to enjoy them or to derive from them a sense of personal competence. They might not attend to positive feelings experienced during these activities, or they might not get such feelings because they either have negative thoughts while engaged in activity or simply do things they do not enjoy. If the client is doing primarily things she or he never liked, the therapist should ask why. Many depressed clients believe they do not deserve to engage in pleasurable activities, particularly if they have not achieved work-related goals (Beck et al., 1979). If this is the problem, the therapist might want to emphasize the role that pleasant events can play in improving mood, which in turn would facilitate increased activity of all kinds.

An instrument such as the Pleasant Events Schedule (MacPhillamy & Lewinsohn, 1982) can aid a therapist in deciding which activities can be used to increase mastery and pleasure feelings for the client. As with activity scheduling, detailed plans are made for what the client will do each day. Besides recording activities performed and accompanying thoughts and feelings, the client is asked to rate on a 0 to 5 scale the pleasure and sense of mastery associated with each activity. The 0 to 5 scale should help the client recognize partial successes rather than put everything into dichotomous bins of successes and failures (see earlier discussion of absolutistic, all-or-none thinking).

Clients are encouraged to base their mastery ratings on their current levels of functioning rather than on their peaks or ideal levels. Thus, whereas preparing a modest meal can be a small feat compared to what one used to be able to do, it could be a significant accomplishment in the light of the handicap under which one operates while depressed.

Graded Task Assignment. Therapist and client first discuss the problem to be addressed by way of a task assignment; for instance, it might be a client's belief that he or she is incapable of achieving meaningful goals. The assignment will be designed to disconfirm this belief, with tasks set at an easy enough level that the client is likely to succeed in carrying them out. Overall goals are broken down into discrete, manageable chunks, with easier assignments undertaken first.

If the project is successful, the therapist calls attention to this success and its implications. She or he might first ask for the client's reactions to the project. If the client has discounted the achievement, the therapist would want to discourage this tendency. One way to do so and to encourage the client to evaluate his or her capabilities more positively would be to refer to the client's prediction regarding the experiment and illustrate how it was disconfirmed by success. To foster the belief that the client can achieve such results independently in the future, the therapist emphasizes that success was a result of the client's skills and effort. Finally, therapist and client plan more difficult assignments to be tried next. It is hoped that these progressive successes and discussions of their implications will undermine the client's image of himself or herself as a "loser."[4]

Cognitive Rehearsal. Prior to carrying out a task assignment, a client could go through it step by step in imagination, to try to see what obstacles might prevent its completion. Thus, if the goal were to get up in the morning and go shopping, the client would visualize potential obstacles (e.g., might want to go back to bed, might be raining). Therapist and client together try to come up with ways to get around each barrier and complete the assignment. Then the client would imagine going through the whole assignment successfully, including coping with the obstacles, before undertaking the assignment in real life.

Role Playing. The therapist might want to reverse roles with a client during a discussion of a situation the client faces. The therapist might think aloud, "I did not get all my plans accomplished; I'm a failure." The client, acting

---

[4]We are moved to remind the reader that effecting such cognitive change is *difficult!* The client would probably not be depressed if she or he were readily convinced by mastery experiences that she or he is an OK individual, with a right to feel pleasure and pride. Our account of cognitive therapy, then, should be read as a guide or outline for how a therapist can go about trying to make therapeutic changes. Clients are rarely persuaded to construe themselves differently with the ease that is implied in a textual account of therapy.

as therapist, could be better able than usual to see the inappropriateness of such a conclusion, as depressed clients often demand less of others than of themselves.

In implementing any of these behavioral techniques, it might be useful to suggest that the client may call the therapist if he or she experiences difficulty. The therapist's advice, encouragement, and questioning while the client actually faces the relevant situation might promote better learning and generalization than if the matter were not discussed until the next treatment session. Also, the CT therapist can recommend that a client call when finished with a homework assignment, as a way of increasing the incentive to attempt the assignment.[5] (Goldfried, 1982, discussed this tactic as a way of combatting noncompliance.)

Cognitive Techniques

CT attempts to identify and modify maladaptive thoughts, defined as "ideation that interferes with the ability to cope with life experiences, unnecessarily disrupts internal harmony, and produces inappropriate or excessive emotional reactions that are painful" (Beck, 1976, p. 235). As we understand it, "thought" in this definition can refer to cognitions at any of the three levels described in Table 7.1. Beck argues that the therapist's notions of what is a maladaptive thought should not be imposed on the client. The two work together to reach agreement on what thoughts impede the client's goal attainment and satisfaction. Still, it would be well to bear in mind that targeting maladaptive thoughts calls for considerable judgment on the part of a therapist; therapists may differ, for instance, on what constitutes "inappropriate or excessive" emotional reactions.

Although the client plays a role in the design and implementation of behavioral CT techniques, the therapist has been fairly directive to this point. If a depressed client is reluctant to engage in activity, the therapist needs to urge such activity in rather one-sided communications. With the use of cognitive techniques in CT, though, the true spirit of the treatment program, *collaborative empiricism*, comes into play. Therapist and client are co-investigators attempting to uncover and examine any maladaptive interpretations of the world that could be aggravating the client's problems.

---

[5]The conduct of therapy entails enormous professional, moral, and personal responsibility. Doing therapy is not easy work! Therapy is particularly trying with depressed, often suicidal, clients and can seldom be restricted to the traditional 50-minute hour. Telephone contacts between sessions add significantly to the therapist's burden, but the therapist must be prepared to accept this onus if he or she is to deal responsibly and humanely with depressed individuals.

This is seen as an important difference between CT and RET. The CT therapist certainly has preconceptions about the forms maladaptive thinking often takes (e.g., overgeneralization), but working with an individual client is a collaborative, inductive procedure by which client and therapist attempt to discover the particular dysfunctional assumptions underlying the client's negative thoughts. RET therapists, in contrast, adopt a deductive approach. They are confident, based on rational-emotive theory, that a distressed person probably subscribes to one or more of a finite list of common irrational beliefs, the content of which the therapist can point out (Beck et al., 1979; Davison & Neale, 1982).

The inductive-deductive difference informs a striking difference in style between CT and standard RET practice. Beck et al. suggest that the CT therapist avoid being overly didactic. Extensive use of Socratic questioning, rather than lectures or parables, models for the client a questioning, nonrigid, "Where's the evidence?" approach to life. Ellis often uses minilectures and didactic speeches. Beck et al. suggest that therapists use terms such as *unproductive ideas* in discussing negative thoughts, to promote rapport with clients. They do not favor the use of words such as *irrational* or *nutty*, which might be heard (with humor, it must be pointed out) from Ellis. Finally, CT theory recommends that the therapist begin by acknowledging the client's frame of reference and asking for elaboration on it (again, What's the evidence for that belief?). Having had a chance to present his or her case and feel understood, the client might be more willing to consider the anomalous data that are already available or that they will together generate in trying to undermine these beliefs. Ellis, on the other hand, believes that quite forceful interventions are necessary to disrupt a well-learned maladaptive pattern of thinking; he therefore confronts the client's irrational beliefs strongly, sometimes within the first few minutes of the first session.[6]

The major tasks of the cognitive phase of CT are identifying automatic

---

[6]The implementation of therapy ideas, as well as the very choice a person makes of a favored approach, would seem to depend a good deal on one's style and personality. Some of these CT versus RET contrasts could be related to the respective personalities of Aaron Beck and Albert Ellis. As is obvious to their colleagues, acquaintances, friends, and even to workshop and lecture participants, Beck is a generally soft-spoken person; Ellis, on the other hand, is more forceful. Both show warmth and caring to their clients, but in different ways. Beck moves slowly in confronting and interpreting; Ellis, much more quickly, even harshly (especially for a client who is not a New Yorker). Informal discussions among colleagues about CT and RET often touch on the roles these rather different personalities play in the actual format of their respective therapies.

thoughts, modifying automatic thoughts, uncovering dysfunctional assumptions, and modifying dysfunctional assumptions.

Identifying Automatic Thoughts. To identify the client's idiosyncratic automatic thoughts, the therapist trains her or him to observe and record such thoughts. First, the therapist should explain what is meant by an automatic thought, namely a verbal or pictorial thought that seems to come to mind automatically. It should be pointed out that these thoughts might not have been noticed previously, though they are within awareness. Next, the therapist assigns homework of collecting and recording automatic thoughts in situations of interest. It is best to record immediately after the relevant situation, but sometimes the client needs to reconstruct the situation later in imagination and recall what she or he had been thinking and feeling at the time. The idea is to record an automatic thought in the manner in which it occurred (e.g., I am a lousy parent), not in a more distanced fashion (e.g., I was thinking that I was a lousy parent). Thoughts are recorded on a sheet with parallel columns, the number depending on the purpose of the assignment. Typically, the date, activating situation, automatic thought, and resulting emotion are listed. When the client has learned how to respond to her or his automatic thoughts, columns for Rational Responses and Outcome are included. Outcome includes the degree of belief the client has in the original automatic thought and in the rational response and the effect of the rational response on the client's mood.

Modifying Automatic Thoughts. In the next session, the CT therapist reviews these records of automatic thoughts and questions the client about evidence in support of a thought. If, for example, an automatic thought were "I'm lousy at parenting," the CT therapist would ask for the evidence: What does your spouse think? How often have your children complained about you in the last month? It is worth noting that the CT therapist does not begin by questioning the belief that might underlie such a thought (perhaps, "I must be competent in all endeavors") but first focuses on the accuracy of the thought itself. Beck et al. believe that leaving the possibly inaccurate perception alone (the A in Ellis's scheme) to work on the belief would be to miss an opportunity to show the client how to check out thoughts against data. Failing this, the client might continue to misinterpret experiences in the future.

What if the client's automatic thought appears to be accurate? For instance, what if the client's spouse and children continually complain about his or her parenting skills and interest? The CT therapist then would ask about the *meaning* of an event or conclusion for the client, that is, What does being a lousy parent mean to you? If it means "I am worthless," the therapist can then explore with the client the reality basis for this personal meaning. The invalidity of self-worth ratings (see earlier discussion in

RET section) can be mentioned, or the meaning could be seen as an over-generalization (that is, parenting, although obviously important, is nevertheless but one characteristic, not the whole, of a person's competencies).[7]

Note that, in exploring personal meanings of automatic thoughts, the therapist can get clues about dysfunctional schemata, but the two are not identical. For instance, another client with the same dysfunctional schema, say, "My self-worth depends on others' evaluations of my competence," might not be upset by the thought "I am a lousy parent" if the personal meaning attached to the thought were "I'm not much of a parent, but I am competent because people say I'm a great lawyer."

In the course of recording automatic thoughts and examining them with the therapist, the client is likely to gain distance from them. That is, he or she will see increasingly that a thought is not a fact, that thoughts or inferences can be checked against data. In exploring the data regarding a thought or the meaning a client attaches to it, the therapist demonstrates (and should make explicit) that events are open to various interpretations and that a depressed client might have exacerbated her or his condition by subscribing to the worst of these alternative interpretations.

Techniques for modifying a negative automatic thought that is not immediately extinguished by the therapist's challenges include *reattribution* and *alternative conceptualizations*. Reattribution, a.k.a. *de-responsibilitizing*, helps a client stop assigning himself or herself 100% of the blame for negative events. A careful collaborative review of the facts of a situation could uncover other sources partially to blame. Also, the therapist might ask the client to devise criteria for making an attribution of total blame to someone else, again taking advantage of the self-other double standard frequently maintained by depressed people. So, if the client thinks, "It's all my fault; I ruined the project," the therapist could ask for a list of the criteria by which the client would judge whether failure were entirely the fault of a coworker. Then the two can examine whether the client meets all these criteria and, if not, decrease the self-blame.

Alternative conceptualization involves examining the evidence and perhaps obtaining new data bearing on a more favorable reinterpretation of an event. So, if the client thinks "I am a lousy parent," consider an alternative

---

[7]This parenting example reveals once again the ethical dimension of therapy. Some readers might in fact believe that it *is* terrible for the client to be a lousy parent. Some readers might base their judgment on whether the client is male or female, employed outside the home or not, deeply involved or not in outside philanthropic activities such as charities for others. The considerations are endless, but they all point to the need for the therapist, at some juncture, to come to terms with what he or she considers really important in his or her own life as well as in the life of the client.

view, perhaps that she or he is a fine parent who, however, has not attended to or sought enough feedback from the family. To check out this alternative conceptualization, she or he could talk to spouse and children to find out what they think.

Uncovering Dysfunctional Assumptions (Schemata). Modifying specific automatic thoughts alone is unlikely to suffice for long-lasting change. The underlying dysfunctional assumptions that give rise to negative automatic thoughts must also be uncovered and changed.

Identifying such assumptions is more difficult and involves higher levels of inference than does identifying automatic thoughts, which are more readily accessible to the client. A useful way to identify such assumptions is to look for themes common to many of the client's automatic thoughts. For instance, if a client reported automatic thoughts such as "X is angry with me," "I should not have offended him," "Wonder how she'll take it?" the therapist might detect a theme of concern about the reactions of others. The therapist would then infer a schema that expresses the meaning of such a theme to the client, for example, "I must please everyone I meet." This rule would then be presented to the client as a hypothesis, not as a fact.

Other clues to dysfunctional assumptions include

1. *Type of cognitive distortion shown by the client.* If she or he tends toward overgeneralization, the underlying assumptions could be in the form of sweeping generalizations.
2. *Words the client uses frequently, especially global words.* If a client describes many people, acts, or situations as "stupid," he or she may show dysfunctional assumptions regarding competence.
3. *Client's justifications of negative automatic thoughts or explanations of occasional positive moods.* If an improvement in mood, for example, is explained by something like "My boss paid me a compliment," this could reflect an assumption that approval from others is necessary for happiness.
4. *Clients' attributions of the well-being of others.* This can yield similar information as clue 3. "My friend is happy of course—he's married" might mean that the client depends on others for how she or he feels.

Modifying Dysfunctional Assumptions. Modifying dysfunctional assumptions once they are identified and agreed upon often involves the previously outlined techniques for challenging automatic thoughts, examining their validity, and considering alternatives. Additionally, some special techniques for altering dysfunctional assumptions are available.

Many dysfunctional assumptions appear in the form of shoulds, much like the irrational beliefs of RET theory. Words like *should*, *must*, and *have to* recur in the automatic thoughts of clients believing in such rules. Beck et al. (1979) recommend response prevention as a measure to discourage shoulds and musts, that is, what would happen if the client were to force himself or herself not to do whatever she or he believes must be done? The client predicts what will happen, implements response prevention and collects the data, and evaluates the rule under which he or she had operated in light of the data. For instance, a man might have assumed that he must defer to his wife in all situations in order to maintain a relatively peaceful home life. The therapist might suggest that he force himself not to defer, to calmly assert his opinions at the next sign of conflict. If the incident does not result in disaster (and the therapist needs to assess this likelihood in advance), this datum can be used to illustrate the inappropriateness of the client's initial assumption.

Acting counter to the assumption is considered the most powerful technique for modifying a dysfunctional assumption, but there are others. The CT therapist might want to have a client list the advantages and disadvantages of holding and of giving up an assumption. Therapist and client then could examine the lists with an eye toward correcting any cognitive distortions involved, such as exaggeration of the problems associated with giving up a belief. This sort of list can help the therapist see obstacles to the client's willingness to part with an assumption that would seem to an observer to be self-destructive.

General Considerations

Considerably more detail on CT practice than we could include in this space can be found in Beck et al. (1979), including session-by-session outlines of typical courses of treatment. One helpful suggestion made by these writers is to utilize whatever course the client's mood should take and construe it in a positive, optimistic way. If mood improves, the CT therapist encourages a client to specify what techniques were helpful. Consideration of what worked might help the client continue to improve and could encourage him or her to apply CT techniques after therapy is terminated. If, as is likely with depression, mood occasionally worsens, the CT therapist suggests viewing this decline in mood as a chance to practice the techniques, as well as a source of data regarding what factors—automatic thoughts, for instance—worsen mood.

Descriptions of the use of CT in groups (Covi, Roth, & Lipman, 1982) and with couples (Rush, Shaw, & Khatami, 1980) are available. These formats might enable the therapist to observe interactional styles of the client that maintain cognitive distortions. Spouses or fellow group members can also serve to illustrate to clients the viability of alternative ways of conceptualizing situations.

Empirical Status

There is probably no approach to psychotherapy that has received as much attention in the past decade from clinical researchers as has Beck's cognitive therapy. Many experiments lend general support to the efficacy of the treatment package for depressed clients (e.g., Blackburn, Bishop, Glen, Whalley, & Christie, 1981; Rush, Beck, Kovacs, & Hollon, 1977; Shaw, 1977). The impact of CT on depression and hopelessness seems to be maintained for at least 1 year after treatment (Kovacs, Rush, Beck, & Hollon, 1981). Further, evidence is emerging that indicates the joint importance of both the cognitive and the behavioral components (Taylor & Marshall, 1977; Wilson, Goldin, & Charbonneau-Powis, 1983). One sign of the importance of cognitive therapy is a large ongoing collaborative study funded by the National Institute of Mental Health, results from which should provide more data on the strengths and limitations of the therapy approach.

Much of the interest in CT on the part of researchers probably resulted from the Rush et al. (1977) data comparing CT to imipramine treatment for moderate to severe unipolar depression. CT consisted of a maximum of 20 interviews in 12 weeks, whereas imipramine was administered at 250 mg per day for 12 weeks. Both groups showed significant improvement on self-report and clinician-rated depression measures, the CT group significantly more so. The CT group's mean Beck Depression Inventory score, for example, declined from 30.21 to 7.26 (a score between 0 and 9 is typically considered nondepressed), compared with a drop from 30.09 to 17.45 for the imipramine group. The CT group also showed lower dropout and were less likely to return to treatment within 6 months.[8]

SOCIAL PROBLEM SOLVING

Experimental psychologists have long been interested in how people solve problems—indeed, their purview has extended to infrahuman species as well (see Köhler, 1925). Our attention in this section is on the utility of problem-solving approaches in therapy.

---

[8] Possible limitations of the Rush et al. data have been discussed. First, the drug treatment with which CT was compared might have been suboptimal (Becker & Schuckit, 1978). However, drug therapy is not suitable for all patients, so even if the superiority of CT to drug therapy is open to question, demonstration of its effectiveness is important (Rush, Hollon, Beck, & Kovacs, 1978). Second, drug-refractory patients, for whom an effective psychotherapy for depression is perhaps most needed, were excluded from the Rush et al. study; some preliminary evidence suggests that CT has a lesser impact on these patients (Fennell & Teasdale, 1982).

D'Zurilla and Goldfried (1971) described such a model of problem solving dealing with social rather than impersonal, intellectual problems. Social problem solving (SPS) is not limited to interpersonal problems, however; one can also apply the model to intrapersonal problems such as financial, educational or career-related ones (D'Zurilla & Nezu, 1982).

D'Zurilla and Goldfried (1971) defined a problem as a situation in which "No effective response alternative is immediately available to the individual confronted with the situation" (p. 108). Problem solving, in turn, was defined as "a behavioral process, whether overt or cognitive in nature, which (a) makes available a variety of potentially effective response alternatives for dealing with the problematic situation and (b) increases the probability of selecting the most effective response from among these various alternatives" (p. 108). Problem solving, in this model, is successfully completed when the situation is no longer problematic to the person and when other consequences of the solution are reasonably good.

SPS training seeks to teach a client a general procedure to use in solving problems, as opposed to alleviating only the client's most pressing current problem. Goldfried (1980) noted that clients frequently enter therapy expecting rapid help in solving a particular problem, not generalized training in problem-solving procedures. Many also think therapy will involve an expert doing something to or for them. SPS training, in which the therapist is a model and consultant, and the client is a student learning a generally applicable self-control technique, contradicts these expectations. Besides emphasizing the idea behind SPS training at the start of therapy, it is important for therapists to watch for any behavior suggesting that the client views what is learned in therapy as pertinent only when the presenting problem is causing distress.

Stages

Five stages are distinguished in social problem solving, primarily for clarity in training and in research on the model. In practice, clients and therapists no doubt proceed in a less tidy, orderly manner than the one described by the model (D'Zurilla & Nezu, 1982). Clinical transcripts illustrating this process can be found in Goldfried and Davison (1976, pp. 194–205). The stages of the SPS model follow.

Problem Orientation

The therapist tries to foster in a client a set that will facilitate successful problem solving. Such a set should include

1. Ability to identify problematic situations. Feelings of frustration, for instance, can be used by the client as cues that there must be a problem to which he or she should attend.

2. Regarding of problems as a normal part of life and recognizing that SPS techniques provide an appropriate way of dealing with them.
3. Feelings of self-efficacy (Bandura, 1977), which should facilitate both initiation of problem-solving attempts and persistence when some fail at first.
4. The habit of stopping and thinking before taking action to try to solve a problem, as opposed to either acting impulsively on the first idea that comes to mind or resigning oneself to the problem and doing nothing.

In trying to develop this set in clients, the clinician presents the rationale behind SPS, that distress and maladaptive behavior often result from ineffective problem solving. She or he might point out that problems ranging from the imposing to the trivial are prominent in daily living, so any way a client can learn to deal with them successfully will be quite useful. It would also be appropriate at this stage to have the client practice identifying problems by keeping a record of situations that seem troubling.

Problem Definition and Formulation

Most problems in the social world are ambiguous and difficult to formulate clearly. Effectiveness at later stages of problem solving depends on defining the problem clearly at this stage. To do so, therapist and client try to (a) obtain all available information about the problem in concrete, specific terms; (b) separate the information that seems relevant from that which is irrelevant to problem solving and try to distinguish facts from possibly inaccurate inferences or assumptions; (c) identify the problematic aspects of the situation—the threats and frustrations inherent in it, subproblems within it, conflicts between incompatible goals, and so on; (d) set realistic goals for the SPS process and specify the desired outcomes. It is important that the goals be attainable, for ending the SPS cycle depends on a satisfactory match between obtained outcomes and desired outcomes. If goals are set impossibly high, the client will never be satisfied with the results.

Generation of Alternatives

The aim is to list a range of potentially effective solutions to the problem. Three principles guide work at this stage.

1. *Deferred judgment.* Good solutions are more apt to be found if clients are initially uncritical in brainstorming for alternatives than if they consider only good solutions.
2. *Quantity breeds quality.* Good solutions are more likely to arise if one seeks to think of many potential solutions.
3. *Strategies–tactics.* Problem solvers will arrive at better solutions if they distinguish between strategies (general alternative directions to take) and

tactics (specific alternatives for implementing strategies). Good strategies are those likely to resolve major aspects of the problem, whereas tactics are evaluated on how well they implement the strategies. Typically, strategies are generated first; then, client and therapist move on to the decision-making stage, select the best strategy, and generate alternative tactics that might be useful in implementing the preferred strategy.

Decision Making

The utility of a strategy or tactic is estimated by the likely consequences of selecting that alternative and the utility of those consequences for dealing with the problem. Determining probable consequences involves considering how likely a solution alternative would be to have the specified effects if implemented properly *and* how likely the client would be to implement it properly.

Consequences to be considered include short- and long-term effects of the solution and effects on the client and on others. Needless to say, such judgments of utility are heavily subjective and influenced by the therapist's and client's value systems.

Solution Implementation and Verification — w+ loss plan

This final stage takes the problem solver into the world of overt behavior and out of a strictly cognitive mode. Elements of it include

1. *Performance.* The client tries out the chosen solution.
2. *Observation.* The client records results, monitoring situations, problem-solving attempts, and emotional consequences.
3. *Evaluation.* The observed results are compared to goals specified at the problem-definition stage. If the client is dissatisfied, he or she must decide along with the therapist whether the difficulty lies in problem-solving errors (in which case they return to generation of alternatives), overly high standards (return to problem definition and formulation), or behavioral skill deficits blocking execution of a suitable solution (instigate behavior rehearsal, skill training, etc.).

If, on the other hand, the client is satisfied with the fit between obtained results and desired results, she or he is encouraged to reinforce herself or himself with positive self-statements and tangible rewards. Self-reinforcement for successful problem solving is thought to improve a client's sense of self-efficacy and to increase the likelihood of further use of SPS, though no data are available to bear out this assumption (D'Zurilla & Nezu, 1982).

In teaching a client the SPS model, the therapist could start by modeling the process, thinking aloud while moving through the stages. Gradually, though, the client is given more responsibility for the process, with the therapist fading his or her level of activity and becoming more of a consultant.

Evaluation

Conceptual

Kanfer and Busemeyer (1982) contended that the SPS model described above is relevant primarily to static decision-making situations, in which a decision is to be made once and for all (e.g., whether or not to have surgery). Many clients' problems might better be thought of as dynamic. The client's goals can change over time. The environment, and therefore the likely consequences of solution strategies, can also change over time.

Perhaps the most important difference between the static and dynamic problem-solving models is that in the dynamic model evaluation occurs not only in the final stage, solution implementation and verification. Instead, feedback is garnered at each stage of the model. Clients test hypotheses about actions that might bring them closer to their goals, which are themselves open to reevaluation at all times. Rather than looking at the problem-solving process as one large decision to make about how to reach the overall goal, to be evaluated in the end as a success or a failure, the dynamic model sees problem solving as a series of small decisions about how to move closer to a satisfactory solution. In making later decisions in the sequence, one can draw on feedback regarding the outcomes of earlier decisions. Kanfer and Busemeyer (1982) made specific suggestions about how to reach and evaluate the small decisions made in this dynamic problem-solving process.

Empirical

Outcome studies provide some support for SPS training in the D'Zurilla-Goldfried model. Alcoholic patients trained with the model performed better than did a no-treatment control group or an attention-placebo group on a situational competency test (e.g., a hypothetical alcohol-related situation is presented; what would you do or say to handle it?) and in actual drinking behavior (e.g., number of days drunk) at 1-year follow-up (Chaney, O'Leary, & Marlatt, 1978).

Depressed elderly patients given SPS training did better on a problem-solving measure and in lowering their Beck Depression Inventory scores and improving Hospital Adjustment Scale scores than did patients in social reinforcement groups (Hussian & Lawrence, 1981).

Treatment outcome research has begun to support the efficacy of the SPS model as a whole, whereas process research has elucidated the importance of various aspects of the program. For example, training in problem definition and formulation helped students, given a goal and a list of possible solutions from which to choose for each of eight social problems, make decisions rated as better than those of students not receiving such training (Nezu & D'Zurilla, 1981a).

In similar studies, each stage of the SPS model appeared to be important

(D'Zurilla & Nezu, 1980; Nezu & D'Zurilla, 1979, 1981b), though no data are available on the role of the solution implementation and verification stage. It is not yet clear whether training in more than one of the stages is needed. An inherent limitation of the laboratory studies is that they cannot capture some of the idiographic aspects of SPS training. For instance, in choosing among alternative solutions, one must decide whether such a course of action is (a) within his or her range of competence and (b) consistent with his or her ethics. These considerations are not available to an external judge rating the quality of a decision or of an alternative generated.

Applications

SPS training is potentially applicable to any client whose troubles seem to stem from ineffectiveness in handling a *range* of problematic situations. It seems particularly appropriate for dependent clients, who may have the performance skills they need but do not effectively solve problems on their own. It is important for therapists not simply to feed such clients one "answer" after another, thereby inducing continued dependence. More beneficial for such clients would be the acquisition of SPS skills, enabling them to cope by themselves with a variety of novel problems.

SPS training might also be appropriate for any client nearing the end of therapy, as a way of promoting maintenance of gains made in treatment. Finally, SPS training seems useful for clients facing overwhelming problems (e.g., clients contemplating suicide), where determined seeking of optimal solutions is well worth the time and effort involved.

Some Basic Reservations About the SPS Approach

The SPS model provides a useful, thorough overview of problem solving, but we suspect that its widespread, literal application to most or all daily problems would prove unworkable and for some clients even detrimental.

Goldfried (1980) pointed out that SPS training implicitly advocates very high perceived control on the part of clients. One should stop and think but then act, avoiding the tendency to do nothing. If it does not work, reevaluate where you went wrong and then go back and try it again. Be persistent. Life is full of problems best viewed as challenges.

Underestimating one's control over situations can indeed perpetuate problems and dissatisfactions. However, the attitude instilled in clients during SPS training can lead to considerable frustration and to fruitless struggles to change the unchangeable. This determination to exert control at all times may be an aspect of the Type A behavior pattern, predictive of coronary problems (Friedman & Rosenman, 1959).

Second, the SPS model, especially insofar as the clinician presents it by pointing out the ubiquity of problems in life and the utility of viewing them through this framework, seems to endorse an extremely calculating approach to daily life. Clients are taught rather doggedly to generate and evaluate alternative solutions to problematic situations and to monitor thoroughly the results of their efforts. It might be wiser for therapists to suggest instead that although life is replete with problems, only a subset merits cranking up the full-blown SPS apparatus to arrive at a solution. Leibenstein (1980) described *calculatedness* as a variable, a component of rationality but not identical to it. When the stakes are relatively low, it is rational to expend less than a complete effort at calculating the consequences and utilities of various alternative actions. Calculating is considered effortful, albeit to different degrees, by most people, and a clinician might do well to promote discrimination on the part of clients, so that they allocate effort and calculatedness in problem solving only when it really counts.

Problem-Solving as an Attitude:
A Different Perspective

> *Son:* "Can I have a motorcycle when I get old enough?"
> *Father:* "If you take care of it. . . . "
> *Son:* "Is it hard?"
> *Father:* "Not if you have the right attitudes. It's having the right attitudes that's hard." (Pirsig, 1974, p. 405)

Our own approach to problem solving emphasizes the initial, orientation, phase of the SPS model, elaborating the remaining stages only for especially refractory problems. To be sure, for certain pivotal, difficult problems the laborious, thorough SPS approach might be called for.

> When I think of formal scientific method an image sometimes comes to mind of an enormous juggernaut, a huge bulldozer — slow, tedious, lumbering, laborious but invincible. It takes twice as long . . . as informal . . . techniques, but you know in the end you're going to *get* it. (Pirsig, 1974, p. 100)

For most problems encountered in the course of living, though, we suspect that one should pay most attention not to the particular thought process and stages passed through on the way to a solution but to the *attitude* taken toward whatever process is used. Pirsig (1974) suggested that the most important problem-solving tool we need is "gumption," which he called "the psychic gasoline that keeps the whole thing going. If you haven't got it there's no way the motorcycle can possibly be fixed. But if you *have* got it and know how to keep it there's absolutely no way in this whole world that motorcycle can *keep* from getting fixed" (p. 297). Although nonmechanical problems sometimes find a way to keep from getting fixed by even the most gumption-filled problem solver (see earlier discussion of Goldfried, 1980, and the perils of assuming every problem can be solved), this still seems an appropriate approach for a problem solver. To maintain gumption it could be necessary at times to reconsider one's whole framework in approaching the problem. The SPS model suggests that if a solution fails to meet the client's standard, she or he should decide whether deficient skills, unrealistic standards, or deficient problem solving was at fault, and then correct the error. We acknowledge the frequent utility of these lines of attack but would like to add a fourth possibility to consider, in particular when none of the first three is obviously to blame for the unsatisfactory outcome.

The fourth angle from which to look at a solution that does not work considers that perhaps the question or problem itself needs to be "unasked." Maybe the attempt at a solution is neither a success nor exactly a failure but simply wrongheaded, in that the "solution" lies in a context beyond the one in which the problem has been formulated. The whole approach needs to be rethought, not simply recycled for another try. One way of reconsidering in this fashion is to avoid desperately trying another potential solution to the problem as formulated or returning to the generation-of-alternatives stage.

Rather, the therapist and the client might want to let go of the model temporarily and, metaphorically speaking, simply sit and stare at the problem for a while (Pirsig, 1974). Be interested in it and immerse yourself in looking at it. When you are feeling "stuck," the methods of science and perhaps of the SPS model are not necessarily the answer. Rather, *what* information do I need to collect and state concretely? *Where* do I find the right alternatives to generate? SPS can tell us some general principles (try for a lot of alternatives; be uncritical; go from general strategies to specific tactics), but it cannot prescribe a way of coming up with those alternatives we need when the problem is truly sticky. It is at this point that one's only recourse could be to stare at it, accept being stuck for the time being, and remain open to the possibility that approaches will emerge other than the framework within which client and therapist have been working to this point.

ATTRIBUTION THERAPY

Psychologists have been interested for some time in the explanations people develop for the causes of their behavior (thinking, feeling, acting). The assumption has been that these explanations, or attributions, play a central role in subsequent behavior. This focus received considerable impetus from the work of Schachter and Singer (1962) in their classic experiments on what Mandler (1962) termed the *plasticity of emotion*. The basic argument was that, given a level and kind of autonomic arousal, a person would have emotions as radically different as joy and fear, depending on the attributions he or she was induced to make about the arousal.

Soon social and experimental-clinical psychologists began to apply attributional ideas to the modification of clinically relevant analogues. An early study by Ross, Rodin, and Zimbardo (1969) can serve as a paradigmatic example. Subjects were persuaded to attribute physiological symptoms normally associated with fear, such as tremors, palpitations and hyperventilation, to an emotionally irrelevant source, noise. All subjects were first made afraid by being told they would be shocked, with one group (noise attribution) told that side effects of noise bombardment include the above fear-related symptoms. *Shock attribution* subjects were told that noise often produces side effects, such as dull headache, presumably unrelated to fear. When feeling aroused after the shock warning, the noise attribution subject could suppose that this arousal was a side effect of the noise, with no implications for her or his emotional state. A shock attribution subject, on the other hand, would not conclude that the arousal resulted from noise and so might attribute it to fear and therefore behave more fearfully. Subjects in the shock attribution group did behave more fearfully, spending significantly more of their available time (78% vs. 49% on average) on a puzzle whose completion would enable them to avoid shocks, as against one that would enable them to obtain monetary rewards.

Many other experiments appeared at the same time and thereafter (e.g., Davison & Valins, 1969; Storms & Nisbett, 1970; Valins & Ray, 1967), strengthening the supposition that human psychological problems could be altered by changing the ways people construed the reasons for their predicaments. However, conceptual and methodological critiques also began to appear, some of them unsuccessful attempts at replicating the original studies.

For instance, a replication of the Ross et al. shock avoidance study (Calvert-Boyanowsky & Leventhal, 1975) suggested that information, rather than attribution, was the crucial variable. In the replication study, suggestion of arousal symptoms, whether attributed to noise or to a subject's fear of shock, led to less avoidant behavior than did suggestion of irrelevant symptoms (e.g., dizziness, ringing in the ears, dull headache) attributed to either noise or fear. It could be that veridical information about what symptoms will be experienced helps subjects cope with these symptoms better, and/or that nonveridical information (e.g., you will feel a dull headache) arouses a subject, who may be wondering what is happening and why she or he feels agitated and not as the doctor promised. This information hypothesis as a reinterpretation of the misattribution results of Ross et al. has not been refuted and remains a plausible alternative explanation (Reisenzein, 1983).

In our view, the situation with misattribution resembles the debates in the desensitization literature 15 years ago (e.g., Mathews, 1971; Wilson &

Davison, 1971). There is probably some truth or at least clinical utility in the idea, but the empirical support is weaker than was once thought.

New, Improved Attribution Therapy

Responses to replication failures and theoretical reinterpretations of misattribution findings have taken two general approaches: (a) Do a better job of presenting a convincing misattribution to neutral stimuli, or (b) change the goal of the attributional manipulation.

Pill attributions, often employed in misattribution research, may not be strong enough to overcome a subject's previous history with a problem (Lowery, Denney, & Storms, 1979). A long history of nighttime arousal and insomnia, for instance, might undermine the credibility of an experimenter's claim that arousal on experimental nights is due solely to a pill (or, Why is this night different from all other nights?). As an alternative to the placebo attribution, Lowery et al. devised a *nonpejorative self attribution*, namely, that subjects' sleep difficulties result from basal autonomic arousal that is high, though within normal limits. For this group the symptom was normalized: They were told that people with high basal arousal have more trouble getting to sleep but are otherwise no different from other people.

The nonpejorative self-attribution group reported having an easier time getting to sleep, and only this group actually got to sleep more quickly (30 min vs. 43 min average) than a control group on days 3 through 7 of the experiment (nonsignificant differences on first two days). These results suggest that an innocuous source to which a client can attribute a problem might be most useful if the source is continually in effect and therefore a plausible cause of a long-standing problem.

Rather than thinking of a better emotionally neutral source to which subjects can attribute their problems, some therapists have tried to use attributional principles for other ends. For example, instead of inducing an external, innocuous attribution for a problem (e.g., it's the pill that does this to me; I'm not really neurotic), one might wish to get clients to attribute a problem to a source that is changeable, thereby inspiring hope that progress is possible. Subjects selected to try out such an attributional strategy were college freshmen who reported having done worse than they thought they could have done in their first semester of college, whose current grade point averages (GPA) were not over 3.5 and who exceeded the median in a large sample for self-reported worry about academic performance. Half of the subjects were informed by way of GPA group averages of previous students, as well as videotaped interviews with upperclassmen, that students often do poorly in the first year of college but improve later. This one-time, relatively simple induction of an innocuous (it happens to everybody; I'm not the only one who has had trouble the first year), unstable (I can expect to do better in future years) attribution showed strong, lasting effects on students' expectancies and performance. GPA-informed subjects did better than noninformed subjects on sample items from the Graduate Record Exam a week later (70% vs. 58% of items correct), were less likely than noninformed subjects to drop out of school within the next year (5% vs. 25%), and, among those still in school, showed a greater GPA gain from first-semester freshman year to second-semester sophomore year (.34 vs. −.05). Informed subjects also showed significantly higher expectations of future academic improvement by the time they graduated (GPA increase of .45 vs. .24 predicted), though no improvement was found on mood measures (Wilson & Linville, 1982).

A Clinical Example

An early clinical report by Davison (1966) represents an amalgam of the implications of such studies as those of Lowery et al. (1979) and Wilson and Linville (1982) in that a patient was led to reattribute a symptom to a source that was both nonpejorative (and more normal) and changeable. A hospitalized patient who had been diagnosed as a paranoid schizophrenic felt tension from "pressure points" above his right eye, which he viewed as caused by a spirit either inside or outside his body. He had had a cyst removed over the eye in an attempt to get rid of the pressure points, to no avail. Davison suggested to the patient that these pressure points might reflect tension arising from anxiety-provoking situations (the normalizing and unstable attribution). In CT-like fashion, he invited the patient to test this new attribution of the symptom as a hypothesis. By contracting his forearm muscles, the patient was able to observe the similarity of muscle tension whose origin was obviously not supernatural. Deep muscle relaxation and its ameliorating effects on the pressue points and on his general anxiety level also helped convince the patient, and he came to think and speak of the "pressure points" as ordinary "sensations." His overall paranoid picture improved.

Note that in this case the suggested therapeutic attribution of a symptom was not a misattribution; deception is by no means always necessary in order to employ attribution methods in therapy (Valins & Nisbett, 1976). Typically the origins of a client's problem are, strictly speaking, unknown and unknowable. It seems therefore ethical to emphasize those likely causes that suggest a client can do something about the problem.

Maintenance

A separate series of studies has looked at the uses of attributions regarding gains made in therapy, in contrast with the studies we have looked at so far, which attempted to manipulate subjects' attributions of the causes of their problems.

Subjects with insomnia problems recorded their sleep patterns during a 4-day baseline period. They then underwent 7 days of treatment featuring self-initiated procedures such as consistent scheduling of lying down to sleep and a relaxation induction upon going to bed. They were also provided with a low dose of chloral hydrate (Davison, Tsujimoto, & Glaros, 1973). Immediately after this treatment phase, half of the subjects were told they had received an optimal dose of the drug, permitting them to attribute any improvement they had noticed during the week to the drug. The other subjects were informed that they had received too low a dose to do any good, leaving the self-controlled psychological procedures as the most plausible attribution for behavioral change.

There were no significant differences between groups in treatment response, but the group that was told they had received a minimal, ineffective dose maintained their improvement significantly better during the 4 days of posttreatment monitoring. The optimal-dose group improved from an average sleep onset time of 55 min at baseline to 17 min during the treatment week but completely relapsed ($M = 63$ min) during posttreatment. Subjects who were told they had gotten a minimal dose improved from 44 min at pretest to 23 min during treatment and 37 min at posttest. The proposed mechanism accounting for these results, self-attribution of gains, was supported by a direct check: Subjects in the minimal group attributed their improvement about 70% to psychological procedures, 30% to the drug, with roughly the reverse percentages attributed by the optimal group.

The utility of attributing treatment gains to oneself for maintaining change has been supported in research on smoking (Chambliss & Murray, 1979) and weight control (Jeffrey, 1974; Sonne & Janoff, 1979). Chambliss and Murray found the internal attribution of change helpful only for smokers reporting internal locus of control. It could be that external subjects were less ready to accept an experimenter's message that they had been responsible for their improvement.

Overview: What Types of Attributions for Whom?

Perhaps the most consistently applicable use of attributions in therapy is attempts to induce clients to attribute therapeutic improvements to themselves and not to drugs or the actions of their therapists (Davison & Valins, 1969). Anything that makes the client feel more responsible for her or his improvement in therapy ought to facilitate independence from the therapist and ability to maintain treatment gains on one's own.

With respect to attributions of causes of the problem in the first place, therapists would do well to be more flexible in their thinking (Brehm, 1976; Forsterling, 1980). Rather than assume that all clients are best helped by the induction of, say, an internal unstable attribution, the clinician should consider each client's difficulties in the context of her or his current attributional pattern and what might seem to be a more desirable attribution. Forsterling (1980) analyzed attributions of problems according to a 2 (internal or external) × 2 (variable or stable) table and suggested that trying to help a client shift from any of these attributions to any of the others could at some point be useful with some clients. As examples, consider:

1. A bright client who attributes failures to stupidity might be encouraged to think of failures as resulting from lack of effort (internal stable to internal variable).
2. A client who thinks she or he cannot manage interpersonal relationships because of some previous unsatisfactory ones might be persuaded to think of these experiences as an insufficient sample for drawing that conclusion and probably a result of bad luck (internal stable to external variable).
3. A client who feels pressured to work to the point of exhaustion for fear that she cannot otherwise meet her responsibilities might be persuaded to think about the evidence and realize that she is very competent and need not exert superhuman effort every time to succeed (internal variable to internal stable).
4. A client who believes he can exert control over the uncontrollable and gets into trouble as a result, for example, a compulsive gambler, could be led to recognize the chance nature of some outcomes and the futility of trying to control them (internal variable to external variable).

What can the attribution-minded therapist do if simply suggesting an attribution to a client ("Your problem, sir, is lack of effort") is not enough? Real clients with long-standing problems presumably have some notions about what caused the problem, how it is maintained, and how it can or cannot be changed. They could be more difficult to convince of the therapist's preferred attribution than are experimental subjects who are told that a pill was or was not therapeutically effective.

One advantage a therapist has over an experimenter is in the use of mere repetition of an idea. Persuasion research suggests that a moderate level of repetition is most effective (Petty & Cacioppo, 1981). Forsterling (1980) suggested several other possibilities as well. Therapists can use Socratic dialogue to undermine clients' dysfunctional attributions and elaborate preferred ones, in much the same way that a rational-emotive therapist would try to replace an irrational belief with a rational one. As in cognitive therapy, behavioral assignments can be employed as experiments to gather evidence for or against attributions.

In designing either in-session verbal arguments or behavioral experiments, the therapist needs to bear in mind the following three variables suggested by Kelley (1967) as crucial to attribution formation. Clients can be questioned about the degree of *consensus* surrounding their attributions (e.g., You say that your boss is impossible to get along with and put all the blame on him. Would every one of 100 other people in your situation behave and feel the same way and reach the same conclusion?). Or he or she might be asked about *consistency* (You say you are a failure. Have you always failed at every task you have set for yourself?). Finally, questions about *covariation* might help to convince a client of a particular attribution advocated by a therapist. Consider a client whom the therapist wishes to convince that the internal, variable factor of effort is important in his or her problem. The therapist might ask if she or he could succeed in overcoming or avoiding the problem by deliberately *not* putting forth any effort. If the client agrees that not trying would not overcome the problem, effort and success have been established as covarying. (Consider, here, the similarities to Beck's therapeutic suggestions.)

GENERAL CONSIDERATIONS IN COGNITIVE CHANGE METHODS

Are There Any Nonscientists Left?

Several cognitive therapy writers have employed the metaphor of a scientist for describing people (e.g., Bedrosian & Beck, 1980; Guidano & Liotti, 1983; Kelly, 1955; Mahoney, 1974). The client is said to be a personal scientist whose beliefs are analogous to scientific theories. These beliefs operate within a personal paradigm, the altering of which resembles in its difficulty the paradigm shifts and scientific revolutions discussed on a grander scale by Kuhn (1962). An important part of therapy involves teaching the client to be a better scientist, to collect data and perform experiments in order to test and perhaps disconfirm maladaptive ideas.

We recognize that these theorists use the personal scientist image metaphorically and that it might be a useful metaphor whether or not everyday life actually resembles scientific inquiry very closely. Nonetheless, we would like to question how hard the metaphor should be pushed. Much of our behavior is probably carried on without a great deal of thoughtful consideration, hypothesis testing, or theory building (Thorngate, 1976), involving much habit and ritual. To be sure, the habitual, nonreflective nature of much maladaptive behavior could be part of the problem, so that training as a thoughtful personal scientist might be needed to induce change (Meichenbaum, 1977). However, a potential pitfall in assuming that everybody tries to assign causality and only lacks training in how to do it better is that we might overlook the possibility that what psychologists tend to find enjoyable and worthwhile (e.g. experimentation, reflection, attribution) could be regarded as quite effortful and aversive, perhaps even irrelevant, by others.

> The attribution literature makes the basic assumption that people *care* what the causes of their behavior are. This central idea is the brainchild of psychologists whose business it is to explain behavior. It may be that psychologists (and psychiatrists) have projected their own need to explain behavior onto other people! Laypeople may simply not reflect on why they act and feel as they do to the same extent that psychologists do (Davison & Neale, 1982, p. 247n).

Resistance

One consequence of skepticism about the assumption that all clients are at home in the role of personal scientist is that it could help us appreciate our own procedures as possible causes of resistance. In a discussion of countercontrol, Davison (1973) called attention to the high level of client cooperation necessary for the successful implementation of any behavior therapy procedure. Indeed, homework assignments, often detailed and extensive, are prominent in cognitive therapies. If a client is less than enthusiastic about collecting data, he or she will find it difficult to comply with, say, a cognitive therapist's request for hourly ratings of the mastery and pleasure associated with activities. Such data-gathering activities are likely to help clients and are important therapeutic tools, but it is well to expect some clients to need a very persuasive rationale for such a burdensome undertaking.

Cognitive therapists might encounter resistance (or what J. Brehm, 1966, terms reactance) particularly as they try to change clients' cognitive structures (rules, assumptions, etc.), perhaps more than in their attempts to elicit compliance with specific behavioral procedures. People have a stake in their implicit ideas about how the world works and what one can expect from life, ideas that afford security and a sense of stability (Didion, 1979; Goodman, 1979).[9] They should not be expected completely to abandon

---

[9] As difficult as it is to change behavior, it is all the more difficult to change cognitions. History is replete with examples of overt behavioral changes without accompanying changes in people's thoughts and ideals. Davison (1973), with only the tip of his tongue in cheek, referred to this as *the Kol Nidre effect*, in reference to the forgiveness Jews sought from God after overtly converting to Catholicism during the Spanish Inquisition lest they be slaughtered, all the while maintaining their Jewish identity. The Kol Nidre prayer basically proclaims to God that "all vows" (made to Catholicism) were not truly intentioned or genuine and hence should be ignored by God.

them as soon as a therapist arranges a potentially disconfirmatory experience.[10] Moreover, no matter how maladaptive a cognitive structure might seem to an observer, it undoubtedly helps the troubled client organize his or her life. Such structures are partially self-confirming (Sollod & Wachtel, 1980). For instance, assuming oneself to be incompetent affects not only one's interpretation of available evidence but also the nature of this evidence. One might come to perform incompetently because of self-defeating expectancies, fail to enter situations that might provide contrary experiences, be treated therefore as incompetent by others, and so forth. So it makes sense to suppose that clients' entire ways of viewing the world, supported by emotional investment and by the self-confirming data that are noted because of these views, might not yield to a single cogent argument from a therapist or to a single corrective experiment. More detailed discussion of these and related practical and conceptual issues regarding resistance appears in Beck et al. (1979; see especially chapter 14) and in Wachtel (1982).

Cognitive Assessment and Cognitive Change Methods

Miller and Berman (1983) recently published a quantitative review of outcome studies employing cognitive behavior therapies. A noteworthy aspect of this review concerns the subject variables assessed for possible subject-treatment interactions. Available data enabled the authors to evaluate such variables as diagnostic category of subjects; whether they were student volunteers, community volunteers or outpatients; and subjects' age, gender, and level of education. This is all well and good, but it seems more likely that important subject-treatment matching variables will be discovered through the consistent use of cognitive assessment tools as measures of change and as subject selection criteria.

For example, it might be that depressed clients who show a high level of cognitive distortion would benefit most from Beck's cognitive therapy, whereas others might process and interpret experiences in adaptive ways but simply not engage in enough pleasant events and might, therefore, be better served by a treatment that focuses on increasing pleasant experiences (Lewinsohn, 1974). This kind of idiographic information would not be detected by sorting subjects according to diagnostic category or demographic

---

[10]Scientists themselves are hardly exemplars of rational information-seekers who change their views just as soon as disconfirming data are available!

variables. What is needed are procedures specifically designed for the collection of verbal reports that reflect the cognitive activities of clients in particular situations. For example, what is the depressed person thinking about as he or she views his or her carefully planned outdoor barbecue come to naught as a thunderstorm strikes unexpectedly? A variety of cognitive assessment methods have been recently developed, such as the Automatic Thoughts Questionnaire (Hollon & Kendall, 1980) and, in our own laboratory, the Articulated Thoughts During Simulated Situations method (Davison, Robins, & Johnson, 1983). Any therapy as specific and target oriented as a cognitive change method will not achieve outcomes any more favorable than the assessment on which it is based.

CONCLUSION

In this chapter we have critically described the rationales for, the common procedures of, and some underlying problems with the principal methods for clinical cognitive change: the rational-emotive therapy of Albert Ellis, the cognitive therapy of Aaron T. Beck, social problem solving, and several approaches employing reattribution. Proponents of each approach have an abiding faith in the power of our conscious, rational minds to direct and redirect our emotions and behavior. Empirical findings, some of them analogical, provide reason to continue operating under this assumption. At the same time, however, we saw how important to the major theorists behavioral, or performance-based, procedures remain. The distinction between workers like Ellis and Beck, on the one hand, and the less cognitive of behavior therapists, on the other hand, would seem to be that, for the former, behavioral change is important not only as a major outcome measure but also as a strong vehicle for altering cognitions. For it is the change of people's constructions of their worlds that will maintain and extend beneficial overt behavioral modifications. Moreover, such cognitive changes will allow people not only to adapt to and change their current life situations but also to deliberate effectively about the broad range of life's challenges that none of us can foresee with certainty.

A final observation concerns the essentially *phenomenological* nature of cognitive change methods. Like Rogers (1951) and Perls (1969), Ellis and Beck exhort therapists to take the client's frame of reference as the ultimate determinant of reality. Differences exist between the work examined in this chapter and the writings of the humanists and existentialists, differences in epistemology, in theory, and in procedure. But it seems just as important to appreciate the similarity, as we direct our and our clients' attention to the stories they tell themselves and the variations they might see fit to introduce into their life scripts.

REFERENCES

Alden, L., & Safran, J. (1978). Irrational beliefs and nonassertive behavior. *Cognitive Therapy and Research, 2,* 357-364.

Arnkoff, D. B., & Glass, C. R. (1982). Clinical cognitive constructs: Examination, evaluation, and elaboration. In P. C. Kendall (Ed.), *Advances in cognitive-behavioral research and therapy* (Vol. 1, 1-34). New York: Academic Press.

Bandura, A. (1969). *Principles of behavior modification.* New York: Holt, Rinehart and Winston.

Bandura, A. (1977). Self-efficacy: Toward a unifying theory of behavioral change. *Psychological Review, 84,* 191-215.

Beck, A. T. (1967). *Depression: Clinical, experimental and theoretical aspects.* New York: Harper and Row.

Beck, A. T. (1976). *Cognitive therapy and the emotional disorders.* New York: International Universities Press.

Beck, A. T., Rush, A. J., Shaw, B. F., & Emery, G. (1979). *Cognitive therapy of depression.* New York: Guilford.

Becker, J., & Schuckit, M. A. (1978). The comparative efficacy of cognitive therapy and pharmacotherapy in the treatment of depression. *Cognitive Therapy and Research, 2,* 193-197.

Bedrosian, R. C., & Beck, A. T. (1980). Principles of cognitive therapy. In M. J. Mahoney (Ed.), *Psychotherapy process: Current issues and future directions* (pp. 127-152). New York: Plenum.

Bernard, M. E. (1981). Private thought in rational emotive psychotherapy. *Cognitive Therapy and Research, 5,* 125-142.

Blackburn, I. M., Bishop, S., Glen, A. I. M., Whalley, L. J., & Christie, J. E. (1981). The efficacy of cognitive therapy in depression: A treatment trial using cognitive therapy and pharmacotherapy, each alone and in combination. *British Journal of Psychiatry, 139,* 181-189.

Block, J. (1980). Effects of rational emotive therapy on overweight adults. *Psychotherapy: Theory, Research and Practice, 17,* 277-280.

Brehm, J. W. (1966). *A Theory of psychological reactance.* New York: Academic Press.

Brehm, S. S. (1976). *The application of social psychology to clinical practice.* New York: John Wiley.

Calvert-Boyanowsky, J., & Leventhal, H. (1975). The role of information in attenuating behavioral responses to stress: A reinterpretation of the misattribution phenomenon. *Journal of Personality and Social Psychology, 32,* 214-221.

Chambliss, C., & Murray, E. J. (1979). Cognitive procedures for smoking reduction: Symptom attribution versus efficacy attribution. *Cognitive Therapy and Research, 3,* 91-95.

Chaney, E. F., O'Leary, M. R., & Marlatt, G. A. (1978). Skill training with alcoholics. *Journal of Consulting and Clinical Psychology, 46,* 1092-1104.

Cohen, L. J. (1981). Can human irrationality be experimentally demonstrated? *Behavioral and Brain Sciences, 14,* 317-370.

Covi, L., Roth, D., & Lipman, R. S. (1982). Cognitive group psychotherapy of depression: The close-ended group. *American Journal of Psychotherapy, 36,* 459-469.

Coyne, J. C. (1982). A critique of cognitions as causal entities with particular reference to depression. *Cognitive Therapy and Research, 6,* 3-13.

Davison, G. C. (1966). Differential relaxation and cognitive restructuring in therapy with a "paranoid schizophrenic" or "paranoid state." *Proceedings of the*

74th Annual Convention of the American Psychological Association. Washington, DC: American Psychological Association.

Davison, G. C. (1968). Systematic desensitization as a counterconditioning process. *Journal of Abnormal Psychology, 73,* 91–99.

Davison, G. C. (1973). Counter control in behavior modification. In L. A. Hamerlynck, L. C. Handy, & E. J. Mash (Eds.), *Behavior change: Methodology, concepts and practice* (pp. 153–167). Champaign, IL: Research Press.

Davison, G. C. (1976). Homosexuality: The ethical challenge. *Journal of Consulting and Clinical Psychology, 44,* 157–162.

Davison, G. C., & Neale, J. M. (1982). *Abnormal psychology: An experimental clinical approach* (3rd Ed.). New York: John Wiley.

Davison, G. C., Robins, C., & Johnson, M. K. (1983). Articulated thoughts during simulated situations: A paradigm for studying cognition in emotion and behavior. *Cognitive Therapy and Research, 7,* 17–40.

Davison, G. C., Tsujimoto, R. N., & Glaros, A. G. (1973). Attribution and the maintenance of behavior change in falling asleep. *Journal of Abnormal Psychology, 82,* 124–133.

Davison, G. C., & Valins, S. (1969). Maintenance of self-attributed and drug-attributed behavior change. *Journal of Personality and Social Psychology, 11,* 25–33.

Davison, G. C., & Zighelboim, V. (1984). *Irrational beliefs in the articulated thoughts of socially anxious college students.* Unpublished manuscript. University of Southern California, Los Angeles.

Didion, J. (1979). *The white album.* New York: Simon & Schuster, Pocket Books.

D'Zurilla, T. J., & Goldfried, M. R. (1971). Problem solving and behavior modification. *Journal of Abnormal Psychology, 78,* 107–126.

D'Zurilla, T. J., & Nezu, A. (1980). A study of the generation-of-alternatives process in social problem solving. *Cognitive Therapy and Research, 4,* 67–72.

D'Zurilla, T. J., & Nezu, A. (1982). Social problem solving in adults. In P. C. Kendall (Ed.), *Advances in cognitive-behavioral research and therapy* (Vol. 1, pp. 201–274). New York: Academic Press.

Egan, G. (1982a). *Exercises in helping skills* (2nd ed.). Monterey, CA: Brooks/Cole.

Egan, G. (1982b). *The skilled helper* (2nd ed.). Monterey, CA: Brooks/Cole.

Ellis, A. (1962). *Reason and emotion in psychotherapy.* New York: Lyle Stuart.

Ellis, A. (1977). Psychotherapy and the value of a human being. In A. Ellis & R. Grieger (Eds.), *Handbook of rational-emotive therapy* (pp. 99–112). New York: Springer.

Ellis, A. (1984). Rational-emotive therapy. In R. J. Corsini (Ed.), *Current psychotherapies* (3rd ed., pp. 196–238). Itasca, IL: F. E. Peacock.

Ellis, A., & Bernard, M. E. (1983). An overview of rational-emotive approaches to the problems of childhood. In A. Ellis & M. E. Bernard (Eds.), *Rational-emotive approaches to the problems of childhood* (pp. 3–43). New York: Plenum.

Ellis, A., & Harper, R. A. (1975). *A new guide to rational living.* Englewood Cliffs, NJ: Prentice-Hall.

Eschenroeder, C. (1982). How rational is rational-emotive therapy? A critical appraisal of its theoretical foundations and therapeutic methods. *Cognitive Therapy and Research, 6,* 381–392.

Fennell, M. J. V., & Teasdale, J. D. (1982). Cognitive therapy with chronic, drug-refractory depressed outpatients: A note of caution. *Cognitive Therapy and Research, 6,* 455–460.

Forsterling, F. (1980). Attributional aspects of cognitive behavior modification: A theoretical approach and suggestions for technique. *Cognitive Therapy and Research, 4,* 27-37.

Friedman, M., & Rosenman, R. (1959). Association of specific overt behavior pattern with blood and cardiovascular findings. *Journal of the American Medical Association, 169,* 1286-1296.

Gagnon, J. H., & Davison, G. C. (1976). Asylums, the token economy, and the metrics of mental life. *Behavior Therapy, 7,* 528-534.

Goldfried, M. R. (1980). Psychotherapy as coping skills training. In M. J. Mahoney (Ed.), *Psychotherapy process: Current issues and future directions* (pp. 89-119). New York: Plenum.

Goldfried, M. R. (1982). Resistance and clinical behavior therapy. In P. L. Wachtel (Ed.), *Resistance: Psychodynamic and behavioral approaches* (pp. 95-113). New York: Plenum.

Goldfried, M. R., & Davison, G. C. (1976). *Clinical behavior therapy.* New York: Holt, Rinehart & Winston.

Goldfried, M. R., Decenteceo, E. T., & Weinberg, L. (1974). Systematic rational restructuring as a self-control technique. *Behavior Therapy, 5,* 247-254.

Goldfried, M. R., Linehan, M. M., & Smith, J. L. (1978). Reduction of test anxiety through cognitive restructuring. *Journal of Consulting and Clinical Psychology, 46,* 32-39.

Goldfried, M. R., & Sobocinski, D. (1975). Effect of irrational beliefs on emotional arousal. *Journal of Consulting and Clinical Psychology, 43,* 504-510.

Goodman, E. (1979). *Turning points.* New York: Ballantine Books, Fawcett Crest.

Guidano, V. F., & Liotti, G. (1983). *Cognitive processes and emotional disorders: A structural approach to psychotherapy.* New York: Guilford Press.

Hollon, S. D., & Beck, A. T. (1979). Cognitive therapy of depression. In P. C. Kendall & S. D. Hollon (Eds.), *Cognitive-behavioral interventions: Theory, research, and procedures* (pp. 153-203). New York: Academic Press.

Hollon, S. D., & Kendall, P. C. (1980). Cognitive self-statements in depression: Development of an automatic thoughts questionnaire. *Cognitive Therapy and Research, 4,* 383-395.

Hussian, R. A., & Lawrence, P. S. (1981). Social reinforcement of activity and problem solving training in the treatment of depressed institutionalized elderly patients. *Cognitive Therapy and Research, 5,* 57-69.

Jeffrey, D. B. (1974). A comparison of the effects of external control and self-control on the modification and maintenance of weight. *Journal of Abnormal Psychology, 83,* 404-410.

Jones, R. (1968). *A factored measure of Ellis' irrational belief systems with personality and maladjustment correlates.* Unpublished doctoral dissertation, Texas State Technical Institute, Waco.

Kanfer, F. H., & Busemeyer, J. R. (1982). The use of problem solving and decision making in behavior therapy. *Clinical Psychology Review, 2,* 239-266.

Kanter, N. J., & Goldfried, M. R. (1979). Relative effectiveness of rational restructuring and self-control desensitization in the reduction of interpersonal anxiety. *Behavior Therapy, 10,* 472-490.

Kelley, H. H. (1967). Attribution theory in social psychology. In D. Levine (Ed.), *Nebraska symposium on motivation, 1967.* Lincoln, NE: University of Nebraska Press.

Kelley, G. A. (1955). *The psychology of personal constructs.* New York: W. W. Norton.

Kendall, P. C. (1984). Cognitive processes and procedures in behavior therapy. In G. T. Wilson, C. M. Franks, K. D. Brownell, & P. C. Kendall, *Annual review of behavior therapy: Theory and practice* (pp. 132-139). New York: Guilford Press.

Kendall, P. C., & Bemis, K. M. (1983). Thought and action in psychotherapy: The cognitive-behavioral approaches. In M. Hersen, A. Kazdin, & A. Bellack (Eds.), *The clinical psychology handbook* (pp. 565-592). Elmsford, NY: Pergamon Press.

Köhler, W. (1925). *The mentality of apes.* New York: W. W. Norton, Liveright.

Kovacs, M., Rush, A. J., Beck, A. T., & Hollon, S. D. (1981). Depressed outpatients treated with cognitive therapy or pharmacotherapy: A one-year follow-up. *Archives of General Psychiatry, 38*, 33-39.

Kuhn, T. S. (1962). *The structure of scientific revolutions.* Chicago, IL: University of Chicago Press.

Lazarus, R. S. (1980). Cognitive behavior therapy as psychodynamics revisited. In M. J. Mahoney (Ed.), *Psychotherapy process: Current issues and future directions* (pp. 121-126). New York: Plenum.

Leibenstein, H. (1980). *Beyond economic man: A new foundation for microeconomics.* Cambridge, MA: Harvard University Press.

Lewinsohn, P. M. (1974). A behavioral approach to depression. In R. J. Friedman & M. M. Katz (Eds.), *The psychology of depression: Contemporary theory and research.* Washington, DC: John Wiley, V. H. Winston.

Linehan, M. M., Goldfried, M. R., & Goldfried, A. P. (1979). Assertion therapy: Skill training or cognitive restructuring. *Behavior Therapy, 10*, 372-388.

Lipsky, M. J., Kassinove, H., & Miller, N. J. (1980). Effects of rational-emotive therapy, rational role reversal, and rational-emotive imagery on the emotional adjustment of community mental health center patients. *Journal of Consulting and Clinical Psychology, 48*, 366-374.

Lohr, J. M., & Bonge, D. (1982). Relationships between assertiveness and factorially validated measures of irrational beliefs. *Cognitive Therapy and Research, 6*, 353-356.

London, P. (1964). *The modes and morals of psychotherapy.* New York: Holt, Rinehart and Winston.

Lowery, C. R., Denney, D. R., & Storms, M. D. (1979). Insomnia: A comparison of the effects of pill attributions and nonpejorative self-attributions. *Cognitive Therapy and Research, 3*, 161-164.

MacPhillamy, D. J., & Lewinsohn, P. M. (1982). The Pleasant Events Schedule: Studies on reliability, validity, and scale intercorrelation. *Journal of Consulting and Clinical Psychology, 50*, 363-380.

Mahoney, M. J. (1974). *Cognition and behavior modification.* Cambridge, MA: Ballinger.

Mahoney, M. J. (1980). Psychotherapy and the structure of personal revolutions. In M. J. Mahoney (Ed.), *Psychotherapy process: Current issues and future directions* (pp. 157-180). New York: Plenum.

Malkiewich, L. E., & Merluzzi, T. V. (1980). Rational restructuring versus desensitization with clients of diverse conceptual levels: A test of a client-treatment matching model. *Journal of Counseling Psychology, 27*, 453-461

Mandler, G. (1962). Emotion. In R. Brown, E. Galanter, E. H. Hess, & G. Mandler (Eds.), *New directions in psychology.* New York: Holt, Rinehart & Winston.

Marzillier, J. S. (1980). Cognitive therapy and behavioural practice. *Behaviour Research and Therapy, 18*, 249-258.

Mathews, A. M. (1971). Psychophysiological approaches to the investigation of desensitization and related procedures. *Psychological Bulletin, 76*, 73–91.

Maultsby, M. C., Jr. (1977). Rational-emotive imagery. In A. Ellis & R. Grieger (Eds.), *Handbook of rational-emotive therapy* (pp. 225–230). New York: Springer.

Meichenbaum, D. (1977). *Cognitive-behavior modification: An integrative approach.* New York: Plenum.

Miller, R. C., & Berman, J. S. (1983). The efficacy of cognitive behavior therapies: A quantitative review of the research evidence. *Psychological Bulletin, 94*, 39–53.

Mischel, W. (1968). *Personality and assessment.* New York: John Wiley.

Nelson, R. E. (1977). Irrational beliefs in depression. *Journal of Consulting and Clinical Psychology, 45*, 1190–1191.

Nezu, A., & D'Zurilla, T. J. (1979). An experimental evaluation of the decision-making process in social problem-solving. *Cognitive Therapy and Research, 3*, 269–277.

Nezu, A., & D'Zurilla, T. J. (1981a). Effects of problem definition and formulation on decision making in the social problem-solving process. *Behavior Therapy, 12*, 100–106.

Nezu, A., & D'Zurilla, T. J. (1981b). Effects of problem definition and formulation on the generation of alternatives in the social problem-solving process. *Cognitive Therapy and Research, 5*, 265–271.

Perls, F. S. (1969). *Gestalt therapy verbatim.* Moab, UT: Real People Press.

Petty, R. E., & Cacioppo, J. T. (1981). *Attitudes and persuasion: Classic and contemporary approaches.* Dubuque, IA: Wm. C. Brown.

Pirsig, R. M. (1974). *Zen and the art of motorcycle maintenance: An inquiry into values.* New York: William Morrow.

Prochaska, J. O. (1984). *Systems of psychotherapy: A transtheoretical analysis.* Homewood, IL: Dorsey.

Reisenzein, R. (1983). The Schachter theory of emotion: Two decades later. *Psychological Bulletin, 94*, 239–264.

Rogers, C. R. (1951). *Client-centered therapy.* Boston: Houghton Mifflin.

Ross, L., Rodin, J., & Zimbardo, P. G. (1969). Toward an attribution therapy: The reduction of fear through induced cognitive-emotional misattribution. *Journal of Personality and Social Psychology, 12*, 279–288.

Rotter, J. B. (1954). *Social learning and clinical psychology.* Englewood Cliffs, NJ: Prentice-Hall.

Rush, A. J., Beck, A. T., Kovacs, M., & Hollon, S. D. (1977). Comparative efficacy of cognitive therapy and pharmacotherapy in the treatment of depressed outpatients. *Cognitive Therapy and Research, 1*, 17–37.

Rush, A. J., Hollon, S. D., Beck, A. T., & Kovacs, M. (1978). Depression: Must pharmacotherapy fail for cognitive therapy to succeed? *Cognitive Therapy and Research, 2*, 199–206.

Rush, A. J., Shaw, B., & Khatami, M. (1980). Cognitive therapy of depression: Utilizing the couples system. *Cognitive Therapy and Research, 4*, 103–113.

Schachter, S., & Singer, J. E. (1962). Cognitive, social and physiological determinants of emotional state. *Psychological Review, 69*, 379–399.

Shaw, B. F. (1977). Comparison of cognitive therapy and behavior therapy in the treatment of depression. *Journal of Consulting and Clinical Psychology, 45*, 543–551.

Smith, T. W. (1983). Change in irrational beliefs and the outcome of rational-emotive psychotherapy. *Journal of Consulting and Clinical Psychology, 51,* 156–157.

Sollod, R. N., & Wachtel, P. L. (1980). A structural and transactional approach to cognition in clinical problems. In M. J. Mahoney (Ed.), *Psychotherapy process: Current issues and future directions* (pp. 1–27). New York: Plenum.

Sonne, J. L., & Janoff, D. (1979). The effect of treatment attributions on the maintenance of weight reduction: A replication and extension. *Cognitive Therapy and Research, 3,* 389–397.

Storms, M. D., & Nisbett, R. E. (1970). Insomnia and the attribution process. *Journal of Personality and Social Psychology, 16,* 319–328.

Sutton-Simon, K., & Goldfried, M. R. (1979). Faulty thinking patterns in two types of anxiety. *Cognitive Therapy and Research, 3,* 193–203.

Taylor, F. G., & Marshall, W. L. (1977). Experimental analysis of a cognitive-behavioral therapy for depression. *Cognitive Therapy and Research, 1,* 59–72.

Thorngate, W. (1976). Must we always think before we act? *Personality and Social Psychology Bulletin, 2,* 31–35.

Trexler, L. D., & Karst, T. O. (1972). Rational-emotive therapy, placebo, and no-treatment effects on public-speaking anxiety. *Journal of Abnormal Psychology, 79,* 60–67.

Valins, S., & Nisbett, R. E. (1976). Attribution processes in the development and treatment of emotional disorders. In J. T. Spence, R. C. Carson, & J. W. Thibaut (Eds.), *Behavioral approaches to therapy* (pp. 261–274). Morristown, NJ: Silver Burdett, General Learning Press.

Valins, S., & Ray, A. A. (1967). Effects of cognitive desensitization on avoidance behavior. *Journal of Personality and Social Psychology, 7,* 345–350.

Vestre, N. D. (1984). Irrational beliefs and self-reported depressed mood. *Journal of Abnormal Psychology, 93,* 239–241.

Wachtel, P. L. (1977). *Psychoanalysis and behavior therapy.* New York: Basic Books.

Wachtel, P. L. (Ed.). (1982). *Resistance: Psychodynamic and behavioral approaches.* New York: Plenum.

Walen, S. R., DiGiuseppe, R., & Wessler, R. L. (1980). *A practitioner's guide to rational-emotive therapy.* New York: Oxford University Press.

Wilson, G. T., & Davison, G. C. (1971). Processes of fear-reduction in systematic desensitization: Animal studies. *Psychological Bulletin, 76,* 1–14.

Wilson, P. H., Goldin, J. C., & Charbonneau-Powis, M. (1983). Comparative efficacy of behavioral and cognitive treatments of depression. *Cognitive Therapy and Research, 7,* 111–124.

Wilson, T. D., & Linville, P. W. (1982). Improving the academic performance of college freshmen: Attribution therapy revisited. *Journal of Personality and Social Psychology, 42,* 367–376.

Wise, E. H., & Haynes, S. N. (1983). Cognitive treatment of test anxiety: Rational restructuring versus attentional training. *Cognitive Therapy and Research, 7,* 69–78.

Wolpe, J. (1958). *Psychotherapy by reciprocal inhibition.* Stanford, CA: Stanford University Press.

Zajonc, R. B. (1984). On the primacy of affect. *American Psychologist, 39,* 117–123.

8

Self-Management Methods

Frederick H. Kanfer and Lisa Gaelick

The traditional concepts underlying the activities of mental health workers imply an *administrative* model of treatment. This model presumes that clients seek assistance in an earnest effort to change their current problem situations. The helper administers a treatment to which the client submits and which eventuates in improvement in the client's life conditions. The model assigns a caretaking or administrative function to the clinician and a relatively passive, accepting, and trusting role to the client.

In some conceptual models, for example, those that rely heavily on the modification of the environment as a means of bringing about change (chapters 4 and 6), the client's participation in the helping process is relatively limited. In other approaches that rely heavily on changing cognitive behaviors (chapter 7) there is a basic presumption that the client is highly motivated to utilize the presented techniques and accepts changes in life orientation with full cooperation. The view of the client either as a passive recipient, be it of drugs, conditioning treatments, or cognitive reorganizations, or as a person who is eager to change often runs into difficulty because of the paradox of the many clients who seek help on the one hand but resist external control or guidance toward change on the other hand. A *participant* model emphasizes the importance of client responsibility in treatment. It represents a shift from the provision of a protective treatment environment toward the offering of rehabilitative experiences in which the client accepts increasing responsibilities for his or her own behavior, for dealing with the environment, and for planning the future. The therapeutic environment is viewed as a transitory support system that prepares the client to handle common social and personal demands more effectively. Although treatment methods that emphasize environmental control of behavior rest on the cooperation of another person, a teacher, a helper, a therapist, or a friend, self-management techniques are prescriptive methods that place the burden of engaging in the change process heavily on the client.

In the current literature there is increasing recognition that treatment failures could be due to two important factors (Foa & Emmelkamp, 1983). First, the methods could be ineffective. Second, the client might fail to comply with the prescribed regimen, and the methods might never be given an opportunity to operate. Clients nowadays have less confidence in unquestioned professional practices and increased sophistication about the nature and objectives of the helping process (Coyne & Widiger, 1978). They increasingly demand a participating role in the selection of treatment objectives. The self-management framework presented in this chapter rests on the following rationale:

1. Many behaviors are not easily accessible for modification by anyone but the client. For example, some intimate and sexual behaviors or some emotional reactions can lead to client discomfort even though other people do not notice their occurrence. Continuing observation and arrangement of conditions for change might require institutionalization for long periods of time, a highly uneconomical and unrealistic procedure. Therefore participation of the client as a change agent is essential in these cases.

2. Problematic behaviors are often closely associated with self-reactions and with such cognitive activities as thinking, fantasizing, imagining, or planning. These covert behaviors are essentially inaccessible to direct observation. If a client possesses an adequate behavioral repertoire for acting on the basis of her or his thoughts, changing the cognitive responses can become the primary task of the helping process. To monitor and alter these behaviors, the helper must shift major responsibility to the client.

3. Changing behavior is difficult and often unpleasant. Many clients seek assistance, but often they are motivated not so much to change as to alleviate current discomforts or threats, preferably without altering their behavior or life-styles. The client's acceptance of a program for change as desirable, feasible, and worth working for is a basic motivational requirement. This orientation constitutes the first and most critical target in a self-management program.

4. The utility of a change program lies not just in removing situation-specific problems or particular symptoms. What is learned in therapy should include a set of generalizable skills such as coping strategies, ability to assess situations and behavioral outcomes, and development of rules of conduct for common problem situations, all of which aid the client in avoiding or handling future problems more effectively than in the past.

The acceptance of responsibility in treatment requires that the client develop a strong motivation to change. Therefore a critical task of the helper is to motivate the client to actively seek change. In contrast with programs based solely on environmental control or on the helper-client relationship as the exclusive vehicle for change, the early phase of self-management therapy is designed to help the client accept the necessity for change and to develop clear objectives for treatment. Modeling, work assignments, and learning to analyze problems and work toward their resolution help the client to plan and to engage in more effective cognitive and interpersonal actions. By altering the social and physical environment, the client can alleviate the difficulty of changing and ease the maintenance of new behavior patterns. Without established incentives for change and environments in which they can be carried out, treatment effects cannot be expected to last long beyond treatment termination. As new behaviors are carried out by the individual in his or her daily life and in the absence of the therapist, the helper fades into a role of diminishing guidance. In this sense, the goal of the treatment process is its termination, and the helper follows a "principle of least intervention," providing only as much assistance as is needed to enable the client to resume control over his or her life.

Self-management methods help the client acquire new behaviors. The techniques should be viewed as temporary devices. They facilitate the learning process, but they do not necessarily become part of the person's everyday repertoire. In learning to use a typewriter, auxiliary charts, mnemonic devices, and self-instructions that guide a finger to the correct key are critical in the learning process. But the accomplished typist uses none of these assists. Similarly, such techniques as self-observation, contingent self-rewards, problem solving, or contracts serve the function of facilitating acquisition. As the person settles into a new and satisfying behavior pattern there is decreasing need for their use. However, they are available on future occasions when the client faces difficulties.

The common element in the various forms of self-management methods is the therapist's role as an instigator and motivator to help the client start a change program. Sometimes the therapist makes special arrangements to insure that the client's efforts are further supported by the natural environment at home, at school, or at work. Combined with the client's increasing skills to use a variety of techniques in future problem situations, her or his ability to alter environments can extend the durability of treatment effects beyond the time of treatment (Goldstein & Kanfer, 1979).

The change process is conducted within a negotiation model. The therapist serves as a consultant and expert who negotiates with the client how to produce change and to what end. The interactions are future oriented in that they focus on the development of general repertoires for dealing with problem situations. They deal with past experiences only as they are needed to help the client recognize the inappropriateness of his or her current behaviors or to facilitate a behavioral analysis by providing information about the conditions under which a maladaptive behavior has developed.

Earlier clinicians have tended to disregard the client's thoughts and fantasies in planning therapy programs. Indeed, in circumstances where strict control of behaviors is exercised by clearly established rules, as in some institutions, in military organizations, and in cases where the individual is totally dependent on the social or physical environment, arrangements of environmental contingencies can be consistently applied, yielding extensive behavior change. In such environments, the person's reaction to control and her or his cognitive activities contribute little to the shaping of behavior. A small child who is totally dependent for satisfaction of his physical needs on the adults in the environment can easily be taught to change her or his behavior by simple rearrangement of reinforcement contingencies. Similarly, if the social environment consistently reinforces behavior that is executed in a strictly prescribed fashion, the person will adopt the required conduct in order to obtain what positive reinforcement the environment offers.

In our everyday experience, environmental controls are much less stringent, often contradictory, and frequently resented. Children are often rewarded or punished for the same behavior on different occasions and sometimes even in similar situations by different people. Verbal instructions, adult models in the family, and television screens frequently demonstrate both the punishments and the benefits of aggressive behavior. Similarly, assertiveness, sexual behaviors, alcohol consumption, smoking, and amoral behaviors are under the control of conflicting social and physical consequences. A still larger group of behaviors, often called *neurotic*, include many interpersonal strategies for controlling other persons or for reducing the anxiety and discomfort of conflicting self-reactions. These behaviors are often determined by combinations of positive and aversive consequences. It is in the case of these conflicting controls that a person's thinking, fantasies, and other covert reactions exert the greatest influence in modifying the simple input-output relationships, that is, the relationships between the environmental, discriminative, and reinforcing stimuli and the behavior that they aim to regulate.

The framework outlined in this chapter views behavior as the product of three sources of control: the immediate environment, the person's biological system, and the cues originating from the person's repertoire of cognitive and self-directive variables. These three spheres of influence interact, and it is their joint effect at a particular point in time that ultimately shapes behavior. Although the influence of a given factor can never be reduced to zero, the relative importance of each factor shifts across time and changing environments. For example, eating behavior is sometimes primarily under the control of the biological system, and, at other times, environmental variables such as the smell of fresh bread or the sight of other people eating are more important. Training in self-regulation can reduce the effect of temporary fluctuations in biological and environmental variables on a person's behavior, thereby freeing the individual to pursue self-imposed goals with some consistency across time and situations. It is clear, however, that such control would break down when the strength of variables originating in the environment or in the person's biological system was substantially increased.

The methods described in this chapter provide a general structure for behavioral interview therapy. The procedures can be used in most cases but are supplemented for the individual client with other, problem-specific methods. Specific complaints, such as anxiety, low assertiveness, depression, sexual dysfunction, and phobias, are attacked with programs designed specifically for these problems. But the general context of the change process is created by combining problem-specific techniques with the present methods.

A THEORETICAL FRAMEWORK OF SELF-REGULATION

To understand the general framework from which various self-management techniques have been derived, it is helpful to consider some of the psychological processes that occur in self-regulation (Karoly & Kanfer, 1982). Social-learning theory assumes that everyday behavior often consists of chains of responses that have been previously built up so that a given response is automatically cued by completion of the immediately preceding response. For example, typing, driving a car, shaving, preparing breakfast, and many other activities are associated with well-learned repertoires stored in long-term memory, and their proper execution does not require continuous decision making about how to proceed. These well-learned sequences are related to the *automatic* mode of cognitive processing, which has been extensively studied by cognitive psychologists (Fisk & Schneider, 1984; Posner & Snyder, 1975; Schneider & Shiffrin, 1977).

Automatic processes do not require attention, can be carried out in parallel with other activities and are difficult to change because they are so well established. However, in other situations, well-learned response repertoires are not available, or previously learned repertoires are no longer effective. When new behavior chains need to be learned, when choices among alternate responses need to be made, or when habitual response sequences are interrupted or ineffective, self-regulation processes are called into play. A qualitatively different mode of cognitive functioning, called *controlled processing*, marks the onset of self-regulation. Controlled processing demands focused attention and continuous decision making among alternate responses. When learning to drive, for example, a person must devote attention to each acceleration, turn, and gear shift: Overall performance is slow and deliberate. This is in sharp contrast with the expert driver, who not only engages in effortless driving behavior but is also able to carry on a conversation at the same time. Automatic processes are efficient because they ease the execution of many familiar behaviors without drawing upon attentional resources. However, the effort involved in controlled processing is offset by the advantage of freedom from rigid, habitual behavior patterns. The individual has greater flexibility in selecting response alternatives, in developing novel responses, and in executing thoughtful, deliberate plans. Many maladaptive behaviors are associated with well-learned repertoires that are executed in an automatic fashion. The helper's task often involves assisting the individual to "deautomatize" troublesome behavior patterns, making them accessible to the self-regulation process, and to then "reautomatize" newly learned and more adaptive behavior chains.

Once initiated, the self-regulation process is characterized by three distinct stages (Kanfer, 1970b; 1971). To illustrate these, consider a social drinker who had never given much thought to his alcohol consumption, until his wife verbalized her intention to divorce him unless he stopped drinking. This event could startle the man, prompting him to attend more closely to his drinking behavior. This first stage is called the *self-monitoring stage* and involves deliberately and carefully attending to one's own behavior. For example, the social drinker might monitor the number of drinks he consumes each day or his behavior while drinking. On the basis of past experience, the drinker has built up expectations about acceptable drinking behavior. These might be called *performance criteria or standards*, the rules by which a person judges his or her own behavior. These rules are influenced by social values and personal experience.

The second stage of self-regulation consists of a comparison between the information obtained from self-monitoring and the person's standards for the given behavior. We have called this stage the *self-evaluation stage*. It involves a discrimination response, a matching that reveals the discrepancy between what one is doing and what one ought to be doing. Self-evaluation based on inappropriate or insufficient self-monitoring or on a vague and unrealistic standard interferes with effective self-regulatory behavior, because the comparison does not yield the most effective guide for corrective action. For example, the social drinker might not detect a discrepancy if his standards for acceptable alcohol consumption were excessive or if he failed to accurately monitor his behavior.

The third stage in the self-regulation process is called *self-reinforcement* and refers to the individual's reactions to the information obtained from the self-evaluation process. The reinforcement operations occurring during this stage refer primarily to emotional and cognitive reactions of satisfaction or dissatisfaction with the preceding sequence, rather than to self-administered external stimuli. The major function of the self-reinforcement stage is motivational. If a discrepancy is not detected or if behavior exceeds standards, the person will feel satisfied with herself or himself and will not be motivated to change. For example, if the social drinker determines that he does not drink more than other people, he continues to drink as before, dismissing his wife's criticisms as unjustified. Behavior that falls short of performance standards yields dissatisfaction and leads the individual to attempt new behavior that is more consistent with the established criteria. As the person tries new responses, the self-regulation process is repeated until the standard is approximated or the person abandons the whole sequence. However, if the discrepancies are very large or if the person responds to them with intense self-punishment, her or his unpleasant affective state could motivate escape behavior rather than behavior designed to correct the discrepancy.

The self-regulation model has recently been elaborated to include important attributional processes that influence movement through the three stages (Kanfer & Hagerman, 1981). For self-regulation to begin at all, the individual must view the behavior in question as being under her or his control. It would make little sense, for example, to *self*-regulate the offensive behavior of a supervisor, although aspects of one's reactions to the supervisor could be under the person's control and therefore within the purview of self-regulatory efforts. The behavior is also evaluated with respect to its relevance to the individual's short- and long-term goals. Trivial behaviors are not expected to become the focus of self-regulatory activity. Finally, during the self-reinforcement stage, the person can attribute the cause of a discrepancy to some aspect of herself or himself or to some external factor. Internal attributions create more arousal and stronger motivation for change, but they can also interfere with the change effort if they implicate global, negative, and unalterable characteristics of the person.

A sketch of the working model of self-regulation is given in Figure 8.1. This model has been derived from laboratory research, and it has been useful in developing clinical techniques for problems ranging from obesity (Mahoney, 1974) to depression (Fuchs & Rehm, 1977) and study skills (Greiner & Karoly, 1976). This does not mean that the model represents the actual and universal presence of discrete psychological processes. In fact, it is quite likely that the total sequence of criteria setting, self-observation, evaluation, reinforcement, and planning of new actions proceeds rather quickly. Nevertheless, the model provides a framework for understanding the processes by which an individual organizes his or her own behavior and for pinpointing specific deficits that underlie self-regulation failures. The setting of excessively high standards, the failure to monitor one's own behavior accurately, and the inappropriate assignment of self-reward or

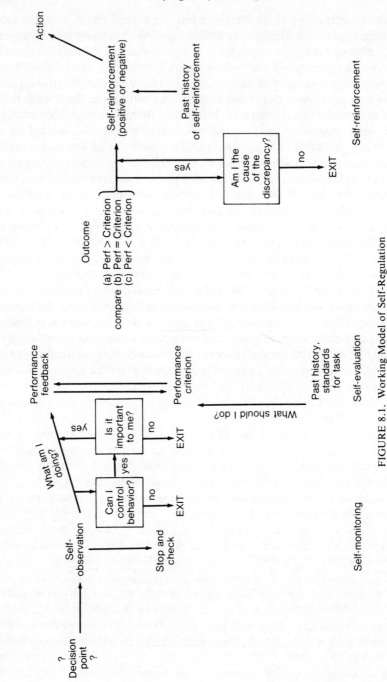

FIGURE 8.1. Working Model of Self-Regulation

self-punishment contingencies are frequently encountered in the histories of clients. For example, Grimm and Yarnold (1984) reported that type A individuals evaluate their behavior against excessively high standards. In clinical situations, numerous methods have been used to increase the effectiveness of behavior at each stage of the self-regulation process. We will describe these methods in the following sections, remembering that the design of an individual program would focus on any combination of these components, depending on the client's skill and particular problem.

The self-regulation model describes the initial stages of behavior change, focusing on the detection of maladaptive behavior and the early sources of motivation for change. Separate sets of variables determine whether the self-regulation process will culminate in (a) a commitment to behavior change and (b) the execution of new behavior (Kanfer & Karoly, 1972). Table 8.1 describes some of the factors that lead people to make intention statements about behavior change. Intentions are an important step in the initiation of new behavior, but, as shown in Table 8.1, not all intentions mark the onset of a commitment to change. Intentions can function to elicit social approval or to reduce guilt over the recent occurrence of maladaptive behavior. For example, intentions to stop gambling might be made after a large loss at the poker table. Similarly, the alcoholic's intentions to stop drinking might function to elicit the approval of a spouse or an employer, and the student's promise of "I'll do it tomorrow" might serve to appease an advisor. Commitment to change is more likely if the intention is specific;

Table 8.1. Factors That Might Influence the Commitment to
Execute a Self-Control Program

COMMITMENT EASIER	COMMITMENT DIFFICULT
1. Delayed program onset	1. Program begins immediately
2. History of pos. Rf. for promise-making	2. Past failure to keep promises was punished
3. Recent indulgence to satiation	3. Problematic behavior is not perceived to be under client's control — "can't be helped"
4. Guilt, discomfort, and fear over action (aversive effects of response) is high	
5. Escape from social disapproval	4. Pos. Rf. for problem behavior is high
6. Presence of others making promises (modeling and social pressure)	5. Criteria for change too high
	6. Consequences of nonfulfillment harsh
7. Behavior to be changed is private and cannot be easily checked	7. Behavior publicly observable
8. Promise is vaguely phrased	8. Support for program planning not anticipated
9. Promise-making leads to social approval or immediate benefits	

Note: Expression of commitment does not guarantee execution of the program. Other factors, such as program requirements and reinforcement for execution in its early stages, determine fulfillment of a commitment after it is made.

refs to publicly observable, concrete behavior; and is motivated by moderate, but not extreme, levels of distress. Also, intentions are more likely to lead to change if rewards are contingent on execution, rather than on verbalizing intentions (Kanfer, Cox, Greiner, & Karoly, 1974).

However, commitment to change does not guarantee the execution of new behavior. Execution is mediated by variables that act at the time of execution and relate to the conditions under which the action must be initiated and the nature of the required behavior. For example, a cigarette smoker might intend to quit after a night of heavy smoking and at the urging of friends. However, later in the day, when alone and experiencing the physiological effects of nicotine withdrawal, the smoker might abandon his or her commitment to change. Self-management techniques can help clients reduce the impact of temporary environmental or biological events that undermine commitment to behavior change. Many of these techniques, such as stimulus control, anxiety management, and self-reinforcement, are discussed in the remainder of this chapter. Clients can also be taught cognitive strategies to increase the probability of response execution. Distraction, attending to the nonconsummatory aspects of tempting stimuli, focusing on the activity to be executed rather than on one's current state or past failures are all specific techniques that increase the likelihood of response execution (Kuhl, 1984; Mischel & Moore, 1980). By now it should be clear that self-management is much more complex than the learning of operant responses that are selectively reinforced by the environment. In environmentally arranged contingencies, the individual's intentions and commitment to the change process are not an issue. In self-regulation, these are of primary importance, and a key role of the therapist involves helping the client to create stable incentives for change and to use self-management skills to facilitate program fulfillment.

The term *self-regulation* applies to the general case in which a person directs her or his own behavior. The behavior might not be very conflictual, as in the learning of a new skill or in problem solving. When the behavior to be executed or avoided is conflictual, we speak of the redirection as *self-control*. In clinical problems, it is this special case of self-regulation that is most frequently encountered and to which self-management methods are most often applied.

Self-Control as a Special Case of Self-Management

In common speech, such terms as *self-control, will power,* and *self-discipline* are used interchangeably. Such behavioral dispositions have been considered to be personality traits resulting from the person's biological constitution or experiences in learning to control his or her actions and impulses. On the other hand, the behavioral view advocated in this chapter reserves the term *self-control* to describe a person's actions in a specific situation, rather than a personality trait. Our definition of self-control requires that (a) the behavior in question has nearly equal positive and aversive consequences; (b) prior to the occurrence of the behavior, that is, earlier in the chain leading up to it, a controlling response be introduced that alters the probability of the response to be controlled; (c) at the time of execution, the controlling response be initiated by self-generated cues and not under the direct control of the social or physical environment. Thus, when a person exercises self-control we talk about the fact that, in the absence of immediate external control, he or she engages in the behavior (the controlling response) that originally had a lower probability than that of a more tempting behavior (the controlled response) in such a way that the controlled response is less likely to occur (Kanfer, 1971; Thoreson & Mahoney, 1974).

This does not mean that self-control is viewed as behavior that unfolds in individual development, independent of environmental influences. On the contrary, its history is related to the person's earlier training, and its success is related to the ultimate consequences supplied by the social environment. It is only at the moment of initiating the response that the person is not under direct environmental control. However, the likelihood that a person will begin a self-control program can be influenced by the environment. Feedback from the social or physical environment often underscores a discrepancy between behavior and standards, setting the self-regulation process in motion. For example, the decision to start a weight control program can be heavily influenced by (a) information from a physician that excessive weight is affecting one's health, (b) aftereffects of overeating during a holiday period, (c) inability to fit into most of one's clothing, (d) the decision of a friend to diet, and/or (e) criticism from a partner or spouse.

There are two types of self-control situations, differing in their time span and in the nature of their response requirements (Kanfer, 1977). In *decisional self-control*, a person is faced with a single choice in which a tempting goal-object or an escape from an aversive situation is given up in favor of an alternative that has greater ultimate (but usually delayed) utility. Making the decision terminates the behavioral sequence. Leaving one's cigarettes in the office, checking into a substance abuse center, passing up dessert when the waiter offers it, deciding to board an airplane or a roller coaster that one fears, all are examples of this type of self-control. Once the choice has been made, it cannot be reversed. The conflict element that, by definition, is a component of self-control is removed as a determinant of future behavior. The shorter the time available for the decision, the smaller the influence of fluctuating considerations and variations on the attractiveness of the available reward. In contrast, resistance to temptation or tolerance of an aversive situation over a prolonged interval constitutes the protracted self-control situation. Concentrating on one's studies while a noisy party is in progress in a friend's adjacent apartment, attempting to reduce caloric intake when working in a pastry shop, controlling aggressive behavior while caring for an obstinate, uncooperative child, or continuing to jog or engage in heavy exercise as fatigue increases are examples of this continuing self-control problem. In these situations the conflict between the two alternatives can continue over an extended time. The desirable response must be executed even though momentary fluctuations in thoughts and emotional or bodily states increase temptation to abandon the controlling response at any moment.

The decisional self-control situation, in which a single choice terminates conflict, is easier to negotiate than the *protracted self-control* situation, which requires continued resistance to temptation. For example, it is easier to turn down an invitation to go to a tavern than to sit in a tavern all evening and refrain from drinking alcohol. Techniques to master both types of situations are necessary in a complete program. However, in the beginning it is easier to help the client master decisional self-control situations and to avoid prolonged exposure to temptation. An individual might be instructed to avoid friends who smoke during the first few days of a smoking cessation program. During this time new patterns of behavior can be learned, providing alternate responses to the cues that previously elicited smoking behavior. When the individual does interact with friends who smoke, his or her new behavioral repertoire will decrease the probability that smoking behaviors will be automatically executed. Because self-control is easier in the decisional situation, the individual will be more likely to succeed in change efforts. This early success could also be important in bolstering client motivation and perceived control over the problem behavior.

Behaviorally oriented clinicians have always emphasized the importance of functional analysis in the design of change programs. We have expanded the traditional S-O-R-K-C framework (Kanfer & Phillips, 1970) to encompass the network of interrelated biological, cognitive, and environmental events in which the problem behavior is embedded. A detailed knowledge of this network often leads to the realization that the problem behavior can be influenced through multiple pathways and that the target of a change program need not be equivalent to the behavior one ultimately wishes to affect. It is often possible to identify a response that covaries with the problem behavior but is easier for the client to control. For example, glucose metabolism is related to the activity of the autonomic system, leading to the hypothesis that behavioral interventions that reduce autonomic activity would be useful in the management of diabetes. Relaxation procedures have proven effective in reducing insulin requirements and might also have desirable effects on other areas of the diabetic's life, such as reducing blood pressure and increasing subjective well-being (Surwit, Feingloss, & Scovern, 1983).

A number of issues should be considered when selecting a target behavior and planning a change program such as client acceptance of the program, its ease of execution and likelihood of success, and the secondary effects of the program (Kanfer, 1985). In a self-control program, the target behavior must be primarily under the client's control, and the client must believe in her or his ability to exert such control (either before or as a result of early treatment sessions). Maladaptive behavior that functions as an escape response from an aversive emotional state is not a good choice for an initial target behavior. Instead, interventions should target on responses that are easier for the client to control such as those occurring very early in the chain of events leading up to the maladaptive behavior. For example, a change program for a child abuser should target on the initial feelings of mild hostility, rather than on the final aggressive behavior toward the child.

One never changes an isolated behavior: Change in one area of the client's life always introduces secondary changes that affect the functioning of the entire life system. The success or failure of a change program can depend on whether these secondary effects support the initial treatment goals. For example, drug withdrawal programs often involve avoidance of environmental cues associated with drug use, in order to reduce the automatic execution of consummatory responses. These cues can also function to elicit physiological responses that increase craving for the drug. Thus, avoidance of drug-related environments is an excellent intervention, as it impacts on both the psychological and physiological systems in ways that support treatment goals.

Unfortunately, the secondary effects of change often interfere with the client's efforts. For example, drastic reductions in calorie intake can lead to decreases in metabolic activity, with the paradoxical effect that weight loss becomes more difficult (Rodin, 1982). Similarly, the alcoholic who successfully avoids a favorite bar might find that his or her social network is substantially diminished. Careful assessment allows the helper to anticipate these secondary effects and to help the client avoid them or develop coping strategies to ameliorate their impact.

A continuing assessment of relevant system parameters is often necessary, as the impact of an intervention can be delayed or change over time. For example, in the weeks following cessation of smoking, physiological changes in the gastrointestinal and metabolic systems can cause weight gain, despite earnest efforts by the client to avoid this undesirable outcome (Rodin, 1982). Such weight gain could have a demoralizing effect on the client, perhaps causing a return to smoking, unless he or she is prepared for this possibility and preventive measures are taken, such as increasing metabolic rate through aerobic exercise. The relapse rate for many addictive behaviors peaks during the first 6 months after treatment, suggesting that continued monitoring of the effects of treatment on related behaviors is essential for maintaining earlier gains. Change introduces further change, and it is critical to the success of the program that these additional changes support the initial goals. The fact that change has multiple effects is not necessarily disadvantageous. But it has important consequences for the maintenance of new behaviors, as maladaptive habits are often woven into many facets of the client's life, and changing a set of behaviors can require widespread change in the individual's life-style.

Although behavior change can be made easier through a carefully developed program, the self-control situation still requires considerable effort by the client. The therapist can facilitate change by helping the client maintain commitment and motivation for desired goals. Motivation can be increased by discussing the benefits of change and by helping the client vividly imagine what life would be like if the particular behavior pattern were altered (Anderson, 1983; Schefft & Kanfer, 1985). For many clients the main obstacle is to overcome the immediate rewards or negative reinforcements associated with the problem behavior. A sexual exhibitionist, for example, could find himself in a tempting situation that promises sexual fulfillment from carrying out the act. Although the prospect of apprehension by the police might make him anxious, this possible outcome is distant and uncertain. The therapist can help to alter the balance by making the aversive consequences more salient to the client, perhaps by discussing these consequences in therapy or by exposing the individual to environments or people related to the undesirable outcomes. It is particularly important to introduce variables that produce or increase the conflict in cases in which a client has been referred for treatment by another person or an agency, such as the court, for a problem that the client does not recognize. An increase in the client's concern over the problem behavior might be needed before she or he could accept the treatment program.

Training in self-management requires strong early support from the helper, with the client gradually relying more and more on his or her newly learned skills. These include skills in (a) self-monitoring, (b) establishment of specific rules of conduct by contracts with oneself or others, (c) seeking support from the environment for fulfillment, (d) self-evaluation, and (e) generating strong reinforcing consequences for engaging in behaviors that achieve the goals of self-control. These techniques are temporary devices, used only until new behavior patterns are well-established and execution becomes automatic. Also, if an individual thoroughly enjoys an activity, even though it has long-range aversive consequences, no conflict is created and the question of self-control does not apply. For example, the person who indulged in heavy smoking prior to knowledge of the aversive consequences, or who fully recognizes the dangers but is unwilling to sacrifice immediate pleasure for a longer life, is not engaging in behavior that falls within the self-control analysis. Similarly, the person who had at one time engaged in excessive eating but who, over many years, has acquired new eating habits and rarely finds himself or herself torn between dieting and indulging in heavy food is not exercising self-control when he or she eats in moderation. In other words, we speak of self-control only when the person initiates some behavior that attempts, successfully or not, to alter a highly probable but undesirable behavior chain.

Persons who successfully cope with their difficulties do not seek help. Inquiry among persons who have achieved control over conflicting behaviors on their own suggests an overlap between the techniques that have evolved from self-control research and the many methods that people use spontaneously and successfully (DiClemente & Prochaska, 1982; Prochaska & DiClemente, 1982). Delaying an undesirable act, engaging in competing cognitive or motor behaviors, setting up challenges for oneself, rehearsing the positive consequences of self-control, and using contingent self-praise or self-criticism are widely used methods. But there are differences between those who are successful and those who are unsuccessful with naturally occurring self-control. Successful self-controllers differ from their unsuccessful peers in using more techniques for a longer period of time, in rating themselves as more committed to personal change, in generating more plans and schedules to facilitate change, and in using the methods more frequently and consistently (Baer, Foreyt, & Wright, 1977; Heffernan & Richards, 1981; Perri, Richards, & Schultheis, 1977). Further, the specific techniques used by successful self-controllers vary according to the particular problem. These data and similar clinical experiences suggest that clients often have the required skills, or can easily learn them. Most frequently, what is needed is the encouragement of deliberate and systematic use of various methods and the development of positive expectation of their utility.

Individuals who have difficulties in resisting temptation or controlling their behavior in one situation do not necessarily experience similar difficulties in others. From our discussion of self-regulation it should be clear that each situation presents conflicts of differing strengths; varies in the importance of reaching standards and in the concomitant involvement of emotional and biological factors; and differs in what the person is able to do to reach a compromise solution. But skill in self-regulation is neither totally dependent on the situation nor a general personality trait. It is presumed that some skills can be acquired. Training should help a client to cope with self-control conflicts in later situations, even though some elements have changed. The generalization effect has been noted in the clinic, but its demonstration in controlled research has been relatively weak (Richards & Perri, 1977; Turkewitz, O'Leary, & Ironsmith, 1975). Recent concern with maintenance of the benefits of behavior change programs is

resulting in growing efforts to build preparation for posttreatment maintenance into the intervention strategy (Goldstein & Kanfer, 1979; Karoly &
Steffen, 1980).

Self-management techniques frequently involve methods of self-control.
The helper's role can be concentrated in four different areas:

1. Collecting information about the problem behavior and planning an
   optimal change program (assessment and program design).
2. Helping the individual establish favorable conditions for carrying out a
   self-control program and providing the initial reinforcement to alter the
   balance in favor of changing the undesirable behavior (motivation).
3. Helping the individual acquire specific behavior change techniques that
   ease the process of change (training).
4. Reinforcing the client's efforts and successes in carrying out a self-
   management program (support and maintenance).

The importance of the helper's role in the early stages of treatment suggests that the various factors that influence the helper-client relationship
(reviewed in chapters 2 and 3) must also be considered.

The Role of Perceived Control
in Self-Management Methods

In addition to the practical advantages of involving a client in the change
program, there are indications from different areas of research that a person's actions are influenced by her or his beliefs about the causes of the
behavior. When a person believes that she or he has responsibility for some
action; that a successful outcome is due to personal competence; that the
behavior is voluntary and not controlled by external threats or rewards;
and that she or he has chosen voluntarily among alternate courses of
action, the person tends to learn more easily, to be more highly motivated,
and to report more positive feelings than when operating under perceived
external pressures. The available research also suggests that perceived control reduces problems of resistance and reactance in therapy and enhances
maintenance of treatment gains. An increased sense of responsibility and
control over one's problems could be a critical element underlying all forms
of successful psychotherapy (Liberman, 1978; Saltzman, Luetgert, Roth,
Creaser, & Howard, 1976) but these processes become explicit goals in self-
management methods. From the initial interview, therapy is structured to
enhance the client's perceived control over personal problems and to help
her or him accept responsibility for the change process.

Perceived control is a broad construct, encompassing at least three more
specific dimensions that are relevant to change in the therapeutic context:
(a) perceived choice over target behavior selection and program develop-

ment (decisional control), (b) perceived control over program execution (self-efficacy), and (c) perceived control over program outcomes. For example, decisional control in a treatment program for a phobia can be established by allowing the client to participate in the choice of specific intervention techniques. If the use of self-directed desensitization is negotiated and agreed on, the client then actively shares in planning the details of the relaxation procedure, the nature and ordering of the items in the anxiety hierarchy, and the time and frequency of at-home practice sessions. Self-efficacy requires the client to have confidence in his or her ability to execute the desensitization program. Perceived outcome control means that he or she believes that its execution will yield the desired effect.

Before using techniques to enhance perceptions of control, the therapist should evaluate the actual constraints operating in the client's life and the appropriateness of the treatment for the client's problem. For example, if a client's weight problem is due to an endocrine disorder, then an exercise regimen will not lead to weight loss, regardless of how strongly the client believes in the effectiveness of this treatment. Similarly, self-efficacy beliefs will soon be undermined if a client lacks critical skills. For example, in overcoming test anxiety, the belief in one's ability must be supplemented with study skills and preparation time. Bolstering client perceptions of control when they in fact lack such control can lead to failure, eroding self-esteem and creating doubts about the very possibility of change. The client's actual control over the problem behavior and treatment plan should be an early target of assessment. If deficits are noted, needed skills can be taught or the change program can be modified accordingly.

Whenever possible, the client should be given decisional control over the nature of the treatment plan. The available research suggests that perceived choice serves to reduce anxiety (Stotland & Blumenthal, 1964), increase tolerance of painful stimuli (Averill, 1973; Kanfer & Seidner, 1973; Langer, Janis, & Wolfer, 1975), and enhance task performance and persistence (Brigham & Stoerzinger, 1976; Felixbroad & O'Leary, 1974; Liem, 1975). For example, Kanfer and Grimm (1978) asked college students to complete a reading task and found that perceived choice significantly facilitated performance and effort. Similarly, when residents in a home for the aged were given greater choice in their daily routines, they showed a significant improvement in alertness, active participation and self-rated well-being (Langer & Rodin, 1976; Rodin & Langer, 1977). In most programs, there are many parameters that permit opportunities for choice. Clients can exert decisional control over the nature of the target behaviors, the order in which multiple targets are addressed, the pace of the program, or the involvement of other people. Even with standardized programs, the client can still be given choices about how the treatment will be tailored to the details of her or his day-to-day life. The perception of decisional control can also be enhanced by the therapist's interpersonal behavior with the client. The client's preferences, opinions, and goals should always be considered. Negotiation and cooperation rather than didactic and authoritarian proscription is the hallmark of the approach.

Another important dimension of perceived control concerns the client's feelings of self-efficacy, or his or her confidence in his or her ability to execute the change program. Self-efficacy is often low at the beginning of therapy because people typically seek help only after repeatedly failing to solve problems on their own. Because low self-efficacy interferes with the initiation and maintenance of new behavior repertoires (Bandura, 1977), enhancing client confidence should be an early intervention target. Bandura (1977) identified four sources of information that influence self-efficacy beliefs: past performance accomplishments, watching the behavior of others, exposure to verbal persuasion efforts, and emotional arousal related to task performance. Past performance is the most heavily weighted information source, suggesting that successful execution has the greatest impact on self-efficacy beliefs. Therapeutic tasks should therefore be designed to guarantee success by insuring that task demands not exceed the client's capacities at the time. Self-efficacy can also be strengthened by adequately preparing the client for execution of the change program. For example, role-plays and behavioral rehearsal can provide preliminary success experience with a task before it is executed in natural settings. The client can also be taught strategies to control emotional arousal such as cue-controlled relaxation or coping self-statements. Another way to enhance self-efficacy involves helping the client prepare alternate plans of action in case the original plan cannot be executed or is unsuccessful. A more flexible plan of action and a backup alternative make the client feel more confident about his or her chances for success.

Clients often hold stable beliefs about their inability to execute certain behaviors, and success experience can be easily forgotten or discounted against the weightier evidence of past failure. The therapist can help the client to cognitively process success experiences in ways that maximize their impact on self-efficacy beliefs (Goldfried & Robins, 1982). For example, clients should be encouraged to evaluate success against past behavior in similar situations. Comparisons with other people, with behavior in other settings, or with ultimate goals provide less satisfying anchor points for assessing change. The client should also be encouraged to attribute her or his success to stable, internal qualities. This can be done by focusing discussion on the ways in which the client's behavior directly led to success. Also, research suggests that participants and observers differ in their attributions of the cause of a behavior, with observers emphasizing qualities of the person more than qualities of the environment (Jones & Nisbett, 1971). Therefore, the client might be better able to see herself or himself as the causal agent in her or his success if she or he adopts a more objective or external view of a positive experience. Change in self-efficacy beliefs requires readjustment in stable cognitive representations, and these changes often lag behind objective measures of behavioral accomplishments. The helper can reduce this lag by initiating frequent discussions of past success, perhaps using objective indexes of improvement such as graphs or self-monitoring records for emphasis.

Perceived outcome control concerns the client's perception of the contingency between the treatment program and the consequences of the program, in terms of its impact on the problem behavior and on the general quality of the client's life. The therapist should first insure that the treatment is appropriate for the client's particular problem. For example, systematic desensitization is an effective way to alter phobic behaviors but might not provide an appropriate treatment for a client who cannot tolerate the accompanying loss of control (Borkovec, 1985). If the treatment is appropriate, its effectiveness can be increased by bolstering the client's expectations for change. For example, the helper should provide a clear and convincing rationale for the treatment effects and offer success stories about clients who have been helped by the treatment in the past.

In general, motivation is increased if the client has decisional control over the treatment, has confidence in his or her ability to execute the plan, and believes that treatment will lead to desirable outcomes. Decisional control is also important in establishing *intrinsic motivation*, or the belief that one is behaving in a certain way because one really wants to do so (Deci, 1980). Research suggests that intrinsic motivation facilitates the learning process: Subjects who are internally motivated generally select harder tasks, are more creative, produce performance of higher quality, and are subsequently more interested in working at the task than subjects working for external rewards on the same problem (Condry, 1977). External rewards decrease intrinsic motivation, encouraging individuals to view their behavior as purely instrumental for obtaining rewards. They are also less likely to maintain the behavior once the external contingency is no longer in effect. However, this does not mean that external rewards have no place in the treatment program. When employed with care, external rewards can be very useful in the initial stages of the change program, when the client requires additional incentives to initiate new behaviors. The negative effects of external rewards can be minimized if the client retains decisional control over the change program and if the reward conveys information about the client's competence at the new task. Rewards can also be more effective if their content is related to the task, such as rewarding weight loss with a new dress instead of with money or other general reinforcers. Of course, the crucial transition to integrating new behavior into the person's repertoire (internalization) requires that the newly developed skills eventually be maintained and reinforced by the client.

In our society in which autonomy, independence, and individuality are strongly emphasized, the client who requires the assistance of a helper to resolve psychological difficulties is presented with a dilemma. On the one hand, the client often actively seeks professional assistance, recognizing her or his inability to cope and the need to comply with the helper's prescriptions and programs. On the other hand, turning over control over one's life decisions to another person elicits opposition. Sufficient evidence has been accumulated in the literature on reactance (Brehm, 1966) and clinical discussions of resistance and countercontrol phenomena (Davison, 1973; Wachtel, 1982) to suggest that a therapist's assumption of full control and responsibility for the change program can hamper progress. In fact, in the medical literature, compliance with a therapeutic regimen is often remarkably poor even with patients whose survival depends on execution of a doctor-prescribed program (DiNicola & DiMatteo, 1982; Haynes, Taylor, & Sackett, 1979). Taken together, the research findings suggest that an optimal treatment program provides clients with extensive opportunities to participate in the selection of treatment procedures and to attribute the cause of behavior change to themselves. Such a course of treatment does not free the helper from responsibility to assist the client and guide her or him toward proper choices, nor does it relegate the helper to a nondirective role. It speaks for a judicious balance between client and helper participation in such a way that the client never perceives the helper as imposing objectives or strategies. It further emphasizes a continuing need for training the client to develop motivation toward jointly established objectives and for reinforcing her or his progress.

Clients and therapists may hold beliefs and expectations about the helping process that undermine the adoption of a self-management perspective. Helping implies that someone needs help, and both client and therapist adopt roles that are congruent with this definition of the situation. The client might see himself or herself in a passive and subordinate role, viewing the therapist as the powerful expert who will "cure" him or her. Other clients might enter treatment with skeptical attitudes toward psychotherapy or with visions of lying on a couch and free-associating. The initial sessions of the self-management program often involve exploring the client's general beliefs about the helping process and establishing new expectations that emphasize the mutual responsibility of therapist and client. Helpers might also hold beliefs about clients and the helping process that interfere with progress. Wills (1978) found that helpers adopt a frame of reference that is biased toward pathology. In comparison with control groups of laypersons, therapists overattributed dependency and helplessness to other people, even if the rated target behavior was depicted as normal. Therapists who hold these beliefs about those they assist might deliver mixed messages, endorsing responsibility at a verbal level but reinforcing dependency through subtle, nonverbal behaviors. These therapists can find it difficult to operate within the self-management paradigm.

The acceptance of responsibility in treatment is frequently related to the very problem for which the client seeks help. We have observed at least five patterns that suggest sources of reluctance on the part of the client to assume responsibility. Self-management treatment requires that these sources of reluctance be viewed as prior targets for change before other programs can be initiated. These sources are

1. Clients who have developed life-long habitual dependency patterns are skillful in eliciting caretaking behaviors, maintaining passivity, avoiding decision making, and maneuvering others to take responsibility. Consequently, they tend to reject the therapist's invitation to participate in the change process. For example, Baltes (1978) found that residents in a nursing home were quite effective in exerting control over their environment through passive behaviors and were reluctant to participate actively, even though increased activity was associated with positive psychological and physiological consequences. In such cases, alterations of interpersonal patterns in small steps and by gradual increases from a very low level of responsible behavior might represent the focus of treatment during early sessions.

2. Clients who have maintained a fairly consistent and rigid pattern of behavior and who have suffered from the consequences of their psychological difficulties for a long time might be afraid to give up their known, though distressing, state for a new and possibly worse one. These clients are afraid of risks and of the unknown involved in changing. Therapeutic attention must first be focused on reducing the aversiveness to change before a specific program can be undertaken.

3. Clients who have previously learned that their own actions have no strong influence on the eventual outcomes of events often show both an unwillingness and an inability to commit themselves to change or to engage in therapeutic tasks. Such learned incompetency due to past experiences of helplessness requires involvement in tasks of increasing difficulty that permit clients to alter their self-perception and increase their behavior in controlling their environments.

4. Clients who might be genuinely interested in change but lack the skills for initiating it. Deficits in decision-making, planning, or interpersonal skills might have blocked previous efforts to break out of their ruts. For these clients, training and practical exercises in gradually changing their life patterns increases motivation and skills for changing.

5. Clients who present themselves for treatment because they are involved in socially unacceptable behaviors that nevertheless provide strong satisfaction such as addictions or antisocial activities, or clients who are supported by a partner, friend, or agency for maintaining the current ineffective behavior (a conflict between desiring change and maintaining some element of the status quo) can be reluctant to assume responsibility for change. For such clients, clarification of objectives and discussion of benefits associated with change are probably required before a change process is undertaken.

METHODS FOR THERAPEUTIC CHANGE

Providing the Conditions for Change

Self-management techniques are most easily applied when the client is concerned about a present problem and can anticipate some improvement by its resolution. In the use of self-management techniques, it is therefore crucial to make change appear possible and desirable. The helper must communicate very early the limitations of his or her own role to the client. He or she must convey his or her expectations that the client will carry out some of the exercises associated with the program and will take responsibility for initiating and maintaining behavior change. At the same time, the helper assures the client that he or she will be available to train the client in techniques that make change easier and to provide guidance in formulating the change program and treatment goals. Self-management therapy can be structured by providing information about the nature of the program, but this structure must be bolstered by the helper's actions throughout the program. For example, the therapist should make consistent efforts to help the client handle decisions and choices in ways that promote the overall change plan. A helper would not respond to direct inquiry by the client about the advisability of changing a job or selecting a friend. However, he or she would work with the client so that the elements of the decision are clearly labeled, and the outcomes of each alternative are stated in terms of their effects on the client and on other people. The choice is then made by the client.

Although clients enter therapy with a desire to alter certain behavior patterns, they often lack sufficient motivation to endure the temporary discomfort and uncertainty that accompanies change. Goal and value clarification is a useful method for establishing and maintaining motivation throughout the course of treatment. During initial sessions, the therapist should encourage the client to discuss long-range goals and to imagine what life would be like if these goals were obtained. For example, a student who has trouble completing class assignments might be engaged in a discussion of her or his ultimate career choice as a lawyer. She or he could be asked to describe the kind of lawyer she or he would be, to imagine a typical day as a lawyer, or to speculate on the changes that would result in relationships with family and friends. Clients are often overwhelmed by the misery of their day-to-day troubles and rarely speculate on broad life goals or the possibility of a better future. By encouraging the client to work out future scenarios, the therapist can help relate the strong incentives often associated with distant goals to the requirements for smaller changes in the client's daily routine which can provide the necessary motivation to initiate them. Long-range goals provide a context for the difficult task of behavior change. Discussion of distant goals should occur regularly, both to insure that the treatment plan is on track and to enhance flagging motivation as therapy continues. Finally, goal and value clarification strengthens the therapeutic relationship. Clients who believe that their therapist understands and accepts their basic life orientation are more likely to trust the therapist and to actively participate in the change process. The helper might find it useful to consult one of the many popular books that contain specific exercises for generating discussions on goals and values (e.g., Koberg & Bagnall, 1976; Lakein, 1973; Lee, 1978).

Self-management methods rely heavily on tasks and assignments to serve the dual purpose of enhancing client motivation and structuring the change program. In the next section, some general comments are made on the use of homework assignments in self-management therapy. This is followed by a more detailed consideration of contracting and self-monitoring, two types of assignments that play a pivotal role in most treatment programs.

Tasks and Assignments

Assignment of particular tasks has long been used as an adjunct therapeutic technique (e.g., Herzberg, 1945; Shelton, 1979; Shelton & Levy, 1981). However, in a self-management program, this feature takes on a central role. The assignment of tasks that are graded in difficulty gives meaning to the helper's description of self-management methods as procedures that require the client to take responsibility for changing her or his own behavior. These tasks stress the importance of changing habitual behaviors outside the helping relationship and help the client perceive the continuity between treatment sessions and daily life experiences. In addition, homework assignments yield information about the client's motivations and skills and the pragmatic feasibility of tentative treatment objectives.

Homework assignments can also increase commitment to change. Ideally, treatment objectives represent current concerns, or short- and long-term goals that the individual is actively striving to obtain (Klinger, Barta, & Maxeiner, 1979). Current concerns serve to heighten attention to goal-relevant cues, to increase the utilization of skills, and to motivate fantasies and thoughts related to goal attainment. Increasing a current concern can sensitize an individual to search his or her own repertoire and the environment for ways of achieving his or her goal and to channel thoughts and fantasies to the same end. Tasks and assignments can help to transform therapeutic objectives into current concerns that significantly influence the client's daily life. For example, when an elderly woman complains of loneliness, increased frequency of social interactions can be a therapeutic objective. Assignments can help to increase her sensitivity to possible opportunities for establishing social contacts. The client might be asked to observe others, to obtain information about where social activities take place, or to initiate brief social contacts or attend social functions. A task for a client looking for work might involve asking friends for information about jobs, searching newspapers, imagining himself in the position of other persons at work, and asking himself while shopping for services or goods what opportunities for work there might be for him. Tasks and assignments can thus intensify the client's involvement in the change process by creating specific incentives and by increasing alertness to opportunities for change in day-to-day life, in addition to the benefits derived from their therapeutic aspects (e.g., practice of skills, reduction of anxiety, and collection of information).

Homework assignments are often presented as tentative (and safe) efforts to acquire new behavioral repertoires. They can also provide opportunities to experience new life patterns, in the guise of tryouts for which there are no aversive consequences. It is important that the client participate in planning the particular forms that the assigned behavior takes. Goals should be realistic, to minimize the possibility of failure.

There are four steps to follow whenever a client is asked to complete a task or assignment, to try a new response, or to execute a specific technique: (a) information provision, (b) anticipatory practice or *prehearsal*, (c) execution in natural settings, and (d) review. Inclusion of all four steps increases the probability of success and maximizes the learning potential of the experience. During the information stage, the requirements of the homework assignment are clarified. This could involve didactic instruction about a particular technique or discussion of how the technique can be tailored to fit the client's daily routine. The helper should also provide relevant information about the time course of the treatment plan and about secondary effects of change on physical or environmental variables.

During prehearsal, the client imagines and practices the assigned task within the safety of the therapy environment. Prehearsal provides opportunities for the helper to model various behaviors, to clarify the details of the situation and the behavior to be executed, and to rehearse and prepare the client, in order to reduce surprises and extinguish some of the anxiety associated with the task. Role-plays are commonly used during prehearsal. They can involve scenarios of interpersonal situations or rehearsals of what the client will later think, fantasize, or say to herself or himself. Through varying the specific details of a series of role plays, the client can be taught to approach the task in a flexible fashion, increasing the ability to execute the task in the face of changing external factors. The helper's role initially is to provide guidance and structure both for the role-play in the session and for preparing the behavior associated with the assigned task. As the client shows increased competence in developing future scenarios, the helper reduces participation, except to maintain encouragement and reinforcement. In addition to serving as a technique for rehearsing and training new skills, role-plays have also been used to assess existing behavioral skills and are a common component of some social skills programs.

After a task has been executed in a natural setting, it should be reviewed in detail during the following therapy session. Memories of task execution are likely to be experiential or *episodic* (Tulving, 1972). Such memories are tied to a specific spatial and temporal context, are difficult to retrieve, and are usually discounted if they are inconsistent with other knowledge. As the client discusses his or her experience, he or she begins to form semantic memories or verbal codes representing basic knowledge about himself or herself. Semantic memories are easier to recall and are therefore more likely to influence thoughts and behaviors on future occasions. Semantic memories are formed slowly, and can require the successful execution and discussion of many similar tasks before they are established and integrated with other knowledge. In reviewing a task, the helper should also direct the discussion so as to promote the client's sense of self-efficacy, according to the guidelines offered above. The review and evaluation of the task often leads directly to the next assignment, whether the client reports progress or discovery of special elements in a situation that has presented difficulties. The helper must be careful to offer encouragement and reinforcement only for those accomplishments that can be attributed to the client's execution of the previously planned behavior and not for success or failure that has been caused by the behaviors of others. When a shy client approaches another person she or he has accomplished her or his task. Whether the person accepts or rejects the overture is beyond the client's control and is irrelevant to the achievement of the task objective.

When the client is fearful about some component of a situation, the task could emphasize a contrived purpose in order to bring about initial emission of the behavior. For example, a client with fears of social interaction could be given a highly specific task that would help him or her overcome the initial fear. With an extremely withdrawn client, we have used such contrived tasks as going to a drugstore for a cup of coffee and specifically recording the number and types of interactions of people sitting at the counter for a 15-minute period. A shy and insecure young woman was asked to attend a social gathering for the specific purpose of obtaining information about the occupational background and current jobs of several (two male and one female) guests. Another reticent client was asked to go to a tavern, order one bottle of beer, and keep a count of the number and approximate age and sex of customers who entered and left the bar. In all these cases, the tasks served several purposes. First, they provided an opportunity for execution of behaviors that had been a problem in the past. At times this helps to dispel the client's expectations that something terrible will occur. Second, the client's self-observation and later discussion with the helper give the client greater efficiency and comfort in his or her newly acquired role. The client can also be asked to say what he or she thought his or her impact was on the behavior of others and to discuss his or her feelings during the interactions witnessed (Kopel & Arkowitz, 1975). These new experiences permit the individual to reevaluate his or her perceptions of self and of his or her skills. They also make possible the utilization of problem-solving skills in the interview sessions and ultimately in the client's daily life.

As the change program progresses, the client should be given increasing responsibility in the planning and execution of tasks that contribute to overcoming her or his problems. Gradually the assignment of tasks can be faded, as the change progress is completed. During training, helpers often complain that in the initial interviews they cannot think of a proper task for the client, but even a first interview offers the opportunity for numerous assignments. Whenever a person is not clear about some aspect of the problem that she or he describes, whenever a person expresses uncertainty about her or his ability to carry out some behavior, or whenever a person indicates that she or he has thought of but never tried a particular behavior strategy, the helper has themes for possible assignments. The tasks might be relatively simple at first, for example, to list desirable outcomes of some relationship, to observe how the client responds to other people's anger, to try to respond positively or not to respond to a partner. All these are appropriate assignments in a first interview and serve the dual purpose of providing information relevant to treatment and structuring therapy as a situation that requires the client's active participation.

Contracts

The psychological contract is a written statement that outlines specific actions that the client has agreed to execute and establishes consequences for fulfillment and nonfulfillment of the agreement. Contracts are commonly used in self-management programs, and they serve a number of functions. Contracts can be used to (a) help the client initiate specific actions, (b) establish clear-cut criteria for achievement, and (c) provide a mechanism for clarifying the consequences of engaging in the behavior. Contracting provides both the helper and the client with a record of what has been agreed upon and an opportunity to evaluate progress by comparison against the terms of the agreement. It also provides the client with both a set of rules that govern the change process and practice in the process of clearly defining goals and instrumental acts to reach them. Negotiating the contract requires a careful review of the behavioral requirements and can be embedded within the information and prehearsal stages of the learning model. Finally, the explicit and public nature of the contract enhances the client's commitment to execute the intended behaviors.

Contracts can be unilateral, when the client obligates himself or herself to a change program without expecting specific contributions from another person, or they can be bilateral. Bilateral contracts, commonly used in marriage counseling, in families, or between teacher and child, specify obligations and mutual reinforcements for each of the parties. Contracts can also be made by an individual with himself or herself, with the helper, with others when the helper serves as a monitor and negotiator, or with a group such as a classroom or family.

There are seven elements that should be considered in every behavioral contract. Each of these elements should be spelled out in detail, arrived at by negotiation, and accepted fully by the client. Good contracts should have short-range goals and should be written. The behaviors required in the contract should be rehearsed prior to execution, and all efforts should be made to avoid a contract that might be difficult or impossible for the person to attain. The seven elements in the contract provide that

1. A clear and detailed description of the required instrumental behavior be stated.
2. Some criterion be set for the time or frequency limitations constituting the goal of the contract.
3. The contract specify positive reinforcements, contingent upon fulfillment of the criterion.
4. Provisions be made for some aversive consequences, contingent upon nonfulfillment of the contract within a specified time or with a specified frequency.
5. A bonus clause indicate the additional positive reinforcements obtainable if the person exceeds the minimal demands of the contract.
6. The contract specify the means by which the contract response is observed, measured, and recorded: a procedure is stated for informing the client of his or her achievements over the duration of the contract.
7. The timing for delivery of reinforcement contingencies be arranged to follow the response as quickly as possible.

Clinical examples of successful behavioral contracting, combined with other self-management techniques, come from the treatment of obesity, excessive smoking, homosexual fantasies, and alcoholism. In each case, the behavioral contract is helpful because the client is not faced with the overwhelming task of eliminating the undesirable behavior all at once. For example, one client reported excessive worries about sexual potency. At first the man could not accept the notion that he would ever be sexually competent. A contract between his wife and him introduced stimulus control procedures that attempted to limit, rather than eliminate, the periods of worry to times when they would not directly interfere with sexual behavior. Subsequent contracts introduced sexual courtship behaviors that were specifically unrelated to achievement of orgasm. Following the general approach of Masters and Johnson (1970), these contracts outlined gradual increases in the instrumental behaviors that constitute the early part of the lovemaking chain. The behavioral contracts served to reduce the client's fear that he would never overcome his problems, by requiring only small behavior changes at first and by providing a framework within which other self-management techniques could be carried out. Reports of successful contract use are available in cases of addictive behaviors (Bigelow, Sticker, Leibson, & Griffiths, 1976; Boudin, 1972), weight control (Jeffery, Gerber, Rosenthal, & Lindquist, 1983), excessive smoking (Spring, Sipich, Trimble, & Goeckner, 1978), marital discord (Jacobson, 1977), and other problem behaviors.

Behavioral contracts can be enhanced if the contract is associated with public commitment to either a friend, a spouse, a class, or a group of coworkers. However, caution must be exercised in the use of public commitment, because the client might set the criterion for the contracted behavior higher than she or he can reasonably achieve, in order to impress others. Furthermore, the client's difficulties in fulfilling the contract might lead her or him to avoid a person who knows of the commitment or to engage in actions that might even endanger the relationship with someone who is party to the client's unfulfilled contract. This effect is related to the problem of intrinsic motivation and perception of control.

Self-Monitoring

Self-monitoring (SM) was initially proposed as an operation that parallels the measurement of behavior in situations where a client is under the continuous observation of a therapist or an experimenter. However, later research indicated that the accuracy of SM, when compared with independent measures of the same behavior, varies widely across different situations (Kazdin, 1974). The schedule on which the behavior is monitored, competition from concurrent responses, awareness that SM is independently assessed by an observer, the valence of the target behavior, reinforcement for accurate SM and the nature of the instructions are among the variables that affect SM accuracy (Kanfer, 1970a; McFall, 1977; Nelson, 1977). Thus there are restrictions on the use of SM when precise, numerical data about a target behavior are required. However, if certain conditions are met, SM data can still be used to provide estimates of behavior or to monitor relative change in behavior over time.

SM also serves a number of functions that do not require absolute accuracy in recording. SM can be used to obtain qualitative information that is relevant to diagnosis and treatment planning. For example, clients might be asked to monitor the antecedents and consequences of a target behavior or to record their emotional states while engaging in the behavior. SM can also serve to increase client motivation for change. Baseline data, collected before treatment implementation, can provide an incentive for future change. Later in the program, the achievement of a criterion can be graphically displayed and can provide a visual guide for the administration of reinforcement, by the therapist and by the client. For example, various common self-indulgences, such as buying a luxury item, engaging in pleasurable activity, or taking a brief rest, can be tied directly to the achievement of a change in the target behavior.

Another important feature of SM, often deliberately used by helpers, is that its use can be incompatible with continuation of an undesirable behavior. For example, in a case of the author's, a husband and wife with severe marital problems were asked to monitor hostile and aggressive thoughts toward each other. The monitoring task included making a tape recording of any interactions that threatened to develop into a fight. The couple reported reduced frequency of fighting and explained laughingly that on several occasions the tape recorder had not been handy. The clients then jointly set up the recorder. By that time, the hostile interpersonal interaction had been interrupted, and the couple could no longer remember what they were going to fight about.

In some instances, self-monitoring assignments have produced favorable change in the target behavior. Subsequent research and clinical practice have therefore attempted to utilize SM as a therapeutic technique in its own right. Studies with obese patients (Romanczyk, 1974), with smokers motivated to stop (Abrams & Wilson, 1979), with school children (Broden, Hall, & Mitts, 1971), with students having study problems (Johnson & White, 1971; Richards, 1975), with agoraphobics (Emmelkamp, 1974), and with retarded adults (Nelson, Lipinski, & Black, 1976) have reported reductions in undesirable behaviors. However, other investigators (e.g., Mahoney, Moura, & Wade, 1973) have failed to reproduce these findings.

The processes underlying SM reactivity appear to be complex and to reflect the operation of many variables. The valence and importance of the behavior, the level of task mastery, the availability of performance feedback and goals, and the delay between response execution and the SM activity all influence the extent to which the SM task is reactive (Fremouw & Brown, 1980; Kirschenbaum & Tomarken, 1982; Komaki & Dore, 1978; McFall, 1977). Also, these variables do not function in a simple fashion. For example, monitoring successful execution produces favorable change if the responses is poorly mastered, but it interferes with performance if the response is well mastered.

The research on reactivity can be clarified by considering the data in the context of the self-regulation model. According to the model, change in the target behavior results when the SM task triggers the self-regulation process. Thus, SM tasks most likely to be reactive are those that require the individual to attend closely to her or his behavior, thereby disrupting ongoing automatic processes. The critical role of increased self-attention is supported by research in which instructions to increase "self-awareness" produce reactive effects similar to those obtained from instructions to self-monitor (Kirschenbaum & Tomarken, 1982). The self-regulation model also explains the finding that favorable behavior change can result when another person monitors the target behavior (Hayes & Nelson, 1983). External monitoring is effective only if clear, obtrusive feedback is given to the person, thereby disrupting ongoing automatic processes. Finally, consider the data on the differential impact of self-monitoring on well-mastered versus poorly mastered tasks. Well-mastered tasks are already automatized, and interventions that disrupt the behavior sequence would be expected to interfere with response execution. However, poorly mastered tasks require close attention to behavior and would benefit from controlled processing. The self-regulation model integrates many seemingly disparate findings on SM reactivity and also provides a guide for helpers who wish to maximize these effects.

However, the mere mechanics of SM do not lead to favorable behavior change unless other conditions of self-regulation are met. For example, change does not occur if the person lacks standards for a given behavior or if there is no discrepancy between these standards and the monitored behavior. Further, reactivity is influenced by the causal attributions the person makes about the behavior and by the importance he or she assigns to the behavior (e.g., see Ewart, 1978). A frequent observation concerns the temporary nature of the change associated with SM tasks. Over time, the execution of the SM task can become increasingly automatic and might no longer trigger self-regulatory processes. To maintain the effectiveness of SM interventions, therapists should modify the SM task from time to time.

A critical feature of SM is the specific behavior selected for monitoring and the temporal relationship between the behavior and the monitoring. Investigators have reported the use of SM for ruminating thoughts, for urges to engage in a problematic behavior, for simple motor behaviors like skin picking or object throwing, for complex social behaviors such as self-deprecatory statements, and many others. SM can also be carried out prior to the execution of the undesirable behavior, immediately following it, or at a much later time. In choosing among these alternatives, the therapist should carefully consider the functions the SM task is intended to serve. The need for accuracy suggests a simple monitoring task, executed immediately after the target behavior has occurred. Assignments designed to provide information about the target behavior might involve more detailed observations of environmental antecedents and consequences. To maximize the reactive effects of SM, the task should require high attention to one's actions and the disruption of ongoing activity. For example, daily monitoring of body weight might be an accurate measure of weight loss, but instructions to count mouthfuls swallowed produce greater behavior change (Green, 1978). The latter intervention occurs in close temporal proximity to the target behavior and is therefore more effective in interrupting eating behavior. In general, summary recording of the target behavior after several hours or at the end of the day introduces a long delay and weakens any reactive effects of SM.

SM tasks that emphasize the negative effects of a target behavior can also increase reactivity (Hayes & Nelson, 1983). For example, one might monitor excess food intake with packages of lard representing body fat, or record cigarettes smoked with a metric based on the smoking habits of the average lung cancer patient. Premonitoring, or monitoring the urge to engage in a maladaptive behavior, is a promising intervention for addictive behaviors (Fremouw & Brown, 1980). Urges that occur early in the chain of events leading to the consummatory response are easier to control than later events in the chain, because a wider range of alternative behaviors is available. Another possibility, which has proven successful in reducing smoking behavior, involves monitoring conquered urges, or instances where an incompatible behavior is executed in response to an urge to engage in undesirable action (O'Banion, Armstrong, & Ellis, 1980). The conquered urge can also elicit feelings of self-satisfaction, introducing a reinforcement component to this technique.

Establishing SM in Individual Adult Programs

In introducing SM to the client, the therapist should begin by discussing its general nature and by giving examples of its utility in the therapeutic program. Together with the client, the helper should clearly specify the class of behaviors to be observed and should discuss examples to illustrate the limits of this class. A good rule is to use frequency counts for behaviors that are clearly separable, such as smoking a cigarette or making a specific positive self-statement, and to use time intervals for behaviors that are continuous. For example, duration of studying or of obsessive ruminations is clocked by recording the time started and stopped. If the target behavior is very frequent or extends over a long period of time, it is possible to use a time-sampling technique. This method requires that the person make self-observations only during previously specified time intervals. To insure adequate sampling of the behavior, the helper can develop a program, best based on randomization of all periods during which the behavior occurs, and ask for SM during specified periods only. For persons who interact with others during much of their working day as part of their occupation, the occurrence of particular responses such as aggressive behaviors or subassertive responses can be sampled by randomly selecting half-hour periods during each of a number of days for observation. Of course, if the goals of SM are to foster behavior change, selection of time periods would invoke consideration of the intervals in which change most easily occurs.

Next, the helper should discuss with the client the selection of a recording method. Care must be taken to select a recording instrument that is always available where and when the behavior is likely to occur. When the therapist wishes to maximize accuracy, the recording instrument should be simple, unobtrusive, and convenient. For this purpose, gold counters, worn like wristwatches, can be used for frequency counts. For low-frequency behaviors a client can carry a small supply of pennies in the right pocket and move one to the left when the behavior occurs, transferring the score to a written record at regular intervals (Watson & Tharp, 1977). More complex monitoring procedures, such as written accounts of thoughts or emotional reactions, can be involved when emphasis is placed on the reactive effects of SM.

Finally, the therapist should role-play and rehearse the entire self-monitoring sequence with the client. It is advisable to provide the client with record sheets or to have her or him purchase the recording devices so that she or he can rehearse the actual procedure with the instruments at hand. The therapist should also demonstrate the graphing of a set of frequency recordings or time intervals for visual inspection. Self-monitoring assignments should be reviewed during the interviews following the session in which they were assigned. At this time, problems with implementation can be discussed, and the task can be modified if needed.

Variations of SM include the use of the graph for display, either as a reminder to the client or for social recognition and support in a small group. The graph serves as a concise summary of improvement over the course of therapy, and it is often helpful to review the graph when motivation flags. It is sometimes beneficial to make the graph available to others.

For example, SM data have been displayed by institutionalized clients at their bedside, by family members in an accessible part of the home, or by children in classrooms. Rutner and Bugle (1969) reported a case of behavior change with SM in a hallucinating patient who recorded the duration of his hallucinations and posted a graph on the wall. Social reinforcement for progress can certainly add to the effectiveness of this technique. However, great care must be taken to insure that the record not emphasize the client's deficiencies, violate confidentiality, or embarrass the client.

There are other modifications of SM techniques that require more elaborate equipment. For example, audiotape and videotape playback have been used widely as a means by which clients can observe their own behavior. Later, these self-observations serve as a base for attempts to improve the actions. This type of self-observation is generally an integral part of a more complex intervention program. It often involves participation of group members and helpers who initiate a self-correcting process by helping the client to discriminate and pinpoint particular problematic aspects of his or her interaction behavior. Other helpers then model more desirable behaviors and reinforce the client's approximations to these (see chapter 3 for discussion of these techniques). Videotapes of interpersonal interactions also provide feedback to the therapist, sensitizing him or her to desirable changes in his or her own behavior. Although originating from a different perspective, biofeedback techniques also function as useful SM techniques. Clients are helped to recognize variations in physiological activities by means of visual or auditory displays of their heart rates, electrical skin resistance, brain waves, or other physiological outputs. These methods are described in detail in chapter 10.

In summary, SM is a useful component of a total self-management program. It does not always provide a sufficiently reliable assessment technique, but it can serve as an important program component and motivating device. SM can also directly produce change when the task is carefully designed. When SM is employed as an agent of behavior change, it is important to add additional techniques, such as contracting, self-reinforcement, and stimulus control and to insure that the self-evaluative and self-reinforcement stages of the self-regulation process occur.

Modification of the Environment

The client whose problems are suitable for treatment by self-management techniques has probably made repeated previous attempts to alter her or his behavior. Failure might have been due to lack of environmental support, lack of knowledge of specific behavior change methods, or lack of sufficient, self-generated incentives and reinforcement for trying to change. The techniques described in the following two sections require only a minimal self-initiated step by the client, namely to trigger a change in the environment in such a way that many subsequent behaviors naturally follow. For example, once a person steps off the edge of a swimming pool, subsequent events are programmed by the laws of physics and no longer require self-regulation. Similarly, the alcoholic who calls a fellow AA member to accompany her or him on a walk through the park is programming environmental conditions that will reduce the need for generating self-controlling responses to compete with the urge for a quick trip to the liquor store.

The following techniques are summarized under the concept of *stimulus control*. These procedures set up environmental conditions that make it either impossible or unfavorable for the undesired behavior to occur. Stimulus control methods include such extremes as physical prevention of the undesired behavior, which could include voluntary confinement in an institution, locking oneself in a room, or turning car keys over to a friend. In each case, some undesirable behavior is avoided simply by the fact that the individual has relinquished control over the behavior to an external controlling agent. Unfortunately, the effects of such control are usually only temporary. In addition, the client frequently develops avoidance or hostility toward the agent to whom he or she has given control. At the other extreme, stimulus control methods include training of self-generated verbal responses without changing the physical environment or the physical possibility of executing the undesirable behavior. For example, repeated self-instructions that emphasize long-range aversive consequences of the behavior, statements about the positive aspects of tolerating an unpleasant situation or resisting a temptation, self-rewarding statements about one's will power, or similar verbal cues can serve as stimuli that exert powerful control over subsequent action. Self-generated verbal instructions are discussed in detail in chapter 9.

In the following section we will consider stimulus control techniques that involve manipulations of the physical environment, rearrangement of the social environment, and self-generation of controlling stimuli and controlling responses. They are similar in principle to those discussed in chapter 9 but somewhat different in method. The techniques to be covered in a later section on covert conditioning considerably overlap stimulus control methods, because training a person to generate stimuli in fantasy or imagination represents an example of altering controlling stimuli. However, unlike alteration of external physical stimuli or reprogramming of the social environment, covert conditioning methods require continued activity by the person in rearranging her or his own behavior and in reorganizing her or his habitual ways of thinking.

Stimulus control techniques can be separated according to their function in (a) altering the physical environment so that execution of the undesirable response is impossible, (b) altering the social environment so that opportunities for execution are heavily controlled by other persons, (c) changing discriminative stimulus functions so that the target behavior is specifically restricted to particular environments or the presence of distinctive external cues, or (d) altering the physical condition of the person so that changes in the target behavior are produced. As with most self-control techniques, these methods could reduce the problem behavior, but their effects can be substantially increased if a new behavioral repertoire is built up at the same time. This dual approach is especially important when the target behavior can be suppressed or eliminated only through temporary rearrangement of the environment.

Environmental Stimulus Control

Numerous clinical reports have described the use of alteration of physical or social environments to prevent a response. For example, cigarette cases or refrigerators have been equipped with time locks that make access impossible except at preset intervals. Persons on weight reduction programs have been advised to keep only as much food in the house as can be consumed in a short time, thus eliminating late evening snacking. The ancient use of chastity belts (and other confining garments) represents a use of stimulus control to make sexual contact difficult by altering accessibility. In everyday life most persons use this technique incidentally. Mothers put mittens on small children to reduce thumb sucking, students find isolated areas for study, some persons reject opening charge accounts or carrying charge cards, others play loud music or flee from houses that hold past memories, all in order to control undesired behaviors or fantasies.

For most people, the presence of other persons is a strong determinant of behavior. By selecting the appropriate person or social environment, the client can relieve himself or herself of much of the burden of generating his or her own controlling responses. For example, in a smoking-cessation program, an individual might give his or her cigarettes to a friend who has agreed to help. Smoking behavior then becomes more difficult, as the individual must exert effort and endure feelings of embarrassment before obtaining a cigarette. A more subtle use of the social environment to control smoking might involve deliberate interactions with adamant nonsmokers. In this case, social control over behavior operates indirectly, mediated by knowledge of the attitudes and typical reactions of others to smoking. Similarly, socializing with tea drinkers, calorie counters, or exercise buffs can facilitate certain types of behavior without incurring the costs of relinquishing control to another person. In these social environments, aversive affective and self-evaluative reactions provide a strong deterrent to the execution of certain behaviors. In today's society, one can select environments in which social, physical, and legal factors combine to control undesirable behavior. For example, smoking is not allowed in libraries, elevators, certain sections of restaurants, or some apartment complexes.

Stimulus Narrowing

This technique involves strengthening the association between a behavior and a specific environmental setting; that is, the behavior is put under S^d control. Undesirable behavior can be reduced by gradually decreasing the range of stimulus conditions in which the behavior occurs. For example, overweight clients are requested to eat only in the dining room, at a table with a particular color tablecloth, or in the presence of other family members (Ferster, Nurnberger, & Levitt, 1962; Stuart & Davis, 1972). Over a period of time, the numerous cues previously associated with eating gradually lose control over the response. The relationship between a desirable behavior and a certain set of stimulus conditions can be strengthened by gradually decreasing the range of other behaviors that occur in that setting. For example, insomniacs can be taught to restrict the bedroom environment to sleeping (and sexual behavior) and to avoid sleep-incompatible behaviors such as worrying, watching TV, eating, or reading (Bootzin & Nicassio, 1978; Nicassio & Buchanan, 1981). Similarly, study habits have been improved by setting up specific environments in which no other activities take place. In establishing S^d control, the client is asked to leave the study area when daydreaming or engaging in other activities. Among the most powerful and convenient S^ds are clocks and watches. Specific time intervals have been employed as cues for engaging in assertive behaviors, smoking, daydreaming, worrying, skin picking, or nail biting. A program for chronic worriers requires that clients postpone all worry behavior until a preset "worry period," occurring at the same time and place every day (Borkovec, Wilkinson, Folensbee, & Lerman, 1983). The treatment package involves other components, such as monitoring worry behavior and substituting present-oriented thoughts, but its essence involves stimulus control techniques. The association between worrying and a myriad of environmental and internal stimuli is reduced, and the behavior is restricted to a preset, limited time interval.

When a target behavior is to be reduced, stimulus control techniques are frequently combined with the method of increasing response cost. For example, in addition to requiring that the behavior occur only in a certain place or at a given time, one can gradually increase other demands so that preparation for execution of the behavior becomes more and more cumbersome. Ultimately, the ritual is sufficiently aversive that the effort outweighs the anticipated consequences of the target behavior. For example, in establishing control over smoking, clients might deliberately place the pack in a distant place, remove matches from the usual location, remove all ashtrays, and, finally, seat themselves in a "smoking chair." On several occasions, clients who have been helped to arrange these procedures have reported that the undesirable behavior dropped out "because it was just too much trouble to go through all that."

Another use of stimulus narrowing focuses on the association between a target behavior and certain bodily cues. Before using this approach, it might first be necessary to teach the client to discriminate somatic stimuli through self-monitoring procedures and through emphasis on the characteristic events surrounding or preceding certain physiological states. Clients can be taught to eat only when hungry, to respond to anxiety with relaxation, or to recognize sexual arousal and make appropriate responses. Other procedures operate to reduce somatic cues that trigger maladaptive behavior. For example, low-calorie, high-bulk foods can reduce cues for eating; for an alcoholic the intake of nonalcoholic fluids prior to a party can control the internal thirst cues that sometimes justify drinking. Finally, the client's interpretation of bodily cues can be altered, reducing the association between these cues and maladaptive behavior. For example, Antabuse can tinge cravings for alcohol with the anticipation of illness; relabeling *social anxiety* as a normal fear of strangers can reduce negative self-statements and lead to more adaptive behavior in new settings.

The methods described above help the client recognize the environmental and somatic variables that control behavior. Stimulus control techniques have also been used to help the client change the nature of self-generated verbal cues. In contrast with the preceding methods, the control of self-generated stimuli is relatively tenuous, because the individual can easily remove or shut out such cues as verbal instructions, imagined sequences, or thoughts. In altering external controlling stimuli, the individual needs to make only one step, the initiation of a chain of events. The subsequent sequence is then determined by the natural environment or by the behavior of others. In the case of self-produced controlling stimuli, the individual must often maintain these cues over time and in the presence of an environment that encourages and supports the problem behavior. We will be dealing with these self-control methods in a later section of this chapter, and they are also described in chapter 9.

Changing Self-Generated Behavioral Consequences

Feelings of satisfaction or dissatisfaction with one's behavior, which constitute the self-reinforcement stage of the self-regulation process, allow individuals to maintain many everyday behaviors in the absence of immediate external consequences. However, these naturally occurring reactions are not always effective in regulating behavior. For some people, low rates of positive self-reinforcement limit the achievement of goals. Other clients might believe that self-reinforcement is undesirable or immodest; they could be highly self-critical or show excessive criteria for achievement, so that positive self-reinforcement rarely occurs. In addition, some behaviors are associated with strong physiological or environmental consequences that oppose and overpower self-reactions. In these cases, it is often helpful to use self-administered reinforcement techniques to establish stronger incentives for desirable behavior. These procedures involve the introduction of additional reinforcing stimuli, which the individual administers to herself or himself only when previously established contingencies are met. The use of this technique also requires that the target behavior, performance criteria, reinforcing stimuli, and contingency relationships be clearly specified. This clarification offers opportunities to correct problematic components of the self-regulation process and also facilitates the disruption of automatic processes by encouraging the individual to pay closer attention to her or his behavior.

Positive self-reinforcement, or self-reward (SR), is most commonly used in self-management programs and has been the focus of most research. Other types of self-administered reinforcement have been used, paralleling the various forms of external reinforcement contingencies. These procedures are summarized in Table 8.2. Aversive self-reinforcement could follow a response, delivered in the form of self-criticism, self-punishment, or withholding of positive self-reinforcement. For example, a person can deny himself or herself a night at the movies if he or she fails to complete preparation for the next day's work. Withholding of a positive SR after previous continued administration and self-imposed extinction have also been used in self-management programs. Finally, a person can present himself or herself with an aversive stimulus that is removed or terminated only when the self-prescribed escape or avoidance response is carried out. Although the self-administered techniques overlap the externally administered techniques, there is controversy over whether they share a common underlying mechanism (e.g., Castro, Perez, Albanchez & de Leon, 1983; Nelson, Hayes,

Table 8.2. Some Combinations of Self-Reinforcement

QUALITY OF CONSEQUENCE	CONSEQUENCE OPERATION	
	GIVE	TAKE AWAY
Positive	Positive Self-Reinforcement (a) self-administered (b) verbal-symbolic	Covert Extinction self-imposed time out (temporary)
Aversive	Self-Punishment (a) self-administered (b) verbal-symbolic	Negative Self-Reinforcement (a) self-administered (b) verbal symbolic

Spong, Jarret, & McKnight, 1983). However, few theorists would argue with the general conclusion that these techniques serve a motivational function and also facilitate the disruption of automatic processes.

Positive self-administered reinforcement encompasses two different operations: (a) approaching or consuming a material reinforcer that is freely available in the person's environment. For example, when a person rewards herself or himself for hard work by a cup of coffee or by treating herself or himself to a good meal, he or she is applying a self-administered consequence; or (b) delivery of contingent verbal-symbolic self-reinforcement such as self-praise for a completed task. The first procedure involves the administration of external reinforcement by the client to herself or himself. Two types of external reinforcers are often used: (a) self-presentation of a new reinforcer that is outside the everyday life of the client such as a luxury item of clothing or attendance at a special event; and (b) initial denial of some pleasant everyday experience and later administration of it only as a contingent reinforcer for a desired behavior (Thoreson & Mahoney, 1974). For example, making an enjoyable phone call, going to a movie, talking to a friend, or having a cup of coffee might be initially postponed, carried out only as a reward for the accomplishment of a prescribed task. As Thoreson and Mahoney suggested, this requires that the person initially deny herself or himself the experience, introducing the conflict elements of a self-control situation. The therapist can help the client postpone easily available rewards by introducing very small delays at first and only gradually increasing the behavioral requirements for the reward.

Verbal-symbolic SRs consist of such verbal statements as "I did well," "That was good," and other positive self-statements by which the individual clearly labels his or her own satisfactions with his or her own achievement. These procedures help the client acknowledge the fact that he or she has successfully negotiated a given task and also give him or her permission to feel satisfied and proud. Although verbal statements are difficult to examine in the laboratory and probably hard for the client to describe and remember, they are useful because they are freely available and require no external support. In a change program, deliberate programming of such verbal-symbolic self-rewards can be carried out by first asking the person to say these positive statements aloud in sessions and by only later making them contingent upon a specified event.

Several studies have reported that the addition of SR improves behavior change programs (Bellack, Schwartz, & Rozensky, 1974; Mahoney et al., 1973; Rehm & Kornblith, 1979; Tressler & Tucker, 1980). There have been reports of effective use of self-reinforcement to improve study skills, enhance weight reduction, increase dating skills and assertive behavior, raise activity levels in depressed patients, and reduce homosexual fantasies. Although training the administration of SR contingencies is more difficult than exposure of a client to external consequences, SR procedures have the advantage that the individual can eventually apply them independently of the helper and that she or he can also use the same procedures for problems that are not related to the central complaint. Laboratory research with children and adults has demonstrated that self-reinforcing operations show the two characteristic properties of reinforcing stimuli: They alter the probability of occurrence of the response that precedes them, and they motivate new learning (Bandura & Perloff, 1967; Kanfer & Duerfeldt, 1967; Montgomery & Parton, 1970). In comparisons with the administration of the same reinforcement by another person, positive SR has been shown to be generally equal, if not slightly superior, in effectiveness (Johnson & Martin, 1973; Lovitt & Curtiss, 1969). The growing literature on the self-reinforcement concept, most of it carried out with positive SR, has also demonstrated that self-reinforcement is not always independent of the environment (Jones, Nelson, & Kazdin, 1977). Although SR operations make it possible for a client to be temporarily independent, ultimate positive consequences from the environment would seem to be necessary to maintain the newly developed behavior in the long run.

Establishing SR in Individual Adult Programs

As we have suggested, the goal of the helper is to start a behavior change program that is carried out by the client and to achieve changes that are maintained without continuing social reinforcement. Most such self-management programs incorporate SR as a treatment component, either to bolster naturally occurring self-reactions or to correct deficits in the individual's self-regulatory processes. The nature of the program often depends on which of these goals is given stronger emphasis. For example, the self-administration of valued material rewards might be effective in creating incentives for behavior, whereas positive self-statements might be more useful in helping a highly self-critical client. As with other techniques, a thorough functional analysis is necessary to pinpoint the nature of the problem and to guide construction of the treatment plan. The following steps summarize the usual procedures in aiding an individual toward effective use of positive SR.

Selection of Appropriate Reinforcers

Although some questionnaires can aid in the preliminary selection of reinforcers (e.g., see Cautela, 1977), it is desirable to discuss and negotiate individual reinforcers in interviews with the client. Asking the client about her or his current practices of self-reward, both symbolic and material; inquiring about luxury items that the client would like to acquire; and obtaining verbal statements that would express self-satisfaction frequently yield suggestions for appropriate SRs. What is often most effective is a rearrangement of behavioral contingencies for self-rewards that the person normally administers noncontingently or only in conjunction with behaviors other than the problem responses. Some novel material SRs can be added as a special incentive for a prolonged program. The list of material reinforcers, enjoyable activities, and positive self-statements is compiled on the basis of the client's current behaviors. For example, acquisition of inexpensive luxury items that the client has wanted but never obtained might include the purchase of a paperback book, a small item of jewelry, clothing accessories, or cosmetics. Among activities, the individual's preference might be to take a trip to a museum, go to a rock concert, go away for a weekend vacation, or spend time at hobbies.

Verbal-symbolic reinforcers include positive self-statements that are employed in self-praise; reaffirmation of one's adequacy, self-worth, or competence; congratulating oneself on physical appearance, physical strength, social attractiveness, interpersonal skill, or any other appropriate content. It is crucial that the selected reinforcers relate to the client's personal history. They must be acceptable to him or her as something he or she wants, could easily acquire or do, and would feel good about. If a complex and long-range program is designed, several reinforcing stimuli should be equated for approximate value, so that they can be interchanged. This prevents satiation with a single item or statement. In a long-term program, a series of small reinforcers should also be exchangeable for one larger reinforcer at infrequent intervals. A person who has accumulated a predetermined number of symbolic SRs because he or she has shown improvement in the target response might work toward a larger material reinforcer such as purchase of a luxury item, contingent upon achievement of a desired goal within a fixed time period. The list of exchangeable reinforcers, therefore, should contain both small items obtained from the person's current activities and larger items that are just outside the range of daily enjoyments.

Definition of Specific Response-Reinforcement Contingencies

The client is encouraged to list variations within the target response class and to indicate the precise conditions and methods for delivery of SR. For example, if the person is on a weight control program, a verbal-symbolic reinforcer might be used for such target behaviors as rejecting offers of food, staying within the allotted daily caloric intake, or choosing an alternate low calorie food. In addition, a larger SR, such as buying a new dress or wardrobe accessory, might be made contingent upon achieving a predetermined weight loss within a specified time period.

In establishing the response-reinforcement contingency, care must be taken to select a good match. For example, not all SRs are equally appropriate for all responses. It would obviously be foolish to choose the eating of a rich dessert as an SR for weight loss for an obese client. It has been pointed out (Seligman, 1970) that there are predispositions for some reinforcers to be more effective with particular behaviors. Whenever possible, the SR should be one that is essentially compatible with the target behavior. For example, the ex-smoker might select the purchase of new perfume or having teeth cleaned and polished, because such rewards emphasize the positive aspects of not smoking in terms of whiter teeth and increased sensitivity to smell. An appropriate reinforcing stimulus for assertive behavior might be one that enhances the person's feelings of adequacy, self-worth, or physical attractiveness, consistent with the goal of helping the person develop a sense of equality and personal confidence in relation to others.

After the appropriate contingencies are established, specific provisions should be made for the occurrence of both the delivery and the recording of SR. On occasion, high frequency of the desired behavior or involvement in a long-term program might require use of intermittent schedules of reinforcement. For instance, one client who had set small material SRs as his rewards for improving his study habits decided to add both interest value and effectiveness to his SR schedule by setting up an intermittent reinforcement schedule. He accomplished this by using a deck of playing cards. He assigned SR values only to cards with values above 10. Prior to administering a material SR, he would shuffle and cut a deck of cards and reward himself only if a card of 10 or higher appeared.

Practice of Procedures

After selecting appropriate reinforcers and establishing reward contingencies, the helper should rehearse with the client several instances of occurrence of the target behavior and the self-reinforcing sequence. In these role-playing sessions the helper can improve, simplify, and reinforce the client for execution of the behavioral sequence until it is performed smoothly. These role-playing sessions are also important because they provide the client with a model and the initial experience in an activity about which he or she might have doubts or in which he or she might feel uncomfortable. Of course, the helper's presence, encouragement, and approval not only strengthen the likelihood that the client will carry out the behavior, but might also eliminate the common misconception that such simple mechanics for self-management don't require effort, careful programming, or diligent practice.

Checking and Revising Procedures

The client should bring in records of the target behavior and contingent SRs for discussion with the helper and for necessary adjustments of the procedure. For example, if the target is a general increase is positive self-statements, it would be desirable to change their specific content rather frequently in order to extend the program over a wide range of the client's daily activities. The monitoring sessions can also be used by the helper to model adminstration of SRs under different conditions. This helps the client to develop a repertoire of appropriate verbal-symbolic stimuli and permits the gradual decrease of small material reinforcers. The ultimate goal of the programs is not to eliminate long-range luxury reinforcers completely but to make them sufficiently infrequent and to increase the demand for achievement to the point where they can be maintained by the client. The real purpose of the program is to help the client utilize the techniques of self-produced reinforcers as a means of handling psychological difficulties that might arise after contacts with the helper have terminated.

Self-Generated Aversive Consequences

There are essentially two different types of self-generated aversive consequences that can be used in the control of behavior — self-punishment and negative self-reinforcement. These two sets of operations differ in that *self-punishment* is aimed at interrupting or decelerating a response, whereas *negative reinforcement* is aimed at increasing a response that serves to terminate or avoid an unpleasant stimulus. The former is illustrated by executing a boring chore as self-punishment for aggressive behavior. The negative SR paradigm is exemplified by lowering the temperature in one's home at 11:00 to promote an earlier bedtime. In this case, feeling cold is the unpleasant stimulus that is escaped by going to bed. Thus, aversive consequences can be used either to decrease the preceding response or to increase a new target behavior. In addition, just as for self-generated positive consequences, the aversive event can consist of verbal-symbolic SRs such as self-criticism or self-deprecatory statements.

Self-punishment can also involve the removal of a positive stimulus following an undesirable behavior. For example, a person could leave a party as self-punishment for having acted foolishly. A more complex procedure involves levying a fine (removal of money, widely held to be a positive reinforcer) following a response that has been targeted for decrease. For example, in the control of smoking behaviors, some clinicians have requested that the client donate $1 to her or his most disliked political organization after smoking a cigarette. The use of withdrawal of a positive reinforcer has been infrequently reported. In a weight control program, Mahoney et al. (1973) found that this procedure was not very effective when used alone. There are, however, some logical advantages to this technique, though there is limited evidence that it works. Because aversive stimuli are not used, the many problems associated with techniques such as self-administered punishment are avoided. At the same time, the practical problems of persuading a person to give away or destroy a valued item as a contingency are not known. This technique has not been sufficiently explored to warrant wide clinical application.

A variety of aversive stimuli have been used in applications of self-punishment. Self-critical verbal statements, presumably conditioned to earlier aversive consequences, can be systematically attached to the undesired behavior. Unfortunately, self-punishing responses are often common in a client's repertoire and frequently do not decelerate target behaviors. Strong self-criticism can create an aversive emotional state, leading to escape behavior rather than constructive efforts at behavior change. For other clients, self-punishment might merely remove the guilt and anxiety accompanying the performance of the undesirable behavior. One of the authors saw a client for whom mild electric shock (administered by a portable battery-operated device) was used as self-punishment. The student, who had complained of sexual rumination during study, was instructed to give himself mild shocks whenever the fantasies occurred. However, after an initial period of success, the frequency of the ruminations increased to pretreatment levels. A closer analysis of the procedure indicated that the client had begun to reverse the sequence. He would shock himself briefly after the start of the ruminations. Then, feeling that "he had already paid the price of his bad behavior," he would continue his fantasies and shock himself at intermittent intervals.

Many clients have a long history of childhood experiences in which they discovered that one way to "have your cake and eat it too" was to carry out the undesired behavior and suffer punishment as well. Helpers who work with parents are familiar with the problem of children who fail to respond to physical punishment. Frequently, the externally administered and eventually self-generated punishing response serves to alleviate guilt and anxiety associated with the behavior, clearing the way for repetition. Also, unusual individual histories in which punishment served as a positive reinforcer, or as an S^d for affect, led some clients to use physical self-punishment excessively. For these reasons, both verbal-symbolic and physical methods of punishment should be used only when no alternative is possible.

Another example of self-administered punishment is the use of an aversive conditioned reinforcer in the thought-stopping technique (Cautela, 1969; Cautela & Wisocki, 1977). In this procedure, the therapist asks the client to think aloud about ruminations, hallucinations, or fantasies that are targeted for decrease. When the client is fully immersed in these thoughts, the clinician shouts "Stop!" loudly enough to evoke a startled reaction from the client. After several trials and explanations of the procedure, the client initiates the shout, first aloud and then in his or her imagination. Frequent practice is suggested at first, in addition to actual use of the procedure whenever the problem behavior occurs. This method has been reported to be helpful in eliminating disturbing thoughts.

A similar technique has been suggested by Mahoney (1971). A client was instructed to wear a heavy rubber band around his wrist. Upon occurrence of obsessive ruminations that were the target for deceleration, the client snapped the rubber band to produce mild pain. Self-administered aversive consequences, much like other SRs, are effective not because of their capacity for producing pain but because they make the undesirable response clearly stand out from the total flow of behavior. They serve as cues for self-monitoring and self-correction, described earlier as essential ingredients of the self-regulation sequence.

The utilization of aversive SR in escape paradigms is best illustrated by *covert sensitization*, a procedure described in the next section. In essence, the client is trained to imagine an unpleasant event and make its removal contingent upon carrying out the desired behavior. Aversive SRs have been used in a simpler way in some weight control programs. The client is instructed to place a large piece of lard or beef fat in the refrigerator as a continually present aversive stimulus representing her or his own excess poundage. With successive weight losses the client cuts away pieces of the lard, gradually removing the aversive stimulus.

When a response of high frequency is to be modified, *satiation* has been suggested as a behavior change technique. This procedure consists of deliberate repetition of a behavior past the point of desire. For example, an excessive cigarette smoker might be instructed to light and smoke cigarettes continuously until she or he feels physically ill. Thus, the positive stimulus can lose its reinforcing properties with frequent repetition and acquire an aversive character. After a long and intensive smoking session, lighting a cigarette might actually become a cue for feeling ill or dizzy. The procedure is most frequently used in conjunction with other aversive stimuli, such as confining the person in a small room where the increased smoke level itself becomes noxious, or in conjunction with relief responses (see discussion of the aversion-relief technique in chapter 6). Finally, *self-deprivation* can constitute a self-imposed aversive consequence. This procedure is illustrated by withholding a positive reinforcer when a person feels that she or he has not behaved appropriately. Giving up an invitation to dinner or imposing a ban on smoking, on sexual activity, or on alcohol intake have all been used as self-imposed aversive consequences.

Covert Conditioning

Covert conditioning (Cautela, 1973) is based on the rationale that covert operants, or coverants, can be treated much like operant responses, even though the exact nature of the coverant is difficult to ascertain because it is not publicly observable (Homme, 1965). The various paradigms of covert conditioning parallel those of operant conditioning except for the use of client imagery as stimuli, responses, or reinforcing events. We have differentiated these techniques from the use of spoken verbal cues because covert processes usually include verbal, symbolic, and imaginal representations that are produced by the client on instruction of the helper. The use of these techniques is justified by rather modest empirical data and some support for clinical utility (Kazdin, 1977). In this section we will illustrate the most widely used techniques, including covert sensitization, covert reinforcement, and covert modeling.

Covert Sensitization

This technique has been used to reduce undesirable behaviors, including addictive behaviors that are generally difficult to attack. The client is asked to imagine a scene that portrays the undesirable behavior and that currently offers some satisfaction. After the positive image is built up to high intensity, the client is requested to change abruptly to imagining a highly aversive event. Both physical and social aversive imagery are usually used and modified according to the client's personal history. Then the client is asked to imagine fleeing the problem situation and the aversive events associated with it. After the escape, he or she visualizes relief and reduction of discomfort. Strong positive reinforcement by the helper, and eventually by the client, is offered for escaping or avoiding the situation, and verbal statements are used to summarize the implications of the experience. Thus, the maladaptive behavior is paired with aversive consequences, and escape from the total situation is rewarded by the relief experience. All of these events take place with guidance by the helper.

To illustrate the procedure, consider a case in which the target behavior is excessive alcohol consumption. The helper first explains the rationale of the technique and obtains detailed descriptions of the setting in which excessive drinking occurs and of positive and aversive consequences that are meaningful to the client. The client might be asked to imagine aloud a scene in which she or he is comfortably seated at her or his favorite bar. When the client appears to be immersed in the imagery, perhaps describing her or his enjoyment when raising a full glass to her or his lips, the helper introduces the aversive event. For instance, it can be suggested that the client suddenly gets sick and begins to vomit. The helper's description is detailed, and the client is asked to imagine, visualize, smell, and feel the aversive scene as vividly as possible. When the client appears to be experiencing the aversive consequences, she or he is asked to imagine turning away in disgust from the bar and rushing out to get a breath of fresh air. As she or he does so, a previously established positive event is imagined. For example, a handsome or pretty young person smiles at the client as she or he breathes fresh air and experiences pride because of the escape from her or his alcohol habit. Favorable summaries are offered that the client can use as a self-statement, such as "Why do I do silly things like drinking?

It only makes me sick." Initially, client and therapist work through a number of different scenes in about 10 trials each. The scenes should be varied to encompass different settings and consequences, and some scenes might involve training in avoidance. For example, the alcoholic might imagine being offered a drink and responding, "No, I won't have any alcohol" and then sensing relief. After learning the procedure, the client is asked to present the scenes to herself or himself aloud and to practice repeatedly between sessions. Variations of the procedure have involved tape-recorded presentations of scenes that can be used with groups of people who share a similar problem.

Clinical experience suggests that careful preparation of the client is needed for successful use of the technique. If the client lacks skill in imagining the suggested scene, his or her ability can be deliberately built up by practice and training in imagining and describing various events. In addition, the client must be highly motivated and cooperative, and the scenes must be varied sufficiently to provide generality of effect. It is also important that strong personal reinforcers be used. For instance, if the alcoholic in our example is socially oriented, his or her vomiting could be portrayed as accidentally soiling an outraged, attractive person on the next bar stool. Nausea can be an especially effective aversive event for alcohol problems, as research suggests that individuals are biologically "prepared" to form associations between nausea and consummatory behavior (Seligman, 1970). Although both in vivo and covert production of nausea have been used to treat alcohol problems, the covert procedure is easier to use and is associated with fewer side effects (Elkins, 1980).

Covert sensitization provides a useful clinical tool because it requires no particular stimulus settings, can be carried out fairly unobtrusively by the client, and has been reported to be effective after only a few sessions. However, it is best used to temporarily suppress undesired behavior and should be combined with other techniques to build and maintain new behavioral repertoires. A limited body of research supports its effectiveness, although most studies have focused on the use of nausea imagery for alcohol problems (Elkins, 1980; Little & Curran, 1978). Treatment effects are mediated by the extent to which nausea is established as a conditioned response to alcohol cues, suggesting that vivid imagery involving descriptions of visual, olfactory, gustatory, and tactile sensations should be used. A stronger association is formed if the person imagines that she or he actually tastes the alcohol before the nausea imagery is introduced (Anant, 1967). In contrast with the classical conditioning explanation of covert sensitization, other authors argue that the essential ingredient involves the disruption of the imagined behavior chain that is caused by the introduction of the aversive event (Foreyt & Hagan, 1973). According to this view, any event, positive or negative, would serve equally well in the effective use of the technique. Based on this idea, Cautela (1983) developed a variant of covert sensitization in which thought stopping is substituted for the aversive event. However, no research is available to document the effectiveness of this technique or the adequacy of the underlying rationale. Until such research is available, the helper would be wise to employ events that are both disruptive and aversive in covert sensitization.

Covert Reinforcement

This method generally parallels the operations carried out in self-administered reinforcement. The technique differs only in that it involves self-presentation of an imagined scene rather than a verbal statement. The client is trained to imagine a well-practiced scene that is objectively experienced as happy or pleasant. A verbal cue, such as the word *reinforcement*, might be attached to the positive imagery to help the client recall the scene. As with any reinforcing stimulus, the imagery is evoked contingent on the occurrence of a target response. The imagined scenes are first practiced with the helper, and eventually the client is instructed to deliver the reinforcement to himself or herself.

Covert negative reinforcement consists of practice in imagining an unpleasant situation that can later be used in place of other aversive reinforcers. In addition to use of covert negative reinforcement for deceleration of a target response, it can be used as a noxious stimulus for escape conditioning. In this procedure the client first imagines the rehearsed unpleasant scene. Subsequently, she or he imagines the response to be increased. For example, after imagining herself or himself experiencing a very distasteful situation, the client visualizes walking into a room full of people and feeling comfortable, calling up someone for a date, or engaging in whatever behaviors represent the deficiency in her or his repertoire. Covert negative reinforcement should be used judiciously, because aversive scenes can leave residual unpleasant feelings that could become associated with the behavior to be increased. For instance, a client who selects feeling anxious or vomiting as an aversive event might not be able to terminate the imagery quickly. If the desirable escape response is one that had previously produced great anxiety, detrimental effects might follow. Thus this technique must be used with caution.

The use of imagery in covert conditioning can be extended to include not only scenes that the person has actually experienced but also imagery about ideal situations, feared situations, or other fantasy constructions. In all of these procedures care must be taken to rehearse the self-presented scenes in detail, to ascertain that the necessary elements are indeed self-presented. Despite rehearsal, however, some problems in dealing with imagery techniques remain. The helper has little control over the nature of the stimuli and responses that the client employs, because these events are by definition inaccessible to objective observation and measurement. The helper is therefore limited in her or his ability to insure that the client is following instructions or using adequate visualizations. These problems have also made research on covert procedures quite difficult.

Covert Modeling

Cautela (1976), Kasdin (1979; Kasdin & Mascitelli, 1982), and others have reported the use of imagined stimuli as substitutes for live or film models in the reduction of fearful behavior. The procedure combines covert methods with those of modeling techniques (see chapter 3). The client practices imagining the problematic situation in detail for a series of trials. Then, he or she is asked to imagine another person, the model, performing the desirable behavior, such as stroking a dog or entering a crowded room. The helper describes the model as initially hesitant and uncertain, but as gradually overcoming his or her fear and executing the behavior in a smooth and competent fashion. Research supports the use of covert modeling for increasing assertiveness, acquiring social skills, and reducing phobic behavior. For example, Kazdin and Mascitelli (1982) asked subassertive adults to imagine 35 scenes that called for assertive behavior and a model who executed the appropriate response. The authors reported that covert modeling produced stable increases in assertive behavior, as measured by self-report and role-plays. They also reported that the technique is most effective when combined with overt rehearsal and homework assignments. Other authors found that the use of imagined models who emit coping self-statements increases the effectiveness of the technique (Tearman, Lahey, Thompson, & Hammer, 1982).

A variation of covert modeling has been described by Susskind (1970) as the idealized self-image technique. With this procedure, the client visualizes her or his ideal self as she or he competently performs the desired behavior. The client is first helped to formulate an ideal self-image, perhaps by asking that she or he recall an incident or experience that yielded a strong feeling of accomplishment or satisfaction. The client then imagines the desired behavior and gradually superimposes her or his idealized self-image on her or his current self-image, observing the gradual change in her or his actions. Thus, the client is requested to act, feel, and see herself or himself in ways that are consistent with her or his idealized self-image. Both the idealized self-image and other covert modeling methods bear some relationship to the use of role-play and Kelly's fixed role therapy (Kelly, 1955). In the course of visualizing the actions of a model (either herself or himself or another person), the client begins to think about the new behavior and acquires some information and experience about what it would be like to perform the sequence. Covert modeling is essentially a prehearsal tool, used to increase the client's familiarity with a new response. The imagined scenes can also serve as standards toward which the client aspires, helping to guide behavior change outside therapy.

OTHER SELF-MANAGEMENT METHODS

Self-management methods vary widely in the degree to which the client is responsible for learning and executing specific techniques. Some techniques are taught and practiced in therapy sessions, under the assumption that this experience will produce changes in the target behavior. Other techniques, the *self-directed* procedures, are discussed in session, but the burden is on the client to self-administer or implement the technique on his or her own. Benefit from these procedures is expected only to the extent that the client applies them to problem situations in his or her daily life. For example, in self-directed desensitization, the client is instructed in the use of systematic desensitization and provided with a standard relaxation tape. She or he is then responsible for self-administering the treatment at home. The self-directed procedures allow a more economical use of therapy time and offer increased opportunities to enhance the client's perceptions of control and self-efficacy beliefs. As with any other technique, self-directed procedures should be used in conjunction with self-monitoring, self-reinforcement, and regular reports to the helper, who must maintain the client's progress by encouragement and support.

In addition to self-directed desensitization, several other self-directed procedures for anxiety control have emerged from the traditional desensitization paradigm (Rosenbaum & Merbaum, 1984). Many of these procedures, such as anxiety-management training and cue-controlled relaxation, aim to reduce anxiety whenever the client notes inner signs of tension, rather than in response to specific fear stimuli. It is critical that the client initiate the technique as soon as she or he detects the onset of anxiety, as these procedures are not effective once the feeling has progressed. In anxiety-management training (Suinn & Richardson, 1971), the client is taught to recognize physical signs of anxiety and to apply relaxation whenever these signs are perceived. After training in deep relaxation, specific cues for anxiety and relaxation are identified and rehearsed. Anxiety is then induced and quickly followed by imagining a happy or relaxed scene. Deep breathing serves as a cue for relaxation. While the client is relaxed, the anxiety cues are presented and terminated by a rapid shift to instructions for relaxation. These sequences can be taped with appropriate sounds or background music to accompany them. Cue-controlled relaxation is a similar technique, which involves the self-presentation of cue words for relaxation whenever anxiety reduction is desired. Training involves repeatedly pairing a deeply relaxed state with a cue word, such as *relax* or *peace*. The client then self-presents the cue word whenever she or he detects the initial signs of anxiety in her or his daily life. The effectiveness of this technique has not been well demonstrated (Grimm, 1980), and research has yet to evaluate the classical conditioning rationale for treatment effects.

Time-management, problem-solving and decision-making skills have also been incorporated into self-directed treatment packages. As with other self-directed techniques, the client is instructed in the basic principles of the method but is expected to implement the procedure alone, with support and reinforcement from the helper. For example, in time-management training (Lakein, 1973), the client is taught to prioritize goals and rearrange daily schedules so that important goals can be accomplished. The client must then apply these principles to the way she or he structures her or his daily routine. Problem-solving and decision-making skills are discussed in chapter 7. These techniques not only help the client to deal with circumscribed problems, but also provide general coping skills that can be used in a variety of life situations.

Self-Help Resources

Self-help resources refer to instructional materials and support groups that are designed to facilitate or maintain behavior change without the direct involvement of a mental health professional. Recent growth in the self-help movement has led to increased availability of books, tapes, films, and other instructional devices (Gartner & Riessman, 1984). However, these programs vary widely in quality, and there is little empirical evidence for their effectiveness and validity (Glasgow & Rosen, 1978; 1979). In fact, self-help programs can have detrimental consequences (Rosen, 1982). Consumers can incorrectly diagnose their problems, select inappropriate methods, or fail to comply with key program requirements. These errors in procedure can result in failure and, more significantly, demoralization and lowered efficacy expectations. However, under close guidance of a helper, carefully chosen self-help resources can be integrated into the total self-management program. It is a basic requirement that the helper be familiar with their content and that the materials and exercises be discussed in session.

There are three major functions of self-help materials in self-management programs:

1. Written self-help books or programs can aid the client as he or she considers the utility and feasibility of the change program and can increase belief in the possibility of change. Inspirational literature and illustrations of the accomplishments of persons who previously carried out the program can increase the client's commitment to a change program.

2. Selected self-help materials can extend the range of situations and activities in which new behavioral skills can be explored. Self-help manuals or books can provide supplementary cues for new behaviors, incentives to take inventory of current repertoires, and suggestions of situations in which new approaches can be tested. In this way a book can stimulate or quicken the pace of change and focus the direction of treatment. When a client follows the program or reads the material, he or she also increases the thinking about the treatment and brings in new ideas and reevaluations for discussion with the helper.

3. Some self-help books and manuals can be used directly as part of the change program to guide the development of specific skills. Clients who need to learn relaxation, anxiety reduction, increased assertiveness, or altered sexual responsiveness can utilize available self-help programs directly under supervision of the helper.

Self-help books, programs, and organizations represent resources that can supplement common therapeutic interventions beyond the limits of the typical 1-hour office session. These activities create a bridge to the client's daily activities. But other activities can also be integrated into a therapy program. For example, cultural, religious, educational, and recreational programs are not utilized fully in most behavior change programs. A client's involvement in a physical training program, a consciousness-raising group, a church-based or synagogue-based social group, or an adult education class can provide excellent opportunities for personal growth, for improvement of behavioral repertoires, and for testing new skills in different settings. Although these resources have been much undervalued, it should be clear that benefits do not occur simply through the client's participation in such activities. Careful joint planning and clear justification of the relationship of the prescribed activity or exercise for the main therapeutic objectives and current abilities and limitations of the client are essential in selecting the resources. It is not simply self-management that is sought. Effective and goal-directed self-management is the aim of the approach to the behavior change process.

Self-Management and Self-Control

In our introduction we referred to the difference between problems of self-control and problems of self-regulation. Now that the reader is familiar with a variety of techniques for self-management, let us review the applicability of self-management techniques to self-control problems. When we speak of self-control problems we emphasize the client's dilemma in embarking upon a behavior change when her or his current actions give her or him at least some degree of gratification. It is the building of a controlling response and the conflicting consequences of the current behavior that differentiate self-control problems from those in which self-management is used to rearrange behavioral schedules, to learn to identify and solve problems, to acquire new skills, or to engage in activities that do not alter the behavioral consequences very much. First, increases in self-control can be obtained by providing a controlling response that eventually replaces the undesirable activity and becomes a habitual response. We have summarized numerous techniques that can be used to achieve this goal, such as stimulus control, strengthening of competing responses, and contingency management. The second feature of the self-control problem is the fact that a problem behavior has conflicting consequences. Self-generated aversive consequences for an undesired response, increased positive SR, or similar techniques can be used to help alter the balance of these response-contingency conflicts. A third feature of self-control concerns the fact that the individual must initiate the new behavioral sequence by herself or himself. Self-instructions, discrimination training and labeling, and self-monitoring are among the methods that can be used to accomplish this. Self-control programs can utilize many of the methods described above, but these methods are applied to problems that fit the specific definition of the self-control phenomenon. In all self-control programs, many essential elements of self-management are employed. For example, helping the client to set goals, to monitor and evaluate behavior, and to reward herself or himself are common features in most programs. Invariably it is the helper's task to provide the initial motivation for behavior change, by interviews, contracts, self-monitoring, and other methods and to withdraw support gradually as the client becomes more proficient in self-management methods. What differentiates self-control from self-management methods is the nature of the problem to which they are applied, not the methods themselves.

Limitations and Cautions

We have suggested that self-management techniques should not be used unless the client accepts the treatment goals as desirable and is motivated toward their achievement. Research evidence for the effectiveness of the programs described in this chapter, although still limited, is generally favorable (Schefft & Kanfer). The theoretical framework on which self-management techniques rest is still tentative and incomplete. Some investigators have achieved success with certain methods, whereas others, drawing from the same theoretical assumptions but employing slightly different procedures, have been unable to achieve similar results. In part, the difficulty lies in the fact that self-management programs require the skillful combination of many elements in matching the program to the needs of each individual client, whereas research usually tests the effects of only one element at a time. Interactions between various components can produce effects that could not have been foreseen from research on the isolated elements.

The combining of individual elements into a program requires thorough behavioral analysis of the problem before the program is undertaken, as well as a helper-client relationship that can promote the change process. Because targeted behaviors for self-management are often behaviors that are difficult to observe, the helper's reliance on the cooperation of the client is greater than it is in other behavior change methods. It is not infrequent that clients, because of their past history, are unwilling, ashamed, or afraid to describe target behaviors that are of greatest concern to them until they are sure that they can trust the helper. If the circumstances under which the client is referred for help are unfavorable for a trusting relationship, as when a client is referred by a court, pressured into treatment by others, or too disturbed to enter interpersonal relationships, self-management methods are not immediately applicable. Under these conditions it is still possible to work toward creating an atmosphere in which prerequisites of self-management are met. However, the appropriate self-management methods can be introduced only after this prior goal is accomplished. Clients with low intellectual skills can be trained in some self-management methods, albeit at a slower pace and with simplified procedures (Guralnick, 1976; Litrownik, 1982). The use of methods based on our model of self-regulation has also been reported with psychotic clients (Breier & Strauss, 1983).

At the beginning of the chapter, we stressed the importance of self-attribution in the self-management program. If a client perceives himself or herself as controlled by the helper, the active cooperation necessary to accomplish the treatment goals can turn into opposition. Research from social psychology (Brehm, 1966) has led to a description of the nature and effects of reactance, the development of opposition to influence. With increased skill in management of behavior control, more attention has been paid to the conditions under which countercontrol can and should be exercised (London, 1969). Essentially, self-management techniques are based on the assumption that the helper plays only a temporary and supportive role in guiding the client toward changing his or her behavior. It is often tempting for the helper to assume too much of the burden of arranging the environment, or establishing reinforcement contingencies, or influencing criteria and goals without first obtaining the client's cooperation, or at least his or her agreement. In such a case, a client's opposition to the helper's influence can appear as failure to carry out the program. It is therefore of prime importance that the helper, from the very beginning of treatment, insure that the target behaviors and techniques are developed in collaboration with the client.

SUMMARY

In this chapter we have presented methods of behavior change based on the assumption that a client can alter her or his own behavior through the use of newly learned skills and rearrangements of her or his environment (see also Karoly & Kanfer, 1982). A brief outline of the theoretical framework of self-regulation was presented, and it was pointed out that even in self-management the client requires initial support and help from her or his environment. The importance of the client's perception as controlling the behavior change process was discussed. Self-control problems were defined as relating to situations in which the person is enjoying positive consequences of a behavior that ultimately has both positive and aversive consequences. The resolution of such problems was outlined as consisting of the establishment of controlling responses that eventually change the occurrence of a response that needs to be controlled. Such situations might involve the execution of a response, such as smoking or overeating, or the avoidance or withdrawal from a necessary but unpleasant activity such as working or tolerating mild pain.

Prior to the training of particular self-management techniques, the conditions for instigating behavior change must be created. Contracts, role-play, self-monitoring, and assignment of tasks aid in motivating the client toward change. Self-administered positive or aversive consequences, whether of the material or verbal-symbolic type, can be used to provide additional incentives. Similarly, self-produced satiation and deprivation have been described as techniques in the service of behavior change. One group of change strategies has been classified under the term *stimulus control*. They involve rearrangement of the social and physical environment or the use of self-generated behaviors. A special case of rearrangement of self-generated reinforcing consequences, the covert conditioning techniques, involves the use of imaginal presentation of stimuli and responses.

The typical treatment plan incorporates multiple techniques that are tailored to the client's particular problem and life situation. However, most effective treatments include the following general sequence of steps (Kanfer & Grimm, 1980):

Step 1. Establish a working relationship with the client including basic rapport building and educating the client about the instigative model of therapy.

Step 2. Create motivation for change through goal and value clarification, self-monitoring, or general discussions about possible positive outcomes.

Step 3.   Employ behavioral analysis that describes the network of biological, environmental, and psychological variables controlling the target behavior and identify the optimal point of intervention. This often involves self-monitoring.

Step 4.   Develop a plan for behavior change. Negotiate a contract with clear specification of the goals to be achieved, the time allowed for the program, the consequences of achieving it, and the methods for producing change.

Step 5.   Introduce a self-reinforcement program that relies increasingly on the client's self-reactions, is sufficiently varied to avoid satiation, and is effective in changing the target behavior.

Step 6.   Prerehearse the change strategy, providing information about the treatment and opportunities for modeling and role-play.

Step 7.   Ask the client to execute new behaviors in his or her natural environment, with discussion and correction of performance as needed. Include a system for recording qualitative and quantitative data documenting change.

Step 8.   Review progress, helping the client to solidify semantic memories of his or her experience. Discuss the nature of procedural effects, the means by which they are achieved, and situations to which they can be applied in the future.

Step 9.   Continue strong support for any activity in which the client assumes increasing responsibility for following the program accurately and extending it to other problematic behaviors.

Step 10. Summarize what has been learned in the change process and prepare the client to transfer the new knowledge and skills to future situations.

REFERENCES

Abrams, D. B., & Wilson, G. T. (1979). Self-monitoring and reactivity in the modification of cigarette smoking. *Journal of Consulting and Clinical Psychology, 47,* 243–251.

Anant, S. S. (1967). A note on the treatment of alcoholics by verbal aversion techniques. *Canadian Psychologist, 8,* 12–22.

Anderson, C. A. (1983). Imagination and expectation: The effect of imagining behavioral scripts on personal intentions. *Journal of Personality and Social Psychology, 45,* 293–305.

Averill, J. R. (1973). Personal control over aversive stimuli and its relationship to stress. *Psychological Bulletin, 80,* 286–303.

Baer, P. E., Foreyt, J. P., & Wright, S. (1977). Self-directed termination of excessive cigarette use among untreated smokers. *Journal of Behavior Therapy and Experimental Psychiatry, 8,* 71–74.

Baltes, M. M. (1978). Environmental factors in dependency among nursing home residents: A social ecology analysis. In T. A. Wills (Ed.), *Basic processes in helping relationships*. New York: Academic Press.

Bandura, A. (1977). Self-efficacy: Toward a unifying theory of behavioral change. *Psychological Review, 84*, 191–215.

Bandura, A., & Perloff, B. (1967). Relative efficacy of self-monitored and externally imposed reinforcement systems. *Journal of Personality and Social Psychology, 7*, 111–116.

Bellack, A. S., Schwartz, J., & Rozensky, R. H. (1974). The contribution of external control to self-control in a weight reduction program. *Journal of Behavior Therapy and Experimental Psychiatry, 5*, 245–249.

Bigelow, G., Sticker, O., Leibson, I., & Griffiths, R. (1976). Maintaining disulfram ingestion among outpatient alcoholics: A security deposit contingency contracting program. *Behaviour Research and Therapy, 14*, 378–380.

Bootzin, R. R., & Nicassio, P. (1978). Behavioral treatment for insomnia. In M. Hersen, R. Eisler, & P. Miller (Eds.), *Progress in behavior modification* (Vol. 6). New York: Academic Press.

Borkovec, T. D. (1985). The role of cognitive and somatic cues in anxiety and anxiety disorders: Worry and relaxation induced anxiety. In A. H. Tuma & J. D. Maser (Eds.), *Anxiety and the anxiety disorders*. Hillsdale, NJ: Lawrence Erlbaum.

Borkovec, T. D., Wilkinson, L., Folensbee, R., & Lerman, C. (1983). Stimulus control applications to the treatment of worry. *Behaviour Research and Therapy, 21*, 247–251.

Boudin, H. M. (1972). Contingency contracting as a therapeutic tool in the deceleration of amphetamine use. *Behavior Therapy, 3*, 604–608.

Brehm, S. (1966). *The application of social psychology to clinical practice*. Washington, DC: Hemisphere.

Breier, A., & Strauss, J. S. (1983). Self-control in psychotic disorders. *Archives of General Psychiatry, 40*, 1141–1145.

Brigham, T. A., & Stoerzinger, A. (1976). An experimental analysis of children's preference for self-selected rewards. In T. A. Brigham, R. Hawkins, J. Scott, & T. F. McLaughlin (Eds.), *Behavior analysis in education: Self-control and reading*. Dubuque, IA: Wm. C. Brown, Kendall/Hunt.

Broden, B., Hall, R. V., & Mitts, B. (1971). The effect of self-recording on the classroom behavior of two eighth grade students. *Journal of Applied Behavior Analysis, 4*, 191–199.

Castro, L., Perez, G. C., Albanchez, D. B., & de Leon, E. P. (1983). Feedback properties of "self-reinforcement": Further evidence. *Behavior Therapy, 14*, 672–681.

Cautela, J. R. (1969, September). *The use of imagery in behavior modification*. Paper presented at the annual meeting of the Association for the Advancement of Behavior Therapy, Washington, DC.

Cautela, J. R. (1973). Covert processes and behavior modification. *Journal of Nervous and Mental Diseases, 157*, 27–36.

Cautela, J. R. (1976). The present status of covert modeling. *Journal of Behavior Therapy and Experimental Psychiatry, 6*, 323–326.

Cautela, J. R. (1977). *Behavior analysis forms for clinical intervention*. Champaign, IL: Research Press.

Cautela, J. R. (1983). The self-control triad: Description and clinical applications. *Behavior Modification, 7*, 299–315.

Cautela, J. R., & Wisocki, P. A. (1977). The thought-stopping procedure: Description, application, and learning theory interpretations. *The Psychological Record, 1*, 255-264.

Condry, J. (1977). Enemies of exploration: Self-initiated versus other-initiated learning. *Journal of Personality and Social Psychology, 35*, 459-477.

Coyne, J. C., & Widiger, T. A. (1978). Toward a participatory model of psychotherapy. *Professional Psychology, 9*, 700-710.

Davison, G. C. (1973). Counter-control in behavior modification. In L. A. Hamerlynck, L. C. Handy, & F. J. Mash (Eds.), *Behavior change: Methodology, concepts and practice*. Champaign, IL: Research Press.

Deci, E. L. (1980). *The psychology of self-determination*. Lexington, MA: Lexington Books.

DiClemente, C., & Prochaska, J. (1982). Self-change and therapy change of smoking behavior: A comparison of processes of change in cessation and maintenance. *Addictive Behaviors, 7*, 133-142.

DiNicola, D. D., & DiMatteo, M. R. (1982). Communication, interpersonal influence and resistance to medical treatment. In T. A. Wills (Ed.), *Basic processes in helping relationships*. New York: Academic Press.

Elkins, R. L. (1980). Covert sensitization treatment of alcoholism: Contributions of successful conditioning to subsequent abstinence maintenance. *Addictive Behaviors, 5*, 67-89.

Emmelkamp, P. M. G. (1974). Self-observation versus flooding in the treatment of agoraphobia. *Behaviour Research and Therapy, 12*, 229-237.

Ewart, C. K. (1978). Self-observation in natural settings: Reactive effects of behavior desirability and goal setting. *Cognitive Therapy and Research, 2*, 39-56.

Felixbroad, J. J., & O'Leary, K. D. (1974). Self-determination of academic standards by children: Toward freedom from external control. *Journal of Educational Psychology, 66*, 845-850.

Ferster, C. B., Nurnberger, J. L., & Levitt, E. B. (1962). The control of eating. *Journal of Mathetics, 1*, 87-109.

Fisk, A. D., & Schneider, W. (1984). Memory as a function of attention, level of processing and automatization. *Journal of Experimental Psychology: Learning, Memory and Cognition, 10*, 181-197.

Foa, E. B., & Emmelkamp, P. M. G. (Eds.). (1983). *Failures in behavior therapy*. New York: John Wiley.

Foreyt, J. P., & Hagan, R. L. (1973). Covert sensitization: Conditioning or suggestion? *Journal of Abnormal Psychology, 82*, 17-23.

Fremouw, W. J., & Brown, J. P. (1980). The reactivity of addictive behaviors to self-monitoring: A functional analysis. *Addictive Behaviors, 5*, 209-217.

Fuchs, S. Z., & Rehm, L. P. (1977). A self-control behavior therapy program for depression. *Journal of Consulting and Clinical Psychology, 45*, 206-215.

Gartner, A., & Riessman, F. (Eds.). (1984). *The self-help revolution*. New York: Human Sciences Press.

Glasgow, R. E., & Rosen, G. M. (1978). Behavioral bibliotherapy: A review of self-help behavior therapy manuals. *Psychological Bulletin, 85*, 1-23.

Glasgow, R. E., & Rosen, G. M. (1979). Self-help behavior therapy manuals: Recent developments and clinical usage. *Behavior Therapy Review, 1*, 1-20.

Goldfried, M. R., & Robins, C. (1982). On the facilitation of self-efficacy. *Cognitive Therapy and Research, 6*, 361-380.

Goldstein, A. P., & Kanfer, F. H. (Eds.). (1979). *Maximizing treatment gains: Transfer enhancement in psychotherapy*. New York: Academic Press.

Green, L. (1978). Temporal and stimulus dimensions of self-monitoring in the treatment of obesity. *Behavior Therapy, 9*, 328–341.

Greiner, J. M., & Karoly, P. (1976). Effects of self-control training on study activity and academic performance: An analysis of self-monitoring, self-reward and systematic planning components. *Journal of Counseling Psychology, 23*, 495–502.

Grimm, L. G. (1980). The evidence for cue-controlled relaxation. *Behavior Therapy, 11*, 283–293.

Grimm, L. G., & Yarnold, P. P. (1984). Performance standards and the type A behavior pattern. *Cognitive Therapy and Research, 8*, 59–66.

Guralnick, M. J. (1976). Solving complex discrimination problems: Techniques for the development of problem solving strategies. *American Journal of Mental Deficiency, 81*, 18–25.

Hayes, S. C., & Nelson, R. C. (1983). Similar reactivity produced by external cues and self-monitoring. *Behavior Modification, 7*, 183–196.

Haynes, R. B., Taylor, D. W., & Sackett, D. L. (Eds.). (1979). *Compliance in health care*. Baltimore, MD: Johns Hopkins University Press.

Heffernan, T., & Richards, C. S. (1981). Self-control of study behavior: Identification of natural methods. *Journal of Counseling Psychology, 28*, 361–364.

Herzberg, A. (1945). *Active psychotherapy*. New York: Grune & Stratton.

Homme, L. E. (1965). Perspectives in psychology—XXIV. Control of coverants: The operants of the mind. *Psychological Record, 15*, 501–511.

Jacobson, N. S. (1977). Problem-solving and contingency contracting in the treatment of marital discord. *Journal of Consulting and Clinical Psychology, 45*, 92–100.

Jeffery, R. W., Gerber, W. M., Rosenthal, B. S., & Lindquist, R. A. (1983). Monetary contracts in weight control: Effectiveness of group and individual contracts of varying size. *Journal of Consulting and Clinical Psychology, 51*, 242–248.

Johnson, S. M., & Martin, S. (1973). Developing self-evaluation as a conditioned reinforcer. In B. Ashem & E. G. Poser (Eds.), *Behavior modification with children*. Elmsford, NY: Pergamon Press.

Johnson, S. M., & White, G. (1971). Self-observation as an agent of behavioral change. *Behavior Therapy, 2*, 488–497.

Jones, R. T., Nelson, R. E., & Kazdin, A. E. (1977). The role of external variables in self-reinforcement: A review. *Behavior Modification, 1*, 147–178.

Jones, E. E., & Nisbett, R. E. (1971). *The actor and observer: Divergent perceptions of the causes of behavior*. New York: Silver Burdett, General Learning Press.

Kanfer, F. H. (1970a). Self-monitoring: Methodological limitations and clinical applications. *Journal of Consulting and Clinical Psychology, 35*, 148–152.

Kanfer, F. H. (1970b). Self-regulation: Research, issues and speculations. In C. Neuringer & J. L. Michael (Eds.), *Behavior modification in clinical psychology*. New York: Appleton-Century-Crofts, 178–220.

Kanfer, F. H. (1971). The maintenance of behavior by self-generated stimuli and reinforcement. In A. Jacob & L. B. Sachs (Eds.), *The psychology of private events*. New York: Academic Press.

Kanfer, F. H. (1977). The many faces of self-control, or behavior modification changes its focus. In P. B. Stuart (Ed.), *Behavioral self-management*. New York: Brunner/Mazel.

Kanfer, F. H. (1985). Target behavior selection for clinical change programs. *Behavioral Assessment, 7*, 7–20.

Kanfer, F. H., Cox, L. E., Greiner, J. M., & Karoly, P. (1974). Contracts, demand characteristics and self-control. *Journal of Personality and Social Psychology, 30,* 605-619.

Kanfer, F. H., & Duerfeldt, P. H. (1967). Motivational properties of S-R. *Perceptual and Motor Skills, 25,* 237-246.

Kanfer, F. H., & Grimm, L. G. (1978). Freedom of choice and behavioral change. *Journal of Consulting and Clinical Psychology, 46,* 873-878.

Kanfer, F. H., & Grimm, L. G. (1980). Managing clinical change: A process model of therapy. *Behavior Therapy, 4,* 419-444.

Kanfer, F. H., & Hagerman, S. (1981). The role of self-regulation. In L. P. Rehm (Ed.), *Behavior therapy for depression: Present status and future directions.* New York: Academic Press.

Kanfer, F. H., & Karoly, P. (1972). Self-control: A behavioristic excursion into the lion's den. *Behavior Therapy, 3,* 378-416.

Kanfer, F. H., & Phillips, J. S. (1970). *Learning foundations of behavior therapy.* New York: John Wiley.

Kanfer, F. H., & Seidner, M. L. (1973). Self-control: Factors enhancing tolerance of noxious stimulation. *Journal of Personality and Social Psychology, 25,* 381-389.

Karoly, P., & Kanfer, F. H. (Ed.). (1982). *Self-management and behavior change: From theory to practice.* Elmsford, NY: Pergamon Press.

Karoly, P., & Steffen, J. J. (Eds.). (1980). *Improving the long-term effects of psychotherapy.* New York: Gardner Press.

Kazdin, A. E. (1974). Self-monitoring and behavior change. In M. J. Mahoney & C. E. Thoreson (Eds.), *Self-control: Power to the person.* Monterey, CA: Brooks/Cole.

Kazdin, A. E. (1977). Research issues in covert conditioning. *Cognitive Therapy and Research, 1,* 45-58.

Kazdin, A. E. (1979). Imagery elaboration and self-efficacy in the covert modeling treatment of assertive behavior. *Journal of Consulting and Clinical Psychology, 47,* 725-733.

Kazdin, A. E., & Mascitelli, S. (1982). Covert and overt rehearsal in homework practice in developing assertiveness. *Journal of Consulting and Clinical Psychology, 52,* 250-258.

Kelly, G. A. (1955). *The psychology of personal constructs.* New York: W. W. Norton.

Kirschenbaum, D. S., & Tomarken, A. J. (1982). On facing the generalization problem: The study of self-regulatory failure. In P. C. Kendall (Ed.), *Advances in cognitive-behavioral research and therapy* (Vol. I, pp. 119-200). New York: Academic Press.

Klinger, E., Barta, S. G., & Maxeiner, M. E. (1979). Current concerns: Assessing therapeutically relevant motivation. In P. C. Kendall & S. D. Hollon (Eds.), *Cognitive-behavioral interventions: Assessment.* New York: Academic Press.

Koberg, D., & Bagnall, J. (1976). *The polytechnic school of values: Values Tech.* Los Altos, CA: William Kaufmann Inc.

Komaki, J., & Dore, B. K. (1978). Self-recording: Its effects on individuals high and low in motivation. *Behavior Therapy, 9,* 65-72.

Kopel, S., & Arkowitz, H. (1975). The role of attribution and self-perception in behavior change: Implications for behavior therapy. *Genetic Psychology Monographs, 92,* 175-212.

Kuhl, J. (1984). Volitional aspects of achievement motivation and learned helplessness: Toward a comprehensive theory of action control. In B. A. Maher (Ed.),

Progress in experimental personality research (Vol. 13). New York: Academic Press.

Lakein, R. (1973). *How to get control of your time and your life.* New York: New American Library, Signet.

Langer, E. J., Janis, I. L., & Wolfer, J. A. (1975). Reduction of physiological stress in surgical patients. *Journal of Experimental Social Psychology, 11*, 155-165.

Langer, E. J., & Rodin, J. (1976). The effect of choice and enhanced personal responsibility for the aged: A field experiment in an institutional setting. *Journal of Personality and Social Psychology, 34*, 191-198.

Lee, W. (1978). *Formulating and reaching goals.* Champaign, IL: Research Press.

Liberman, B. L. (1978). The role of mastery in psychotherapy: Maintenance of improvement and prescriptive change. In J. D. Frank, R. Hoehn-Saric, D. D. Imber, B. L. Liberman, & A. R. Stone (Eds.), *The effective ingredients of successful psychotherapy.* New York: Brunner/Mazel.

Liem, G. R. (1975). Performance and satisfaction as affected by personal control over salient decisions. *Journal of Personality and Social Psychology, 31*, 232-240.

Little, L. M., & Curran, J. P. (1978). Covert sensitization: A clinical procedure in need of some explanations. *Psychological Bulletin, 85 (3)*, 513-531.

Litrownik, A. J. (1982). Special considerations in the self-management of training of the developmentally disabled. In P. Karoly & F. H. Kanfer (Eds.), *Self-management and behavior change: From theory to practice.* Elmsford, NY: Pergamon Press.

London, P. (1969). *Behavior control.* New York: Harper & Row.

Lovitt, T. C., & Curtiss, K. A. (1969). Academic response rate as a function of teacher and self-imposed contingencies. *Journal of Applied Behavioral Analysis, 2*, 49-53.

Mahoney, M. J. (1971). The self-management of covert behavior: A case study. *Behavior Therapy, 2*, 575-578.

Mahoney, M. J. (1974). *Cognition and behavior modification.* Cambridge, MA: Ballinger.

Mahoney, M. J., Moura, N. G. M., & Wade, T. C. (1973). Relative efficacy of self-reward, self-punishment, and self-monitoring techniques for weight loss. *Journal of Consulting and Clinical Psychology, 40*, 404-407.

Masters, W. H., & Johnson, V. E. (1970). *Human sexual inadequacy.* Boston: Little, Brown.

McFall, R. M. (1977). Parameters of self-monitoring. In P. B. Stuart (Ed.), *Behavioral self-management: Strategies, techniques and outcomes.* New York: Brunner/Mazel.

Mischel, W., & Moore, B. (1980). The role of ideation in voluntary delay for symbolically presented rewards. *Cognitive Therapy and Research, 4*, 211-221.

Montgomery, G. T., & Parton, D. A. (1970). Reinforcing effect of self-reward. *Journal of Experimental Psychology, 84*, 273-276.

Nelson, R. O. (1977). Methodological issues in assessment via self-monitoring. In J. D. Cone & R. P. Hawkins (Eds.), *Behavioral assessment: New directions in clinical psychology.* New York: Brunner/Mazel.

Nelson, R. O., Hayes, S. C., Spong, R. T., Jarret, R. B., & McKnight, D. L. (1983). Self-reinforcement: Appealing misnomer or effective mechanism? *Behaviour Research and Therapy, 21*, 557-566.

Nelson, R. O., Lipinski, D. P., & Black, J. L. (1976). The reactivity of adult retardates' self-monitoring: A comparison among behaviors of different valences, and a comparison with token reinforcement. *Psychological Record, 26*, 189-201.

Nicassio, P. M., & Buchanan, D. C. (1981). Clinical application of behavior therapy for insomnia. *Comprehensive Psychiatry, 22,* 512–521.

O'Banion, D., Armstrong, B. K., & Ellis, J. (1980). Conquered urge as a means of self-control. *Addictive Behaviors, 5,* 101–106.

Perri, M. G., Richards, C. S., & Schultheis, K. R. (1977). Behavioral self-control and smoking reduction: A study of self-initiated attempts to reduce smoking. *Behavior Therapy, 8,* 360–365.

Posner, M. I., & Snyder, C. R. R. (1975). Attention and cognitive control. In R. L. Solso (Ed.), *Information-processing and cognition: The Loyola symposium* (pp. 55–85). Hillsdale, NJ: Lawrence Erlbaum.

Prochaska, J. D., & DiClemente, C. O. (1982). Transtheoretical therapy: Toward a more integrative model of change. *Psychotherapy: Theory, Research, and Practice, 19,* 276–288.

Rehm, L. P., & Kornblith, S. J. (1979). Behavior therapy for depression: A review of recent developments. In M. Hersen, R. M. Eisler, & P. M. Miller (Eds.), *Progress in behavior modification* (Vol. 7). New York: Academic Press.

Richards, C. S. (1975). Behavior modification of studying through study skills advice and self-control procedures. *Journal of Counseling Psychology, 22,* 431–436.

Richards, C. S., & Perri, M. G. (1977). Do self-control treatments last? An evaluation of behavioral problem solving and faded counselor maintenance strategies. Paper presented at the eleventh annual meeting of the Association for Advancement of Behavior Therapy, Atlanta, GA.

Rodin, J. (1982). Biopsychosocial aspects of self-management. In P. Karoly & F. H. Kanfer (Eds.), *Self-management and behavior change: From theory to practice.* Elmsford, NY: Pergamon Press.

Rodin, J., & Langer, E. J. (1977). Long-term effects of a control-relevant intervention with the institutionalized aged. *Journal of Personality and Social Psychology, 35,* 897–902.

Romanczyk, R. G. (1974). Self-monitoring in the treatment of obesity: Parameters of reactivity. *Behavior Therapy, 5,* 531–540.

Rosen, G. M. (1982). Self-help approaches to self-management. In K. R. Blankstein, & J. Polivy (Eds.), *Self-control and self-modification of emotional behavior.* New York: Plenum.

Rosenbaum, M., & Merbaum, M. (1984). Self-control of anxiety and depression: An evaluative review of treatments. In C. M. Franks (Ed.), *New developments in practical behavior therapy: From research to clinical application* (pp. 105–154). New York: Howarth Press.

Rutner, I. T., & Bugle, C. (1969). An experimental procedure for modification of psychotic behavior. *Journal of Consulting and Clinical Psychology, 33,* 651–653.

Saltzman, C., Luetgert, M. J., Roth, C. H., Creaser, J., & Howard, L. (1976). Formation of a therapeutic relationship: Experiences during the initial phase of psychotherapy as predictors of treatment duration and outcome. *Journal of Consulting and Clinical Psychology, 44,* 546–555.

Schefft, B. K., & Kanfer, F. H. Self-management therapy: A comparative study of treatment and generalization effects. Manuscript submitted for publication.

Schneider, W., & Shiffrin, R. M. (1977). Controlled and automatic human information processing: I. Detection, search and attention. *Psychological Review, 84,* 1–66.

Seligman, M. E. P. (1970). On the generality of the laws of learning. *Psychological Review, 77,* 406–418.

Shelton, J. L. (1979). Instigation therapy: Using therapeutic homework to promote treatment gains. In A. P. Goldstein & F. H. Kanfer (Eds.), *Maximizing treatment gains*. New York: Academic Press.

Shelton, J. L., & Levy, R. L. (1981). *Behavioral assignments and treatment compliance: A handbook of clinical strategies*. Champaign, IL: Research Press.

Spring, F. L., Sipich, J. F., Trimble, R. W., & Goeckner, D. J. (1978). Effects of contingency and noncontingency contracts in the context of a self-control-oriented smoking modification program. *Behavior Therapy, 9*, 967–968.

Stotland, E., & Blumenthal, A. L. (1964). The reduction of anxiety as a result of the expectation of making a choice. *Canadian Journal of Psychology, 18*, 139–145.

Stuart, R. B., & Davis, B. (1972). *Slim change in a fat world: Behavioral control of obesity*. Champaign, IL: Research Press.

Suinn, R. M., & Richardson, R. (1971). Anxiety management training: A nonspecific behavior therapy for anxiety control. *Behavior Therapy, 2*, 498–510.

Susskind, D. J. (1970). The idealized self-image (ISI): A new technique in confidence training. *Behavior Therapy, 1*, 538–541.

Surwit, R. S., Feingloss, M. N., & Scovern, A. N. (1983). Diabetes and behavior: A paradigm for health psychology. *American Psychologist, 38*, 255–262.

Tearman, B. H., Lahey, B. B., Thompson, J. K., & Hammer, D. (1982). The role of coping self-instructions combined with covert modeling in specific fear reduction. *Cognitive Therapy and Research, 6*, 185–190.

Thoreson, C. E., & Mahoney, M. J. (1974). *Behavioral self-control*. New York: Holt, Rinehart & Winston.

Tressler, D. P., & Tucker, R. D. (1980, November). *The comparative effects of self-evaluation and self-reinforcement training in the treatment of depression*. Paper presented at the meeting of the Association for Advancement of Behavior Therapy, New York, NY.

Tulving, E. (1972). Episodic and semantic memory. In E. Tulving & W. Donaldson (Eds.), *Organization of memory*. New York: Academic Press.

Turkewitz, H., O'Leary, K. D., & Ironsmith, M. (1975). Generalization and maintenance of appropriate behavior through self-control. *Journal of Consulting and Clinical Psychology, 43*, 577–583.

Wachtel, P. L. (Ed.). (1982). *Resistance: Psychodynamic and behavioral approaches*. New York: Plenum.

Watson, D. L., & Tharp, R. G. (1977). *Self-directed behavior: Self-modification for personal adjustment* (2nd ed.). Monterey, CA: Brooks/Cole.

Wills, T. A. (Ed.). (1978). *Basic processes in helping relationships*. New York: Academic Press.

9

Cognitive-Behavior Modification

Donald Meichenbaum

The field of cognitive-behavior modification (CBM) has grown immensely during the last decade. For example, a recent survey by Klesges, Sanchez, and Stanton (1982) revealed that 40% of new clinical faculty members described their theoretical orientation as cognitive-behavioral, as compared with only 18% who described their orientation as behavioral. Both of these percentages exceeded any other theoretical preference. One reason for such interest is that CBM has tried to *integrate* the clinical concerns of psychodynamically oriented psychotherapists and the technology of behavior therapy into a comprehensive clinically sensitive treatment approach. Although the reported efficacy of CBM procedures can only be characterized as promising at this stage, a great deal of research is underway to assess the clinical value of this method with a variety of diverse populations. This chapter will consider some of the major concepts, illustrate CBM treatment approaches with both child and adult populations, and, it is hoped, whet the reader's appetite so he or she can pursue the topic further.

WHAT CBM IS

CBM is not an easy term to define. Subsumed under the heading of CBM is a host of different treatment procedures including such techniques as cognitive therapy (Beck, 1970, 1976; Beck, Rush, Hollon, & Shaw, 1979); cognitive restructuring procedures such as rational-emotive therapy (Ellis & Grieger, 1978); skills training programs such as stress-inoculation training (Meichenbaum, 1977) and anxiety management training (Suinn & Richardson, 1971); problem-solving training (D'Zurilla & Goldfried, 1971); self-control procedures (Karoly & Kanfer, 1982); and self-instructional training procedures (Meichenbaum, 1977). These various CBM procedures differ in several ways. They

1. Focus on different aspects of the cognitive experience (e.g., beliefs, expectations, images, problem-solving cognition, coping self-statements).
2. Offer different prescriptions as to the best point of intervention in the cognition-affect-behavior-consequences chain.
3. Emphasize different strategies for intervention, ranging from didactic assaults of clients' irrational beliefs to Socratic dialogues designed to foster coping skills.

Even though there is diversity in how CBM is implemented, some common features can be identified. CBM interventions are usually active, time-limited, and fairly structured. They are designed to enlist the client (and in some instances significant others such as spouse, parents, peers) in a collaborative process, whereby the client becomes her or his own "personal scientist" (Mahoney, 1974), engaging in what has been called a *collaborative empiricism* (Beck et al., 1979). The cognitive therapist works with clients to

1. Help them better understand the nature of their presenting problems.
2. View their cognitions ("automatic" thoughts, images) and accompanying feelings as hypotheses worthy of testing rather than as facts or truths.
3. Encourage them to perform "personal experiments" and review the consequences of their actions as "anomalous data" or "evidence" that is contrary to their prior expectations and beliefs.
4. Learn new behavioral, interpersonal, cognitive and emotional-regulation skills.

In short, CBM refers not only to a set of therapeutic techniques, but also to a conceptualization of behavior change. We will be better able to understand the CBM theory of change and CBM treatment techniques if we first pause to consider briefly how the concept of cognition has been conceptualized from a CBM perspective.

WHAT COGNITION WITHIN A COGNITIVE-BEHAVIORAL FRAMEWORK MEANS

The concept of cognition has been used in three different ways: as cognitive events, cognitive processes, and cognitive structures. Let us consider each in turn.

Cognitive events are conscious thoughts and images that occur in an individual's stream of consciousness or that can be readily retrieved upon request. Beck (1976) has referred to them as *automatic thoughts* and

Meichenbaum (1977) has described them as *internal dialogue*. Cognitive events incorporate, among other things, attributions, expectancies, and task-irrelevant thoughts. Such automatic cognitive events are not limited to cognitions, but can involve images, symbolic "words," and gestures and *their accompanying affect*. These cognitive events can at times be affectively laden or constitute what Zajonc (1980) has described as "hot," as compared with "cold," cognitions.

It should be noted, however, that people do *not* go around talking to themselves all the time. In fact, most of our behavior is "mindless" or "scripted," occurring in an automatic fashion with little accompanying intentional thought. But on some occasions we do "talk to ourselves," and the content of our self-talk can influence how we behave, feel, and appraise the outcome of our behavior. Moreover, as we will see, there are instances, such as with impulsive children, when it is therapeutic to encourage and teach clients to talk to themselves in a self-guiding fashion.

Some hint as to how this is accomplished comes from consideration of when we naturally talk to ourselves or are "mindful" of our behavior. Cognitive events are likely to occur when an individual (a) constructs and integrates new thought and action structures such as learning a new motor skill when learning to drive a car; (b) has to exercise choices and judgments, as in uncertain or novel situations, like covert trial and error conditions or when one's plans are interrupted; and (c) anticipates and/or experiences an intense emotional experience.

Cognitive processes are the ways we process information. Because we are bombarded with more information (both internal and external cues) than we can process, we are selective in what we attend to in the present, the past, and the future. We are also selective in how we appraise information, the meaning we attribute to it, and so forth. In the same way that we don't attend to how we speak, walk, or breathe (although our attention can be drawn to such acts), we don't readily attend to how we process information (i.e., search, store, retrieve, and infer). Such processes operate in an automatic or unconscious fashion (see Meichenbaum and Gilmore, 1984, for a more complete discussion). In later sections we will consider two such cognitive processes, metacognition and cognitive distortions, and note their implications for treatment.

Cognitive structures are tacit assumptions and beliefs that give rise to habitual ways of construing the self and the world. The individual's personal schemata, current concerns, hidden agenda, and personal goals influence the way information is processed and the way behavior is organized. George Kelly (1969) anticipated the current interest in cognitive structures in his personal construct theory. As Kelly noted, cognitive structures act as perceptual sets that serve a *gating function*. It is important to appreciate that each cognitive structure or schema embodies both an ideational component and an affective component. Not only information is coded and stored, but affect is also (Bower, 1981). Such schemata operate like Kuhn's (1962) paradigms and Polanyi's (1958) tacit knowledge in influencing behavior. They act like "selective filters," influencing how we appraise events.

A MODEL OF BEHAVIOR CHANGE

Now that the concepts of cognitive events, processes, and structures have been introduced, let us briefly consider how these are employed in helping people change. A basic premise of the CBM approach is that one cannot change behavior without having individuals increase their awareness, raise their consciousness, or notice a behavioral pattern (how they think, feel, and behave and the impact they have on others). There is a need to have clients interrupt the automaticity of their acts or the scripted nature of their behavior. Such an interruption is the occasion for people to talk to themselves, to appraise the situation and their behavior.

The CBM therapist attempts to influence the content and nature of the client's internal dialogue. Moreover, the CBM therapist attempts to aid clients in becoming aware of the beliefs, current concerns, hidden agendas, and personal goals (i.e., cognitive structures) that influence how they appraise and process events. Moreover, the CBM therapist insures that clients have the variety of behavioral, cognitive, affective, and interpersonal skills needed to perform "in vivo personal experiments" (try out new behaviors) and then works with clients to consider how they will appraise the results of their efforts.

Do the clients take the "data" (results of their efforts) as "evidence" that will change their prior expectancies and beliefs? The CBM therapist focuses on how clients view possible setbacks and frustrations that might occur in the future. Such setbacks must come to be viewed as constructive feedback rather than the occasion for "catastrophizing" ideation, dysfunctional emotions, and relapse. The therapist needs to help the client anticipate the occasional lapses that could occur. No matter how successful the treatment, there are very likely occasions in which "slips" or "relapses" occur. Inoculation for failure by means of identifying high-risk situations and training specific coping skills can help clients maintain improvement. Thus, a key feature of CBM treatment is the inclusion of relapse prevention (Marlatt & Gordon, 1980).

This abbreviated description of the complex and dynamic learning experience of CBM treatment can now be illustrated in the treatment of children and adults. More detailed accounts of CBM therapy have been offered by Beck et al. (1979); Ellis and Bernard (1984); Ellis and Grieger (1978); Freeman (1983); Kendall and Braswell (1984); Meyers and Craighead (1984); Meichenbaum (1977); Meichenbaum and Jaremko (1983); Novaco (1975);

Sank and Shaffer (1984); Turk, Meichenbaum, and Genest (1983); and Williams (1984). In short, there are many recent publications in which cognitive behavior therapists have "gone public" in describing their treatment approach, so others can attempt to replicate and extend their efforts. The present list of CBM manual-type books is *not* exhaustive but illustrative of the current activity that is now underway. None of these manuals deserves a Good Housekeeping seal of approval, but, rather, each bears careful critical appraisal. These efforts deserve consideration and further empirical validation.

COGNITIVE BEHAVIOR MODIFICATION WITH CHILDREN

The major use of CBM procedures with children has involved the training of self-control skills, especially with hyperactive, impulsive, and aggressive children. CBM procedures have also been employed with children who are socially withdrawn, mentally retarded, psychotic, learning disabled, and delinquent, as well as with "normal" children, to enhance academic and interpersonal skills (Meyers & Craighead, 1984). For purposes of illustration, this discussion will focus on work with hyperactive, impulsive children, or what has recently been described as children with attentional deficit disorders.

Hyperactive, Impulsive Children

A major social problem in schools is the high incidence of hyperactive, impulsive children. According to O'Malley and Eisenberg (1973), for example, 5% to 10% of school-age children are diagnosed as hyperactive. It has been estimated (Grinspoon & Singer, 1973) that 200,000 schoolchildren in the United States daily receive some form of medication for treatment of hyperactivity. The second major mode of treatment for these children is environmental control by such means as operant conditioning. A CBM treatment intervention called *self-instructional training* was developed to supplement the pharmacological and behavioral treatments.

The impetus for the self-instructional training procedure was the theoretical work of the Soviet psychologists Luria (1961) and Vygotsky (1962). Luria (1959) proposed a developmental model of self-control consisting of three stages by which the initiation and inhibition of children's voluntary motor behaviors come under verbal control. During the first stage, the speech of others, usually adults, controls and directs a child's overt behavior. The second stage is characterized by the child's speech becoming an effective regulator of her or his behavior. Finally, the child's covert or inner speech comes to assume a self-governing role. From this hypothetical developmental sequence, a treatment paradigm was developed and success-fully used to train impulsive children to talk to themselves as a means of developing self-control (Meichenbaum & Goodman, 1971). The training regimen included the following procedural steps:

1. An adult model performed a task while talking to himself out loud (cog-nitive modeling).
2. The child performed the same task under the direction of the model's instructions (overt, external guidance).
3. The child performed the task while instructing himself aloud (overt self-guidance).
4. The child whispered the instructions to himself as he went through the task (faded, overt self-guidance).
5. The child performed the task while guiding his performance via inaudible or private speech or nonverbal self-direction (covert self-instruction).

Over a number of training sessions, the package of self-statements modeled by the tutor and rehearsed by the child (initially aloud and then covertly) was enlarged by means of response chaining and successive ap-proximation procedures. For example, in a task that required the copying of line patterns, the examiner performed the task while cognitively model-ing as follows:

> Okay, what is it I have to do? You want me to copy the picture with the differ-ent lines. I have to go slowly and carefully. Okay, draw the line down, down, good; and then to the right, that's it; now down some more and to the left. Good, I'm doing fine so far. Remember, go slowly. Now back up again. No, I was supposed to go down. That's okay. Just erase the line carefully. . . . Good. Even if I make an error I can go on slowly and carefully. I have to go down now. Finished. I did it! (Meichenbaum & Goodman, 1971, p. 117)

In this thinking-out-loud phase, the model displayed several performance-relevant skills: (a) problem definition ("What is it I have to do?"); (b) attention focusing and response guidance ("Carefully. . . . Draw the line down"); (c) self-reinforcement ("Good, I'm doing fine"); and (d) self-evaluative coping skills and error correcting options ("That's okay. . . . Even if I make an error I can go on slowly").

A variety of tasks was employed to train the child to use self-instructions to control his nonverbal behavior. The tasks varied from simple sensorimo-tor abilities to more complex problem-solving abilities. The sensorimotor tasks (such as copying line patterns and coloring figures within bound-aries) provided first the model, then the child, with the opportunity to pro-duce a narrative description of the behavior, both preceding and accom-panying performance. Over the course of a training session, the child's overt self-statements about a particular task were faded to the covert level. The difficulty of the training tasks was increased over the training sessions, using more cognitively demanding activities. Hence, there was a progression from tasks such as reproducing designs and following sequential instructions, taken from the Stanford-Binet Intelligence Test, to completing such pictorial series as those in the Primary Mental Abilities Test, to solving conceptual tasks such as Raven's Matrices. The experimenter modeled appropriate self-verbalizations for each of these tasks and then had the child follow the fading procedure.

The self-instructional training procedure, relative to placebo and assessment control groups, resulted in significantly improved performance on Porteus Maze, performance IQ on the WISC, and increased cognitive reflectivity on the Matching Familiar Figures Test (MFF). The improved performance was evident in a 1-month follow-up. Moreover, it was observed that 60% of the self-instructionally trained impulsive children were talking to themselves spontaneously in the posttest and the follow-up sessions (Meichenbaum & Goodman, 1971).The cognitive behavioral paradigm has now been used successfully to establish inner speech control over the disruptive behavior of hyperactive children (Douglas, Parry, Martin, & Garson, 1976) and aggressive children (Camp, Blom, Hebert, & Van Doorninck, 1977); cheating behavior of kindergartners and first graders (Monahan & O'Leary, 1971); Porteus Maze performance of hyperactive boys (Palkes, Stewart & Freedman, 1972; Palkes, Stewart, & Kahana, 1968); and the conceptual tempo of emotionally disturbed boys (Finch, Wilkinson, Nelson, & Montgomery, 1975), as well as that of normal children (Bender, 1976; Meichenbaum & Goodman, 1971).

The Douglas et al. (1976) study nicely illustrates the general treatment approach. Hyperactive children were initially exposed to a model who verbalized the cognitive strategies, described later. The child could in turn rehearse these strategies initially aloud and then covertly. The cognitive strategies included stopping to define a problem and the various steps within it, considering and evaluating several possible solutions before acting on any one, checking one's work throughout and calmly correcting any errors, sticking with a problem until everything possible had been tried to solve it correctly, and giving oneself a pat on the back for work well done. Verbalizations modeled by the trainer to illustrate these strategies included

"I must stop and think before I begin." "What plans can I try?" "How would it work out if I did that?" "What shall I try next?" "Have I got it right so far?" "See, I made a mistake there—I'll just erase it." "Now let's see, have I tried everything I can think of?" "I've done a pretty good job!" (Douglas et al., 1976, p. 408)

Training was applied across tasks to insure that the children did *not* just develop task-specific responses, but instead developed generalized cognitive strategies.

Metacognition

The task of teaching children to think before they act is nicely illustrated when we consider the cognitive process of metacognition. Metacognitive development refers to the child's awareness of her or his own cognitive machinery and the way this machinery works. A quote from Flavell nicely describes this cognitive process.

Metacognition refers to one's knowledge concerning one's own cognitive processes and products or anything related to them, e.g., the learning-relevant properties of information or data. For example, I am engaging in metacognition (meta-memory, meta-learning, meta-attention, meta-language, or whatever) if I notice that I am having more trouble learning A than B; if it strikes me that I should double-check C before accepting it as a fact; if it occurs to me that I had better scrutinize each and every alternative in any multiple-choice type task situation before deciding which is the best one; if I sense that I had better make a note of D because I may forget it. . . . Metacognition refers, among other things, to the active monitoring and consequent regulation and orchestration of these processes in relation to the cognitive objects or data on which they bear, usually in the service of some concrete goal or objective. (1976, p. 232)

A further illustration of metacognition comes from our own experience. Introspect for a moment about the cognitive and behavioral acts in which you engage to retrieve a bit of information, such as a name, that you have forgotten (i.e., the tip-of-the-tongue phenomenon). Consider how you try to retrieve the missing name, the way in which you use imagery, mnemonic devices, and so on. This knowledge of your metamemory processes and how you monitor and control these cognitive processes is what is meant by the term *metacognition*.

Although the developmental work on metacognition began in the area of memory, it has been quickly extended to a variety of areas including attention (Miller & Bigi, 1978), reading comprehension (Meyers & Paris, 1978), self-control (Mischel, Mischel, & Hood, 1978), communication (Markman, 1977), and peer relationship (Asarnow & Callan, in press). For example, Meyers and Paris found that children could benefit from instruction regarding the means, goals, and parameters of proficient reading.

For the purposes of CBM, metacognition can be conceptualized as *both* the knowledge one has of his or her cognitive processes and the ability to guide and control those processes. It can be thought of as the self-communication one engages in or the internal dialogue one emits before, during, and after performing a task. In most instances this occurs in an automatic, unconscious fashion, but for children who have difficulties, such metacognitive skills can enhance performance and engender self-control (Meichenbaum & Asarnow, 1979). The teaching of such skills as self-interrogation, planning, and self-monitoring represent important CBM treatment goals. Borkowski and Cavanaugh (1979) have described what should go into a training regimen designed to teach metacognitive skills:

First, we need to identify several strategies each of which is operative in different learning situations. Second, we need to train children on several strategies, making sure that they know when and how to apply them. Third, we need to train the instructional package so that common elements between training and generalization contexts are evident, and distractors minimal. Fourth, we need to develop child-generated search routines, probably through the use of self-instructional procedures, that encourage the child to analyze a task, scan his or her available strategic repertoire, and match the demands of the task with an appropriate strategy and retrieval plan. Fifth, we need to instruct children in such a way that we utilize whatever skills they possess, in order to bring each child to an awareness of the advantage of executive monitoring and decision-making in solving problems. Finally, we may need to reinforce, in a very explicit way, successful executive functioning in order for it to come under the control of natural environmental contingencies, such as a child's good feelings about solving a difficult problem. (p. 54)

Table 9.1 provides a more detailed list of treatment guidelines to follow in order to teach metacognitive skills that will be internalized; that will generalize across situations, tasks, skills; and that will be maintained over time. These guidelines underscore the important role of *collaboration* in all forms of cognitive behavioral interventions. More specifically, there is a need to insure that the child

1. Understands the reasons why he or she is being seen and perceives that he or she does indeed have a problem.
2. Collaborates in the selection of the skills to be worked on.
3. Appreciates how the skills that will be worked on in the training will be helpful in changing behaviors in the criterion situations.

TABLE 9.1. GUIDELINES FOR DEVELOPING A TRAINING PROGRAM

1. Analyze target behaviors. Conduct both a performance and a situation analysis. Identify component processes and capacity requirements to perform target behaviors.
2. Assess for client's existing strategies, behavioral competencies, and affect-laden thoughts, images, and feelings that could inhibit performance.
3. Collaborate. Have client collaborate in analysis of the problem and in development, implementation, and evaluation of the training package.
4. Select training tasks carefully. Make training tasks similar to the criterion.
5. Insure that the component skills needed to perform in the criterion situation are in the client's repertoire and then teach metacognitive or executive planning skills.
6. Insure that the client receives and recognizes feedback about the usefulness of the training procedures.
7. Make the need and means for generalizing explicit. Don't expect generalization — train for it.
8. When possible, train in multiple settings with multiple tasks and trainers. Have clients engage in multiple graded assignments in clinic and in vivo.
9. Anticipate and incorporate possible and real failures into the training program.
10. Make the termination of training performance-based, not time-based. Include follow-through booster sessions and follow-up assessments.

4. Considers when and how he or she will practice these skills in other situations.
5. Anticipates and reacts constructively to possible setbacks.

Moreover, in many instances, the CBM treatment has to go beyond the "targeted" child to include the child's peers and family members. For example, in treating socially withdrawn children, the CBM intervention should *not* only be focused on helping the child develop social skills, but also on influencing the child's acceptance in her or his peer group (Ladd & Keeney, 1983). Bierman (1981) has demonstrated that the combination of social skills training and providing the peer group with supraordinate goals (e.g., making a movie), so the socially withdrawn child can be more readily accepted, increased the efficacy and generalizability of treatment effects.

As Stokes and Baer (1977) have noted, therapists should *not* lament the fact that their treatments do not achieve generalization, but rather should train for generalization explicitly as described in Table 9.1.

Treatment Effectiveness

How effective is CBM with children? A number of major review papers on CBM with children have been written (Abikoff, 1979; Craighead, Craighead-Wilcoxon, & Meyers, 1978; Harris, 1982; Hobbs, Moguin, Tyroler, & Lahey, 1980; Karoly, 1977; Kendall, 1977; Kendall & Finch, 1979; Mash & Dalby, 1978; Meichenbaum & Asarnow, 1979; Meyers & Craighead, 1984; and Pressley, 1979) as well as an entire issue of the *Exceptional Education Quarterly*, 1980. It is difficult to summarize so many diverse reviews of CBM applied to such diverse populations in one short statement. Nevertheless, a common theme does seem to be emerging, namely, the results of CBM interventions are most encouraging, but demonstrations of long-term improvements that generalize across settings have *not* yet been forthcoming. As Meyers and Craighead (1984) noted in a recent review, such CBM training programs as social problem solving, self-instructional training, and self-control training, with their emphasis on the modification of thinking, have demonstrated remediative effects with a variety of child populations.

A consideration of several CBM studies will illustrate the current state of the art and the sometimes contradictory results, especially in terms of evidence for generalization. In the Douglas et al. (1976) study, the effects of modeling, self-verbalization, and self-reinforcement techniques on hyperactive boys were examined. The training period covered 3 months in which the children were seen for two, 1-hour sessions per week, for a total of 24 sessions. In addition, 6 sessions were conducted with each child's teacher and 12 with the child's parents. The results indicated that, relative to an assessment control group, the children who received CBM treatment evidenced improvement on a variety of cognitive and motor tasks such as listening, spelling, and oral comprehension tests, but they did *not* improve on the Connors' Teacher Rating Scale. Whereas improvement was evident on a number of academic tasks, improvement in classroom behavior was not noted.

In contrast, Camp et al. (1977) found evidence of generalization. They employed a "think aloud" program to teach young aggressive boys to develop answers to four basic questions: "What is my problem?" "What is my plan?" "Am I using my plan?" and "How did I do?" The CBM training yielded significant improvement relative to control groups on a variety of measures, including Porteus Maze, the Matching Familiar Figures Test, WISC performance IQ, reading achievement and also in classroom behavior (teacher ratings).

Several other studies have also indicated the relative effectiveness of CBM procedures with children. Watson and Hall (1978) successfully employed self-control training (relaxation plus Camp et al.'s think aloud program, 1977) in the treatment of hyperactive fifth- and sixth-grade boys. Relative to placebo-control training, improvement was not only evident on teachers' ratings (Connors' Abbreviated Rating Scale), but also generalized to reading comprehension scores. Barkley, Copeland, and Sivage (1978) also found that a self-control treatment program that involved self-instruction, self-monitoring, and self-reinforcement was effective in improving hyperactive children's misbehavior and attention to tasks, but the improvement did *not* extend to achievement scores. Both Watson and Hall and Barkley et al. commented on how readily classroom procedures can be modified to include self-instructional training.

Snyder and White (1977) successfully applied CBM training to institutionalized adolescents. Relative to contingency-awareness and assessment-control groups, the adolescents trained in self-instruction reduced impulsive behaviors and increased school attendance and self-care responsibilities. The changes were maintained at a 6-week follow-up. The impulsive behaviors included drug taking, physical aggression toward residents and staff, stealing, and destruction of property. The CBM training focused on problematic self-control situations that were encountered by the adolescents. The analysis of these situations in training highlighted the role of private speech as a contributor to conflicts. The modeling of means-ends problem solving was included in the CBM training regimen.

Problem-Solving Training

The use of problem-solving training has emerged as an important mode of CBM treatment. As in the case of self-instructional training procedures, the problem-solving approach to teaching children self-control has received only recent attention, and extensive comparative studies with adequate follow-up are few. The problem-solving-training approach attempts to teach children to become sensitive to interpersonal problems, to develop the ability to generate alternative solutions, and to understand means-end relationships and the effects of one's social acts on others. The research by Douglas (1972, 1975) and Spivack, Platt, and Shure (1976) indicates that children with behavior problems often benefit from such problem-solving training.

The deficits such children often show include a tendency to select the first solution that occurs to them, often without developing alternatives or examining consequences, and a failure to conceptualize alternative options of action. To compensate for these deficiencies, Spivack and Shure (1974) provided training in two types of social reasoning over some 30 lessons. One type of reasoning involved the child's thinking of alternative solutions to simple conflict situations with peers. A related ability was the child's prediction of likely consequences should her or his solution be put into effect. The focus of the training, which takes the form of a variety of games, was not *what* to think, but rather *how* to think, about interpersonal problems. The initial games dealt with developing specific language and attentive skills, identifying emotions, thinking about how people have different likes and dislikes, and learning to gather information about other people. Final games posed the problem of finding several alternative solutions to interpersonal problems and evaluating cause and effect in human relationships. The training resulted in significant increases in social reasoning abilities, and most importantly — and rather uniquely for a training study — the children showed significant and enduring positive effects in social behaviors with peers, changes that were maintained at a 1-year follow-up in kindergarten. A most important aspect of the training program is that positive results were obtained when teachers trained children and when mothers trained their own children. In a personal communication, Spivack described his training as follows:

> Training reduces socially maladaptive behavior by enhancing certain mediating interpersonal cognitive skills of direct relevance to social adjustment. . . . These skills involve the capacity to generate alternative solutions and consequences, and in older individuals the ability to generate means-ends thought. (Spivack, 1977, personal communication)

Recently, a number of programs tailored after Spivack and Shure have been developed to teach children a variety of skills, including self-control. These programs have been conducted by Allen, Chinsky, Larcen, Lochman, and Selinger (1976); Elardo (1974); Gesten, de Apodaca, Rains, Weissberg, and Cowen (1979); McClure, Chinsky, and Larcen (1978); Meijers (1978); Poitras-Martin and Stone (1977); Russell and Thoresen (1976); and Stone, Hinds, and Schmidt (1975). To teach such skills, several teaching modes are used, including verbal, behavioral, videotape vignettes, and cartoon-workbook, poster-pictorial, and flash-card activities. The pedagogical potential of problem-solving training procedures has been nicely illustrated in the recent work on the CBM treatment of academic problems.

CBM Treatment of Academic Problems

Recently there has been increasing research on the possible application of cognitive behavioral procedures to traditional academic concerns such as reading comprehension, arithmetic, interpersonal problem solving and creativity. In the same way that the CBM procedures with hyperactive children found impetus in the work of Soviet psychologists, the CBM-training approach with academic problems was guided by the work of the American psychologist Gagné. Gagné (1964) proposed a task-analysis approach to education by emphasizing the need for explicit operational statements of the instructional objectives. He then determined the prerequisite behaviors or component skills that the child must possess in order to perform each of the desired terminal behaviors. For each of the identified behaviors, the same question is asked, and a hierarchy of objectives is thereby generated. Gagné was proposing that an individual's learning of a complex behavior is contingent on his or her prior acquisition of a succession of simpler behaviors. Thus the instruction can be based on the cumulative learning process.

The cognitive-behavior-training approach follows a similar strategy, except that each step in the hierarchy is translated into cognitive strategies that can be taught by means of discovery learning on well-engineered tasks and modeled by the instructor and rehearsed by the student. Practically, this means that the teacher must be sensitive, in performing a task analysis, not only to the behaviors, but also to the cognitions, strategies, and accompanying feelings required to do a task. The instructor can use a variety of experiential and investigative techniques to discover the hierarchy of cognitive abilities, strategies, and feelings required to perform a task. These techniques include observing his or her own thinking processes while performing the task; observing and interviewing children who do poorly or well on the task; conducting an error analysis; and so forth (see Meichenbaum, Burland, Gruson, & Camerson, 1984, for discussion of these assessment techniques). The instructor can then translate these cognitive strategies into sets of self-statements that can be modeled and rehearsed by a student. Moreover, the teacher can cognitively model not only task-relevant, problem-solving self-statements, but also coping self-statements. Teachers at all levels very infrequently, if at all, model how they cope with frustrations and failures while doing a particular task (i.e., they are mastery, not coping, models). They rarely share with their students the thinking processes and other events that are involved in how they performed the task.

The student is told to perform a task, but is rarely shown (a) how to break the task down into manageable units, (b) how to determine the hierarchy of skills required to do the task, or (c) how to translate these skills into self-statements and images that can be rehearsed.

One illustration of such a CBM intervention is a study that attempted to enhance creative problem solving by modifying what college students say to themselves (Meichenbaum, 1975). Each of three major conceptualizations of creativity represented in the literature was translated into a set of self-statements that was modeled by the trainer and then practiced by the subjects on meaningful self-selected tasks. Table 9.2 illustrates the variety of self-statements used in training.

The use of such self-statements not only enhanced performance on creativity measures, but also engendered a generalized set to handle life situations more creatively. Following training, the clients reported that they had spontaneously applied the problem-solving training to a variety of personal and academic problems. This observation suggests that psychotherapy clients could benefit from such a problem-solving approach as described by D'Zurilla and Goldfried (1971).

It should be noted that subjects or clients are not merely given a list of self-statements and told that just saying these things to themselves will make everything better. Such a strategy would be reminiscent of the exhortative techniques espoused by those who endorse the power of positive thinking. For example, the once-popular French psychiatrist Emile Coue enjoined his patients to say "Every day, in every way, I'm getting better and better." Such verbal palliatives were designed to self-induce a beneficial state. The present CBM treatment approach is quite different in its objectives. It is designed to have the client

1. Become aware of the habits of thought and thinking styles that impede performance and that lead to dysfunctional emotions that interfere with task-relevant activities.
2. Generate, in collaboration with the trainer, a set of incompatible, task-relevant specific behavioral and cognitive (self-statements) strategies and accompanying feelings of self-efficacy about implementing such skills.
3. Systematically implement the skills and learn from his or her mistakes.

Clinical Implementation of CBM with Children

Since the initial self-instructional training study (Meichenbaum & Goodman, 1971), we have learned a good deal about how to teach children to talk to themselves. A few of these implementation techniques include

1. Using the child's own medium of play to initiate and model self-talk

TABLE 9.2. EXAMPLES OF SELF-STATEMENTS USED IN CREATIVITY TRAINING

Self-statements arising from an attitudinal conceptualization of creativity

Set-inducing self-statements
What to do:
　Be creative, be unique.
　Break away from the obvious, the commonplace.
　Think of something no one else will think of.
　Just be free-wheeling.
　If you push yourself, you can be creative.
　Quantity helps breed quality.
What not to do:
　Hold onto internal blocks.
　Make judgments.
　Worry what others think.
　Put everything on a right-or-wrong basis.
　Give the first answer you think of.
　Make negative self-statements.

Self-statements arising from a mental abilities conceptualization of creativity

Problem analysis — what you say to yourself before you start a problem
　Size up the problem; what is it you have to do?
　You have to put the elements together differently.
　Use different analogies.
　Do the task as if you were Osborn brainstorming or Gordon doing Synectics training.
　Elaborate on ideas.
　Make the strange familiar and the familiar strange.
　Task execution — what you say to yourself while doing a task
　You're in a rut — okay try something new.
　How can you use this frustration to be more creative?
　Take a rest now; who knows when the ideas will visit again.
　Go slowly — no hurry, no need to press.
　Good, you're getting it.
　This is fun.
　That was a pretty neat answer; wait till you tell the others!

Self-statements arising from a psychoanalytic conceptualization of creativity

Release controls, let your mind wander.
Free-associate, let ideas flow.
Relax — just let it happen.
Let your ideas play.
Refer to your experience, just view it differently.
Let your ego regress.
Feel like a bystander through whom ideas are just flowing.
Let one answer lead to another.
Almost dreamlike, the ideas have a life of their own.

2. Using tasks that have a high "pull" for the use of sequential cognitive strategies
3. Using peer teaching by having children cognitively model while performing for another child

4. Moving through the program at the child's own rate and building up the package of self-statements to include self-talk of a problem-solving variety as well coping and self-reinforcing elements
5. Guarding against the child's using the self-statements in a mechanical, noninvolved fashion and nurturing the child's spontaneity and involvement
6. Including a therapist who is animated and responsive to the child
7. Learning to use the self-instructional training with low intensity responses
8. Supplementing the training with imagery practice such as the *turtle technique* (Schneider & Robin, 1976)
9. Supplementing the self-instructional training with correspondence training (Rogers-Warren & Baer, 1976)
10. Supplementing the self-instructional training with operant procedures such as a response-cost system (Kendall & Finch, 1976, 1978; Nelson & Birkimer, 1978; Robertson & Keeley, 1974)

The CBM treatment can be introduced during ongoing play activities. The therapist can teach the hyperactive, impulsive child the concept of talking to herself or himself and gain the child's attention by using her or his play activities. For example, while playing with one young hyperactive child, the therapist said, "I have to land my airplane: now slowly, carefully, into the hangar." The therapist then encouraged the child to have the control tower tell the pilot to go slowly, and so on. In this way, the therapist is able to have the child build a repertoire of self-statements to be used on a variety of tasks. Training begins on a set of tasks (games) in which the child is somewhat proficient and for which she or he does not have a history of failures and frustrations. The therapist employs tasks that lend themselves to a self-instructional approach and have a high "pull" for the use of cognitive strategies. For example, the therapist can have the impulsive child verbally direct another person (e.g., the therapist) to perform a task such as a finger maze while the child sits on her or his own hands. In this way, the child has to learn to use language in an instrumental fashion in order to direct another person to perform the task and eventually to direct her or his own behavior.

Another technique designed to enhance self-control is to have an older, impulsive child teach a younger child how to do a task. The older, impulsive child, whose own behavior is actually the target of modification, is employed as a "teaching assistant" to model self-instructions for the young child.

In using such CBM procedures, it is important to insure that the child not say the self-statements in a mechanical, rote, or automatic fashion without the accompanying meaning and inflection. This would approximate the everyday experience of reading aloud or silently when one's mind is elsewhere. One can read a paragraph aloud without recalling the content. What is needed instead is modeling and practice in synthesizing and internalizing the meaning of one's self-statements.

One strength of the training procedure is its *flexibility*. The rate at which the therapist proceeds with the CBM training procedure can be individually tailored to the needs of each child. Some children require many trials of cognitive modeling and overt self-instructional rehearsal, whereas others may proceed directly to the stage of covert rehearsal after being exposed to a model. For some children, the phase of having the child do the task while the therapist instructs the child can foster dependency. In such cases cognitive modeling followed by covert rehearsal might suffice. In some cases, it is not necessary to have the child self-instruct aloud.

The CBM approach also provides some flexibility in how quickly the therapist and the child rehearse comprehensive packages of self-statements. Usually, the CBM training follows the principle of successive approximations. Initially, the therapist models and has the child rehearse simple self-statements such as "Stop! Think before I answer." Gradually the therapist models (and the child rehearses) more complex sets of self-statements.

A key feature of self-instructional training is to view the child as a *collaborator* in generating and implementing the training package. The trainer can tap the child's strategies by asking him or her what advice he or she might have for another child who wants to play the same game but who wants to make as few errors as possible. For example, consider the impulsive child's answer after taking the MFF Test. This test requires the child to find one of six variant figures (e.g., cowboys) that is identical to a standard figure. When asked what another child would do so he or she would make as few errors as possible on the MFF test, some impulsive children suggested that the other child should look at each of the alternatives on the MFF and systematically check each alternative against the standard. But, when we monitored the impulsive child's eye movements while doing the MFF, he did not do this at all. Instead his search strategy while doing the MFF was quite haphazard. Thus, the correct strategy was in the impulsive child's repertoire, but he did not spontaneously employ it while doing the task.

The trainer can then indicate that the advice offered seems worthwhile and that she or he would like to "try on" these suggestions. In this way the child is involved in teaching the trainer. This exchange can then be developed across both impersonal and interpersonal tasks. For example, Goodwin and Mahoney (1975) used a circle game to teach CBM skills to aggressive children. In the circle game, children are placed around a circle and asked to taunt and tease the trainer, who is in the middle of the circle. The therapist acts as a cognitive coping model, manifesting behaviors and self-statements by which she or he can handle the provocations. The children in turn rehearse similar coping skills by following the lead of the therapist. They then consider, rehearse, and practice these same self-control skills in their school and home environments. An example of the clinical use of such self-control training was offered recently by Hinshaw, Henker, and Whalen (1984). Importantly, they discussed some of the risks involved in such direct peer provocation training, and they underscored the clinical skill required on the part of the trainers in keeping the boys oriented toward mutual self-help goals.

The CBM training regimen can also be supplemented with imagery manipulations, especially in treating young children. One can train the impulsive child to imagine and to subsequently self-instruct: "I will not go faster than a slow turtle, slow turtle." Robin, Schneider, and Dolnick (1976) have used such a turtle-imagery procedure in an ingenious way to foster self-control in hyperactive, disruptive school children. Robin et al. incorporated the turtle image into a story that was read to the class. Following the story, the students imitated the turtle, who withdrew into its shell when it felt it was about to lose self-control. This was followed by relaxation and self-instructional and problem-solving exercises to teach self-control. The teachers and the other classmates would remind each other to "do turtle" whenever a child was behaving inappropriately. In the Robin et al. study, the teacher spent 15 minutes each day for approximately 3 weeks in training, and, as a result, the children evidenced reduced aggressive behavior and fewer frustration responses. One could use a variety of different stories and cognitive techniques to teach such self-control behaviors.

The CBM approach to treating impulsivity directly focuses on the child's conscious self-regulatory ability. The same would apply to the treatment of impulsive adolescents and adults. The child's behavior pattern is broken down into smaller, manageable units, and, in this way, the therapist tries to make the client aware of the chain of events of external and internal events that trigger impulsive and aggressive behavior. This treatment process is enhanced by performing a diagnostic evaluation of the conditions under which self-control is deficient. By becoming aware of the sequence of events, the client can be helped to interrupt them early in the chain and to employ self-control coping procedures.

The CBM approach can be contrasted with other therapy approaches employed with problems of impulsivity. Bergin (1976) indicated

> Impulse control problems are often treated by aversive methods, by analysis of psychodynamics via transference, by modification of self-perceptions and relationships with others, by altering values, etc., but seldom are they dealt with by direct treatment of the self-regulatory defect per se. (p. 116)

The present CBM approach focuses on the self-regulation process.

One final note needs to be added to this consideration of CBM with children. There has been increasing recognition that child maladjustment and child behavior problems are often accompanied by family conflict and marital discord (e.g., Fergeson & Allen, 1978). A good deal of CBM work is now directed at affecting the parent-child unit (e.g., Blechman, Olson, & Hellman, 1976; Robin et al., 1971). A CBM problem-solving approach with parents is designed to teach them the transactional nature of their behavior (namely, how their behavior influences and is influenced by their child) and what they can do to anticipate, prevent, and interrupt conflictual parent-child interactions. The parents are taught (a) to recognize the manner in which their cognitions (i.e., hidden agendas, current concerns, expectations, appraisals, attributions), feelings, and behavior contribute to the escalation of parent-child conflicts; (b) to interrupt this pattern; and (c) to employ problem-solving and communication skills (which are the focus of intervention). Moreover, CBM therapy focuses on the impact of marital discord on the parent-child relationship. In recent years CBM treatment procedures have been extended to the treatment of distressed couples. The research has indicated a need to go beyond the "targeted" child in formulating a treatment approach.

✓ COGNITIVE BEHAVIOR MODIFICATION WITH ADULTS

The focus of our discussion thus far has been on the application of CBM with children. A similar discussion of CBM with adults is more difficult in this limited space, because so many different procedures have been subsumed under the CBM heading. The adult populations and problems that have received CBM treatment include clients who have problems with interpersonal anxiety (Goldfried, 1977; Heppner, 1978; Lange & Jakubowski, 1976; Thorpe, 1975), with test anxiety (Denney, 1982; Wine, 1982), with anger control (Novaco, 1975, 1977), with pain (Turk et al. 1983), with depression (Beck et al., 1979), with addictions (Marlatt & Gordon, 1980; Rychtarik & Wollersheim, 1978), with sexual dysfunction (Rook & Hammen, 1977), and with alcohol abuse (Chaney, O'Leary, & Marlatt, 1978; Intagliata, 1978). Also, a number of behavior therapy procedures, such as desensitization, modeling, operant and aversive conditioning, imagery, and behavioral rehearsal have been altered to highlight the role of cognitive factors (see Meichenbaum, 1977). Thus, a comprehensive review of CBM with adults is beyond the scope of the present chapter. Instead, a descriptive account of the communalities that seem apparent across the respective CBM treatment approaches follows, indicating how behavioral and cognitive factors have been integrated into a therapeutic approach.

An Overview of CBM with Adults

For descriptive purposes, the CBM therapy process can be viewed as consisting of three phases. These phases do not form a lock-step progression but can be repeated or returned to as necessary for therapy progress. The first phase is concerned with helping the client understand the nature of her or his problem(s) and enlisting her or his collaboration in formulating a treatment plan. In this phase, the client and the therapist begin to evolve a common view of the problem from which a variety of therapeutic interventions naturally follow. A motivating factor for a number of clients is the need to make sense of their behaviors, to understand what is happening and why, to receive assurances that they are not going to "lose their minds," and to realize that something can be done to help them change. It is partly in response to these concerns and also as a way of preparing clients to actively engage in the change procedures that the conceptualization process receives so much attention in CBM. During the second phase of treatment the therapist helps the client to explore, try on, and consolidate the conceptualization of the presenting problem.

Whereas the first two phases of therapy involve preparing the client for change, it is during the third phase of CBM training that the therapist helps the client to modify his or her internal dialogue (self-statements, images, and accompanying feelings) and to produce new, more adaptive behaviors to be performed in vivo. As noted previously, these behaviors (or personal experiments) lead to consequences that the client and therapist can then consider in light of the client's prior expectancies and beliefs. This "reappraisal" can give rise to the production of further new behaviors and so forth. The third phase of therapy is designed to begin the process of affecting the ongoing reciprocal interactions between cognition, affect, behavior, and environmental consequences.

The length of time for each of the three phases varies, depending on the client's problem, the therapist's style and skill, the goals of therapy, and so forth. In research studies with clients who had similar problems (e.g., phobias, interpersonal and evaluative anxiety), the three phases were successfully completed in eight sessions, whereas some individual therapy has required as many as 40 sessions.

Phase I: Conceptualization of the Problem

The role of the conceptualization process in psychotherapy has received insufficient attention, especially from behavior modifiers. For example, what goes on in therapy before a behavior modification technique such as desensitization is applied is rarely discussed (see chapter 1, however). How do we prepare the patient to accept the rationale and the treatment intervention? One way is to try to modify what the client says to herself or himself and her or his images about the problem or symptom, that is, modify the client's perceptions, expectations, and attributions. The client usually enters therapy with some conceptualization or definition of her or his problem. If the client is depressed, she or he might complain of being a victim of mood changes; if anxious and phobic, external events are viewed as causing the malady. Rarely does the client see the role of her or his own thinking processes and the interpersonal meaning of her or his behavior as sources of disturbance. Rarely does the client recognize the transactional nature of her or his behavior, how she or he inadvertently often creates and engenders the very reactions she or he so readily complains about. Rarely does the patient recognize how her or his own reactions play a role in maintaining this maladaptive behavior.

The first goal of CBM treatment is to enlist the client in a collaborative investigative effort to understand and reconceptualize the nature of his or her problem(s). The CBM therapist can use interviews with the client and significant others, client self-monitoring, questionnaires, tests, and homework assignments as means of data collection. In this way the client can collect information that will help him or her redefine his or her problems in terms that yield a sense of control and responsibility and feelings of hope that will lead to specific behavioral interventions. Thus, the therapist tries to understand the client's description and definition of the problem, but the therapist does *not* merely uncritically accept the client's view of the problem. Instead, the therapist and the client attempt to redefine the problem in terms that are acceptable to both of them. It is this reformulation or conceptualization phase that provides the basis for behavior change. There are a variety of ways in which the client and the therapist can evolve a common (re)conceptualization. Some therapists are very directive in forcing upon the client a particular conceptualization by power of their personality, jargon, or position. In some cases such a hard-sell approach might prove successful.

A preferred way to proceed is to have the client and the therapist evolve a common reconceptualization, so that the client feels that she or he is an active participant and contributor. The initial phase of CBM therapy with adults is designed to have such a common conceptualization evolve. The manner in which the therapist discusses the presenting problem, the kinds of questions the therapist asks, the types of assessment procedures the therapist employs, the content of the therapy rationale, and the kinds of homework assignments given are all used to help evolve a common client-therapist conceptualization.

The initial session of CBM training begins with the therapist exploring the extent and duration of the client's problem. The therapist performs a situational analysis of the client's problem, ascertaining the range of situations, both present and past, where the client has similar difficulties (maladaptive thoughts and dysfunctional emotions). It should be noted that this type of assessment and reconceptualization process can be facilitated if CBM treatment is conducted on a group basis, where various members can self-disclose and search collaboratively as to the transactional nature of their behaviors. Clients often benefit from a group discussion of their faulty thinking styles, namely, their tendency to think in black-and-white terms, to "catastrophize," to draw arbitrary conclusions, to view their automatic thoughts as "truths," and so forth. The group can be used effectively to help clients become aware of how their mental habits or cognitive processes contribute to their problems.

In some cases it is helpful to have a client close his or her eyes and "run a movie through his or her head" of a recent incident involving his or her problem, reporting the sequence of thoughts, feelings, and behaviors. Such an imagery procedure is a useful adjunct to the standard interview in eliciting internal dialogue. Usually when an individual describes a situation, the focus is on the circumstances involved. Only rarely does the individual recognize his or her own contribution to the problem. The imagery-recall procedure is designed to tap the client's reactions and help him or her appreciate their impact on the behavioral sequence.

Another interesting means of tapping the client's reactions is the use of videotaping. Clients are given a behavioral assessment relevant to their problem (e.g., making a speech, handling a phobic object, interacting with a spouse, tolerating laboratory-induced pain) while being videotaped. The behavioral assessment can also involve a test sample of behavior elicited in a role-playing situation. Immediately after the assessment, both the client and the therapist view of the videotape while the client tries to reconstruct the thoughts and feelings she or he was experiencing on the tape. The therapist can then explore with the client whether she or he has the same or similar reactions in other situations and assess the impact of such reactions on the client's behavior. In this way, by means of Socratic dialogue and systematic inquiry, the therapist is enlisting the client in a collaborative venture and helping the client to reconceptualize her or his presenting problem(s).

During this initial phase of therapy, the therapist also helps clients realize the irrational, self-defeating, and self-fulfilling aspects of their thinking style, self-statements, and images. One way to help clients become aware of such processes is to have them self-monitor their thoughts or listen to themselves with a "third ear." Therapists differ in how demanding and structured they make this self-monitoring assignment. Some therapists encourage explicit monitoring, recording, and graphing of specific behaviors, thoughts, urges, moods, whereas others have asked clients merely to keep an informal diary to be filled in at the end of each day. A common self-monitoring procedure is to ask clients to use a double-column technique whereby they record the specific situation in which they are upset (column 1); the dysfunctional emotion, or how they felt (column 2); the automatic thought(s) they had in the situation and how much they believed that thought on a 0 to 100 scale (column 3); and, later, in therapy, incompatible thoughts they could have in that situation (column 4).

It should be noted, however, that, prior to treatment, it is unlikely that the client tells himself or herself various things, consciously or deliberately, when confronted by problem situations. Rather, as Goldfried, Decenteceo, and Weinberg (1974) have indicated, because of the habitual nature of one's expectations or beliefs, it is likely that such thinking processes become automatic and seemingly involuntary, like most overlearned acts. The client's negative self-statements become a habitual style of thinking, in many ways similar to the automatization of thought that accompanies the mastery of a motor skill such as driving a car or skiing. The therapist can make the client aware of such cognitive processes and increase the likelihood that the client will in the future notice similar self-statements. The client's faulty cognition can also take a pictorial form instead of a verbal form. Beck (1970) reported that a woman with a fear of walking alone found that her spells of anxiety followed images of having a heart attack and being left helpless; a college student discovered that her anxiety at leaving the dormitory was triggered by visual fantasies of being attacked.

In summary, the purpose of the four steps in this initial phase of therapy—assessment procedures, group discussion, situational analysis, and homework assignment—is to secure information about the client's problems, to lay the groundwork for the therapist and the client to evolve a common conceptualization of the presenting problem, and to decide upon the means of therapeutic intervention.

Phase II: "Trying on" the Conceptualization

The second phase of CBM training with adults is designed to have clients try on and consolidate the conceptualizations of their problems. Included in this phase is a discussion of the therapy rationale and the therapy plan.

The phase begins with the clients reporting on their self-monitoring efforts of recording cognitive events, (automatic thoughts, images) and the impact of their styles of thinking (cognitive processes). Moreover, the therapist can help clients determine if any specific themes or current concerns cut across the various situations in which they become upset. Is a client particularly preoccupied with issues of control, equity, social acceptance, and so forth? What is the nature of this client's beliefs, assumptions, and cognitive structures that influence how situations are appraised and how one believes? As the client begins to report these, the therapist can ask tactfully, "Are you saying that part of your problem is what you are telling yourself? How so?" Such questions should not be posed until clients have explored the content of their cognitions and the self-defeating and self-fulfilling prophecy aspects of their styles of thinking. In fact, one can use clients' behavior in the therapy session as a basis for further exploring the impact of their cognitions. For example, if a client does not participate in the group, the therapist can ask him or her to describe how he or she is feeling and then to explore the thoughts and feelings that are keeping him or her from participating. In this manner, clients will work to convince the therapist, each other, and themselves that a key aspect of their problem is their thinking styles. Clients are beginning to discover that their fears and anxieties are not a property of external events, but rather that it is their own thoughts that help to elicit and maintain dysfunctional emotions and maladaptive behavior.

At this point the therapist might introduce the therapy rationale. Throughout the presentation of the rationale, there is a dialogue between the therapist and the clients. The exact wording, vocabulary level, and format can be adapted to each group. For example, consider the rationale offered in the cognitive behavior modification treatment of test anxiety (Meichenbaum, 1972; Meichenbaum & Genest, 1977). The therapist says to the group

> As I listen to you discuss your test anxiety I am struck by some of the similarities in how each of you is feeling and what you are thinking. On the one hand there are reports of quite a bit of tenseness and anxiety in exam situations and in evaluative situations. This seems to take many forms such as stomachs and necks becoming tense, pounding hearts, sweaty palms, heavy breathing, and so on (the therapist should use the specific reactions offered by group members). At the same time — and correct me if I am wrong — several of you described how difficult it was for you to focus attention on only the task before you. Somehow, your attention wandered away from what you had to do (such as studying, or taking the exam) to something irrelevant. (Once again the therapist should use reactions offered by group members.) Your thinking, or self-statements and images, seem to get in the way of what you had to do. Your thoughts about catastrophes and how awful the consequences will be because of your not doing well got in the way. (Pause). Have I heard you correctly?

The therapist might decide to have the group return to the description of their test anxiety, specifically, to their reactions in exam situations. What kinds of thoughts and feelings, what self-statements and images did the clients emit?

The therapy rationale continues.

> In the therapy sessions we will be working on ways to control how you feel, on ways of controlling your anxiety and tenseness. We will do this by learning how to relax in order to control your arousal and tenseness.
>
> In addition to learning relaxation skills, we will learn how to control our thinking processes and attention. The control of our thinking, or what we say to ourselves, comes about by first becoming aware of when we are producing negative self-statements, catastrophizing, being task irrelevant, and so forth. (Once again, the therapist and the clients should give examples of the negative thinking style.) The recognition that we are in fact doing this will be a step forward in changing. This recognition will also act as a reminder, a cue, a bell-ringer for us to produce different thoughts and self-instructions, to challenge

and dispute our self-statements. In this way we will come to produce task-relevant self-instructions and new, adaptive behaviors. (Pause) I'm wondering about your reactions to what I have described. Do you have any questions? (The therapist should determine how the rationale matches the clients' expectations and conceptualization for change.)

Perhaps another example, taken this time from the CBM "stress-inoculation" treatment of phobics, will illustrate how the therapist incorporates and shares the theory for change with the client. The training was designed to accomplish three goals: (a) to "educate" phobic clients about the nature of stressful or fearful reactions, (b) to have the clients rehearse various coping behaviors, and (c) to give the clients an opportunity to practice their new coping skills in a stressful situation (Meichenbaum, 1977).

The educational phase of the stress-inoculation treatment began with a discussion of the nature of each client's fears. Discussion topics included how she or he felt and what she or he thought about when confronted by the phobic objects, how she or he was coping with stress in general, and her or his phobias in particular. Interestingly, even clients who appear incapacitated can often describe coping techniques that they have employed in other stressful areas (e.g., visits to the dentist). The therapist had the group discuss these skills and explore why they were not employed in overcoming their problems.

As part of the therapy rationale, the therapist conceptualized each client's anxiety in terms of Schachter's model of emotional arousal (Schachter, 1966). That is, the therapist stated that the client's fear reaction seemed to involve two major elements: (a) heightened physiological arousal, and (b) a set of anxiety-producing, avoidant thoughts and self-statements (e.g., disgust evoked by the phobic object, a sense of helplessness, panic thoughts of being overwhelmed by anxiety, a desire to flee). After laying this groundwork, the therapist noted that the client's fear seemed to fit Schachter's theory that an emotional state such as fear is in large part determined by the thoughts in which the client engages when physically aroused.

It should be noted that the Schachter and Singer (1962) theory of emotion was used for purposes of conceptualization only. Although the theory and the research upon which it is based have been criticized (Lazarus, Averill, & Opton, 1970; Plutchik & Ax, 1967), the theory has an aura of plausibility that clients tend to accept: The logic of the treatment plan is clearer to clients in light of this conceptualization.

To prepare each client further for training, the therapist helped the client change his perception of how he behaved in the phobic situation. Instead of viewing his response as a massive panic reaction, the therapist suggested that the client's response seemed to include several phases. In the course of the discussion, the following four phases were suggested: preparing for the stressor, confronting or handling the stressor, possibly being overwhelmed by the stressor, and, finally, reinforcing oneself for having coped.

The client was encouraged to offer examples of cognitive strategies or self-statements that he could use for coping during each phase. With some support, a package of self-statements similar to that listed in Table 9.3 emerged. The cognitive strategies encouraged clients to (a) assess the reality of the situation; (b) control negative, self-defeating, anxiety-engendering ideation; (c) acknowledge, use, and possibly relabel the anxiety they were experiencing; (d) "psych" themselves to perform the task; (e) cope with the intense fear they might experience; and (f) reinforce themselves for having

TABLE 9.3. EXAMPLES OF COPING SELF-STATEMENTS REHEARSED
IN STRESS INOCULATION TRAINING

Preparing for a stressor
What is it you have to do?
You can develop a plan to deal with it.
Just think about what you can do about it.
That's better than getting anxious.
No negative self-statements: just think rationally.
Don't worry; worry won't help anything.
Maybe what you think is anxiety is eagerness to confront the stressor.

Confronting and handling a stressor
Just "psych" yourself up — you can meet this challenge.
Reason your fear away.
One step at a time; you can handle the situation.
Don't think about fear; just think about what you have to do. Stay relevant.
This anxiety is what the doctor said you would feel.
It's a reminder to use your coping exercises.
This tenseness can be an ally, a cue to cope.
Relax, you're in control. Take a slow deep breath.
Ah, good.

Coping with the feeling of being overwhelmed
When fear comes, just pause.
Keep the focus on the present; what is it you have to do?
Label your fear from 0 to 10 and watch it change.
You should expect your fear to rise.
Manageable.

Reinforcing self-statements
It worked; you did it.
Wait until you tell your therapist (or group) about this.
It wasn't as bad as you expected.
You made more out of your fear than it was worth.
Your damn ideas — that's the problem.
When you control them, you control your fear.
It's getting better each time you use the procedures.
You can be pleased with the progress you're making.
You did it!

coped. The cognitive coping reconceptualization provides preparation for the needed in vivo and participant modeling procedures.

Once the client became proficient in the relaxation exercises and the self-instructional techniques, the therapist suggested that the client should test and practice his coping skills by actually employing them under graded stressful conditions. The therapist could also use imagery procedures as a supplement to in vivo graded exposure. In collaboration with the client, the therapist develops a hierarchy of scenes from least to most fear engendering and then has the client imagine employing the variety of coping responses. This coping imagery procedure differs from the imagery procedure employed in systematic desensitization by including the client's own symptoms and his or her ability to notice, interrupt, and cope with such reactions. Such imagery rehearsal, as well as behavioral procedures, can be employed in the application phase.

In summary, the stress-inoculation training involved discussing the nature of emotion and stress reactions, rehearsing coping skills, and testing these skills under actual stress conditions. In some sense, the emphasis of treatment switches from trying to totally reduce the client's anxiety to training her or him to function despite anxiety. With continued practice, further anxiety reduction tends to occur. This is illustrated by the statements offered by a phobic client who reported that, following treatment, she reassured herself by talking to herself. She said

> It (self-instructing) makes me able to be in the situation, not to be comfortable, but to tolerate it. . . . I don't talk myself out of being afraid, just out of appearing afraid. . . . You immediately react to the thing you're afraid of and then start to reason with yourself. I talk myself out of panic.

Following a series of such successful attempts, she reported that even the feeling of fear dissipated, and the amount of anxiety was reduced.

Given the increasing demands on individuals to deal with daily stress, the possibility of using inoculation training for prophylactic purposes is most exciting. For example, Novaco (1977) has used stress-inoculation training on a preventative basis with policemen, who often must control their own anger. The possibility of explicitly teaching persons to cope cognitively by such diverse techniques as information seeking, anticipatory problem solving, imagery and behavior rehearsal, task organization, attribution and self-label altering, attention shifting or cognitive reevaluation and relaxation seems to hold much promise (Meichenbaum & Novaco, 1977). An explicit training program that would teach coping skills and then provide training in handling various stressful situations contrasts sharply with the haphazard way in which most individuals now learn to cope with stress. Meichenbaum and Jaremko (1983) described the application of stress-inoculation to a variety of diverse populations including rape victims, victims of terrorist attacks, burn and pain patients, patients about to undergo noxious medical examination and surgery, Type A businessmen, military recruits, and others.

Phase III: Modifying Cognitions and Producing New Behaviors
The first two phases of CBM treatment serve the purpose of having the therapist understand the client's problems and concerns and of having the client and the therapist evolve a common conceptualization. The third phase of CBM treatment is designed to help the client modify her or his cognitions and to produce new behaviors. How one proceeds at this point varies, depending in part on the nature of the problem, the goals of therapy, and the orientation of the CBM therapist.

One way to conceptualize these different modes of intervention is to recognize that a variety of different foci is available. Some CBM therapists, such as those who adopt a rational-emotive (RET) approach, tend to frontally attack the "irrational" attitudes and faulty beliefs of their clients. The somewhat different focus and style of CBM intervention is to have the client examine the nature of his or her problem-solving and coping skills. A variety of behavioral and imagery procedures such as rational restructuring and coping desensitization, as well as a host of other behavior therapy techniques, can be employed to teach such cognitive and behavioral skills. A host of behavior therapy procedures can be modified in order to change the client's cognitions and behaviors. For example, the systematic desensitization procedure can be altered, both in its rationale and in how the imagery rehearsal procedures are employed. From a CBM perspective, a coping, self-control orientation is used in describing the desensitization process, and both a cue-controlled relaxation and a coping imagery approach are used.

Similarly, modeling procedures can be altered to include a coping CBM orientation. CBM modeling approaches deliberately emphasize a model's verbalizations of the problem-solving steps, coping attitudes, and other self-instructions and images needed to help the client learn the "how to" elements in generating strategies and response alternatives, not just "what is" an appropriate response. Bruch (1978) has summarized data for the relative efficacy of cognitive modeling versus exemplar modeling alone.

Another focus of intervention for CBM therapists has been on behavior itself. Beck et al. (1979), when working with depressed patients, attempted to have the client engage in graded homework task assignments. In this way, the CBM therapist can help the client collect data that is incompatible with her or his prior expectations about the outcomes. In turn, the CBM therapist has the client come to recognize the range of situations in which she or he has similar expectations, appraisals, and attributions and to recognize and change the faulty aspects of her or his thinking (e.g., magnification, arbitrary inferences, overgeneralization, dichotomous reasoning, and the like). The use of such graded in vivo exposure and behavioral exercises represents a central feature of all CBM work. For example, rational-emotive therapists regularly have clients engage in "shame exercise," whereby the clients receive feedback that will cause them to question and dispute their belief systems or cognitive structures.

The point, as noted above, is that to characterize a therapy as being *either* cognitive *or* behavioral is too simplistic. The CBM therapist is as concerned with using environmental consequences as is the behavior therapist. But for the CBM therapist, such consequences represent informational feedback trials that provide the client with an opportunity to question, reappraise, and gain distance from his or her cognitions, feelings, and maladaptive behavior. The CBM treatment approach can intervene at various points, namely, at the point of cognitive structures (beliefs, meaning systems), cognitive processes (automatic thoughts and images, problem-solving coping skills), behavioral acts, and environmental consequences. The CBM approach can also intervene by influencing the content of the client's thoughts and the client's style of thinking. Wherever the initial focus of intervention is, if durable and generalizable change is to occur, then several different foci must be involved. For example, although one can begin CBM therapy with behavioral acts, this will then have reverberating results affecting the environmental consequences and how they are appraised. This reappraisal will affect the preceding and accompanying internal dialogue that will, in turn, affect behavior. Such changes will in turn lead to new consequences in the client that will cause him or her to further reevaluate his or her thinking style and beliefs. Similarly, if one intervenes at the point of cognitions, it is important that this result in the client's generating and implementing new behaviors or conducting in vivo personal experiments.

A FINAL WORD

Rathjen, Rathjen, and Hiniker (1978) have summarized well over 20 different CBM procedures designed to effect the *reciprocal determinism* cycle, or the interaction between cognition, affect, behavior, and environmental consequences. In fact, the list of CBM intervention procedures is becoming as long as the classic list of behavior therapy procedures once was (Ullmann & Krasner, 1965). If progress is to be made, however, the CBM approach must not develop a preoccupation with techniques per se, but must instead struggle with developing a testable theory of behavior change. Some recent attempts toward such theory development have been offered by Bandura (1977), Meichenbaum (1977), Meichenbaum and Gilmore (1984), and Mischel (1973). It is to be hoped that continued attempts will mature into a cognitive social-learning theory that will explain behavior change and that will have implications for how best to intervene. Perhaps there is no more fitting epilogue to offer than to share this hope and to indicate the task before us.

REFERENCES

Abikoff, H. (1979). Cognitive training interventions in children: Review of a new approach. *Journal of Learning Disabilities, 12*, 65–77.

Allen, G., Chinsky, J., Larcen, S., Lochman, J., & Selinger, W. (1976). *Community psychology and the schools: A behaviorally oriented multi-level preventive approach*. Hillsdale, NJ: Lawrence Erlbaum.

Asarnow, J. R., & Callan, J. W. (in press). Boys with peer adjustment problems: Social cognitive processes. *Journal of Consulting and Clinical Psychology*.

Bandura, A. (1977). Self-efficacy: Toward a unifying theory of behavioral change. *Psychological Review, 84*, 191–215.

Barkley, R., Copeland, A., & Sivage, C. (1978). A self-control classroom for hyperactive and impulsive children. Unpublished manuscript, Milwaukee Children's Hospital. Milwaukee, WI.

Beck, A. (1970). Cognitive therapy: Nature and relation to behavior therapy. *Behavior Therapy, 1*, 184–200.

Beck, A. (1976). *Cognitive therapy and emotional disorders*. New York: International Universities Press.

Beck, A., Rush, J., Hollon, S., & Shaw, B. (1979). *Cognitive therapy of depression*. New York: Guilford Press.

Bender, N. (1976). Self-verbalization versus tutor verbalization in modifying impulsivity. *Journal of Educational Psychology, 68*, 347–354.

Bierman, K. (1981). *Enhancing generalization of social skills training with peer involvement and superordinate goals*. Paper presented at the Biennial Meeting of the Society for Research in Child Development, Boston.

Blechman, E., Olson, D., & Hellman, I. (1976). Stimulus control over family problem-solving behavior: The family contract game. *Behavior Therapy, 7*, 686–692.

Borkowski, J., & Cavanaugh, J. (1979). Maintenance and generalization of skills and strategies by the retarded. In N. Ellis (Ed.), *Handbook of mental deficiency: Psychological theory and research* (2nd ed.). Hillsdale, NJ: Lawrence Erlbaum.

Bower, G. (1981). Mood and memory. *American Psychologist, 36*, 129–148.

Bruch, M. (1978). Type of cognitive modeling, imitation of modeled tactics, and modification of test anxiety. *Cognitive Therapy and Research, 2*, 147–164.

Camp, E., Blom, G., Herbert, F., & Van Doorninck, W. (1977). "Think aloud": A program for developing self-control in young aggressive boys. *Journal of Abnormal Child Psychology, 8*, 157–169.

Chaney, E., O'Leary, M., & Marlatt, G. (1978). Skill training with alcoholics. *Journal of Consulting and Clinical Psychology, 46*, 1092–1104.

Craighead, E., Craighead-Wilcoxon, L., & Meyers, A. (1978). New directions in behavior modification with children. In M. Hessen, R. Eisler, & P. Miller (Eds.), *Progress in behavior modification* (Vol. 6). New York: Academic Press.

Denney, D. (1982). Self-control approaches to the treatment of test anxiety. In I. Sarason (Ed.), *Test anxiety: Theory, research and application*. Hillsdale, NJ: Lawrence Erlbaum.

Douglas, V. (1972). Stop, look and listen: The problem of sustained attention and impulse control in hyperactive and normal children. *Canadian Journal of Behavioral Science, 4*, 259-281.

Douglas, V. (1975). Are drugs enough? To treat or to train the hyperactive child. *International Journal of Mental Health, 5*, 199-212.

Douglas, V., Parry, P., Martin, P., & Garson, C. (1976). Assessment of a cognitive training program for hyperactive children. *Journal of Abnormal Child Psychology, 4*, 389-410.

D'Zurilla, T., & Goldfried, M. (1971). Problem-solving and behavior modification. *Journal of Abnormal Psychology, 78*, 107-126.

Elardo, P. (1974). *Project AWARE: A school program to facilitate social development of children.* Paper presented at the Fourth Annual Blumberg Symposium, Chapel Hill.

Ellis, A., & Bernard, M. E. (1984). *Rational-emotive approaches to the problems of childhood.* New York: Plenum.

Ellis, A., & Grieger, R. (1978). *RET: Handbook of rational emotive therapy.* New York: Springer.

Exceptional Education Quarterly. (1980). Cognitive behavior modification with children, *1*.

Finch, A., Wilkinson, M., Nelson, W., & Montgomery, L. (1975). Modification of an impulsive cognitive tempo in emotionally disturbed boys. *Journal of Abnormal Child Psychology, 3*, 49-52.

Flavell, J. (1976). Metacognitive aspects of problem-solving. In L. Resnick (Ed.), *The nature of intelligence.* Hillsdale, NJ: Lawrence Erlbaum.

Furgeson, L. R., & Allen, D. (1978). Congruence of parental perception, marital satisfaction, and child adjustment. *Journal of Consulting and Clinical Psychology, 46*, 345-346.

Gagné, R. (1964). Problem solving. In A. Melton (Ed.), *Categories of human learning.* New York: Academic Press.

Gesten, E. L., de Apodaca, R. F., Rains, M., Weissberg, R. P., & Cowen, E. I. (1979). Promoting peer-related social competence in school. In M. W. Kent & J. E. Rolf (Eds.), *The primary prevention of psychopathology* (Vol. 3). Hanover, NH: University Press of New England.

Goldfried, M., Decenteceo, E., & Weinberg, L. (1974). Systematic rational restructuring as a self-control technique. *Behavior Therapy, 5*, 247-254.

Goodwin, S., & Mahoney, M. (1975). Modification of aggression via modeling: An experimental probe. *Journal of Behavior Therapy and Experimental Psychiatry, 6*, 200-202.

Grinspoon, L., & Singer, S. (1973). Amphetamines in the treatment of hyperactive children. *Harvard Educational Review, 43*, 515-565.

Harris, K. (1982). Cognitive behavior modification: Application with exceptional children. *Focus on Exceptional Children, 15*, 1-16.

Heppner, P. (1978). A review of problem-solving literature and its relationship to the counseling process. *Journal of Counseling Psychology, 25*, 366-375.

Hinshaw, S. P., Henker, B., & Whalen, C. W. (1984). Self-control in hyperactive boys in anger-inducing situations: Effects of cognitive-behavioral training and of methylphendate. *Journal of Abnormal Child Psychology, 12*, 55-78.

Karoly, P. (1977). Behavioral self-management in children: Concepts, methods, issues and directions. In M. Hersen, R. Eisler, & P. Miller (Eds.), *Progress in behavior modification* (Vol. 5). New York: Academic Press.

Karoly, P., & Kanfer, F. H. (Eds.). (1982). *Self management and behavior change.* Elmsford NY: Pergamon Press.

Kelly, G. (1969). Personal construct theory and the psychotherapeutic interview. In B. Maher (Ed.), *Clinical psychology and personality: The selected papers of George Kelly.* New York: John Wiley.

Kendall, P. (1977). On the efficacious use of verbal self-instructional procedures with children. *Cognitive Therapy and Research, 1,* 331–341.

Kendall, P., & Braswell, L. (1984). *Cognitive-behavioral intervention with impulsive children.* New York: Guilford Press.

Kendall, P., & Finch, A. (1976). A cognitive-behavioral treatment for impulse control: A case study. *Journal of Consulting and Clinical Psychology, 44,* 852–859.

Kendall, P., & Finch, A. (1978). A cognitive-behavioral treatment for impulsivity: A group comparison study. *Journal of Consulting and Clinical Psychology, 46,* 110–118.

Klesges, R. C., Sanchez, V. C., & Stanton, A. L. (1982). Obtaining employment in academia: The hiring process and characteristics of successful applicants. *Professional Psychology, 13,* 577–586.

Kuhn, T. (1962). *The structure of scientific revolutions.* Chicago: University of Chicago Press.

Ladd, G. W., & Keeney, B. F. (1983). Intervention strategies and research with socially isolated children: An ecological-systems perspective. *Small Group Behavior, 14,* 175–185.

Lange, A., & Jakubowski, P. (1976). *Responsible assertive behavior: Cognitive-behavioral procedures for trainees.* Champaign, IL: Research Press.

Lazarus, R., Averill, J., & Opton, E. (1970). Toward a cognitive theory of emotions. In M. Arnold (Ed.), *Feelings and emotions.* New York: Academic Press.

Luria, A. (1959). The directive function of speech in development. *Word, 15,* 341–352.

Luria, A. (1961). *The role of speech in the regulation of normal and abnormal behaviors.* New York: Liveright.

Mahoney, M. (1974). *Cognition and behavior modification.* Cambridge, MA: Ballinger.

Markman, E. (1977). Realizing that you don't understand: A preliminary investigation. *Child Development, 48,* 986–992.

Marlatt, G., & Gordon, J. (1980). Determinants of relapse: Implications for the maintenance of behavior change. In P. Davidson (Ed.), *Behavior of medicine: Changing health lifestyles.* New York: Brunner/Mazel.

Mash, E., & Dalby, J. (1978). Behavioral interventions for hyperactivity. In R. Trites (Ed.), *Hyperactivity in children: Etiology, measurement and treatment implications.* Baltimore: University Park Press.

McClure, L., Chinsky, J., & Larcen, S. (1978). Enhancing social problem-solving performance in an elementary school setting. *Journal of Educational Psychology, 70,* 504–513.

Meichenbaum, D. (1972). Cognitive modifications of test anxious college students. *Journal of Consulting and Clinical Psychology, 39,* 370–382.

Meichenbaum, D. (1975). Enhancing creativity by modifying what subjects say to themselves. *American Educational Research Journal, 12,* 129–145.

Meichenbaum, D. (1977). *Cognitive-behavior modification: An integrative approach.* New York: Plenum.

Meichenbaum, D., & Asarnow, J. (1979). Cognitive-behavior modification and metacognitive development: Implications for the classroom. In P. Kendall & S. Hollon (Eds.), *Cognitive behavioral interventions: Theory research and procedures.* New York: Academic Press.

Meichenbaum, D., Burland, S., Gruson, L., & Camerson, R. (1984). Metacognitive assessment. In S. Yassen (Ed.), *The growth of insight in children*. New York: Academic Press.

Meichenbaum, D., & Genest, M. (1977). Treatment of anxiety. In G. Harris (Ed.), *The group treatment of human problems: A social learning approach*. New York: Grune & Stratton.

Meichenbaum, D., & Gilmore, J. B. (1984). The unconscious: A cognitive-behavioral perspective. In K. Bowers & D. Meichenbaum (Eds.), *The unconscious reconsidered*. New York: John Wiley.

Meichenbaum, D., & Goodman, J. (1971). Training impulsive children to talk to themselves: A means of developing self-control. *Journal of Abnormal Psychology, 77*, 115–126.

Meichenbaum, D., & Jaremko, M. (1983). *Stress reduction and prevention*. New York: Plenum.

Meichenbaum, D., & Novaco, R. (1977). Stress inoculation: A preventative approach. In C. Spielberger & I. Sarason (Eds.), *Stress and anxiety* (Vol. 5). New York: Halsted Press.

Meijers, J. (1978). *Problem-solving therapy with socially anxious children*. Amsterdam, The Netherlands: Alblasserdam-Kanters, B. V.

Meyers, A. W., & Craighead, W. E. (1984). *Cognitive behavior therapy with children*. New York: Plenum.

Meyers, M., & Paris, S. (1978). Children's metacognitive knowledge about reading. *Journal of Educational Psychology, 70*, 680–690.

Miller, P., & Bigi, L. (1978). Children's understanding of attention, or You know I can't hear you when the water's running. Unpublished manuscript, University of Michigan, Ann Arbor, MI.

Mischel, W. (1973). Toward a cognitive social learning reconceptualization of personality. *Psychological Review, 80*, 252–283.

Mischel, W., Mischel, H., & Hood, S. (1978). The development of knowledge of effective ideation to delay gratification. Unpublished manuscript, Stanford University, Stanford, CA.

Monahan, J., & O'Leary, D. (1971). Effects of self-instruction on rule-breaking behavior. *Psychological Reports, 29*, 1059–1066.

Nelson, W., & Birkimer, J. (1978). Role of self-instruction and self-reinforcement in the modification of impulsivity. *Journal of Consulting and Clinical Psychology, 46*, 183.

Novaco, R. (1975). *Anger control: The development and evaluation of an experimental treatment*. Lexington, MA: Lexington Books.

Novaco, R. (1977). A stress inoculation approach to anger management in the training of law enforcement officers. *American Journal of Community Psychology, 5*, 327–346.

O'Malley, J., & Eisenberg, L. (1973). The hyperkinetic syndrome. *Seminars in Psychiatry, 5*, 95–103.

Palkes, H., Stewart, M., & Freedman, J. (1972). Improvement in maze performance on hyperactive boys as a function of verbal training procedures. *Journal of Special Education, 5*, 237–342.

Palkes, H., Stewart, M., & Kahana, B. (1968). Porteus maze performance after training in self-directed verbal commands. *Child Development, 39*, 817–826.

Plutchik, R., & Ax, A. (1967). A critique of "Determinant of emotional states" by Schachter and Singer (1962). *Psychophysiology, 4*, 79–82.

Poitras-Martin, D., & Stone, G. (1977). Psychological education: A skill-oriented approach. *Journal of Counseling Psychology, 24*, 153–157.

Polanyi, M. (1958). *Personal knowledge: Towards a post-critical philosophy.* Chicago, IL: University of Chicago Press.

Pressley, M. (1979). Increasing children's self-control through cognitive interventions. *Review of Educational Research, 49*, 319-370.

Rathjen, D., Rathjen, E., & Hiniker, A. (1978). A cognitive analysis of social performance. In J. Foreyt & D. Rathjen (Eds.), *Cognitive behavior therapy: Research and application.* New York: Plenum.

Robertson, D., & Keeley, S. (1974). *Evaluation of a mediational training program for impulsive children by a multiple case study design.* Paper presented at American Psychological Association.

Robin, A., Kent, R., O'Leary, D., Foster, S., & Prinz, R. (1971). An approach to teaching parents and adolescents problem solving communication skills: A preliminary report. *Behavior Therapy, 8*, 639-643.

Robin, A., Schneider, M., & Dolnick, M. (1976). The turtle technique: An extended case study of self-control in the classroom. *Psychology in the Schools, 13*, 449-453.

Rook, K., & Hammen, C. (1977). A cognitive perspective on the experience of sexual arousal. *Journal of Social Issues, 33*, 7-29.

Russell, M., & Thoresen, C. (1976). Teaching decision-making skills to children. In J. Krumboltz & C. Thoresen (Eds.), *Counseling methods.* New York: Holt, Rinehart & Winston.

Rychtarik, R., & Wollersheim, J. (1978). The role of cognitive mediators in alcohol addiction with some implications for treatment. *Journal Supplement Abstract Service.* Manuscript number 1763.

Sank, L. I., & Shaffer, C. S. (1984). *A therapist's manual for cognitive behavior therapy in groups.* New York: Plenum Press.

Schachter, S. (1966). The interaction of cognitive and physiological determinants of emotional state. In C. Spielberger (Ed.), *Anxiety and behavior.* New York: Academic Press.

Schachter, S., & Singer, J. (1962). Cognitive social and physiological determinants of emotional state. *Psychological Review, 69*, 379-399.

Schneider, M., & Robin, A. (1976). The turtle technique: A method for the self-control of impulsive behavior. In J. Krumboltz & C. Thoresen (Eds.), *Counseling methods.* New York: Holt, Rinehart & Winston.

Snyder, J., & White, M. (1977). *The use of cognitive self-instruction in the treatment of behaviorally disturbed adolescents.* Unpublished manuscript, Wichita State University, Wichita, KS.

Spivack, G., Platt, J., & Shure, M. (1976). *The problem solving approach to adjustment.* San Francisco: Jossey-Bass

Spivack, G., & Shure, M. (1974). *Social adjustment of young children: A cognitive approach to solving real-life problems.* San Francisco: Jossey-Bass.

Stokes, T., & Baer, D. (1977). An implicit technology of generalization. *Journal of Applied Behavior Analysis, 10*, 349-367.

Stone, G., Hinds, W., & Schmidt, G. (1975). Teaching mental health behaviors to elementary school children. *Professional Psychology, 6*, 34-40.

Suinn, R. M., & Richardson, F. (1971). Anxiety management training: A nonspecific behavior therapy program for anxiety control. *Behavior Therapy, 2*, 498-510.

Thorpe, G. (1975). Desensitization, behavioral rehearsal, self-instructional training and placebo effects on assertive-refusal behavior. *European Journal of Behavioral Analysis and Modification, 1*, 30-44.

Turk, D., Meichenbaum, D., & Genest, M. (1983). *Pain and behavioral medicine.* New York: Guilford Press.

Ullmann, L., & Krasner, L. (1965). *Case studies in behavior modification.* New York: Holt, Rinehart & Winston.

Vygotsky, L. (1962). *Thought and language.* New York: John Wiley.

Watson, D., & Hall, D. (1978). *Self-control of hyperactivity.* Unpublished manuscript, LaMesa School District, LaMesa, CA.

Williams, J. (1984). *The psychological treatment of depression.* London: Crown Helm.

Wine, J. (1982). Cognitive attentional theory of test anxiety. In I. Sarason (Ed.), *Test anxiety: Theory, research and application.* Hillsdale, NJ: Lawrence Erlbaum.

Zajonc, R. (1980). Feeling and thinking: Preferences need no inferences. *American Psychologist, 35,* 151-175.

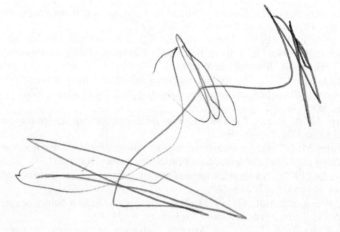

10

Biofeedback and Behavioral Medicine

Sheila D. Reed, Edward S. Katkin, and Steve Goldband

Biofeedback refers to any technique that uses instrumentation to provide an individual with immediate and continuous information concerning the activity of that individual's physiological functions. Usually feedback is provided for physiological functions of which the individual is not normally aware, such as activity from visceral organs (heart, blood vessels) or the central nervous system (brain waves), but it is also used to provide information about physiological functions of which the individual is usually but not currently aware, such as peripheral striate muscular activity that might not be providing normal feedback (after a stroke, for instance). Feedback loops are the single most important source of information for normal functioning.

Normal homeostatic mechanisms depend on feedback channels to stabilize the internal environment. Also, all learning of skills depends on knowledge of results feedback. Miller (1975) has pointed out that learning to control visceral responses can be likened to learning to shoot a basketball. Whereas the muscles used to shoot baskets provide the learner with immediate and usable feedback, the smooth muscles, glands, and blood vessels that are the typical target organs of biofeedback researchers do not provide readily usable feedback. Through external sensory pathways, biofeedback provides alternate feedback channels by augmenting inherent feedback that is either not strong enough or disabled. Using the feedback from physiological responses the learner can modify previously uncontrollable functions, according to the same principles used to increase the field goal percentage of a basketball player.

BRIEF HISTORY

Biofeedback, a specific form of treatment, together with a variety of behavior modification techniques, is the basis for the new field of behavioral medicine. The origins of behavior therapy can be linked rather directly to learning theory and the experimental analysis of behavior. Biofeedback was derived from the scientific fields of psychophysiology, learning theory, and the experimental analysis of behavior, having emerged rather directly from basic research on the instrumental conditioning of autonomically mediated behavior (Crider, Schwartz, & Shnidman, 1969; Katkin & Murray, 1968; Katkin, Murray, & Lachman, 1969).

Instrumental Control of Autonomic Responses

Traditionally, learning theorists had assumed that "for autonomically mediated behavior, the evidence points unequivocally to the conclusion that such responses can be modified by classical, but not instrumental, training methods" (Kimble, 1961, p. 100). Explanations for the apparent inability to condition autonomic nervous system (ANS) responses instrumentally usually were founded upon the observation that the ANS did not interact directly with the external milieu; thus it was assumed to be incapable of functioning instrumentally. It was also thought that the ANS was solely a motor system, and, lacking an afferent function, it was incapable of learning by reinforcement principles (Smith, 1954).

Yet, a number of empirical investigations carried out in both the United States and the Soviet Union suggested that autonomically mediated responses *could* be shaped by instrumental conditioning (Kimmel, 1967). The key to these early studies was the introduction of appropriate technology that allowed the autonomic responses to interact directly with the environment. With the use of electronic devices and logic circuitry, it was possible to create conditions in which changes in skin resistance, heart rate (HR), or blood flow could be detected, differentially reinforced, and conditioned. Early reports from the laboratories of Kimmel (Kimmel & Kimmel, 1963; Kimmel & Hill, 1960; Kimmel & Sternthal, 1967), Shapiro (Birk, Crider, Shapiro, & Tursky, 1966; Crider, Shapiro, & Tursky, 1966; Shapiro, Crider, & Tursky, 1964), and Miller (DiCara & Miller, 1968; Miller, 1969; Miller & DiCara, 1967) all signaled the end of a scientific era in which the distinction between motor learning and autonomic learning was considered fundamental.

The new findings were not accepted without controversy, however, the most intense of which focused on the so-called "mediation" issue. Katkin and Murray (1968) argued that there were no unequivocal data on the instrumental conditioning of ANS responses that could be shown to be independent of skeletal or cognitive mediators, and they suggested further that it was probably impossible to design experiments to obtain such data. Although Miller and his colleagues had demonstrated instrumental conditioning in the curarized rat, a finding that seemed to rule out the possibility that such responses were skeletally mediated, later reports (Dworkin & Miller, 1977; Miller & Dworkin, 1974) indicated that the findings on curarized rats could not be replicated. This failure to replicate has been discussed in terms of certain undetermined peripheral autonomic and central nervous system effects of curare and of difficulties in maintaining a stable animal preparation with artificial respiration (Hahn, 1974; Roberts, 1974).

Whereas investigators such as Miller attempted to develop strategies to demonstrate the instrumental conditionability of ANS responses independent of potential mediators, other investigators argued that the mediation issue was totally irrelevant to the issue of using reinforcement to modify autonomic responses (Crider et al., 1969). Black (1974) pointed out that a distinction must be drawn between the *conditioning* of ANS responses (a theoretical concept) and the *controlling* of ANS responses (a technological problem); and Katkin and Murray (1968), although arguing strongly that instrumental ANS conditioning could not be demonstrated, suggested that the technology that had emerged from the controversial research was already on its way to making a clinical, applied contribution: "For those . . . whose primary goal is to gain control over ANS function, and for whom theoretical problems concerning possible mediators and underlying phenomena are less important, it may be unnecessary to demonstrate the pure phenomenon of instrumental conditioning" (p. 66). Later, Katkin (1971) suggested a strategy for clinicians that would exploit possible mediators rather than trying to eliminate them.

> For those who want to control autonomic activity for clinical or therapeutic reasons an alternative procedure would be first to determine accurately the relationship between certain voluntary skeletal actions and their associated autonomic response patterns, and then to reinforce the voluntary response. Similarly, . . . relationships between cognitive activity and autonomic responses can be determined, and subjects may then be reinforced for certain specified thoughts. (p. 23)

Out of this milieu there emerged a pragmatic approach to the problem of instrumental control of autonomic functions that was based upon the skills acquisition model (Lang, 1974) implied by Miller's analogy of learning to throw a basketball through a hoop.

Role of Biofeedback in Behavioral Medicine

Biofeedback has had a crucial historical role in the development of the field of behavioral medicine. According to Blanchard (1982), two general trends led to the development of behavioral medicine. First, medical problems were emerging in which the changing of behavior was crucial to treatment. During the late 1960s and early 1970s most of the major acute diseases had been arrested, which left chronic diseases as the major concern. As stress related disorders began to emerge, the need to modify behavior as a technique for stress prevention or reduction was recognized. The second general trend was the development of techniques for changing behavior. Behavioral techniques emerged that were useful in changing overt behaviors.

Initially biofeedback was employed in the realm of psychosomatic medicine. Until biofeedback was introduced, psychosomatic medicine had been based on ill-defined personality processes and had few behavioral strategies for changing behavior or relieving symptoms. Biofeedback techniques were used to control the physical symptoms of psychosomatic disorders. Today it is recognized that behavioral processes can enter into any disease; therefore biofeedback is applicable to all medical disorders, not just the traditional psychosomatic ones (Shapiro & Katkin, 1980).

PHYSIOLOGICAL INDEXES

Physiological activity is electrical, mechanical, or chemical. Different methodology is used to measure different forms of activity. Biofeedback consists of the continuous measurement of these physiological responses and the transformation of the raw signals into signals that (a) can provide immediate feedback to the client, (b) are usable by the individual and (c) can be varied to shape the desired response. The physiological responses to be measured, the method of measurement, and the form of the biofeedback signal all need to be considered when doing biofeedback. An understanding of the basic principles of psychophysiology is therefore invaluable for the safe and effective use of biofeedback instrumentation. In this section we will present material on safety and the use of instrumentation, as well as a brief discussion of the rationale and techniques behind measurements of clinically relevant biological functions.

Safety

The physical safety of both client and therapist should always be an overriding concern in the use of biofeedback instrumentation (Pope, 1978). The greatest potential hazard from instrumentation is, of course, electric shock; anytime an electrode is attached to a client, the possibility exists of a current flow through the client's body. Current flow is usually considered to be the index of danger in electric shock. A dangerous level of current flow can arise from improperly designed equipment, failure in equipment, or operator error.

From the standpoint of the clinician, electrical safety is largely a matter of purchasing proper instruments, using them according to instructions, and employing common sense. The executive board of the Biofeedback Society of America and the National Association of Biofeedback Instrument manufacturers have adopted the Safe Current Limits Standard for medical apparatus of the Association for the Advancement of Medical Instrumentation. This standard guards against design problems that might lead to shock hazard. The purchase only of devices carrying a notation that they abide by the standard is a first step toward safety. In addition, the manufacturer's directions for connecting the case of line-powered equipment to a proper earth ground should be strictly followed to prevent dangerous ground loop hazards. If connectors are modified between the electrodes and the apparatus, they should be designed so that it is impossible to accidentally connect the client to a source of current. Finally, it is good practice to arrange the therapy room so that the client cannot accidentally touch any conductive object connected to ground, such as appliances, water pipes, and telephones.

Electrical Measurements

For those measures that detect electrical activity, it is necessary to attach electrodes to the subject. The electrodes usually employed are either stainless steel or composed of a hybrid material such as silver-silver chloride. In addition, an electrolyte, or conductive gel, is usually placed between the electrode and the skin to improve contact conductance and reduce measurement artifacts. Finally, the electrode is attached to the subject by either an adhesive disk or "collar," tape, or an elastic band of some type. The site for electrode attachment is sometimes prepared by washing with mild soap, rubbing with acetone, or abrading lightly with sandpaper, to remove dead skin, skin oils, and other material that could interfere with good contact.

Electrocardiography

Measurement of heart rate is usually accomplished by the attachment of electrodes in such a way as to detect the electrical activity of the beating heart, or electrocardiogram (EKG). The EKG is characterized by a complex waveform, a part of which is a sharp voltage spike called the R-wave, which corresponds to contraction of the left ventricle. In biofeedback for heart rate, this spike is usually detected by a circuit that is sensitive to a given voltage level, called a Schmitt trigger. If the interval between spikes is measured in seconds, the heart rate can be readily computed in beats per minute as 60/inter-beat interval. It is this rate that is commonly displayed on feedback devices.

For biofeedback of heart rate, two measurement electrodes and one reference (ground) electrode are commonly used. The two signal electrodes may be placed at any two sites that straddle the heart; a convenient placement is on the client's left ankle and right forearm with the ground electrode on the client's right ankle. This configuration gives the most pronounced R-wave. Site preparation for EKG measurement is not critical. The site does not need to be specially prepared, but an electrolyte between the electrodes and the skin is recommended.

Electrodermal Activity

Electrodermal activity (EDA) is due to perspiration and is considered a measure of emotional sweating. The cavities of sweat ducts have a negative potential with respect to the surrounding tissue. When sympathetic activation increases the secretion of sweat, the negative potential is increased. The change in electrical potential can be measured by measuring the conductive properties of the skin.

Measurement of skin conductance for biofeedback application is done by attaching two electrodes on the palmar surface of the same hand (palms have the most sweat glands). The two most widely used sets of placements are the thenar and hypothenar eminences, or the medial digits of the first and second fingers. Electrode placement for EDA measurement is critical, as both electrodes must be placed over areas that receive the same innervation. Also, site preparation, appropriate electrodes, and an appropriate electrolyte are very important. The skin surface should be cleaned with mild soap but should not be abraded or washed with chemicals (such as acetone). The electrolyte should be of a physiological saline composition, because other chemicals can alter the electrical properties of the skin, and the electrodes are usually of an Ag/AgCl composition, to reduce the polarization tendencies of electrodes.

Electroencephalography

The electroencephalogram (EEG) measures electrical activity of the cerebral cortex. Electrodes placed on or just below the skin of the scalp pick up very low amplitude signals. These signals are usually amplified and filtered so that waves of only certain frequencies will pass through. Some feedback device is then activated by the presence or absence of waves at the critical frequencies. Researchers have defined the presence of signals in at least four frequency bands in the human EEG: (a) delta waves of 1–3 Hz in deep sleep, (b) theta waves of 4–7 Hz in early sleep stages, (c) alpha waves of 8–13 Hz in relaxed wakefulness, and (d) beta waves of 14–30 Hz during mental activity. Early biofeedback focused on the alpha state, based largely on optimistic reports that subjects producing high alpha density felt peaceful and meditative. Later work, however, called into question these early hopes, finding that alpha was not always experienced pleasurably (Walsh,

1974) and that production of alpha might be primarily associated with visual rather than attentional phenomena (Plotkin, 1976).

As with electrodermal measures, the electrode placement and site preparation are critical in the measurement of EEG. The electrodes need to be quite small, so that there is a solid connection with the skin, in order to reduce movement artifacts. The skin surface is often washed with alcohol and abraded to facilitate contact. The electrodes are usually an Ag/AgCl compound, and an NaCl compound is used as an electrolyte. Attachment of the electrodes to the scalp is much more difficult than with other measures. The electrodes can be glued to the skin, or a conductive clay, Bentonite, can be used as both an adhesive and an electrolyte. Another method of electrode placement is to use head gear that presses electrode needles into the skull.

Placement of electrodes on the scalp has been standardized with the International 10–20 system (Jasper, 1958). This system allows precise placement of electrodes, taking into account individual differences in head size. EEG recording can be monopolar or bipolar. Monopolar recording employs one electrode over an active site and one electrode over an inactive size (ear, nose). Bipolar recording uses two electrodes, each placed on an active site. With this procedure, only those rhythms that are not common to both sites are seen.

Electrogastrography

The stomach spontaneously generates rhythmic electrical potentials at an approximate rate of three per minute. These spontaneous electrical potentials are accompanied by stomach contractions. These relatively small, very slow potentials can be recorded from the surface of the abdomen and used to reflect stomach contractions. The frequency of this electrogastrogram (EGG) wave is a valid indicator of the frequency of contractions.

Site preparation is important, and electrode composition and placement are critical. The size of the electrodes is not important, but electrical stability is, therefore Ag/AgCl electrodes are recommended. The site area should be shaved, cleaned with alcohol, and lightly abraded to reduce resistance. The electrolyte can be any conductive gel. The active electrode is placed at the intersection of the midline and epigastric line (line connecting lowest ribs). The reference electrode is usually placed on a leg (an arm reference gives a greater EKG artifact).

Electromyography

The detection of muscle activity is usually accomplished by measurement of electrical activity of the muscle fibers. This is called the electromyogram, or EMG. When a single muscle fiber contracts, an electrical potential — the muscle action potential (MAP) — is produced. Although the measurement of single-fiber MAPs has been important in certain basic research, clinical biofeedback is ordinarily addressed to the relaxation or tension of whole groups of such cells. If surface electrodes are used to measure EMG, as is usually the case, the MAPs from many cells beneath the electrode sites are detected. Most biofeedback instruments use some technique for integrating or averaging these MAPs to produce an output that reflects the overall level of muscle contraction beneath the electrodes. During nonstrenuous activity, there is a linear relationship between the actual force exerted by a muscle and the EMG record.

Electrodes for EMG recording should be small, lightweight, and non-polarizing (Ag/AgCl). The placement site should be cleaned with alcohol and lightly abraded to remove high impedance from dead surface skin. The electrolyte can be any conductive gel. Both electrodes should be placed over the same muscle, on a line parallel with the muscle fiber. The distance between the two electrodes is restricted by the length of the muscle fibers.

Particularly in EMG biofeedback, the clinician must be aware of the correspondence between the conceptually important measurement and the measurement provided by a given technique at a given site. For example, it is often reported that feedback from the frontalis muscle (a muscle in the forehead) is given to augment relaxation, using electrodes on the temples. Such a placement, however, provides feedback from numerous muscles besides the frontalis. Nevertheless, if one is using feedback to teach general relaxation, it is probably just as well to give information about a variety of muscles simultaneously. On the other hand, relaxation of one muscle group does not necessarily spread to relaxation of other groups. Thus it might be useful to provide EMG feedback from several sites, to maximize a general relaxation effect.

Electrooculography

The electrooculogram (EOG) is a recording of electrical potentials generated by eye movement, but it is not a measure of action potentials of the eye muscles. The cornea is electrically positive relative to the retina. The EOG measures the difference in potential between the front and the back of the eyeball. The orientation of the corneoretinal potential shifts as the eye changes position, creating a change in the electrical potential being recorded.

Miniature Ag/AgCl electrodes are used to measure EOG. The placement site should be lightly abraded, but chemical cleansers such as alcohol are not used because they could hurt the eyes. To measure horizontal eye movements, an electrode is placed on the outer edge of each eye, as near to the eye as possible. Vertical eye movements are measured by placing the electrodes above and below one eye. A major difficulty in measuring EOG is distinguishing between eye movements and head movements, both of which cause a shift in the electrical potential.

Mechanical Measurements

Recording of mechanical activity includes measuring changes in volume of blood or air and in blood pressure, physical movements of sphincters, gastric motility, or eye blinks. Transducers, which translate pressure, heat, or light into electrical events that can be recorded, are used to record these mechanical activities.

Plethysmography (Volume Measurement)

In a variety of clinical biofeedback applications, the biological response of interest is the volume of blood flow at a peripheral site. This volume is primarily determined by the state of constriction or dilation of peripheral blood vessels. Similarly, respiration rate, depth, or irregularities that are reflected in air volume changes might be of clinical interest. The transducer that assesses volume is called a plethysmograph. Plethysmographs are either pressure plethysmographs or photoplethysmographs. A strain gauge is a pressure plethysmograph consisting of a thin electrical conductor that decreases its resistance when stretched. It is used most effectively to measure changes in respiration, where the chest cavity expands and contracts, or for measuring penile tumescence when giving feedback for the erectile response. A second type of pressure plethysmograph is a pneumograph or pneumatic tube consisting of a closed column of air that is arranged so that the response (usually respiration) changes the pressure in, or mechanically stretches, a transducer. This change is converted into a varying voltage that is amplified and fed back.

Another pressure plethysmograph is the piezo-electric crystal, which produces a small voltage proportional to mechanical strain in the crystal. If the crystal is mounted so that movement of a sensor causes it to bend, the sensor can be mounted over an artery, and the blood flow through the artery can be indexed by the changing voltage of the crystal. Piezo-electric devices are probably more useful for measurement of fast-changing (phasic) blood flow, such as pulse pressure, than slower changing (tonic) flow, such as peripheral dilation. They cannot easily provide absolute indexes of change, but they are fast responding and can be used at some sites (the temporal artery for example) where other techniques are more prone to artifacts.

The use of photoplethysmography in the measurement of blood flow is based on the fact that phasic changes in the reflectance of, or permeability to, light of tissue result primarily from changes in blood flow. A transmission plethysmograph is a device with a light source and a photocell on opposite sides of the tissue of interest (the ear lobe, for example). The amount of light transmitted from the light source through the tissue to the photocell is proportional to the blood volume in the tissue. Similarly, a reflectance plethysmograph provides a source of light and a photodetector, but they are mounted side by side. The device is attached to the skin, and the amount of light reflected from the skin is an index of blood volume.

A plethysmograph can ordinarily provide information only about changes, not about absolute level, and so it can be used only for measuring changes within a session. This makes its use in long-term treatment somewhat problematic, because the client and the therapist have no objective means of tracking the client's progress across sessions. On the other hand, plethysmograph measurement is very simple, inexpensive, and comfortable.

Temperature Sensing

Measuring temperature is yet another technique used to assess blood volume changes. When blood courses through vessels, it warms the surrounding tissues, and the heat is simultaneously dissipated to the cooler environment. Thus the more blood that flows through tissue, the higher the temperature of the tissue. Furthermore, even though it is not a direct volume measure, the measurement system can be calibrated so that it yields absolute units (degrees) that can be compared from session to session.

Air in the lungs is warmed by the blood and the surrounding tissues. Therefore, air flowing past the nostrils during inspiration will be cooler than the airflow during expiration. Therefore, respiration rates and relative measures of respiration depth can be calculated, and respiration irregularities can be identified using temperature sensing techniques.

The most common temperature sensing devices are thermocouples and thermistors. A thermocouple generates a variable electrical potential as a function of its temperature. A thermistor has the property of having its electrical resistance reduced in proportion to elevations of its temperature; if a small current is passed through a thermistor placed against tissue, the amount of current flow is an index of the temperature of the tissue.

Pressure Measurement

Although mechanical pressure measurements are used as indexes of volume, the index of interest in *blood pressure measurement* is *pressure*, not volume. Blood volume or blood flow can remain constant or nearly constant, whereas pressure can change due to several variables, including peripheral resistance. Although the reduction of blood pressure in hypertensive individuals has been one of the greatest hopes of the biofeedback movement, as yet, technical and theoretical barriers have prevented widespread clinical use of feedback for blood pressure. The measurement of blood pressure is based on the fact that sound is produced by the turbulence of a partially occluded artery. This sound, called a *Korotkoff*, or *K-sound*, can be detected by a human or electronic sensor when an occluding cuff is inflated to a pressure between the diastolic (resting) and systolic (peak) pressure of an artery. Measurement is obtained by inflating the cuff to a pressure greater than systolic pressure and deflating it slowly until the first sound is heard. The pressure at that point is systolic blood pressure. The cuff is further deflated until the last sound is heard. This is diastolic blood pressure.

The standard technique can be automated so that the inflation, listening for K-sounds, and deflation are all electronically controlled. But even with automation, the time for a measurement is typically about 30 seconds. Thus feedback can only be given infrequently. Tursky, Shapiro, and Schwartz (1972) devised a cuff that remains constantly inflated at the subject's systolic blood pressure on the previous trial. The presence or absence of K-sounds on each beat is then fed back to the subject as feedback for either increasing or decreasing blood pressure. Refinements of this system have made it possible to provide feedback of a more continuous nature by the use of a computer, which controls the cuff to track the subject's pressure. However, the complexity and expense of this system have meant that it is still an experimental tool.

An alternative technique that holds some promise for blood pressure feedback is called *R-wave to pulse interval (RPI) feedback*. This technique is based on the observation that the velocity of blood pumped by the heart in its travel to a peripheral site is proportional to its pressure. Thus, if a device senses the heart beat (R-wave), followed by the pulse wave, say, at the wrist, and computes the time between them, it can feed back this indirect measure of blood pressure to the client on a beat-to-beat basis.

Although studies have found that the RPI is highly correlated with systolic blood pressure under certain conditions (Obrist, Light, McCubbin, Hutcheson, & Hoffer, 1978; Steptoe, Smulyan, & Gribbin, 1976), widespread clinical adoption of RPI as an index of blood pressure awaits more research with clinical populations under controlled conditions. It is important to note, though, that RPI holds the promise of a noninvasive, relatively inexpensive measure that can provide beat-by-beat information in an absolute, analog form.

Mechanical Movement Measurements

Three major physiological responses involve mechanical movement: sphincters, gastric motility, and eye blinks. Using strain gauge measurements, Engel, Nikoomanesh, and Schuster (1974) have reported successful treatment of fecal incontinence through the use of feedback from the internal and external rectal sphincters.

Until the discovery of the EGG, gastric motility had been measured by one of several uncomfortable techniques. The earliest technique for measuring intragastric pressure consisted of swallowing a balloon connected to a pressure-sensitive device. Gastric movement exerted variable pressure on the balloon. Subjects were also asked to swallow magnets that could be used to trace movement of contents within the stomach. Telemetry capsules, which contained a battery, a transmitter, and a pressure transducer, measured intragastric pressure. Again, subjects were required to swallow the device. All of these techniques, besides being unpleasant and dangerous, had several major problems: Putting something into the stomach stimulates the stomach and causes contractions, the recording site is unknown, and retrieval of expensive equipment is difficult.

Periodic involuntary eye blinks, the rate of which can change with subjective state or degree of mental tension, are measured by gluing a thread to the eyelid. The thread is then attached by rods to a mechanical counter. Another procedure uses special glasses with a light source and a photoelectric cell attached to them. The photoelectric cell measures the light reflected from the eyes, and this changes when the eye blinks. Both procedures interfere with or cause blinking and are uncomfortable for the subject.

Chemical Measurements

The pH of the stomach is related to ulcer formation. Through the use of rather cumbersome techniques, some work has been done to train ulcer patients to reduce stomach pH (Welgan, 1974; Whitehead, Renault, and Goldiamond, 1975). Although other disorders, such as diabetes, involve chemical imbalances, the feedback normally provided is for relaxation and not direct feedback of chemical composition itself.

CLINICAL PROCEDURES

Symptom Assessment

Perhaps the most important phase of treatment planning for biofeedback is the careful assessment of the problem to be treated. At the simplest level this requires a determination of the type of biofeedback to be applied. Will EMG, skin temperature, or peripheral vascular feedback be the treatment of choice? These decisions cannot be based exclusively on the patient's report of symptomatology, but must also be based on careful analyses of the underlying process leading to the symptoms. For example, if a patient complains of a headache, it is important to take a careful history and do a thorough diagnostic evaluation to determine whether the headache is attributable to gross muscle tension or whether it is a specific vascular headache such as migraine or a histamine headache. It is particularly important when dealing with pain symptomatology that a careful analysis of the underlying source of pain be carried out before attempting any specific treatment.

A case study taken from the files of our clinic might be instructive to illustrate this point. Mrs. X, a 54-year-old woman, contacted our clinic requesting biofeedback help for migraine headaches, with which she had been suffering for over 30 years. She described a typical story of migraine, including unilateral pain, associated with visceral distress, visual aura preceding onset of the headache, and some relief from vasoconstrictive drugs. Furthermore, the client told us that her headaches began during her young adulthood and followed a regular pattern for more than 30 years. At about the time of menopause a number of stressful events occurred simultaneously. Her father died of cancer, and her husband was stricken with a progressively deteriorative cancer that necessitated a series of major surgeries over the next few years. Although still living, her husband was in very poor health, and she was experiencing enormous psychological stress. During these years, she reported, the intensity of her migraines decreased and underwent what she believed was a minor qualitative change, but their frequency had increased to the point where she was totally debilitated and unable to function. Given the increased responsibilities placed upon her by her husband's illness, the debilitating migraine was particularly maladaptive, and she felt increasingly unable to cope with the demands placed upon her. She had been to a series of physicians, who had prescribed varying vasoconstrictive drugs, painkillers, tranquilizers, and perhaps even placebos, none of which alleviated her continuing migraine distress.

Mrs. X was an experienced migraine sufferer who was fairly familiar with most of the treatments available, and she had read more than the average layperson might concerning biofeedback treatment. When she came to the clinic, she asked for hand warming or head cooling therapy because she was familiar with the research literature that indicated that temperature feedback was the indicated form of therapy for migraine. During the diagnostic interviewing, however, it became apparent that although Mrs. X had undoubtedly suffered from migraine most of her adult life, the headaches she was describing at the current time did not conform to the standard description of migraine. Furthermore, Mrs. X indicated, as mentioned above, that the frequency had increased and the quality of headache had changed somewhat in the past few years, coincident with her menopause. Given that female migraine sufferers frequently become symptom free after menopause and that there was a radical increase in life stress coincident with her menopause, it began to appear that the client had developed a pattern of chronic muscle tension headache that she was accustomed by habit to describing as migraine. The change in quality and intensity that she described could be explained as the development of a different source for the headache discomfort, that is, a shift from vascular headache to muscular headache. The increase in frequency could be attributed to the fact that her life stress had elicited from her an almost continuing state of chronic elevated muscle tension. Consequently, the clinical team decided that immediate relief might be obtained more directly from biofeedback for muscle tension around the head than from hand warming or head cooling. At this point the clinicians were faced with a patient management credibility problem. Upon presenting information to the client, we had to tell her we did not perceive migraine to be the major problem. This is a difficult bit of information to communicate to someone who has admittedly suffered from migraine for many years; consequently a treatment decision was made to provide the patient with both biofeedback for hand warming and biofeedback for frontal area muscle tension reduction. To the extent that the effective therapeutic agent in skin temperature feedback for migraine is really the induction of relaxation, the addition of this skin temperature feedback could only be seen as an adjunct to our presumed main goal—tension reduction. But what if we were wrong in our diagnosis, and Mrs. X was in fact suffering from an unusual variation of a true migraine disorder? In that case, skin temperature feedback might be a more appropriate treatment, and we included it.

The point of this case study is that even in situations with a seemingly clear diagnostic label, it is important to recognize that there might be several factors that could lead to a misdiagnosis and a potentially inappropriate form of treatment. One cannot always assume that the syndrome to be treated can be understood through past history. Assessment of current functioning of a client and careful attention to the specific description of the syndrome pattern are fundamentally important.

In treating complex phenomena such as cardiac arrhythmias there are similarly important diagnostic questions that must be addressed. Weiss and Engel (1971) have noted that the mechanisms of cardiac control are quite complex, involving at least two underlying physiological processes. The implications of this are clear; if a patient produces, for instance, premature ventricular contractions only through a sympathetically mediated route, and biofeedback of heart rate leads to learned control of that heart rate via parasympathetic vagal control, then it is unlikely that the biofeedback would have any facilitative effect on reducing the symptoms. Shapiro and Surwit (1976) have noted that precise knowledge of the underlying mechanism of a symptom can have clear implications for treatment choice. As they have pointed out, if a cardiac symptom is exacerbated by increased sympathetic tone, then the object of treatment might be to reduce sympathetic tone, and cardiac feedback might not be the most efficient means to the end. In other words, the appropriate selection of a biofeedback treatment is integrally related to a proper understanding of the relationship of the underlying psychophysiological process to the clinical symptom.

Casual diagnosis of the specific cause of a patient's symptoms does not necessarily lead to an obvious choice of location for biofeedback treatment. For instance, a patient who suffers from tension headaches might or might not derive maximum therapeutic benefit from EMG feedback to muscles of the head. It is possible that biofeedback for muscle tension reduction in the head muscles is an effective treatment, but it is also possible that, for certain patients, biofeedback treatment for general muscle relaxation in the arms or in the trunk might be equally effective or in some cases more effective.

The clinician must be prepared to make individual judgments based upon the mode of tension expression of the individual patient, and to revise those judgments as treatment progresses. For instance, more careful assessment of the source of the symptoms might require that, before treatment begins, a series of baseline muscle potential recordings be taken from various sites that might be possible contributors to the pain. The frontal area, as well as the neck and masseter (jaw) areas, might be examined. The clinician can note which of these muscle groups appears to be manifesting the most tension, and, by testing with relaxation instructions, he or she can observe the degree to which the patient has differential voluntary control over relaxation. Next, it is essential to monitor the frequency and intensity of reported symptoms, preferably by having the patient keep a detailed log. If you are getting excellent results in the biofeedback, but no reduction of symptomatology, then there is good reason to assume that the particular physiological function that is being controlled is not a contributor to the symptom. Like the behavioral psychologist searching for the effective reinforcer, the biofeedback therapist is constantly in search of the clinically relevant physiological function.

The neatness of the treatment package presented by biofeedback instrumentation can easily lull clinicians into a false sense of security about their treatment choices. It is essential that accurate behavioral assessment be employed in decision making about biofeedback therapy, for there is always the risk that the client is presenting symptomatology for which there are alternative, more effective somatic treatments or alternative, less obvious, but equally important, avenues of psychotherapeutic intervention that might be indicated. It is important for the clinician to assess the background of the patient's problems and to be certain that the particular form of treatment to be employed represents a rational choice. What we are particularly concerned about is the seductive but nevertheless ever present danger that the clinician will become overly technique-oriented when faced with the glittering and interesting electronic instruments normally employed in the biofeedback procedures.

Finally, the clinician must assess the particular purpose of the biofeedback treatment. Is he or she going to employ a strategy that will lead to per-

manent change in physiological response levels or a strategy that is directed
toward teaching the patient to modify responses to specific situations?

Treatment Planning

Having decided that a client's symptoms are amenable to biofeedback
treatment, and having decided also upon the specific form of treatment
being employed, the clinician must face a number of serious procedural
issues concerning the administration and ultimate evaluation of therapeutic
success including (a) establishment of an appropriate baseline against which
to compare the treatment effect, (b) appropriate criteria for reinforcement
of the patient's responses, (c) decisions about the modality of feedback,
and (d) creation of conditions for appropriate assessment of therapeutic
outcome. None of these issues is unique to biofeedback; all of them are
commonly discussed in the literature on self-management and self-control.
The goal of effective biofeedback therapy is to enable the patient to control
or modify her physiological responses without continuous feedback of
those responses. Thus, if the patient is to be freed from bioelectric connec-
tions, she must acquire the skills necessary for self-management of the targeted autonomic responses. No less important, the patient must also
acquire the motivation to use these self-management skills and the ability to
discriminate situations that might elicit undesirable physiological
responses.

One characteristic that distinguishes biofeedback from other forms of
self-management, however, is that the necessary skills needed might not be
readily available to the client before treatment. Therefore emphasis must be
placed on the *acquisition* of specific skills. This is not necessarily true in all
forms of self-management training. For instance, if an obese patient wants
to learn to control his eating habit, the client must learn to identify situations that provoke excessive eating. In addition, he must learn specific
responses that may alter his motivation to eat. However, it is not likely that
the therapist will be required to teach an obese person the specific motor
skills needed to keep the mouth closed to prevent the entry of food. In
biofeedback therapy, however, the client must not only learn to identify
provocative situations and be motivated to alter responses, but she or he
must also learn to recognize what those responses are. The therapist must
pay special attention to helping patients discover their baselines of responding in order to identify changes from them.

Baseline Measurement

The therapist should be alerted to the fact that the introduction of
biofeedback techniques themselves can elicit elevated levels of responding;
thus an arbitrarily high baseline might be observed in the first few sessions.

It is important, therefore, that the therapist obtain multiple resting baseline levels of the physiological response in order to be certain of reasonable reliability and in order to feel confident that the initial level from which treatment will begin represents a valid assessment of the subject's true baseline. In addition, the therapist will often discover that elevated levels of muscle tension, for instance, can be reduced substantially by simple verbal instructions for either general or specific muscle relaxation. It is important to remember that the primary purpose of biofeedback is to provide help in learning to control functions over which normal control is absent. Thus, baseline measures should be assessed *after* the patient has already achieved as much control as possible without biofeedback. A case study might illustrate this point more clearly.

Mr. S was referred to our biofeedback clinic from a distinguished cardiac clinic in the Midwest. Mr. S was a 28-year-old factory worker who suffered an apparent heart attack while at work and was rushed to the emergency room of his local hospital, in a state of semiconsciousness, complaining of a crushing pain in the chest and radiating pain and numbness down through his left arm. He was taken to an intensive care unit where, in a matter of hours, he showed a complete recovery. Cardiological examination in the local hospital could find no evidence of cardiac disease, and a neurological exam revealed no problems. Mr. S showed repeated episodes of the "heart attack" over the next few weeks and was referred to a cardiac care center where, over the course of a week, he was examined carefully and had extensive neurological and cardiological exams. The results of those exams, as well as psychiatric evaluations, suggested that his pain and numbness were being caused by excess tension, and he was told to contact our biofeedback clinic. It should be noted that before we received this client, we obtained a complete medical record from the cardiac center, to be sure that we were not dealing with a subtle neurological or cardiological problem. After studying the records and interviewing Mr. S for a few hours, we were convinced that we were dealing with a rather complicated psychiatric disorder that expressed itself through unusually high levels of body tension, which might have resulted in the experience of pain. We proposed to the client, who was extremely resistive to psychotherapy and who, in many ways, was typical of "insightless" patients, that we would use biofeedback to teach him muscle relaxation and that we were optimistic that, when he had learned to gain total control of his striate musculature and relax it at will, he might lose his symptomatology.

Before beginning the treatment, we took some baseline measures of electromyographic voltage levels of the frontal area of Mr. S's head. Much to our surprise, we found that during a 10-minute rest period, with Mr. S in a reclining chair, his eyes closed in a darkened room, and having received instructions designed to induce deep relaxation, he manifested a mean muscle tension level of 50 mv. (The typical patient in a similar situation can be expected to show levels between 1 and 3 mv.) To understand more clearly the enormous level of tension this figure represented, note that a number of workers in our clinic tried to tighten up their jaw, head, and neck muscles sufficiently to generate 50 mv over a 10-minute period. Not one clinician was successful in doing so, and all reported that after 2 to 3 minutes of such tension, they experienced intense pain. Yet Mr. S reported that he found the experience of reclining in the chair with his eyes closed and listening to the relaxation instructions quite pleasant and that he felt he was as relaxed as he had ever been. He did not seem to be aware that he was generating an enormous amount of muscle tension. Close scrutiny of Mr. S during these relaxation periods indicated that his jaw muscles were clenched tightly, and visible signs of muscle tension in the face were obvious.

Before proceeding with any biofeedback treatment, the clinician simply indicated to Mr. S what had been observed and told him that he might consider paying special attention to the muscles in his jaw — unclenching his teeth, allowing his chin to droop slightly, and just letting the tension flow out of his jaw muscles. He was then asked to sit back again for 10 more minutes, concentrating on keeping his jaw unclenched. During the next 10-minute rest period, the mean microvoltage level recorded from Mr. S was below 5 mv — only one-tenth of the previous amplitude. Astonishingly, Mr. S reported that he could not feel the difference between the two conditions. Yet when he was presented with the record obtained from the EMG machine, he was impressed that there was in fact a serious change in the level of his muscle tension. It was explained to him that the clinician considered the new level as a starting point and that the biofeedback machine would now be used to give him more refined feedback to enable him to reduce the voltage below the level of 5 mv.

The point of this case study is obvious. Had the clinician begun the biofeedback before he had administered to Mr S the simple instructions about relaxing his jaw muscles, he might have discovered what appeared to be a magnificent treatment effect (as indeed it would have been, but the real treatment and the real value of the biofeedback begins at the point where the patient cannot normally gain control without biofeedback). In this case study, as you can see, significant treatment effects were obtained by the use of simple instructions based on simple but intelligent observations. Biofeedback becomes useful after that point, not before.

As treatment progresses, the therapist will note that he can structure the format so that he can evaluate therapeutic progress by comparing the patient's initially determined baseline response level to the patient's baseline level in any given session. In addition to using initially determined baseline and session-to-session baselines, the therapist might want to measure trial-by-trial baselines *within* a given session. For instance, the biofeedback program can be structured so that the patient receives alternate "time-in" and "time-out" sessions in which feedback is available and then not available. The patient's level of physiological responsivity can be assessed continuously, and, within a given feedback session, physiological responses during the time in, time out can be evaluated with time-out periods functioning as trial-by-trial baseline measures. In this manner, the therapist can evaluate not only the long-term progress of the patient but also the short-term rate of progress within a given session. The evaluation of therapeutic progress can be based either upon sequential changes in the time-out periods or upon the basis of changes in the degree of discrimination between time-in and time-out periods. The subject who is successfully acquiring self-management skills might continue to show self-control during the time-out periods, whereas the patient who is learning to respond well to feedback but is not learning effective self-management might show large discrepancies between response levels during the time-in and time-out periods. These individual assessments can be particularly useful in indicating to the therapist whether his ultimate goals of teaching the patient self-control outside the clinical situation are being obtained. Thus, the careful assessment of baselines throughout the therapeutic procedure allows the therapist to evaluate not only the patient's ability to use biofeedback effectively but more importantly, the patient's ability to self-control his physiological responses in the absence of contingent biofeedback.

Criteria for Reinforcement

If the therapeutic goal in biofeedback is, for instance, the reduction of a hypertensive patient's systolic blood pressure from 180 mm Hg to 120 mm Hg, it is important not only to provide the subject with continuous feedback of his or her blood pressure level, but also to give him or her some veridical information concerning the time at which his or her blood pressure has been reduced by a significant amount. Although it is not necessary for the clinician to calculate standard deviations of blood pressure level for any given session, it is important that he or she be able to discriminate the difference between a patient whose blood pressure normally varies 20 mm Hg/min around his or her baseline and a patient whose blood pressure varies only 5 mm Hg/min around his or her baseline. There are great differences from patient to patient, and the therapist must be sensitive to establishing criteria for reinforcement that are consistent with an individual patient's variability. The assessment of baseline variability, therefore, is an essential component in determining the criteria for reinforcement in the treatment program.

Although laboratory research on biofeedback has often used monetary incentives for facilitating self-control of physiological responses, in clinical practice a patient's own knowledge of successful self-control constitutes the primary reinforcement. Typically, in a biofeedback treatment situation subjects receive continuous feedback about their physiological responses. Consequently, they receive a constantly changing array, reflecting the variability of their baselines. How is the subject to know when the perceived changes represent significant therapeutic progress rather than random variation? It is the therapist's responsibility to establish criteria for reinforcement that provide the subject with the information necessary to evaluate when responses are therapeutically meaningful.

At the simplest level, the therapist can provide the patient with a verbal statement of what his goal for the session will be. This verbal statement can be based upon the therapist's knowledge of the patient's expected variability, so that, for instance, if a subject has a baseline heart rate of 100 bpm and an expected range between 90 and 110 bpm, the therapist can indicate to the patient that the goal for the session is to keep his heart beating at, say, a level somewhere in the low 90s. Consequently, if a subject sees a decrease in heart rate level from 110 to 105, he will not misinterpret this as therapeutic progress, whereas a change in heart rate level of similar magnitude, but from 100 to 95, can be interpreted as progress, because of the verbal instructions from the therapist. Thus the goal is to reinforce the subject for changes from his mean baseline level, not to reinforce responses that are simply in the appropriate direction. Of course, the therapist must reassess the baseline on a regular basis, and the reinforcement criterion must be updated as the baseline changes. In the early stages of training, the subject will be reinforced for small responses that are below the mean but still within his normal range of variability. As training progresses, the criteria for reinforcement can become more stringent, with reinforcement defined as changes that exceed the normal range of variability.

The reader will note that the rules that govern the therapist's criterion setting for reinforcement are identical in principle with the rules for the shaping of any operant response. Similarly, the therapist must be sensitive to all the principles that underlie operant response shaping and must be prepared to modify criteria in accordance with the individual behavioral record of the subject. As the patient begins to develop increasingly greater approximations to the desired physiological response level, the criteria for reinforcement can be made increasingly stringent. It is likely that, as the therapy progresses, the degree to which the reinforcement criterion becomes more stringent will represent, in and of itself, another source for evaluating therapeutic progress.

The criteria employed for reinforcement have implications not only for the acquisition of self-control, but also for the enhancement or debilitation of motivation for success. If the therapist sets initial reinforcement criteria that are too stringent for the subject, it might result in a variety of counterproductive negative self-statements that could lead the subject to adopt a pessimistic attitude and withdraw prematurely from continuing treatment. If, on the other hand, the therapist applies reinforcement criteria that are too lenient, the patient might be disappointed to discover that, although he or she is apparently doing well, he or she is enjoying little or no symptom reduction. This also can lead to negative consequences with respect to motivation for continuing therapy.

It is difficult, if not impossible, to advise a biofeedback therapist about the specific establishment of reinforcement criteria for any given patient, but it is never impossible to recommend sensitivity in making initial determinations. One arbitrary rule of thumb is that, at the beginning of the treatment program, a criterion for reinforcement be established so that a subject on average receives reinforcing feedback about half the time for any given session. This brings us back again to the importance of discriminating between a session baseline and a treatment program baseline. Although the patient might be receiving reinforcement approximately half the time in any given session, this is based upon her or his baseline for *that* session. With respect to the *initial pretreatment baseline*, the patient might be functioning at a far more effective level, and she or he should be apprised of that fact as she or he makes such progress. Thus, reinforcement criteria are probably best based upon session baselines and not upon initial pretreatment baseline assessment. If reinforcement were based on initial pretreatment baseline assessment, it is likely that as therapy progressed, the criteria for reinforcement would become far too lenient.

Sensory Modality of Feedback

Most of the commercially available biofeedback equipment allows the patient to obtain biofeedback in an auditory or a visual mode, or both. Although at first glance the distinction between a visual or an auditory analogue of the physiological response might seem to be trivial, the therapist will discover that there are important reasons to choose either one or the other type of feedback, depending upon both the inherent nature of the response being modified and the patient's individual preferences. A striking example of a case in which auditory feedback would be much preferred over visual feedback is found in the use of an alpha feedback machine to increase a subject's ability to maintain a high level of alpha density and/or amplitude. It is well known that ocular activity can create artifactual contamination of alpha wave recordings and lead to inaccurate and misleading interpretations of the EEG record. Plotkin (1976) has demonstrated that alpha feedback in general can be explained more by ocular activity than by brain wave activity. Although the ultimate interpretation of alpha wave biofeedback still awaits more intensive research, it is obvious that it would be preferable to use analogue auditory feedback of the alpha signal rather than visual feedback, so that eye movement can be controlled adequately.

On the other hand, if the therapist using EMG feedback wants to establish a goal level toward which the patient should strive, it is generally easier to provide the patient with a visual, rather than an auditory, representation of that goal level. Different manufacturers have provided a variety of formats for visual feedback, including light bars, light circles, video screens with various monochromatic and polychromatic displays. Less exotic and less expensive visual displays include pointer needles on a voltmeter or digitized readings on a digital voltmeter to provide subjects with continuous feedback about the voltage level of their responses. Auditory feedback is generally designed so that subjects hear continuous tones whose pitch varies proportionately with the level of their responses. Alternately, volume can be varied, but most therapists have chosen to manipulate the pitch of an auditory signal, rather than the volume of such a signal, for providing feedback.

Whether the therapist ultimately decides to use visual or auditory feedback depends of course upon the availability of equipment, but ideally it should depend on more than that. Some initial discussion with the client about differences in comfort with the modalities should be taken into consideration. If the primary purpose of the biofeedback training is to facilitate general relaxation, an eyes-closed auditory feedback modality might be preferable to an eyes-open visual feedback modality. Yet it should be noted that some of the more elaborate visual displays commercially available are similar to modern video computer games and are engaging and interesting; they could enhance the subject's motivation for participating in the biofeedback therapy and could be more attractive to some patients than the relatively monotonous eyes-closed auditory feedback modality.

Scientific evidence at this time suggests that there is no difference in effectiveness between auditory and visual feedback (Gaudette, Prins, & Kahane, 1983; Janman & Daniels, 1983; O'Connell, Frerker, & Russ, 1979; Schandler & Grings, 1978) for heart rate control, hand temperature control, or frontalis EMG control. Nor has there been any more effectiveness using combined visual and auditory feedback rather than simple auditory or visual feedback (Chen, 1981). There has been little exploration of the use of other sensory modalities as effective feedback vehicles. For instance, it is quite possible that one could provide subjects with tactile sensations proportional to their physiological responses. Such a technique would have obvious advantages for providing biofeedback to people with visual or hearing impairments, but these are not the only reasons for inquiring into their efficacy.

It is important to note that, in deciding upon a sensory modality, the therapist should keep in mind that the ultimate effectiveness of the treatment depends upon the subject's knowledge of the results. Thus it is likely that clients who feel more comfortable interpreting visual feedback should receive it, whereas clients who feel more comfortable with auditory feedback should be so treated. If the client feels comfortable, there is no reason not to give both visual and auditory feedback simultaneously.

Assessment of Outcome

After all the procedural issues concerning baseline assessment, reinforcement criterion, and feedback modality have been ironed out, the therapist comes to the bottom line — evaluating the success or failure of the treatment. In evaluating therapeutic outcome, an important distinction must be made. There are some syndromes in which the physiological responses constitute the malady itself. An example would be essential hypertension. In this disorder, sometimes referred to as "the silent killer," the definition of the disorder *is* the elevated blood pressure. Most patients do not have subjective awareness of their elevated blood pressure, and, if they report symptoms of distress, they are more likely to be secondary phenomena rather than primary. Consequently, successful outcome of a biofeedback treatment program for high blood pressure can be readily defined by changes in blood pressure level. Other syndromes, such as migraine headache, are defined by subjective report of pain and associated symptoms. Biofeedback for migraine is not directed to the symptoms but to the presumed underlying mechanisms (i.e., vascular control). It is possible in treating someone for migraine with, say, skin temperature biofeedback, that one can teach the person to achieve excellent control of the skin temperature but fail to have any impact on the frequency and intensity of the migraine episodes. Thus the biofeedback can be seen to be a great success for training physiological self-control but a complete failure for alleviating the syndrome in question. In addition to making a clear distinction between the success of self-control and the success of symptom reduction, the biofeedback therapist must also be aware of the distinction between success in the clinic and success outside the clinic.

Placebo Effects

Biofeedback, as much as any other form of psychological treatment, and perhaps more so, is potentially susceptible to nonspecific placebo effects. Although the practicing clinician might find it unimportant to distinguish whether the client has improved because of an active treatment effect or a nonspecific effect, the ability to differentiate one from the other has important implications for the eventual refinement of techniques and generalizability to other patients. Consequently, although relatively unimportant for the individual client, it remains extremely important for the therapist to have some insight into the relative contribution of specific and nonspecific factors in the treatment process. There are also certain unique considerations that distinguish biofeedback from other forms of behavior modification.

Strictly speaking, the concept of placebo refers to the use of a pharmacologically inactive agent that is administered to a patient for a variety of reasons, including the failure to identify a diagnosable disorder. Often, but not always, the placebo administration results in symptom reduction. It must be understood that the positive therapeutic results of placebo administration should be relatively random. That is, it is expected that a placebo will show neither disease specificity nor interpatient reliability. If either of these events occurred, the agent would lose its definition as a placebo and be reclassified as an active treatment, even if its mechanism were not well understood. It is not the case that a treatment is classified as a placebo because its mechanism is not understood; rather, it is classified as a placebo precisely when its mechanism is well understood, and there is no pharmacologically valid reason for it to succeed.

In the area of psychotherapy, the term *placebo* has been borrowed from medicine and employed frequently. In the psychotherapeutic sense, therefore, a placebo should refer to a type of treatment that is known to have no valid specific treatment effect but that superficially appears to the patient to be an active form of psychotherapy. In other words, placebo psychotherapy should look like therapy, should sound like therapy, and *should cause the patients to expect that they are receiving therapy*. Nevertheless, the treatment should be understood to have no valid theoretical mechanism by which it could actually *be* therapy.

Among the many reasons for the rapid development of the field of behavior modification in the past two decades has been the greater precision with which outcome studies of its effectiveness could be designed. Many forms of behavior modification, and especially biofeedback, specify precise theoretical mechanisms, supposedly independent of therapist characteristics, that are expected to produce operationally defined symptom reduction. Within the context of the greater definitional precision, a variety of placebo possibilities present themselves.

Controlled research on placebo effects in behavior modification technique has usually focused on the issue of patient expectancy for success. The general strategy has been to present a placebo therapy to patients with instructions that lead them to expect success as much as they would with the actual treatment. Careful steps are usually taken to equate time and effort of the therapist and to create conditions that are similar to the actual therapy. Finally, care is usually taken to insure that there are no experimenter bias or demand characteristics associated with the outcome evaluation.

As careful as these procedures have been, it is not clear that they have been entirely effective. Kazdin and Wilcoxon (1976) have suggested that the procedures of the treatments themselves, rather than any characteristics of the therapist or demands of the evaluation, generate different expectancies for success because of differential credibility. Lick and Bootzin (1975) have focused on the mechanisms by which expectancy effects work in systematic desensitization. Assuming that there is no magical or mystical manner by which expectancy leads to therapeutic success, Lick and Bootzin stated that to "the extent to which placebo manipulations work they must operate by mechanisms different from those traditionally proffered to explain the efficacy of (systematic desensitization)" (p. 926). They then suggested the following possible mechanisms. First, expecting to be cured of fear, the patient might test the expectancy by exposing himself or herself to the feared object, thus leading to some increment in extinction of the fear. Second, expectancy changes might encourage greater attention to cues that represent improvement, leading to greater *report* of gain. Third, because the expectancy of improvement would be cognitively dissonant with knowledge that one still has symptoms, the dissonance might create heightened drive to continue testing reality as described above, further facilitating the actual desensitization process. Lick and Bootzin have speculated that any or all of these mechanisms might lead to changes in a patient's self-report of therapeutic gain as well as to a change in overt behavior indicative of such gain.

Even if a placebo therapy for biofeedback should lead to differential expectancy, it is unlikely that the mechanisms postulated by Lick and Bootzin would be applicable. First, self-reports of symptom reduction are rarely the primary criteria for success in biofeedback; quantitative changes in psychophysiological response activity are. Second, if the effect of the placebo is to cause the subject voluntarily to test the therapeutic hypothesis, it is less likely to be carried out in the visceral arena. A patient can approach a feared object in a runway more readily than he can reduce his blood pressure just to test a hypothesis.

Biofeedback for tension headaches, migraine headaches, or other forms of *subjective distress* is theoretically presumed to work via specific measurable alterations of muscle tension, vasoconstriction, skin temperature, and so on. Although a placebo treatment can significantly alter a patient's subjective report of symptom reduction, it is not likely that it would similarly result in altered physiological patterns. To be sure, it is still possible that proper placebo control research on biofeedback is contaminated. Nevertheless, our thesis is that biofeedback therapy, by its very nature, is a better candidate for careful evaluation with placebo control than other forms of behavior modification, and the results of placebo studies of biofeedback should be relatively easy to interpret. With that in mind, the following section will review the current research literature on the classical effectiveness of biofeedback therapy along a number of dimensions, specifically analyzing the degree to which treatment effectiveness has been demonstrated to be greater than that attributable to a placebo.

RESEARCH ON THERAPEUTIC EFFECTIVENESS

A survey of the research literature on biofeedback as an effective therapeutic tool reveals that virtually every organ system and every syndrome have been subject to attempts at modification through feedback. The most extensive work, however, has been addressed to three broad categories: (a) anxiety disorders, (b) cardiovascular disorders, and (c) neuromuscular disorders.

Anxiety Disorders

Generalized Anxiety

The most popular form of biofeedback therapy for the treatment of general anxiety is EMG biofeedback, specifically, EMG biofeedback of the frontalis muscles. The rationale for the use of frontalis EMG biofeedback in the treatment of anxiety is based on two assumptions: (a) EMG biofeedback of the frontalis muscles is an effective procedure for inducing general body relaxation, and (b) deep relaxation leads to the subjective experience of relaxation. Reviews of early studies on the use of frontalis EMG biofeedback for the reduction of anxiety (Alexander & Smith, 1979; Burish, 1981; Katkin & Goldband, 1979) concluded that there was no conclusive evidence that muscle tension biofeedback treatment is effective in reducing anxiety.

Recent studies that have attempted to control for nonspecific factors have found that EMG biofeedback is no better than relaxation or simple instructions in reducing EMG levels (Burish, Hendrix, & Frost, 1981; LeBoeuf, 1980; Raskin, Bali, & Peeke, 1980) and that EMG levels are not related to the self-report of anxiety (Burish et al., 1981; LeBoeuf, 1980; Raskin et al., 1980; Rupert, Dobbins, & Mathew, 1981). Lavellee, Lamontagne, Annable, and Fontaine (1982) are the only researchers who have reported a correlation between EMG levels and self-reports of anxiety, but only for those subjects who reported a decrease in anxiety. These studies suggest that not only is biofeedback no more effective than other techniques in reducing anxiety, but also that the assumptions underlying the use of frontalis EMG biofeedback for the reduction of anxiety may be invalid.

Levels of frontalis EMG activity have been compared with the activity levels of other muscles and to other indexes of autonomic nervous system such as heart rate, finger pulse volume, or blood pressure in order to test the validity of using frontalis EMG levels as an index of general relaxation. Some of the earlier studies suggested that frontalis EMG levels might be correlated with autonomic nervous system measures (Gatchel, Korman, Weiss, Smith, & Clarke, 1978) or with other striate muscular activity (Freedman & Papsdorf, 1976; O'Connell & Yeaton, 1981; Stoyva & Budzynski, 1974), but these have been criticized for not using proper control groups or for reaching conclusions not supported by the data (Kotses & Glaus, 1982). The majority of studies have found no relationship between frontalis EMG activity and other muscle activity (Alexander, White, & Wallace, 1977; Fridlund, Fowler, & Pritchard, 1980; Jones & Evans, 1981; Kotses & Glaus, 1982; Sheidivy & Kleinman, 1977) or other autonomic nervous system indexes of arousal (Alexander et al., 1977; Siddle & Wood, 1978).

It appears that, although EMG biofeedback of the frontalis muscles produces reductions in frontalis muscle activity, it is not the appropriate treatment for anxiety reduction. Simple instructions or relaxation procedures produce the same reduction in frontalis muscle activity. Reduction in frontalis activity does not produce decreases in the activity of other muscles nor does it reduce general autonomic nervous system arousal, and it is not related to subjective reports of anxiety. If biofeedback is to be useful in the treatment of anxiety, other methods need to be investigated more thoroughly.

A second biofeedback technique for anxiety reduction and tension reduction is discrete brainwave (EEG) feedback, usually involving alpha wave and/or theta wave feedback (Glueck & Stroebel, 1975). Although this type of biofeedback was quite popular in the early development of the field, it is not as widely used today, partly because of the methodological complications inherent in its use and partly because of some controversies about its actual clinical effectiveness (Kamiya, 1968; Plotkin, 1976; Plotkin & Cohen, 1976; Travis, Kondo, & Knott, 1975; Valle & Levine, 1975). Also, studies have failed to support any intrinsic or consistent relationship between alpha levels and anxiety (Garrett & Silver, 1972; Orne & Paskewitz, 1974; Plotkin, 1978; Reeves & Mealiea, 1975; Wickramasekera, 1972). More recently, Plotkin and Rice (1981) have shown that anxiety was unrelated to either direction or magnitude of alpha changes, but that there was a high correlation between anxiety and perceived success.

An attempt by Rupert and Holmes (1978) to reduce anxiety levels using heart rate biofeedback was not successful. Not only was HR not related to subjective anxiety levels, but also subjects given biofeedback for HR reduction did not reduce their heart rates any more than subjects who sat still for the same period.

At this time it does not appear that biofeedback is useful in the treatment of generalized anxiety. New approaches such as using multiple EMG recording sites, or more carefully controlled studies need to be developed and tested.

Phobia

The rationale for using biofeedback for the treatment of specific phobias is that phobias are accompanied by anxiety. Most reports of biofeedback treatment for phobias combine biofeedback with either systematic desensitization (Budzynski & Stoyva, 1973) or progressive relaxation (Benjamins, 1976; Reeves & Mealiea, 1975; Wickramasekera, 1972). The biofeedback of choice is usually frontalis EMG biofeedback (Budzynski & Stoyva, 1973; Chiari & Mosticoni, 1979; Garrett & Silver, 1972; Reeves & Mealiea, 1975; Wickramasekera, 1972) although Benjamins (1976) has used alpha biofeedback with snake phobics, and Nunes and Marks (1975) and Prignatano and Johnson (1972) used HR biofeedback with spider phobics. Although most of the studies reported positive results, they did not test the efficacy of biofeedback. Most of the studies are case reports; there have not been any sufficient control techniques employed, and the biofeedback is always used in conjunction with some other technique.

Cardiovascular Disorders

Cardiac Rate Disorders

Most of the earliest basic research on instrumental autonomic conditioning involved the modification of HR because of the ease of measurement and quantification. A great deal of experimental work aimed at controlling the human heart rate has been done with normal subjects. A typical experimental design for this research consists of subjects' attempting to raise or lower their heart rates using a variety of kinds of feedback reinforcement — lights, oscilloscope patterns, slides of landscapes, or pictures of nudes. These studies have typically shown that normal subjects can raise and lower their heart rates to some extent and can decrease heart rate variability, but there are some limitations on how the results of these studies can be interpreted. It is difficult to assess whether the small decreases in rate obtained were the results of the feedback process itself or could be accounted for by general relaxation, or even whether the reduction could have been more efficiently obtained by other methods. Studies of physiological changes associated with transcendental meditation (Wallace, 1970; Wallace & Benson, 1972) and progressive relaxation (Paul, 1969), for instance, have found heart rate decreases that equaled and sometimes exceeded changes obtained in biofeedback experimentation.

Clinicians have adopted cardiac rate biofeedback techniques for the purpose of treating specific types of cardiac dysfunctions. The major use of cardiac rate biofeedback has been in the treatment of premature ventricular contractions (PVC). The early work of Engel and his associates (Engel & Bleecker, 1974; Engel & Melmon, 1968; Weiss & Engel, 1970, 1971) reported case studies of patients with PVCs. The two Weiss and Engel studies devoted a great many sessions to treatment and did extended follow-up (up to 21 months later). On follow-up, half of the patients maintained a low PVC frequency.

The other major use of cardiac rate biofeedback has been for treatment of tachycardia. Engel and Bleecker (1974) reported the successful treatment of three patients with tachycardia; Scott, Blanchard, Edmunson, and Young (1973) were successful with two tachycardia patients, and Janssen (1983b) has recently reported success in treating a single patient with tachycardia. Bleecker and Engel (1973) also reported the successful biofeedback treatment of a patient with Wolff-Parkinson-White syndrome, a heart conduction defect. The patient eventually learned to maintain normal conduction without feedback.

These case studies have not employed controls for nonspecific effects, nor have they employed some of the single case study design elements discussed by Hersen and Barlow (1976). Although it is difficult to disagree with the dramatic results obtained, it is clear that almost half of the subjects treated for arrhythmias did not show success. These case reports do not show a specific treatment effect of biofeedback.

Hypertension

Excessively high blood pressure for which there is no apparent physiological cause, that is, *essential hypertension*, is a vascular disorder for which psychological stress is presumed to be an etiological factor. Although there are antihypertensive medications available that are often successful in reducing blood pressure, there are a number of reasons why alternative behavioral treatments need to be developed: (a) Some individuals will not use the available drugs, (b) many of the drugs have unpleasant side effects, (c) alternative methods might allow individuals to reduce their medications or become drug free, and (d) some individuals do not respond to the drugs. Because stress is thought to have an etiological role in the onset of hypertension, and biofeedback is believed to mediate stress responses, biofeedback is one of the alternative behavioral techniques that has been developed. The most common form of biofeedback for hypertension is direct blood pressure biofeedback (systolic, diastolic, or mean BP). However, other types of biofeedback, such as EMG or temperature biofeedback, which help induce relaxation, are also used.

Most of the early studies that employed systolic blood pressure (SBP) biofeedback reported successful results. In 1971, Benson, Shapiro, Tursky, and Schwartz reported that within feedback sessions, five out of seven hypertensives were able to reduce their SBP as much as 16 mm Hg but were not successful in reducing their diastolic blood pressure (DBP). Kristt and Engel (1975) reported that four patients trained to raise and lower their SBP showed a significant decrease in both SBP and DBP. Blanchard,

Young, and Haynes (1975) reported on four hypertensive patients who were able to reduce their SBP but not their DBP using SBP biofeedback, and Datey (1976) had 20 patients show SBP reductions. Goldman, Kleinman, Snow, Bidus, and Korol (1975), using SBP feedback with seven hypertensives, found that, within sessions, patients showed a substantial SBP decrease and a DBP decrease across sessions. Kleinman, Goldman, Snow, and Korol (1977) obtained similar results with eight hypertensive subjects; SBP was reduced within sessions, and DBP was reduced across sessions. Although these results looked promising, none of the studies employed adequate controls. One control-group outcome study (Shoemaker & Tasto, 1975) compared SBP biofeedback with relaxation. It found that, although there was no substantial reduction in BP, the relaxation group did significantly better than the biofeedback group.

The results of recent studies have not been as promising. Surwit, Shapiro, and Good (1978) compared a combination of SBP and HR biofeedback with simple relaxation or frontalis EMG biofeedback. Although there were significant systolic and diastolic BP reductions within sessions, there were no significant reductions across sessions. Also, there were no significant differences among treatments, although the relaxation treatment appeared more effective. Blanchard, Miller, Abel, Haynes, and Wicker (1979) also compared SBP biofeedback to simple relaxation or frontalis EMG biofeedback. Their results were similar to Surwit, Shapiro, and Good's (1978); all subjects showed SBP decreases, there were no significant differences among groups, and the relaxation treatment appeared slightly more effective (8.1 mm Hg decrease for SBP group and 9.5 mm Hg decrease for the relaxation group). Unlike the Surwit, Shapiro, and Good (1978) study, Blanchard et al. (1979) did not find any significant reductions in DBP.

Luborsky et al. (1982) compared four treatment groups; SBP biofeedback, mild exercise, relaxation, and antihypertensive medication. The drug treatment showed the most significant decreases in both SBP and DBP. The three behavioral treatments were not different from one another. The SBP feedback and relaxation decreased SBP equally, but only slightly more than the exercise. There were no significant decreases in DBP on any of the three behavioral treatments, although relaxation appeared to be more effective. Glasgow, Gaarder, and Engel (1982) reported a similar finding. They compared SBP feedback with relaxation and a no-treatment control and found that relaxation reduced both SBP and DBP, but SBP biofeedback only reduced SBP. Richter-Heinrich et al. (1981) combined SBP with relaxation and found decreases in BP equivalent to changes found using beta-blockers.

With studies using more appropriate controls, it appears that SBP feedback is not any more effective than simple relaxation in reducing SBP and perhaps less effective than relaxation in reducing DBP. Glasgow et al. (1982) argued that relaxation achieves lower BP primarily through a reduction in cardiac output, whereas feedback acts primarily by lowering peripheral vascular resistance.

Treatment of hypertension using diastolic blood pressure feedback has not been as successful as that using systolic blood pressure biofeedback. Miller (1972) reported a case study in which a patient reduced his DBP by 19 mm HG, but he was unable to replicate this finding with 19 additional hypertensive patients (Miller, 1975). Elder, Ruiz, Deabler, and Dillenkoffer (1973) reported on hospitalized patients who showed reductions in DBP but not SBP, and Elder and Eustis (1975) reported DBP reductions of 6–8 mm Hg, but neither of these studies used a control group. Schwartz and Shapiro (1973), combining relaxation with DBP biofeedback, found that only one of seven subjects showed any DBP reduction. Weston (1974) compared DBP biofeedback with a combined treatment of frontalis EMG feedback, DBP feedback, and relaxation and also with a treatment package of frontalis EMG feedback and DBP feedback without relaxation. All of the treatment groups showed a significant decrease in both SBP and DBP, with no differences among groups. Unfortunately this study did not have any control for nonspecific effects. Friedman and Taub (1977) compared DBP biofeedback with hypnosis. Although the decreases were not clinically significant, both groups reduced SBP and DBP, and hypnosis appeared slightly more effective. Frankel, Patel, Horwitz, Friedewald, and Gaarder (1978) combined DBP biofeedback with frontalis EMG biofeedback, autogenic training, and progressive relaxation and compared the treatment to sham DBP feedback and a no-treatment control group. There were no significant changes in either SBP or DBP, although some individuals did show decreases. Two of seven subjects in the active treatment group decreased their BP, whereas five of seven subjects in the sham treatment group showed BP decreases.

There have not been many adequately controlled studies using DBP feedback. What has been done suggests that DBP feedback is probably not effective for controlling hypertension, and it is certainly less effective than SBP feedback or simple relaxation.

Other Biofeedback Techniques

Other biofeedback techniques that have been used to treat hypertension include EMG, EDA, and temperature biofeedback. Moeller (1976) compared frontalis EMG biofeedback to combined frontalis EMG biofeedback and relaxation. Both treatment groups reduced SBP and DBP significantly more than a no-treatment control group. Orlando (1974) found significant decreases in both SBP and DBP in a group of hypertensives treated with a combination of frontalis EMG biofeedback and relaxation. Surwit,

Shapiro, and Good (1978) found EMG biofeedback to be no different from either SBP biofeedback or simple relaxation, and Blanchard et al. (1979) found it to be less effective.

Patel and her associates (Patel, 1973, 1976; Patel, Marmot, & Terry, 1981; Patel & North, 1975) have done a number of studies using EDA feedback combined with yoga, relaxation, or EMG biofeedback to reduce blood pressure. Patel reported that all of her experimental groups were able to reduce both SBP and DBP. Datey (1977, 1978) also reported success in reducing BP using EDA biofeedback. However, BP reductions were no different from those found using yoga (Datey, 1977) or hypnosis (Datey, 1978). Datey (1976, 1977) also reported positive results using temperature biofeedback as a treatment for hypertension. Green, Green, and Norris (1980), using temperature biofeedback combined with relaxation, found clinically significant BP decreases in nine hypertensives, but Bertilson, Bartz, and Zimmerman (1979) reported that hand temperature biofeedback did not increase hand temperature beyond that attained with relaxation, although there was an additional 2.5 mm Hg decrease in SBP during temperature biofeedback. Sedlacek and Cohen (1978) combined frontalis EMG feedback, hand temperature feedback, and several relaxation techniques and found significant SBP and DBP decreases.

Although many of these studies appear to have positive results, many of them combined treatments, so that specific treatment effects are impossible to determine (Bertilson et al., 1979; Green et al., 1980; McGrady, Yonker, Tan, Fine, & Woerner, 1981; Orlando, 1974; Patel, 1973, 1976; Patel et al., 1981; Patel & North, 1975; Sedlacek & Cohen, 1978), or there were no differences between biofeedback and relaxation groups (Datey, 1977, 1978; Orlando, 1974; Patel & North, 1975). The initial positive results reported from case studies do not appear to hold up under more controlled conditions. There does not appear to be any specific effect of biofeedback of systolic or diastolic blood pressure, or EMG feedback, for the treatment of hypertension, beyond that achieved through simple relaxation.

Migraine

Migraine headaches are classified as a vascular disorder; they result from a dysfunction of the cranial arteries. The specific mechanisms by which a migraine occurs are still not known, but it is believed that sympathetic arousal initiates excessive cerebral vasoconstriction, which, due to an insufficient blood supply to the brain, results in a rebound dilation. Although the etiology of the initial dysfunction is still unknown, the resultant symptoms are easily recognized. During the early vasoconstrictive phase, the patient reports any of a variety of visual disturbances including scintillating scotoma, hemianopia, and, for many, a distinctive pattern of radiating gridlike visual illusions. As the cerebral vasculature shifts from a constricted to a dilated stage, the visual disturbance clears up and is followed by extreme pain on one side of the head, often over the eye but frequently radiating throughout the entire side of the head. In some cases the pain is bilateral, and, in many cases, the head pain is associated with nausea, photophobia, and/or phonophobia.

The pharmacological treatment for migraine attacks is the administration of vasoconstrictive drugs, such as ergotamine tartrate, to prevent the rebound vasodilation and the associated pain. However, if the drugs are administered after the dilation has begun, they are usually ineffective; therefore, the patient must receive the drugs during the early constrictive phase of the episode. Too strong a dose of a vasoconstrictor, given while the cerebral blood vessels are already constricting, could be fatal. Therefore, many physicians tend to prescribe such low-level doses as to be ineffective in relieving the symptoms. In addition, there are a variety of negative side effects associated with the use of vasoconstrictive drugs, including nausea, dependency, tolerance, and withdrawal effects. Given the limitations of medical interventions, a behavioral treatment for migraine is desirable.

Common sense would suggest that biofeedback for blood flow to the head would be a reasonable starting point for migraine treatment, and, indeed, early research on the phenomenon began there. Although plethysmographic recording allows direct measurement of blood flow, many investigators have chosen to use the simple, equally valid measure of skin temperature as an index of blood volume. Sargent, Green, and Walters (1972, 1973) reported great success in treating migraine patients by teaching them to warm their hands relative to their heads. The general strategy was to train patients to decrease vasodilation in the head, and to simultaneously increase vasodilation at the hands, thereby training the patient to create an integrated shift of blood volume from central to peripheral sites. Following these reports, several case studies (Johnson & Turin, 1975; Kentsmith, Strider, Copenhaver, & Jacques, 1976; Turin, 1977; Turin & Johnson, 1976; Wickramasekera, 1973) and group outcome studies (Diamond & Franklin, 1974; Medina, Diamond, & Franklin, 1976; Mitch, McGrady, & Iannone, 1976; Weinstock, 1973) supported the conclusion of Sargent et al. (1972, 1973) that temperature biofeedback was useful in treating migraine. Turin and Johnson (1976) also suggested that training for increased vasodilation at the hands was sufficient to result in therapeutic effectiveness.

Since the initial enthusiasm, several areas of research have developed to test the specific efficacy of hand warming biofeedback in the treatment of migraine. One area has attempted to compare hand warming biofeedback to other behavioral techniques such as hypnosis (Graham, 1974), autogenic training or relaxation (Barrios & Karoly, 1983; Beasley, 1976; Hart, 1984; LaCroix et al., 1983), or frontalis EMG biofeedback (Hart, 1984; LaCroix et al., 1983; Sargent, 1984). With the exception of Beasley (1976), all of these studies reported that the different treatment groups showed significantly greater reductions in migraine activity than control groups, but there were no differences among treatments. Hand warming biofeedback was no more effective in reducing migraine activity than was hypnosis, general relaxation, or even frontalis EMG biofeedback. Beasley (1976) reported that hand warming biofeedback alone was ineffective in reducing migraine activity, but when combined with relaxation it was better than a no-treatment control.

Other researchers have done controlled studies using thermal biofeedback combined with some form of relaxation. Andreychuk and Skriver (1975) compared thermal biofeedback combined with autogenic training to alpha EEG biofeedback and to hypnosis. All three groups showed a significant reduction in migraine activity, but there were no differences among them. Thompson (1977) reported that, although a group of migraineurs trained to increase their finger temperatures with biofeedback and autogenic training demonstrated greater finger temperature control than a group not trained, both groups reported equal reductions in migraine activity. When Blanchard et al. (1978) compared a combination of thermal biofeedback and autogenic training to progressive relaxation and to a waiting list control group, they found that both experimental groups reported significant migraine improvement, and, although it was not statistically significant, the relaxation group reported slightly more improvement. Similarly, Daly, Donn, Galliher, and Zimmerman (1983) compared relaxation plus autogenic training to EMG biofeedback plus autogenic training and to thermal biofeedback plus autogenic training. Once again, all three groups learned the appropriate responses, and all three groups reported a decrease in migraine activity with no differences among the groups. The only report that appears to support the use of thermal biofeedback comes from Blanchard, Andrasik, Neff, Arena, et al. (1982). All of their migraine subjects initially received relaxation training. Those subjects who did not show a substantial improvement in migraine activity were then given thermal biofeedback. Blanchard, Andrasik, Neff, Arena, et al. (1982) reported that a substantial percentage of these remaining subjects showed additional improvement. They concluded that, for some subjects, thermal biofeedback adds something beyond simple relaxation.

The effects of hand cooling have also been compared to the effects of hand warming. Early case reports suggested that hand cooling either exacerbated migraine activity (Johnson & Turin, 1975; Largen et al., 1979; Turin, 1977) or had no effect on migraine activity (Turin & Johnson, 1976; Wickramasekera, 1973). Recent controlled studies, however, suggested that there is no difference between hand warming biofeedback and hand cooling biofeedback in effects on migraine activity (Claghorn, Mathew, Largen,

& Meyer, 1981; Gauthier, Bois, Allaire, & Drolet, 1981; Jessup, 1978; Kewman & Roberts, 1980; Mullinix, Norton, Hock, & Fishman, 1978). Whether subjects were trained to increase hand temperature or decrease it, all reported significant reductions in migraine activity.

Several researchers have also reported finding no correlation between migraine activity and finger temperatures, whether hand cooling was effective in reducing migraine activity (Gauthier et al., 1981; Jessup, 1978; Mullinix et al., 1978) or not (Turin & Johnson, 1976). Also, using only hand warming, LaCroix et al. (1983) and Hart (1984) reported no correlations between finger temperature changes and migraine improvement.

The rationale behind using finger temperature biofeedback for the treatment of migraine was that an increase in hand temperature would be associated with a decrease in the dilation of the cephalic arteries; however, this reciprocal relationship has not been demonstrated. In fact, the data suggest that the effectiveness of thermal biofeedback is not specific to the feedback itself but is simply a reduction in autonomic nervous system arousal. This is supported by studies that found that EMG biofeedback was as effective in relieving migraine as was thermal biofeedback (Daly et al., 1983; Hart, 1984; LaCroix et al., 1983; Sargent, 1984) or simple relaxation (Barrios & Karoly, 1983; Blanchard et al., 1978; Daly et al., 1983; Hart, 1984; LaCroix et al., 1983; Sargent, 1984).

An alternative procedure for migraine treatment is training for constriction of the cephalic arteries. Early reports suggested that blood volume pulse (BVP) biofeedback of the cephalic extracranial arteries is a useful technique in treating migraine (Adams, Webster, & Graham, 1976; Christie & Kotses, 1973; Feuerstein & Adams, 1975; Koppman, McDonald, & Kunzel, 1974; Pearse, Walters, Sargent, & Meers, 1975; Price & Tursky, 1976; Savill & Koppman, 1975; Sturgis, Tollison, & Adams, 1978). However, BVP feedback from the fingers does not appear to be useful in treating migraine (Allen & Mills, 1982; Friar, 1974; Friar & Beatty, 1976). When compared with relaxation (Zamani, 1974) or frontalis EMG biofeedback (Bild, 1976; Bild & Adams, 1980; Feuerstein & Adams, 1977), cephalic BVP feedback appears to be significantly more effective.

Although most of the studies appear to support the efficacy of cephalic BVP feedback for treating migraines, Feuerstein, Adams, and Beiman (1976) found that even though subjects were unable to reduce either EMG levels or cephalic BVP, both groups reported reductions in frequency, intensity, and duration of migraines. Friar and Beatty (1976) reported finding no correlation between pulse amplitudes and measures of migraine activity, and Knapp (1982), comparing cephalic BVP with a cognitive technique, found that all subjects reported significant migraine relief, but there were no differences among the treatment groups.

The best support for the use of cephalic BVP feedback in treating migraines comes from Allen and Mills (1982). They trained migraine patients in bidirectional control of both finger and cephalic BVP amplitude, then asked subjects to use the control techniques during an actual migraine. There was no difference in headache pain between attempts to vasoconstrict or vasodilate the finger. However, subjects reported migraine relief when vasoconstricting the cephalic arteries but not when vasodilating.

The data for cephalic BVP feedback are quite equivocal. Although it appears promising, several studies suggest it may also be no more than simple relaxation. More controlled studies need to be done, and more attention needs to be given to the usefulness of biofeedback as a relief for migraine and as a preventative measure.

Raynaud's Syndrome

Raynaud's syndrome, a functional disorder of the peripheral cardiovascular system, is characterized by intermittent spasms of small arteries and/or arterioles. These cutaneous vasospasms most frequently occur in the hands or feet but are also seen in the face, the nose, and the ears. A Raynaud's attack involves a three-stage color change of the affected area: (a) blanching, due to digital artery vasospasms and the resulting depletion of blood in the cutaneous vessels; (b) cyanotic phase with bluish color due to the slow blood flow in dilated capillaries; and (c) bright red, which is reactive hyperemia, manifested by redness, painful throbbing, and a burning sensation, terminating the vasospasms.

Although the specific mechanism responsible for Raynaud's syndrome is not known, it is believed to be a result of a hyperactive or hyperreactive sympathetic nervous system, and it is precipitated by exposure to cold or emotional stress. Raynaud's *disease* refers to the primary form of the disorder, where the symptoms cannot be attributed to any identifiable disease process. Raynaud's *phenomenon* refers to the secondary form, where the Raynaud's symptoms are secondary to other diseases such as scleroderma, rheumatoid arthritis, traumatic vibration disease, occlusive artery disease, or thoracic outlet syndrome. Pharmacological treatments that involve vasodilating drugs to increase peripheral blood flow are often not effective, and all have negative side effects. Hand temperature biofeedback seems an ideal behavioral intervention because increased hand temperature indicates increased blood flow.

Early studies of the use of biofeedback in treating Raynaud's syndrome reported success. However, most of these early studies were only single or multiple case reports (Blanchard & Haynes, 1975; Jacobson, Hackett, Surman, & Silverberg, 1973; Sappington, 1977; Sedlacek, 1976, 1979; Stephenson, 1976; Sundermann & Delk, 1978; Surwit, 1973; Taub, 1977). They often combined biofeedback with other forms of relaxation (Jacobson et al., 1973; Sedlacek, 1976, 1979; Stephenson, 1976; Surwit, 1973).

Freedman and his associates (Freedman, Ianni, Hale, & Lynn, 1979; Freedman, Ianni, & Wenig, 1983; Freedman, Lynn, & Ianni, 1978; Freedman, Lynn, Ianni, & Hale, 1981) have reported the greatest success using finger temperature biofeedback, reporting that subjects who control their finger temperatures show a concomitant decrease in Raynaud's symptoms. Although Freedman and his colleagues' earlier studies did not control for any nonspecific factors, Freedman et al. (1983), using autogenic training and EMG biofeedback control groups, found that Raynaud's subjects trained with thermal biofeedback showed better finger temperature control during feedback sessions, better finger temperature control under stress, and greater reduction of Raynaud's symptoms than either the autogenic-trained subjects or the EMG-trained subjects. Freedman et al. (1983) also reported finding a significant correlation between the degree of temperature control and the degree of symptom reduction. Stroebel, Ford, Strong, and Szarek (1981) also reported that between 40% and 70% of Raynaud's sufferers reported relief after temperature biofeedback therapy. However, Stroebel et al. (1981) did not treat the data statistically, and the biofeedback was combined with other types of relaxation and EMG biofeedback.

Other researchers have found that finger temperature biofeedback was no better than relaxation for increasing finger temperature and reducing Raynaud's symptoms. Surwit, Pilon, and Fenton (1978) compared a combination of autogenic training and temperature biofeedback to autogenic training alone. They concluded that the biofeedback made no further contribution to the autogenic training. Jacobson, Manschreck, and Silverberg (1979) combined temperature feedback with relaxation and compared it with relaxation alone. They also concluded that the biofeedback added nothing beyond the relaxation. Similarly, Keefe, Surwit, and Pilon (1980) compared autogenic training, relaxation, and a combination of autogenic training and temperature biofeedback. They found no differences among the groups; all reported symptom relief.

Whether or not Raynaud's patients even learn to control their finger temperatures has been questioned (Keefe et al., 1980; Surwit, Pilon, & Fenton, 1978), but, more importantly, finger temperature changes have not been correlated with symptom relief. Jacobson, Silverberg, Hackett, and Manschreck (1978) reported on eight cases given a combination of biofeedback and relaxation therapy. The clinical response obtained was poorly correlated with ability to control finger temperature. Keefe, Surwit, and Pilon (1979), in a 1-year follow-up study, found that, although symptoms remained improved, finger temperatures had returned to pretreatment baselines. Jacobson et al. (1979) also found that the clinical benefit obtained was not correlated with the ability to warm fingers. Guglielmi, Roberts, and Patterson (1982), in a double-blind study, gave subjects feedback, either for increasing their finger temperatures or for reducing EMG tension levels. They then separated subjects into learners and nonlearners, based on their ability to control finger temperature or EMG tension levels. They found that all the experimental groups reported a decrease in the frequency of Raynaud's attacks, with no differences among the groups, regardless of whether they learned their task or not.

Although Raynaud's symptoms improve significantly after finger temperature biofeedback, it does not appear that the improvement results from any specific effect of biofeedback. Identical results, which are as robust as temperature biofeedback, can be obtained using relaxation procedures.

Neuromuscular Disorders

Bruxism

Bruxism is the habit of clenching or grinding the teeth, which can lead to serious dental damage, neck and facial pain, or even muscle contraction headaches. Although the exact etiology of bruxism remains unclear, recent correlational studies suggest that stress, anxiety, fear, and frustration play a major role (Rugh & Solberg, 1975). Also, clinical observations suggest that daytime stress and anxiety increases nocturnal bruxism. Dental treatment, usually occlusal appliances such as bite plates or splints, have been found to be of limited effectiveness and are cumbersome for patients.

Bruxism is most prevalent during sleep. Therefore, biofeedback for bruxism usually consists of a loud tone that is intended to awaken the patient, presented contingent on the patient's oral activity. Oral activity is measured either with a pressure plate placed between the teeth or with masseter EMG levels. DeRisi (1970) found that biofeedback was effective but that the bruxism returned once the feedback was removed. Heller and Strang (1973) and Rugh and Solberg (1975) reported similar results. Biofeedback reduced bruxism, but only during treatment; once feedback was discontinued, the grinding returned. Rappaport, Cammer, Cannistraci, Gelb, and Strong (1975) also reported clinical success using a combination of progressive relaxation, meditation, and EMG biofeedback. Although all of these studies reported a reduction in bruxism activity during treatment, none of the studies were controlled experimental studies, and most reported no long-term changes.

Recent reports, which are better controlled, have been less promising. Clark, Beemsterboer, and Rugh (1981) reported a significant decrease in masseter muscle activity during EMG biofeedback in 10 patients; however, they did not use a control group and, at a 3-month follow-up, four of seven subjects reported that their symptoms had returned. Rugh and Johnson (1981) reported a significant reduction in the *duration* of bruxism episodes for five subjects but found no differences in the *frequency* of episodes. Funch and Gale (1980), in a case study, reported a decrease in both duration and frequency of episodes during treatment. They used an A-B-A design and found a rebound effect after the withdrawal of treatment, such that bruxism was five times greater than the initial baseline activity.

Piccione, Coates, George, Rosenthal, and Karzmark (1982), using masseter EMG biofeedback in an A-B-A-B design, found no decrease in either duration or frequency in two subjects. Casas, Beemsterboer, and Clark (1982), in a controlled experiment, compared masseter EMG biofeedback to cognitive therapy, to a combination of cognitive therapy and biofeedback, and to a no-treatment waiting list control group. All three treatment groups reduced their EMG levels, but both of the counseling treatments were superior to EMG alone, and EMG added nothing to the counseling.

In summary, the few studies that have looked at the efficacy of biofeedback for the treatment of bruxism are either case studies or uncontrolled group outcome studies. They do not support the usefulness of biofeedback for the long-term treatment of bruxism. Casas et al. (1982) have suggested that cognitive interventions might be more useful.

Temporomandibular Joint (TMJ) Syndrome

TMJ syndrome refers to the limitation of mandibular movement caused by muscle tension and often accompanied by muscle pain or tenderness around the jaw. Dental treatments for TMJ syndrome are often directed toward structures of the masticatory system, including equilibration of the dentition and bite guards. The pain is assumed to be a result of hyperactivity of the masticatory muscles. Gessel and Alderman (1971) measured EMG activity in TMJ patients and found a pronounced elevation in muscle activity on the affected side. Biofeedback treatment for TMJ pain usually involves masseter muscle EMG feedback to reduce muscle tension.

Case studies and single-group outcome studies suggest that reduction in masseter muscle tension results in symptom reduction (Carlsson & Gale, 1977; Carlsson, Gale, & Ohman, 1975; Dohrman & Laskin, 1978; Gessel, 1975). Similar results have also been obtained using frontalis muscle biofeedback (Beaton, 1984; Principato & Barwell, 1978). Stenn, Mothersill, and Brooke (1979), in a comparison of a cognitive behavioral intervention with a combination of cognitive intervention and masseter biofeedback, found that both groups reduced muscle tension significantly, and both reported significant reductions in pain, but the clinical improvement was significantly greater for the biofeedback group.

Carlsson and Gale (1977), however, reported finding little relationship between outcome and ability to relax the masseter muscle. Dahlstrom, Carlsson, Gale, and Jansson (1984), in a well-controlled experiment, compared frontalis muscle biofeedback to masseter muscle biofeedback. They found that both groups showed a significant reduction in activity of the target muscle, and both groups showed significant clinical improvement.

There were no differences between the two groups on any outcome measures, and there was no significant correlation between muscle response and outcome.

Although the number of controlled experimental studies is limited, it appears as if there is no substantial support for the use of masseter EMG biofeedback in the treatment of TMJ pain. There is no clear relationship between EMG levels and measures of the disorder.

Tension Headache

The primary source of pain in tension or muscle contraction headaches is believed to be from sustained contractions of the skeletal muscles of the head and neck. Several researchers have found that, on average, headache-prone individuals, during headache-free periods, have substantially higher frontalis EMG levels than nonheadache individuals (Haynes, Griffin, Mooney, & Parise, 1975; Hutchings & Reinking, 1976; Philips, 1977b; Pozniak-Patewicz, 1976; Sainsbury & Gibson, 1954; Vaughn, Pall, & Haynes, 1977), but, during an actual headache, their EMG levels are not significantly higher than their already high resting EMG levels (Hutchings & Reinking, 1976; Philips, 1977b; Philips, 1978). Because EMG levels were believed to be the specific cause of tension headaches, biofeedback treatment of tension headaches has focused on reducing frontalis EMG levels. Nuechterlein and Holroyd (1980), in an extensive review of the research literature through 1978, concluded that "EMG biofeedback training, *on the average*, leads to a statistically significant and clinically meaningful reduction of tension headache activity . . . [which] often continues to show improvement over at least several weeks or months subsequent to treatment" (p. 872). They went on, however, to point out that not all tension headache subjects showed improvement using EMG biofeedback. More importantly, they found that, when EMG biofeedback was compared with relaxation techniques, the "evidence suggests that these two modalities are equally effective in the treatment of tension headache . . . [and] issues of cost effectiveness become especially important" (p. 872). The research they reviewed suggests that, although EMG biofeedback is useful, it does not appear to be a specific treatment and is no more useful than general relaxation.

Research conducted since Nuechterlein and Holroyd's (1980) review continues to cast doubt on the efficacy of frontalis EMG biofeedback as a treatment for tension headaches, although not all of the reports are negative. Holroyd, Andrasik, and Noble (1980) compared frontalis EMG biofeedback to meditation and to a self-monitoring control group. They found that only the feedback group reduced EMG levels, and only the feedback group reported significant improvement in headache activity. Although they appeared to have found support for the use of EMG biofeedback, Holroyd et al. (1980) argued that the results did not support the specific efficacy of biofeedback because the two treatments differed on many dimensions other than the use of biofeedback. When they compared frontalis EMG biofeedback to a placebo treatment group, Carrobles, Cardona, and Santacreu (1981) found that, although both groups reduced EMG tension levels, only the feedback group reduced headache activity. Unfortunately, their placebo treatment group consisted of simply telling the subjects, when they came in for EMG measurements, that they would get better. Carrobles et al. (1981) did not include any credibility check to see if subjects believed they were receiving treatment. Also, this study suggested that there was no relationship between EMG levels and headache activity, because both groups reduced EMG, but only the biofeedback group reported relief.

Just as only a few studies support the efficacy of biofeedback, only a few studies tend to find totally negative results using biofeedback. Kremsdorf, Kochanowicz, and Costell (1981) reported that EMG biofeedback was not useful in reducing tension headaches, although it was useful in maintaining headache reduction once it was achieved. They reached these conclusions after treating two patients with different combinations of multiple presentations of EMG biofeedback and a cognitive training task. Russ, Hammer, and Adderton (1979) did not find any significant decrease in headache activity when they combined frontalis EMG biofeedback with relaxation. This negative result could be explained, in part, by the fact that many of their headache patients also had migraine headaches. Cott, Goldman, Pavloski, Kirschberg, and Fabich (1981) also combined frontalis EMG biofeedback with relaxation and compared it to simple relaxation. They found equivalent symptom reduction in both groups and concluded that there was no specific main effect of biofeedback.

Other researchers have focused on the relationship between EMG tension levels and headache activity because many of the earlier studies had not found a consistent relationship between EMG levels and headache activity (Cox, Freundlich, & Meyer, 1975; Epstein & Abel, 1977; Haynes et al., 1975; Holroyd & Andrasik, 1978; Holroyd, Andrasik, & Westbrook, 1977; Kremsdorf, 1978; Martin & Mathews, 1978; Philips, 1977a; Philips, 1978). Hart and Cichanski (1981) trained patients in either frontalis EMG biofeedback or biofeedback for neck EMG levels. Although both groups were able to control the appropriate muscle and both groups reported a reduction in headache activity, neither set of EMG changes was significantly correlated with headache symptoms. Cram (1980) trained patients either to decrease frontalis EMG levels or to maintain EMG at the current levels; both groups reported a decrease in headache activity. Andrasik and Holroyd (1980) went one step further. They trained subjects to increase, decrease, or maintain frontalis EMG tension levels. Compared to a control group that monitored their headache activity, all of the treatment groups learned the appropriate EMG control, and all reported significant decreases in headache activity, with no differences among the three groups.

Philips and Hunter (1981), aware that some tension headaches were not associated with elevated EMG levels (Bakal & Kaganov, 1977; Hart & Cichanski, 1975; Martin & Mathews, 1978; Philips, 1977b), used only subjects who did show elevated resting EMG levels and trained them either to raise or to lower their EMG levels. They reported finding no differences in headache activity between the two groups and no correlation between EMG levels on intensity, duration, or frequency of tension headaches. One of the few, if not the only, report of a correlation between EMG level and headache activity came from Janssen (1983a), in a comparison of frontalis EMG biofeedback with a combination of feedback and relaxation and to a waiting list control group.

Blanchard and his associates (Blanchard et al., 1983; Blanchard, Andrasik, Neff, Teders, et al., 1982) took still another approach. Assuming relaxation was as efficient as biofeedback in reducing tension headaches, they questioned whether biofeedback would add anything beyond that attained from relaxation alone. In a very sophisticated study using a large number of subjects, Blanchard, Andrasik, Neff, Teders, et al. (1982) used relaxation procedures to treat subjects with tension headaches. At the end of training, any subject who had not achieved at least 60% improvement was then given frontalis EMG biofeedback training. Blanchard, Andrasik, Neff, Teders, et al. (1982) reported that a substantial number of these subjects showed an additional improvement beyond that achieved with relaxation alone. This suggested that biofeedback could be useful at the point where relaxation stops. On closer inspection, however, Blanchard, Andrasik, Neff, Teders, et al. (1982) discovered that only those individuals who had already shown some improvement with relaxation showed additional improvement with biofeedback; if the relaxation had not helped at all, neither did the biofeedback. Because they did not have a control group that continued to get relaxation therapy, one cannot conclude that the additional improvement was due specifically to biofeedback. Subjects given additional relaxation might have shown parallel improvement.

Blanchard et al. (1983) reported finding no correlation between EMG levels and measures of headache activity. They also designed their study to test other nonspecific effects. They reported that level of therapist training had no effect on clinical improvement, and subject's perception of the therapist as being warm or cold did not effect clinical improvement. There was, however, a significant correlation between headache activity and the regularity with which subjects practiced home relaxation procedures.

The data do not support the efficacy of frontalis EMG biofeedback in the treatment of tension headaches. Any number of relaxation techniques appear to be as useful as EMG biofeedback and considerably more cost efficient.

CONCLUSION

Shapiro and Surwit (1976), in an early review of the biofeedback literature, arrived at the gloomy conclusion that "there is *not one* well controlled scientific study of the effectiveness of biofeedback and operant conditioning in treating a particular physiological disorder" (p. 113). Four years later, in their review of the literature, Katkin and Goldband (1980) concluded that there was "little reason to revise that conclusion" (p. 570). Another 5 years later, it appears, at last, that Shapiro and Surwit's (1976) conclusions can be revised. Serious researchers have been conscientious in their attempts to design well-controlled experiments. Although they are not all as thorough as the double-blind studies of Guglielmi et al. (1982) and Kewman and Roberts (1980), the majority of the recent studies have employed procedures designed to control nonspecific factors. That is the good news. The bad news is that, now that studies are being controlled more adequately, researchers are finding no specific effect of biofeedback, and, in some cases, the data suggest that the particular form of biofeedback most often employed might not be the most appropriate (i.e. hand warming for migraine).

This is not to say that biofeedback is ineffective, only that there appears to be no treatment effect specific to biofeedback. The same results, or often more significant results, can usually be obtained through simpler, less costly relaxation procedures. Taking individual differences into account, it could be the case that certain individuals profit more from biofeedback than from relaxation, not because of any specific effect of biofeedback but because of expectancy effects.

In 1980, Katkin and Goldband concluded their review of biofeedback with a final comment concerning the enormous attention that it has received within the professional community. That message is no less relevant now. Despite the clear lack of experimental evidence to support assertions of its effectiveness as therapy, increasing numbers of clinicians are incorporating biofeedback into their practice. Workshops to train clinical biofeedback practitioners are heavily attended, and many cassette-tape-trained biofeedback practitioners are gainfully employed from one end of the continent to another. It is not uncommon to see secondary sources describe Miller's and Shapiro's remarkable success in treating essential hypertension, even as these authors take great pains to publish clear statements of caution about the actual effectiveness of their treatments. The pattern of enthusiasm is similar in some ways to the enthusiasm shown about the introduction of projective testing, various forms and varieties of psychotherapy, and, within modern medicine, the flirtations with vitamin treatments for cancer and cholesterol reduction for the prevention of heart disease. There is a powerful desire among health and health-related professionals to be able to provide treatment. It is incumbent upon the serious professional to temper that desire with an appreciation of the value of hard evidence and the need for caution and patience.

REFERENCES

Adams, H. E., Webster, J. S., & Graham, L. E. (1976). *Cephalic vasomotor response feedback as a method for modifying migraine headache: Two case studies*. Paper presented at the meeting of the Southeastern Psychological Association, New Orleans, LA.

Alexander, A. B., & Smith, D. D. (1979). Clinical applications of EMG biofeedback. In R. J. Gatchel & K. P. Price (Eds.), *Clinical applications of biofeedback: Appraisal and status* (pp. 112-113). Elmsford, NY: Pergamon Press.

Alexander, A. B., White, P. D., & Wallace, H. M. (1977). Training and transfer of training effects in EMG biofeedback assisted muscular relaxation. *Psychophysiology, 14*, 551-559.

Allen, R. A., & Mills, G. K. (1982). The effects of unilateral plethysmographic feedback of temporal artery activity during migraine head pain. *Journal of Psychosomatic Research, 26*, 133-140.

Andrasik, F., & Holroyd, K. A. (1980). A test of specific and nonspecific effects in the biofeedback treatment of tension headache. *Journal of Consulting and Clinical Psychology, 48*, 575-586.

Andreychuk, T., & Skriver, C. (1975). Hypnosis and biofeedback in the treatment of migraine headache. *International Journal of Clinical and Experimental Hypnosis, 23*, 172-183.

Bakal, D. A., & Kaganov, J. A. (1977). Muscle contraction and migraine headache: A psychophysiological comparison. *Headache, 5*, 208-216.

Barrios, F. X., & Karoly, P. (1983). Treatment expectancy and therapeutic change in treatment of migraine headache: Are they related? *Psychological Reports, 52*, 59-68.

Beasley, J. (1976). Biofeedback in the treatment of migraine headaches. *Dissertation Abstracts International, 36*, (11-B) 5850B-5851B (abstract).

Beaton, R. D. (1984). Frontal, trapezius, and afflicted masseteric electromyographic levels and variability in patients with orofacial/temporomandibular pain-dysfunction prior to and following multimodal biofeedback treatment. *Biofeedback and Self-Regulation, 9*, 90 (abstract).

Benjamins, J. K. (1976). The effectiveness of alpha feedback training and muscle relaxation procedures in systematic desensitization. *Proceedings of the Biofeedback Research Society Seventh Annual Meeting.* Colorado Springs, CO. (p. 5) (abstract).

Benson, H., Shapiro, D., Tursky, B., & Schwartz, G. E. (1971). Decreased systolic blood pressure through operant conditioning techniques in patients with essential hypertension. *Science, 173*, 740-742.

Bertilson, H. S., Bartz, A. E., & Zimmerman, A. D. (1979). Treatment program for borderline hypertension among college students: Relaxation, finger temperature biofeedback, and generalization. *Psychological Reports, 44*, 107-114.

Bild, R. (1976). Cephalic vasomotor response biofeedback as a treatment modality for vascular headache of the migraine type. *Dissertation Abstracts International, 37* (5-B), 2494B (abstract).

Bild, R., & Adams, H. E. (1980). Modification of migraine headaches by cephalic blood volume pulse and EMG biofeedback. *Journal of Consulting and Clinical Psychology, 48*, 51-57.

Birk, L., Crider, A., Shapiro, D., & Tursky, B. (1966). Operant electrodermal conditioning under partial curarization. *Journal of Comparative and Physiological Psychology, 62*, 165-166.

Black, A. H. (1974). Operant autonomic conditioning: The analysis of response mechanisms. In P. A. Obrist, A. H. Black, J. Brener, & L. V. DiCara (Eds.), *Cardiovascular psychophysiology.* Chicago, IL: Aldine.

Blanchard, E. B. (1982). The role of biofeedback in behavioral medicine. *American Journal of Clinical Biofeedback, 5*, 126-130.

Blanchard, E. B., Andrasik, F., Neff, D. F., Arena, J. G., Ahles, T. A., Jurish, S. E., Pallmeyer, T. P., Saunders, N. L., & Teders, S. J. (1982). Biofeedback and relaxation training with three kinds of headache: Treatment effects and their prediction. *Journal of Consulting and Clinical Psychology, 50*, 562-575.

Blanchard, E. B., Andrasik, F., Neff, D. F., Saunders, N. L. Arena, J. G., Pallmeyer, T. P., Teders, S. J., Jurish, S. E., & Rodichok, L. (1983). Four process studies in the behavioral treatment of chronic headache. *Behaviour Research and Therapy, 21*, 209-220.

Blanchard, E. B., Andrasik, F., Neff, D. F., Teders, S. J., Pallmeyer, T. P., Arena, J. G., Jurish, S., Saunders, N. L., Ahles, T. A., & Rodichok, L. (1982). Sequential comparisons of relaxation training and biofeedback in the treatment of three kinds of chronic headaches or, the machines may be necessary some of the time. *Behaviour Research and Therapy, 20*, 469-481.

Blanchard, E. B., & Haynes, M. (1975). Biofeedback treatment of a case of Raynaud's disease. *Journal of Behavior Therapy and Experimental Psychiatry, 6*, 230-234.

Blanchard, E. B., Miller, S. T., Abel, G. G., Haynes, M. R., & Wicker, R. (1979). Evaluation of biofeedback in the treatment of borderline essential hypertension. *Journal of Applied Behavior Analysis, 12*, 99-109.

Blanchard, E. B., Theobald, E. E., Williamson, D. A., Silver, B. V., & Brown, D. A. (1978). Temperature biofeedback in the treatment of migraine headaches: A controlled evaluation. *Archives of General Psychiatry, 35*, 581-588.

Blanchard, E. B., Young, L. D., & Haynes, M. R. (1975). A simple feedback system for the treatment of elevated blood pressure. *Behavior Therapy, 6*, 241-245.

Bleecker, E. R., & Engel, B. T. (1973). Learned control of cardiac rate and cardiac conduction in the Wolff-Parkinson-White syndrome. *New England Journal of Medicine, 288*, 560-562.

Budzynski, T., & Stoyva, J. (1973). Biofeedback techniques in behavior therapy. In D. Shapiro, T. X. Barber, L. V. DiCara, J. Kamiya, N. E. Miller, & J. Stoyva (Eds.), *Biofeedback and self-control 1972: An Aldine annual on the regulation of bodily processes and consciousness.* Chicago: Aldine.

Burish, T. G. (1981). EMG biofeedback in the treatment of stress-related disorders. In C. K. Prokop & L. A. Bradley (Eds.), *Medical psychology: Contributions to behavioral medicine* (pp. 315-421). New York: Academic Press.

Burish, T. G., Hendrix, E. M., & Frost, R. O. (1981). Comparison of frontal EMG biofeedback and several types of relaxation instructions in reducing multiple indices of arousal. *Psychophysiology, 18*, 594-602.

Carlsson, S. G., & Gale, E. N. (1977). Biofeedback in the treatment of long-term temporomandibular joint pain. *Biofeedback and Self-Regulation, 2,* 161–171.

Carlsson, S. G., Gale, E. N., & Ohman, A. (1975). Treatment of temporomandibular joint syndrome with biofeedback training. *Journal of American Dental Association, 91,* 602–605.

Carrobles, J. A. I., Cardona, A., & Santacreu, J. (1981). Shaping and generalization procedures in the EMG biofeedback treatment of tension headache. *British Journal of Clinical Psychology, 20,* 49–56.

Casas, J. M., Beemsterboer, P., & Clark, G. T. (1982). A comparison of stress-reduction behavioral counseling and contingent nocturnal EMG feedback for the treatment of bruxism. *Behaviour Research and Therapy, 20,* 9–15.

Chen, W. (1981). Comparison of sensory modes of biofeedback in relaxation training of frontalis muscle. *Perceptual and Motor Skills, 53,* 875–880.

Chiari, G., & Mosticoni, R. (1979). The treatment of agoraphobia with biofeedback and systematic desensitization. *Journal of Behavior Therapy and Experimental Psychiatry, 10,* 109–113.

Christie, D. J., & Kotses, H. (1973). Bi-directional operant conditioning of the cephalic vasomotor response. *Psychosomatic Research, 17,* 167.

Claghorn, J. L., Mathew, R. J., Largen, J. W., & Meyer, J. S. (1981). Directional effects of skin temperature self-regulation on regional cerebral blood flow in normal subjects and migraine patients. *American Journal of Psychiatry, 138,* 1182–1187.

Clark, G. T., Beemsterboer, P., & Rugh, J. D. (1981). The treatment of nocturnal bruxism using contingent EMG feedback with an arousal task. *Behaviour Research and Therapy, 19,* 451–455.

Cott, A., Goldman, J. A., Pavloski, R. P., Kirschberg, G. J., & Fabich, M. (1981). The long-term therapeutic significance of the addition of electromyographic biofeedback to relaxation training in the treatment of tension headaches. *Behavior Therapy, 12,* 556–559.

Cox, D., Freundlich, A., & Meyer, R. G. (1975). Differential effectiveness of EMG feedback, verbal relaxation instructions, and medication placebo with tension headaches. *Journal of Consulting and Clinical Psychology, 43,* 892–898.

Cram, J. R. (1980). EMG biofeedback and the treatment of tension headache: A systematic analysis of treatment components. *Behavior Therapy, 11,* 699–710.

Crider, A., Schwartz, G. E., & Shnidman, S. (1969). On the criteria for instrumental autonomic conditioning: A reply to Katkin and Murray. *Psychological Bulletin, 71,* 455–461.

Crider, A., Shapiro, D., & Tursky, B. (1966). Reinforcement of spontaneous electrodermal activity. *Journal of Comparative and Physiological Psychology, 61,* 20–27.

Dahlstrom, L., Carlsson, S. G., Gale, E. N., & Jansson, T. G. (1984). Clinical and electromyographic effects of biofeedback training in mandibular dysfunction. *Biofeedback and Self-Regulation, 9,* 37–47.

Daly, E. J., Donn, P. A., Galliher, J. J., & Zimmerman, J. S. (1983). Biofeedback applications to migraine and tension headaches: A double-blinded outcome study. *Biofeedback and Self-Regulation, 8,* 135–152.

Datey, K. K. (1976). Temperature regulation in the management of hypertension. *Proceedings of the Biofeedback Research Society Seventh Annual Meeting,* Colorado Springs, CO. (p. 11) (abstract).

Datey, K. K. (1977). *Biofeedback training and Shavasan in management of hypertension.* Paper presented at the meeting of the Biofeedback Society, Orlando, FL.

Datey, K. K. (1978). Biofeedback training and hypnosis in the management of hypertension. *Biofeedback and Self-Regulation, 3*, 206-207 (abstract).

DeRisi, W. J. (1970). A conditioning approach to the treatment of bruxism. University Microfilms, Ann Arbor, MI.

Diamond, S., & Franklin, M. (1974). *Indications and contraindications for the use of biofeedback therapy in headache patients.* Paper presented at the Biofeedback Research Society Fifth Annual Meeting, Colorado Springs, CO.

DiCara, L. V., & Miller, N. E. (1968). Changes in heart rate instrumentally learned by curarized rats as avoidance responses. *Journal of Comparative and Physiological Psychology, 65*, 8-12.

Dohrman, R. J., & Laskin, D. M. (1978). An evaluation of electromyographic biofeedback in the treatment of myofascial pain-dysfunction syndrome. *Journal of the American Dental Association, 96*, 656-662.

Dworkin, B. R., & Miller, N. E. (1977). Visceral learning in the curarized rat. In G. E. Schwartz & J. Beatty (Eds.), *Biofeedback: Theory and research.* New York: Academic Press.

Elder, S. T., & Eustis, N. K. (1975). Instrumental blood pressure conditioning in out-patient hypertensives. *Behaviour Research and Therapy, 13*, 185-188.

Elder, S. T., Ruiz, Z. R., Deabler, H. L., & Dillenkoffer, R. L. (1973). Instrumental conditioning of diastolic blood pressure in essential hypertensive patients. *Journal of Applied Behavior Analysis, 6*, 377-382.

Engel, B. T., & Bleecker, E. R. (1974). Application of operant conditioning techniques to the control of the cardiac arrhythmias. In P. A. Obrist, A. H. Black, J. Brener, & L. V. DiCara (Eds.), *Cardiovascular psychophysiology.* Chicago, IL: Aldine.

Engel, B. T., & Melmon, L. (1968). Operant conditioning of heart rate in patients with cardiac arrhythmias. *Conditional Reflex. 3*, 130.

Engel, B. T., Nikoomanesh, P., & Schuster, M. M. (1974). Operant conditioning of rectosphincteric responses in the treatment of fecal incontinence. *New England Journal of Medicine, 290*, 646-649.

Epstein, L. H., & Abel, G. G. (1977). An analysis of biofeedback training effects for tension headache patients. *Behavior Therapy, 8*, 37-47.

Feuerstein, M., & Adams, H. E. (1975). *Cephalic vasomotor feedback for the treatment of migraine headache: An alternative therapeutic approach.* Paper presented at the meeting of the Association for Advancement of Behavior Therapy, San Francisco, CA.

Feuerstein, M., & Adams, H. E. (1977). Cephalic vasomotor feedback in the modification of migraine headache. *Biofeedback and Self-Regulation, 2*, 241-254.

Feuerstein, M., Adams, H. E., & Beiman, I. (1976). Cephalic vasomotor and electromyographic feedback in the treatment of combined muscle contraction and migraine headaches in a geriatric case. *Headache, 16*, 232-237.

Frankel, B. L., Patel, D. J., Horwitz, D., Friedewald, W. T., & Gaarder, K. K. (1978). Treatment of hypertension with biofeedback and relaxation techniques. *Psychosomatic Medicine, 40*, 276-293.

Freedman, R. R., Ianni, P., Hale, P., & Lynn, S. (1979). Treatment of Raynaud's phenomenon with biofeedback and cold desensitization. *Psychophysiology, 16*, 182 (abstract).

Freedman, R. R., Ianni, P., & Wenig, P. (1983). Behavioral treatment of Raynaud's disease. *Journal of Consulting and Clinical Psychology, 51*, 539-549.

Freedman, R. R., Lynn, S. J., & Ianni, P. (1978). Biofeedback treatment of Raynaud's phenomenon. *Biofeedback and Self-Regulation, 3*, 320 (abstract).

Freedman, R. R., Lynn, S. J., Ianni, P., & Hale, P. A. (1981). Biofeedback treatment of Raynaud's disease and phenomenon. *Biofeedback and Self-Regulation, 6*, 355-365.

Freedman, R. R., & Papsdorf, J. (1976). Generalization of frontalis EMG biofeedback training to other muscles. *Biofeedback and Self-Regulation, 1*, 333 (abstract).

Friar, L. (1974). Operant training with biofeedback of pulse amplitude decreases in normal and migraine subjects. *Dissertation Abstracts International, 35*, (74-18, 770) 1046B-1048B (abstract).

Friar, L., & Beatty, J. (1976). Migraine: Management by trained control of vasoconstriction. *Journal of Consulting and Clinical Psychology, 44*, 46-53.

Fridlund, A. J., Fowler, S. C., & Pritchard, D. A. (1980). Striate muscle tensional patterning in frontalis EMG biofeedback. *Psychophysiology, 17*, 47-55.

Friedman, H., & Taub, H. A. (1977). The use of hypnosis and biofeedback procedures for essential hypertension. *International Journal of Clinical and Experimental Hypnosis, 25*, 335-347.

Funch, D. P., & Gale, E. N. (1980). Factors associated with nocturnal bruxism and its treatment. *Journal of Behavioral Medicine, 3*, 385-397.

Garrett, B., & Silver, M. (1972). *The use of EMG and alpha biofeedback to relieve test anxiety in college students.* Paper presented at the meeting of the American Psychological Association, Washington, DC.

Gatchel, R. J., Korman, M., Weiss, C. B., Smith D., & Clarke, L. (1978). A multi-response evaluation of EMG biofeedback performance during training and stress-induction conditions. *Psychophysiology, 15*, 253-258.

Gaudette, M., Prins, A., & Kahane, J. (1983). Comparison of auditory and visual feedback for EMG training. *Perceptual and Motor Skills, 56*, 383-386.

Gauthier, J., Bois, R., Allaire, D., & Drolet, M. (1981). Evaluation of skin temperature biofeedback training at two different sites for migraine. *Journal of Behavioral Medicine, 4*, 407-419.

Gessel, A. H. (1975). Electromyographic biofeedback and tricyclic antidepressants in myofascial pain-dysfunction syndrome. Psychological predictors of outcome. *Journal of the American Dental Association, 91*, 1048-1052.

Gessel, A. H., & Alderman, M. M. (1971). Management of myofascial pain dysfunction syndrome of the temporomandibular joints by tension control training. *Psychosomatics, 12*, 302-309.

Glasgow, M. S., Gaarder, K. R., & Engel, B. T. (1982). Behavioral treatment of high blood pressure. II: Acute and sustained effects of relaxation and systolic blood pressure biofeedback. *Psychosomatic Medicine, 44*, 155-170.

Glueck, B. C., & Stroebel, C. F. (1975). Biofeedback and meditation in the treatment of psychiatric illnesses. *Comprehensive Psychiatry, 16*, 303-321.

Goldman, H., Kleinman, K. M., Snow, M. V., Bidus, D. R., & Korol, B. (1975). Relationship between essential hypertension and cognitive functioning: Effects of biofeedback. *Psychophysiology, 12*, 569-573.

Graham, G. (1974). Hypnosis and biofeedback as treatments for migraine headaches. *Dissertation Abstracts International, 35* (5-B) 2428B-2429B (abstract).

Green, E. E., Green, A. M., & Norris, P. A. (1980, March). Self-regulation training for control of hypertension. *Primary Cardiology*, 126-127.

Guglielmi, R. S., Roberts, A. H., & Patterson, R. (1982). Skin temperature biofeedback for Raynaud's disease: A double-blind study. *Biofeedback and Self-Regulation, 7*, 99-120.

Hahn, W. W. (1974). The learning of autonomic responses by curarized animals. In

P. A. Obrist, A. H. Black, J. Brener, & L. V. DiCara (Eds.), *Cardiovascular psychophysiology*, Chicago, IL: Aldine.

Hart, J. D. (1984). Temperature biofeedback, frontal EMG biofeedback, and relaxation training in the treatment of migraine. *Biofeedback and Self-Regulation, 9*, 84–85 (abstract).

Hart, J. D., & Cichanski, K. A. (1975). *Biofeedback as a treatment for headaches: Conceptual and methodological issues.* Paper presented at the meeting of the Association for Advancement of Behavior Therapy, San Francisco, CA.

Hart, J. D., & Cichanski, K. A. (1981). A comparison of frontal EMG biofeedback & neck EMG biofeedback in the treatment of muscle-contraction headache. *Biofeedback and Self-Regulation, 6*, 63–74.

Haynes, S. N., Griffin, P., Mooney, D., & Parise, M. (1975). Electromyographic biofeedback and relaxation instructions in the treatment of muscle contraction headaches. *Behavior Therapy, 6*, 672–678.

Heller, R., & Strang, H. (1973). Controlling bruxism through automated aversive conditioning. *Behaviour Research and Therapy, 11*, 327–329.

Hersen, M., & Barlow, D. M. (1976). *Single case experimental designs.* Elmsford, NY: Pergamon Press.

Holroyd, K. A., & Andrasik, F. (1978). Coping and the self-control of chronic tension headache. *Journal of Consulting and Clinical Psychology, 46*, 1036–1045.

Holroyd, K. A., Andrasik, F., & Noble, J. (1980). A comparison of EMG biofeedback and a credible pseudotherapy in treating tension headache. *Journal of Behavioral Medicine, 3*, 29–39.

Holroyd, K., Andrasik, F., & Westbrook, T. (1977). Cognitive control of tension headache. *Cognitive Therapy Research, 1*, 721–733.

Hutchings, D. F., & Reinking, R. H. (1976). Tension headaches: What form of therapy is most effective? *Biofeedback and Self-Regulation, 1*, 183–190.

Jacobson, A. M., Hackett, T. P., Surman, O., & Silverberg, E. (1973). Raynaud's phenomenon: Treatment with hypnotic and operant technique. *Journal of the American Medical Association, 225*, 739–740.

Jacobson, A. M., Manschreck, T. C., & Silverberg, E. (1979). Behavioral treatment for Raynaud's disease: A comparative study with long-term follow-up. *American Journal of Psychiatry, 136*, 844–846.

Jacobson, A. M., Silverberg, E., Hackett, T., & Manschreck, T. (1978). Treatment of Raynaud's disease: Evaluation of a behavioral approach. *Psychiatria Clinica, 11*, 125–131.

Janman, K., & Daniels, D. (1983). Feedback modality and dimension in voluntary skin temperature control. *Journal of Behavioral Medicine, 6*, 329–333.

Janssen, K. (1983a). Differential effectiveness of EMG-feedback versus combined EMG-feedback and relaxation instructions in the treatment of tension headache. *Journal of Psychosomatic Research, 27*, 243–253.

Janssen, K. (1983b). Treatment of sinus tachycardia with heart-rate feedback. *Journal of Behavioral Medicine, 6*, 109–114.

Jasper, H. H. (1958). Report of committee on methods of clinical examination in EEG: Appendix: The ten-twenty electrode system of the international federation. *Electroencephalography and Clinical Neurophysiology, 10*, 371–375.

Jessup, B. (1978). *Autogenic feedback for migraine: A bidirectional control group study.* Unpublished paper, University of Western Ontario, London, Ontario.

Johnson, W. G., & Turin, A. (1975). Biofeedback treatment of migraine headache: A systematic case study. *Behavior Therapy, 6*, 394–397.

Jones, G. E., & Evans, P. A. (1981). Effectiveness of frontalis feedback training in producing general body relaxation. *Biological Psychology, 12,* 313-320.

Kamiya, J. (1968). Conscious control of brain waves. *Psychology Today, 1,* 57-60.

Katkin, E. S. (1971). *Instrumental autonomic conditioning.* Morristown, NJ: Silver Burdett, General Learning Press.

Katkin, E. S., & Goldband, S. (1979). The placebo effect and biofeedback. In R. Gatchel & K. Price (Eds.), *Clinical applications of biofeedback: Appraisal and status.* Elmsford, NY: Pergamon Press.

Katkin, E. S., & Goldband, S. (1980). Biofeedback. In F. H. Kanfer & A. P. Goldstein (Eds.), *Helping people change* (2nd ed.). Elmsford, NY: Pergamon Press, pp. 537-578.

Katkin, E. S., & Murray, E. N. (1968). Instrumental conditioning of autonomically mediated behavior: Theoretical and methodological issues. *Psychological Bulletin, 70,* 52-68.

Katkin, E. S., Murray, E. N., & Lachman, R. (1969). Concerning instrumental autonomic conditioning: A rejoinder. *Psychological Bulletin, 71,* 462-466.

Kazdin, A. E., & Wilcoxon, L. A. (1976). Systematic desensitization and nonspecific treatment effects: A methodological evaluation. *Psychological Bulletin, 83,* 729-758.

Keefe, F., Surwit, R., & Pilon, R. (1979). A 1-year follow-up of Raynaud's patients treated with behavioral therapy techniques. *Journal of Behavioral Medicine, 2,* 385-391.

Keefe, F. J., Surwit, R. S., & Pilon, R. N. (1980). Biofeedback, autogenic training, and progressive relaxation in the treatment of Raynaud's disease: A comparative study. *Journal of Applied Behavior Analysis, 13,* 3-11.

Kentsmith, D., Strider, F., Copenhaver, J., & Jacques, D. (1976). Effects of biofeedback upon suppression of migraine symptoms and plasma dopamine-B-hydroxylase activity. *Headache, 16,* 173-177.

Kewman, D., & Roberts, A. H. (1980). Skin temperature biofeedback and migraine headache: A double-blind study. *Biofeedback and Self-Regulation, 5,* 327-345.

Kimble, G. A. (1961). *Hilgard and Marquis' conditioning and learning* (2nd ed.). New York: Appleton-Century.

Kimmel, E., & Kimmel H. D. (1963). A replication of operant conditioning of the GSR. *Journal of Experimental Psychology, 65,* 212-213.

Kimmel, H. D. (1967). Instrumental conditioning of autonomically mediated behavior. *Psychological Bulletin, 67,* 337-345.

Kimmel, H. D., & Hill, F. A. (1960). Operant conditioning of the GSR. *Psychological Reports, 7,* 555-562.

Kimmel, H. D., & Sternthal, H. S. (1967). Replication of GSR avoidance conditioning with concomitant EMG measurement and subjects matched in responsivity and conditionability. *Journal of Experimental Psychology, 74,* 144-146.

Kleinman, K. M., Goldman, H., Snow, M. V., & Korol, B. (1977). Relationship between essential hypertension and cognitive functioning. II. Effects of biofeedback training generalize to non-laboratory environment. *Psychophysiology, 14,* 192-197.

Knapp, T. W. (1982). Treating migraine by training in temporal artery vasoconstriction and/or cognitive behavioral coping: A one-year follow-up. *Journal of Psychosomatic Research, 26,* 551-557.

Koppman, J. W., McDonald, R. D., & Kunzel, B. A. (1974). Voluntary regulation of temporal artery diameter by migraine patients. *Headache, 14,* 133.

Kotses, H., & Glaus, K. D. (1982). Generalization of conditioned muscle tension: Sharpening the focus. *Psychophysiology, 19*, 498-500.

Kremsdorf, R. R. (1978). *Biofeedback and cognitive skills training: An evaluation of their relative efficacy.* Paper presented at the Ninth meeting of the Biofeedback Society of America, Albuquerque, NM.

Kremsdorf, R. R., Kochanowicz, N. A., & Costell, S. (1981). Cognitive skills training versus EMG biofeedback in the treatment of tension headache. *Biofeedback and Self-Regulation, 6*, 93-102.

Kristt, D. A., & Engel, B. T. (1975). Learned control of blood pressure in patients with high blood pressure. *Circulation, 51*, 370-378.

LaCroix, M., Clarke, M. A., Bock, J. C., Doxey, N., Wood, A., & Lavis, S. (1983). Biofeedback and relaxation in the treatment of migraine headaches: Comparative effectiveness and physiological correlates. *Journal of Neurology, Neurosurgery, and Psychiatry, 46*, 525-532.

Lang, P. J. (1974). Learned control of human heart rate in a computer directed environment. In P. A. Obrist, A. H. Black, J. Brener, & L. V. DiCara (Eds.), *Cardiovascular psychophysiology.* Chicago, IL: Aldine.

Largen, J. W., Mathew, R. J., Dobbins, K., Meyer, J. S., Sakai, F., & Claghorn, J. L. (1979). *The effects of direction of skin temperature self-regulation on migraine activity and cerebral blood flow.* Paper presented at the meeting of the Biofeedback Society of America, San Diego, CA.

Lavellee, Y., Lamontagne, Y., Annable, L., & Fontaine, F. (1982). Characteristics of chronically anxious patients who respond to EMG feedback training. *Journal of Clinical Psychiatry, 43*, 229-230.

LeBoeuf, A. (1980). Effects of frontalis biofeedback on subjective ratings of relaxation. *Perceptual and Motor Skills, 50*, 99-103.

Lick, J., & Bootzin, R. (1975). Expectancy factors in the treatment of fear: Methodological and theoretical issues. *Psychological Bulletin, 82*, 917-931.

Luborsky, L., Crits-Christoph, P., Brady, J. P., Kron, R. E., Weiss, T., Cohen, M., & Levy, L. (1982). Behavioral versus pharmacological treatments for essential hypertension: A needed comparison. *Psychosomatic Medicine, 44*, 203-213.

Martin, P. R., & Mathews, A. M. (1978). Tension headache: A psychophysiological investigation. *Journal of Psychosomatic Research, 22*, 389-399.

McGrady, A. V., Yonker, R., Tan, S. Y., Fine, T. H., & Woerner, M. (1981). The effect of biofeedback-assisted relaxation training on blood pressure and selected biochemical parameters in patients with essential hypertension. *Biofeedback and Self-Regulation, 6*, 343-353.

Medina, J. L., Diamond, S., & Franklin, M. A. (1976). Biofeedback therapy for migraine. *Headache, 16*, 115-118.

Miller, N. E. (1969). Learning of visceral and glandular responses. *Science, 163*, 434-445.

Miller, N. E. (1972). Learning of glandular and visceral responses: Postscript. In D. Singh & C. T. Mogan (Eds.), *Current status of physiological psychology: Readings.* Monterey, CA: Brooks/Cole.

Miller, N. E. (1975). Clinical applications of biofeedback: Voluntary control of heart rate, rhythm, and blood pressure. In H. I. Russek (Ed.), *New horizons in cardiovascular practice.* Baltimore, MD: University Park Press.

Miller, N. E., & DiCara, L. (1967). Instrumental learning of heart rate changes in curarized rats: Shaping and specificity to discriminative stimulus. *Journal of Comparative and Physiological Psychology, 63*, 12-19.

Miller, N. E, & Dworkin, B. R. (1974). Visceral learning: Recent difficulties with curarized rats and significant problems for human research. In P. A. Obrist, A. H. Black, J. Brener, & L. V. DiCara (Eds.), *Cardiovascular psychophysiology.* Chicago, IL: Aldine.

Mitch, P. S., McGrady, A., & Iannone, A. (1976). Autogenic feedback training in migraine: A treatment report. *Headache, 15,* 267–270.

Moeller, L. E. (1976). EMG biofeedback facilitation of progressive relaxation and autogenic training: A comparative study. *Dissertation Abstracts International, 36,* 4168B (abstract).

Mullinix, J. M., Norton, B. J., Hock, S., & Fishman, M. A. (1978). Skin temperature biofeedback and migraine. *Headache, 17,* 242–244.

Nuechterlein, K. H., & Holroyd, J. C. (1980). Biofeedback in the treatment of tension headache: Current status. *Archives of General Psychiatry, 37,* 866–873.

Nunes, J., & Marks, I. (1975). Feedback of true heart rate during exposure to vivo. *Archives of General Psychiatry, 32,* 933–936.

Obrist, P. A., Light, K. C., McCubbin, J. A., Hutcheson, J. S., & Hoffer, J. L. (1978). Pulse transit time: Relationship to blood pressure. *Behavior Research Methods & Instrumentation, 10,* 623–626.

O'Connell, M. F., Frerker, D. L., & Russ, K. L. (1979). The effects of feedback sensory modality, feedback information content, and sex on short-term biofeedback training of three responses. *Psychophysiology, 16,* 438–444.

O'Connell, M. F., & Yeaton, S. P. (1981). Generalized muscle changes during EMG relaxation training. *Psychophysiology, 18,* 56–61.

Orlando, A. B. (1974). *Learned self-regulation of arterial hypertension utilizing biofeedback and relaxation training.* Unpublished doctoral dissertation, University of Florida, Gainesville, FL.

Orne, M. T., & Paskewitz, D. A. (1974). Aversive situational effects on alpha feedback training. *Science, 186,* 458–460.

Patel, C. H. (1973). Yoga and biofeedback in the management of hypertension. *Lancet, 7837,* 1053–1055.

Patel, C. H. (1976). Biofeedback as therapy with particular emphasis on hypertension. *Proceedings of the Biofeedback Research Society Seventh Annual Meeting,* Colorado Springs, CO. p. 57 (abstract).

Patel, C., Marmot, M. G., & Terry, D. J. (1981). Controlled trial of biofeedback-aided behavioural methods in reducing mild hypertension. *British Medical Journal, 6281,* 2005–2008.

Patel, C. H., & North, W. R. S. (1975). Randomized controlled trial of yoga and biofeedback in management of hypertension. *Lancet, 2,* 93–99.

Paul, G. L. (1969). Physiological effects of relaxation training and hypnotic suggestion. *Journal of Abnormal Psychology, 74,* 425–437.

Pearse, B., Walters, E., Sargent, J., & Meers, M. (1975). *Exploratory observations of the use of an intensive autogenic biofeedback training (IAFT) procedure in a follow-up study of out-of-town patients having migraine or tension headaches.* Paper presented at the meeting of the Biofeedback Research Society, Monterey, CA.

Philips, C. (1977a). The modification of tension headache pain using EMG biofeedback. *Behaviour Research and Therapy, 15,* 119–129.

Philips, C. (1977b). A psychological analysis of tension headaches. In S. Rachman (Ed.), *Contributions to medical psychology* (Vol I, pp. 91–113). Oxford: Pergamon Press.

Philips, C. (1978). Tension headache: Theoretical problems. *Behaviour Research and Therapy, 16*, 249–261.

Philips, C., & Hunter, M. (1981). The treatment of tension headache. I: Muscular abnormality and biofeedback. *Behaviour Research and Therapy, 19*, 485–498.

Piccione, A., Coates, T. J., George, J. M., Rosenthal, D., & Karzmark, P. (1982). Nocturnal biofeedback for nocturnal bruxism. *Biofeedback and Self-Regulation, 7*, 405–419.

Plotkin, W. B. (1976). On the self-regulation of the occipital alpha rhythm: Control strategies, states of consciousness, and the role of physiological feedback. *Journal of Experimental Psychology: General, 105*, 66–99.

Plotkin, W. B. (1978). Long-term eyes-closed alpha-enhancement training: Effects on alpha amplitude and on experiential state. *Psychophysiology, 15*, 40–52.

Plotkin, W. B., & Cohen, R. (1976). Occipital alpha and the attributes of the "alpha experience." *Psychophysiology, 13*, 16–21.

Plotkin, W. B., & Rice, K. M. (1981). Biofeedback as a placebo: Anxiety reduction facilitated by training in either suppression or enhancement of alpha brainwaves. *Journal of Consulting and Clinical Psychology, 49*, 590–596.

Pope, A. T. (1978). Electrical safety in the use of biofeedback instruments. *Behavior Research Methods & Instrumentaion, 10*, 627–631.

Pozniak-Patewicz, E. (1976). "Cephalgic" spasm of head and neck muscles. *Headache, 15*, 261–266.

Price, K. P., & Tursky, B. (1976). Vascular reactivity of migraineurs and non-migraineurs: A comparison of responses to self-control procedures. *Headache, 16*, 210.

Prignatano, G., & Johnson, H. (1972). Biofeedback control of heart rate variability to phobic stimuli: A new approach to treating spider phobia. *Proceedings of the 80th Annual American Psychological Association Convention* (pp. 403–404). Washington, DC.

Principato, J. J., & Barwell, D. R. (1978). Biofeedback training and relaxation exercises for treatment of temporomandibular joint dysfunction. *Journal for Oto-Rhino-Laryngology and its Borderlands, 86*, 766–769.

Rappaport, A. F., Cammer, L., Cannistraci, A. J., Gelb, H., & Strong, D. (1975). *EMG feedback for the treatment of bruxism: A stress control program.* Paper presented at the Sixth Meeting of the Biofeedback Research Society, Monterey, CA.

Raskin, M., Bali, L. R., & Peeke, H. V. (1980). Muscle biofeedback and transcendental meditation: A controlled evaluation of efficacy in the treatment of chronic anxiety. *Archives of General Psychiatry, 37*, 93–97.

Reeves, J. L., & Mealiea, W. L. (1975). Biofeedback assisted cue-controlled relaxation for the treatment of flight phobias. *Journal of Behavior Therapy and Experimental Psychiatry, 6*, 105–109.

Richter-Heinrich, E., Homuth, V., Heinrich, B., Schmidt, K. H., Wiedemann, R., & Gohlke, H. R. (1981). Long-term application of behavioral treatments in essential hypertension. *Physiology and Behavior, 26*, 915–920.

Roberts, L. E. (1974). Comparative psychophysiology of the electrodermal and cardiac control systems. In P. A. Obrist, A. H. Black, J. Brener, & L. V. DiCara (Eds.), *Cardiovascular psychophysiology.* Chicago: Aldine.

Rugh, J. D., & Johnson, R. W. (1981). Temporal analysis of nocturnal bruxism during EMG biofeedback. *Journal of Periodontology, 52*, 263–265.

Rugh, J. D., & Solberg, W. K. (1975). Electromyographic studies of bruxist behavior before and during treatment. *California Dental Association Journal, 3,* 56–59.

Rupert, P. A., Dobbins, K., & Mathew, R. J. (1981). EMG biofeedback and relaxation instructions in the treatment of chronic anxiety. *American Journal of Clinical Biofeedback, 4,* 52–61.

Rupert, P. A., & Holmes, D. S. (1978). Effects of multiple sessions of true and placebo heart rate biofeedback training on the heart rates and anxiety levels of anxious patients during and following treatment. *Psychophysiology, 15,* 582–590.

Russ, K. L., Hammer, R. L., & Adderton, M. (1979). Clinical follow-up: Treatment and outcome of functional headache patients treated with biofeedback. *Journal of Clinical Psychology, 35,* 148–153.

Sainsbury, P., & Gibson, J. G. (1954). Symptoms of anxiety and tension and the accompanying physiological changes in the muscular system. *Journal of Neurology, Neurosurgery, and Psychiatry, 17,* 216–224.

Sappington, J. T. (1977). *Operant conditioning of peripheral vasodilation in Raynaud's disease: A case study.* Paper presented at the meeting of the Southeastern Psychological Association, Hollywood, FL.

Sargent, J. D. (1984). Results of a controlled, experimental, outcome study of non-drug treatments for the control of migraine headache. *Biofeedback and Self-Regulation, 9,* 106 (abstract).

Sargent, J. D., Green, E. E., & Walters, E. D. (1972). The use of autogenic feedback training in a pilot study of migraine and tension headaches. *Headache, 12,* 120–125.

Sargent, J. D., Green, E. E., & Walters, E. D. (1973). Preliminary report on the use of autogenic feedback training in the treatment of migraine and tension headaches. *Psychosomatic Medicine, 35,* 129–135.

Savill, G. E., & Koppman, J. W. (1975). *Voluntary temporal artery regulation compared with finger blood volume and temperature.* Paper presented at the Sixth Meeting of the Biofeedback Research Society, Monterey, CA.

Schandler, S. L., & Grings, W. W. (1978). Feedback modalities as a consideration in biofeedback application. *Behavior Research Methods and Instrumentation, 10,* 597–606.

Schwartz, G. E., & Shapiro, D. (1973). Biofeedback and essential hypertension: Current findings and theoretical concerns. *Seminars in Psychiatry, 5,* 493–503.

Scott, R. W., Blanchard, E. B., Edmunson, E. D., & Young, L. D. (1973). A shaping procedure for heart rate control in chronic tachycardia. *Perceptual and Motor Skills, 37,* 327–338.

Sedlacek, K. (1976). EMG and thermal feedback as a treatment for Raynaud's disease. *Biofeedback and Self-Regulation, 1,* 318 (abstract).

Sedlacek, K. (1979). Biofeedback for Raynaud's disease. *Psychosomatics, 20,* 535–541.

Sedlacek, K. W., & Cohen, J. (1978). Biofeedback treatment in essential hypertension. *Biofeedback and Self-Regulation, 3,* 207 (abstract).

Shapiro, D., Crider, A. B., & Tursky, B. (1964). Differentiation of an autonomic response through operant reinforcement. *Psychonomic Science, 1,* 147–148.

Shapiro, D., & Katkin, E. S. (1980). Psychophysiological disorders. In A. E. Kazdin, A. S. Bellack, & M. Hersen (Eds.), *New perspectives in abnormal psychology* (pp. 227–243). New York: Oxford University Press.

Shapiro, D., & Surwit, R. S. (1976). Learned control of physiological functions and disease. In H. Leitenberg (Ed.), *Handbook of behavior modification and behavior therapy.* Englewood Cliffs, NJ: Prentice-Hall.

Sheidivy, D. J., & Kleinman, K. M. (1977). Lack of correlation between frontalis EMG and either neck or verbal ratings of tension. *Psychophysiology, 14,* 182-186.

Shoemaker, J. E., & Tasto, D. L. (1975). The effects of muscle relaxation on blood pressure of essential hypertensives. *Behaviour Research and Therapy, 13,* 29-43.

Siddle, D. A. T., & Wood, L. (1978). Effects of frontalis EMG feedback on frontalis tension level, cardiac activity and electrodermal activity. *Biological Psychology, 7,* 169-173.

Smith, K. (1954). Conditioning as an artifact. *Psychological Review, 61,* 217-225.

Stenn, P. G., Mothersill, K. J., & Brooke, R. I. (1979). Biofeedback and a cognitive behavioral approach to treatment of myofascial pain dysfunction syndrome. *Behavior Therapy, 10,* 29-36.

Stephenson, N. E. (1976). Two cases of successful treatment of Raynaud's disease with relaxation and biofeedback training and supportive psychotherapy. *Biofeedback and Self-regulation, 1,* 318-319 (abstract).

Steptoe, A., Smulyan, H., & Gribbin, B. (1976). Pulse wave velocity and blood pressure change: Calibration and applications. *Psychophysiology, 13,* 488-493.

Stoyva, J., & Budzynski, T. (1974). Cultivated low arousal—an antistress response? In L. DiCara (Ed.), *Limbic and autonomic nervous system research.* New York: Plenum.

Stroebel, C. F., Ford. M. R., Strong, P., & Szarek, B. L. (1981). *Quieting response training: Five-year follow-up of a clinical biofeedback practice.* Paper presented at the Twelfth Meeting of the Biofeedback Society of America, Louisville, KY.

Sturgis, E. T., Tollison, C. D., & Adams, H. E. (1978). Modification of combined migraine-muscle contraction headaches using BVP and EMG biofeedback. *Journal of Applied Behavior Analysis, 11,* 215-223.

Sundermann, R. H., & Delk, J. L. (1978). Treatment of Raynaud's disease with temperature biofeedback. *Southern Medical Journal, 71,* 340-342.

Surwit, R. (1973). A possible treatment for Raynaud's disease. *Seminars in Psychiatry, 5,* 483-489.

Surwit, R. S., Pilon, R. N., & Fenton, C. H. (1978). Behavioral treatment of Raynaud's disease. *Journal of Behavioral Medicine, 1,* 323-335.

Surwit, R. S., Shapiro, D., & Good, J. I. (1978). Comparison of cardiovascular biofeedback, neuromuscular biofeedback, and meditation in the treatment of borderline essential hypertension. *Journal of Consulting and Clinical Psychology, 46,* 252-263.

Taub, E. (1977). Self-regulation of human tissue temperature. In G. Schwartz & J. Beatty (Eds.), *Biofeedback: Theory and Research.* New York: Academic Press.

Thompson, C. (1977). Autogenic feedback training: The effect of outcome and accessibility of hand temperature biofeedback on the reduction of migraine headaches. *Dissertation Abstracts International, 37* (7-B), 3635B-3636B.

Travis, T. A., Kondo, C. Y., & Knott, J. R. (1975). Alpha enhancement research: A review. *Biological Psychiatry, 10,* 69-89.

Turin, A. C. (1977). Biofeedback and suggestion in finger temperature training: An effect for the controls but not the "treatment." *Biofeedback and Self-Regulation, 2,* 296.

Turin, A., & Johnson, W. G. (1976). Biofeedback therapy for migraine headaches. *Archives of General Psychiatry, 33,* 517-519.

Tursky, B., Shapiro, D., & Schwartz, G. E. (1972). Automated constant cuff-pressure system for measuring average systolic and diastolic blood pressure in man. *IEEE Transactions on Biomedical Engineering, 19,* 271-275.

Valle, R. S., & Levine, J. M. (1975). Expectation effects in alpha wave control. *Psychophysiology, 12*, 306–310.

Vaughn, R., Pall, M. L., & Haynes, S. N. (1977). Frontalis response to stress in subjects with frequent muscle-contraction headaches. *Headache, 16*, 313–317.

Wallace, R. K. (1970). Physiological effects of transcendental meditation. *Science, 167*, 1751–1754.

Wallace, R. K., & Benson, H. (1972). The physiology of meditation. *Scientific American, 226*, 85–90.

Walsh, D. H. (1974). Interactive effects of alpha feedback and instructional set on subjective state. *Psychophysiology, 11*, 428–435.

Weinstock, S. (1973). A tentative procedure for control of pain: Migraine and tension headaches. In D. Shapiro, T. Barber, L. DiCara, J. Kamiya, N. Miller, & J. Stoyva (Eds.), *Biofeedback and self-control*. Chicago, IL: Aldine.

Weiss, T., & Engel, B. T. (1970). Voluntary control of premature ventricular contractions in patients. *American Journal of Cardiology, 26*, 666 (abstract).

Weiss, T., & Engel, B. T. (1971). Operant conditioning of heart rate in patients with premature ventricular contractions. *Psychosomatic Medicine, 33*, 301–321.

Welgan, P. R. (1974). Learned control of gastric acid secretions in ulcer patients. *Psychosomatic Medicine, 36*, 411–419.

Weston, A. (1974). *Perception of autonomic processes, social acquiescence, and cognitive development of a sense of self-control in essential hypertensives trained to lower blood pressure using biofeedback procedures*. Unpublished doctoral dissertation, Nova University, Fort Lauderdale, FL.

Whitehead, W. E., Renault, P. E., & Goldiamond, I. (1975). Modification of human gastric acid secretion with operant-conditioning procedures. *Journal of Applied Behavior Analysis, 8*, 147–156.

Wickramasekera, I. (1972). Instructions and EMG feedback in systematic desensitization: A case report. *Behavior Therapy, 3*, 461–465.

Wickramasekera, I. (1973). Temperature feedback for the control of migraine. *Journal of Behavior Therapy and Experimental Psychiatry, 4*, 343–345.

Zamani, R. (1974). Treatment of migraine headache through operant conditioning of vasoconstriction. University Microfilms, Ann Arbor, MI.

11

Group Methods

Sheldon D. Rose

The group consisted of five women and three men in their late 20s and 30s. All were unmarried. This was the fifth session of the group designed to help "singles" cope more effectively with their unique stresses. As the group settled into places on the floor or on chairs, Harriet, the group therapist, welcomed them and asked each member to review what he or she had done throughout the week to complete the assignment of the previous week. One at a time, members described their social achievements, their success in coping with anxiety, and the frequency with which they used the relaxation exercise. Several also related unusually stressful situations they had experienced during the week.

After each had summarized her or his experiences, amid a great deal of praise and support from group members for achievements, Delores volunteered to describe in some detail her situation, in which her ever present feelings of helplessness were intensified. Her supervisor at her office, she stated, was always giving her instructions on the least little thing. "It was as if she thought I was stupid and, frankly, I'm beginning to believe it." The other members inquired as to the nature of her job, which was quite complicated. They noted that she did receive good feedback from her peers, who often consulted with her with various problems. She also noted that in a previous job no one gave her more than the briefest instructions, and she did fine. Charles wondered whether she couldn't conclude that there was a problem between her and her supervisor and not with her as a person. There was just no evidence that she was dumb in any way; in fact, she appeared to be uniquely qualified to do the job. The others agreed.

Delores said she guessed they were right, but she didn't know what to do about it, and it was making her miserable. She had thought about quitting, but it was in other ways a good job; and besides, she added, "good jobs were hard to get these days."

The other clients then provided her with a number of strategies she could employ to deal with the situation and suggested what she could specifically say to herself and to her supervisor. She evaluated and selected several from among these for practice in the group.

This excerpt is taken from the beginning of a behavior group therapy session. Such therapy within the context of the group focuses on the development of cognitive, affective, and social coping skills necessary to improve

437

the quality of each client's relationships with others and to help each to cope more effectively with the numerous stress and problematic situations with which he or she is confronted. Through such procedures, a client is helped to learn not only a wide variety of verbal and nonverbal coping behaviors and cognitive skills, but also to differentiate among those situations that require the application of such skills. Essential in this process is the mutual support, teaching, demonstrations, and feedback of the clients to each other. However, this does not mean that complex problems cannot be dealt with in a group. Behavior and cognitive-behavior group therapy can be looked upon as a continuum from short-term training to intensive long-term therapy (Shoemaker, 1977). At the training end of the continuum, groups focus on teaching a narrow range of highly specific behaviors such as assertion, parenting skills, marital communication, and stress reduction. The tools are brief lecture, specific social interactive exercises, and a limited range of the earlier-mentioned interventions, especially social skill training. Because of the restricted number of sessions, a highly specific agenda at each meeting is used, and only limited flexibility is permitted. Most research on small group therapy has evaluated this type of program.

At the intensive therapy end of the continuum, all the interventions mentioned are used as needed, but individualization is much greater. Group problems and processes are dealt with as learning experiences, and the structured exercises used in training are also included if the group members reveal a common need. Moreover, the problems are usually more complex and more varied in therapy groups than in the training groups. Because of greater individualization, more attention is also given to pregroup assessment in the long-term therapy groups than in short-term training groups. In general, however, both groups at different extremes of the continuum follow many of the same principles described in this chapter.

What kinds of clients are seen in behavioral group therapy? Most group members present at least one and often several of the following problems: social skill deficits, depression, phobias, anxiety, stress, sexual disorders, pain management, anger or violence control, obesity or weight control, alcohol and drug abuse, and child management. In the short-term groups, most members are referred or refer themselves for one of these problems in response to a group specifically available for that given problem, that is, a parent-training group, an assertiveness group, a weight loss group. Because all members have similar problems, the assumption is that one can work more quickly on the specific area if everyone has similar goals. In the longer term groups a more heterogeneous composition in terms of presenting problems is possible.

What all these groups of clients hold in common is the use of the group as the context of therapy. This context provides a number of unique possibilities (discussed later) that the group therapist assumes can enhance (but can also hinder) the therapeutic process. Therapists tend to vary in their use of group strategies and in their dealing with group phenomena. The approach described in this chapter emphasizes how the more common behavioral and cognitive-behavioral strategies can be uniquely applied in the group context and how an assortment of strategies unique to the group can be incorporated into the approach.

To survive in a group and in social situations in general, a minimum of social skills is necessary. For these reasons, in almost every type of behavioral group therapy, some form of social skill training is required. For those clients who have social skill deficiencies, social skill training could represent the major intervention strategy.

Early evidence suggests that social skill deficits are related to major psychiatric problem areas. Lewinsohn and his associates have demonstrated a link between interpersonal deficits and such clinical phenomena as depression (Lewinsohn, Weinstein, & Alper, 1970; Libet & Lewinsohn, 1973). Argyle (1969) has analyzed how social skill deficits can precede a variety of other clinical syndromes. Many strategies are used to reduce these deficits, one of the most important of which is the social skill training sequence. This sequence includes modeling, behavior rehearsal, coaching, and group feedback. Examples of all these are found throughout this chapter.

Of course, some persons who might not be deficient in social skills are still unable to perform these skills that enable them to relate to others or to solve social problems without high levels of anxiety or other distress. For these clients, it appears that certain interpersonal and intrapersonal events are accompanied by or evoke distorted cognitions, which in turn elicit anxiety and other strong emotions. Under intense anxiety, the performance of adaptive or coping behavior is limited or even inhibited. For these persons, cognitive procedures such as stress inoculation (Meichenbaum, 1977) or cognitive restructuring (Mahoney & Arnkoff, 1978) can be combined with social skill training procedures to enhance social functioning and reduce anxiety (Thorpe, 1975).

A general cognitive strategy that is used alone or incorporated into social skill training or cognitive restructuring is systematic problem solving. Problem solving is a procedure used in all behavior therapy groups in one form or another.

Several studies have shown that emotionally distressed individuals are not very efficient at solving problems (see, for example, Platt, Scuro, & Hammon, 1973; Spivack & Levine, 1963). Emotionally distressed individuals tend to use more impulsive and aggressive solutions to problematic situations and are less capable of means-ends thinking than their "normal" peers (Shure & Spivack, 1972). The term *problem solving* has been used to explain a particular systematic process that leads step by step to the resolution of problematic situations experienced by the client.

In problem-solving training, the client learns to systematically work through a set of steps for analyzing a problem, discovering new approaches, evaluating those approaches, and developing strategies for implementing those approaches in the real world. In groups, problem solving is taught through exercises in which each person brings a problem to the group, and the group goes explicitly through the various steps. This technique is also demonstrated when group problems arise and must be dealt with. Moreover, a review of Figures 11.1 and 11.2 reveals that both social skill training and cognitive restructuring involve the client in the major steps of the problem-solving process. For further information and a review of empirical support for the efficacy of the problem-solving process, the reader is referred to Heppner (1978). Thus, behavior group therapy, as it is described here, permits the integrated use of (a) social skills training; (b) cognitive therapy, especially cognitive restructuring and stress inoculation; (c) systematic problem-solving; and (d) group theory as four major sources of intervention to enhance client social functioning. Let us examine in some detail other characteristics and assumptions about the nature of the group in which these procedures take place.

THE GROUP CONTEXT

The most crucial aspect of group therapy is the context in which it takes place. A number of advantages and limitations of the group are assumed that both guide and constrain the therapist's role. The most fundamental assumption is that the presence of other clients provides a unique opportunity for practicing new social interactional skills with peers in a protected setting.

The group provides clients with an opportunity to recognize and change many behaviors and cognitions as they respond to the constantly changing group demands and challenges. The group structure encourages clients to offer other clients feedback about their behavior and to offer advice about new behaviors. As a result, clients in groups develop important skills for leadership and self-therapy. Furthermore, by helping others, clients are also afforded practice in the skills required to help themselves.

As clients interact with each other, powerful norms are developed that serve to enhance protherapeutic behavior. If these norms (informal agreements among members as to preferred modes of action and interaction in the group) are introduced and effectively maintained by the group therapist, they serve as efficient therapeutic tools. The group will pressure its members who manifest deviant behaviors to conform to such group norms

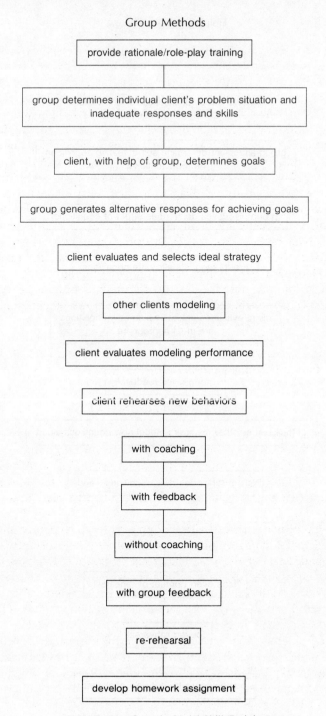

FIGURE 11.1. Steps in Social Skill Training

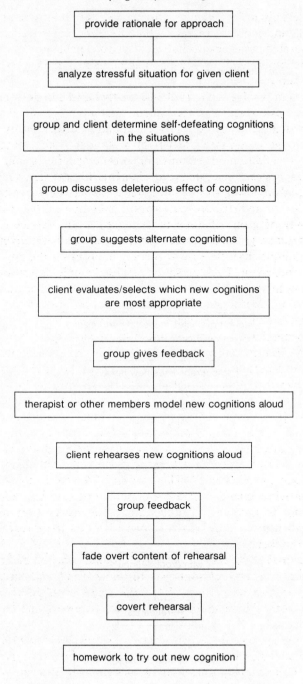

provide rationale for approach

analyze stressful situation for given client

group and client determine self-defeating cognitions in the situations

group discusses deleterious effect of cognitions

group suggests alternate cognitions

client evaluates/selects which new cognitions are most appropriate

group gives feedback

therapist or other members model new cognitions aloud

client rehearses new cognitions aloud

group feedback

fade overt content of rehearsal

covert rehearsal

homework to try out new cognition

FIGURE 11.2. Steps in Cognitive Restructuring

as honest self-disclosing, regular attendance, peer reinforcement of those who do well, and problem analysis. Of course, antitherapeutic norms might also be generated in groups, as indicated by such behaviors as erratic attendance, noncompletion of agreed-upon assignments, and excessive criticism of other group members.

To prevent or resolve such problems, the therapist can draw upon a modest body of basic research about norms and other group phenomena in which individual behavior both influences and is influenced by the various attributes of the group (see Cartwright & Zander, 1968, for an extensive summary). In addition to establishing protherapeutic or antitherapeutic norms, therapists can facilitate the attainment of both individual and group treatment goals by using strategies designed to increase the cohesiveness of the group or to redistribute patterns of communication. Much of the unique power of group therapy is harnessed to the service of defeating change if negative group attributes are not dealt with effectively.

Another unique characteristic of therapy in groups is the opportunity for mutual reinforcement. Each person is afforded ample opportunity to learn or to improve his or her ability to mediate rewards for others in social interactive situations (with family, friendship groups, the work group). The therapist can structure a therapeutic situation in which each person has frequent opportunities, instructions, and even rewards for reinforcing others in the group. Reinforcement is a valued skill in our society. Research suggests that, as a person learns to reinforce others, he or she is reciprocally reinforced by others, and mutual liking increases (Lott & Lott, 1961).

Opportunity for more precise assessment is another advantage of group therapy. As group members assess an individual's report about a situation, many aspects of that situation that would escape even the most sensitive therapist are often clearly revealed during the intensive group discussion. This is helpful, especially when clients cannot readily pinpoint what is problematic in their behavior. The group, more effectively than a single therapist, provides clients with a major source of feedback about what in their behavior is annoying to others and what makes them attractive to others. Furthermore, feedback from peers is often more readily accepted than from the therapist.

The group makes available a variety of models, coaches, and role-players for behavioral rehearsal, personpower for monitoring, and partners for use in a buddy system or pairing off of one client with another for work between sessions. These supportive roles are learned as part of the therapeutic process.

Because the group supplies so many of its own therapeutic needs and offers simultaneous treatment to a number of people, this type of therapy appears to be less costly than individual treatment in terms of staff and money. Almost all research has shown that group therapy is at least as effective as, and less expensive than, individual treatment (see the discussion of relevant research).

Finally, the group serves as a check to keep the group therapist from imposing his or her values on individual clients. Clients in groups appear to be less accepting of the arbitrary values proposed by therapists than clients in dyads. A group of people can readily support each other in their disagreement with the therapist. The group therapist is constantly forced by group members to make his or her values explicit.

Several disadvantages of groups have also been noted. First, as already mentioned, antitherapeutic norms can develop, especially in highly cohesive groups. This atmosphere could work against effective treatment. If identified early, however, it is possible to examine the norms and work together to change them.

When the group is highly structured, as it is in behavioral group therapy, additional disadvantages can be noted. Although a group contract might prevent excessive wandering to irrelevant topics, it could also serve to deter exploration of the idiosyncratic needs of any one individual. Each person needs to be allotted some time at every meeting to discuss unique problems. Therefore, no one or two persons can be permitted to dominate an entire session. For the clients whose needs are pressing, it might be difficult to wait a turn.

Another potential disadvantage of the group is the difficulty of guaranteeing confidentiality. Although all clients are urged to hold in confidence any discussion of individual problems in the group, they are not necessarily committed to the professional ethics of the therapist. The limits of any guarantee of confidentiality can also restrict the degree to which some clients are willing to self-disclose. It could even restrict the degree to which the therapist should urge the members to self-disclose in the group. However, it should be noted that, in the author and his colleagues' experience, actual breaches of confidentiality have been rare.

The disadvantage for those few clients whose anxiety in social situations is so great that they cannot function in a group without panic is that the group is not the preferred context of therapy for them.

Now that we have reviewed the major advantages and disadvantages of groups, let us examine what therapists actually do in cognitive-behavioral group therapy to facilitate the learning of social and cognitive skills by the clients within the constraints of the assumptions just discussed.

THERAPIST FUNCTIONS

At least 10 major categories of functions can be identified in cognitive-behavioral group therapy. Although there is considerable overlap, each category is sufficiently unique to describe separately. These categories include organizing the group, orienting the members to the group, building group attraction, assessing the problem and the possibilities for resolving it, monitoring the behaviors determined as problematic, evaluating the progress of treatment, planning for and implementing specific change procedures, assessing group problems, modifying group attributes, and establishing transfer and maintenance programs for behavior changes occurring in the group. Each functional category consists of a series of still more specific activities, some of which will be described.

Beginning The Group

In the initial phase of group therapy, the therapist focuses on three major activities: organizing the group, orienting the clients, and building group attraction.

Organizational activities involve discussion and decision making about type of group, duration of group, length of meetings, number of therapists, location of meetings, nature of fees or deposits, and similar structural concerns. In the pregroup interview, clients decide whether the therapist's description of the group's focus adequately meets what they perceive to be their needs. Most intensive therapy groups involve a pregroup interview, 14 to 18 full-length weekly sessions, and several "booster" sessions at 1 to 6 month intervals. Short-term training groups are 8 to 12 sessions, with 1 booster session 1 to 3 months after treatment. The short-term group could involve a pregroup interview as well. Some therapists have successfully used open-ended groups for intensive therapy. In open-ended groups, clients terminate when they achieve treatment goals or no longer feel the need for group support. New members are added as old members terminate, usually one at a time. The more experienced members orient the new members, which provides experienced clients an opportunity for leadership.

Orientation refers to those activities in which the therapist informs the client of the group's purposes and content and of the responsibilities of the clients to themselves and to the others. It also involves the process of negotiating the content of the general treatment contract. As part of this function, the group is oriented toward the philosophy of treatment and its empirical foundations. In the orientation process, the therapist is the major contributor, who provides information and case studies as examples. The major therapist activities of the pretreatment interview and the first session are, to a large degree, concerned with orientation and development of initial group structure, that is, rules for the group.

Building group attraction focuses on increasing the positive attitudes of the group members toward each other, the therapist, and the content of the program. Initially, the group is merely an assembly of strangers who often are quite frightened of one another. There are many advantages to increasing group cohesion from this early state.

High group cohesion has been found to be positively associated with group effectiveness (Flowers & Borraem, 1980; Liberman, 1970). Flowers and Borraem (1980, p. 302) have identified eight correlates of cohesion.

1. Increased attending to the speaker
2. Increased problem disclosure
3. Increased proportion of negative feedback
4. Decreased frequency of group members in negative input or output roles
5. Increased role flexibility during group sessions
6. Increased percentage of client-client interactions
7. Increased number of group members trusted
8. Increased self-reported session or group satisfaction

Research by Liberman (1970) demonstrated that a group therapist can directly influence the level of group cohesion. By using extensive social reinforcements, the therapists in Liberman's study effectively shaped, modified, and facilitated verbal behavior reflecting cohesiveness.

Other strategies employed to increase group cohesion include providing food at meetings, varying the content of meetings, providing audiovisual aids, providing incentives for attendance, using humor judiciously, using interactive group exercises, employing goal-oriented interactive games, and providing sociorecreational activities for adolescents and children.

Assessment, monitoring, and evaluation are also a part of the beginning phase of the group, but because these activities continue throughout treatment and require distinct activities, they are discussed under a separate section.

Assessment, Monitoring, and Evaluating

As defined earlier, assessment is the group activity concerned with defining problem situations and the behavior and cognitions required to deal with those situations. The resources of the individual and his or her environment that facilitate remediation of the problem situations are also explored in the course of group discussions.

The assessment process in group therapy is continuous throughout therapy. Preliminary information and initial complaints are first used to decide whether the group is appropriate for a given individual and, if appropriate, to ascertain the particular kind of group that is appropriate—a stress management group, a long-term group therapy, or an assertiveness training program. Later this information and other facts that have come up in group sessions are used to determine the interventions most likely to be successful, the types of goals the client can aim at while in the group, and the evaluation of whether session and treatment goals are attained. Effective assessment is facilitated by pregroup interviews in which the therapist explores with the client the unique problematic situations clients are experiencing and their behavioral, cognitive, and affective responses to those situations. From these interviews and subsequent contacts, information is obtained about resources and barriers that impinge on the effectiveness of treatment. Interviews are often supplemented by role-play tests, behavioral inventories, checklists, and observations in and out of the group, as a means of zeroing in on specific target areas.

Although pregroup interviews and tests are useful, most of the required data are obtained in the group discussion, as members bring to the group descriptions of the problematic or stressful situations they encountered since the previous session. The members, in interviewing each other, help each other to spell out the relevant details of situations before going on to problem solving or other treatment approaches. To facilitate this process, clients are asked to keep a diary containing all critical events.

Group members can be further involved in assessment by interviewing one another in the group; by serving as observers, as judges, of each other's role-plays; and by giving feedback to each other. Such involvement not only increases the relevance of the assessment process, because it provides multiple perceptions, but it also increases interpersonal attraction.

Also included in group assessment is the collection of group data such as participation, satisfaction, attendance, and assignment completion. These rates provide a basis for evaluating whether group problems exist and whether group goals are being attained. For example, if the average rate of satisfaction at a giving meeting is 2.2 on a 5-point scale, and the average assignment completion is 30%, a group problem exists that needs to be dealt with in the group (for greater detail on this subject, see Rose, 1984).

Although assessment begins in the pregroup interview, it constantly shifts emphasis throughout treatment. In the pregroup interview and in the initial group sessions, members are encouraged to present the problem situations, complaints, and reasons why they have come to the group. Clients are later taught how to define their problems in terms of specified criteria (discussed later in the chapter).

One of the most crucial steps in ongoing assessment is the analysis of situations that are viewed as problematic or stressful by the client. In this analysis, an attempt is made to define a time-limited event in terms of what was happening, who was involved, and where it occurred. Additionally, clients are asked which moment in time was the most difficult for them. This is called the *critical moment*.

Clients are asked to describe their behavior, affect, and cognitions for these critical moments. Among specific affect responses are the clients' satisfaction with their behavioral responses and their anxiety or anger. If the client is not at least somewhat dissatisfied with the response, the problem might not warrant targeting for change.

Once defined, behaviors, and the situations in which they occur, are systematically observed and measured in some way. The client, and occasionally others, serve as recorders. Only after such assessment is an explicit change procedure started. For example, in anxiety management groups, clients first rate their anxiety levels three to four times a day. After treatment is begun, data collection is continued until the follow-up interview. The group therapist uses the data as it is collected to evaluate the effectiveness of specific treatment procedures, the group meetings, and the course of therapy. Effectiveness is determined on the basis of whether the goals of a given technique, a given meeting, or a given therapy have, indeed, been achieved. If it is discovered that the format of a given meeting has been partially or totally unsuccessful (because of the high frequency of critical comments on the session's evaluation, low participation in the meeting, and failure of most members to complete their weekly assignments), the format can be changed. Thus, changes are initiated on the basis of a review of data, not on intuitive hunches. Because of the abundance of data and the regularity of feedback, change procedures can be designed and carried out as soon as a specific problem has been identified.

As a consequence of assessment, the therapist and the client can also evaluate the degree to which individual treatment goals are achieved. By keeping a record of ongoing progress, the therapist and others with whom he or she shares the data can ascertain what kinds of clients can best use the procedures commonly found in various models of group therapy. Each therapist can expand the knowledge base further if he or she establishes research controls. In behavior group therapy, if all treatment steps and problems are explicated, the total treatment of each group and each client can be viewed as an experiment in which the client and group are observed before, during, and after treatment. Variations of this time-series model without a control group have been suggested by a number of authors (Hersen & Barlow, 1976) as a means of strengthening the conclusion of a casual connection between treatment and outcome. Such designs as the multiple-baseline, the A-B-A-B model, and other time-series designs (see Hersen & Barlow, 1976) are especially suited to small samples and to data-based group therapy. Unfortunately, they have been rarely used in group therapy research.

To plan for the kind of individualized intervention to be used, a review of the assessment data is first required for all of the members. Common treatment goals permit common intervention plans. For example, if all the members or many of the members have some problems with agoraphobia, then group exposure could be the appropriate strategy, because empirical support exists for its use in groups (Emmelkamp, 1982). Similarly, if all or most of the members have difficulty talking with members of the opposite sex, social situations could be created in which members must observe, then practice, a variety of common conversations. If the group is homogeneous in reference to a problem, common intervention strategies are possible. Even when the specific complaints are quite diverse, there are a number of common skills that must be taught in order to mediate the achievement of solutions to the diverse problems. For example, most programs contain exercises in the giving and receiving of feedback, in systematic problem solving, in systematic relaxation, and in role-playing.

No matter how diverse the presenting problems in a group are, it is possible to individualize them. As each person presents a given problem situation, the group and the group therapist together can design an idiosyncratic training program for that individual. Although it requires more time, an individualized program is required for complex psychological problems. Even when the problems are not too complex, individualization is desirable and possible through the highly individualized homework assignments developed by each member for himself or herself, with another member as consultant and through individual presentations.

In one instance, the client brought in a situation that required problem solving in that the group needed to generate ideas as to what the client could say to the garage owner and what the client could say to himself. The situation also required social skill training and cognitive restructuring in that the client needed to have modeled and practiced the words he was to use overtly to the garage owner and covertly to himself. It could have also been necessary in that situation for the client to use relaxation or avoidance strategies as a means of coping with the situation. If these general strategies had already been taught to the group in common, the specific words and cognitions could have been taught individually to Eric. Of course, if the intervention strategies were not yet in the repertoire of the group members, they would first have to be demonstrated and explained by the group therapist. In this example, we see a meshing of the common and the individualized intervention plan.

Planning for and Implementing Specific Change Procedures

Because social skill training, cognitive restructuring, problem solving, and group intervention are the major intervention strategies used, let us examine each of these more closely in terms of how they are applied in groups.

Social Skill Training

Combs and Slaby (1977) defined social skills as "the ability to interact with others in a given social context in specific ways that are societally acceptable or valued and at the same time personally beneficial, mutually beneficial, or beneficial primarily to others" (p. 162).

Social skills development involves several critical assumptions (Bellack & Hersen, 1978). The first is that interpersonal behavior is based on a distinct set of skills that are primarily learned behaviors. Thus, how one behaves in an interpersonal situation depends on the individual's repertoire of effective social behaviors. The second aspect is that socially skilled behavior is situationally specific. It is important to recognize that cultural and situational factors determine social norms or what is expected of an individual. Third, effective functioning (e.g., carrying on a conversation with a new acquaintance) depends on an individual's repertoire of social skills and, if effective, is a powerful source of reinforcement. Social skills facilitate receiving reinforcement and avoiding problematic behavior.

Further, Bellack and Hersen (1978) described three general categories that are the components of social skills: conversational skills, social perception skills, and skills necessary for special problem situations. With regard to conversational skills, Hersen and Bellack point out that every social interaction is dependent on one's ability to initiate, maintain, and terminate a conversation. With regard to social perception, that is, accurate perception of the social situation, the following skills have been identified as relevant: listening, timing, getting clarification, maintaining relevancy, and identifying emotions. Lastly, it is important to attend to special problem situations that are particularly difficult because they are stressful even though they could be infrequent. Such situations place unique demands on the individual such as dealing with impositions of others, handling job interviews, or dealing with an oppressive boss.

Research on social skills training has revealed no specific components that are universally effective across different subject populations and difficult problems. Whereas McFall and Twentyman (1973) found coaching (instructing a client how to perform in a specific situation) and rehearsal (role-played practice) to be important components of assertive training, and symbolic modeling (observing others) contributing little to effective social skills training, Eisler, Hersen, and Miller (1973) found modeling and instructions to be the most critical elements in social skills training with psychiatric clients. It appears that different training components are effective in producing different aspects of social skills (Edelstein & Eisler, 1976; Hersen, Eisler, Miller, Johnson, & Pinkston, 1973), and that results have different effects, depending on the subject population (Eisler, Fredericksen, & Peterson, 1978). In general it appears that a comprehensive treatment package is important when teaching complex response patterns

(Hersen et al., 1973; Rimm, Snyder, Depue, Haanstand, & Armstrong, 1976).

Social skill training in groups involves the application of those behavioral procedures already mentioned, usually in the order identified in Figure 11.1. Because few of the above references refer to group therapy, let us look at what each of these steps entails as it is applied in a group context.

Prior to the initiation of social skill training, the therapist discusses with members the rationale of the procedures and provides examples. When possible the therapist draws upon those members who have used the procedures to share their experiences with the group.

If the members have had no previous experience with role-play or other simulation procedures, the group therapist might have to train them in the technique. Prepared situations are presented to the group in which the therapist and an experienced member or a member from a previous group demonstrate how to role-play. The group is divided into pairs. Each pair role-plays the same or a similar situation in one corner of the room. Later each pair demonstrates their role-play to the entire group, and each person receives positive feedback on what she or he role-played well.

Once the group members have demonstrated role-play skills, they are trained to develop situations that lend themselves to social skill training. These are brief situations with a clear-cut beginning and end. The place, the persons involved, the content of the interaction, and the time it took place are clearly delineated. The client should be dissatisfied with what she or he did or said in the situation. Finally, each event should have a critical moment, that is, a point in time in which the client is expected to respond or expects herself or himself to respond. An example of a situation amenable to social skill analysis is the following:

> The client, when he was at work the day before the session, was unable to complete the assignment his employer had given him because he simply did not understand the instructions. When his boss asked him how it was going he said, "fine," even though he wanted to ask for help. In this example we know when it occurred, where, and with whom. It is interactive, and the critical moment occurred when the boss asked how it was going and the client was dissatisfied with his response.

The therapist provides, first, a number of examples of situations, such as the one just given, that meet the criteria. The group then discusses these situations. Later the therapist might provide situations that do not meet the criteria and let the group modify them to meet the criteria. Later the members are asked to develop in pairs at least one new situation of their own that meets the criteria. Each of the situations is evaluated in terms of whether the criteria have been met.

Once the group is trained in the development of problem situations, they keep a diary of such situations as they occur in the course of the week. Each week, one such situation by each member is handled in the group.

When the situation is presented, the member either states her or his goals, or if she or he requests it, is helped by the group to develop goals for the situation. In the situation given earlier, the goals at the critical moment were to explain in a clear voice, with reasonable eye contact, that the client had not understood the original instructions and to ask whether the supervisor might not explain them again.

Once the goals are agreed upon and evaluated in terms of potential risk and reasonableness, the members are asked to propose the exact things the client could do or say to achieve these goals. Effective problem-solving techniques prohibit evaluation of suggestions until *after* all suggestions have been presented. The group then helps the client evaluate the list of suggestions in reference to relative risk, appropriateness, compatibility with personal style, and probable effectiveness. Ultimately it is the client with the problem situation who decides upon an overall strategy.

Usually the therapist or another group member models the desired verbal and nonverbal behavior in a brief role-played demonstration. The given client evaluates how realistic the modeled situation was and states what he or she finds useful in the performance of the model.

The client then practices or rehearses her or his own role in the situation, utilizing the agreed-upon behaviors. In subsequent rehearsals the difficulty and complexity of the situation can be gradually increased. When the client has difficulty carrying out the strategy in the rehearsal, she or he can be coached or assisted by the therapist or another member, or even through the use of cue cards. If coaching is used, it is usually eliminated in subsequent rehearsals. Following each rehearsal, the client receives feedback from the group as to what was done well and what might be done differently.

After several increasingly difficult rehearsals, the client assigns to himself or herself a homework assignment, to try out some of the new behaviors learned in the group, role-play, observe one's self in a new situation and/or keep a diary in which problematic or stressful situations are recorded. Homework is an essential part of this approach and is used as a means of increasing time spent on therapeutic endeavors, as well as for transferring therapeutic activities to the real world.

Let us look briefly at the sequence of these procedures as they applied in a group.

Evelyn had been upset when her colleague gave her advice whether she asked for it or not. Evelyn did nothing about it except get upset. Her goal was to ask Annie politely and firmly to stop it. In the group, the members recommended a number of things she could say. The particular suggestion Evelyn liked best was to say in a firm tone that she appreciated all the help she had been given, but now it was important for her to do everything on her own. Whenever she needed help, she'd be sure to ask. Otherwise, please, no help needed! When Evelyn was asked about what risk she might incur if she was assertive with her colleague, Annie, she thought the risk was far greater if she did nothing. Sticking up for herself, she added, wasn't her style, but it was a style, she said, she would like to acquire. Karin demonstrated in a roleplay how Evelyn might say it (modeling). Evelyn role-played the situation herself in her own role (behavioral rehearsal), with Janet playing the role of the colleague. Most group members thought she was quite impressive and pointed to specific things she did well. Glenda and Jean added that she might speak a little more slowly and emphatically (group feedback). After a second rehearsal, Evelyn said she couldn't wait for her real colleague to give her advice, so she could try out what she had just learned; but, just in case, she'd practice a half dozen more times with her buddy Karin during the week.

Most of these same procedures such as modeling, rehearsal, and homework are used in the modification of cognitions. In addition, a number of specific adaptations and uniquely cognitive procedures are used.

Cognitive Restructuring

In describing their cognitive responses during stress or problem situations, clients often reveal self-defeating thoughts or severely distorted beliefs about themselves in relation to the world about them. For example, in the excerpt just cited, Evelyn implied that some catastrophe might befall her if anyone became angry or upset with her. In some cases these cognitions seem to generate so much anxiety for an individual that she or he is unable to make use of social skill training in developing and trying out specific alternatives for coping with stress as it occurs in the real world. Under these conditions some form of restructuring of cognitions could be necessary. Cognitive restructuring refers to the process of identifying and evaluating one's own cognitions, recognizing the deleterious effect of maladaptive cognitions, and replacing these cognitions with more appropriate ones (Beck, 1976). Much of the data suggesting the usefulness of cognitive restructuring has come from a series of studies conducted by Fremouw and associates (Fremouw & Harmatz, 1975; Fremouw & Zitter, 1978; Glogower, Fremouw, & McCroskey, 1978) and from the work of Meichenbaum, 1977. Cognitive restructuring has been used to help anxious clients cope with test anxiety (Goldfried, Linehan, & Smith, 1978; Meichenbaum, 1972), speech anxiety (Fremouw & Harmatz, 1975; Fremouw & Zitter, 1978; Thorpe, Amatu, Blakey, & Burns, 1976), social interaction anxiety (Elder, 1978; Glass, Gottman, & Shmurak, 1976) and treating depression (Taylor & Marshall, 1977) and pain-related stress (Langer, Janis, & Wolfer, 1975; Turk, 1975). This procedure also is used in conjunction with other therapeutic strategies when the client's belief system becomes part of the change target. The major steps in cognitive restructuring as they are used in a group are described in Figure 11.2.

Just as in social skill training, offering a rationale for cognitive restructuring is an imperative first step (Meichenbaum, 1977). As a part of this step, clients are provided with examples, evidence of effectiveness, and an overview of the major steps. Members are encouraged to provide others with their own examples of the relationship between cognitions, anxiety, and behavior. An example of a rationale that the author and his colleagues have commonly used is the following:

> No one is free from stress or anxiety. The way we view ourselves, what we say to ourselves, and what we expect from ourselves can strongly influence how much anxiety is produced in a given situation. One person might view getting a ticket for a parking violation as a terrible tragedy and brood about it for a week; another person in the same situation might reflect casually that it was an expensive parking fee, pay the fine, and go off on his or her own business without further concern. The situation is the same, but the anxiety experienced is dramatically different! Changing the first person's view of the situation to more realistic proportions in this and similar situations could result in reduced anxiety, better problem solving, and generally more comfortable living. That is one of the things group therapy is all about, helping each person to discover inefficient, or harmful—or a word we'll use a lot, *self-defeating*—thoughts and replace them with coping thoughts and actions that work better for that person, as well as for the rest of us.

The following serves to identify each client's particular self-defeating or irrational cognitions through analysis of logical inconsistencies and long-range consequences of pervasive cognitions. In order to analyze cognitive responses to stress, situations are brought in by the clients, who are interviewed by the other members of the group. The group provides each participant feedback on the accuracy of her or his cognitions. This step of identifying self-defeating statements is exemplified in the group's work with Karl in an early session.

> Karl had told about a situation in which he had wanted to ask a girl in his class for a date. He knew what to say, but he failed to say it because, as he thought, "She'll never go out with a slob like me, and, if she says no, I'll not be able to stand it!" The group members pointed out to Karl two apparent self-defeating cognitions. The first implied "if she refused him he would be devastated" and the second that he considered himself a socially inept individual. Janine (therapist) had the group deal with each cognition, one at a time. The members interviewed Karl. Terry asked Karl if he had had any successes at all in approaching and talking to women. Karl gave a couple of examples. Janine asked if the women in the group had experienced Karl as a "slob." "To the contrary," Ellie said, "you make me feel quite comfortable." (The discussion continued with both Karl and the group providing evidence inconsistent with Karl's self-description).

Group exercises can be used first to teach clients to differentiate between self-defeating and coping statements (see Rose et al., 1984, exercise 26). Additional exercises are sometimes used to encourage clients to learn how to identify and analyze their own cognitions. Group participants provide each other not only with feedback but also with repeated and varied models of a cognitive analysis.

Often, repeated recognition that one is consumed by a given set of self-defeating cognitions is sufficient to warrant change (Beck, 1976; Ellis, 1970), but more often, in the author and his colleagues' experience and that of Meichenbaum and Cameron (1973), further steps must be employed. Thus the subsequent step is to solicit ideas from the client and from other group members as to potential self-enhancing or coping cognitions that facilitate problem solving or effective actions. The following is a continuation of Karl's group interview:

> *Janine:* What else might Karl say in a similar situation to himself that would accurately portray his response, instead of, "I'm such a slob that she would never go out with me"?
>
> *Gerard:* I've got to admit lots of people don't view me as a slob, and maybe she won't either.
>
> *Analisa:* Everyone's a slob once in a while, and in the group I'm learning how to approach people. Let's try it out now. The worst that can happen is that she'll say, no, and that's not so terrible.
>
> *Sylvia:* What do you think about. . . . "So what if I feel slobby. I can do something about it, like asking her for a date."

After the client decides on a set of accurate and comfortable cognitive statements, cognitive modeling is used in which the client imagines the stressful situation, experiences the initial self-defeating statements, stops herself or himself, and replaces the self-defeating statement with a coping statement, as the previous example continues:

> *Janine:* Gerard, would you demonstrate to Karl how he might handle himself in that situation? I'll help you if you get stuck.
>
> *Gerard:* OK, I imagine I see this girl in the library, OK? She seems real nice. I know her from class. There's a movie tonight at the student union. I'd really like to ask her to go with me. Got the picture? But I think Oh, she'd *never* go out with a slob like me. Wait a minute! (note the shift statement) I feel like a slob sometimes, but other people find me attractive. (Gerard seems at a loss so Janine coaches him at this time.) Oh yes, and I have been working on making friends in the group so, damn it, I'll ask her for a date. If she says no, she says no, it's not so awful.
>
> *Janine:* OK, Karl, how does that sound?

With cognitive rehearsal the client goes through the same steps as the model but adapts these steps to her or his own style. Afterward the client gets feedback from the group. The client might need to be coached during the first few trials. Finally, when feeling comfortable, the client practices the entire process silently (covert rehearsal). After the example just given, Karl duplicated in a cognitive rehearsal much of what Gerard had said. Now Janine asks the group for positive feedback.

Janine: Well, what did Karl say to himself or how did he say it in ways that should prove useful to him?

Theresa: He sounded like he believed it.

Sparky: He was really into the situation.

Gerard: For sure, he improved on my version. I especially liked the way he switched from the self-defeating statements.

Janine: (After a pause) What might he have done or said differently?

Karl: I forgot to say, "After all, plenty of people don't think I'm a slob."

It should be noted that Janine focused first on positive feedback, before asking for ways of improving. Now, after several practices, Janine shifts to a covert rehearsal.

Ok, let's try again, only this time let's do it silently. All of you might practice your own situation at the same time.

Usually, after several trials in the group, an assignment to practice a number of time at home is developed with the client. Ultimately it must be tried out in the real world.

Thus, in the final step, just as in social skill training homework, an assignment is developed at the end of one session and is monitored at a subsequent session. Assignments are usually developed in pairs and discussed in the larger groups. Homework is developed at successive levels of difficulty each week. For example, it might initially focus on learning to discriminate in general between self-defeating and self-enhancing or coping cognitions. Later the focus might be on identifying and evaluating the clients' cognitive responses to their own situations or shifting from the practice of self-defeating responses to coping skills, with the addition of praise to one's self for one's achievements. Homework can be carried out with "buddies" from the group, with a friend, or with a family member.

Of course, with most problems, just learning to perceive or evaluate oneself differently in a situation is probably not enough. Social skill training might be necessary to help Karl with the actual words he needed to talk with women. And additional coping skills such as relaxation (or deep breathing) might be necessary to create an internal state that facilitates thinking or speaking appropriately. The entire package of all these skill training procedures has been referred to as *stress inoculation*. This procedure is quite similar to cognitive restructuring but goes beyond it in teaching physical, as well as cognitive and social coping, skills. Designed by Meichenbaum and Cameron (1973), stress inoculation aims to provide a client with a set of skills to deal with future stress situations. Stress inoculation works on situations in each of three important phases: prior to, during, and immediately following a stressful situation. This approach has been used to aid abusive clients and law enforcement personnel with anger control (Novaco, 1975; 1977) and to teach others how to manage anxiety, stress, tension, headaches, and pain (for a review of this research, see Mahoney & Arnkoff, 1978).

Because most of these procedures have already been explained, except physical or active coping skills, let us look briefly at these skills.

Coping Skill Training

In addition to overt interactive responses, which are usually taught through social skill training procedures, a number of other more general behavioral strategies have been found effective in coping with both specific and general stress situations (Horan, Hackett, Buchanan, Stone & Demchik-Stone, 1977). These include relaxation, deep breathing, inquiry, and (in some cases) avoidance of the stress situation. (See Barrios & Shigetomi, 1979, for a review of the research on coping skill training.)

Relaxation and deep breathing are taught in groups in which anxiety-related problems are prominent. The skills are demonstrated and members then practice the skills in pairs and give each other feedback. Finally, with the help of instructional tapes, they practice the skills at home. Once learned, the group discusses when and where such procedures should be used.

When to use inquiry (collection of information) in stress situations is taught as each person brings in a stress situation. The question is always asked, What information do you need to reduce the ambiguity of this situation?

Avoidance, too, is often looked upon as one alternative response in every stress situation. However, the question is usually discussed in the group of whether the costs or risks of avoidance are greater than the risks of a more confrontative or cognitive coping or physical coping strategy.

In summary, behavior group therapy includes three main strategies of intervention: social skill training, cognitive restructuring, and coping skill training. All are integrated within a problem-solving framework. Clients learn the social, coping, and cognitive skills they need to deal with themselves, their thoughts, their anxiety, and the world about them. An additional set of procedures uniquely characteristic of group therapy must still be discussed called *group procedures*.

Group Procedures

A number of intervention techniques can be used solely in a small-group context. These group procedures involve dividing the group into subunits and/or involving the group in interactive exercises in which the members must communicate in prescribed ways. The purposes of such group procedures are to increase the interaction, modify the general pattern of interaction, increase responsibility to members, provide leadership opportunities, and/or provide greater opportunities for autonomous functioning. Let us examine the commonly used group procedures in more detail.

Recapitulation is a group technique used to slow down the pace of interaction and increase listening to others. With this procedure, a participant summarizes what the previous speaker has said before he or she expresses his or her own opinion. The problem with the procedure is that the discussion often loses its spontaneity, and some members are afraid to speak at all. The author has found it useful only when he limited the activity to several 5-minute exercises throughout the group meeting. As persons appear to be listening more effectively, the technique is eliminated.

A case study can be presented to the group for discussion whenever the therapist wants the group members to discuss an issue without first talking directly about themselves. In early sessions, when the group is hesitant to self-disclose, this technique is especially useful. In the first session, the author and his colleagues often present the group with two cases of persons who are similar to, but not the same as, a composite of several persons in the group. We ask the members to describe how each feels he or she is different from one or both of the cases.

In very large groups, 10 or more, we occasionally make use of a *fishbowl procedure*. Half the group is placed in a tight inner circle, and the remainder are seated in an outer circle surrounding the others. The inner circle usually discusses an issue while the outer circle observes. The outer circle is not permitted to interact until the inner circle is finished. At that time, the outer circle provides feedback to the members of the inner circle.

The *buddy system* was mentioned earlier in this chapter. The members select partners for mutual monitoring during the week between sessions. Contacts can be in person or by telephone. They are usually quite brief. This arrangement provides members the opportunity to be helper as well as client and to practice their newly learned leadership skills. The assignments for the partners are highly specific and limited in scope, so that clients will not deal with areas for which they are not prepared. Contact outside the group also serves to extend treatment into everyday life. It should be noted that, in contrast with our suggestion, some authors do not recommend extragroup contact among members (e.g., Lawrence & Sundell, 1972).

The author and his colleagues also use numerous *small group exercises* specific to each topic. For example, clients are taught feedback first by everyone's writing down one feedback statement to the group therapist about his or her behavior. Then, each statement is evaluated in terms of a specific set of criteria, its content, and the way it was delivered. Finally, each member does the same thing with the person on his or her right, who in turn gives him or her feedback on the feedback.

The handing out to clients of a list of self-defeating statements was mentioned before. Members then clarify why each statement is self-defeating and change it into a coping or self-enhancing statement. Members then discuss each of the statements in the group. Following this part of the exercise, members describe to the group their own self-defeating statements, and the group suggests alternative coping thoughts. Other exercises are to be found in the exercise manual (Rose, Tolman, Hanusa, & Tallant, 1984).

Resolving Group Problems

Because of the diversity of clients who make up any given group, there are diverse patterns of interaction, varied norms, differing levels of group cohesion, and unique patterns of conflict among groups. Some of these patterns or structures facilitate the achievement of treatment goals whereas others interfere with them. One of the unique characteristics of group therapy, in contrast with individual therapy, is the possibility of modifying group structure or resolving group problems in such a way as to enhance problem-solving and feedback skills and to provide practice in a protected setting for the members to deal with complex social situations. These particular conditions often function as interactive barriers to goal attainment.

Instead of group problems being viewed as limitations of group therapy, they should be considered therapeutic opportunities. In the identification of a problem, in discovering each individual's contribution to that problem, in planning for and carrying out intervention to resolve a problem, and in evaluating the outcome of the entire process, the group worker models and gives members multiple occasions to practice a systematic problem-solving approach around a significant common issue. Members have the opportunity to view their own unique patterns of behavioral, cognitive, and affective response to interactive events of the group. In the group, the individual can evaluate with the help of the others those responses to problems that are ineffective. In the group, members design together new strategies of remediation for group problems and observe and evaluate the consequences of their plans in terms of problem remediation.

Although, in the case of a group problem, no one person in the group can escape partial responsibility, no one should assume sole responsibility for it. Because blame can be avoided, members are more readily able to participate openly and actively in the process. In the world outside of the group, responsibility for most communication problems is shared with others. Learning to deal with mutual problems is an important task in its own right.

Assessing Group Interactive Problems

One of the major characteristics of group or interactive problem solving is its reliance on data in determining whether or not a problem exists. Do the observation data indicate limited participation by many members? Do the satisfaction data suggest only moderate satisfaction? Is the weekly rate of assignment completion less than 75%? The answer of yes to several of these questions often indicates a group or interactive problem or the existence of an undesirable norm. The data, of course, must be interpreted by the therapist and the group, as is exemplified later in this chapter. Such data make it possible to define group problems in quantifiable terms. To do so requires that data be collected on a regular basis.

A major source of group data comes from a postsession questionnaire (see Rose, 1984) that is administered at the end of every meeting. This questionnaire has proven valuable in ascertaining a number of different group problems.

To get an estimate of perceived satisfaction and perceived usefulness, members are asked to evaluate the issues just mentioned on 5-point scales. A rating of low satisfaction from two or more persons is often indicative of a number of different group or subgroup problems. A rating of low usefulness (if it remains low over time) is also indicative of failure to provide relevant materials or failure to link the material to concrete problems of the members.

Without a sophisticated observation instrument, one way of obtaining information about self-disclosure is to ask members their perceptions not only of their own self-disclosure, but also that of others. This provides evidence as to whether members perceive too much or too little self-disclosure as a group problem. The therapist can check her or his own subjective impression against these data.

A question concerned with the interrelations of members gives us further insight into the level of perceived group cohesion of the entire group and of subgroups.

Other ways to provide information about group states include an adjective list on which participants are asked to describe their moods in the group. If there is any persistent negative attitude across members, this is regarded as a group problem to be dealt with in the group.

Two other questions concern the relevance of problems discussed in the group, both the members' own problems and others' problems. Again, an average low level of relevance of problems discussed seems to be an indicator of a group problem.

Finally, open-ended questions are asked about what members found useful or interesting, what they wanted more or less of, and what they found annoying. Responses to these questions provide specific direction for adjustments in the program or discussion in the group.

The entire questionnaire takes about 3 minutes to fill in. The time for the leaders to analyze the data is somewhat longer, but the method is extremely valuable for detecting general group problems and specific member concerns.

The second set of data is derived from direct observations. In most groups, data is collected every 10 seconds on who is speaking. Noting the frequency of who speaks every time the speaker changes is another method. The first method gives a better estimate of length of speaking time. The second gives some insight into sequences. Both are easy to learn, and one can use former members, present members, visitors, or students as the observers. Because the method is simple, observers can be reliably trained in about 10 minutes.

Other more sophisticated (and hence more costly) observational methods can also be used to classify the content of interaction. The reader is referred to Mash and Terdal (1976, pp. 261–352) for a critical review and detailed presentation of still more elaborate systems. Because these usually are too costly for the practitioner to train observers, carry out the data analysis, and interpret in the typical clinical group program, they are not included here.

The rate of assignment completion, which also has been shown to correlate with behavioral change in a role-play test (Rose, 1981), is a good index of ongoing productivity. Low productivity is a major group problem and requires dramatic action as soon as it is detected. One way it can be assessed is to collect data on all assignments agreed upon at the end of one meeting and completed by the beginning of the next. The rate is computed by the number of assignments completed, divided by the number of assignments given. One problem with this index is that all assignments are assumed to be equal. An assertive task, such as talking to a new person, might be far more important than describing in writing a stressful situation. Some leaders give more weight to the completion of such tasks. Others consider only the completion of tasks in ascertaining productivity, because these assignments alone represent transfer of learning to the real world.

The fourth set of data commonly collected is on attendance, which was also correlated with outcome, though not significantly in Rose's study (1981). Promptness was not considered in the earlier study, but the same principle applies. The more time spent in the treatment, the more likely treatment goals will be achieved.

Modifying Group Attributes

Modification of a group problem was illustrated in a group the author supervises. The data revealed that 2 of 6 members spoke almost 60% of the time and one less than 5% of the time. Average satisfaction had dropped from 4.5 to 3.5 on a 5-point scale. After the data were presented to the group, they agreed that the uneven distribution of participation was a problem, and they developed a plan through systematic problem solving, which they agreed to implement at that meeting. The more active members stated they would reformulate the previous speaker's position before making a point of their own (recapitulation), whereas the less active members agreed to write down any thoughts they had relevant to each subject. The group therapist would then call upon them to review their notes, if they had not spoken. The group practiced the complex plan for the following 5 minutes and decided to use it only twice per meeting for 20 minutes because it was somewhat disruptive. They also agreed to end it once the distribution of participation was somewhat more even. Thus, the plan utilized problem solving, recapitulation, self-monitoring, cuing by the leader, and rehearsal.

Another group with a similar problem utilized primarily cognitive procedures, which they had recently been working on in the group. The members decided to analyze their thinking whenever they were expected to participate, and, in a later discussion, the group helped each member to determine whether a given thought was individually and group self-enhancing. Other procedures commonly used have been verbal reinforcement of inactive participants for even brief contributions and role-play practice with a buddy prior to a meeting regarding what might be said at that meeting (for further examples, see Rose, 1977b).

As clients respond to the unique and often complex group problems, the group therapist often discusses with the group the typical responses of each of the members and how each has learned to respond in more flexible and appropriate ways. By looking at the general pattern, the group therapist facilitates the generalization of changes learned in the group to situations outside the group. Teaching the general pattern is only one approach to facilitating generalization. The following section discusses other ways in which the group can increase the likelihood of generalization and maintenance of learning.

Generalization and Maintenance of Behavioral Change

Generalization strategies involve the application of those procedures designed to facilitate the transfer of learning occurring in the treatment situation to the real world of the client. There are two major types of procedures for generalization. The first type comprises intragroup procedures such as behavioral rehearsal, which simulates the real world and represents a preparatory step toward performance outside the group. The second type are extragroup procedures such as the behavioral assignment or homework in which the client tries out the rehearsed behavior in the community. Other extragroup techniques include meeting in the homes of the clients and using the buddy system outside the group.

Some strategies involve procedures oriented toward maintaining the goal level or quality of behavior achieved during the course of group therapy for a significant period after treatment is terminated. Several techniques uniquely designed for this purpose are used. Among them are gradual fading of the treatment procedures and thinning of the reinforcement schedules, that is, reducing frequency and regularity of rewards. Overlearning the new behavior through frequent trials has been used but probably is not sufficient by itself. It is also necessary to review summary rules or cognitive strategies in order that the more complex patterns of functioning be maintained (Rosenthal & Bandura, 1978). In groups, this review is often carried out at the end of each meeting, and the members are asked to participate.

In preparing for termination, the attraction of other groups is increased relative to the therapy groups. Clients are encouraged to join nontherapeutic groups in order to practice their newly learned skills under less controlled conditions. Greater reliance is placed on the decisions of the clients as they increasingly perform the major leadership tasks in the group. The role of the therapist shifts from direct therapist to consultant. These activities not only serve to make termination easier on the clients, but they also permit clients to function independently of a therapist. This independence is necessary not only for the maintenance of changes beyond the end of the group, but also for making the client more comfortable in dealing with new problems as they occur.

Clients are prepared for potential setbacks, unsympathetic relatives and friends, and unpredicted pressure through role-play of situations simulating the above conditions. It should be noted that preparation for generalization and maintenance of change is found throughout treatment. As early as the third or fourth meeting, partners are working with each other outside of the group, rehearsals are occurring within the group, and behavioral assignments are given for practicing the desired behavior outside of the group (see Goldstein, Heller, & Sechrest, 1966, for further discussion of these principles).

RELEVANT RESEARCH

Throughout this chapter, I have reported on some of the empirical support for each of the behavioral components of group therapy. In putting a behavioral and cognitive behavioral group package together for various problems, a large number of experimental studies can be identified. All of the studies have components of the package developed in this chapter, but none are exactly the same. Most of the studies have been on homogeneous groups of clients with a common major problem such as social skills deficits, depression, anxiety and stress, agoraphobia, and sexual disorders. Most of the studies failed to mention group conditions such as group cohesion or group structure as a concern of the experimenter. Several studies compared the effectiveness of group behavioral intervention strategies with individual ones. To my knowledge, only two studies attempted to measure the effects of group process, and none have attempted to manipulate the group process. Yet most clinicians working with groups would usually view the group as a variable as important as the major intervention strategies in behavioral change.

Let us review some of the major findings here. In the group treatment of social skill deficits, Linehan, Goldfried, and Goldfried (1979) found that a combined behavioral and cognitive restructuring approach in groups was superior to behavioral rehearsal alone, cognitive-behavioral alone, relationship therapy (all of which were in groups), and a waiting list control in the development of social skills.

It is interesting to note that, often when authors compared behavioral or cognitive-behavioral group packages with nondirective group therapy of the same duration, the nonbehavioral group package often did as well on the behavioral measures and occasionally even better. For example, LaPointe and Rimm (1980) compared Beck's cognitive-behavioral group approach with both an assertive training group and an insight-oriented group. All three treatments resulted in significant improvements in depression, rationality, and assertiveness measures. Unexpectedly, the insight group and the assertiveness group made significantly more gains in rationality regarding self. Hodgson (1981) also found an interpersonal skills approach in groups. Other experimenters found that Beck's cognitive approach in groups was superior in the reduction of depression to other group approaches (Shaw, 1977) and to an interest support group (Shipley & Fazio, 1973). Shaffer, Shapiro, Sank, and Coghlen (1981) also found that a mixed behavioral and cognitive restructuring approach in groups was effective, but no more effective than a nondirective treatment group (this study is described further later). Interpretation of these mixed findings is difficult. But one cannot underestimate the importance of the group as a component, even in the absence of the behavioral or cognitive-behavioral intervention package. From the description of the Beck approach as applied in groups, it is not clear if and how the experimenters made use of the unique characteristics and potential of the group.

In the treatment of depression in groups, several studies compared a group cognitive-behavioral approach to an individual one. When the psychoeducational group model of Brown and Lewinsohn (1984) was compared with individual tutoring, Teri and Lewinsohn (1981) found that both the group and the individual approaches were equally effective but that the individualized treatment requires 12 contact hours per client, the group, only 3 contact hours per client. Thus group treatment was clearly far more cost effective. Schaffer et al. (1981), in the study just mentioned, compared three conditions: a cognitive-behavioral group, individual cognitive-behavioral treatment, and a nondirective group approach. The behavioral condition consisted of progressive relaxation, cognitive restructuring, and assertion training. All three conditions resulted in a significant reduction of depression, but there were no significant differences among conditions.

Rush and Watkins (1981) compared a group cognitive-behavioral approach with individual ones with and without medication. All conditions improved significantly on Beck's Depression Inventory (BDI) and the Hamilton Rating Scale for Depression, but the individual conditions improved significantly more than the group condition. There is no evidence that either of the last two studies made use of unique characteristics of the group. Nor did either study control for therapist time. Similar inconclusive results were found in the behavioral treatment (group in-vivo exposure) of agoraphobia (Emmelkamp & Emmelkamp-Benner, 1975). The group and individually treated patients made significant gains, but there were no apparent differences in outcome between the two approaches. Similar findings were obtained in two separate studies in the group treatment of sexual dysfunction (Golden, Price, Heinreich, & Lobitz, 1978; Nemetz, Craig, & Reith, 1978). In almost every study in which group cognitive-behavioral or behavioral treatment is compared with individual treatment, both conditions show significant gains without either being significantly better. At least, in most cases, the group is less costly (in terms of staff time in achieving the same level of behavioral change) than the individual approach.

In many other studies examining group therapy, the group seemed to be used merely as a convenience for dealing with a large number of clients at the same time rather than a therapeutic tool in its own right. Fortunately, several researchers have attempted to examine the contribution of the group in exploratory parts of their studies. D'Alelio and Murray (1981) compared 8-week groups to 4-week groups in the treatment of anxiety. They found that 8 weeks of group behavioral treatment was consistently superior to 4 weeks on the self-report component of anxiety. The study went further in exploring group process by asking each client at the end of therapy what each thought was most useful in treatment. Specifically, 73% reported "seeing that others were going through the same thing" was the most important component. Only 45% thought that the behavioral learning techniques were of equal importance. A similar questionnaire with groups of depressives was used by Roth, Bielski, Jones, Parker, and Osborne (1982) with similar client responses that emphasized the importance of the group in contributing to outcome.

Antonuccio, Lewinsohn, and Steinmetz (1982) studied 106 subjects in eight groups, all of which followed a Brown and Lewinsohn (1984) cognitive-behavioral or psychoeducational model for the treatment of depression. Although they did not control for group process, they did examine homework compliance rates, rates of attendance, participation levels of each individual, and level of group cohesion. Leadership behavior, style, and leadership characteristics were also assessed. Not only did all groups improve on Beck's Depression Inventory after twelve 2-hour sessions, but there were also significant effects on participation levels, group cohesiveness, leadership style differences and differences on several other group dimensions. However, these differences had no effect on outcome.

In conclusion, although there is growing empirical support for the utility of various components of a behavioral and cognitive behavioral group therapy, only modest evidence exists on the advantage of integrating various behavioral techniques and group methods. Although most authors and clients believe that the group itself is a significant component of group therapy, few authors have attempted to investigate this dimension within the context of the therapeutic group. Group therapy, thus far, has been demonstrated to be at least as effective as individual treatment and, in most cases, much less costly. Obviously, further research is necessary, not only on comparative outcome of different approaches and on who can use what kind of treatment best, but also on the contribution of group process to outcome.

REFERENCES

Antonuccio, D. O., Lewinsohn, P. M., & Steinmetz, J. (1982). Identification of therapist differences in a group treatment for depression. *Journal of Consulting and Clinical Psychology, 50*, 433–435.

Argyle, M. (1969). *Social interaction*. Chicago, IL: Aldine.

Barrios, B. A., & Shigetomi, C. C. (1979). Coping skills training for the management of anxiety: A critical review. *Behavior Therapy, 10*, 491–522.

Beck, A. T. (1976). *Cognitive therapy and the emotional disorders*. New York: International Universities Press.

Bellack, A. S., & Hersen, M. (1978). Chronic psychiatric patients and social skills training. In M. Hersen & A. S. Bellack (Eds.), *Behavior therapy in the psychiatric setting*. Baltimore, MD: Williams & Wilkins.

Brown, R., & Lewinsohn, P. M. (1984). A psycho-educational approach to the treatment of depression: Comparison of group, individual, and minimal contact procedures. *Journal of Consulting and Clinical Psychology*.

Cartwright, D., & Zander, A. (Ed.). (1968). *Group dynamics: Research and theory*. New York: Harper & Row.

Combs, M. L., & Slaby, D. A. (1977). Social skills training with children. In B. B. Lahley & A. E. Kazdin (Eds.), *Advances in clinical child psychology* (Vol 1). New York: Plenum.

D'Alelio, W. A., & Murray, E. J. (1981). Cognitive therapy for test anxiety. *Cognitive Therapy and Research, 5*, 299–307.

Edelstein, B. A., & Eisler, R. M. (1976). Effects of modeling and modeling with instructions and feedback on the behavioral components of social skills. *Behavior Therapy, 7*, 382–389.

Eisler, R. M., Frederiksen, L. W., & Peterson, G. L. (1978). The relationships of cognitive variables to the expression of assertiveness. *Behavior Therapy, 9*, 419–427.

Eisler, R. M., Hersen, M., & Miller, P. M. (1973). Effects of modeling on components of assertive behavior. *Journal of Behavior Therapy and Experimental Psychiatry, 4*, 1-6.

Elder, J. (1978). *Comparison of cognitive restructuring and response acquisition in the enhancement of social competence in college freshmen.* Unpublished doctoral dissertation, West Virginia University, Morgantown, WV.

Ellis, A. C. (1970). *The essence of rational psychotherapy: A comprehensive approach to therapy.* New York: Institute for Rational Living.

Emmelkamp, P. M. G. (1982). *Phobic and obsessive-compulsive disorders.* New York: Plenum.

Emmelkamp, P. M. G., & Emmelkamp-Benner, A. (1975). Effects of historically portrayed modeling and group treatment on self-observation: A comparison with agoraphobics. *Behaviour Research and Therapy, 13*, 135-139.

Flowers, J. V., & Booraem, C. D. (1980). Three studies toward a fuller understanding of behavioral group therapy: Cohesion, client flexibility and outcome generalization. In D. Upper & S. M. Ross (Eds.), *Behavior Group Therapy*, Champaign, IL: Research Press.

Fremouw, W. J., & Harmatz, M. G. (1975). A helper model for behavioral treatment of speech anxiety. *Journal of Consulting and Clinical Psychology, 43*, 652-660.

Fremouw, W. J., & Zitter, R. E. (1978). A comparison of skills training and cognitive restructuring-relaxation for the treatment of speech anxiety. *Behavior Therapy, 9*, 248-259.

Glass, C. R., Gottman, J. M., & Shmurak, S. H. (1976). Response-acquisition and cognitive self-statement modification approaches to dating-skills training. *Journal of Counseling Psychology, 23*, 520-525.

Glogower, F. D., Fremouw, W. J., & McCroskey, J. C. (1978). A component analysis of restructuring. *Cognitive Therapy and Research, 2*, 209-223.

Golden, J. S., Price, S., Heinreich, A. G., & Lobitz, W. C. (1978). Group versus couple treatment of sexual dysfunctions. *Archives of Sexual Behavior, 7*, 593-602.

Goldfried, M. R., Linehan, M. M., & Smith, J. L. (1978). Reduction of test anxiety through cognitive restructuring. *Journal of Consulting and Clinical Psychology, 46*, 32-39.

Goldstein, A., Heller, K., & Sechrest, L. B. (1966). *Psychotherapy and the psychology of behavior change.* New York: John Wiley.

Heppner, P. P. (1978). A review of the problem-solving literature and its relationship to the counseling process. *Journal of Counseling Psychology, 25*, 366-375.

Hersen, M., & Barlow, D. H. (1976). *Single case experimental designs.* New York: Pergamon Press.

Hersen, M., Eisler, R. M., Miller, P. M., Johnson, M. B., & Pinkston, S. G. (1973). Effects of practice, instructions and modeling on components of assertive behavior. *Behaviour Research and Therapy, 11*, 443-451.

Hodgson, J. (1981). Cognitive versus behavioral interpersonal approaches to the group treatment of depressed college students. *Journal of Counseling Psychology, 28*, 243-249.

Horan, J. J., Hackett, G., Buchanan, J. D., Stone, C. I., & Demchik-Stone, D. (1977). Coping with pain: A component analysis of stress inoculation. *Cognitive Therapy and Research, 1*, 211-221.

Langer, E. J., Janis, I. L., & Wolfer, J. A. (1975). Reduction of psychological stress in surgical patients. *Journal of Experimental Social Psychology, 11*, 155-165.

LaPointe, K., & Rimm, D. (1980). Cognitive, assertive, and insight-oriented group therapies in the treatment of reactive depression in women. *Psychotherapy: Theory, Research, and Practice, 17*, 312–321.

Laurence, H., & Sundel, M. (1972). Behavior modification in adult groups. *Social Work, 17*, 34–43.

Lewinsohn, P. M., Weinstein, M. S., & Alper, T. A. (1970). A behavioral approach to the group treatment of depressed persons: A methodological contribution. *Journal of Clinical Psychology, 26*, 525–632.

Libet, I., & Lewinsohn, P. M. (1973). The concept of social skill with special references to the behavior of depressed persons. *Journal of Consulting and Clinical Psychology, 40*, 304–312.

Lieberman, R. P. (1970). A behavioral approach to group dynamics: I. Reinforcement and prompting of cohesiveness in group therapy. *Behavior Therapy, 1*, 141–175.

Linehan, M. M., Goldfried, M. R., & Goldfried, A. P. (1979). Assertion therapy skill training or cognitive restructuring. *Behavior Therapy, 10*, 372–388.

Lott, A. J., & Lott, B. E. (1961). Group cohesiveness, communication level and conformity. *Journal of Abnormal and Social Psychology, 62*, 408–412.

Mahoney, M. J., & Arnkoff, D. (1978). Cognitive and self-control therapies. In S. L. Goldfried & A. E. Bergin (Eds.), *Handbook of psychotherapy and behavior change* (2nd ed.). New York: John Wiley.

Mash, E. J., & Terdal, L. G. (Eds.). (1976). *Behavior-therapy assessment: Diagnosis, design, and evaluation.* New York: Springer.

McFall, R. M., & Twentyman, C. T. (1973). Four experiments on the relative contributions of rehearsal, modeling and coaching to assertion training. *Journal of Abnormal Psychology, 81*, 198–218.

Meichenbaum, D. (1972). Cognitive modification of test anxious college students. *Journal of Consulting and Clinical Psychology, 39*, 370–380.

Meichenbaum, D. (1977). *Cognitive behavior modification.* New York: Plenum.

Meichenbaum, D., & Cameron, R. (1973). Training schizophrenics to talk to themselves: A means of developing attentional controls. *Behavior Therapy, 4*, 515–534.

Nemetz, G. H., Graig, K. D., & Reith, G. (1978). Treatment of female sexual dysfunction through symbolic modeling. *Journal of Consulting and Clinical Psychology, 46*, 62–73.

Novaco, R. W. (1975). *Anger control: The development and evaluation of an experimental treatment.* Lexington, MA: D. C. Heath.

Novaco, R. W. (1977). Stress inoculation: A cognitive therapy for anger and its application to a case of depression. *Journal of Consulting and Clinical Psychology, 45*, 600–608.

Platt, J., Scuro, W. C., & Hammon, J. R. (1973). Problem-solving thinking of youthful incarcerated heroin addicts. *Journal of Community Psychology, 1*, 278–281.

Platt, J., & Spivack, G. (1972a). Problem-solving thinking of psychiatric patients. *Journal of Consulting and Clinical Psychology, 39*, 148–151.

Platt, J., & Spivack, G. (1972b). Social competence and effective problem-solving thinking in psychiatric patients. *Journal of Clinical Psychology, 28*, 3–5.

Rimm, D. C., Snyder, J. J., Depue, R. A., Haanstad, M. J., & Armstrong, D. P. (1976). Assertive training versus rehearsal and the importance of making assertive response, *Behaviour Research and Therapy, 14*, 315–321.

Rose, S. D. (1977a). Assertive training in groups: Research in clinical settings. *Scandinavian Journal of Behavior Therapy, 6*, 61–86.

Rose, S. D. (1977b). *Group therapy: A behavioral approach.* Englewood Cliffs, NJ: Prentice-Hall.

Rose, S. D. (1981). Assessment in groups. *Social Research and Abstracts, 17,* 29–37.

Rose, S. D. (1984). The use of data in resolving group problems. *Social Work with Groups, 7,* 119–130.

Rose, S. D., Tolman, R., Hanusa, P., & Tallant, R. (1984). Leader's manual for stress management training. University of Wisconsin, Madison, WI: School of Social Work.

Rosenthal, T., & Bandura, A. (1978). Psychological modeling: Theory and practice. In S. L. Garfield & A. E. Bergin (Eds.), *Handbook of psychotherapy and behavior change* (2nd ed.). New York: John Wiley.

Roth, D., Bielski, R., Jones, M., Parker, W., & Osborn, G. (1982). A comparison of self-control therapy and combined self-control therapy and anti-depressant medication in the treatment of depression, *Behavior Therapy, 13,* 133–144.

Rush, J., & Watkins, J. (1981). Group versus individual cognitive therapy: A pilot study. *Cognitive Therapy and Research, 1,* 95–103.

Shaffer, C., Shapiro, J., Sank, L., & Coghlen, D. (1981). Positive changes in depression, anxiety, and assertion following individual and group cognitive-behavior therapy intervention. *Cognitive Therapy and Research, 5,* 149–157.

Shaw, B. (1977). Comparison of cognitive therapy and behavior therapy in the treatment of depression. *Journal of Consulting and Clinical Psychology, 45,* 543–551.

Shipley, C., & Fazio, A. (1973). Pilot study of a treatment for psychological depression, *Journal of Abnormal Psychology, 2,* 372–376.

Shoemaker, M. E. (1977). Developing assertiveness: Training or therapy? In R. E. Alberti (Ed.), *Assertiveness innovation, applications, issues.* San Luis Obispo, CA: Impact.

Shure, M. B., & Spivack, G. (1972). Means-ends thinking, adjustment and social class among elementary school-aged children. *Journal of Consulting and Clinical Psychology, 38,* 348–353.

Spivack, G., & Levine, M. (1963). *Self-regulation in acting-out and normal adolescents* (Report M-4531). Washington, DC.: National Institute of Mental Health.

Taylor, F. G., & Marshall, W. L. (1977). Experimental analysis of a cognitive-behavioral therapy for depression. *Cognitive Therapy and Research, 1,* 59–72.

Teri, L., & Lewinsohn, P. M. (1981). *A comparison of individual and group treatments for depression.* Paper presented at the meeting of the Association for Advancement of Behavior Therapy.

Thorpe, G. L. (1975). Desensitization, behavior rehearsal, self-instructional training and placebo effects on assertive-refusal behavior. *European Journal of Behavioural Analysis and Modification, 1,* 30–44.

Thorpe, G. L., Amatu, H. I., Blakey, R. S., & Burns, L. E. (1976). Contributions of overt instructional rehearsal and "specific insight" to the effectiveness of self-instructional training: A preliminary study. *Behavior Therapy, 7,* 504–511.

Turk, D. (1975). *Cognitive control of pain: A skills training approach for the treatment of pain.* Unpublished master's thesis, University of Waterloo, Waterloo, Ontario, Canada.

Author Index

Subject Index

About the Editors and Contributors

Frederick H. Kanfer (PhD, Indiana University) is professor of psychology and director of clinical training at the University of Illinois. His primary interest is in developing the necessary conceptualizations and methods to provide a broad behavioral framework for application to personal and social problems.

He was awarded a Diplomate in Clinical Psychology from the American Board of Examiners in Professional Psychology. He is a Fellow of the American Psychological Association and has held office in the Division of Clinical Psychology and in the Association for the Advancement of Behavior Therapy.

Dr. Kanfer has taught at Washington University, St. Louis; at Purdue University; in the Department of Psychiatry at the University of Oregon Medical School; and at the University of Cincinnati. (He is currently Professor of Psychology at the University of Illinois.) He was a Fulbright Scholar to Europe and has been visiting professor and consultant to various agencies dealing with psychological problems, both in the United States and in Europe. In addition, he has served on editorial boards of several psychological journals and has published over 120 articles. He is co-author of *Learning Foundations of Behavior Therapy*, and co-editor of *Maximizing Treatment Gains* and of *Self-Management and Behavior Change*. His experimental work is primarily in the area of self-regulation, self-control, and altruism.

Arnold P. Goldstein (PhD, Pennsylvania State University) is professor of special education and director of the Center for Research on Aggression at Syracuse University. His primary interest is behavior modification, skill training, and interpersonal relationships. He is a Fellow of the American Psychological Association and a member of the International Society for Research on Aggression and the Correctional Education Association.

Dr. Goldstein has taught at the University of Pittsburgh Medical School and served as a research psychologist at the VA outpatient research laboratory in Washington, DC. He was a visiting professor at the Free University of Amsterdam, Holland, in 1970, and at the University of Hawaii in the summer of 1972. He has published over 40 articles and is author, co-author or editor of *Therapist-Patient Expectancies in Psychotherapy; Psychotherapy and the Psychology of Behavior Change; The Investigation of Psychotherapy; Psychotherapeutic Attraction; The Lonely Teacher; Structured Learning Therapy; Changing Supervisor Behavior; Skill Training for Community Living; Prescriptive Psychotherapies; Prescriptions for Child Mental Health and Education; Police Crisis Intervention; Hostage; Police and the Elderly; Maximizing Treatment Gains; Skillstreaming the Adolescent;* and *In Response to Aggression.*

THE CONTRIBUTORS

Gerald C. Davison
Department of Psychology
University of Southern California
Seely Mudd Building
University Park
Los Angeles, CA 90089

M. Judith Furukawa, MS
University of Washington
Seattle, WA

Lisa Gaelick, MS
Psychology Department
University of Illinois
Champaign, IL

Steve Goldband, PhD
Instruments Division
IBM Corporation
Buffalo, NY

Arnold P. Goldstein, PhD
Special Education
805 S. Crouse Ave.
Syracuse University
Syracuse, NY 13210

David A. Haaga, MS
Psychology Department
University of Southern California
Los Angeles, CA

Anne Harris, PhD
Psychology Department
Arizona State University
Tempe, AZ 85281

Frederick H. Kanfer, PhD
Psychology Department
University of Illinois
Champaign, IL

Paul Karoly
Department of Psychology
Arizona State University
Tempe, AZ 85281

Edward S. Katkin
Psychology Department
SUNY–Buffalo
4230 Ridge Lea Road
Buffalo, NY 14226

Donald H. Meichenbaum
Department of Psychology
University of Waterloo
Waterloo, Ontario, Canada
N2L 3G1

Richard J. Morris
Special Education
College of Education
University of Arizona
Tucson, AZ 85721

Charles R. Myers, MS
Psychology Department
Syracuse University
Syracuse, NY 13210

Martha Perry
Psychology Department
University of Washington
Seattle, WA 98195

Sheila D. Reed, MS
Psychology Department
SUNY–Buffalo
Buffalo, NY 14226

Sheldon D. Rose
School of Social Work
University of Wisconsin
425 Henry Mall
Madison, WI 53706

Jack Sandler
Department of Psychology
University of South Florida
Tampa, FL 33620

Pergamon General Psychology Series

Editors: Arnold P. Goldstein, Syracuse University
Leonard Krasner, SUNY at Stony Brook